# WEBSTER'S II
## New Riverside Pocket Dictionary

The Riverside Publishing Company

# CONTENTS

Library of Congress Cataloging-in-Publication Data

Webster's II new Riverside pocket dictionary.
    1. English language — Dictionaries.   I. Riverside Publishing Company.   II. Title: Webster's two new Riverside pocket dictionary.   III. Title: Webster's 2 new Riverside pocket dictionary.
PE1628.W55167   1986   423   86-13762
ISBN 0-395-52379-6

Manufactured in the United States
of America

# HOW TO USE THE RAPID WORD FINDER

To locate the section in which you want to look up a word, find the number that corresponds to the first letter of the word and flip through the pages of the dictionary until you find that number.

The Rapid Word Finder index system contained in this volume is used under license from Mr. Tracy Mathis, patent holder. It may not be reproduced or used in any way without permission of the publisher and the patent holder.

| A-1 | I-9 | Q-17 |
| B-2 | J-10 | R-18 |
| C-3 | K-11 | S-19 |
| D-4 | L-12 | T-20 |
| E-5 | M-13 | U-21 |
| F-6 | N-14 | V-22 |
| G-7 | O-15 | W-23 |
| H-8 | P-16 | XYZ |

**Houghton Mifflin Company**

*Editorial Director*
Fernando de Mello Vianna

*Supervising Editor*
Anne D. Steinhardt

*Associate Editor*
Pamela DeVinne

*Assistant Editor*
Carole La Mond

*Reference Editor*
Kaethe Ellis

*Project Editor*
Tim Baehr

*Contributing Editors*
Mark Boyer
Walter Havighurst

*Art Director*
Geoffrey Hodgkinson

# HOW TO USE THIS DICTIONARY

## The Main Entry

Entry words, divided into syllables by centered dots, appear in alphabetical order. Two or more entries that are identical in spelling but have different histories are entered separately, each bearing a superscript number:

> game¹
> game²

## Variants

When two or more different spellings of a single word are entered, they are set in boldface type. If a variant follows the main entry, separated from it by only a comma, the two forms are used with almost equal frequency:

> ax, axe

If one spelling is distinctly preferred, the variant is introduced by the word "Also":

> glam·our ... Also glam·or.

## Inflected Forms

Irregular inflected forms or those offering possible spelling problems are entered in boldface type, often in shortened form:

> base ... baser, basest.
> gam·ble ... -bled, -bling.
> well ... better, best.

Although regular inflections are normally not entered, the regular plural of a noun is shown when there is an irregular variant plural or when the spelling of the regular plural might present difficulty:

> cac·tus ... *pl.* -ti (-tī′) or -tuses.
> gal·lows ... *pl.* -lowses or -lows.
> pi·an·o ... *pl.* -os.

The inflected forms of verbs are given in the following order: past tense, past participle (if it differs from the past tense), and present participle:

> fly ... flew, flown, flying.

## Labels

The labels below are used to indicate parts of speech:

| | |
|---|---|
| n. | noun |
| adj. | adjective |
| adv. | adverb |
| pron. | pronoun |
| conj. | conjunction |
| prep. | preposition |
| v. | verb |
| interj. | interjection |

The following additional labels are used to indicate additional forms:

| | |
|---|---|
| pl. | plural |
| sing. | singular |
| fem.n. | feminine noun |
| masc.n. | masculine noun |
| pres.p. | present participle |
| p,t. | past tense |
| p.p. | past participle |
| compar. | comparative |
| superl. | superlative |
| pl.n. | plural noun |

## Pronunciation

All pronunciations, indicated in parentheses following the forms to which they apply, are acceptable in all circumstances. When more than one is given, the first is assumed to be the most common, although the difference in frequency may be insignificant.

Below is a list of the symbols used in the pronunciations in this dictionary:

| Spellings | Symbols |
|---|---|
| pat | ă |
| pay | ā |
| care | âr |
| father | ä |
| bib | b |
| church | ch |
| deed, milled | d |
| pet | ĕ |
| bee | ē |
| fife, phase | f |
| gag | g |
| hat | h |
| which | hw |
| pit | ĭ |
| pie, by | ī |
| pier | îr |
| judge | j |
| kick, cat, pique | k |
| lid, needle | l |
| mum | m |
| no, sudden | n |
| thing | ng |
| pot, horrid | ŏ |
| toe, hoarse | ō |
| caught, paw, for | ô |
| noise | oi |
| took | ŏŏ |
| boot | ōō |
| out | ou |
| pop | p |
| roar | r |
| sauce | s |
| ship, dish | sh |
| tight, stopped | t |
| thin | th |
| this | th |
| cut | ŭ |
| urge, term, firm, word, heard | ûr |

| Spellings | Symbols |
|---|---|
| valve | v |
| with | w |
| yes | y |
| zebra, xylem | z |
| vision, pleasure, garage | zh |
| about, item, edible, gallop, circus | ə |
| butter | ər |

A *y* between slashes (/y/) indicates that the sound is present in the pronunciation of some speakers and absent from the pronunciation of others, as in the word *duty*, where two pronunciations may occur, (dōō′tē) and (dyōō′tē). In this dictionary both pronunciations are represented: (d/y/ōō′tē).

*Stress*, the relative degree of loudness with which the syllables of a word are spoken, is indicated in three different ways. An unmarked syllable has the weakest stress in the word. The strongest, or *primary*, stress is marked with a bold mark (′). An intermediate level of stress, called *secondary*, is marked with a similar but lighter mark (′). Words of one syllable show no stress mark, since there is no other stress level to which the syllable is compared.

Primary stress ′
  **bi·ol′o·gy**  (bī-ŏl′ə-jē)

Secondary stress ′
  **bi′o·log′i·cal** (bī′ə-lŏj′ĭ-kəl)

consideration. —v. To consider or esteem.
—**account for. 1.** To make a reckoning; report. **2.** To give the reason for; explain. **3.** To be answerable for. —**ac·count'a·bil'i·ty** n. —**ac·count'a·ble** adj.

**ac·count·ing** (ə-koun'tĭng) n. The occupation, process, or methods of keeping the financial records of a business. —**ac·count'ant** n.

**ac·cred·it** (ə-krĕd'ĭt) v. **1.** To attribute to. **2.** To certify as meeting a prescribed standard. —**ac·cred'i·ta'tion** n.

**ac·crue** (ə-krōō') v. **-crued, -cruing.** To increase by regular growth, as interest on capital. —**ac·cru'al** n.

**ac·cu·mu·late** (ə-kyōōm'yə-lāt') v. **-lated, -lating.** To amass; mount up. —**ac·cu'mu·la'tion** n.

**ac·cu·rate** (ăk'yər-ĭt) adj. Having no errors; exact; correct. —**ac'cu·ra·cy** n. —**ac'cu·rate·ly** adv.

**ac·cuse** (ə-kyōōz') v. **-cused, -cusing. 1.** To charge (someone) with an error; blame. **2.** In law, to bring charges against. —**ac'cu·sa'tion** n.

**ac·cus·tom** (ə-kŭs'təm) v. To familiarize.

**ace** (ās) n. **1.** A playing card, domino, etc., having one spot. **2.** In tennis, a point scored for an unreturned serve. **3.** An expert in any field, esp. a fighter pilot. —adj. First-rate.

**ache** (āk) v. **ached, aching. 1.** To suffer a dull pain. **2.** To yearn. —n. A dull, steady pain.

**a·chieve** (ə-chēv') v. **achieved, achieving.** To accomplish successfully; attain. —**a·chieve'ment** n.

**ac·id** (ăs'ĭd) n. A substance capable of dissolving certain metals to form salts, reacting with bases or alkalis to form salts, or having a sour taste. —adj. Biting; ill-tempered. —**a·cid'i·ty** n.

**ac·knowl·edge** (ăk-nŏl'ĭj) v. **-edged, -edging. 1.** To admit the existence or truth of. **2.** To report the receipt of. **3.** To express gratitude for. —**ac·knowl'edg·ment** n.

**ac·me** (ăk'mē) n. The point of utmost attainment.

**ac·ne** (ăk'nē) n. A skin disease characterized by pimples.

**a·corn** (ā'kôrn', ā'kərn) n. The nut of the oak tree.

**a·cous·tic** (ə-kōō'stĭk) adj. Also **a·cous·ti·cal.** Of sound, the sense of hearing, or the science of sound. —n. **acoustics. 1.** (takes sing. v.). The science of sound. **2.** (takes pl. v.). The effect of sound, esp. in an enclosed space.

**ac·quaint** (ə-kwānt') v. **1.** To make familiar.

**2.** To inform. —**ac·quain'tance** n. —**ac·quaint'ed** adj.

**ac·qui·esce** (ăk'wē-ĕs') v. **-esced, -escing.** To consent passively. —**ac'qui·es'cence** n. —**ac'qui·es'cent** adj.

**ac·quire** (ə-kwīr') v. **-quired, -quiring.** To gain possession of. —**ac'qui·si'tion** n. —**acquis'i·tive** adj.

**ac·quit** (ə-kwĭt') v. **-quitted, -quitting.** To clear of a charge. —**ac·quit'tal** n.

**a·cre** (ā'kər) n. A unit of land area equal to 4,840 square yards. —**a'cre·age** n.

**ac·ri·mo·ny** (ăk'rə-mō'nē) n. Animosity in speech or manner. —**ac'ri·mo'ni·ous** adj.

**ac·ro·bat** (ăk'rə-băt') n. One skilled in feats of agility and balance. —**ac'ro·bat'ic** adj.

**a·cross** (ə-krôs', ə-krŏs') prep. **1.** On, at, or from the other side of. **2.** From one side of to the other. —adv. **1.** From one side to the other. **2.** On or to the opposite side.

**act** (ăkt) n. **1.** The process of doing something. **2.** Something that is done. **3.** A legislative enactment. **4.** A major division of a play, opera, etc. **5.** A pose. —v. **1.** To perform, as in a play. **2.** To behave. **3.** To do something.

**act·ing** (ăk'tĭng) adj. Temporarily assuming another's duties. —n. The occupation of an actor.

**ac·tion** (ăk'shən) n. **1.** The state or process of doing. **2.** An act or deed. **3. actions.** Behavior. **4.** The operating parts of a mechanism. **5.** The plot of a story or play. **6.** A lawsuit. **7.** Combat.

**ac·ti·vate** (ăk'tə-vāt') v. **-vated, -vating. 1.** To set in motion. **2.** To make active.

**ac·tive** (ăk'tĭv) adj. **1.** In action; moving. **2.** Functioning. **3.** Participating. **4.** Characterized by energetic action. **5.** Denoting that the subject of a sentence is performing the action expressed by the verb. —**ac·tiv'i·ty** n.

**ac·tor** (ăk'tər) n. A theatrical performer. —**ac'tress** fem.n.

**ac·tu·al** (ăk'chōō-əl) adj. In existence; real. —**ac·tu·al'i·ty** n. —**ac'tu·al·ly** adv.

**a·cu·men** (ə-kyōō'mən) n. Keenness of insight.

**a·cute** (ə-kyōōt') adj. **1.** Sharp. **2.** Keenly perceptive. **3.** Sensitive; critical. **4.** Extremely severe. **5.** Designating angles less than 90°. —**a·cute'ly** adv.

**ad·age** (ăd'ĭj) n. A short proverb.

**ad·a·mant** (ăd'ə-mənt) adj. Unyielding; stubborn.

**a·dapt** (ə-dăpt') v. To adjust to new or different conditions. —**a·dapt'a·bil'i·ty** n. —a·dapt-

**dapt'a·ble** *adj.* — **ad·ap·ta'tion** *n.* — **a·dap'tive** *adj.*

**add** (ăd) *v.* **1.** To join so as to increase. **2.** To combine to form a sum. **3.** To say further.

**ad·dict** (ə-dĭkt') *v.* To give (oneself) habitually to; depend on. —*n.* (ăd'ĭkt). A person who is addicted, esp. to narcotics. — **ad·dic'tion** *n.*

**ad·di·tion** (ə-dĭsh'ən) *n.* **1.** The act or process of adding. **2.** Something added; a supplement. — **ad·di'tion·al** *adj.*

**ad·dle** (ăd'l) *v.* **-dled, -dling. 1.** To make or become confused. **2.** To spoil, as an egg.

**ad·dress** (ə-drĕs') *v.* **1.** To speak to. **2.** To mark with a destination. **3.** To direct one's efforts to. —*n.* **1.** A formal speech. **2.** The indication of destination on mail. **3.** The location of an organization or person. — **ad'dress·ee'** *n.*

**ad·e·noids** (ăd'n-oidz') *pl.n.* Tissue growths above the throat in the nose.

**a·dept** (ə-dĕpt') *adj.* Highly skilled. —**a·dept'ly** *adv.*

**ad·e·quate** (ăd'ĭ-kwĭt) *adj.* **1.** Able to satisfy a requirement. **2.** Satisfactory or sufficient. — **ad'e·qua·cy** *n.* — **ad'e·quate·ly** *adv.*

**ad·here** (ăd-hîr') *v.* **-hered, -hering. 1.** To stick to as if glued. **2.** To maintain loyalty; follow without deviation. — **ad·her'ence** *n.* — **ad·her'ent** *adj. & n.*

**ad·he·sive** (ăd-hē'sĭv) *adj.* Tending to adhere; sticky. —*n.* An adhesive substance. — **ad·he'sion** *n.*

**ad·ja·cent** (ə-jā'sənt) *adj.* Next to; adjoining.

**ad·jec·tive** (ăj'ĭk-tĭv) *n.* A word used to modify a noun. — **ad·jec·ti'val** *adj.*

**ad·join** (ə-join') *v.* To be next to.

**ad·journ** (ə-jûrn') *v.* To suspend until a later stated time. — **ad·journ'ment** *n.*

**ad·just** (ə-jŭst') *v.* **1.** To regulate or adapt. **2.** To settle a debt or claim). — **ad·just'a·ble** *adj.* — **ad·just'er** *n.* — **ad·just'ment** *n.*

**ad·ju·tant** (ăj'ōō-tənt) *n.* A military assistant to a commander.

**ad·lib** (ăd-lĭb') *v.* **-libbed, -libbing.** To improvise. — *n.* Something ad-libbed.

**ad·min·is·ter** (ăd-mĭn'ĭs-tər) *v.* **1.** To manage. **2.** To give or dispense. **3.** To mete out. — **ad·min'is·tra'tor** *n.*

**ad·min·is·tra·tion** (ăd-mĭn'ĭs-trā'shən) *n.* **1.** The act of administering. **2.** Management. **3.** The executive body of a government. — **ad·min'is·tra'tive** *adj.*

**ad·mi·ral** (ăd'mər-əl) *n.* A naval officer of next-to-highest rank.

**ad·mire** (ăd-mīr') *v.* **-mired, -miring. 1.** To regard with wonder and approval. **2.** To esteem; respect. — **ad'mi·ra·ble** *adj.* — **ad'mi·ra'tion** *n.* — **ad·mir'er** *n.*

**ad·mis·si·ble** (ăd-mĭs'ə-bəl) *adj.* Allowable. — **ad·mis'si·bil'i·ty** *n.*

**ad·mis·sion** (ăd-mĭsh'ən) *n.* **1.** The act of admitting. **2.** An acknowledgment or confession. **3.** The right to enter. **4.** An entrance fee.

**ad·mit** (ăd-mĭt') *v.* **-mitted, -mitting. 1.** To permit to enter. **2.** To allow; permit (with *of*). **3.** To acknowledge; confess. **4.** To concede. — **ad·mit'tance** *n.*

**ad·mon·ish** (ăd-mŏn'ĭsh) *v.* **1.** To reprove. **2.** To counsel against; warn. — **ad·mo·ni'tion,** **ad·mon'ish·ment** *n.* — **ad·mon'i·to'ry** *adj.*

**a·do** (ə-dōō') *n.* Bustle; bother.

**ad·o·les·cence** (ăd'l-ĕs'əns) *n.* The period between puberty and maturity. — **ad'o·les'cent** *adj. & n.*

**a·dopt** (ə-dŏpt') *v.* **1.** To take (a child) into one's family and raise as one's own. **2.** To take up and use or follow. — **a·dop'tion** *n.*

**a·dore** (ə-dôr', ə-dōr') *v.* **adored, adoring. 1.** To worship. **2.** To love deeply. — **a·dor'a·ble** *adj.* — **a·do·ra'tion** *n.*

**a·dorn** (ə-dôrn') *v.* **1.** To enhance. **2.** To decorate, as with ornaments. — **a·dorn'ment** *n.*

**ad·re·nal gland** (ə-drē'nəl). One of two endocrine glands located above the kidneys.

**ad·ren·a·lin** (ə-drĕn'əl-ĭn) *n.* Also **a·dren·a·line.** Epinephrine.

**a·drift** (ə-drĭft') *adv.* Floating; without direction. — **a·drift'** *adj.*

**a·droit** (ə-droit') *adj.* Dexterous. — **a·droit'ly** *adv.*

**a·dult** (ə-dŭlt', ăd'ŭlt') *n.* One who is fully grown or of legal age. —*adj.* Fully developed and mature. — **a·dult'hood** *n.*

**a·dul·ter·ate** (ə-dŭl'tə-rāt') *v.* **-ated, -ating.** To make impure, as by adding improper ingredients. — **a·dul'ter·a'tion** *n.*

**a·dul·ter·y** (ə-dŭl'tər-ē, -trē) *n.,* pl. **-ies.** Marital infidelity. — **a·dul'ter·ous** *adj.*

**ad·vance** (ăd-văns', -väns') *v.* **-vanced, -vancing. 1.** To move forward. **2.** To propose. **3.** To make progress or aid the progress of. **4.** To raise or rise in rank, amount, etc. **5.** To pay (money) beforehand. —*n.* **1.** The act of moving forward. **2.** Improvement; progress. **3.** A rise in price or value. **4.** Payment of money before legally due. —*adj.* **1.** Prior. **2.** Going before. — **ad·vance'ment** *n.*

**ad·van·tage** (ăd-văn′tĭj, ăd-vän′-) n. **1.** A favorable position or factor. **2.** Benefit; gain. — **ad·van·ta′geous** adj.

**ad·ven·ture** (ăd-věn′chər) n. **1.** A risky undertaking. **2.** An exciting experience. — **ad·ven′tur·ous** adj.

**ad·verb** (ăd′vûrb′) n. A word used to modify a verb, an adjective, or another adverb. — **ad·ver′bi·al** adj.

**ad·ver·sar·y** (ăd′vər-sĕr′ē) n., pl. **-ies.** An opponent; enemy.

**ad·verse** (ăd-vûrs′, ăd′vûrs′) adj. **1.** Actively opposed; hostile. **2.** Unfavorable.

**ad·ver·si·ty** (ăd-vûr′sə-tē) n., pl. **-ties.** Hardship; misfortune.

**ad·ver·tise** (ăd′vər-tīz′) v. **-tised, -tising.** To call public attention to so as to promote sales. — **ad·ver·tise′ment** n. — **ad·ver′tis·ing** n.

**ad·vice** (ăd-vīs′) n. Opinion about a course of action; counsel.

**ad·vis·a·ble** (ăd-vī′zə-bəl) adj. Prudent; expedient. — **ad·vis·a·bil′i·ty** n.

**ad·vise** (ăd-vīz′) v. **-vised, -vising. 1.** To offer advice to; recommend. **2.** To inform. — **ad·vis′er, ad·vi′sor** n. — **ad·vi′so·ry** adj.

**ad·vo·cate** (ăd′və-kāt′) v. **-cated, -cating.** To speak in favor of; recommend. —n. (-kĭt, -kāt′). **1.** One who argues for a cause or person; a supporter. **2.** A lawyer. — **ad′vo·ca·cy** n.

**aer·ate** (âr′āt′) v. **-ated, -ating.** To supply or charge with air or gas. — **aer·a′tion** n.

**aer·i·al** (âr′ē-əl) adj. **1.** Of, in, or caused by the air. **2.** Lofty. **3.** Airy. —n. An antenna.

**aer·ie** (âr′ē, ĭr′ē) n. A high nest, as of an eagle.

**aer·o·nau·tics** (âr′ə-nô′tĭks) n. **1.** The design and construction of aircraft. **2.** Aircraft navigation. — **aer′o·nau′tic, aer′o·nau′ti·cal** adj.

**aer·o·space** (âr′ō-spās′) adj. **1.** Of the earth's atmosphere and the space beyond. **2.** Of the science or technology of flight. — **aer′o·space′** n.

**aes·thete, es·thete** (ĕs′thēt′) n. One who cultivates a superior appreciation of the beautiful.

**aes·thet·ic, es·thet·ic** (ĕs-thĕt′ĭk) adj. **1.** Of aesthetics. **2.** Of the beautiful; artistic. —n. **aesthetics, esthetics.** (takes sing. v.). The philosophical study of the beautiful and of the fine arts.

**af·fa·ble** (ăf′ə-bəl) adj. **1.** Amiable. **2.** Mild; gentle. — **af′fa·bil′i·ty** n.

**af·fair** (ə-fâr′) n. **1.** Anything done or to be done. **2. affairs.** Business matters. **3.** A sexual involvement.

**af·fect**[1] (ə-fĕkt′) v. **1.** To bring about a change in. **2.** To touch the emotions of.

**af·fect**[2] (ə-fĕkt′) v. **1.** To simulate so as to impress; feign. **2.** To fancy; prefer. — **af·fec·ta′tion** n. — **af·fect′ed** adj.

**af·fec·tion** (ə-fĕk′shən) n. A tender feeling toward another; fondness. — **af·fec′tion·ate** adj.

**af·fi·da·vit** (ăf′ə-dā′vĭt) n. A written statement made under oath.

**af·fil·i·ate** (ə-fĭl′ē-āt′) v. **-ated, -ating. 1.** To adopt as a subordinate associate. **2.** To associate (with). —n. (-ĭt). An associate or subordinate. — **af·fil′i·a′tion** n.

**af·fin·i·ty** (ə-fĭn′ĭ-tē) n., pl. **-ties. 1.** An attraction. **2.** Relationship; kinship.

**af·firm** (ə-fûrm′) v. **1.** To maintain to be true. **2.** To confirm. — **af·fir·ma′tion** n.

**af·firm·a·tive** (ə-fûr′mə-tĭv) adj. **1.** Giving assent. **2.** Confirming. —n. A word signifying assent.

**af·fix** (ə-fĭks′) v. **1.** To attach. **2.** To append. —n. (ăf′ĭks′). Something attached or added, esp. a prefix or suffix.

**af·flict** (ə-flĭkt′) v. To inflict suffering upon; cause distress to. — **af·flic′tion** n.

**af·flu·ence** (ăf′lōō-əns) n. Wealth; abundance. — **af′flu·ent** adj.

**af·ford** (ə-fôrd′, ə-fōrd′) v. **1.** To have the financial means for. **2.** To be able to spare or give up. **3.** To provide.

**af·front** (ə-frŭnt′) v. To offend. —n. An insult.

**a·fraid** (ə-frād′) adj. **1.** Filled with fear. **2.** Reluctant; averse.

**a·fresh** (ə-frĕsh′) adv. Anew; again.

**aft** (ăft, äft) adv. At, in, or toward the stern of a vessel. —adj. Situated near or at the stern.

**af·ter** (ăf′tər, äf′-) prep. **1.** Behind in place or order. **2.** In pursuit of. **3.** At a later time than. **4.** In the style of. **5.** Past the hour of. —adv. **1.** Behind. **2.** Later. —adj. Later; following. —conj. Subsequent to the time than.

**af·ter·math** (ăf′tər-măth′, äf′-) n. A consequence or result.

**af·ter·noon** (ăf′tər-nōōn′, äf′-) n. The day from noon until sunset.

**af·ter·ward** (ăf′tər-wərd, äf′-) adv. Also **af·ter·wards.** In or at a later time; subsequently.

**a·gain** (ə-gĕn′) adv. **1.** Once more. **2.** To a previous place or position. **3.** Furthermore.

**a·gainst** (ə-gĕnst′) prep. **1.** In a direction or course opposite to. **2.** So as to come into contact with. **3.** In opposition to.

**age** (āj) n. **1.** The length of time someone or

something has existed. **2.** The time in life when one officially assumes certain rights. **3.** A distinctive period or stage. **4.** The state of being old. —v. **aged, aging** or **ageing.** To grow or cause to grow old. —**a′ged** adj.

**a·gen·cy** (ā′jən-sē) n., pl. **-cies. 1.** Action; operation. **2.** A means. **3.** A business or service acting for others.

**a·gen·da** (ə-jĕn′də) pl.n. Sing. **-dum.** A list of things to be done.

**a·gent** (ā′jənt) n. **1.** One that acts. **2.** One that acts as the representative of another. **3.** A means; instrument.

**ag·glom·er·ate** (ə-glŏm′ə-rāt′) v. **-ated, -ating.** To form into a rounded mass. —**ag·glom′er·a′tion** n.

**ag·gra·vate** (ăg′rə-vāt′) v. **-vated, -vating. 1.** To make worse. **2.** To annoy.—**ag′gra·va′tion** n.

**ag·gre·gate** (ăg′rə-gĭt′) adj. Gathered together into a mass. —n. A collective mass; total. —v. (-gāt′) **-gated, -gating.** To gather into a mass. —**ag′gre·ga′tion** n.

**ag·gres·sion** (ə-grĕsh′ən) n. **1.** An assault. **2.** Hostile action or behavior. —**ag·gres′sive** adj. —**ag·gres′sor** n.

**a·ghast** (ə-găst′, ə-gäst′) adj. Horror-stricken; appalled.

**ag·ile** (ăj′əl, ăj′īl) adj. Quick; nimble. —**a·gil′i·ty** n.

**ag·i·tate** (ăj′ə-tāt′) v. **-tated, -tating. 1.** To stir up violently. **2.** To upset; disturb. **3.** To arouse public interest. —**ag′i·ta′tion** n. —**ag′i·ta′tor** n.

**ag·nos·tic** (ăg-nŏs′tĭk) n. One who doubts the possibility of knowing the existence of God. —**ag·nos′tic** adj. —**ag·nos′ti·cism′** n.

**a·go** (ə-gō′) adj. & adv. Gone by; past.

**ag·o·nize** (ăg′ə-nīz′) v. **-nized, -nizing.** To suffer great distress.

**ag·o·ny** (ăg′ə-nē) n., pl. **-nies.** Intense pain or distress.

**a·gree** (ə-grē′) v. **agreed, agreeing. 1.** To consent. **2.** To be in accord. **3.** To have the same opinion. **4.** To be beneficial. **5.** To correspond, as in grammatical number. —**a·gree′ment** n.

**a·gree·a·ble** (ə-grē′ə-bəl) adj. **1.** Pleasing; pleasant. **2.** Willing. —**a·gree′a·bly** adv.

**ag·ri·cul·ture** (ăg′rĭ-kŭl′chər) n. Cultivation of crops and raising livestock; farming. —**ag′ri·cul′tur·al** adj. —**ag′ri·cul′tur·ist** n.

**a·head** (ə-hĕd′) adv. **1.** At or to the front. **2.** Before; in advance. **3.** Onward; forward.

**aid** (ād) v. To help; assist. —n. **1.** Help; assistance.

**aide** (ād) n. An assistant.

**aim** (ām) v. **1.** To direct (a weapon, blow, etc.). **2.** To direct one's efforts or purpose. —n. **1.** The act of aiming. **2.** The direction of something aimed. **3.** Purpose; intention. —**aim′less** adj.

**ain't** (ānt). Contraction of am not, is not, has not, and have not.

**air** (âr) n. **1.** A gaseous mixture that surrounds the earth. **2.** An impression; appearance. **3.** airs. Affectation. **4.** A melody. —v. **1.** To expose to air. **2.** To give public utterance to.

**air-con·di·tion** (âr′kən-dĭsh′ən) v. To control, esp. lower, the temperature and humidity of (an enclosure). —**air conditioner.** —**air conditioning.**

**air·craft** (âr′krăft′, -krăft′) n., pl. **-craft.** Any machine or device capable of flight.

**air·plane** (âr′plān′) n. A winged, heavier-than-air flying machine propelled by jet engines or propellers.

**air·port** (âr′pôrt′, -pōrt′) n. A place with cargo and passenger facilities where aircraft take off and land.

**air·y** (âr′ē) adj. **-ier, -iest. 1.** Of or like air. **2.** Breezy. **3.** Graceful or delicate. —**air′i·ly** adv.

**aisle** (īl) n. A passageway between rows of seats.

**a·jar** (ə-jär′) adv. & adj. Partially open.

**a·kim·bo** (ə-kĭm′bō) adj. & adv. With the hands on the hips.

**a·kin** (ə-kĭn′) adj. **1.** Related. **2.** Similar.

**a·lac·ri·ty** (ə-lăk′rə-tē) n. Cheerful eagerness; sprightliness.

**a·larm** (ə-lärm′) n. **1.** A sudden feeling of fear. **2.** A warning of danger. **3.** A device sounded to warn people of danger. —v. To fill with alarm; frighten. —**a·larm′ing** adj. —**a·larm′ing·ly** adv.

**al·ba·tross** (ăl′bə-trôs′, -trŏs′) n. A large, web-footed sea bird.

**al·bi·no** (ăl-bī′nō) n., pl. **-nos.** A person or animal having abnormally pale skin, very light hair, and lacking normal eye coloring.

**al·bum** (ăl′bəm) n. **1.** A blank book for stamps, photographs, etc. **2.** One or more phonograph records in one binding.

**al·bu·men** (ăl-byōō′mən) n. The white of an egg.

**al·che·my** (ăl′kə-mē) n. An early kind of chemistry concerned primarily with changing common metals into gold. —**al′che·mist** n.

**al·co·hol** (ăl′kə-hôl′) n. **1.** Any of a series of

chemically related organic compounds. **2.** An intoxicating liquor. —**al·co·hol·ic** *adj.* & *n.* —**al·co·hol·ism'** *n.*

**al·cove** (ăl'kōv') *n.* A recess of a room.

**al·der·man** (ôl'dər-mən) *n.* A member of a municipal legislative body. —

**ale** (āl) *n.* A beverage similar to beer.

**a·lert** (ə-lûrt') *adj.* **1.** Vigilant; watchful. **2.** Mentally responsive; quick. —*n.* **1.** A warning signal. **2.** The period during which such a warning is in effect. —*v.* To warn. —**a·lert'ness** *n.*

**al·fal·fa** (ăl-făl'fə) *n.* A cloverlike plant cultivated for forage.

**al·gae** (ăl'jē) *pl.n.* Mostly aquatic plants, as the seaweeds.

**al·ge·bra** (ăl'jə-brə) *n.* A form of mathematics dealing with symbols, equations, etc. —**al'ge·bra'ic** *adj.*

**a·li·as** (ā'lē-əs, āl'yəs) *n.* An assumed name. —*adv.* Otherwise named.

**al·i·bi** (ăl'ə-bī') *n.* **1.** A legal defense in which a defendant tries to prove he was elsewhere when a crime was committed. **2.** An excuse.

**a·li·en** (ā'lē-ən, āl'yən) *adj.* **1.** Foreign; unfamiliar. **2.** Repugnant. —*n.* An unnaturalized resident of a country.

**a·li·en·ate** (āl'yən-āt', ā'lē-ən-) *v.* -ated, -ating. To make unfriendly or indifferent. —**al'ien·a'tion** *n.*

**a·light¹** (ə-līt') *v.* alighted or alit, alighting. **1.** To come down and settle. **2.** To dismount.

**a·light²** (ə-līt') *adj.* & *adv.* Burning; lighted.

**a·lign** (ə-līn') *v.* **1.** To arrange in a line. **2.** To ally (oneself) with; take sides. —**a·lign'ment** *n.*

**a·like** (ə-līk') *adj.* Similar. —*adv.* In the same way.

**al·i·mo·ny** (ăl'ə-mō'nē) *n., pl.* -nies. An allowance for support paid to a former spouse.

**a·lit** (ə-līt') *p.t.* & *p.p.* of alight.

**a·live** (ə-līv') *adj.* **1.** Having life; living. **2.** In operation; active. **3.** Full of life; lively.

**all** (ôl) *adj.* **1.** The total extent, number, or quantity of. **2.** Every. **3.** Any. **4.** Nothing but. —*pron.* Each and every one. —*n.* The whole number; totality. —*adv.* Wholly; entirely.

**al·lay** (ə-lā') *v.* **1.** To lessen; relieve. **2.** To calm; pacify.

**al·lege** (ə-lěj') *v.* -leged, -leging. To assert, esp. without proof. —**al'le·ga'tion** *n.* —**al·leg'ed·ly** *adv.*

**al·le·giance** (ə-lē'jəns) *n.* Loyalty to a nation, sovereign, or cause.

**al·le·go·ry** (ăl'ə-gôr'ē, -gōr'ē) *n., pl.* -ries. A story in which the characters represent abstract qualities. —**al'le·gor'ic, al'le·gor'i·cal** *adj.*

**al·ler·gy** (ăl'ər-jē) *n., pl.* -gies. Hypersensitive reaction to a substance harmless to most people. —**al·ler'gic** *adj.*

**al·le·vi·ate** (ə-lē'vē-āt') *v.* -ated, -ating. To make more bearable. —**al·le'vi·a'tion** *n.*

**al·ley** (ăl'ē) *n., pl.* -leys. A narrow passageway between or behind buildings.

**al·li·ance** (ə-lī'əns) *n.* **1.** An agreement to join forces or work together. **2.** A connection; union.

**al·li·ga·tor** (ăl'ə-gā'tər) *n.* A large reptile with a shorter snout than the related crocodiles.

**al·lit·er·a·tion** (ə-lĭt'ə-rā'shən) *n.* The occurrence of two or more words having the same initial sound. —**al·lit'er·a'tive** *adj.*

**al·lo·cate** (ăl'ō-kāt', ăl'ə-) *v.* -cated, -cating. To allot; assign. —**al·lo·ca'tion** *n.*

**al·lot** (ə-lŏt') *v.* -lotted, -lotting. To distribute; give. —**al·lot'ment** *n.*

**al·low** (ə-lou') *v.* **1.** To let happen; permit. **2.** To acknowledge or admit. **3.** To make provision. **4.** To provide. —**al·low'a·ble** *adj.*

**al·low·ance** (ə-lou'əns) *n.* A regular provision, as of money.

**al·loy** (ăl'oi', ə-loi') *n.* A mixture of metals. —**al·loy'** *v.*

**all right.** **1.** Satisfactory; average. **2.** Correct. **3.** Uninjured. **4.** Very well; yes.

**al·lude** (ə-lōōd') *v.* -luded, -luding. To refer to indirectly. —**al·lu'sion** *n.*

**al·lure** (ə-lōōr') *v.* -lured, -luring. To entice; tempt. —*n.* The power to entice. —**al·lur'ing·ly** *adv.*

**al·ly** (ə-lī', ăl'ī') *v.* -lied, -lying. To unite or join for a specific purpose. —*n.* (ăl'ī') *pl.* -lies. A nation or person that is allied to another.

**al·ma·nac** (ôl'mə-năk', ăl'-) *n.* A calendar with weather forecasts and other useful information.

**al·might·y** (ôl-mī'tē) *adj.* Omnipotent. —*n.* —**the Almighty.** God.

**al·mond** (ä'mənd, ăm'ənd) *n.* An oval, edible nut with a light-brown shell.

**al·most** (ôl'mōst', ôl-mōst') *adv.* Nearly; not quite.

**alms** (ämz) *pl.n.* Money or goods given to the poor.

**a·lone** (ə-lōn') *adj.* **1.** Apart from other people; single; solitary. **2.** Sole; only. —**a·lone'** *adv.*

**a·long** (ə-lông', ə-lŏng') *adv.* **1.** In a line

with. **2.** Forward. **3.** In association; together-er. —*prep.* In a line with; by the length of.

**a·long·side** (ə-lông'sīd', ə-lŏng'-) *adv.* Along, at, or to the side. —*prep.* By the side of.

**a·loof** (ə-lōof') *adj.* Distant; reserved. —**a·loof'ness** *n.*

**al·pha·bet** (ăl'fə-bĕt', -bǐt) *n.* The letters of a language, arranged in a fixed order. —**al'pha·bet'i·cal** *adj.* —**al'pha·bet'i·cal·ly** *adv.* —**al'pha·bet·ize'** *v.*

**al·read·y** (ôl-rĕd'ē) *adv.* By this time.

**al·so** (ôl'sō) *adv.* Besides; in addition.

**al·tar** (ôl'tər) *n.* An elevated structure used in religious ceremonies.

**al·ter** (ôl'tər) *v.* To change; modify. —**al'ter·a'tion** *n.*

**al·ter·nate** (ôl'tər-nāt', ăl'-) *v.* -nated, -nating. **1.** To do, use, occur, etc., in turn. **2.** To go back and forth. —*adj.* (-nĭt). **1.** Happening or following in turns. **2.** Every other. **3.** Substitute. —*n.* (-nĭt). A substitute. —**al'ter·na'tion** *n.*

**al·ter·na·tive** (ôl-tûr'nə-tĭv, ăl-) *n.* A choice between possibilities. —*adj.* Allowing or furnishing a choice.

**al·though** (ôl-thō') *conj.* Also **al·tho.** Regardless of the fact that.

**al·ti·tude** (ăl'tə-t/yōod') *n.* Height, esp. above the earth's surface.

**al·to** (ăl'tō) *n., pl.* **-tos.** A low female singing voice.

**al·to·geth·er** (ôl'tə-gĕth'ər, ôl'tə-gĕth'ər) *adv.* Entirely.

**al·tru·ism** (ăl'trōō-ĭz'əm) *n.* Selfless concern for others. —**al'tru·ist** *n.* —**al'tru·is'tic** *adj.*

**a·lu·mi·num** (ə-lōo'mə-nəm) *n.* A metallic element used to form many hard, light alloys.

**a·lum·na** (ə-lŭm'nə) *n., pl.* **-nae.** A female graduate of a school, college, or university.

**a·lum·nus** (ə-lŭm'nəs) *n., pl.* **-ni.** A male graduate of a school, college, or university.

**al·ways** (ôl'wāz, -wĭz) *adv.* **1.** On every occasion. **2.** Continuously.

**am** (ăm; *unstressed* əm). 1st person sing. present indicative of **be.**

**a·mass** (ə-măs') *v.* To accumulate.

**am·a·teur** (ăm'ə-chŏor', -ə-tər, -ə-t/yŏor') *n.* **1.** One who engages in an activity for pleasure, not pay. **2.** An inept practitioner. —**am'a·teur'ish** *adj.*

**a·maze** (ə-māz') *v.* **amazed, amazing.** To surprise; astound. —**a·maze'ment** *n.*

**am·bas·sa·dor** (ăm-băs'ə-dər, -dôr') *n.* A diplomat of the highest rank. —**am·bas·sa·do'ri·al** *adj.*

**am·bi·ance** (ăm'bē-əns) *n.* Surroundings; atmosphere.

**am·bi·dex·trous** (ăm'bĭ-dĕk'strəs) *adj.* Able to use both hands with equal facility.

**am·big·u·ous** (ăm-bĭg'yōō-əs) *adj.* Having more than one meaning; unclear. —**am·big'u·i·ty, am·big'u·ous·ness** *n.*

**am·bi·tion** (ăm-bĭsh'ən) *n.* **1.** A strong desire to achieve something; will to succeed. **2.** A goal. —**am·bi'tious** *adj.*

**am·biv·a·lence** (ăm-bĭv'ə-ləns) *n.* The existence of conflicting feelings about a person or thing. —**am·biv'a·lent** *adj.*

**am·bu·lance** (ăm'byə-ləns) *n.* A vehicle to transport the sick or wounded.

**am·bu·la·to·ry** (ăm'byə-lə-tôr'ē, -tōr'ē) *adj.* Involving or capable of walking.

**am·bush** (ăm'bŏosh') *n.* **1.** A surprise attack from a concealed position. **2.** The concealed position from which such an attack is made. —**am'bush'** *v.*

**a·men** (ä-mĕn', ā-) *interj.* So be it.

**a·me·na·ble** (ə-mē'nə-bəl, ə-mĕn'ə-) *adj.* Agreeable; responsive.

**a·mend** (ə-mĕnd') *v.* **1.** To improve. **2.** To correct; rectify. **3.** To alter (a law) formally. —**a·mend'ment** *n.*

**a·mends** (ə-mĕndz') *pl.n.* Compensation for insult or injury; redress.

**a·men·i·ty** (ə-mĕn'ə-tē, ə-mē'nə-) *n., pl.* **-ties. 1.** Pleasantness. **2.** A comfort or convenience. **3.** **amenities.** Social courtesies.

**am·e·thyst** (ăm'ə-thĭst) *n.* A purple quartz used as a gemstone.

**a·mi·a·ble** (ā'mē-ə-bəl) *adj.* **1.** Goodnatured. **2.** Cordial; friendly. —**a'mi·a·bil'i·ty** *n.*

**am·i·ca·ble** (ăm'ĭ-kə-bəl) *adj.* Friendly. —**am'i·ca·bly** *adv.*

**a·mid** (ə-mĭd') *prep.* Also **a·midst.** Among.

**a·miss** (ə-mĭs') *adj.* Wrong. —*adv.* In an improper way.

**am·i·ty** (ăm'ə-tē) *n.* Friendly relations.

**am·mo·nia** (ə-mōn'yə) *n.* A colorless, pungent gas.

**am·mu·ni·tion** (ăm'yə-nĭsh'ən) *n.* Bullets, shells, etc. that can be fired from guns.

**am·ne·sia** (ăm-nē'zhə) *n.* Loss of memory.

**am·nes·ty** (ăm'nə-stē) *n., pl.* **-ties.** A general pardon, esp. for political offenders.

**a·moe·ba, a·me·ba** (ə-mē'bə) *n., pl.* **-bas** or **-bae.** A one-celled organism that has a changeable form. —**a·moe'bic** *adj.*

**a·mong** (ə-mŭng') *prep.* Also **a·mongst. 1.** In or through the midst of. **2.** In the group or

company of. **3.** With portions to each of.
**4.** Between one another.

**a·mor·phous** (ə-môr′fəs) *adj.* Lacking definite form or shape.

**am·or·tize** (ăm′ər-tīz′, ə-môr′tīz′) *v.* **-tized, -tizing.** To pay off (as a debt) by installments. — **am′or·ti·za′tion** *n.*

**a·mount** (ə-mount′) *n.* **1.** A total or sum. **2.** Quantity. — *v.* **1.** To reach as a total. **2.** To be equivalent.

**am·phib·i·an** (ăm-fĭb′ē-ən) *n.* **1.** An animal, as a frog, that can live in water and on land. **2.** A vehicle that can travel in water and on land. — *adj.* Amphibious.

**am·phib·i·ous** (ăm-fĭb′ē-əs) *adj.* Able to live or operate both in water and on land.

**am·phi·the·a·ter** (ăm′fə-thē′ə-tər) *n.* An oval structure with tiers of seats rising around an arena.

**am·ple** (ăm′pəl) *adj.* **-pler, -plest. 1.** Large. **2.** Sufficient; abundant. — **am′ply** *adv.*

**am·pli·fy** (ăm′plə-fī′) *v.* **-fied, -fying. 1.** To enlarge, extend, or increase. **2.** To make louder. — **am′pli·fi·ca′tion** *n.* — **am′pli·fi′er** *n.*

**am·pli·tude** (ăm′plə-t/y/ōōd′) *n.* **1.** Abundance; fullness. **2.** Greatness of size; extent.

**am·pu·tate** (ăm′pyōō-tāt′) *v.* **-tated, -tating.** To cut off, as a limb. — **am′pu·ta′tion** *n.* — **am′pu·tee′** *n.*

**a·muck** (ə-mŭk′) *adv.* Also **a·mok.** In a fit of wildness.

**am·u·let** (ăm′yə-lĭt) *n.* A charm worn against evil or injury.

**a·muse** (ə-myōōz′) *v.* **amused, amusing.** To entertain; divert. — **a·muse′ment** *n.*

**an** (ăn, ən) A form of *a* used before words beginning with a vowel.

**a·nach·ro·nism** (ə-năk′rə-nĭz′əm) *n.* Something that is out of its proper time. — **a·nach′ro·nis′tic** *adj.*

**an·al·ge·sic** (ăn′əl-jē′sĭk) *n.* A drug that relieves pain.

**a·nal·o·gy** (ə-năl′ə-jē) *n., pl.* **-gies.** Correspondence in some respects; partial similarity. — **a·nal′o·gous** *adj.*

**a·nal·y·sis** (ə-năl′ĭ-sĭs) *n., pl.* **-ses. 1.** The separation of a whole into its parts for study and interpretation. **2.** Psychoanalysis. — **an′a·lyst** *n.* — **an′a·lyt′ic, an′a·lyt′i·cal** *adj.* — **an′a·lyze′** *v.*

**an·ar·chy** (ăn′ər-kē) *n., pl.* **-chies. 1.** Absence of political authority. **2.** Disorder and confusion. — **an·ar′chic** *adj.*

**a·nat·o·my** (ə-năt′ə-mē) *n., pl.* **-mies. 1.** The structure of an organism. **2.** The science of the structure of organisms. — **an′a·tom′ic, an′a-**

**a·tom′i·cal** *adj.*

**an·ces·tor** (ăn′sĕs′tər) *n.* A person from whom another has descended. — **an′ces′try** *n.*

**an·chor** (ăng′kər) *n.* A heavy metal device cast overboard to keep a ship in place. — *v.* To hold or be held fast or secure.

**an·cient** (ān′shənt) *adj.* **1.** Very old. **2.** Belonging to times long past.

**and** (ənd, ən; *stressed* ănd) *conj.* **1.** Together with; as well as. **2.** Added to; plus. **3.** As a result.

**and·i·ron** (ănd′ī′ərn) *n.* One of a pair of metal supports for logs in a fireplace.

**an·ec·dote** (ăn′ĭk-dōt′) *n.* A short account of an interesting or humorous incident. — **an′ec·do′tal** *adj.*

**a·ne·mi·a** (ə-nē′mē-ə) *n.* Also **a·nae·mi·a.** A deficiency in the oxygen-carrying material of the blood. — **a·ne′mic** *adj.*

**a·nem·o·ne** (ə-nĕm′ə-nē) *n.* A plant having cup-shaped flowers.

**an·es·the·sia** (ăn′ĭs-thē′zhə) *n.* Also **an·aes·the·sia.** Loss of sensation.

**an·es·thet·ic** (ăn′ĭs-thĕt′ĭk) *adj.* Also **an·aes·thet·ic.** Causing anesthesia. — *n.* An anesthetic agent. — **an·es′the·tist** *n.* — **an·es′the·tize′** *v.*

**an·gel** (ān′jəl) *n.* **1.** One of the immortal beings attendant upon God. **2.** A kind and lovable person. — **an·gel′ic** *adj.*

**an·ger** (ăng′gər) *n.* Wrath; rage. — *v.* To make or become angry.

**an·gle¹** (ăng′gəl) *v.* **-gled, -gling.** To fish with a hook and line. — **an′gler** *n.*

**an·gle²** (ăng′gəl) *n.* **1.** The figure formed by two lines diverging from a common point. **2.** A point of view. — *v.* **-gled, -gling.** To move or turn at an angle.

**an·gry** (ăng′grē) *adj.* **-grier, -griest. 1.** Feeling or showing anger. **2.** Having a menacing aspect. — **an′gri·ly** *adv.*

**an·guish** (ăng′gwĭsh) *n.* Great physical or mental pain; torment. — **an′guished** *adj.*

**an·gu·lar** (ăng′gyə-lər) *adj.* **1.** Having an angle or angles. **2.** Bony and lean. — **an′gu·lar′i·ty** *n.*

**an·i·mal** (ăn′ə-məl) *n.* **1.** An organism distinguished from a plant by such characteristics as the ability to move. **2.** A bestial person; brute. — *adj.* **1.** Of animals. **2.** Sensual or physical as distinguished from spiritual.

**an·i·mate** (ăn′ə-māt′) *v.* **-mated, -mating. 1.** To give life to. **2.** To enliven. **3.** To make (a cartoon) so as to convey the illusion of motion. — *adj.* (-mĭt). Living. — **an′i·ma′tion**

*n.*

**an-kle** (ăng′kəl) *n.* The joint that connects the foot with the leg.

**an-nex** (ə-něks′, ăn′ěks′) *v.* To add or join, esp. to a larger thing. —*n.* (ăn′ěks′). A building added on to a larger one. —**an′nex-a′tion** *n.*

**an-ni-hi-late** (ə-nī′ə-lāt′) *v.* -**lated, -lating.** To destroy completely. —**an-ni′hi-la′tion** *n.*

**an-ni-ver-sa-ry** (ăn′ə-vûr′sər-ē) *n., pl.* -**ries.** The annual return, often celebrated, of the date of an important event.

**an-no-tate** (ăn′ō-tāt′) *v.* -**tated, -tating.** To furnish with explanatory notes. —**an′no-ta′tion** *n.*

**an-nounce** (ə-nouns′) *v.* -**nounced, -nouncing.** To bring to public notice; proclaim. —**an-nounce′ment** *n.* —**an-nounc′er** *n.*

**an-noy** (ə-noi′) *v.* To bother or irritate. —**an-noy′ance** *n.*

**an-nu-al** (ăn′yōō-əl) *adj.* Yearly. —*n.* **1.** A yearly periodical. **2.** A plant that lives for one year or season.

**an-nul** (ə-nŭl′) *v.* -**nulled, -nulling.** To nullify or cancel, as a marriage. —**an-nul′ment** *n.*

**a-nom-a-ly** (ə-nŏm′ə-lē) *n., pl.* -**lies.** A deviation from the normal; abnormality. —**a-nom′a-lous** *adj.*

**a-non** (ə-nŏn′) *adv.* In a short time; soon.

**a-non-y-mous** (ə-nŏn′ə-məs) *adj.* Having an unknown or withheld name. —**an′o-nym′i-ty,** **a-non′y-mous-ness** *n.*

**an-oth-er** (ə-nŭth′ər) *adj.* **1.** Additional; one more. **2.** Different; some other. —*pron.* **1.** An additional or different one. **2.** One of the same kind.

**an-swer** (ăn′sər, ăn′-) *n.* **1.** A reply, as to a question. **2.** A solution or result. —*v.* **1.** To reply to. **2.** To respond correctly to. **3.** To serve (a purpose). **4.** To be responsible. —**an′swer-a-ble** *adj.*

**ant** (ănt) *n.* An insect, usually wingless, living in colonies.

**an-tag-o-nism** (ăn-tăg′ə-nĭz′əm) *n.* Opposition; hostility. —**an-tag′o-nist** *n.* —**an-tag′o-nis′tic** *adj.*

**an-tag-o-nize** (ăn-tăg′ə-nīz′) *v.* -**nized, -nizing.** To arouse the hostility of.

**an-te-ce-dent** (ăn′tə-sēd′ənt) *adj.* Going before; preceding. —*n.* **1.** One that precedes another. **2.** A word or phrase to which a pronoun refers.

**an-te-lope** (ăn′tə-lōp′) *n.* A swift-running, long-horned hoofed mammal.

**an-ten-na** (ăn-těn′ə) *n.* **1.** *pl.* -**nae.** One of the feelers on the head of an insect, crustacean,

etc. **2.** *pl.* -**nas.** A metallic apparatus for sending and receiving electromagnetic waves; aerial.

**an-te-ri-or** (ăn-tîr′ē-ər) *adj.* **1.** Located in front. **2.** Earlier.

**an-them** (ăn′thəm) *n.* A patriotic or religious song.

**an-thol-o-gy** (ăn-thŏl′ə-jē) *n., pl.* -**gies.** A collection of literary pieces.

**an-thro-pol-o-gy** (ăn′thrə-pŏl′ə-jē) *n.* The study of the origin, culture, and development of man. —**an′thro-po-log′ic, an′thro-po-log′i-cal** *adj.* —**an′thro-pol′o-gist** *n.*

**an-ti-bi-ot-ic** (ăn′tĭ-bī-ŏt′ĭk, ăn′tĭ-) *n.* A substance, often produced by fungi or bacteria, that destroys or inhibits the growth of microorganisms.

**an-ti-bod-y** (ăn′tĭ-bŏd′ē) *n., pl.* -**ies.** A protein in the blood generated to combat foreign substances.

**an-tic** (ăn′tĭk) *n.* A playful or ludicrous act; a caper.

**an-tic-i-pate** (ăn-tĭs′ə-pāt′) *v.* -**pated, -pating.** **1.** To realize beforehand; foresee. **2.** To look forward to. **3.** To prevent; forestall. —**an-tic′i-pa′tion** *n.*

**an-ti-cli-max** (ăn′tĭ-klī′măks′) *n.* A decline in disappointing contrast to what has preceded.

**an-ti-dote** (ăn′tĭ-dōt′) *n.* Something that counteracts a poison or injury.

**an-tip-a-thy** (ăn-tĭp′ə-thē) *n., pl.* -**thies.** An intense dislike.

**an-tique** (ăn-tēk′) *adj.* Belonging to an earlier period. —*n.* An object having special value because of its age. —*v.* -**tiqued, -tiquing.** To give the appearance of an antique to.

**an-tiq-ui-ty** (ăn-tĭk′wə-tē) *n., pl.* -**ties.** **1.** Ancient times. **2.** Great age. **3. antiquities.** Relics and monuments of former times.

**an-ti-sep-tic** (ăn′tĭ-sĕp′tĭk) *adj.* **1.** Capable of destroying harmful bacteria. **2.** Thoroughly clean. **3.** Austere; drab. —*n.* An antiseptic substance.

**ant-ler** (ănt′lər) *n.* One of the paired bony growths on the head of a deer.

**an-to-nym** (ăn′tə-nĭm′) *n.* A word opposite in meaning to another.

**a-nus** (ā′nəs) *n., pl.* **anuses.** The excretory opening of the digestive system.

**an-vil** (ăn′vĭl) *n.* A block on which metals are shaped by hammering.

**anx-i-e-ty** (ăng-zī′ə-tē) *n., pl.* -**ties.** A feeling of uneasiness; worry.

**anx-ious** (ăngk′shəs, ăng′shəs) *adj.* **1.** Worried about some uncertainty. **2.** Desirous;

eager. — **anx'ious·ly** adv.

**an·y** (ĕn'ē) adj. **1.** One, no matter which, from three or more. **2.** Some. —pron. **1.** Any one or ones. **2.** Any quantity or part.

**an·y·bod·y** (ĕn'ē-bŏd'ē, -bŭd-ē) pron. Anyone.

**an·y·how** (ĕn'ē-hou') adv. **1.** In any way. **2.** In any case.

**an·y·one** (ĕn'ē-wŭn', -wən) pron. Any person.

**an·y·thing** (ĕn'ē-thĭng) pron. Any object or matter whatever.

**an·y·way** (ĕn'ē-wā') adv. **1.** In any manner. **2.** Nevertheless.

**an·y·where** (ĕn'ē-hwâr') adv. To, in, or at any place.

**a·or·ta** (ā-ôr'tə) n., pl. **-tas** or **-tae.** The main artery carrying blood away from the heart.

**a·part·ment** (ə-pärt'mənt) n. A room or suite of rooms for dwelling.

**a·pa·thy** (ăp'ə-thē) n. Lack of emotion or interest; indifference. — **ap'a·thet'ic** adj.

**ape** (āp) n. A large primate such as a chimpanzee. —v. **aped, aping.** To mimic.

**aph·o·rism** (ăf'ə-rĭz'əm) n. A maxim; adage.

**a·pi·ar·y** (ā'pē-ĕr'ē) n., pl. **-ies.** A place where bees are raised.

**a·piece** (ə-pēs') adv. To or for each one.

**a·plomb** (ə-plŏm', ə-plŭm') n. Self-confidence; poise.

**a·pol·o·gy** (ə-pŏl'ə-jē) n., pl. **-gies. 1.** An expression of regret. **2.** A formal justification or defense. — **a·pol'o·get'ic** adj. — **a·pol'o·gist** n. — **a·pol'o·gize'** v.

**a·pos·tle** (ə-pŏs'əl) n. **1. Apostle.** One of Christ's 12 original disciples. **2.** One who leads a new cause.

**a·pos·tro·phe** (ə-pŏs'trə-fē) n. The sign (') used to indicate the omission of a letter or letters from a word, the possessive case, and certain plurals.

**ap·pall** (ə-pôl') v. To fill with dismay. — **ap·pall'ing** adj.

**ap·pa·ra·tus** (ăp'ə-rā'təs, -răt'əs) n., pl. **-tus** or **-tuses.** The equipment needed to perform a specific function; machine or device.

**ap·par·el** (ə-păr'əl) n. Clothing. —v. To clothe; dress.

**ap·par·ent** (ə-păr'ənt, ə-pâr'-) adj. Readily perceived; evident; plain. — **ap·par'ent·ly** adv.

**ap·pa·ri·tion** (ăp'ə-rĭsh'ən) n. A ghost.

**ap·peal** (ə-pēl') n. **1.** An earnest request. **2.** Attraction; allure. **3.** In law, a request for a new hearing by a higher court. —v. **1.** To make an earnest request. **2.** To be attractive.

**3.** To apply to transfer (a case) to a higher court for rehearing.

**ap·pear** (ə-pîr') v. **1.** To become visible. **2.** To come into existence. **3.** To seem or look. **4.** To come before the public. — **ap·pear'ance** n.

**ap·pease** (ə-pēz') v. **-peased, -peasing. 1.** To placate, esp. by granting concessions. **2.** To satisfy. — **ap·pease'ment** n.

**ap·pend** (ə-pĕnd') v. To attach; add.

**ap·pend·age** (ə-pĕn'dĭj) n. An attached organ or part.

**ap·pen·dec·to·my** (ăp'ən-dĕk'tə-mē) n., pl. **-mies.** Surgical removal of the appendix.

**ap·pen·di·ci·tis** (ə-pĕn'də-sī'tĭs) n. Inflammation of the appendix.

**ap·pen·dix** (ə-pĕn'dĭks) n., pl. **-dixes** or **-dices. 1.** Supplementary material at the end of a book. **2.** A tubular projection attached to the large intestine.

**ap·pe·tite** (ăp'ə-tīt') n. A desire or craving, esp. for food or drink.

**ap·pe·tiz·er** (ăp'ə-tī'zər) n. A food or drink served before a meal.

**ap·plaud** (ə-plôd') v. To express approval, esp. by clapping the hands. — **ap·plause'** n.

**ap·ple** (ăp'əl) n. A rounded, often redskinned edible fruit.

**ap·pli·ance** (ə-plī'əns) n. A machine or device, esp. one for household use.

**ap·pli·cant** (ăp'lĭ-kənt) n. One who applies, as for a job.

**ap·pli·ca·tion** (ăp'lĭ-kā'shən) n. **1.** The act of applying. **2.** Something that is applied, as a cosmetic. **3. a.** A request, as for a job. **b.** A form on which such a request is made.

**ap·ply** (ə-plī') v. **-plied, -plying. 1.** To put on or upon. **2.** To adapt for a special use. **3.** To devote (oneself or one's efforts). **4.** To be pertinent. **5.** To make a request, as for a job. — **ap'pli·ca·ble** adj. — **ap'pli·ca·bil'i·ty** n.

**ap·point** (ə-point') v. **1.** To name for a position. **2.** To fix or set, as a time. **3.** To furnish; equip. — **ap·point·ee'** n. — **ap·point'ive** adj. — **ap·point'ment** n.

**ap·por·tion** (ə-pôr'shən, ə-pōr'-) v. To divide and assign; allot. — **ap·por'tion·ment** n.

**ap·praise** (ə-prāz') v. **-praised, -praising.** To evaluate. — **ap·prais'al** n. — **ap·prais'er** n.

**ap·pre·ci·a·ble** (ə-prē'shə-bəl) adj. Capable of being noticed or measured; noticeable. — **ap·pre'ci·a·bly** adv.

**ap·pre·ci·ate** (ə-prē'shē-āt') v. **-ated, -ating. 1.** To value highly. **2.** To realize. **3.** To be thankful for. **4.** To go up in value. — **ap·pre'ci·a'tion** n. — **ap·pre'ci·a·tive** adj.

**ap·pre·hend** (ăp′rĭ-hĕnd′) v. **1.** To arrest. **2.** To grasp mentally; understand. **3.** To anticipate with anxiety. —**ap′pre·hen′sion** n. —**ap′pre·hen′sive** adj.

**ap·pren·tice** (ə-prĕn′tĭs) n. **1.** One learning a trade under a skilled craftsman. **2.** Any beginner. —v. **-ticed, -ticing.** To place as an apprentice. —**ap·pren′tice·ship′** n.

**ap·prise** (ə-prīz′) v. **-prised, -prising.** To inform.

**ap·proach** (ə-prōch′) v. **1.** To come near (to). **2.** To approximate. **3.** To make a proposal to. —n. **1.** The act of approaching. **2.** A way of dealing or working with something. **3.** A way of reaching; access.

**ap·pro·pri·ate** (ə-prō′prē-ĭt) adj. Suitable; proper. —v. (-āt′) **-ated, -ating.** **1.** To set apart for a particular use. **2.** To take; seize. —**ap·pro′pri·ate·ly** adv. —**ap·pro′pri·a′tion** n.

**ap·prove** (ə-prōōv′) v. **-proved, -proving.** **1.** To regard favorably. **2.** To consent to. —**ap·prov′al** n.

**ap·prox·i·mate** (ə-prŏk′sə-mĭt) adj. Almost exact or accurate. —v. (-māt′) **-mated, -mating.** To come close to; be nearly the same as. —**ap·prox′i·ma′tion** n.

**a·pri·cot** (ā′prĭ-kŏt′, ăp′rĭ-) n. A yellow-orange peachlike fruit.

**A·pril** (ā′prəl) n. The 4th month of the year.

**a·pron** (ā′prən, ā′pərn) n. A garment worn over the front to protect one's clothes.

**apt** (ăpt) adj. **1.** Exactly suitable; appropriate. **2.** Likely. **3.** Quick to learn.

**ap·ti·tude** (ăp′tə-t/y/ōōd′) n. **1.** A natural talent. **2.** Quickness in learning.

**a·quar·i·um** (ə-kwâr′ē-əm) n., pl. **-ums** or **-ia.** A water-filled enclosure for keeping or displaying fish.

**quat·ic** (ə-kwŏt′ĭk, ə-kwăt′-) adj. Living or happening in water.

**ar·bi·ter** (är′bə-tər) n. A judge; arbitrator.

**ar·bi·trar·y** (är′bə-trĕr′ē) adj. **1.** Determined by whim or caprice. **2.** Based on individual judgment. —**ar′bi·trar′i·ly** adv.

**ar·bi·trate** (är′bə-trāt′) v. **-trated, -trating.** To hear and settle a dispute; mediate. —**ar′bi·tra′tion** n. —**ar′bi·tra′tor** n.

**arc** (ärk) n. A portion of a curve, esp. of a circle. —v. **arced** or **arcked, arcing** or **arcking.** To form an arc.

**ar·cade** (är-kād′) n. **1.** A series of arches supported by columns. **2.** A roofed passageway, esp. one lined with shops.

**arch** (ärch) n. A curved structure forming the upper edge of an opening or a support, as in a bridge or doorway. —v. To form or supply with an arch.

**ar·chae·ol·o·gy, ar·che·ol·o·gy** (är′kē-ŏl′-ə-jē) n. The recovery and study of material evidence of human life and culture in past ages. —**ar′chae·o·log′ic, ar′chae·o·log′i·cal** adj. —**ar′chae·ol′o·gist** n.

**ar·cha·ic** (är-kā′ĭk) adj. **1.** Belonging to a much earlier time. **2.** Suggesting an earlier style or period.

**arch·bish·op** (ärch-bĭsh′əp) n. A bishop of the highest rank.

**arch·di·o·cese** (ärch-dī′ə-sĭs, -sēs′, -sēz′) n. A diocese under an archbishop's jurisdiction.

**arch·er·y** (är′chər-ē) n. The art or skill of shooting with a bow and arrows. —**arch′er** n.

**ar·chi·pel·a·go** (är′kə-pĕl′ə-gō′) n., pl. **-goes** or **-gos.** A large group of islands.

**ar·chi·tec·ture** (är′kə-tĕk′chər) n. The art and science of designing and erecting buildings. —**ar′chi·tect′** n. —**ar′chi·tec′tur·al** adj.

**ar·chives** (är′kīvz′) pl.n. Public records or the place where they are kept.

**arcked** (ärkt). Alternate p.t. & p.p. of **arc.**

**arcking** (är′kĭng). Alternate pres.p. of **arc.**

**ar·dent** (är′dənt) adj. Passionate; fervent. —**ar′dent·ly** adv. —**ar′dor** n.

**ar·du·ous** (är′jōō-əs) adj. Strenuous; difficult.

**are** (är). 2nd person sing. and present tense indicative pl. of **be.**

**ar·e·a** (âr′ē-ə) n. **1.** A space; region. **2.** A range, as of study. **3.** The measure of a region, in square units.

**a·re·na** (ə-rē′nə) n. The area in the center of an amphitheater or stadium where contests are held.

**aren't** (ärnt, är′ənt). Contraction of **are not.**

**ar·gue** (är′gyōō) v. **-gued, -guing. 1.** To put forth reasons for or against. **2.** To dispute; quarrel. —**ar′gu·a·ble** adj. —**ar′gu·ment** n. —**ar′gu·men′ta·tive** adj.

**a·ri·a** (ä′rē-ə) n. A solo vocal piece, as in an opera.

**ar·id** (ăr′ĭd) adj. **1.** Lacking moisture; dry. **2.** Dull.

**a·rise** (ə-rīz′) v. **arose, arisen, arising. 1.** To get up or move upward. **2.** To come into being. **3.** To result or proceed (with *from*).

**ar·is·toc·ra·cy** (ăr′ĭs-tŏk′rə-sē) n., pl. **-cies. 1.** A hereditary ruling class or nobility. **2.** Government by such a class. —**a·ris′to·crat′** n. —**a·ris′to·crat′ic** adj.

**a·rith·me·tic** (ə-rĭth′mə-tĭk) n. Computation involving the addition, subtraction, multiplication, and division of real numbers. —**ar′ith·met′ic, ar′ith·met′i·cal** adj.

**ark** (ärk) n. The boat built by Noah for the Flood.

**arm**[1] (ärm) n. **1.** An upper limb of the human body. **2.** A part similar to an arm.

**arm**[2] (ärm) n. **1.** A weapon. **2.** A branch of a military force. —v. **1.** To equip with weapons. **2.** To prepare for war.

**ar·ma·ment** (är′mə-mənt) n. Often **armaments.** All the military weapons and equipment of a country.

**ar·mi·stice** (är′mə-stĭs) n. A truce.

**ar·mor** (är′mər) n. **1.** A protective covering, as for the body. **2.** The armored vehicles of an army. — **ar′mored** adj.

**ar·mor·y** (är′mər-ē) n., pl. **-ies. 1.** An arsenal. **2.** The headquarters of a military reserve force.

**ar·my** (är′mē) n., pl. **-mies. 1.** A large body of soldiers organized for warfare. **2.** Any large organized group.

**a·ro·ma** (ə-rō′mə) n. A pleasant odor. — **ar′o·mat′ic** adj.

**a·rose** (ə-rōz′). p.t. of **arise.**

**a·round** (ə-round′) adv. **1.** On or to all sides or in all directions. **2.** In a circle. **3.** In or toward the opposite direction. **4.** Close at hand; nearby. —prep. **1.** On all sides of. **2.** So as to surround. **3.** In or to various places within or near. **4.** Approximately at.

**a·rouse** (ə-rouz′) v. **aroused, arousing. 1.** To awaken. **2.** To stir up; stimulate. — **a·rous′al** n.

**ar·raign** (ə-rān′) v. **1.** To call before a court to answer a charge. **2.** To accuse.

**ar·range** (ə-rānj′) v. **-ranged, -ranging. 1.** To put into a deliberate order. **2.** To agree about; settle. **3.** To reset (music) for other instruments or voices. — **ar·range′ment** n.

**ar·ray** (ə-rā′) v. **1.** To arrange or draw up, as troops. **2.** To dress up, esp. in fine clothes. —n. **1.** An orderly arrangement. **2.** An impressive collection. **3.** Splendid attire.

**ar·rear** (ə-rîr′) n. Often **arrears.** An overdue debt. — **in arrears.** Behind in paying debts.

**ar·rest** (ə-rĕst′) v. **1.** To stop or check. **2.** To seize and hold by legal authority. —n. The act of arresting or state of being arrested.

**ar·rive** (ə-rīv′) v. **-rived, -riving. 1.** To reach a destination. **2.** To come at last. **3.** To achieve success. — **ar·riv′al** n.

**ar·ro·gant** (ăr′ə-gənt) adj. Overbearingly proud; haughty. — **ar′ro·gance** n.

**ar·row** (ăr′ō) n. **1.** A pointed shaft, shot from a bow at a target. **2.** A symbol used to indicate direction.

**ar·se·nal** (är′sə-nəl) n. A place for storing or making weapons.

**ar·son** (är′sən) n. The crime of burning buildings or other property. — **ar′son·ist** n.

**art** (ärt) n. **1. a.** The activity of creating beautiful things. **b.** Works, as paintings, poetry, music, etc., resulting from this. **2. arts.** The liberal arts. **3.** A craft; skill. **4.** Cunning.

**ar·ter·y** (är′tər-ē) n., pl. **-ies. 1.** Any of a branching system of tubes that carry blood away from the heart. **2.** A major transport route. — **ar·te′ri·al** adj.

**art·ful** (ärt′fəl) adj. **1.** Skillful; clever. **2.** Crafty; deceitful.

**ar·thri·tis** (är-thrī′tĭs) n. Inflammation of a joint or joints. — **ar·thrit′ic** adj. & n.

**ar·ti·choke** (är′tə-chōk′) n. The edible flower head of a thistlelike plant.

**ar·ti·cle** (är′tĭ-kəl) n. **1.** An individual thing; item. **2.** A section of a document. **3.** A piece of nonfiction writing, as in a magazine. **4.** Any of the words *a, an,* or *the.*

**ar·tic·u·late** (är-tĭk′yə-lĭt) adj. **1.** Able to speak clearly. **2.** Having joints. —v. (-lāt′) **-lated, -lating. 1.** To pronounce distinctly. **2.** To give voice to, as an emotion. — **ar·tic′u·la′tion** n.

**ar·ti·fice** (är′tə-fĭs) n. A clever device or crafty trick.

**ar·ti·fi·cial** (är′tə-fĭsh′əl) adj. **1.** Made by man rather than natural forces. **2.** Not genuine or natural. — **ar′ti·fi′ci·al′i·ty** n.

**ar·til·ler·y** (är-tĭl′ə-rē) n. **1.** Large-caliber mounted guns. **2.** The branch of an army that uses such guns.

**art·ist** (är′tĭst) n. One who creates works of art, esp. a painter or sculptor.

**ar·tis·tic** (är-tĭs′tĭk) adj. **1.** Of art or artists. **2.** Skilled. **3.** Appreciative of the fine arts.

**art·less** (ärt′lĭs) adj. **1.** Without guile; ingenuous. **2.** Natural; simple.

**as** (ăz, əz) adv. **1.** Equally. **2.** For instance. —conj. **1.** To the same degree. **2.** In the same way that. **3.** While. **4.** Since; because. **5.** Though. — **as for** (or to). With regard to; concerning. —pron. That; which; who. —prep. In the capacity of.

**as·cend** (ə-sĕnd′) v. To move upward; climb. — **as·cen′sion** n.

**as·cen·dant** (ə-sĕn′dənt) adj. Also **as·cen·dent. 1.** Rising. **2.** Dominant; superior. — **as·cen′dan·cy** n.

**as·cent** (ə-sĕnt′) n. **1.** The act of ascending. **2.** An upward slope.

**as·cer·tain** (ăs′ər-tān′) v. To find out.

**as·cet·ic** (ə-sĕt′ĭk) adj. Practicing austere

self-discipline. —**as·cet'ic** n. —**as·cet'i·cism** n.

**ash¹** (ăsh) n. The gray or black residue of combustion.

**ash²** (ăsh) n. A tree having strong, durable wood.

**a·side** (ə-sīd') adv. 1. On or to one side. 2. Apart. —**aside from.** Excluding; excepting. —n. 1. A piece of dialogue that other actors on stage are supposed not to hear. 2. A digression.

**as·i·nine** (ăs'ə-nīn') adj. Stupid or silly. —**as'i·nin'i·ty** n.

**ask** (ăsk, äsk) v. 1. To put a question to. 2. To inquire about. 3. To request. 4. To invite.

**a·skew** (ə-skyōō') adj. Crooked. —adv. To one side; awry.

**a·sleep** (ə-slēp') adj. 1. Sleeping. 2. Inactive. 3. Numb. —adv. Into a sleep.

**as·par·a·gus** (ə-spăr'ə-gəs) n. The young, edible stalks of a cultivated plant.

**as·pect** (ăs'pĕkt') n. 1. Appearance; look. 2. A side; facet.

**as·perse** (ə-spûrs', ă-) v. -persed, -persing. To defame; slander. —**as·per'sion** n.

**as·phyx·i·ate** (ăs-fĭk'sē-āt') v. -ated, -ating. To cause or undergo unconsciousness or death from lack of oxygen. —**as·phyx'i·a'tion** n.

**as·pi·ra·tion** (ăs'pə-rā'shən) n. 1. Expulsion of breath in speech. 2. A strong desire, as for high achievement.

**as·pire** (ə-spīr') v. -pired, -piring. To have a great ambition; strive. —**as'pi·rant** n. & adj.

**ass** (ăs) n. 1. A donkey. 2. A silly or stupid person.

**as·sail** (ə-sāl') v. 1. To attack with blows. 2. To attack verbally. —**as·sail'ant** n.

**as·sas·sin** (ə-săs'ĭn) n. A murderer, esp. of a prominent person.

**as·sas·si·nate** (ə-săs'ə-nāt') v. -nated, -nating. To murder (a prominent person). —**as·sas'si·na'tion** n.

**as·sault** (ə-sôlt') n. A violent physical or verbal attack. —v. To attack violently.

**as·say** (ăs'ā', ă-sā') n. A chemical analysis, esp. of an ore. —v. (ă-sā', ăs'ā). 1. To analyze, esp. chemically; test. 2. To attempt.

**as·sem·ble** (ə-sĕm'bəl) v. -bled, -bling. 1. To bring or gather together; congregate. 2. To fit or join together the parts of. —**as·sem'blage** n.

**as·sem·bly** (ə-sĕm'blē) n., pl. -blies. 1. A gathering. 2. A legislative body. 3. The putting together of parts.

**as·sent** (ə-sĕnt') v. To express agreement (with to). —n. Agreement; consent.

**as·sert** (ə-sûrt') v. 1. To state; declare. 2. To defend or maintain. —**as·ser'tion** n. —**as·ser'tive** adj.

**as·sess** (ə-sĕs') v. 1. To estimate the value of (property) for taxation. 2. To charge with a tax or fine. 3. To evaluate. —**as·sess'ment** n. —**as·ses'sor** n.

**as·set** (ăs'ĕt') n. 1. A valuable quality or possession. 2. **assets.** All the property owned by a person, business, etc.

**as·sid·u·ous** (ə-sĭj'ōō-əs) adj. Diligent; industrious.

**as·sign** (ə-sīn') v. 1. To set apart for a particular purpose. 2. To appoint. 3. To give out as a task. 4. To ascribe; attribute. —**as·sign'ment** n.

**as·sim·i·late** (ə-sĭm'ə-lāt') v. -lated, -lating. To consume and incorporate; absorb. —**as·sim'i·la'tion** n.

**as·sist** (ə-sĭst') v. To aid; help. —n. An act of giving aid. —**as·sis'tance** n. —**as·sis'tant** n.

**as·so·ci·ate** (ə-sō'shē-āt', -sē-āt') v. -ated, -ating. 1. To connect or join in a relationship. 2. To connect in the mind. —n. (-ĭt). A partner; colleague. —adj. (-ĭt). Joined with others and having equal or nearly equal status. —**as·so'ci·a'tion** n.

**as·sort·ment** (ə-sôrt'mənt) n. A variety.

**as·sume** (ə-sōōm') v. -sumed, -suming. 1. To undertake. 2. To adopt. 3. To feign; affect. 4. To take for granted; suppose. —**as·sump'tion** n.

**as·sure** (ə-shōōr') v. -sured, -suring. 1. To inform confidently. 2. To make certain. 3. To insure. —**as·sur'ance** n.

**as·ter·isk** (ăs'tə-rĭsk') n. A symbol (*) used to indicate an omission or a reference to a footnote.

**asth·ma** (ăz'mə) n. A chronic disease marked by coughing and labored breathing. —**asth·mat'ic** adj.

**a·stig·ma·tism** (ə-stĭg'mə-tĭz'əm) n. An eye defect that prevents focusing of sharp, distinct images. —**as'tig·mat'ic** adj.

**a·stir** (ə-stûr') adj. Moving about.

**a·ston·ish** (ə-stŏn'ĭsh) v. To fill with wonder; amaze. —**a·ston'ish·ment** n.

**a·stound** (ə-stound') v. To astonish.

**as·trin·gent** (ə-strĭn'jənt) adj. Tending to constrict living tissue. —n. An astringent substance. —**as·trin'gen·cy** n.

**as·trol·o·gy** (ə-strŏl'ə-jē) n. The study of stars, planets, etc., to predict their supposed influence on human affairs. —**as·trol'o·ger**

*n.* — **as·tro·log·ic, as·tro·log·i·cal** *adj.*

**as·tro·naut** (ăs'trə-nôt') *n.* A person trained to participate in a spacecraft's flight.

**as·tron·o·my** (ə-strŏn'ə-mē) *n.* The scientific study of the universe beyond the earth. — **as·tron·o·mer** *n.* — **as·tro·nom'ic, as·tro·nom'i·cal** *adj.*

**as·tute** (ə-styōōt') *adj.* Keen in judgment.

**a·sun·der** (ə-sŭn'dər) *adv.* Apart.

**a·sy·lum** (ə-sī'ləm) *n.* **1.** An institution for the mentally ill or aged. **2.** A place offering safety.

**at** (ăt, ət) *prep.* **1.** Near to; by; in; on. **2.** In the direction of; to. **3.** Engaged in.

**ate** (āt). *p.t.* of **eat.**

**a·the·ism** (ā'thē-ĭz'əm) *n.* Denial of the existence of God. — **a'the·ist** *n.* — **a'the·is'tic** *adj.*

**ath·lete** (ăth'lēt') *n.* One who takes part in competitive sports. — **ath·let'ic** *adj.*

**at·las** (ăt'ləs) *n.* A bound collection of maps.

**at·mos·phere** (ăt'mə-sfîr') *n.* **1.** The air surrounding a celestial body, esp. the earth. **2.** A general feeling or mood. — **at'mos·pher'ic** *adj.*

**a·toll** (ă'tôl', ā'tôl', ā'-) *n.* A ringlike coral island enclosing a lagoon.

**at·om** (ăt'əm) *n.* The smallest part of a chemical element. — **a·tom'ic** *adj.*

**a·tone** (ə-tōn') *v.* **atoned, atoning.** To make amends for. — **a·tone'ment** *n.*

**a·tro·cious** (ə-trō'shəs) *adj.* **1.** Extremely evil or cruel. **2.** Exceptionally bad. — **a·troc'i·ty** *n.*

**at·ro·phy** (ăt'rə-fē) *n., pl.* **-phies.** Shrinking or wasting away of body tissues. — *v.* **-phied, -phying.** To cause or undergo atrophy.

**at·tach** (ə-tăch') *v.* **1.** To fasten on; connect. **2.** To adhere. **3.** To ascribe. **4.** To bind by ties of affection or loyalty. **5.** To seize by legal writ. — **at·tach'ment** *n.*

**at·tack** (ə-tăk') *v.* **1.** To set upon with force. **2.** To denounce; criticize. **3.** To start work on. — *n.* **1.** An assault. **2.** Seizure by a disease.

**at·tain** (ə-tān') *v.* **1.** To accomplish. **2.** To arrive at. — **at·tain'a·ble** *adj.* — **at·tain'ment** *n.*

**at·tempt** (ə-tĕmpt') *v.* To try. — *n.* **1.** An effort. **2.** An attack.

**at·tend** (ə-tĕnd') *v.* **1.** To be present at. **2.** To accompany. **3.** To take care of. **4.** To heed.

**at·ten·dance** (ə-tĕn'dəns) *n.* **1.** The act of attending. **2.** The number of persons present.

**at·ten·dant** (ə-tĕn'dənt) *n.* **1.** One who waits on another. **2.** One who is present. — *adj.* Accompanying or consequent.

**at·ten·tion** (ə-tĕn'shən) *n.* **1.** Concentration of one's mental powers upon an object. **2.** Consideration; notice. — **at·ten'tive** *adj.*

**at·ten·u·ate** (ə-tĕn'yōō-āt') *v.* **-ated, -ating.** To thin; weaken. — **at·ten·u·a'tion** *n.*

**at·test** (ə-tĕst') *v.* **1.** To affirm to be true, correct, etc. **2.** To provide evidence of.

**at·tic** (ăt'ĭk) *n.* A space directly below the roof.

**at·tire** (ə-tīr') *v.* **-tired, -tiring.** To dress; clothe. — *n.* Clothing; array.

**at·ti·tude** (ăt'ə-t/yōōd') *n.* **1.** A posture. **2.** A state of mind or feeling.

**at·tor·ney** (ə-tûr'nē) *n., pl.* **-neys.** A lawyer.

**at·tract** (ə-trăkt') *v.* **1.** To cause to draw near. **2.** To appeal; allure. — **at·trac'tion** *n.* — **at·trac'tive** *adj.*

**at·trib·ute** (ə-trĭb'yōōt) *v.* **-uted, -uting.** To regard as belonging to; ascribe. — *n.* (ăt'rə-byōōt'). A distinctive feature; mark. — **at·trib'ut·a·ble** *adj.* — **at'tri·bu'tion** *n.*

**at·tri·tion** (ə-trĭsh'ən) *n.* **1.** A rubbing away or wearing down by friction. **2.** A gradual, natural reduction in membership or personnel, as through retirement, death, etc.

**at·tune** (ə-t/yōōn') *v.* **-tuned, -tuning.** **1.** To tune. **2.** To bring into harmony.

**auc·tion** (ôk'shən) *n.* A public sale in which items are sold to the highest bidder. — *v.* To sell at an auction. — **auc'tion·eer** *n.*

**au·da·cious** (ô-dā'shəs) *adj.* **1.** Daring; reckless. **2.** Arrogant; impudent. — **au·dac'i·ty** *n.*

**au·di·ble** (ô'də-bəl) *adj.* Capable of being heard. — **au'di·bil'i·ty** *n.* — **au'di·bly** *adv.*

**au·di·ence** (ô'dē-əns) *n.* **1.** A gathering of spectators or listeners. **2.** Those reached by a book, television program, etc. **3.** A formal hearing or conference.

**au·dit** (ô'dĭt) *n.* An examination of records or accounts. — *v.* **1.** To examine and verify (records or accounts). **2.** To attend (a college course) without receiving academic credit. — **au'di·tor** *n.*

**au·di·tion** (ô-dĭsh'ən) *n.* A trial performance, as of an actor. — *v.* To perform in or give an audition.

**au·di·to·ri·um** (ô'də-tôr'ē-əm, -tōr'ē-əm) *n., pl.* **-ums** or **-toria.** A room or building to accommodate an audience.

**aught** (ôt) *n.* **1.** Anything. **2.** Zero.

**aug·ment** (ôg-mĕnt') *v.* To enlarge; increase. — **aug'men·ta'tion** *n.*

**A-1**

**au·gur** (ô′gər) *n.* A seer or prophet. —*v.* **1.** To foretell. **2.** To betoken. —**au′gu·ry** *n.*

**au·gust** (ô-gŭst′) *adj.* Majestic; venerable.

**Au·gust** (ô′gəst) *n.* The 8th month of the year.

**aunt** (ănt, änt) *n.* **1.** The sister of one's father or mother. **2.** The wife of one's uncle.

**au·ra** (ôr′ə) *n.* A distinctive air or quality.

**au·ri·cle** (ôr′ĭ-kəl) *n.* **1.** The external part of the ear. **2.** A chamber of the heart.

**aus·pic·es** (ô′spə-sĕz′) *pl.n.* Sponsorship; patronage.

**aus·pi·cious** (ô-spĭsh′əs) *adj.* Propitious; fortunate. —**aus·pi′cious·ly** *adv.*

**aus·tere** (ô-stîr′) *adj.* **1.** Severe; stern. **2.** Ascetic; frugal. —**aus·ter′i·ty** *n.*

**au·then·tic** (ô-thĕn′tĭk) *adj.* Genuine; real. —**au·then′ti·cal·ly** *adv.*

**au·then·ti·cate** (ô-thĕn′tĭ-kāt′) *v.* **-cated, -cating.** To confirm as authentic. —**au·then′ti·ca′tion** *n.*

**au·thor** (ô′thər) *n.* **1.** A writer. **2.** An originator or creator. —**au′thor·ship′** *n.*

**au·thor·i·tar·i·an** (ə-thôr′ĭ-târ′ē-ən, ə-thŏr′-, ô-) *adj.* Characterized by or favoring absolute obedience to authority. —*n.* One who believes in such policies.

**au·thor·i·ta·tive** (ə-thôr′ĭ-tā′tĭv, ə-thŏr′-, ô-) *adj.* Having or arising from authority.

**au·thor·i·ty** (ə-thôr′ə-tē, ə-thŏr′-, ô-) *n., pl.* **-ties. 1. a.** The power to command, determine, influence, or judge. **b.** A person or group with this power. **2.** An accepted source of expert information.

**au·thor·ize** (ô′thə-rīz′) *v.* **-ized, -izing. 1.** To grant authority to. **2.** To sanction. —**au′thor·i·za′tion** *n.*

**au·to** (ô′tō) *n., pl.* **-tos.** An automobile.

**au·to·bi·og·ra·phy** (ô′tō-bī-ŏg′rə-fē, -bē-ŏg′rə-fē) *n., pl.* **-phies.** The story of a person's life written by himself.

**au·toc·ra·cy** (ô-tŏk′rə-sē) *n., pl.* **-cies.** Government by a person having absolute power. —**au′to·crat′** *n.* —**au′to·crat′ic** *adj.*

**au·to·graph** (ô′tə-grăf′, -grăf′) *n.* A person's own signature or handwriting. —*v.* To sign.

**au·to·mate** (ô′tə-māt′) *v.* **-mated, -mating.** To convert to or operate by self-regulating machinery. —**au′to·ma′tion** *n.*

**au·to·mat·ic** (ô′tə-măt′ĭk) *adj.* **1. a.** Acting or operating by itself. **b.** Self-regulating. **2.** Involuntary; reflex. —*n.* An automatic device.

**au·to·mo·bile** (ô′tə-mō-bēl′, -mō′bēl′, ô′tə-mō-bēl′) *n.* A self-propelled land vehicle. —**au′to·mo′tive** *adj.*

**au·ton·o·mous** (ô-tŏn′ə-məs) *adj.* Independent; self-governing. —**au·ton′o·my** *n.*

**au·top·sy** (ô′tŏp′sē, ô′təp-sē) *n., pl.* **-sies.** The examination of a dead body to determine the cause of death; post-mortem.

**au·tumn** (ô′təm) *n.* The season of the year between summer and winter. —**au·tum′nal** *adj.*

**aux·il·ia·ry** (ôg-zĭl′yər-ē, -zĭl′ər-ē) *adj.* **1.** Giving assistance; aiding; helping. **2.** Subsidiary; supplementary. —*n., pl.* **-ries. 1.** One that gives aid. **2.** Also **auxiliary verb.** A verb that accompanies certain verb forms to express tense, mood, voice, or aspect.

**a·vail** (ə-vāl′) *v.* To be of use; assist; help. —*n.* Use; benefit.

**a·vail·a·ble** (ə-vā′lə-bəl) *adj.* Accessible for use; obtainable. —**a·vail′a·bil′i·ty** *n.*

**av·a·lanche** (ăv′ə-lănch′, -länch′) *n.* A fall of a large mass of snow, rock, or other material down a mountainside.

**av·a·rice** (ăv′ə-rĭs) *n.* Greed for wealth.

**a·venge** (ə-vĕnj′) *v.* **avenged, avenging.** To take revenge for. —**a·veng′er** *n.*

**av·e·nue** (ăv′ə-n/yōō′) *n.* A wide street.

**av·er·age** (ăv′rĭj, ăv′ər-ĭj) *n.* **1.** The sum of a set of quantities divided by the number of quantities in the set; mean. **2.** The usual type, amount, or quality. —*adj.* **1.** Of or constituting the average. **2.** Typical. —*v.* **-aged, -aging. 1.** To calculate, obtain, or amount to an average of. **2.** To distribute proportionally.

**a·verse** (ə-vûrs′) *adj.* Opposed; reluctant.

**a·vert** (ə-vûrt′) *v.* **1.** To turn away. **2.** To ward off or prevent.

**a·vi·a·tion** (ā′vē-ā′shən, ăv′ē-) *n.* The operation of aircraft. —**a′vi·a′tor** *n.*

**av·id** (ăv′ĭd) *adj.* Eager; enthusiastic. —**a·vid′i·ty** *n.* —**av′id·ly** *adv.*

**av·o·ca·do** (ăv′ə-kä′dō) *n., pl.* **-dos.** A tropical fruit with yellow-green pulp.

**av·o·ca·tion** (ăv′ō-kā′shən) *n.* A hobby.

**a·void** (ə-void′) *v.* To keep away from; shun. —**a·void′ance** *n.*

**av·oir·du·pois** (ăv′ər-də-poiz′) *n.* **1.** The system of weights in which 16 ounces equal a pound. **2.** Weight; heaviness.

**a·vow** (ə-vou′) *v.* To acknowledge openly; confess. —**a·vow′al** *n.*

**a·wait** (ə-wāt′) *v.* **1.** To wait for. **2.** To be in store for.

**a·wake** (ə-wāk′) *v.* **awoke, awaked, awaking.** To rouse from sleep; wake up. —*adj.* **1.** Not asleep. **2.** Alert; watchful.

**a·wak·en** (ə-wā′kən) v. To wake up; rouse. **—a·wak′en·ing** adj. & n.

**a·ward** (ə-wôrd′) v. To grant for high performance or quality. —n. **1.** A decision, as by a judge. **2.** A prize.

**a·ware** (ə-wâr′) adj. Conscious; informed. **—a·ware′ness** n.

**a·way** (ə-wā′) adv. **1.** At or to a distance. **2.** To a different place. **3.** From one's possession. **4.** Continuously. —adj. **1.** Absent. **2.** At a distance.

**awe** (ô) n. Mingled reverence, dread, and wonder. —v. awed, awing. To inspire with awe. **—awe′some** adj.

**aw·ful** (ô′fəl) adj. **1.** Extremely bad or unpleasant. **2.** Dreadful; appalling. **—aw′ful·ly** adv.

**awk·ward** (ôk′wərd) adj. **1.** Lacking grace or dexterity; clumsy. **2.** Unwieldy. **3.** Uncomfortable; inconvenient. **4.** Embarrassing. **—awk′ward·ly** adv. **—awk′ward·ness** n.

**a·woke** (ə-wōk′). p.t. of awake.

**a·wry** (ə-rī′) adv. **1.** Askew. **2.** Amiss; wrong. **—a·wry′** adj.

**ax, axe** (ăks) n., pl. axes. A chopping tool with a bladed head mounted on a handle.

**ax·i·om** (ăk′sē-əm) n. A self-evident or accepted principle. **—ax′i·o·mat′ic** adj.

**ax·is** (ăk′sĭs) n., pl. axes. **1.** A straight line about which an object rotates. **2.** A center line or part.

**ax·le** (ăk′səl) n. A shaft on which a wheel turns.

**aye** (ī) n. Also **ay.** An affirmative vote. —adv. Yes.

**az·ure** (ăzh′ər) n. Sky blue. **—az′ure** adj.

# B

**b, B** (bē) n. The 2nd letter of the English alphabet.

**bab·ble** (băb′əl) v. -bled, -bling. **1.** To utter incoherent sound. **2.** To chatter. —n. Babbling sound. **—bab′bler** n.

**ba·boon** (bă-bōōn′) n. A large monkey with a prominent muzzle.

**ba·by** (bā′bē) n., pl. -bies. An infant. —v. -bied, -bying. To pamper; coddle. **—ba′by·hood′** n. **—ba′by·ish** adj.

**bach·e·lor** (băch′ə-lər, băch′lər) n. **1.** An unmarried man. **2. a.** An undergraduate de-

gree. **b.** A person holding such a degree. **—bach′e·lor·hood′** n.

**back** (băk) n. **1.** The part of the body nearest the spine. **2.** The rear. **3.** The reverse side. —v. **1.** To move backward. **2.** To support; strengthen. **3.** To bet on. **4.** To form the back of. **— back down.** To withdraw from a former stand. —adj. **1.** At the rear. **2.** Of a past time. **3.** Backward. —adv. **1.** To or toward the rear. **2.** To or toward a former place, state, or time. **3.** In reserve, concealment, or check. **4.** In return. **—back′er** n. **—back′ing** n.

**back·bone** (băk′bōn′) n. **1.** The vertebrate spine. **2.** A main support. **3.** Strength of character.

**back·fire** (băk′fīr′) n. An explosion of prematurely ignited fuel or of unburned exhaust. —v. **1.** To have a backfire. **2.** To produce an unwanted result.

**back·ground** (băk′ground′) n. **1.** The area, space, or surface against which objects are seen or represented. **2.** A setting. **3.** Relative obscurity. **4.** One's experience or training.

**back·lash** (băk′lăsh′) n. **1.** A sudden backward whipping motion. **2.** An antagonistic reaction.

**back·log** (băk′lôg′, -lŏg′) n. A reserve supply or accumulation.

**back·slide** (băk′slīd′) v. To revert to wrongdoing. **—back′slid′er** n.

**back·track** (băk′trăk′) v. **1.** To retrace one's route. **2.** To reverse one's stand; retreat.

**back·ward** (băk′wərd) adv. Also **back·wards.** **1.** Toward the back. **2.** With the back leading. **3.** In reverse. **4.** Toward a former, often worse, condition. —adj. **1.** Reversed. **2.** Reluctant; unwilling. **3.** Retarded in development. **—back′ward·ness** n.

**ba·con** (bā′kən) n. Salted and smoked meat from a pig's back and sides.

**bac·te·ri·a** (băk-tîr′ē-ə) pl.n. Sing. -terium. Single-celled organisms often causing disease. **—bac·te′ri·al** adj.

**bac·te·ri·ol·o·gy** (băk-tîr′ē-ŏl′ə-jē) n. The study of bacteria. **—bac·te′ri·o·log′ic,** **bac·te′ri·o·log′i·cal** adj. **—bac·te′ri·ol′o·gist** n.

**bad** (băd) adj. worse, worst. **1.** Undesirable; not good. **2.** Inferior; poor. **3.** Unfavorable. **4.** Rotten; spoiled. **5.** Severe; intense. **6.** Sorry; regretful. **—bad′ly** adv. **—bad′ness** n.

**bade** (băd). A p.t. of bid.

**badge** (băj) n. An emblem worn as a sign of rank, membership, or honor.

**badg·er** (băj′ər) n. A burrowing animal with a grizzled coat. —v. To harry; pester.

**baf-fle** (băf'əl) v. **-fled, -fling. 1.** To foil; thwart. **2.** To make helplessly puzzled. —n. A structure that impedes or deflects. — **baf-fle-ment** n. — **baf'fler** n.

**bag** (băg) n. **1.** A nonrigid container, as of paper. **2.** A suitcase or purse. —v. **bagged, bagging. 1.** To hang or bulge loosely. **2.** To capture or kill, as game. — **bag'gy** adj.

**bag-gage** (băg'ĭj) n. Luggage.

**bag-pipe** (băg'pīp') n. Often **bagpipes.** A musical instrument with an inflatable bag attached to pipes.

**bail**[1] (bāl) n. **1.** Money supplied as a guarantee that an arrested person will appear for trial. **2.** Release obtained by such security. —v. To release by providing or taking bail. — **bail'er** n.

**bail**[2] (bāl) v. To empty a boat of water by scooping or dipping. — **bail out.** To parachute from an aircraft.

**bail-iff** (bā'lĭf) n. A courtroom attendant who guards prisoners and maintains order.

**bait** (bāt) n. **1.** Food used to catch fish or trap animals. **2.** An enticement; lure. —v. **1.** To supply with bait. **2.** To lure; entice. **3.** To harass.

**bake** (bāk) v. **baked, baking. 1.** To cook with dry heat, esp. in an oven. **2.** To harden with heat. — **bak'er** n. — **bak'er-y** n.

**bal-ance** (băl'əns) n. **1.** A weighing device having a lever with two pans suspended from it. **2.** Equilibrium. **3.** Equality or difference between totals in the debit and credit sides of an account. **4.** Remainder. **5.** Harmony; symmetry. —v. **-anced, -ancing. 1.** To bring into or be maintained in equilibrium. **2.** To counterbalance. **3.** To compute the difference between the debits and credits of (an account).

**bal-co-ny** (băl'kə-nē) n., pl. **-nies. 1.** A platform projecting from an upper story of a building. **2.** A gallery projecting over the main floor in a theater.

**bald** (bôld) adj. **1.** Lacking hair on the top of the head. **2.** Unadorned; plain. — **bald'ness** n.

**bale** (bāl) n. A large bound package. —v. **baled, baling.** To wrap in bales. — **bal'er** n.

**bale-ful** (bāl'fəl) adj. **1.** Malignant. **2.** Ominous. — **bale'ful-ly** adv. — **bale'ful-ness** n.

**balk** (bôk) v. **1.** To stop short and refuse to go on. **2.** To thwart; check. —n. A hindrance. — **balk'y** adj.

**ball**[1] (bôl) n. **1.** A round object; sphere. **2. a.** A rounded object used in a game. **b.** A game played with such an object.

**ball**[2] (bôl) n. **1.** A formal dance. **2.** An enjoyable time.

**bal-lad** (băl'əd) n. **1.** A narrative poem, often of folk origin and intended to be sung. **2.** A slow, romantic popular song. — **bal'lad-eer** n.

**bal-last** (băl'əst) n. Heavy material put aboard a ship to enhance stability. —v. To stabilize with ballast.

**bal-let** (bă-lā', băl'ā') n. A dance genre with a highly formalized technique. — **bal'le-ri'na** fem.n.

**bal-lis-tics** (bə-lĭs'tĭks) n. **1.** The study of the dynamics of projectiles. **2.** The study of firearms and bullets. — **bal-lis'tic** adj.

**bal-loon** (bə-lōōn') n. A flexible bag that expands when inflated with a gas. —v. To expand like a balloon.

**bal-lot** (băl'ət) n. **1.** A paper or ticket used to cast a vote. **2.** The act or method of voting. **3.** A list of candidates for office. —v. To cast a ballot.

**balm-y** (bä'mē) adj. **-ier, -iest.** Mild and pleasant.

**bal-us-ter** (băl'ə-stər) n. One of the upright supports of a handrail.

**bal-us-trade** (băl'ə-strād') n. A rail and the row of posts that support it.

**bam-boo** (băm-bōō') n. A tall tropical grass with hollow, woody stems.

**ban** (băn) v. **banned, banning.** To prohibit, esp. officially. —n. A prohibition.

**ba-nal** (bə-năl', -näl', bā'nəl) adj. Trite; ordinary. — **ba-nal'i-ty** n.

**ba-nan-a** (bə-năn'ə) n. A crescent-shaped tropical fruit having pulpy flesh and yellow skin.

**band**[1] (bănd) n. **1.** A thin strip of flexible material used to bind together. **2.** A range of numerical values. —v. To bind or identify with a band.

**band**[2] (bănd) n. **1.** A group of people or animals. **2.** A group of musicians. —v. To assemble or unite in a group.

**band-age** (băn'dĭj) n. A strip of material used to protect a wound or other injury. —v. **-aged, -aging.** To apply a bandage to.

**ban-dit** (băn'dĭt) n. A robber.

**ban-dy** (băn'dē) v. **-died, -dying. 1.** To toss back and forth. **2.** To discuss or exchange. —adj. Bent in an outward curve.

**bane** (bān) n. A cause of distress or ruin. — **bane'ful** adj.

**bang** (băng) n. A sudden loud noise. —v. To hit or close noisily.

**ban-ish** (băn'ĭsh) v. **1.** To force to leave a

country; exile. **2.** To drive away; expel. —**ban'ish·ment** *n.*

**ban·is·ter** (băn'ĭ-stər) *n.* **1.** A baluster. **2.** The balustrade of a staircase.

**ban·jo** (băn'jō) *n., pl.* **-jos** or **-joes.** A stringed instrument having a hollow circular body.

**bank¹** (băngk) *n.* **1.** Any piled-up mass. **2.** A natural incline. **3.** An artificial embankment. **4.** The slope of land adjoining a lake, river, or sea. **5.** Lateral tilting of an aircraft in a turn. —*v.* **1.** To border or protect with a bank. **2.** To pile up; amass. **3.** To cover (a fire) with ashes or fuel for low burning. **4.** To tilt (an aircraft) laterally in flight.

**bank²** (băngk) *n.* **1.** An establishment for safekeeping, handling, and lending money. **2.** A supply or stock. —*v.* **1.** To deposit (money) in a bank. **2.** To transact business with a bank. **3.** To operate a bank. —**bank on.** To have confidence in. —**bank'er** *n.*

**bank·rupt** (băngk'rŭpt', -rəpt) *n.* A debtor who is judged insolvent and whose remaining property is administered for his creditors. —*adj.* **1.** Legally declared a bankrupt. **2.** Financially ruined. —*v.* To cause to become bankrupt. —**bank'rupt·cy** *n.*

**ban·ner** (băn'ər) *n.* A flag; standard. —*adj.* Outstanding.

**ban·quet** (băng'kwĭt) *n.* An elaborate feast or ceremonial dinner.

**ban·ter** (băn'tər) *n.* Good-humored teasing. —*v.* To tease or mock gently.

**bap·tism** (băp'tĭz'əm) *n.* A Christian sacrament in which a person is symbolically cleansed of original sin by immersion in or sprinkling with water. —**bap·tis'mal** *adj.* —**bap·tize'** *v.*

**bar** (bär) *n.* **1.** A long, rigid piece of solid material. **2.** A solid oblong block of a substance, as soap. **3.** An obstacle. **4.** A band, as one formed by light. **5.** A system of law courts. **6.** The profession of law. **7.** A vertical line dividing a musical staff into measures. **8.** A counter at which drinks are served. —*v.* **barred, barring.** **1.** To obstruct with or as if with bars. **2.** To exclude. —*prep.* Excluding.

**barb** (bärb) *n.* **1.** A sharp backward-pointing projection. **2.** A cutting remark. —**barbed** *adj.*

**bar·bar·i·an** (bär-bâr'ē-ən) *n.* An uncivilized or uncultured person. —**bar·bar'i·an** *adj.* —**bar·bar'ic, bar'bar·ous** *adj.* —**bar'bar·ism** *n.* —**bar·bar'i·ty** *n.*

**bar·be·cue** (bär'bĭ-kyōō') *n.* **1.** A grill or outdoor fireplace for roasting meat. **2.** Meat

roasted over an open fire. —*v.* **-cued, -cuing.** To cook (meat) over live coals or an open fire.

**bar·ber** (bär'bər) *n.* One whose business is to cut hair or beards.

**bar·bi·tu·rate** (bär-bĭch'ər-ĭt, -ə-rāt', bär'bə-t/yōōr'ĭt, -āt') *n.* A sedative drug.

**bare** (bâr) *adj.* **barer, barest.** **1.** Naked. **2.** Exposed to view; undisguised. **3.** Plain; simple. **4.** Just sufficient. —*v.* **bared, baring.** To make bare. —**bare'ly** *adv.*

**bare-faced** (bâr'fāst') *adj.* Bold; brazen.

**bar·gain** (bär'gĭn) *n.* **1.** An agreement or contract. **2.** Something offered or acquired at a low price. —*v.* To negotiate the terms of an agreement; haggle. —**bar'gain·er** *n.*

**barge** (bärj) *n.* A flat-bottomed freight boat. —*v.* **barged, barging.** To intrude (with *in* or *into*).

**bar·i·tone** (băr'ə-tōn') *n.* A male voice between a bass and a tenor.

**bark¹** (bärk) *n.* The short, harsh sound made by a dog. —*v.* **1.** To utter a bark. **2.** To speak sharply.

**bark²** (bärk) *n.* The outer covering of trees. —*v.* **1.** To remove bark from. **2.** To scrape skin from.

**barn** (bärn) *n.* A farm building for storing produce and sheltering livestock. —**barn'yard'** *n.*

**bar·na·cle** (bär'nə-kəl) *n.* A marine crustacean that adheres to submerged surfaces. —**bar'na·cled** *adj.*

**ba·rom·e·ter** (bə-rŏm'ə-tər) *n.* An instrument for measuring atmospheric pressure. —**bar·o·met'ric, bar·o·met'ri·cal** *adj.* —**ba·rom'e·try** *n.*

**ba·roque** (bə-rōk') *adj.* Of an artistic style marked by elaborate decoration.

**bar·racks** (băr'ĭks) *n.* A building used to house soldiers.

**bar·rage** (bə-räzh') *n.* A heavy curtain of artillery fire.

**bar·rel** (băr'əl) *n.* **1.** A large cask with bulging sides and flat ends. **2.** The cylindrical part of a firearm, through which the bullet travels.

**bar·ren** (băr'ən) *adj.* **1.** Infertile; sterile. **2.** Unproductive.

**bar·ri·cade** (băr'ə-kād', băr'ə-kād') *n.* A barrier set up across a route of access. —*v.* **-caded, -cading.** To block or confine with a barricade.

**bar·ri·er** (băr'ē-ər) *n.* **1.** A structure built to bar passage. **2.** An obstruction; hindrance.

**bar·ter** (bär'tər) *v.* To exchange (goods). —*n.*

The practice of bartering.

**base¹** (bās) *n.* **1.** The lowest part; bottom. **2.** A fundamental principle; basis. **3.** In certain sports, a goal, starting point, or safety area. **4.** A center of organization, supply, or activity. —*v.* **based, basing. 1.** To form or make a base for. **2.** To find a basis for; establish.

**base²** (bās) *adj.* baser, basest. Low; inferior. —**base'ly** *adv.* —**base'ness** *n.*

**base·ball** (bās'bôl') *n.* **1.** A game played with a bat and ball. **2.** The ball used.

**base·ment** (bās'mənt) *n.* The story below the ground floor of a building.

**ba·ses.** *pl. of* basis.

**bash·ful** (băsh'fəl) *adj.* Shy; retiring. —**bash'ful·ly** *adv.* —**bash'ful·ness** *n.*

**ba·sic** (bā'sĭk) *adj.* Fundamental; essential. —*n.* A basic fact or skill. —**ba'si·cal·ly** *adv.*

**ba·sis** (bā'sĭs) *n., pl.* **-ses. 1.** A foundation. **2.** The chief component.

**bask** (băsk, bäsk) *v.* .To warm oneself pleasantly.

**bas·ket** (băs'kĭt) *n.* A container of interwoven material.

**bas·ket·ball** (băs'kĭt·bôl') *n.* **1.** A game in which players try to throw a large ball through an elevated hoop. **2.** The ball used.

**bass** (bās) *n.* The lowest male voice. —**bass** *adj.*

**bas·soon** (bə-sōōn', bă-) *n.* A low-pitched woodwind instrument. —**bas·soon'ist** *n.*

**bas·tard** (băs'tərd) *n.* An illegitimate child. —*adj.* Illegitimate. —**bas'tard·y** *n.*

**baste** (bāst) *v.* **basted, basting. 1.** To sew loosely. **2.** To pour liquid over.

**bas·tion** (băs'chən, băs'tē-ən) *n.* A well-fortified position.

**bat¹** (băt) *n.* A stout wooden stick or club. —*v.* **batted, batting.** To hit with a bat.

**bat²** (băt) *n.* A mouselike flying mammal.

**batch** (băch) *n.* An amount produced at one time.

**bath** (băth, bäth) *n., pl.* baths. **1.** The act of washing the body. **2.** A tub for bathing. **3.** A room with a bath and usually a toilet.

**bathe** (bāTH) *v.* **bathed, bathing. 1.** To take or give a bath. **2.** To go swimming. **3.** To suffuse. —**bath'er** *n.*

**ba·ton** (bə-tŏn', băt'n) *n.* A stick, esp. for conducting an orchestra.

**bat·tal·ion** (bə-tăl'yən) *n.* A large group, esp. a force of several military companies.

**bat·ter¹** (băt'ər) *v.* To pound with heavy blows.

**bat·ter²** (băt'ər) *n.* A mixture of flour and

liquid used in cooking.

**bat·ter·y** (băt'ə-rē) *n., pl.* **-ies. 1.** An unlawful beating. **2.** An array, esp. of artillery. **3.** A device for generating an electric current.

**bat·tle** (băt'l) *n.* A combat; struggle, as between armies. —*v.* **-tled, -tling.** To engage in battle.

**bau·ble** (bô'bəl) *n.* A trinket.

**bawd·y** (bô'dē) *adj.* **-ier, -iest.** Humorously coarse; lewd. —**bawd'i·ness** *n.*

**bawl** (bôl) *v.* To cry out loudly; bellow. —**bawl out.** To scold. —**bawl'er** *n.*

**bay¹** (bā) *n.* A wide body of water partly enclosed by land.

**bay²** (bā) *adj.* Reddish-brown. —*n.* A reddish-brown animal, esp. a horse.

**bay³** (bā) *v.* To bark with long, deep cries.

**bay·o·net** (bā'ə-nĭt, -nĕt', bā'ə-nĕt') *n.* A blade affixed to a rifle. —*v.* **-neted** or **-netted, -neting** or **-netting.** To stab with a bayonet.

**bay·ou** (bī'ōō, bī'ō) *n., pl.* **-ous.** A marsh connected to a lake or river.

**ba·zaar** (bə-zär') *n.* **1.** An Oriental market. **2.** A fair for charity.

**be** (bē) *v.* **1.** To exist. **2.** To occupy a place. **3.** To equal. **4.** To mean; signify. **5.** To have a specified quality.

**beach** (bēch) *n.* A sandy shore.

**bea·con** (bē'kən) *n.* A guiding or signal light.

**bead** (bēd) *n.* **1. a.** A small piece of material pierced for stringing. **b. beads.** A necklace of such pieces. **2.** A drop or globule.

**beak** (bēk) *n.* The horny, projecting mouth parts of a bird; bill.

**beak·er** (bē'kər) *n.* A large drinking cup or glass vessel.

**beam** (bēm) *n.* **1.** A length of timber supporting a structure. **2.** A radio signal for navigational guidance. **3.** A ray of light or particles. —**on the beam.** On the right track. —*v.* **1.** To emit or radiate. **2.** To smile radiantly.

**bean** (bēn) *n.* The edible seed or seed pod of any of various plants.

**bear¹** (bâr) *v.* **bore, borne** or **born, bearing. 1.** To carry; support. **2.** To endure. **3.** To conduct (oneself). **4.** To have; show. **5.** *p.p.* **borne.** To give birth to. **6.** To yield; produce. **7.** To exert pressure. —**bear'a·ble** *adj.* —**bear'er** *n.*

**bear²** (bâr) *n.* A large, burly, shaggy-coated mammal.

**beard** (bîrd) *n.* The hair on the chin and cheeks of a man.

**bear·ing** (bâr'ĭng) *n.* **1.** Deportment; pos-

**belligerent**

ture. **2.** A device that connects and reduces friction between machine parts. **3.** Relationship or relevance. **4.** Direction.

**beast** (bēst) *n.* An animal.

**beat** (bēt) *v.* **beat, beaten** (bēt'n) or **beat, beating. 1.** To strike repeatedly. **2.** To forge. **3.** To tread. **4.** To defeat. **5.** To pulsate; throb. **6.** To mix rapidly. — *n.* **1.** A stroke; blow. **2.** A throb. **3.** A rhythmic stress. **4.** A regular round. — **beat'er** *n.*

**beau·ty** (byōō'tē) *n., pl.* **-ties. 1.** A quality that delights the senses; loveliness. **2.** One possessing this quality. — **beau'te·ous** *adj.* — **beau'ti·ful** *adj.* — **beau'ti·fy** *v.*

**bea·ver** (bē'vər) *n.* A large aquatic rodent.

**be·came** (bǐ-kām') *p.t.* of **become.**

**be·cause** (bǐ-kôz', -kŭz') *conj.* For the reason that; since. — **because of.** On account of.

**beck·on** (běk'ən) *v.* To summon by gesture.

**be·come** (bǐ-kŭm') *v.* **-came, -come, -coming. 1.** To grow or come to be. **2.** To be appropriate to. — **become of.** To be the fate of. — **be·com'ing** *adj.*

**bed** (běd) *n.* **1.** A piece of furniture for sleeping. **2.** A plot of ground. **3.** A layer. **4.** A foundation. — *v.* **bedded, bedding.** To put in a bed.

**bed·ding** (běd'ĭng) *n.* Coverings for a bed.

**bed·lam** (běd'ləm) *n.* Noisy confusion.

**bed·room** (běd'rōōm', -rŏŏm') *n.* A room for sleeping.

**bed·stead** (běd'stěd') *n.* The frame supporting a bed.

**bee** (bē) *n.* **1.** An insect that lives in hives and makes honey. **2.** A gathering for work or competition.

**beef** (bēf) *n.* **1.** The meat of a full-grown steer, bull, ox, or cow. **2.** Human strength; brawn. **3.** A complaint. — *v.* To complain.

**been** (bĭn). *p.p.* of **be.**

**beer** (bîr) *n.* An alcoholic drink brewed from malt and hops.

**bee·tle** (bēt'l) *n.* An insect with horny front wings.

**be·fall** (bǐ-fôl') *v.* **-fell, -fallen, -falling. 1.** To come to pass. **2.** To happen to.

**be·fit** (bǐ-fĭt') *v.* **-fitted, -fitting.** To be suitable to.

**be·fore** (bǐ-fôr', -fōr') *adv.* Earlier; previously. — *prep.* **1.** Ahead of. **2.** Prior to. **3.** In front of. **4.** In the presence of. **5.** Under the consideration of. **6.** In preference to. — *conj.* **1.** In advance of the time when. **2.** Sooner than.

**be·friend** (bǐ-frĕnd') *v.* To act as a friend to.

**be·fud·dle** (bǐ-fŭd'l) *v.* **-dled, -dling.** To confuse. — **be·fud'dle·ment** *n.*

**beg** (běg) *v.* **begged, begging. 1.** To ask for as charity. **2.** To entreat.

**be·gan** (bǐ-găn'). *p.t.* of **begin.**

**be·get** (bǐ-gět') *v.* **-got, -gotten** or **-got, -getting.** To father; sire. — **be·get'ter** *n.*

**beg·gar** (běg'ər) *n.* One who begs for money. — *v.* To impoverish.

**be·gin** (bǐ-gĭn') *v.* **-gan, -gun, -ginning.** To start. — **be·gin'ner** *n.* — **be·gin'ning** *n.*

**be·got** (bǐ-gŏt'). *p.t.* and alternate *p.p.* of **beget.**

**be·got·ten** (bǐ-gŏt'n). *p.p.* of **beget.**

**be·grudge** (bǐ-grŭj') *v.* **-grudged, -grudging. 1.** To envy. **2.** To give with reluctance.

**be·guile** (bǐ-gīl') *v.* **-guiled, -guiling. 1.** To deceive. **2.** To divert; charm. — **be·guile'ment** *n.* — **be·guil'er** *n.*

**be·gun** (bǐ-gŭn'). *p.p.* of **begin.**

**be·half** (bǐ-hăf', -häf') *n.* Interest; benefit.

**be·have** (bǐ-hāv') *v.* **-haved, -having. 1.** To act or function. **2.** To conduct oneself, esp. properly. — **be·hav'ior** *n.* — **be·hav'ior·al** *adj.*

**be·head** (bǐ-hěd') *v.* To kill by cutting off the head of.

**be·hind** (bǐ-hīnd') *adv.* **1.** In or toward the rear. **2.** In arrears; late. — *prep.* **1.** To the rear of. **2.** After. **3.** In support of.

**be·hold** (bǐ-hōld') *v.* **-held** (-hěld'), **-holding.** To look upon; see. — **be·hold'er** *n.*

**beige** (bāzh) *n.* Light grayish brown. — **beige** *adj.*

**be·ing** (bē'ĭng) *n.* **1.** Existence. **2.** One that exists.

**be·lat·ed** (bǐ-lā'tĭd) *adj.* Tardy. — **be·lat'ed·ly** *adv.*

**belch** (bělch) *v.* To expel stomach gas through the mouth. — *n.* A belching. — **belch'er** *n.*

**bel·fry** (běl'frē) *n., pl.* **-fries.** A church bell tower.

**be·lief** (bǐ-lēf') *n.* **1.** Trust; confidence. **2.** A conviction or opinion.

**be·lieve** (bǐ-lēv') *v.* **-lieved, -lieving. 1.** To accept as true or real. **2.** To credit; trust. **3.** To suppose; think. — **be·liev'a·ble** *adj.* — **be·liev'er** *n.*

**be·lit·tle** (bǐ-lĭt'l) *v.* **-tled, -tling.** To speak of as small or unimportant; disparage.

**bell** (běl) *n.* A hollow metal object that rings when struck.

**bel·lig·er·ent** (bə-lĭj'ər-ənt) *adj.* **1.** Aggressively hostile. **2.** Waging war. — *n.* A warring nation. — **bel·lig'er·ence, bel·lig'er·en·cy** *n.* — **bel·lig'er·ent·ly** *adv.*

**bel·low** (bĕl'ō) v. To roar like a bull. —**bel'-low** n.

**bel·lows** (bĕl'ōz, -əz) n. A device for producing and directing a strong current of air.

**bel·ly** (bĕl'ē) n., pl. **-lies**. The abdomen or stomach.

**be·long** (bĭ-lông', -lŏng') v. 1. To be the property of. 2. To be a member of. 3. To have a proper place. —**be·long'ings** pl.n.

**be·low** (bĭ-lō') adv. In or to a lower place. —prep. 1. Lower than. 2. Inferior to.

**belt** (bĕlt) n. 1. A band around the waist. 2. A continuous moving band in machinery or manufacturing. 3. A geographic region. —v. 1. To encircle; gird. 2. To strike with or as if with a belt.

**bench** (bĕnch) n. 1. A long seat. 2. a. The judge's seat in court. b. The court or judges. 3. A craftsman's worktable.

**bend** (bĕnd) v. **bent, bending**. 1. To curve. 2. To coerce or subdue. 3. To yield; submit. —n. Something bent; a curve; crook.

**be·neath** (bĭ-nēth') adv. 1. In a lower place. 2. Underneath. —prep. 1. Below. 2. Unworthy of.

**ben·e·dic·tion** (bĕn'ə-dĭk'shən) n. A blessing.

**ben·e·fac·tor** (bĕn'ə-făk'tər) n. One who gives financial or other aid. —**ben'e·fac'tion** n. —**ben'e·fac'tress** fem.n.

**be·nef·i·cent** (bə-nĕf'ə-sənt) adj. Kind; charitable. —**be·nef'i·cence** n.

**ben·e·fi·cial** (bĕn'ə-fĭsh'əl) adj. Helpful; advantageous. —**ben·e·fi'cial·ly** adv. —**ben'e·fi'ci·ar·y** n.

**ben·e·fit** (bĕn'ə-fĭt) n. 1. An advantage. 2. An aid; help. 3. A payment. 4. A fundraising event. —v. 1. To be helpful or advantageous to. 2. To derive advantage.

**be·nev·o·lence** (bə-nĕv'ə-ləns) n. Charitable good nature. —**be·nev'o·lent** adj.

**be·nign** (bĭ-nīn') adj. 1. Kindly; favorable. 2. Not malignant.

**bent** (bĕnt) p.t. & p.p. of **bend**. —adj. 1. Crooked. 2. Determined. —n. An inclination.

**be·queath** (bĭ-kwēth', -kwĕth') v. 1. To leave by will. 2. To pass on or hand down by will.

**be·quest** (bĭ-kwĕst') n. Something left by will.

**be·rate** (bĭ-rāt') v. **-rated, -rating**. To scold harshly.

**be·reave** (bĭ-rēv') v. **-reaved** or **-reft** (-rĕft'), **-reaving**. To deprive of, as by death. —**be·reave'ment** n.

**ber·ry** (bĕr'ē) n., pl. **-ries**. A small, many-seeded fruit.

**ber·serk** (bər-sûrk', -zûrk') adj. Destructively violent. —**ber·serk'** adv.

**berth** (bûrth) n. 1. A built-in bed. 2. A docking space. 3. A job. —v. To dock.

**be·seech** (bĭ-sēch') v. **-sought** or **-seeched, -seeching**. To request earnestly; implore. —**be·seech'er** n.

**be·set** (bĭ-sĕt') v. **-set, -setting**. To attack from all sides; harass.

**be·side** (bĭ-sīd') prep. 1. Next to. 2. In comparison with. —**beside oneself**. Extremely agitated. —adv. In addition to.

**be·sides** (bĭ-sīdz') adv. 1. In addition; also. 2. Furthermore. 3. Otherwise. —prep. 1. In addition to. 2. Except for.

**be·siege** (bĭ-sēj') v. **-sieged, -sieging**. 1. To encircle; crowd around. 2. To overwhelm; flood. —**be·sieg'er** n.

**be·smirch** (bĭ-smûrch') v. To soil; dishonor.

**be·sought** (bĭ-sôt') p.t. & p.p. of **beseech**.

**be·speak** (bĭ-spēk') v. **-spoke, -spoken** or **-spoke, -speaking**. To be or give a sign of; indicate.

**best** (bĕst) adj. superl. of **good**. Surpassing all others; most excellent. —adv. superl. of **well**. 1. Most advantageously. 2. To the greatest extent. —n. 1. The best one. 2. The best condition. 3. The utmost. —v. To surpass; defeat.

**bes·tial** (bĕs'chəl, bĕst'yəl) adj. Like a beast; savage. —**bes·ti·al'i·ty** n.

**be·stow** (bĭ-stō') v. To present; confer. —**be·stow'al** n.

**bet** (bĕt) n. An agreement between two parties that the party proved wrong will pay the other; wager. —v. **bet, betting**. To make or place a bet. —**bet'tor, bet'ter** n.

**be·tray** (bĭ-trā') v. 1. To be disloyal or faithless to. 2. To reveal, esp. unintentionally. —**be·tray'al** n. —**be·tray'er** n.

**be·troth** (bĭ-trōth', bĭ-trôth') v. To promise in marriage. —**be·troth'al** n. —**be·trothed'** adj. & n.

**bet·ter** (bĕt'ər) adj. compar. of **good**. 1. Greater in excellence or higher in quality. 2. More useful. 3. Healthier. —adv. compar. of **well**. 1. To a greater or higher extent. 2. More. —**had better**. Ought to. —**think better of**. To change one's mind. —n. 1. Something better. 2. Often **betters**. One's superiors. —v. 1. To make or become better. 2. To surpass. —**bet'ter·ment** n.

**be·tween** (bĭ-twēn') prep. 1. In the space or time separating. 2. In the combined effort or ownership of. —adv. In an intermediate space, position, or time.

**bev·er·age** (bĕv′rĭj, bĕv′ə-rĭj) n. A liquid refreshment; drink.

**be·ware** (bĭ-wâr′) v. -wared, -waring. To guard against; be cautious of.

**be·wil·der** (bĭ-wĭl′dər) v. To confuse or befuddle. —**be·wil′der·ment** n.

**be·witch** (bĭ-wĭch′) v. To enchant; fascinate.

**be·yond** (bē-ŏnd′) prep. 1. Farther away than. 2. After. 3. Outside the limits of. —adv. Farther along.

**bi·an·nu·al** (bī-ăn′yōō-əl) adj. Twice each year. —**bi·an′nu·al·ly** adv.

**bi·as** (bī′əs) n. 1. A line cutting diagonally across the grain of fabric. 2. Prejudice. —v. -ased or -assed, -asing or -assing. To prejudice or influence. —**bi′ased** adj.

**Bi·ble** (bī′bəl) n. 1. The sacred book of Christianity. 2. The Old Testament, the sacred book of Judaism. —**Bib′li·cal** adj.

**bib·li·og·ra·phy** (bĭb′lē-ŏg′rə-fē) n., pl. -phies. A list of works by an author or on a subject. —**bib′li·og′ra·pher** n. —**bib′li·o·graph′ic, bib′li·o·graph′i·cal** adj.

**bi·ceps** (bī′sĕps′) n., pl. -ceps or -cepses. The large muscle at the front of the upper arm.

**bick·er** (bĭk′ər) v. To quarrel.

**bi·cy·cle** (bī′sĭk′əl, -sĭ-kəl) n. A two-wheeled vehicle pedaled by the rider. —**bi′cy·cle** v. —**bi′cy·clist** n.

**bid** (bĭd) v. **bid** or **bade, bidden** or **bid, bidding.** a. To direct; command. b. To invite; summon; ask. 2. **bid, bid, bidding.** a. To seek; strive. b. To offer as a price. —n. 1. An offer of a price. 2. An invitation. 3. A try; attempt. —**bid′der** n.

**bide** (bīd) v. **bided** or **bode, bided, biding.** 1. To stay. 2. To await.

**bi·en·ni·al** (bī-ĕn′ē-əl) adj. 1. Lasting two years. 2. Happening every second year. —**bi·en′ni·al** n.

**bier** (bîr) n. A stand for a coffin.

**bi·fo·cal** (bī-fō′kəl) adj. Designed to correct both near and distant vision. —n. **bifocals.** Eyeglasses with bifocal lenses.

**big** (bĭg) adj. **bigger, biggest.** 1. Of great size; large. 2. Grown-up. 3. Important. —**big′gish** adj. —**big′ness** n.

**big·a·my** (bĭg′ə-mē) n., pl. -mies. The crime of marrying one person while still married to another. —**big′a·mist** n. —**big′a·mous** adj.

**big·ot** (bĭg′ət) n. An intolerant person. —**big′ot·ed** adj. —**big′ot·ry** n.

**bile** (bīl) n. 1. A bitter liquid secreted by the liver and aiding in digestion. 2. Ill humor. —**bil′ious** adj.

**bilge** (bĭlj) n. 1. The lowest inner part of a ship's hull. 2. Water that collects in this part. 3. Stupid talk; nonsense.

**bill¹** (bĭl) n. 1. A statement of charges. 2. A list of items offered. 3. An advertising poster. 4. A piece of paper money. 5. A proposed law. —v. To present a statement of costs to.

**bill²** (bĭl) n. The beak of a bird.

**bil·let** (bĭl′ĭt) n. A lodging, as for troops. —v. To assign quarters to.

**bill·fold** (bĭl′fōld′) n. A wallet.

**bil·lion** (bĭl′yən) n. A thousand million. —**bil′lion** adj. —**bil′lionth** n.& adj.

**bil·low** (bĭl′ō) n. 1. A large wave. 2. A great swell or surge. —v. To surge, roll, or rise in billows.

**bin** (bĭn) n. A storage receptacle.

**bi·na·ry** (bī′nə-rē) adj. Based on or having two.

**bind** (bīnd) v. **bound, binding.** 1. To tie or encircle. 2. To bandage. 3. To hold or restrain. 4. To compel; oblige. 5. To enclose and fasten (a book) between covers. —**bind′er** n.

**bin·oc·u·lars** (bə-nŏk′yə-lərz, bī-) pl.n. An optical device with a lens for each eye for magnifying distant objects.

**bi·o·chem·is·try** (bī′ō-kĕm′ĭs-trē) n. The chemistry of biological substances and processes. —**bi′o·chem′i·cal** adj.

**bi·og·ra·phy** (bī-ŏg′rə-fē, bē-) n., pl. -phies. A written account of a person's life. —**bi·og′ra·pher** n. —**bi′o·graph′ic, bi′o·graph′i·cal** adj.

**bi·ol·o·gy** (bī-ŏl′ə-jē) n. The science of living things. —**bi′o·log′i·cal** adj. —**bi·ol′o·gist** n.

**bi·par·ti·san** (bī-pär′tə-zən) adj. Of two parties. —**bi·par′ti·san·ship** n.

**bird** (bûrd) n. A warm-blooded, egg-laying, feathered vertebrate with wings.

**birth** (bûrth) n. 1. The act or condition of being born. 2. Origin; beginning. —**birth′day** n.

**bis·cuit** (bĭs′kĭt) n. 1. A small roll of bread. 2. A cracker or cooky.

**bi·sect** (bī′sĕkt′, bī-sĕkt′) v. To divide or cut into two. —**bi·sec′tion** n.

**bish·op** (bĭsh′əp) n. A Christian clergyman in charge of a diocese.

**bi·son** (bī′sən, -zən) n. A short-horned, oxlike mammal of North America.

**bit¹** (bĭt) n. 1. A small piece or amount. 2. A moment.

**bit²** (bĭt) *n.* **1.** A pointed tool for drilling and boring. **2.** The metal mouthpiece of a bridle.

**bitch** (bĭch) *n.* **1.** A female dog. **2.** A spiteful woman. —*v.* To complain. —**bitch'y** *adj.*

**bite** (bīt) *v.* **bit, bitten** or **bit, biting. 1.** To cut or tear with the teeth. **2.** To sting. **3. a.** A tiny bait. —*n.* **1.** The act of biting. **2.** An injury resulting from biting. **3. a.** A stinging or smarting sensation. **b.** An incisive, penetrating quality. **4.** A mouthful.

**bit·ter** (bĭt'ər) *adj.* **1.** Having a sharp and unpleasant taste. **2.** Painful; resentful. —**bit'ter·ly** *adv.* —**bit'ter·ness** *n.*

**biv·ou·ac** (bĭv'ōō-ăk, bĭv'wăk) *n.* A temporary encampment of soldiers. —*v.* **-acked, -acking.** To encamp in a bivouac.

**bi·zarre** (bĭ-zär') *adj.* Strikingly unconventional; odd.

**blab** (blăb) *v.* **blabbed, blabbing.** To chatter indiscreetly. —**blab'ber** *n.* —**blab'by** *adj.*

**black** (blăk) *adj.* **1.** Of the darkest color. **2.** Having no light. **3.** Negroid. **4.** Evil. **5.** Cheerless. —*n.* **1.** A black color or pigment. **2.** A Negro. —**black'ish** *adj.*

**black·guard** (blăg'ərd, -ärd) *n.* A scoundrel.

**black·jack** (blăk'jăk') *n.* **1.** A small leather-covered club. **2.** A card game.

**black·mail** (blăk'māl') *n.* Extortion by threat of exposing something disgraceful. —**black'mail'** *v.* —**black'mail'er** *n.*

**blad·der** (blăd'ər) *n.* A sac, esp. a sac in the pelvic cavity for storing urine.

**blade** (blād) *n.* **1.** The flat-edged cutting part of a tool. **2.** A leaf of grass. **3.** A dashing young man.

**blame** (blām) *v.* **blamed, blaming. 1.** To hold responsible. **2.** To censure. —*n.* **1.** Responsibility for a fault or error. **2.** Censure.

**blanch** (blănch, blänch) *v.* To make or become pale or white.

**bland** (blănd) *adj.* **1.** Moderate; mild. **2.** Characterless; zestless. —**bland'ness** *n.*

**blan·dish** (blăn'dĭsh) *v.* To coax by flattery; cajole. —**blan'dish·ment** *n.*

**blank** (blăngk) *adj.* **1.** Bearing no writing or marking. **2.** Not filled in. **3.** Expressing nothing; vacant. —*n.* **1.** An empty space. **2.** A space or form to be filled in. **3.** A gun cartridge with no bullet. —**blank'ly** *adv.*

**blan·ket** (blăng'kĭt) *n.* **1.** A thick cloth used as a covering, esp. on a bed. **2.** A thick layer that covers. —*adj.* Covering a wide range of conditions. —*v.* To cover with or as if with a blanket.

**blare** (blâr) *v.* **blared, blaring.** To sound loudly. —*n.* A loud sound.

**blar·ney** (blär'nē) *n.* Smooth, flattering talk.

**blas·pheme** (blăs-fēm') *v.* **-phemed, -pheming.** To speak of irreverently; profane. —**blas'phe·mous** *adj.* —**blas'phe·my** *n.*

**blast** (blăst, blăst) *n.* **1.** A strong gust; rush. **2.** A loud sound, as of a whistle. **3.** An explosion. **4.** A verbal assault. —**(at) full blast.** At full capacity. —*v.* **1.** To explode. **2.** To blight; wither. **3.** To criticize vigorously.

**bla·tant** (blā'tənt) *adj.* Offensively conspicuous; obvious. —**bla'tant·ly** *adv.*

**blaze** (blāz) *n.* **1.** A fire. **2.** Any bright, hot light. **3.** A sudden outburst. —*v.* **blazed, blazing. 1.** To burn brightly. **2.** To shine brightly. **3.** To be deeply excited.

**bleach** (blēch) *v.* To make or become white or colorless. —*n.* A chemical used for bleaching.

**bleak** (blēk) *adj.* **1.** Exposed; barren. **2.** Gloomy and somber.

**blear** (blîr) *v.* To blur; dim. —**blear'i·ness** *n.* —**blear'y** *adj.*

**bleed** (blēd) *v.* **bled** (blĕd), **bleeding. 1.** To lose or extract blood. **2.** To extort money from. **3.** To become mixed or run, as dyes in wet cloth.

**blem·ish** (blĕm'ĭsh) *n.* A flaw; defect. —**blem'ished** *v.*

**blend** (blĕnd) *v.* To combine; mix; merge. —*n.* A combination; mixture.

**bless** (blĕs) *v.* **blessed** or **blest, blessing. 1.** To make holy; sanctify. **2.** To invoke divine favor upon. **3.** To make fortunate; favor. —**bless'ed** *adj.* —**bless'ing** *n.*

**blew** (bloo) *p.t.* of **blow.**

**blight** (blīt) *n.* **1.** A destructive plant disease. **2.** An injurious influence. —**blight** *v.*

**blind** (blīnd) *adj.* **1.** Without sight. **2.** Without reason or evidence. **3.** Hidden from sight. **4.** Closed at one end. —*n.* **1.** Something that shuts out light. **2.** A shelter for concealing hunters. —*v.* To deprive of sight. —**blind'ly** *adv.* —**blind'ness** *n.*

**blind·fold** (blīnd'fōld') *n.* A bandage over the eyes. —**blind'fold'** *v.*

**blink** (blĭngk) *v.* **1.** To close and open (one or both eyes) rapidly. **2.** To flash on and off. —*n.* **1.** The act of blinking. **2.** A flash of light; a glimmer.

**bliss** (blĭs) *n.* Serene happiness. —**bliss'ful** *adj.*

**blis·ter** (blĭs'tər) *n.* A thin, fluid-filled swelling of the skin caused by irritation. —**blis'ter** *v.*

**blithe** (bli*th*, bli*th*) *adj.* Cheerful; carefree.

**bliz·zard** (bliz′ərd) *n.* A heavy snowstorm.

**bloat** (blōt) *v.* To make or become swollen.

**blob** (blŏb) *n.* A rounded mass or splotch.

**bloc** (blŏk) *n.* A group united for common action.

**block** (blŏk) *n.* **1.** A solid, flat-sided piece of wood or other hard substance. **2.** A stand at an auction. **3.** A pulley or a system of pulleys set in a casing. **4.** A set of like items. **5. a.** A section of a town bounded on each side by consecutive streets. **b.** A segment of a street bounded by successive cross streets. **6.** An obstacle. —*v.* **1.** To stop the passage or view of. **2.** To plan roughly; shape. —**block′age** *n.*

**block·ade** (blŏ-kād′) *n.* The closing off of access to an area. —**block·ade′** *v.*

**blond** (blŏnd) *adj.* Also *fem.* **blonde.** Having fair hair. **2.** Light-colored. —*n.* Also *fem.* **blonde.** A blond person.

**blood** (blŭd) *n.* **1.** The red fluid that flows through the body. **2.** Kinship. **3.** Racial or national ancestry.

**blood·shed** (blŭd′shĕd′) *n.* Loss of life; casualties.

**blood·thirst·y** (blŭd′thûr′stē) *adj.* Murderous; cruel.

**blood·y** (blŭd′ē) *adj.* **-i·er, -i·est. 1.** Of, containing, or stained with blood. **2.** Giving rise to bloodshed. **3.** Bloodthirsty; cruel. —*v.* **-ied, -ying.** To stain with blood.

**bloom** (blōōm) *n.* **1.** The flower or blossoms of a plant. **2.** The time of flowering. **3.** A fresh, rosy complexion. **4.** A glow. —*v.* **1.** To bear flowers. **2.** To glow. **3.** To grow or flourish.

**bloom·ers** (blōō′mərz) *pl.n.* Women's wide, loose underpants.

**blos·som** (blŏs′əm) *n.* A flower. —*v.* **1.** To flower; bloom. **2.** To develop; flourish.

**blot** (blŏt) *n.* A spot; a stain. —*v.* **-ted, -ting. 1.** To spot or stain. **2.** To erase; cancel (with *out*). **3.** To dry with absorbent material. —**blot′ter** *n.*

**blotch** (blŏch) *n.* A spot or blot. —**blotch** *v.*

**blouse** (blous, blouz) *n.* A loosely fitting shirtlike garment. —*v.* **bloused, blousing.** To hang loosely.

**blow** (blō) *v.* **blew, blown** (blōn), **blowing. 1.** To move as the wind does. **2.** To carry or be carried by the wind. **3.** To expel a current of air. **4.** To sound or make by expelling a current of air. **5.** To explode. **6.** To melt (a fuse). —*n.* **1.** A blast of air or wind. **2.** The act of blowing. **3.** A hard stroke; impact; hit. **4.** A shock or calamity. —**blow′er** *n.*

**blow-out** (blō′out′) *n.* **1.** A sudden bursting, as of an automobile tire. **2.** The burning out of a fuse.

**blow·torch** (blō′tôrch′) *n.* A gas burner that produces a flame for welding metals.

**blow-up** (blō′ŭp′) *n.* **1.** An explosion. **2.** A photographic enlargement.

**blub·ber** (blŭb′ər) *n.* Fat, esp. whale fat.

**bludg·eon** (blŭj′ən) *n.* A short club. —*v.* **-eoned, -eoning. 1.** To club. **2.** To threaten or bully.

**blue** (blōō) *n.* A color like that of a clear sky. —**the blues. 1.** Low spirits. **2.** A slow, sad style of jazz ballad. —*adj.* **bluer, bluest. 1.** Of the color blue. **2.** Gloomy; dreary.

**blue·print** (blōō′print′) *n.* A detailed plan, as of an architectural design.

**bluff** (blŭf) *v.* To mislead by a false display of boldness. —*n.* **1.** The act of bluffing. **2.** A steep bank; cliff. —*adj.* Blunt. —**bluff′er** *n.*

**blun·der** (blŭn′dər) *n.* A stupid mistake. —*v.* **1.** To move awkwardly or clumsily. **2.** To make a stupid mistake.

**blunt** (blŭnt) *adj.* **1.** Having a thick, dull edge or end. **2.** Outspoken; brusque. —*v.* To make or become blunt. —**blunt′ly** *adv.*

**blur** (blûr) *v.* **blurred, blurring. 1.** To make or become indistinct; obscure. **2.** To smear or stain. **3.** To dim. —*n.* Anything hazy and indistinct. —**blur′ry** *adj.*

**blurt** (blûrt) *v.* To utter impulsively.

**blush** (blŭsh) *n.* A reddening of the face, as from shame. —**blush** *v.*

**blus·ter** (blŭs′tər) *v.* **1.** To blow in violent gusts, as wind in a storm. **2.** To speak boastfully. —**blus′ter·y** *adj.*

**board** (bôrd, bōrd) *n.* **1.** A long, flat piece of wood. **2.** Regularly provided meals. **3.** A group of administrators; council. —**on board.** Aboard. —*v.* **1.** To cover or close with boards. **2.** To furnish with or receive meals. **3.** To enter or go aboard (a vehicle or ship). —**board′er** *n.*

**boast** (bōst) *v.* **1.** To talk about or speak with excessive pride. **2.** To take pride in; enjoy the possession of. —*n.* An instance of bragging. —**boast′er** *n.* —**boast′ful** *adj.*

**boat** (bōt) *n.* A small water craft. **2.** A ship.

**bob** (bŏb) *n.* **1.** A short jerking movement. **2.** A fishing float. **3.** A short haircut. —*v.* **bobbed, bobbing. 1.** To move or jerk up and down. **2.** To cut (hair) short.

**bob·bin** (bŏb′in) *n.* A spool or reel for thread.

**bob·sled** (bŏb′slĕd′) *n.* A racing sled.

**bode**

— bob'sled' v.

**bode¹** (bōd) v. **boded, boding.** To be an omen of.

**bode²** (bōd). Alternate p.t. of **bide.**

**bod·ice** (bŏd'ĭs) n. The fitted upper part of a woman's dress.

**bod·y** (bŏd'ē) n., pl. **-ies. 1. a.** The physical structure, esp. of a human being or animal. **b.** A corpse. **2.** A trunk or torso. **3.** A person. **4.** A number of persons or things; group. **5.** The main or central part. **6.** Any bounded mass. — **bod'i·ly** adj. & adv.

**bog** (bŏg, bôg) n. Soft, water-logged ground; a marsh. —v. **bogged, bogging.** To hinder or be hindered; slow (with down).

**bo·gus** (bō'gəs) adj. Counterfeit; fake.

**boil¹** (boil) v. **1.** To vaporize a liquid by applying heat. **2.** To cook by boiling. **3.** To be in a state of agitation. — **boil down.** To condense; summarize. —n. The state of boiling. — **boil'er** n.

**boil²** (boil) n. A pus-filled skin swelling.

**bois·ter·ous** (boi'stər-əs, -strəs) adj. Noisy and unrestrained; rowdy. — **bois'ter·ous·ly** adv. — **bois'ter·ous·ness** n.

**bold** (bōld) adj. **1.** Fearless; courageous. **2.** Unduly forward; impudent. **3.** Clear and distinct. — **bold'ly** adv. — **bold'ness** n.

**bol·ster** (bōl'stər) n. A long, narrow pillow. —v. To prop up.

**bolt** (bōlt) n. **1.** A sliding bar used to fasten or lock a door. **2.** A threaded metal pin used with a nut to hold parts together. **3.** A flash of lightning. **4.** A sudden movement; dash. **5.** A large roll of cloth. —v. **1.** To secure or lock with a bolt. **2.** To eat hurriedly; gulp. **3.** To desert; abandon. **4.** To move or spring suddenly; dash.

**bomb** (bŏm) n. An explosive weapon dropped on or thrown at a target. —v. To attack with bombs.

**bom·bard** (bŏm-bärd') v. To attack heavily with bombs or missiles. — **bom·bar'dier** n. — **bom·bard'ment** n.

**bom·bast** (bŏm'băst') n. Pompous speech or writing. — **bom·bas'tic** adj.

**bomb·er** (bŏm'ər) n. An aircraft designed to drop bombs.

**bond** (bŏnd) n. **1.** Anything that binds, ties, or fastens together. **2.** A uniting force or tie; a link. **3.** A sum of money paid as bail or surety. **4.** A certificate of debt guaranteeing payment plus interest. —v. **1.** To furnish bond or surety for. **2.** To join securely, as with glue.

**bond·age** (bŏn'dĭj) n. Slavery; servitude.

**bone** (bōn) n. **1.** The rigid, calcified material that makes up the skeleton. **2.** One of the pieces of the skeleton. —v. **boned, boning.** To remove the bones from. — **bon'y** adj.

**bon·fire** (bŏn'fīr') n. A large outdoor fire.

**bon·net** (bŏn'ĭt) n. A hat tied under the chin.

**bo·nus** (bō'nəs) n., pl. **-nuses.** An extra payment or gift.

**book** (bŏŏk) n. **1.** Written or printed material made up of fastened pages between protective covers. **2.** A literary work. **3.** A volume in which financial transactions are recorded. —v. To list, reserve, or schedule in a book. — **book'ish** adj.

**book·keep·ing** (bŏŏk'kē'pĭng) n. The recording of the accounts of a business. — **book'keep'er** n.

**book·let** (bŏŏk'lĭt) n. A small bound book.

**boom¹** (bŏŏm) v. **1.** To make a deep, resonant sound. **2.** To flourish. —n. **1.** A booming sound. **2.** Prosperity; success.

**boom²** (bŏŏm) n. **1.** A long spar extending from a mast to hold a sail. **2.** A long pole, esp. to support or guide objects lifted.

**boo·mer·ang** (bŏŏ'mə-răng') n. A flat, curved missile that can be hurled so that it returns to the thrower. —v. To rebound detrimentally.

**boon** (bŏŏn) n. Something beneficial; a blessing.

**boor** (bŏŏr) n. A rude, clumsy person. — **boor'ish** adj.

**boost** (bŏŏst) v. **1.** To raise by pushing up from below. **2.** To increase; raise. **3.** To promote vigorously. —n. A lift or help. **2.** An increase. — **boost'er** n.

**boot** (bŏŏt) n. **1.** A piece of footwear covering the foot and part or all of the leg. **2.** A kick. —v. **1.** To put boots on. **2.** To kick.

**booth** (bŏŏth) n., pl. **booths.** A small enclosed compartment, stall, or eating area.

**boot·leg** (bŏŏt'lĕg') v. **-legged, -legging.** To make, sell, or transport illegally, as liquor. —adj. Illegal. — **boot'leg'ger** n.

**boo·ty** (bŏŏ'tē) n., pl. **-ties.** Plunder; loot.

**booze** (bŏŏz) n. Intoxicating liquor. —v. **boozed, boozing.** To drink to excess.

**bor·der** (bôr'dər) n. **1.** A surrounding margin; edge. **2.** A geographic boundary. —v. **1.** To provide with a border. **2.** To lie on the border of. **3.** To verge; approach.

**bore¹** (bôr, bōr) v. **bored, boring.** To make a hole in or through; drill; dig. —n. **1.** A hole made by drilling. **2.** The interior diameter of a tube, cylinder, etc.

**bore²** (bôr, bōr) v. **bored, boring.** To tire by dullness; be uninteresting to. —n. A dull person or thing. — **bore'dom** n.

**bore³** (bôr, bōr). p.t. of **bear¹.**

**born** (bôrn). A p.p. of **bear¹.** —adj. From birth; innate.

**borne** (bôrn, bōrn). A p.p. of **bear¹.**

**bor·row** (bŏr'ō, bôr'ō) v. 1. To obtain on loan with intent to return. 2. To adopt or use as one's own. — **bor'row·er** n.

**bos·om** (bŏoz'əm, bōo'zəm) n. 1. The chest or breasts. 2. The center or heart. —adj. Intimate.

**boss** (bôs, bŏs) n. 1. An employer or supervisor. 2. A powerful politician. —v. 1. To supervise. 2. To command in a domineering manner. — **boss'y** adj.

**bot·a·ny** (bŏt'n-ē) n. The science of plants. — **bo·tan'ic, bo·tan'i·cal** adj. — **bot'a·nist** n.

**botch** (bŏch) v. To ruin; bungle. — **botch** n.

**both** (bōth) adj. Two or two together. —pron. The one and the other. —conj. As well; together.

**both·er** (bŏth'ər) v. 1. To irritate, esp. by small annoyances; pester; harass. 2. To trouble or concern oneself. —n. A cause or state of disturbance. — **both'er·some** adj.

**bot·tle** (bŏt'l) n. A container, usually glass, having a narrow neck and a mouth that can be sealed. —v. **-tled, -tling.** To place in a bottle. — **bottle up.** To confine.

**bot·tom** (bŏt'əm) n. 1. The lowest or deepest part. 2. The underside. 3. The basic quality; essence. 4. The buttocks. —adj. Lowest; fundamental. — **bot'tom·less** adj.

**bough** (bou) n. A branch of a tree.

**bought** (bôt). p.t. & p.p. of **buy.**

**bouil·lon** (bŏo'yŏn', bōol'yŏn', -yən) n. A clear meat broth.

**boul·der** (bōl'dər) n. A large rounded rock.

**bounce** (bouns) v. **bounced, bouncing.** 1. To rebound from a collision. 2. To cause to collide and rebound; bound. —n. 1. A bound or rebound. 2. A spring or leap.

**bound¹** (bound) v. To leap or spring. —n. 1. A leap. 2. A bounce.

**bound²** (bound) n. Often **bounds.** A boundary. —v. 1. To limit. 2. To demarcate. — **bound'less** adj.

**bound³** (bound). p.t. & p.p. of **bind.** —adj. 1. Confined by bonds; tied. 2. Under obligation. 3. Equipped with a cover or binding. 4. Certain.

**bound·a·ry** (boun'drē, -də-rē) n., pl. **-ries.** A border or limit.

**boun·te·ous** (boun'tē-əs) adj. 1. Generous. 2. Plentiful. — **boun'te·ous·ly** adv.

**boun·ty** (boun'tē) n., pl. **-ties.** 1. Liberality in giving. 2. A reward or inducement. — **boun'ti·ful** adj.

**bou·quet** (bō-kā', bōō-) n. 1. A bunch of flowers. 2. An aroma.

**bour·bon** (bûr'bən) n. A whiskey distilled from corn.

**bour·geois** (bŏor-zhwä', bŏor'zhwä') n., pl. **-geois.** One belonging to the middle class. — **bour·geois'** adj. — **bour'geoi·sie'** n.

**bout** (bout) n. 1. A contest; match. 2. A period of time; spell.

**bo·vine** (bō'vīn', -vēn') adj. Of or resembling a cow or cattle. — **bo'vine'** n.

**bow¹** (bou) n. The front section of a ship.

**bow²** (bou) v. 1. To bend (the head or body) in order to express greeting or respect. 2. To acquiesce; submit. —n. An inclination of the head or body, as in greeting.

**bow³** (bō) n. 1. Something bent, curved, or arched. 2. A curved stick, strung taut and used to launch arrows. 3. A rod strung with horsehair, used in playing violins, etc. 4. A knot having loose loops. —v. 1. To bend into a bow. 2. To play a stringed instrument with a bow.

**bow·els** (bou'əlz) pl.n. 1. The intestines. 2. The interior; depths.

**bowl¹** (bōl) n. 1. A hemispheric vessel for food or fluids. 2. A curved, hollow part. 3. A bowl-shaped building.

**bowl²** (bōl) v. To throw or roll a ball in bowling. — **bowl'er** n.

**box¹** (bŏks) n. 1. A rectangular container, often with a lid. 2. A separate seating compartment in a theater. —v. To place in a box.

**box²** (bŏks) n. A blow or cuff. —v. To hit or fight with the fists. — **box'er** n. — **box'ing** adj. & n.

**box·car** (bŏks'kär') n. An enclosed railway car for freight.

**boy** (boi) n. A male child or youth. — **boy'hood'** n.

**boy·cott** (boi'kŏt') v. To abstain from dealing with, as a means of protest. — **boy'cott'** n.

**brace** (brās) n. 1. A clamp. 2. Any support. 3. A cranklike device for turning a bit. 4. pl. **brace.** A pair of like things. —v. **braced, bracing.** 1. To support. 2. To prepare for an impact or danger. 3. To invigorate.

**brace·let** (brās'lĭt) n. An ornamental band for the wrist.

**brack·et** (brăk'ĭt) n. 1. A structure projecting to support a shelf or other weight. 2. Either of a pair of symbols, [ ], used to enclose written or printed material. 3. A classification. —v. 1. To support with brackets. 2. To place within brackets. 3. To classify together.

**brack·ish** (brăk'ĭsh) adj. Salty.

**brag** (brăg) v. bragged, bragging. To talk boastfully. —brag'gart n.

**braid** (brād) v. 1. To interweave strands of; plait. 2. To decorate with an ornamental trim. —n. 1. A braided length. 2. An ornamental trim.

**Braille** (brāl) n. Also braille. A system of printing for the blind, using raised dots.

**brain** (brān) n. 1. The gray nerve tissue in the skull responsible for the control of bodily activities and the exercise of emotion and thought. 2. Often brains. Intelligence. —v. To smash in the skull of. —brain'less adj. —brain'y adj.

**brake** (brāk) n. A device for slowing or stopping motion. —v. braked, braking. To slow or stop with a brake.

**bram·ble** (brăm'bəl) n. A prickly plant.

**branch** (brănch, bränch) n. 1. An extension dividing off from the trunk or a limb of a plant. 2. A division, tributary, or unit. —v. 1. To spread out in branches. 2. To subdivide; diverge.

**brand** (brănd) n. 1. A trademark or label. 2. A make; kind. 3. A mark burned on the hide of an animal. 4. A mark of disgrace; stigma. —v. 1. To mark with a brand. 2. To stigmatize.

**bran·dish** (brăn'dĭsh) v. To flourish; display.

**bran·dy** (brăn'dē) n., pl. -dies. A liquor distilled from wine or fruit juice.

**brash** (brăsh) adj. 1. Hasty; rash. 2. Impudent; saucy.

**brass** (brăs, bräs) n. 1. An alloy of copper and zinc. 2. brasses. Wind instruments made of brass. 3. Military officers. —brass adj.

**bras·siere, bras·sière** (brə-zîr') n. A woman's undergarment worn to support the breasts.

**brat** (brăt) n. A disobedient child. —brat'ty adj.

**bra·va·do** (brə-vä'dō) n., pl. -does or -dos. False bravery; swagger.

**brave** (brāv) adj. braver, bravest. Displaying courage. —n. A North American Indian warrior. —v. braved, braving. To face courageously. —brave'ly adv. —brav'er·y n.

**brawl** (brôl) n. A noisy quarrel or fight. —v. To quarrel noisily.

**brawn** (brôn) n. 1. Well-developed muscles. 2. Muscular power. —brawn'y adj.

**bra·zen** (brā'zən) adj. Impudent; bold. —bra·zen·ly adv. —bra'zen·ness n.

**breach** (brēch) n. 1. A violation; infraction. 2. A gap; rift; break. —v. To make a hole or gap in; break through.

**bread** (brĕd) n. 1. A foodstuff made from baked flour dough. 2. The necessities of life; livelihood. —v. To coat with bread crumbs.

**breadth** (brĕdth) n. 1. The measure from side to side; width. 2. Wide extent or scope.

**break** (brāk) v. broke, broken, breaking. 1. To separate into pieces by sudden force; come apart. 2. To make or become unusable. 3. To force or make a way into; pierce. 4. To disrupt. 5. To come into being or notice. 6. To surpass. 7. To tame; subdue. 8. To stop. —break in. 1. To train. 2. To enter forcibly. 3. To interrupt. —break off. To stop suddenly. —break out. 1. To erupt. 2. To escape, as from prison. —n. 1. The act of breaking. 2. A fracture or crack. 3. A disruption. 4. A change. 5. A respite; rest period. —break'age n.

**break·down** (brāk'doun') n. 1. Loss of function; mechanical failure. 2. A collapse in health. 3. An analysis.

**break·fast** (brĕk'fəst) n. The first meal of the day. —break'fast v.

**breast** (brĕst) n. 1. A mammary gland. 2. The chest.

**breath** (brĕth) n. 1. The air inhaled and exhaled in respiration. 2. Respiration. 3. A stirring of air. 4. A trace. —breath'less adj. —breath'tak'ing adj.

**breathe** (brēth) v. breathed, breathing. 1. To inhale and exhale. 2. To live. 3. To pause to rest. 4. To utter. —breath'a·ble adj.

**breath·er** (brē'thər) n. A short rest period.

**breech·es** (brĭch'ĭz) pl.n. Knee-length trousers.

**breed** (brēd) v. bred (brĕd), breeding. 1. To produce (offspring); reproduce. 2. To bring about. 3. To raise (animals). 4. To rear; bring up. —n. 1. A genetic strain. 2. A kind; sort. —breed'ing n.

**breeze** (brēz) n. A gentle wind. —v. breezed, breezing. To move effortlessly. —breez'y adj.

**brev·i·ty** (brĕv'ə-tē) n. Briefness; terseness.

**brew** (brōō) v. 1. To make (ale or beer) from malt and hops. 2. To make by boiling or steeping. 3. To concoct; make. —n. A beverage made by brewing. —brew'er n.

**bribe** (brīb) n. Anything offered or given to induce someone to act dishonestly. —v. **bribed, bribing.** To give or offer a bribe to. —**brib·er·y** n.

**brick** (brĭk) n. A block of baked clay used in construction. —v. To cover with brick. —**brick** adj. —**brick'lay·er** n.

**bride** (brīd) n. A woman recently married or about to be married. —**bri'dal** adj.

**bride-groom** (brīd'grōom', -grŏom') n. A man recently married or about to be married.

**bridge** (brĭj) n. 1. A structure providing passage over a waterway or other obstacle. 2. A connection; link; liaison. 3. The ridge of the nose. 4. A false tooth or set of teeth anchored by the gums. —v. **bridged, bridging.** To build or be a bridge over.

**bri·dle** (brīd'l) n. 1. The harness fitted about a horse's head. 2. Any restraint. —v. **died, -dling.** 1. To put a bridle on. 2. To control or restrain. 3. To display resentment.

**brief** (brēf) adj. Short. —n. A summary, esp. of a legal case. —v. To inform or instruct. —**brief'ly** adv.

**brig** (brĭg) n. 1. A two-masted sailing ship. 2. A ship's prison.

**bri·gade** (brĭ-gād') n. 1. A military unit consisting of a number of combat battalions. 2. Any organized group.

**bright** (brīt) adj. 1. Emitting or reflecting light; shining. 2. Brilliant; vivid. 3. Auspicious. 4. Happy; cheerful. 5. Intelligent. —**bright'en** v. —**bright'ly** adv. —**bright'ness** n.

**bril·liant** (brĭl'yənt) adj. 1. Shining. 2. Brightly vivid in color. 3. Glorious; splendid. 4. Marked by extraordinary intellect. —**bril'liance, bril'lian·cy** n. —**bril'liant·ly** adv.

**brim** (brĭm) n. 1. The uppermost edge of a cup. 2. A projecting edge of a hat.

**brine** (brīn) n. 1. Very salty water. 2. The ocean. —**brin'y** adj.

**bring** (brĭng) v. **brought, bringing.** 1. To take with oneself to a place. 2. To lead into a specified state. 3. To induce. 4. To cause to occur. —**bring about.** To cause to happen. —**bring forth.** To produce. —**bring off.** To accomplish. —**bring out.** 1. To reveal. 2. To produce. —**bring up.** 1. To rear (a child). 2. To mention.

**brink** (brĭngk) n. The edge; verge.

**brisk** (brĭsk) adj. 1. Moving or acting quickly. 2. Keen or sharp. 3. Invigorating. —**brisk'ly** adv.

**bris·tle** (brĭs'əl) n. A short, stiff hair. —v. **-tled, -tling.** 1. To erect the bristles. 2. To

react with anger. 3. To be densely covered. —**bris'tly** adj.

**brit·tle** (brĭt'l) adj. Hard but breakable; fragile. —**brit·tle·ness** n.

**broad** (brôd) adj. 1. Wide from side to side. 2. Spacious. 3. Widely diffused. 4. Covering a wide scope. 5. Liberal; tolerant. 6. Plain; obvious. —**broad'en** v. —**broad'ly** adv.

**broad·cast** (brôd'kăst', -kăst') v. **-cast** or **-casted, -casting.** 1. To transmit (a program) by radio or television. 2. To make known widely. —n. A radio or television program. —adv. Far and wide. —**broad'cast·er** n.

**bro·cade** (brō-kād') n. A fabric with a raised interwoven design. —**bro·cad'ed** adj.

**broc·co·li** (brŏk'ə-lē) n. A plant with an edible flower head.

**bro·chure** (brō-shŏor') n. A pamphlet.

**brogue** (brōg) n. 1. A strong Irish accent. 2. A sturdy oxford shoe.

**broil** (broil) v. To cook by direct radiant heat. —**broil'er** n.

**broke** (brōk). p.t. of **break.** —adj. Lacking funds.

**bro·ken** (brō'kən). p.p. of **break.** —adj. 1. Fractured; shattered. 2. Violated, as promises. 3. Discontinuous. 4. Spoken imperfectly. 5. Defeated; tamed.

**bro·ker** (brō'kər) n. One who buys or sells for another; an agent. —**bro'ker·age** n.

**bro·mide** (brō'mīd') n. 1. A sedative drug. 2. A commonplace saying.

**bron·chus** (brŏng'kəs) n., pl. **-chi.** Either of two main branches of the trachea, leading directly to the lungs. —**bron'chi·al** adj.

**bronze** (brŏnz) n. 1. An alloy of copper and tin. 2. Reddish brown. —v. **bronzed, bronzing.** To give the appearance of bronze to. —**bronze** adj.

**brooch** (brōch, brōoch) n. A large decorative pin.

**brood** (brōod) n. A group of young animals, esp. of birds, hatched at one time. —v. 1. To sit on and hatch (eggs). 2. To ponder moodily. —adj. Kept for breeding.

**brook** (brōok) n. A small freshwater stream.

**broom** (brōom, brŏom) n. A long-handled brushlike implement for sweeping.

**broth** (brôth, brŏth) n. A thin, clear soup; stock.

**broth·er** (brŭth'ər) n. 1. A male having the same parents as another. 2. One who has a close bond with another. 3. A fellow member. —**broth'er·hood'** n. —**broth'er·ly** adv.

**brought** (brôt). p.t. & p.p. of **bring.**

**brow** (brou) n. 1. a. The ridge over the eyes.

**b.** An eyebrow. **c.** The forehead. **2.** The edge of a steep place.

**brown** (broun) *n.* A color between red and yellow. —*v.* To make or become brown. — **brown** *adj.* — **brown'ish** *adj.*

**browse** (brouz) *v.* **browsed, browsing. 1.** To look through books casually. **2.** To feed on vegetation; graze.

**bruise** (brōōz) *v.* **bruised, bruising. 1.** To injure the skin without rupture. **2.** To dent or mar. —*n.* An injury in which the skin is not broken; contusion.

**bru·net** (brōō-nĕt′). Also *fem.* **brunette.** *adj.* Dark or brown in color, as hair. —*n.* A person with brown hair.

**brunt** (brŭnt) *n.* The main impact, as of a blow.

**brush** (brŭsh) *n.* **1.** A device consisting of bristles or other material fastened into a handle, for scrubbing, grooming, etc. **2.** A light touch in passing. **3.** A brief encounter. **4.** A growth of bushes; thicket. —*v.* **1.** To scrub, groom, etc., with a brush. **2.** To apply or remove with or as if with motions of a brush. **3.** To touch lightly in passing.

**brusque** (brŭsk) *adj.* Abrupt; discourteously blunt. — **brusque'ly** *adv.*

**bru·tal** (brōōt′l) *adj.* Cruel; harsh. — **bru·tal'i·ty** *n.* — **bru'tal·ize'** *v.* — **bru'tal·ly** *adv.*

**brute** (brōōt) *n.* **1.** An animal; beast. **2.** A brutal person. —*adj.* Of beasts. — **brut'ish** *adj.*

**bub·ble** (bŭb′əl) *n.* A light, hollow ball, esp. a small globule of gas trapped in a liquid. —*v.* **-bled, -bling.** To form or give off bubbles. — **bub'bly** *adj.*

**buc·ca·neer** (bŭk′ə-nîr′) *n.* A pirate.

**buck** (bŭk) *n.* **1.** An adult male deer or other animal. **2.** A rear; lunge. **3.** A dollar. —*v.* **1.** To leap forward and upward suddenly; rear up. **2.** To struggle against. **3.** To charge into.

**buck·et** (bŭk′ĭt) *n.* A cylindrical container for liquids; pail.

**buck·le** (bŭk′əl) *n.* A clasp for fastening two strap or belt ends. —*v.* **-led, -ling.** To fasten or secure with a buckle.

**bu·col·ic** (byōō-kŏl′ĭk) *adj.* Pastoral; rustic.

**bud** (bŭd) *n.* A small, protruding plant part containing undeveloped flowers, leaves, etc. **2.** An undeveloped or incipient stage. —*v.* **budded, budding. 1.** To form or produce buds. **2.** To develop as from a bud.

**Bud·dhism** (bōō′dĭz′əm, bōōd′ĭz′-) *n.* A religion of Asia. — **Bud'dhist** *n. & adj.*

**budge** (bŭj) *v.* **budged, budging.** To move slightly.

**budg·et** (bŭj′ĭt) *n.* **1.** A plan for meeting expenses. **2.** The total sum of money needed or available. —*v.* To make or plan for in a budget.

**buff** (bŭf) *n.* **1.** A soft, thick leather. **2.** Light yellowish brown. **3.** An enthusiast. —*v.* To polish or shine with a soft cloth. — **buff** *adj.*

**buf·fa·lo** (bŭf′ə-lō′) *n., pl.* **-loes** or **-los** or **buffalo. 1.** An oxlike African or Asian mammal. **2.** The American bison. —*v.* To intimidate.

**buf·fet¹** (bə-fā′, bŏō-) *n.* **1.** A sideboard. **2.** A meal at which guests serve themselves from a table or sideboard.

**buf·fet²** (bŭf′ĭt) *n.* A blow or cuff. — **buf'fet** *v.*

**buf·foon** (bə-fōōn′) *n.* A clown; jester. — **buf·foon'er·y** *n.*

**bug** (bŭg) *n.* **1.** An insect, spider, or similar creature. **2.** A germ. **3.** A defect; flaw. **4.** An enthusiast. **5.** A hidden microphone. —*v.* **bugged, bugging. 1.** To annoy; pester. **2.** To eavesdrop on, esp. with electronic devices.

**bug·a·boo** (bŭg′ə-bōō′) *n., pl.* **-boos.** A persistent annoyance.

**bu·gle** (byōō′gəl) *n.* A trumpetlike instrument without valves. — **bu'gle** *v.* — **bu'gler** *n.*

**build** (bĭld) *v.* **built, building. 1.** To erect; construct. **2.** To fashion; create. **3.** To add to; develop. —*n.* Physical make-up; physique. — **build'er** *n.* — **build'ing** *n.*

**bulb** (bŭlb) *n.* **1.** A rounded underground plant part from which a new plant develops. **2.** An incandescent lamp or its glass housing. — **bul'bous** *adj.*

**bulge** (bŭlj) *n.* An outward swelling. —*v.* **bulged, bulging.** To swell up.

**bulk** (bŭlk) *n.* **1.** Great size, mass, or volume. **2.** The major portion. —*v.* To appear massive; loom. — **bulk'y** *adj.*

**bull** (bŏŏl) *n.* The adult male of cattle or certain other large mammals. —*adj.* **1.** Male. **2.** Marked by rising prices.

**bul·let** (bŏŏl′ĭt) *n.* A projectile fired from a gun.

**bul·le·tin** (bŏŏl′ə-tən, -tĭn) *n.* **1.** A printed or broadcast news statement. **2.** A periodical.

**bul·lion** (bŏŏl′yən) *n.* Gold or silver metal.

**bul·ly** (bŏŏl′ē) *n., pl.* **-lies.** One who is cruel to weaker people. —*v.* **-lied, -lying.** To behave like a bully.

**bum** (bŭm) *n.* A tramp; hobo. —*v.* **bummed, bumming. 1.** To beg. **2.** To loaf. —*adj.* **1.** Of poor quality. **2.** Disabled.

**bum·ble·bee** (bŭm′bəl-bē′) *n.* A large bee.

**bump** (bŭmp) *v.* **1.** To strike or collide with.

**2.** To knock. **3.** To displace; oust. —n. **1.** A light blow. **2.** A lump.

**bump·er** (bŭm'pər) n. An impact-absorbing device, esp. a metal bar attached to an automobile.

**bun** (bŭn) n. **1.** A rounded, often sweetened roll. **2.** A tight roll of hair.

**bunch** (bŭnch) n. A group or cluster. — bunch v. — bunch'y adj.

**bun·dle** (bŭn'dl) n. Anything bound together; package. —v. **-dled, -dling.** To tie or otherwise secure together. — bundle up. To dress warmly.

**bun·gle** (bŭng'gəl) v. **-gled, -gling.** To perform badly; ruin. — bun'gler n.

**bunk** (bŭngk) n. A narrow bed built like a shelf against a wall.

**bunt·ing** (bŭn'tĭng) n. **1.** A light cloth used for making flags. **2.** Flags.

**buoy** (boo'ē, boi) n. **1.** A marker moored in water. —v. **1.** To mark with a buoy. **2.** To keep afloat. **3.** To uplift the spirits of.

**buoy·an·cy** (boi'ən-sē, boo'yən-) n. **1.** The tendency to float. **2.** The ability to recover quickly from setbacks. **3.** Cheerfulness. — buoy'ant adj.

**bur·den** (bûrd'n) n. **1. a.** Something that is carried. **2.** Something that is difficult to bear. **2.** A duty. —v. To load or overload; weigh down; oppress. — bur'den·some adj.

**bu·reau** (byoor'ō) n., pl. **-reaus** or **bureaux.** **1.** A chest of drawers. **2.** A government department. **3.** An office or business.

**bu·reauc·ra·cy** (byoo-rŏk'rə-sē) n., pl. **-cies.** Government marked by numerous offices and inflexible rules of operation. — bu'reau·crat' n. — bu'reau·crat'ic adj.

**bur·geon** (bûr'jən) v. To sprout or grow.

**bur·glar** (bûr'glər) n. One who breaks into a building, esp. to steal. — bur'glar·ize' v. — bur'gla·ry n.

**bur·i·al** (bĕr'ē-əl) n. The burying of a dead body.

**bur·lap** (bûr'lăp') n. A coarsely woven cloth.

**bur·lesque** (bər-lĕsk') n. **1.** Broad or crudely comic imitation. **2.** Vaudeville entertainment, often with nudity. —v. **-lesqued, -lesquing.** To imitate mockingly.

**bur·ly** (bûr'lē) adj. **-lier, -liest.** Heavy and strong.

**burn** (bûrn) v. **burned** or **burnt, burning.** **1.** To be or set on fire. **2. a.** To destroy or be destroyed by fire. **b.** To damage or be damaged by fire or heat. **3.** To use as a fuel. **4.** To feel or look hot. **5.** To be consumed with strong emotion. —n. An injury from fire or heat. — burn'er n.

**bur·nish** (bûr'nĭsh) v. To polish by rubbing. — bur'nish n.

**bur·row** (bûr'ō) n. A hole or tunnel dug by an animal. — bur'row v.

**burst** (bûrst) v. **burst, bursting.** **1.** To force open or fly apart suddenly; explode. **2.** To be full to the breaking point. **3.** To appear or emerge suddenly. —n. A rupture or explosion.

**bur·y** (bĕr'ē) v. **-ied, -ying.** **1.** To place in the ground. **2.** To place in a grave or tomb. **3.** To hide; conceal.

**bus** (bŭs) n., pl. **buses** or **busses.** A large motor vehicle for carrying passengers.

**bush** (boosh) n. **1.** A branching, woody plant; shrub. **2.** Land covered with dense shrubby growth. — bush'y adj.

**bush·el** (boosh'əl) n. A dry measure equal to 4 pecks.

**busi·ness** (bĭz'nĭs) n. **1.** An occupation. **2.** Commercial, industrial, or professional dealings. **3.** Any commercial establishment. **4.** Volume of commercial trade. **5.** One's concern or interest. **6.** An affair or matter. — busi'ness·man n.

**bust¹** (bŭst) n. **1.** A woman's bosom. **2.** A sculpture of the head and shoulders.

**bust²** (bŭst) v. **1.** To burst or break. **2.** To demote. **3.** To punch. **4.** To arrest. —n. **1.** A failure. **2.** An arrest.

**bus·tle** (bŭs'əl) v. **-tled, -tling.** To move energetically. —n. **1.** Flurry; haste. **2.** A pad at the upper back of a woman's skirt.

**bus·y** (bĭz'ē) adj. **-ier, -iest.** **1.** Actively engaged; at work. **2.** Crowded with activity. **3.** Temporarily in use. —v. **-ied, -ying.** To make busy. — bus'i·ly adv.

**but** (bŭt; *unstressed* bət) conj. **1.** On the contrary. **2.** However. **3.** Except. —prep. With the exception of. — but for. Were it not for. —adv. No more than; only; just. — all but. Nearly.

**butch·er** (booch'ər) n. **1.** One who kills and cuts up animals for food. **2.** One who sells meat. **3.** A cruel killer. —v. **1.** To slaughter. **2.** To kill cruelly.

**butt¹** (bŭt) v. To hit with the head or horns. — butt in. To meddle.

**butt²** (bŭt) n. An object of ridicule.

**butt³** (bŭt) n. **1.** The larger end. **2.** A remnant; remainder.

**but·ter** (bŭt'ər) n. A yellowish, fatty food churned from milk or cream. —v. **1.** To put butter on. **2.** To flatter.

**but·ter·fly** (bŭt'ər-flī') *n., pl.* **-flies.** An insect with four broad, usually colorful wings.

**but·tocks** (bŭt'əks) *pl.n.* The two rounded parts of the lower back.

**but·ton** (bŭt'n) *n.* A small disk sewn on a garment as a fastener or trimming. — **on the button.** Exactly. —*v.* To fasten with a button or buttons.

**but·tress** (bŭt'rĭs) *n.* **1.** A structure built against a wall for support. **2.** Any support. — **but'tress** *v.*

**buy** (bī) *v.* **bought, buying. 1.** To acquire for money; purchase. **2.** To bribe. —*n.* Anything bought. — **buy'er** *n.*

**buzz** (bŭz) *v.* To make a droning sound like that of a bee. — **buzz** *n.* — **buzz'er** *n.*

**by** (bī) *prep.* **1.** Next to. **2.** With the use of. **3.** Up to and beyond; past. **4.** Not later than. **5.** To the extent of. **6.** According to. **7.** Through the agency or action of. —*adv.* **1.** On hand; nearby. **2.** Aside; away. **3.** Past. — **by** and **large.** For the most part.

**by·word** (bī'wûrd') *n.* **1.** A proverb. **2.** A notorious example.

# C

**c, C** (sē) *n.* The 3rd letter of the English alphabet.

**cab** (kăb) *n.* **1.** A taxicab. **2.** The compartment in a truck where the driver sits.

**cab·bage** (kăb'ĭj) *n.* A plant having an edible head of leaves.

**cab·in** (kăb'ĭn) *n.* **1.** A small, roughly built house. **2.** An enclosed compartment on a ship or airplane.

**cab·i·net** (kăb'ə-nĭt) *n.* **1.** A cupboardlike repository with shelves or drawers. **2.** The leading ministers in a government. — **cab'i·net** *adj.*

**ca·ble** (kā'bəl) *n.* **1.** A thick steel or fiber rope. **2.** A telegram. —*v.* **-bled, -bling.** To send a telegram to.

**ca·ca·o** (kə-kā'ō) *n.* The seed of a tropical American tree, used in making chocolate and cocoa.

**cack·le** (kăk'əl) *v.* **-led, -ling.** To make the shrill cry of a hen. — **cack'le** *n.* — **cack'ler** *n.*

**cac·tus** (kăk'əs) *n., pl.* **-ti** or **-tuses.** A leafless, fleshy-stemmed desert plant.

**ca·dav·er** (kə-dăv'ər) *n.* A dead body. — **ca·dav'er·ous** *adj.*

**ca·dence** (kād'əns) *n.* Rhythmic flow or movement. — **ca'denced** *adj.*

**ca·det** (kə-dĕt') *n.* A student training to be a military officer. — **ca·det'ship** *n.*

**ca·fé** (kă-fā', kə-) *n.* A small, informal restaurant.

**caf·e·te·ri·a** (kăf'ə-tîr'ē-ə) *n.* A restaurant in which customers carry their meals from a service counter to tables.

**caf·feine** (kă-fēn') *n.* A stimulant found in coffee and tea.

**cage** (kāj) *n.* A barred or grated enclosure for confining animals. —*v.* **caged, caging.** To confine in a cage.

**ca·jole** (kə-jōl') *v.* **-joled, -joling.** To coax; wheedle. — **ca·jole'** *n.* — **ca·jol'er·y** *n.*

**cake** (kāk) *n.* **1.** A sweet food made from baked batter or dough. **2.** A shaped mass, as of soap. —*v.* **caked, caking.** To make into a hard mass.

**ca·lam·i·ty** (kə-lăm'ə-tē) *n., pl.* **-ties.** A disaster. — **ca·lam'i·tous** *adj.* — **ca·lam'i·tous·ly** *adv.* — **ca·lam'i·tous·ness** *n.*

**cal·ci·um** (kăl'sē-əm) *n.* A silvery metallic element that occurs in bone, shells, etc.

**cal·cu·late** (kăl'kyə-lāt') *v.* **-lated, -lating. 1.** To compute; figure. **2.** To estimate. — **cal'cu·la·ble** *adj.* — **cal'cu·la·bly** *adv.* — **cal'cu·la'tion** *n.* — **cal'cu·la'tor** *n.*

**cal·dron** (kôl'drən) *n.* A large kettle.

**cal·en·dar** (kăl'ən-dər) *n.* **1.** A table showing time divisions, esp. the days of a year. **2.** A schedule.

**calf**[1] (kăf) *n., pl.* **calves** (kăvz). The young of cattle or certain other large mammals, as the elephant.

**calf**[2] (kăf) *n., pl.* **calves** (kăvz). The fleshy back part of the leg.

**cal·i·ber** (kăl'ə-bər) *n.* **1.** The diameter of the bore of a gun, bullet, or shell. **2.** Quality.

**cal·i·co** (kăl'ĭ-kō) *n., pl.* **-coes** or **-cos.** A printed cotton cloth.

**cal·is·then·ics** (kăl'əs-thĕn'ĭks) *pl.n.* Simple gymnastic exercises. — **cal·is·then'ic** *adj.*

**call** (kôl) *v.* **1.** To cry or utter loudly. **2.** To summon. **3.** To telephone. **4.** To name. **5.** To pay a brief visit. — **call off.** To cancel. —*n.* **1.** A shout or loud cry. **2.** A summons. **3.** Demand; need. **4.** A short visit. **5.** A communication by telephone. — **call'er** *n.*

**cal·lous** (kăl'əs) *adj.* Hardened; unfeeling. — **cal'lous·ly** *adv.* — **cal'lous·ness** *n.*

**cal·lus** (kăl'əs) *n., pl.* **-luses.** An area of skin that has grown thick and tough. —*v.* To form a callus.

**calm** (käm) *adj.* Quiet; undisturbed. —*n.* Stillness; serenity. —*v.* To make or become calm. —**calm'ly** *adv.* —**calm'ness** *n.*

**cal·o·rie** (kăl'ə-rē) *n.* 1. A unit of heat. 2. A unit of energy that can be derived from food. —**ca·lor'ic** *adj.*

**cal·um·ny** (kăl'əm-nē) *n., pl.* -nies. Slander. —**ca·lum'ni·ous** *adj.*

**calves.** *pl.* of **calf.**

**came** (kām) *v. p.t.* of **come.**

**cam·el** (kăm'əl) *n.* A humped, long-necked desert animal.

**cam·e·o** (kăm'ē-ō') *n., pl.* -os. A gem, medallion, etc., with a carved design.

**cam·er·a** (kăm'ər-ə, kăm'rə) *n.* An apparatus for taking photographs.

**cam·ou·flage** (kăm'ə-fläzh', -fläj') *n.* Concealment of something by making it look like its surroundings. —*v.* -flaged, -flaging. To conceal by such means. —**cam'ou·flag'er** *n.*

**camp** (kămp) *n.* 1. A place where people are temporarily lodged in makeshift shelters. 2. A group supporting a cause. —*v.* To shelter in a camp. —**camp'er** *n.*

**cam·paign** (kăm-pān') *n.* A series of actions taken to achieve a goal, as in warfare or politics. —*v.* To engage in a campaign. —**cam·paign'er** *n.*

**cam·pus** (kăm'pəs) *n., pl.* -puses. The grounds of a school or college.

**can¹** (kăn) *v.* Past tense **could,** present tense **can.** 1. To be able to. 2. To have permission to.

**can²** (kăn) *n.* A metal container used for airtight food storage. —*v.* canned, canning. To preserve in cans or jars. —**can'ner** *n.* —**can'ner·y** *n.*

**ca·nal** (kə-năl') *n.* 1. A man-made channel filled with water. 2. In anatomy, a tube or duct.

**ca·nar·y** (kə-nâr'ē) *n., pl.* -ies. A yellow songbird.

**can·cel** (kăn'səl) *v.* 1. To cross out. 2. To annul or invalidate. 3. To neutralize; offset. —**can'cel·a·ble** *adj.* —**can'cel·er** *n.* —**can'cel·la'tion** *n.*

**can·cer** (kăn'sər) *n.* 1. A malignant tumor that tends to spread. 2. A spreading evil. —**can'cer·ous** *adj.*

**can·did** (kăn'dĭd) *adj.* 1. Straightforward; open. 2. Not posed. —**can'did·ly** *adv.* —**can'did·ness** *n.*

**can·di·date** (kăn'də-dāt') *n.* A person seeking an office, prize, honor, etc. —**can'di·da·cy** *n.*

**can·dle** (kăn'dəl) *n.* A stick of solid wax with an embedded wick, burned for light.

**can·dor** (kăn'dər) *n.* Frankness; sincerity.

**can·dy** (kăn'dē) *n., pl.* -dies. A sweet confection made with sugar. —*v.* -died, -dying. To cook or coat with sugar or syrup.

**cane** (kān) *n.* 1. A hollow woody stem. 2. A walking stick. —*v.* caned, caning. 1. To beat with a cane. 2. To weave with cane.

**ca·nine** (kā'nīn') *adj.* Of dogs. —*n.* 1. One of the conical teeth between the incisors and the bicuspids. 2. A dog.

**can·is·ter** (kăn'ĭs-tər) *n.* A container for holding dry foods.

**can·ker** (kăng'kər) *n.* An ulcerous sore of the mouth. —**can'ker·ous** *adj.*

**can·ni·bal** (kăn'ə-bəl) *n.* A person who eats the flesh of human beings. —**can'ni·bal·ism'** *n.* —**can'ni·bal·is'tic** *adj.*

**can·non** (kăn'ən) *n., pl.* -non or -nons. A heavy mounted gun.

**can·not** (kăn'ŏt, kă-nŏt') *v.* The negative form of **can.**

**ca·noe** (kə-nōō') *n.* A light, slender boat, propelled by paddles. —*v.* -noed, -noeing. To carry or travel by canoe. —**ca·noe'ist** *n.*

**can·on** (kăn'ən) *n.* 1. A church law or code of laws. 2. A secular code of law. —**ca·non'i·cal** *adj.*

**can·o·py** (kăn'ə-pē) *n., pl.* -pies. A covering fastened over a bed, chair, etc. —**can'o·pied** *adj.*

**cant** (kănt) *n.* 1. Insincere or hypocritically pious talk. 2. Jargon. —**cant'ing·ly** *adv.*

**can't** (kănt, känt). Contraction of *cannot.*

**can·tank·er·ous** (kăn-tăng'kər-əs) *adj.* Ill-tempered.

**can·teen** (kăn-tēn') *n.* 1. A store for military personnel. 2. Water flask.

**can·ter** (kăn'tər) *n.* A gait slower than the gallop but faster than the trot. —**can'ter** *v.*

**can·tor** (kăn'tər) *n.* The singer of the liturgy in a synagogue.

**can·vas** (kăn'vəs) *n.* A heavy, closely woven fabric used for making tents and sails.

**can·yon** (kăn'yən) *n.* A narrow valley with steep cliff walls.

**cap** (kăp) *n.* 1. A close-fitting brimless hat. 2. A tight cover; lid. —*v.* capped, capping. To put a cap on.

**ca·pa·ble** (kā'pə-bəl) *adj.* Able; competent. —**ca'pa·bil'i·ty** *n.* —**ca'pa·bly** *adv.*

**ca·pac·i·ty** (kə-păs'ə-tē) *n., pl.* -ties. 1. Volume. 2. A maximum; limit. 3. Ability. 4. Role; position.

**cape¹** (kāp) *n.* A sleeveless garment worn over the shoulders.

**cape²** (kāp) *n.* A point of land projecting into water.

**cap·il·lar·y** (kăp'ə-lĕr'ē) *n., pl.* **-ies.** A minute blood vessel. — **cap'il·lar·y** *adj.*

**cap·i·tal** (kăp'ĭ-təl) *n.* **1.** An official seat of government. **2.** Wealth, esp. invested or available funds. **3.** A large or upper-case letter. — *adj.* **1.** First; chief. **2.** First-rate; excellent. **3.** Punishable by or involving death. **4.** Large; upper-case.

**cap·i·tal·ism** (kăp'ə-təl-ĭz'əm) *n.* An economic system in which goods are produced privately and sold for profit. — **cap'i·tal·ist** *n.* — **cap'i·tal·is'tic** *adj.* — **cap'i·tal·is'ti·cal·ly** *adv.*

**cap·i·tal·ize** (kăp'ə-təl-īz') *v.* **-ized, -izing.** **1.** To write in or begin a word with an upper-case letter. **2.** To seize an advantage. — **cap'i·tal·i·za'tion** *n.*

**ca·pri·cious** (kə-prĭsh'əs, -prē'shəs) *adj.* Unpredictable; impulsive. — **ca·price'** *n.*

**cap·size** (kăp'sīz, kăp-sīz') *v.* **-sized, -sizing.** To overturn or cause to turn over.

**cap·sule** (kăp'səl, -syōol) *n.* **1.** A small case, esp. one containing medicine. **2.** A pressurized compartment, as in a spacecraft. — **cap'su·lar** *adj.*

**cap·tain** (kăp'tən) *n.* **1.** One who commands; leader. **2.** The officer in command of a ship. **3.** A commissioned army or navy officer. — *v.* To command or direct. — **cap'tain·cy** *n.* — **cap'tain·ship'** *n.*

**cap·tion** (kăp'shən) *n.* A short legend or description.

**cap·ti·vate** (kăp'tə-vāt') *v.* **-vated, -vating.** To fascinate. — **cap'ti·va'tion** *n.*

**cap·tive** (kăp'tĭv) *n.* A prisoner. — *adj.* Held prisoner. — **cap·tiv'i·ty** *n.*

**cap·ture** (kăp'chər) *v.* **-tured, -turing.** **1.** To take captive. **2.** To win possession of. — *n.* The act of capturing.

**car** (kär) *n.* **1.** An automobile. **2.** A wheeled vehicle.

**car·a·mel** (kăr'ə-məl, kär'məl) *n.* **1.** A chewy candy. **2.** Burnt sugar, used for coloring.

**car·at** (kăr'ət) *n.* A unit of weight for precious stones.

**car·a·van** (kăr'ə-văn') *n.* A group of travelers, esp. across a desert.

**car·bine** (kär'bīn', -bēn') *n.* A light rifle.

**car·bo·hy·drate** (kär'bō-hī'drāt') *n.* An organic compound, such as sugar or starch, important as a foodstuff.

**car·bon** (kär'bən) *n.* A naturally abundant nonmetallic element.

**car·bu·re·tor** (kär'bə-rā'tər, kär'byə-) *n.* A device used in gasoline engines to mix fuel and air.

**car·cass** (kär'kəs) *n.* A dead body, esp. of an animal.

**card** (kärd) *n.* A small, flat piece of stiff paper, esp.: **a.** One of a set of playing cards. **b.** A post card. **c.** A greeting or business card. — **card'board** *n.*

**car·di·ac** (kär'dē-ăk') *adj.* Of the heart.

**car·di·gan** (kär'dĭ-gən) *n.* A sweater opening down the front.

**car·di·nal** (kärd'n-əl, kärd'nəl) *adj.* **1.** Primary; foremost. **2.** Vivid red. — *n.* **1.** One of the highest ranking Roman Catholic clergymen. **2.** A vivid red. **3.** A crested, bright-red bird.

**care** (kâr) *n.* **1.** Mental distress and grief. **2.** Caution. **3.** Supervision. — **(in) care of.** At the address of. — *v.* **cared, caring.** **1.** To be concerned or interested. **2.** To object; mind. — **care'free** *adj.*

**ca·reer** (kə-rîr') *n.* **1.** A chosen pursuit. **2.** A person's progress in his occupation.

**care·ful** (kâr'fəl) *adj.* **1.** Cautious. **2.** Thorough; painstaking. — **care'ful·ly** *adv.* — **care'ful·ness** *n.* — **care'less** *adj.* — **care'less·ly** *adv.* — **care'less·ness** *n.*

**ca·ress** (kə-rĕs') *n.* A gentle touch or gesture of fondness. — **ca·ress'** *v.*

**car·go** (kär'gō) *n., pl.* **-goes** or **-gos.** The freight carried by a vehicle.

**car·i·ca·ture** (kăr'ĭ-kə-chŏŏr') *n.* A comically exaggerated portrait. — *v.* **-tured, -turing.** To represent in a caricature. — **car'i·ca·tur'ist** *n.*

**car·na·tion** (kär-nā'shən) *n.* A plant having fragrant many-petaled flowers.

**car·ni·val** (kär'nə-vəl) *n.* **1.** A celebration; festivity. **2.** A traveling amusement show.

**car·niv·o·rous** (kär-nĭv'ər-əs) *adj.* Flesh-eating. — **car'ni·vore** *n.* — **car·niv'o·rous·ly** *adv.*

**car·ol** (kăr'əl) *v.* To sing joyously. — *n.* A festive song, esp. for Christmas. — **car·ol·er** *n.*

**ca·rouse** (kə-rouz') *v.* Boisterous, drunken merrymaking. — *v.* **-roused, -rousing.** To go on a drinking spree. — **ca·rous'al** *n.* — **ca·rous'er** *n.*

**car·pen·ter** (kär'pən-tər) *n.* A maker of wooden objects and structures. — **car'pen·ter** *v.* — **car'pen·try** *n.*

**car·pet** (kär'pĭt) *n.* A heavy fabric covering for a floor. — *v.* To cover with a carpet.

**car·riage** (kăr'ĭj) *n.* **1.** A four-wheeled, horse-drawn vehicle. **2.** A machine part for holding or shifting another part. **3.** Posture.

**car·rot** (kăr′ət) n. A plant with an edible, orange root.

**car·ry** (kăr′ē) v. -ried, -rying. 1. To convey; transport. 2. To win over. 3. To have on one's person. 4. To involve; imply. 5. To conduct (oneself); behave. 6. To support. 7. To keep in stock. 8. To reach. —carry on. 1. To continue. 2. To act wildly. —carry out. To put into practice. —car′ri·a·ble, car′ry·a·ble adj. —car′ri·er n.

**cart** (kärt) n. 1. A two-wheeled vehicle. 2. Any small vehicle. —v. To convey in a cart. —cart′a·ble adj. —cart′er n.

**car·tel** (kär-tĕl′) n. A large-scale monopoly.

**car·ti·lage** (kär′tə-lĭj) n. A tough connective tissue attached to the bone joints. —car′ti·lag′i·nous adj.

**car·tog·ra·phy** (kär-tŏg′rə-fē) n. The making of maps. —car·tog′ra·pher n. —car′to·graph′ic adj.

**car·ton** (kärt′n) n. A cardboard box.

**car·toon** (kär-tōōn′) n. 1. A satirical drawing. 2. A short animated film. 3. A comic strip. —car·toon′ist n.

**car·tridge** (kär′trĭj) n. A tubular case containing the powder and projectile for a firearm.

**carve** (kärv) v. carved, carving. 1. To cut and serve meat. 2. To fashion by cutting. —carv′er n.

**cas·cade** (kăs-kād′) n. 1. A waterfall. 2. Profusion; shower. —v. -caded, -cading. To fall in a cascade.

**case¹** (kās) n. 1. An instance; example. 2. A matter. 3. A persuasive argument or justification. 4. The form of a noun that indicates its relation to other words. 5. A legal action. —v. cased, casing. To inspect.

**case²** (kās) n. 1. A container or receptacle. 2. A covering. —v. cased, casing. To put into a case. —cas′ing n.

**cash** (kăsh) n. Ready money. —v. To exchange for money.

**cash·ew** (kăsh′ōō, kə-shōō′) n. A tropical kidney-shaped nut.

**cash·ier** (kă-shîr′) n. A business employee responsible for paying or receiving money.

**cash·mere** (kăzh′mîr′, kăsh′-) n. Fine wool from an Asian goat.

**ca·si·no** (kə-sē′nō) n., pl. -nos. A gambling house.

**cask** (kăsk) n. A barrel for liquids.

**cas·ket** (kăs′kĭt, käs′-) n. 1. A small case for valuables. 2. A coffin.

**cas·se·role** (kăs′ə-rōl′) n. A baking dish or the food cooked in it.

**cas·sette** (kə-sĕt′) n. A small case for film or magnetic tape.

**cast** (kăst, käst) v. cast, casting. 1. To throw. 2. To direct; aim. 3. To give or deposit (a ballot). 4. To assign, as an actor's part. 5. To form by molding. —n. 1. A throw. 2. A mold or form. 3. A rigid plaster dressing for a broken bone. 4. The actors in a play.

**caste** (kăst, käst) n. Any exclusive social class.

**cast·er** (kăs′tər) n. A small swiveled wheel on which a heavy object can be rolled.

**cas·tle** (kăs′əl) n. A large, fortified building.

**cas·trate** (kăs′trāt′) v. -trated, -trating. To remove the testicles of a man. —cas·tra′tion n.

**cas·u·al** (kăzh′ōō-əl) adj. 1. Occurring by chance. 2. Informal. 3. Careless; negligent. —cas′u·al·ly adv. —cas′u·al·ness n.

**cas·u·al·ty** (kăzh′ōō-əl-tē) n., pl. -ties. One injured or killed, as in an accident.

**cat** (kăt) n. 1. A small, domesticated furry mammal. 2. A related animal, as the lion.

**cat·a·clysm** (kăt′ə-klĭz′əm) n. A violent upheaval. —cat·a·clys′mic, cat·a·clys′mal adj.

**cat·a·logue** (kăt′ə-lôg′) n. An itemized list. —v. -logued, -loguing. To list. Also **cat·a·log**. —cat′a·logu′er n.

**cat·a·lyst** (kăt′l-ĭst) n. 1. A substance that modifies a chemical reaction without being consumed. 2. Any person, event, or factor that causes or inspires a sudden change. —ca·tal′y·sis n. —cat·a·lyt′ic adj.

**cat·a·ract** (kăt′ə-răkt′) n. 1. A great waterfall. 2. Opacity of the lens of the eye.

**ca·tas·tro·phe** (kə-tăs′trə-fē) n. A sudden calamity; disaster. —cat·a·stroph′ic adj. —cat·a·stroph′i·cal·ly n.

**catch** (kăch) v. caught, catching. 1. To capture, esp. after a chase. 2. To snare or trap. 3. To surprise. 4. To grasp. 5. To contract; get. —n. 1. The act of catching. 2. A fastening device. 3. Something caught. 4. An unsuspected drawback.

**cat·e·gor·i·cal** (kăt′ə-gôr′ĭ-kəl) adj. Absolute; certain. —cat·e·gor′i·cal·ly adv. —cat′e·gor′i·cal·ness n.

**cat·e·go·ry** (kăt′ə-gôr′ē, -gōr′ē) n., pl. -ries. A division in a system of classification; a class. —cat·e·go·rize′ v. —cat′e·go·ri·za′tion n.

**ca·ter** (kā′tər) v. To provide food, as for a party. —ca′ter·er n.

**cat·er·pil·lar** (kăt′ər-pĭl′ər, kăt′ə-) n. The wormlike larva of a butterfly or moth.

**ca·the·dral** (kə-thē′drəl) n. The principal church of a bishop's see.

**cath·o·lic** (kăth′lĭk, kăth′ə-lĭk) adj. 1. Universal. **2. Catholic.** Of the Roman Catholic Church. —*n.* **Catholic.** A member of the Roman Catholic Church. —**Ca·thol'i·cism'** *n.*

**cat·tle** (kăt'l) *pl.n.* Horned, hoofed mammals; livestock.

**Cau·ca·sian** (kô-kā'zhən) *n.* A person of a light-skinned race. —**Cau·ca'sian** *adj.*

**cau·cus** (kô'kəs) *n., pl.* **-cuses.** A meeting, esp. of the members of a political party. —**cau'cus** *v.*

**caught** (kôt). *p.t.* & *p.p.* of **catch.**

**cau·li·flow·er** (kô'lĭ-flou'ər, kŏl'ĭ-) *n.* A plant with an edible, compact head.

**caulk** (kôk) *v.* Also **calk.** To make watertight by filling cracks. —**caulk'er** *n.*

**cause** (kôz) *n.* **1.** A person or thing responsible for an action or result. **2.** A reason; motive. **3.** A social or political purpose. **4.** A lawsuit. —*v.* **caused, causing.** To bring about. —**caus'al** *adj.* —**cau·sal'i·ty** *n.* —**caus'al·ly** *adv.* —**cau·sa'tion** *n.*

**caus·tic** (kô'stĭk) *adj.* Corrosive; biting.

**cau·ter·ize** (kô'tə-rīz') *v.* **-ized, -izing.** To burn or sear (a wound). —**cau'ter·i·za'tion** *n.*

**cau·tion** (kô'shən) *n.* **1.** Forethought; prudence. **2.** A warning. —*v.* To warn against danger. —**cau'tion·ar'y** *adj.* —**cau'tious** *adj.* —**cau'tious·ly** *adv.*

**cav·a·lier** (kăv'ə-lîr') *n.* **1.** A knight. **2.** A gallant. —*adj.* **1.** Haughty. **2.** Carefree; offhand. —**cav·a·lier'ly** *adv.*

**cav·al·ry** (kăv'əl-rē) *n., pl.* **-ries.** Mounted or motorized troops. —**cav'al·ry·man** *n.*

**cave** (kāv) *n.* A hollow beneath the earth's surface. —**cav'ern** *n.* —**cav'er·nous** *adj.*

**cav·i·ar** (kăv'ē-är') *n.* The salted eggs of a sturgeon.

**cav·il** (kăv'əl) *v.* To quibble or carp. —**cav'il** *n.*

**cav·i·ty** (kăv'ə-tē) *n., pl.* **-ties.** A hollow or hole.

**ca·vort** (kə-vôrt') *v.* To prance.

**cease** (sēs) *v.* **ceased, ceasing.** To discontinue; stop. —*n.* Cessation. —**cease'less** *adj.* —**cease'less·ly** *adv.*

**cede** (sēd) *v.* **ceded, ceding.** To relinquish; transfer.

**ceil·ing** (sē'lĭng) *n.* **1.** The interior upper surface of a room. **2.** A maximum limit.

**cel·e·brate** (sĕl'ə-brāt') *v.* **-brated, -brating. 1.** To observe (a day or event) with festivity. **2.** To perform (a religious ceremony). **3.** To praise. —**cel'e·bra'tion** *n.* —**cel'e·bra'tor** *n.*

**ce·leb·ri·ty** (sə-lĕb'rə-tē) *n., pl.* **-ties. 1.** A famous person. **2.** Fame.

**cel·er·y** (sĕl'ər-ē) *n.* A plant with juicy

edible stalks.

**ce·les·tial** (sə-lĕs'chəl) *adj.* **1.** Of the sky or heavens. **2.** Heavenly; divine.

**cel·i·ba·cy** (sĕl'ə-bə-sē) *n.* The condition of being unmarried. —**cel'i·bate** *adj.* & *n.*

**cell** (sĕl) *n.* **1.** A small, plain room. **2.** A small enclosed space. **3.** The smallest independent unit of living matter. **4.** A device for generating electricity. —**cel'lu·lar** *adj.*

**cel·lar** (sĕl'ər) *n.* An underground storage room.

**cel·lo** (chĕl'ō) *n., pl.* **-los.** Also **'cel·lo.** A violinlike instrument played between the knees. —**cel'list** *n.*

**cel·lo·phane** (sĕl'ə-fān') *n.* A transparent material used for wrapping.

**Cel·si·us** (sĕl'sē-əs, -shəs) *adj.* Of a temperature scale that registers the freezing point of water at 0°C and the boiling point as 100°C.

**ce·ment** (sĭ-mĕnt') *n.* **1.** A construction material made of powdered rock, clay, and water that hardens after pouring. **2.** Any adhesive; glue. —*v.* To bind with or as if with cement.

**cem·e·ter·y** (sĕm'ə-tĕr'ē) *n., pl.* **-ies.** A graveyard.

**cen·sor** (sĕn'sər) *n.* An examiner of printed or other materials, who may prohibit what he considers objectionable. —*v.* To examine and expurgate. —**cen·so'ri·al** *adj.* —**cen'sor·ship'** *n.*

**cen·sure** (sĕn'shər) *n.* Disapproval. —*v.* **-sured, -suring.** To criticize severely; blame. —**cen'sur·a·ble** *adj.* —**cen'sur·er** *n.*

**cen·sus** (sĕn'səs) *n., pl.* **-suses.** An official population count.

**cen·ten·ni·al** (sĕn-tĕn'ē-əl) *adj.* Of 100 years or a 100th anniversary. —*n.* A 100th anniversary. —**cen·ten'ni·al·ly** *adv.*

**cen·ter** (sĕn'tər) *n.* **1.** A middle point. **2.** A place of concentrated activity. —*v.* **1.** To place at the center. **2.** To concentrate or cluster.

**cen·ti·grade** (sĕn'tĭ-grād') *adj.* Celsius.

**cen·tral** (sĕn'trəl) *adj.* **1.** At, near, or being the center. **2.** Essential. —**cen'tral·ly** *adv.*

**cen·tu·ry** (sĕn'chə-rē) *n., pl.* **-ies.** A period of 100 years.

**ce·ram·ics** (sə-răm'ĭks) *pl.n.* **1.** Pottery and other objects made by shaping and baking clay. **2.** (*takes sing. v.*). The art of making such objects. —**ce·ram'ic** *adj.*

**ce·re·al** (sîr'ē-əl) *n.* **1.** An edible grain. **2.** A food prepared from such grain. —**ce're·al** *adj.*

**ce·re·bral** (sə-rē'brəl, sĕr'ə-brəl) *adj.* Of the brain. — **ce·re'bral·ly** *adv.*

**cer·e·mo·ny** (sĕr'ə-mō'nē) *n., pl.* **-nies. 1.** A formal act or set of acts prescribed by ritual or custom. **2.** Formality; etiquette. — **cer·e·mo'ni·al** *adj.* — **cer·e·mo'ni·al·ly** *adv.* — **cer·e·mo'ni·ous** *adj.* — **cer·e·mo'ni·ous·ly** *adv.*

**cer·tain** (sûrt'n) *adj.* **1.** Definite; sure; indisputable. **2.** Inevitable. **3.** Not identified. — **cer'tain·ly** *adv.* — **cer'tain·ty** *n.*

**cer·tif·i·cate** (sər-tĭf'ĭ-kĭt) *n.* A document testifying to a fact or promise.

**cer·ti·fy** (sûr'tə-fī') *v.* **-fied, -fying. 1.** To confirm formally as true. **2.** To guarantee. — **cer'ti·fi'a·ble** *adj.* — **cer'ti·fi'a·bly** *adv.* — **cer'·ti·fi·ca'tion** *n.* — **cer'ti·fied** *adj.*

**cess·pool** (sĕs'pool') *n.* A covered hole for sewage.

**chafe** (chāf) *v.* **chafed, chafing. 1.** To make or become worn or sore from rubbing. **2.** To make or become annoyed.

**cha·grin** (shə-grĭn') *n.* Deep disappointment; humiliation. — *v.* To humiliate.

**chain** (chān) *n.* **1.** A flexible series of connected links. **2.** Any series of related things. — *v.* To bind with a chain. **2.** To confine.

**chair** (châr) *n.* **1.** A seat with a back. **2.** An important office, as of a judge or chairman.

**chair·man** (châr'mən) *n.* One who presides over a meeting. — **chair'man·ship'** *n.* — **chair'·wom'an** *fem·n.*

**chalk** (chôk) *n.* A soft mineral used in pieces for marking on a blackboard. — *v.* To mark with chalk. — **chalk** *adj.* — **chalk'i·ness** *n.* — **chalk'y** *adj.*

**chal·lenge** (chăl'ənj) *n.* **1.** A call to engage in a contest. **2.** A demand for an explanation or identification. **3.** A test of one's abilities. **4.** A formal objection. — *v.* **-lenged, -lenging.** To put or be a challenge to. — **chal'lenge··a·ble** *adj.* — **chal'leng·er** *n.*

**cham·ber** (chām'bər) *n.* **1.** A room. **2.** A judge's office. **3.** A hall, esp. for a legislative assembly.

**cham·pagne** (shăm-pān') *n.* A sparkling white wine.

**cham·pi·on** (chăm'pē·ən) *n.* **1.** One that holds first place. **2.** An advocate; defender. — *v.* To fight for; support. — **cham'pi·on·ship'** *n.*

**chance** (chăns, chäns) *n.* **1.** Randomness; unpredictability. **2.** Luck; fate. **3.** Probability. **4.** An opportunity. **5.** A risk. — *v.* **chanced, chancing. 1.** To happen to be by chance.

**2.** To risk. — **chance** *adj.* — **chanc'y** *adj.*

**chan·cel·lor** (chăn'sə-lər) *n.* **1.** A state official of high rank. **2.** The head of certain universities. — **chan'cel·lor·ship'** *n.*

**chan·de·lier** (shăn'də-lîr') *n.* A branched, hanging fixture for lights.

**change** (chānj) *v.* **changed, changing. 1.** To make or become different; alter. **2.** To exchange. **3.** To put on fresh clothes. — *n.* **1.** The process or condition of changing. **2.** Money given in exchange for money of higher denomination. **3.** Any small coins. — **change'a·ble** *adj.* — **change'less** *adj.* — **chang'er** *n.*

**chan·nel** (chăn'əl) *n.* **1.** The bed of a stream. **2.** The deeper part of a river or harbor. **3.** A strait. **4.** A passage or route. **5.** A specified frequency band, esp. for a TV station. — *v.* **1.** To make or form channels in. **2.** To direct or guide.

**chant** (chănt, chänt) *n.* **1.** A melody in which a number of words are sung on each note. **2.** A monotonous voice. — *v.* To say or sing in a chant. — **chant'er** *n.*

**cha·os** (kā'ŏs') *n.* Total disorder. — **cha·ot'ic** *adj.* — **cha·ot'i·cal·ly** *adv.*

**chap¹** (chăp) *v.* **chapped, chapping.** To roughen, esp. from cold.

**chap²** (chăp) *n.* A man; fellow.

**chap·el** (chăp'əl) *n.* A place of worship subordinate to a church.

**chap·er·on** (shăp'ə-rōn') *n.* An older person who for propriety accompanies young unmarried people. — *v.* To act as chaperon in.

**chap·lain** (chăp'lĭn) *n.* A clergyman attached to a chapel or military unit.

**chap·ter** (chăp'tər) *n.* **1.** A main division of a book. **2.** A branch of a club, fraternity, etc.

**char·ac·ter** (kăr'ĭk-tər) *n.* **1.** A distinguishing feature. **2.** The essential nature of a person or group. **3.** Integrity; fortitude. **4.** Reputation. **5.** An eccentric person. **6.** A person portrayed in a drama, novel, etc. **7.** A symbol in a writing system.

**char·ac·ter·is·tic** (kăr'ĭk-tə-rĭs'tĭk) *adj.* Distinctive; typical. — *n.* A distinguishing feature or attribute. — **char'ac·ter·is'ti·cal·ly** *adv.*

**char·ac·ter·ize** (kăr'ĭk-tə-rīz') *v.* **-ized, -izing. 1.** To describe. **2.** To be a distinguishing trait of. — **char'ac·ter·i·za'tion** *n.*

**char·coal** (chär'kōl') *n.* A black, porous material made by burning wood in an airless kiln.

**charge** (chärj) *v.* **charged, charging. 1.** To entrust. **2.** To command. **3.** To blame or accuse. **4.** To set as a price. **5.** To demand payment from. **6.** To attack violently. **7.** To load or fill. —*n.* **1.** Care; custody. **2.** A command. **3.** An accusation. **4.** Cost; price. **5.** An attack. **6.** A load; burden.

**cha·ris·ma** (kə-rĭz′mə) *n.* Power to attract followers. —**char′is·mat′ic** *adj.*

**char·i·ty** (chăr′ə-tē) *n., pl.* **-ties. 1.** Help given to the poor. **2.** An organization that helps the poor. **3.** A kindly act. —**char′i·ta·ble** *adj.* —**char′i·ta·bly** *adv.*

**char·la·tan** (shär′lə-tən) *n.* A pretender; impostor.

**charm** (chärm) *n.* **1.** The power of pleasing or attracting. **2.** A small ornament worn on a bracelet. **3.** A formula, object, etc., thought to have magical power. —*v.* **1.** To attract; delight. **2.** To bewitch. —**charm′er** *n.* —**charm′ing** *adj.*

**chart** (chärt) *n.* **1.** A map. **2.** A graph or table. —*v.* **1.** To make a chart of. **2.** To plan.

**char·ter** (chär′tər) *n.* **1.** A document creating a corporation, chapter, etc. **2.** The hiring of an aircraft, vessel, etc. —*v.* **1.** To grant a charter to. **2.** To hire or lease.

**chase** (chās) *v.* **chased, chasing. 1.** To pursue; follow. **2.** To hunt. **3.** To drive away. —*n.* The act of chasing. —**chas′er** *n.*

**chas·sis** (shăs′ē) *n., pl.* **-sis. 1.** The rectangular frame of a car. **2.** The framework of a radio, television set, etc.

**chaste** (chāst) *adj.* **1.** Modest. **2.** Abstaining from sexual intercourse. —**chaste′ly** *adv.* —**chaste′ness** *n.* —**chas′ti·ty** *n.*

**chas·tise** (chăs-tīz′) *v.* **-tised, -tising. 1.** To punish. **2.** To criticize severely. —**chas·tise′ment** *n.*

**chat** (chăt) *v.* **chatted, chatting.** To converse lightly and casually. —*n.* An informal conversation. —**chat′ty** *adj.*

**cha·teau** (shă-tō′) *n., pl.* **-teaux.** A French castle.

**chat·ter** (chăt′ər) *v.* **1.** To talk foolishly; babble. **2.** To make a chirping noise. —**chat′ter** *n.* —**chat′ter·er** *n.*

**chauf·feur** (shō′fər, shō-fûr′) *n.* One employed to drive a private automobile. —**chauffeur** *v.*

**cheap** (chēp) *adj.* **1.** Inexpensive. **2.** Of low quality. Stingy. —*adv.* Inexpensively. —**cheap′en** *v.* —**cheap′ly** *adv.* —**cheap′ness** *n.*

**cheat** (chēt) *v.* **1.** To swindle. **2.** To act dishonestly. —*n.* **1.** A fraud or swindle. **2.** One guilty of swindle or dishonesty. —**cheat′er** *n.*

**check** (chĕk) *n.* **1.** An abrupt stop. **2.** A restraint. **3.** A verification. **4.** A bill. **5.** A

written bank draft. **6.** A pattern of small squares. —*v.* **1.** To stop; halt. **2.** To hold in restraint. **3.** To examine for accuracy. **4.** To make a check mark on. **5.** To deposit for temporary safekeeping. —**check′a·ble** *adj.*

**check·ers** (chĕk′ərz) *n.* A board game played by two persons. —**check′er·board′** *n.*

**cheek** (chēk) *n.* **1.** The fleshy part of either side of the face. **2.** Impudence. —**cheek′i·ly** *adv.* —**cheek′i·ness** *n.* —**cheek′y** *adj.*

**cheer** (chîr) *n.* **1.** Gaiety; happiness. **2.** A joyful shout. —*v.* **1.** To fill with happiness. **2.** To encourage with cheers. —**cheer′ful** *adj.* —**cheer′ful·ly** *adv.* —**cheer′ful·ness** *n.* —**cheer′i·ly** *adv.* —**cheer′i·ness** *n.* —**cheer′less** *adj.* —**cheer′y** *adj.*

**cheese** (chēz) *n.* A solid food prepared from milk curd.

**chef** (shĕf) *n.* A chief cook.

**chem·i·cal** (kĕm′ĭ-kəl) *adj.* **1.** Of chemistry. **2.** Involving or produced by chemicals. —*n.* A substance produced by or used in chemistry. —**chem′i·cal·ly** *adv.*

**chem·is·try** (kĕm′ĭs-trē) *n., pl.* **-tries.** The science of the composition and reactions of matter. —**chem′ist** *n.*

**cher·ish** (chĕr′ĭsh) *v.* To hold dear. —**cher′-isher** *n.*

**cher·ry** (chĕr′ē) *n., pl.* **-ries. 1.** A small, rounded fruit. **2.** Deep red. —**cherry** *adj.*

**chess** (chĕs) *n.* A board game for two players. —**chess′man′** *n.*

**chest** (chĕst) *n.* **1.** The part of the body between the neck and abdomen. **2.** A sturdy box. **3.** A bureau.

**chest·nut** (chĕs′nŭt′, -nət) *n.* **1.** An edible nut. **2.** Reddish brown. —**chest′nut** *adj.*

**chew** (chōō) *v.* To grind with the teeth. —**chew′er** *n.*

**Chi·ca·no** (shĭ-kä′nō, chĭ-) *n., pl.* **-nos.** A Mexican-American. —**Chi·ca′no** *adj.*

**chick·en** (chĭk′ən) *n.* The common domestic fowl or its edible flesh. —**chick** *n.*

**chide** (chīd) *v.* **chided, chiding.** To scold. —**chid′er** *n.*

**chief** (chēf) *n.* A leader. —*adj.* Principal; most important. —**chief′ly** *adv.* —**chief′tain** *n.*

**child** (chīld) *n., pl.* **children. 1.** Any person between birth and puberty. **2.** A son or daughter. —**child′hood′** *n.* —**child′ish** *adj.* —**child′ish·ly** *adv.* —**child′ish·ness** *n.* —**child′less** *adj.*

**chill** (chĭl) *n.* **1.** A moderate coldness. **2.** A sensation of coldness; a shiver. —*adj.* Cold. —*v.* To make or become cold. —**chill′y** *adj.* —**chill′i·ness** *n.*

cinnamon

**chime** (chīm) n. Often **chimes**. A set of tuned bells or their sound. —v. chimed, chiming. To sound harmoniously. —chim'er n.

**chim·ney** (chim'nē) n. A passage through which smoke escapes from a fireplace.

**chim·pan·zee** (chim'păn-zē', chĭm-păn'zē) n. A gregarious African ape.

**chin** (chĭn) n. The central portion of the lower jaw. —v. chinned, chinning. To pull oneself up on an overhead bar.

**chi·na** (chī'nə) n. Pottery, esp. high-quality porcelain.

**chip** (chĭp) n. 1. A small piece broken or cut off. 2. A mark; dent. 3. A disk; counter. —v. chipped, chipping. To break so as to form chips. —chip in. To contribute.

**chip·munk** (chĭp'mŭngk') n. A small squirrel-like rodent.

**chi·ro·prac·tic** (kī'rə-prăk'tĭk) n. A system of therapy by manipulation of the spinal column and other bodily structures. —chi'ro·prac'tor n.

**chis·el** (chĭz'əl) n. A cutting and shaping tool with a sharp edge. —v. 1. To shape with a chisel. 2. To swindle. —chis'el·er n.

**chiv·al·ry** (shĭv'əl-rē) n., pl. -ries. Bravery, courtesy, etc., as idealized by knighthood. —chiv'al·rous adj. —chiv'al·rous·ly adv.

**chive** (chīv) n. A grasslike plant with onion-flavored leaves.

**choc·o·late** (chôk'lĭt) n. 1. Roasted and ground cacao seeds. 2. A candy or beverage made from this. —choc'o·late adj.

**choice** (chois) n. 1. The act or right of choosing. 2. Something chosen. —adj. choicer, choicest. Of fine quality.

**choir** (kwīr) n. An organized group of singers, esp. in a church.

**choke** (chōk) v. choked, choking. 1. To interfere with the breathing of; suffocate. 2. To repress or check. 3. To obstruct. —n. The act or sound of choking.

**chol·er·a** (kŏl'ər-ə) n. An acute, often fatal epidemic disease.

**cho·les·ter·ol** (kə-lĕs'tə-rôl', -rōl') n. A soapy crystalline substance, occurring notably in animal fats.

**choose** (chōōz) v. chose, chosen, choosing. 1. To select. 2. To desire. —choos'er n. —choos'y adj.

**chop** (chŏp) v. chopped, chopping. 1. To cut by striking with a sharp tool. 2. To cut into bits. —n. 1. A sharp blow. 2. A small cut of meat from the rib, shoulder, etc. —chop'per n.

**chop·py** (chŏp'ē) adj. -pier, -piest. Shifting abruptly, as waves. —chop'pi·ness n.

**chore** (chôr, chōr) n. A task.

**cho·re·og·ra·phy** (kôr'ē-ŏg'rə-fē) n. The creation of ballets or dances. —chor·e·o·graph' v. —cho're·og'ra·pher n. —cho're·o·graph'ic adj.

**cho·rus** (kôr'əs) n., pl. -ruses. 1. A group of singers. 2. A repeated refrain. —v. To sing or utter together. —cho'ral adj.

**chose** (chōz). p.t. of choose.

**cho·sen** (chō'zən). p.p. of choose. —adj. Preferred above others.

**chow·der** (chou'dər) n. A thick seafood soup.

**chris·ten** (krĭs'ən) v. 1. To baptize. 2. To name. —chris'ten·ing n.

**Chris·ti·an·i·ty** (krĭs'chē-ăn'ə-tē) n. The religion founded on the teachings of Jesus. —Chris'tian adj. & n.

**chron·ic** (krŏn'ĭk) adj. Prolonged; lingering. —chron'i·cal·ly adv.

**chron·i·cle** (krŏn'ĭ-kəl) n. A historical record. —v. -cled, -cling. To record. —chron'i·cler n.

**chro·nol·o·gy** (krə-nŏl'ə-jē) n., pl. -gies. 1. The determination of sequences of events. 2. A list of successive events; order of occurrence. —chron·o·log'i·cal adj. —chron·o·log'i·cal·ly adv.

**chry·san·the·mum** (krĭ-săn'thə-məm) n. A plant with showy flowers.

**chub·by** (chŭb'ē) adj. -bier, -biest. Plump. —chub'bi·ly adv. —chub'bi·ness n.

**chuck·le** (chŭk'əl) v. -led, -ling. To laugh quietly. —chuck'le n. —chuck'ler n.

**chum** (chŭm) n. A close friend. —v. chummed, chumming. To be a close friend. —chum'my adj.

**chunk** (chŭngk) n. A thick piece.

**church** (chûrch) n. 1. A building for public worship. 2. A congregation. 3. Any Christian denomination; sect.

**churn** (chûrn) n. A vessel in which butter is made. —v. 1. To shake. 2. To make (butter). —churn'er n.

**ci·der** (sī'dər) n. Apple juice.

**ci·gar** (sĭ-gär') n. Tobacco leaves rolled into a cylinder for smoking.

**cig·a·rette** (sĭg'ə-rĕt') n. A small roll of tobacco enclosed in paper for smoking.

**cin·der** (sĭn'dər) n. 1. A burned substance not reduced to ashes. 2. cinders. Ashes.

**cin·e·ma** (sĭn'ə-mə) n. 1. A motion picture. 2. A motion-picture theater.

**cin·na·mon** (sĭn'ə-mən) n. A spice made

from the bark of a tropical tree.

**ci·pher** (sī′fər) n. **1.** The mathematical symbol (0); zero. **2.** A code or the key to it.

**cir·cle** (sûr′kəl) n. **1.** A closed curve everywhere equidistant from a central point. **2.** Anything similarly shaped. **3.** A group sharing an interest, activity, etc. —v. **-cled, -cling.** To make a circle around. —**cir′cler** n.

**cir·cuit** (sûr′kĭt) n. **1.** A closed, usually circular, curve. **2.** A repeated route, sequence, or round. **3.** A closed path followed by an electric current.

**cir·cu·lar** (sûr′kyə-lər) adj. **1.** Of or shaped like a circle. **2.** Returning to a starting point. —n. A printed notice for mass distribution. —**cir′cu·lar′i·ty** n.

**cir·cu·late** (sûr′kyə-lāt′) v. **-lated, -lating.** To move about freely or in a circle. —**cir′cu·la′tion** n. —**cir′cu·la′tor** n. —**cir′cu·la·to′ry** adj. —**cir′cu·la·tive** adj.

**cir·cum·cise** (sûr′kəm-sīz′) v. **-cised, -cising.** To remove the foreskin. —**cir′cum·ci′sion** n.

**cir·cum·fer·ence** (sər-kŭm′fər-əns) n. The distance around a circle or other figure.

**cir·cum·spect** (sûr′kəm-spĕkt′) adj. Prudent; cautious. —**cir′cum·spec′tion** n.

**cir·cum·stance** (sûr′kəm-stăns′) n. **1.** One of the conditions or facts attending an event. **2.** Often **circumstances.** Financial means. **3.** A detail. —**cir′cum·stan′tial** adj.

**cir·cus** (sûr′kəs) n. A traveling show of acrobats, clowns, trained animals, etc.

**cite** (sīt) v. **cited, citing. 1.** To quote as an authority or example. **2.** To commend. —**ci·ta′tion** n.

**cit·i·zen** (sĭt′ĭ-zən) n. A person belonging by birth or naturalization to a given place or nation. —**cit′i·zen·ry** n. —**cit′i·zen·ship** n.

**cit·rus** (sĭt′rəs) adj. Of fruit such as the orange, lemon, etc. —n, pl. **-ruses.** A citrus tree.

**cit·y** (sĭt′ē) n, pl. **-ies.** A large town.

**civ·ic** (sĭv′ĭk) adj. Of a city or citizenship. —n. **civics** (takes sing. v.). The study of the rights and duties of citizenship.

**civ·il** (sĭv′əl) adj. **1.** Of citizens. **2.** Of ordinary community life. **3.** Polite. —**civ′il·ly** adv. —**civ′il·ness** n.

**ci·vil·ian** (sə-vĭl′yən) n. A person in civil life, not in the armed forces.

**ci·vil·i·ty** (sə-vĭl′ə-tē) n, pl. **-ties. 1.** Politeness. **2.** A courteous act.

**ci·vil·i·za·tion** (sĭv′ə-lə-zā′shən) n. Any human society having an advanced cultural development. —**civ′i·lize′** v.

**clad** (klăd). Alternate p.t. & p.p. of **clothe.**

**claim** (klām) v. **1.** To demand as one's due. **2.** To state to be true. —n. **1.** A demand. **2.** Title or right. **3.** Something claimed.

**clair·voy·ance** (klâr-voi′əns) n. The power to perceive things beyond the natural range of human senses. —**clair·voy′ant** n. & adj.

**clam** (klăm) n. A mollusk. —v. **clammed, clamming.** To hunt for clams.

**clam·my** (klăm′ē) adj. **-mier, -miest.** Disagreeably moist and cold. —**clam′mi·ly** adv. —**clam′mi·ness** n.

**clam·or** (klăm′ər) n. A loud outcry; hubbub. —v. To make a clamor. —**clam′or·ous** adj.

**clamp** (klămp) n. A device used to fasten or grip things. —v. To fasten with a clamp. —**clamp′er** n.

**clan** (klăn) n. A large family or group of related families. —**clan′nish** adj. —**clan′nish·ly** adv. —**clans′man** n.

**clan·des·tine** (klăn-dĕs′tən) adj. Concealed; secret.

**clap** (klăp) v. **clapped, clapping. 1.** To strike (the hands) together, as in applauding. **2.** To come together with a sharp noise. —n. The act or sound of clapping.

**clap·board** (klăb′ərd, klăp′bôrd′, -bōrd′) n. A board placed in overlapping rows on the outside of houses.

**clar·et** (klăr′ət) n. A red table wine.

**clar·i·fy** (klăr′ə-fī′) v. **-fied, -fying.** To make or become clear. —**clar′i·fi·ca′tion** n.

**clar·i·net** (klăr′ə-nĕt′) n. A tube-shaped woodwind instrument. —**clar′i·net′ist** n.

**clar·i·ty** (klăr′ə-tē) n. Clearness.

**clash** (klăsh) v. **1.** To collide noisily. **2.** To conflict; disagree. —n. **1.** A loud metallic noise. **2.** A conflict.

**clasp** (klăsp, klasp) n. **1.** A fastener; clip. **2. a.** An embrace. **b.** A grip of the hand. —v. **1.** To fasten. **2.** To grip. —**clasp′er** n.

**class** (klăs, klas) n. **1.** A group; kind; sort. **2.** A division by quality or grade. **3.** A social stratum. **4.** A group of students in the same year. —v. To classify.

**clas·sic** (klăs′ĭk) adj. **1.** Of ancient Greece or Rome. **2.** Traditional. **3.** Supreme; exemplary. —n. An artist, author, or work of the highest rank. —**clas′si·cal** adj. —**clas′si·cal·ly** adv.

**clas·si·fy** (klăs′ə-fī′) v. **-fied, -fying.** To put in classes or groupings. —**clas′si·fi·ca′tion** n. —**clas′si·fi′er** n.

**clat·ter** (klăt′ər) v. A rattling sound. —**clat′ter** v.

**clause** (klôz) n. 1. A group of words with a subject and verb that forms part of a sentence. 2. A provision.

**claus·tro·pho·bi·a** (klôs′trə-fō′bē-ə) n. Fear of confined spaces. —**claus′tro·pho′bic** adj.

**claw** (klô) n. 1. A sharp, curved nail on the toe of an animal. 2. A pincerlike part. —v. To scratch with claws.

**clay** (klā) n. A readily molded earth used in making bricks and pottery. —**clay′ey, clay′ish** adj.

**clean** (klēn) adj. 1. Free from impurities. 2. Thorough; complete. —v. To rid of dirt or other impurities. —**clean′er** n. —**clean′ly** adj. —**clean′li·ness** n. —**clean′ness** n.

**cleanse** (klēnz) v. **cleansed, cleansing.** To clean; purify. —**cleans′er** n.

**clear** (klîr) adj. 1. Free from anything that dims or obscures. 2. Unobstructed. 3. Easily perceptible. 4. Free from doubt, burden, or guilt. —adv. 1. Distinctly. 2. Entirely. —v. 1. To make or become clear. 2. To gain as net profit. —**clear′ance** n. —**clear′er** n. —**clear′ly** adv. —**clear′ness** n.

**clear·ing** (klîr′ĭng) n. A tract of land cleared of trees.

**cleat** (klēt) n. A projection used to prevent slipping.

**cleave** (klēv) v. **cleft** or **cleaved, cleaving.** To split or separate. —**cleav′age** n. —**cleav′er** n.

**clef** (klĕf) n. A written musical symbol indicating the pitch of the notes.

**cleft** (klĕft) n. A p.t. & p.p. of **cleave.** —adj. Split. —n. A crack.

**clem·ent** (klĕm′ənt) adj. 1. Merciful. 2. Mild, as the weather. —**clem′en·cy** n.

**clench** (klĕnch) v. To bring together tightly. —n. A tight grip or grasp.

**cler·gy** (klûr′jē) n., pl. **-gies.** Persons ordained for religious service. —**cler′gy·man** n.

**cler·i·cal** (klĕr′ĭ-kəl) adj. 1. Of clerks or office workers. 2. Of the clergy.

**clerk** (klûrk) n. 1. A person who performs office work. 2. A salesperson. —v. To work as a clerk.

**clev·er** (klĕv′ər) adj. 1. Mentally quick and resourceful. 2. Dexterous. —**clev′er·ly** adv. —**clev′er·ness** n.

**cli·ché** (klē-shā′) n. A trite expression.

**cli·ent** (klī′ənt) n. 1. One for whom professional services are rendered. 2. A customer.

**cliff** (klĭf) n. A high, steep face of rock.

**cli·mate** (klī′mĭt) n. The prevailing weather. —**cli·mat′ic, cli·mat′i·cal** adj. —**cli·mat′i·cal·**

**ly** adv.

**cli·max** (klī′măks′) n. The point of greatest intensity or excitement. —v. To reach a climax. —**cli·mac′tic** adj.

**climb** (klīm) v. To move up or ascend. —**climb down.** To descend. —n. The act of climbing. —**climb′a·ble** adj.

**clinch** (klĭnch) v. 1. To fasten securely. 2. To settle decisively; win. 3. To embrace tightly. —n. The act of clinching. —**clinch′er** n.

**cling** (klĭng) v. **clung, clinging.** To hold fast. —**cling′er** n.

**clin·ic** (klĭn′ĭk) n. 1. A specialized hospital. 2. An outpatient division. 3. A center that offers counsel or instruction. —**clin′i·cal** adj.

**clip**[1] (klĭp) v. 1. To cut off. 2. To cut short. —n. A brisk pace. —**clip′per** n.

**clip**[2] (klĭp) n. 1. A clasp. 2. A container. —v. **clipped, clipping.** To fasten.

**clique** (klēk, klĭk) n. An exclusive group.

**cloak** (klōk) n. 1. A loose outer garment. 2. Anything that conceals. —v. To conceal.

**clock** (klŏk) n. An instrument for measuring time. —v. To record the time or speed of. —**clock′wise** adv. & adj.

**clod** (klŏd) n. 1. A lump of earth. 2. A stupid person. —**clod′dish** adj.

**clog** (klŏg) n. 1. An obstacle. 2. A heavy, usually wooden shoe. —v. **clogged, clogging.** 1. To impede. 2. To make or become obstructed. —**clog′gy** adj.

**clois·ter** (klois′tər) n. 1. A covered walk. 2. A monastery or convent. —v. To seclude.

**close** (klōs) adj. **closer, closest.** 1. Near. 2. Compact. 3. Nearly even. 4. Fitting tightly. 5. Complete; thorough. 6. Intimate. 7. Confined. 8. Secretive. 9. Miserly. 10. Lacking fresh air. —v. (klōz) **closed, closing.** 1. To shut. 2. To end; finish. 3. To come near. 4. To agree. —n. (klōz). A conclusion. —adv. (klōs). In a close manner. —**close′ly** adv. —**close′ness** n.

**clos·et** (klŏz′ĭt, klô′zĭt) n. A small room for storage and clothes. —v. To shut up in a private room.

**clot** (klŏt) n. A coagulated mass. —**clot** v.

**cloth** (klôth, klŏth) n., pl. **cloths.** 1. Fabric. 2. A piece of fabric used for a specific purpose, as a tablecloth.

**clothe** (klōth) v. **clothed** or **clad, clothing.** To dress.

**clothes** (klōz, klōthz) pl.n. Articles of dress. —**cloth′ing** n.

**cloud** (kloud) n. 1. A visible body of fine water droplets in the sky. 2. Any hovering mass, as of dust. —v. **1.** To cover with clouds. **2.** To make or become gloomy or troubled. —**cloud'i·ness** n. —**cloud'less** adj. —**cloud'y** adj.

**clout** (klout) n. A blow. —v. To strike heavily.

**clove¹** (klōv) n. A spice from the flower of an Asian tree.

**clove²** (klōv) n. A section of a bulb, as of garlic.

**clown** (kloun) n. **1.** A comic entertainer. **2.** A fool. —v. To behave like a clown. —**clown'ish** adj. —**clown'ish·ly** adv.

**cloy** (kloi) v. To surfeit. —**cloy'ing** adj. —**cloy'ing·ly** adv.

**club¹** (klŭb) n. **1.** A heavy stick. **2.** A playing card marked with a black cloverleaf. —v. clubbed, clubbing. To strike with a club.

**club²** (klŭb) n. A social group or hobby.

**clue** (kloō) n. Also **clew.** Anything that helps solve a problem or mystery.

**clump** (klŭmp) n. **1.** A clustered mass. **2.** A heavy dull sound. —v. To walk with a heavy dull sound.

**clum·sy** (klŭm'zē) adj. **-sier, -siest.** Graceless; awkward. —**clum'si·ly** adv. —**clum'si·ness** n.

**clung** (klŭng) p.t. & p.p. of **cling.**

**clus·ter** (klŭs'tər) n. A close group; bunch. —v. To gather or grow in clusters.

**clutch** (klŭch) v. To grasp or attempt to grasp tightly. —n. **1.** A tight grasp. **2.** clutches. Control. **3.** A device for engaging engine gears.

**clut·ter** (klŭt'ər) n. A disordered state; jumble. —v. To litter.

**coach** (kōch) n. **1.** A closed carriage, bus, train, etc. **2.** One who trains, esp. in athletics. —v. To teach or train.

**co·ag·u·late** (kō-ăg'yə-lāt') v. **-lated, -lating.** To thicken; clot. —**co·ag'u·lant** adj. & n. —**co·ag'u·la'tion** n.

**coal** (kōl) n. A black carbon-containing mineral burned as a fuel.

**co·a·li·tion** (kō'ə-lĭsh'ən) n. An alliance or union. —**co·a·li'tion·ist** n.

**coarse** (kôrs, kōrs) adj. **coarser, coarsest.** **1.** Crude. **2.** Rough-textured. —**coarse'ly** adv. —**coars'en** v. —**coarse'ness** n.

**coast** (kōst) n. The seashore. —v. **1.** To slide down a slope. **2.** To move effortlessly. —**coast'al** adj. —**coast'er** n.

**coat** (kōt) n. **1.** An outer garment with sleeves. **2.** A natural outer covering. **3.** A covering layer. —v. To cover with a coat. —**coat'ed** adj.

**coax** (kōks) v. To urge by pleading or flattery. —**coax'er** n.

**cob** (kŏb) n. The core of an ear of corn.

**cob·ble** (kŏb'əl) v. **-bled, -bling.** To mend (shoes). —**cob'bler** n.

**co·caine** (kō-kān') n. A narcotic drug from the leaves of a tree.

**cock** (kŏk) n. **1.** A male bird, esp. a rooster. **2.** A faucet or valve. **3.** The hammer in a firearm. —v. **1.** To set the hammer of (a gun) for firing. **2.** To tilt or turn up.

**cock·pit** (kŏk'pĭt') n. The pilots' space in an airplane.

**cock·roach** (kŏk'rōch') n. A common flatbodied insect.

**cock·tail** (kŏk'tāl') n. **1.** A mixed alcoholic drink. **2.** An appetizer.

**co·coa** (kō'kō) n. Roasted powdered cacao seeds, or a drink made from this powder.

**co·co·nut** (kō'kə-nŭt', -nət) n. Also **co·coa·nut.** The large, hard-shelled, edible nut of a tropical palm tree.

**co·coon** (kə-koōn') n. The pupal case spun by the larva of a moth or other insect.

**cod** (kŏd) n., pl. cod or cods. Also **cod·fish** n. A food fish of N Atlantic waters.

**cod·dle** (kŏd'l) v. **-dled, -dling.** To pamper.

**code** (kōd) n. **1.** A set of laws or rules. **2.** A system of signals. —v. **coded, coding.** To put in a code.

**co·ed·u·ca·tion** (kō'ĕj-ōō-kā'shən) n. The education of both men and women at the same institution. —**co·ed'** n. & adj. —**co·ed·u·ca'tion·al** adj.

**co·erce** (kō-ûrs') v. **-erced, -ercing.** To compel; force. —**co·erc'er** n. —**co·er'cion** n. —**co·er'cive** adj.

**cof·fee** (kô'fē, kŏf'ē) n. A beverage prepared from the seeds of a tropical tree.

**cof·fin** (kô'fən, kŏf'ən) n. A box in which a corpse is buried.

**cog** (kŏg) n. **1.** A tooth on the rim of a wheel. **2.** A subordinate member of an organization.

**co·gnac** (kōn'yăk', kŏn'-, kŏn'-) n. A fine French brandy.

**cog·ni·zance** (kŏg'nə-zəns) n. Awareness. —**cog'ni·zant** adj.

**co·her·ent** (kō-hîr'ənt, kō-hĕr'-) adj. **1.** Sticking together. **2.** Orderly; intelligible. —**co·her'ence, co·her'en·cy** n.

**co·he·sion** (kō-hē'zhən) n. The condition of sticking together; union. —**co·here'** v. —**co·he'sive** adj. —**co·he'sive·ly** adv. —**co·he'sive·ness** n.

**co·hort** (kō'hôrt') n. **1.** A group or band.

**2.** A companion.

**coll** (koil) *n.* **1.** A series of connected spirals. **2.** A spiral or ring. —*v.* To wind in coils. —**coil'er** *n.*

**coin** (koin) *n.* A piece of metal issued as money. —*v.* **1.** To make (coins) from metal. **2.** To invent (a word or phrase). —**coin'age** *n.*

**co-in-cide** (kō'ĭn-sīd') *v.* **-cided, -ciding. 1.** To happen at the same time. **2.** To correspond exactly. —**co-in'ci-dence** *n.* —**co-in'ci-den'tal, co-in'ci-dent** *adj.*

**coke** (kōk) *n.* The solid residue of coal after removal of gases.

**col-an-der** (kŭl'ən-dər, kŏl'-) *n.* A perforated kitchen bowl for draining.

**cold** (kōld) *adj.* **1.** Having a low temperature. **2.** Uncomfortably chilled. **3.** Lacking warmth; reserved; unemotional. —*n.* **1.** Relative lack of warmth. **2.** A chilly sensation. **3.** A viral respiratory infection. —**cold'ly** *adv.* —**cold'ness** *n.*

**cole-slaw** (kōl'slô') *n.* Also **cole slaw.** Shredded raw cabbage.

**col-lab-o-rate** (kə-lăb'ə-rāt') *v.* **-rated, -rating. 1.** To work together. **2.** To cooperate with an invading enemy. —**col-lab'o-ra'tion** *n.* —**col-lab'o-ra'tive** *adj.* —**col-lab'o-ra'tor** *n.*

**col-lapse** (kə-lăps') *v.* **-lapsed, -lapsing. 1.** To fall down; cave in. **2.** To break down. —**col-lapse'** *n.* —**col-laps'i-ble** *adj.*

**col-lar** (kŏl'ər) *n.* A band of a garment that encircles the neck. —*v.* To seize or detain. —**col'lar-less** *adj.*

**col-lat-er-al** (kə-lăt'ər-əl) *adj.* **1.** Side-by-side. **2.** Secondary. —*n.* Property acceptable as security for a loan.

**col-league** (kŏl'ēg') *n.* A fellow worker or member of a profession.

**col-lect** (kə-lĕkt') *v.* **1.** To assemble; accumulate. **2.** To obtain payment of. —*adj. & adv.* With payment to be made by the receiver. —**col-lec'tion** *n.* —**col-lec'tive** *adj. & n.* —**col-lec'tive-ly** *adv.* —**col-lec'tor** *n.*

**col-lege** (kŏl'ĭj) *n.* A school of higher learning. —**col-le'gian** *n.* —**col-le'giate** *adj.*

**col-lide** (kə-līd') *v.* **-lided, -liding.** To come together violently. —**col-li'sion** *n.*

**col-lie** (kŏl'ē) *n.* A large, long-haired dog.

**col-lo-qui-al** (kə-lō'kwē-əl) *adj.* Used in conversation but not formal writing. —**col-lo'qui-al-ism** *n.* —**col-lo'qui-al-ly** *adv.*

**col-lu-sion** (kə-lōō'zhən) *n.* A secret, deceitful agreement. —**col-lu'sive** *adj.*

**co-logne** (kə-lōn') *n.* A perfumed liquid.

**co-lon¹** (kō'lən) *n.* A punctuation mark (:).

**co-lon²** (kō'lən) *n., pl.* **-lons** or **-la.** A section of the large intestine. —**co-lon'ic** *adj.*

**colo-nel** (kûr'nəl) *n.* An officer ranking above a lieutenant colonel. —**colo'nel-cy, colo'nel-ship'** *n.*

**col-on-nade** (kŏl'ə-nād') *n.* A row of columns.

**col-o-ny** (kŏl'ə-nē) *n., pl.* **-nies. 1.** A group of settlers far from but subject to a parent country. **2.** A region politically controlled by another country. **3.** A group living together. —**co-lo'ni-al** *adj.* —**co-lo'ni-al-ism** *n.* —**col'o-nist** *n.* —**col'o-ni-za'tion** *n.* —**col'o-nize** *v.* —**col'o-niz'er** *n.*

**col-or** (kŭl'ər) *n.* **1.** The perceived quality of the light reflected or emitted by an object. **2.** A dye, paint, etc. **3.** Skin tone; complexion. **4.** colors. A flag. **5.** Vividness or picturesqueness. —*v.* **1.** To impart color to. **2.** To influence. **3.** To misrepresent. **4.** To blush. —**col'or-a'tion** *n.* —**col'or-ful** *adj.* —**col'or-ful-ly** *adv.* —**col'or-less** *adj.* —**col'or-less-ly** *adv.*

**co-los-sal** (kə-lŏs'əl) *adj.* Enormous; gigantic. —**co-los'sal-ly** *adv.*

**colt** (kōlt) *n.* A young male horse.

**col-umn** (kŏl'əm) *n.* **1.** An upright rod-shaped structure; pillar. **2.** A vertical section of print on a page. **3.** A regular feature article. **4.** A long row, as of troops. —**col'um-nist** *n.*

**co-ma** (kō'mə) *n.* A deep, prolonged unconsciousness. —**co'ma-tose** *adj.*

**comb** (kōm) *n.* **1.** A thin, toothed object for arranging the hair. **2.** A fleshy crest on a bird's head. —*v.* **1.** To arrange with a comb. **2.** To search thoroughly.

**com-bat** (kəm-băt', kŏm'băt') *v.* To fight against; contend. —*n.* Fighting, esp. armed battle. —**com-bat'ant** *adj. & n.* —**com-bat'ive** *adj.*

**com-bi-na-tion** (kŏm'bə-nā'shən) *n.* **1.** The act of combining. **2.** A group; aggregate. **3.** A sequence of numbers used to open a lock.

**com-bine** (kəm-bīn') *v.* **-bined, -bining.** To unite; merge; blend. —*n.* (kŏm'bīn'). A machine that harvests and threshes grain. —**com-bin'er** *n.*

**com-bus-ti-ble** (kəm-bŭs'tə-bəl) *adj.* Capable of burning. —*n.* A combustible substance. —**com-bus'ti-bil'i-ty** *n.* —**com-bus'ti-bly** *adv.* —**com-bus'tion** *n.*

**come** (kŭm) *v.* **came, coming. 1.** To advance; approach. **2.** To arrive. **3.** To happen. **4.** To occur; originate.

**com-e-dy** (kŏm'ə-dē) *n., pl.* **-dies. 1.** A humorous drama. **2.** Humor. —**co-me'dic** *adj.* —**co-me'di-an** *n.* —**co-me'di-enne'** *fem. n.*

# C-3

**comely** 44

**come·ly** (kŭm'lē) adj. -lier, -liest. Attractive; handsome. —**come'li·ness** n.

**com·et** (kŏm'ĭt) n. A celestial body having a long, bright tail.

**com·fort** (kŭm'fərt) v. To soothe, console. —n. 1. Ease or well-being. 2. Consolation; solace. 3. One that brings ease. —**com'fort·a·ble** adj. —**com'fort·a·bly** adv. —**com'fort·er** n.

**com·ic** (kŏm'ĭk) adj. Also **com·i·cal.** 1. Of comedy. 2. Amusing; humorous. —n. A comedian. —**com'i·cal·ly** adv.

**com·ma** (kŏm'ə) n. A punctuation mark (,).

**com·mand** (kə-mănd', -mänd') v. 1. To give orders (to). 2. To rule. —n. 1. An order. 2. The authority to command. 3. A unit, etc., under one officer. —**com'man·dant** n. —**com·mand'er** n. —**com·mand'ing** adj. —**com·mand'ing·ly** adv.

**com·mand·ment** (kə-mănd'mənt, kə-mänd'-) n. A command; edict.

**com·mem·o·rate** (kə-mĕm'ə-rāt') v. -rated, -rating. 1. To honor the memory of. 2. To serve as a memorial to. —**com·mem'o·ra'tion** n. —**com·mem'o·ra·tive** adj.

**com·mence** (kə-mĕns') v. -menced, -mencing. To begin; start.

**com·mence·ment** (kə-mĕns'mənt) n. 1. A beginning. 2. A graduation ceremony.

**com·mend** (kə-mĕnd') v. 1. To recommend. 2. To praise. —**com·mend'a·ble** adj. —**com·mend'a·bly** adv. —**com'men·da'tion** n.

**com·ment** (kŏm'ĕnt') n. A remark; observation; note. —v. To make a comment (on).

**com·men·tar·y** (kŏm'ən-tĕr'ē) n., pl. -ies. A series of explanations.

**com·men·ta·tor** (kŏm'ən-tā'tər) n. A radio or television reporter.

**com·merce** (kŏm'ərs) n. The buying and selling of goods; trade.

**com·mer·cial** (kə-mûr'shəl) adj. 1. Of or engaged in commerce. 2. Having profit as a major aim. —n. An advertisement. —**com·mer'cial·ism** n. —**com·mer'cial·ize** v.

**com·mis·er·ate** (kə-mĭz'ə-rāt') v. -ated, -ating. To sympathize. —**com·mis'er·a'tion** n.

**com·mis·sar·y** (kŏm'ĭ-sĕr'ē, -sâr'ē) n., pl. -ies. A food store on a military post.

**com·mis·sion** (kə-mĭsh'ən) n. 1. Authorization to carry out a task. 2. A group authorized to perform certain duties. 3. A committing; perpetration. 4. An allowance to a salesman or agent for his services. 5. A document conferring the rank of a military officer. —v. 1. To grant a commission to. 2. To place an order for.

**com·mis·sion·er** (kə-mĭsh'ən-ər) n. 1. A

member of a commission. 2. An official in charge of a public service.

**com·mit** (kə-mĭt') v. -mitted, -mitting. 1. To do; perform. 2. To consign; entrust. 3. To place in confinement. 4. To pledge; bind. —**com·mit'ment** n.

**com·mit·tee** (kə-mĭt'ē) n. A group delegated to perform a function.

**com·mode** (kə-mōd') n. 1. A low cabinet. 2. A toilet.

**com·mod·i·ty** (kə-mŏd'ə-tē) n., pl. -ties. An agricultural or mining commodity.

**com·mo·dore** (kŏm'ə-dôr', -dōr') n. A naval officer.

**com·mon** (kŏm'ən) adj. 1. Belonging to all; joint. 2. Widespread; prevalent. 3. Ordinary. 4. Average. 5. Vulgar; coarse. —n. A tract of public land. —**com'mon·ly** adv —**com'mon·ness** n.

**com·mon·place** (kŏm'ən-plās') adj. Ordinary; common. —n. Something ordinary, esp. an obvious remark.

**com·mon·weal** (kŏm'ən-wēl') n. The public good.

**com·mon·wealth** (kŏm'ən-wĕlth') n. 1. The people of a nation or state. 2. A republic. 3. A federation.

**com·mo·tion** (kə-mō'shən) n. Violent motion; agitation.

**com·mu·nal** (kə-myōōn'əl, kŏm'yə-nəl) adj. 1. Of a commune or community. 2. Public. —**com'mu·nal'i·ty** n. —**com·mu'nal·ly** adv.

**com·mu·ni·cate** (kə-myōō'nə-kāt') v. -cated, -cating. 1. To make known; impart. 2. To transmit, as a disease. —**com·mu'ni·ca·ble** adj.

**com·mu·ni·ca·tion** (kə-myōō'nə-kā'shən) n. 1. Transmission. 2. The exchange of thoughts, messages, etc. 3. Something communicated. 4. communications. A means of communicating. —**com·mu'ni·ca·tive** adj.

**com·mun·ion** (kə-myōōn'yən) n. 1. A sharing, as of thoughts or feelings. 2. A religious or spiritual fellowship. 3. Communion. The Eucharist.

**com·mu·nism** (kŏm'yə-nĭz'əm) n. 1. An economic system in which factories, farms, etc., are owned in common by the workers. 2. Communism. Revolutionary struggle toward this system. —**com'mu·nist** n. & adj. —**com'mu·nis'tic** adj.

**com·mu·ni·ty** (kə-myōō'nə-tē) n., pl. -ties. A group of people living in the same area.

**com·mute** (kə-myōōt') v. -muted, -muting. 1. To change (a penalty or payment) to a less severe one. 2. To travel to and from work. —**com'mu·ta'tion** n. —**com·mut'er** n.

**comprehend**

**com·pact** (kəm-păkt') *adj.* **1.** Closely packed. **2.** Expressed briefly. —*v.* To pack firmly together. —**com·pact'ly** *adv.*

**com·pact** (kŏm'păkt') *n.* **1.** A small cosmetic case. **2.** An agreement. —**com·pact'ly** *adv.* —**com·pact'ness** *n.*

**com·pan·ion** (kəm-păn'yən) *n.* **1.** A comrade; associate. **2.** One of a pair; mate. —**com·pan'ion·ship'** *n.*

**com·pa·ny** (kŭm'pə-nē) *n., pl.* **-nies.** **1.** A group of people. **2.** A guest or guests. **3.** A business enterprise. **4.** A subdivision of a regiment.

**com·par·a·tive** (kəm-păr'ə-tĭv) *adj.* **1.** Involving comparison. **2.** Compared to others; relative. —**com·par'a·tive·ly** *adv.*

**com·pare** (kəm-pâr') *v.* **-pared, -paring. 1.** To represent as similar (with *to).* **2.** To examine the similarities or differences (with *with).* —*n.* —**beyond** (or **without**) **compare.** Unequaled. —**com'pa·ra·ble** *adj.* —**com·par'er** *n.* —**com·par'i·son** *n.*

**com·part·ment** (kəm-pärt'mənt) *n.* A space or subdivision sectioned off.

**com·pass** (kŭm'pəs, kŏm'-) *n.* **1.** A device for finding direction. **2.** A device for drawing circles. **3.** A range or scope.

**com·pas·sion** (kəm-păsh'ən) *n.* Sympathy toward suffering; pity. —**com·pas'sion·ate** *adj.*

**com·pat·i·ble** (kəm-păt'ə-bəl) *adj.* Capable of living or performing together. —**com·pat'i·bil'i·ty, com·pat'i·ble·ness** *n.* —**com·pat'i·bly** *adv.*

**com·pa·tri·ot** (kəm-pā'trē-ət, -ŏt') *n.* A fellow countryman.

**com·pel** (kəm-pěl') *v.* **-pelled, -pelling.** To force.

**com·pen·sate** (kŏm'pən-sāt') *v.* **-sated, -sating. 1.** To make up for. **2.** To pay. —**com·pen·sa'tion** *n.* —**com·pen'sa·to·ry** *adj.*

**com·pete** (kəm-pēt') *v.* **-peted, -peting.** To contend with another; vie.

**com·pe·tent** (kŏm'pə-tənt) *adj.* **1.** Properly qualified; capable. **2.** Adequate. —**com'pe·tence** *n.* —**com'pe·tent·ly** *adv.*

**com·pe·ti·tion** (kŏm'pə-tĭsh'ən) *n.* **1.** A vying with others; struggle. **2.** A contest of skill. —**com·pet'i·tive** *adj.* —**com·pet'i·tive·ness** *n.* —**com·pet'i·tor** *n.*

**com·pile** (kəm-pīl') *v.* **-piled, -piling.** To compose from diverse sources. —**com·pi·la'tion** *n.* —**com·pil'er** *n.*

**com·pla·cen·cy** (kəm-plā'sən-sē) *n.* Also **com·pla·cence.** Self-satisfaction; smugness. —**com·pla'cent** *adj.* —**com·pla'cent·ly** *adv.*

**com·plain** (kəm-plān') *v.* **1.** To express pain, dissatisfaction, or resentment. **2.** To make a formal accusation. —**com·plain'er** *n.* —**com·plaint'** *n.*

**com·ple·ment** (kŏm'plə-mənt) *n.* **1.** Something that completes or balances. **2.** Full quantity or allowance. —*v.* To complete; balance. —**com'ple·men'ta·ry** *adj.*

**com·plete** (kəm-plēt') *adj.* **1.** Having all parts. **2.** Concluded; ended. **3.** Thorough; perfect. —*v.* **-pleted, -pleting. 1.** To make whole. **2.** To finish. —**com·plete'ly** *adv.* —**com·ple'tion** *n.*

**com·plex** (kəm-plěks', kŏm'plěks') *adj.* **1.** Consisting of interconnected parts. **2.** Intricate; complicated. —*n.* (kŏm'plěks'). **1.** A whole complex. **2.** A painful or disruptive set of fixed ideas. —**com·plex'i·ty** *n.*

**com·plex·ion** (kəm-plěk'shən) *n.* The color and texture of the skin.

**com·pli·cate** (kŏm'plĭ-kāt') *v.* **-cated, -cating.** To make complex or difficult. —**com'pli·ca'tion** *n.*

**com·plic·i·ty** (kəm-plĭs'ə-tē) *n.* The state of being an accomplice, as in wrongdoing.

**com·pli·ment** (kŏm'plə-mənt) *n.* **1.** An expression of praise or admiration. **2.** A formal act of courtesy or respect. —*v.* To pay a compliment to.

**com·pli·men·ta·ry** (kŏm'plə-měn'tər-ē, -trē) *adj.* **1.** Expressing a compliment. **2.** Given free.

**com·ply** (kəm-plī') *v.* **-plied, -plying.** To act in accordance; conform. —**com·pli'ance** *n.* —**com·pli'ant** *adj.*

**com·po·nent** (kəm-pō'nənt) *n.* A part; constituent.

**com·pose** (kəm-pōz') *v.* **-posed, -posing. 1.** To make up the parts of. **2.** To make by putting parts together. **3.** To create or write, esp. music. **4.** To make calm. —**com·pos'er** *n.* —**com·po·si'tion** *n.*

**com·pos·ite** (kəm-pŏz'ĭt) *adj.* Made up of distinct parts. —*n.* A composite structure. —**com·pos'ite·ly** *adv.*

**com·po·sure** (kəm-pō'zhər) *n.* Self-possession.

**com·pound** (kəm-pound') *v.* **1.** To combine; mix. **2.** To increase. —*adj.* (kŏm'pound'). Consisting of two or more parts. —*n.* (kŏm'pound'). **1.** A compound entity. **2.** A combination. **3.** A pure substance consisting of atoms of different elements bound together.

**com·pre·hend** (kŏm'prĭ-hěnd') *v.* **1.** To understand. **2.** To include. —**com'pre·hen'si·ble** *adj.* —**com'pre·hen'sion** *n.*

**com·pre·hen·sive** (kŏm'prĭ-hĕn'sĭv) *adj.* Totally inclusive. — **com'pre·hen'sive·ly** *adv.*

**com·press** (kəm-prĕs') *v.* To press together. —*n.* (kŏm'prĕs'). A pad applied to an injury. — **com·press'i·ble** *adj.* — **com·pres'sion** *n.*

**com·prise** (kəm-prīz') *v.* -**prised**, -**prising**. 1. To consist of. 2. To include; contain.

**com·pro·mise** (kŏm'prə-mīz') *n.* A settlement in which both sides make concessions. —*v.* -**mised**, -**mising**. 1. To settle by compromise. 2. To expose to suspicion. — **com'pro·mis'er** *n.*

**com·pul·sion** (kəm-pŭl'shən) *n.* 1. The act of compelling or the state of being compelled. 2. An irresistible impulse to act. — **com·pul'sive** *adj.* — **com·pul'sive·ly** *adv.*

**com·pul·so·ry** (kəm-pŭl'sə-rē) *adj.* Obligatory; required. — **com·pul'so·ri·ly** *adv.*

**com·punc·tion** (kəm-pŭngk'shən) *n.* Uneasiness caused by guilt; remorse.

**com·pute** (kəm-pyōōt') *v.* -**puted**, -**puting**. To calculate. — **com·put'a·ble** *adj.* — **com'pu·ta'tion** *n.* — **com·put'er** *n.*

**com·rade** (kŏm'răd) *n.* A friend or associate. — **com'rade·ship'** *n.*

**con** (kŏn) *adv.* Against. — **con** *n.*

**con·cave** (kŏn-kāv') *adj.* Curved inward. — **con·cav'i·ty** *n.*

**con·ceal** (kən-sēl') *v.* To keep secret; hide. — **con·ceal'er** *n.* — **con·ceal'ment** *n.*

**con·ceit** (kən-sēt') *n.* 1. Self-importance; vanity. 2. A fanciful comparison or notion. — **con·ceit'ed** *adj.*

**con·ceive** (kən-sēv') *v.* -**ceived**, -**ceiving**. 1. To become pregnant (with). 2. To imagine; understand. — **con·ceiv'a·ble** *adj.* — **con·ceiv'a·bly** *adv.* — **con·ceiv'er** *n.*

**con·cen·trate** (kŏn'sən-trāt') *v.* -**trated**, -**trating**. 1. To draw inward; focus. 2. To think attentively. —*n.* A concentrated substance. — **con'cen·tra'tion** *n.* 3. To make or become more dense.

**con·cept** (kŏn'sĕpt) *n.* An idea.

**con·cep·tion** (kən-sĕp'shən) *n.* 1. The fact of becoming pregnant. 2. A beginning; start. 3. A thought.

**con·cern** (kən-sûrn') *v.* 1. To relate to; affect. 2. To engage the interests of. 3. To cause uneasiness in. —*n.* 1. Something of interest. 2. Earnest regard. 3. Anxiety; worry. 4. A business. — **con·cerned'** *adj.* — **con·cern'ing** *prep.*

**con·cert** (kŏn'sûrt) *n.* 1. A public musical performance. 2. Agreement. —*v.* To plan or arrange together. — **con·cert'ed** *adj.*

**con·cer·to** (kən-chĕr'tō) *n., pl.* -**tos**. A composition for an orchestra and one or more solo instruments.

**con·ces·sion** (kən-sĕsh'ən) *n.* 1. The act of conceding. 2. Something conceded. 3. The privilege of maintaining a subsidiary business within certain premises.

**conch** (kŏngk, kŏnch) *n., pl.* **conchs** or **conches**. A large spiral sea shell.

**con·cil·i·ate** (kən-sĭl'ē-āt') *v.* -**ated**, -**ating**. To overcome the animosity of. — **con·cil·i·a'tion** *n.* — **con·cil'i·a·tor** *n.* — **con·cil'i·a·to'ry** *adj.*

**con·cise** (kən-sīs') *adj.* Expressing much in few words; succinct. — **con·cise'ly** *adv.* — **con·cise'ness** *n.*

**con·clave** (kŏn'klāv, kŏng'-) *n.* A secret meeting.

**con·clude** (kən-klōōd') *v.* -**cluded**, -**cluding**. 1. To bring to an end. 2. To agree. 3. To decide; resolve. — **con·clu'sion** *n.* — **con·clu'sive** *adj.* — **con·clu'sive·ly** *adv.*

**con·cord** (kŏn'kôrd, kŏng'-) *n.* Harmony. — **con·cord'ant** *adj.*

**con·cor·dance** (kən-kôr'dəns) *n.* 1. Agreement. 2. An index of all the words in a book.

**con·course** (kŏn'kôrs, -kōrs, kŏng'-) *n.* A crowd. 2. A large open space for crowds.

**con·crete** (kŏn-krēt') *adj.* 1. Particular; specific. 2. Real; tangible. 3. Hard; solid. —*n.* A construction material made of gravel and mortar or cement. — **con·crete'ly** *adv.* — **con·cre'tion** *n.*

**con·cur** (kən-kûr') *v.* -**curred**, -**curring**. 1. To have the same opinion. 2. To coincide. — **con·cur'rence** *n.* — **con·cur'rent** *adj.*

**con·cus·sion** (kən-kŭsh'ən) *n.* 1. A violent jarring; shock. 2. A brain injury from a blow.

**con·demn** (kən-dĕm') *v.* 1. To express disapproval of; censure. 2. To sentence. 3. To mark for destruction. — **con'dem·na'tion** *n.*

**con·dense** (kən-dĕns') *v.* -**densed**, -**densing**. 1. To compress. 2. To abridge. 3. To form a liquid from a vapor. — **con·den·sa·ble** *adj.* — **con'den·sa'tion** *n.* — **con·den'ser** *n.*

**con·de·scend** (kŏn'dĭ-sĕnd') *v.* To be patronizing; stoop. — **con'de·scen'sion** *n.*

**con·di·tion** (kən-dĭsh'ən) *n.* 1. A state of being. 2. State of health. 3. A disease. 4. A prerequisite. 5. A qualification. 6. Often **conditions**. The existing circumstances. —*v.* 1. To make conditional. 2. To put into a proper condition. — **con·di'tion·al** *adj.*

**con·dole** (kən-dōl') *v.* -**doled**, -**doling**. To express sympathy to one in grief. — **con·do'lence** *n.* — **con·dol'er** *n.*

**conquer**

**con·duct** (kən-dŭkt′) v. **1.** To direct; manage. **2.** To lead or guide. **3.** To transmit. **4.** To behave. —n. (kŏn′dŭkt). **1.** The way a person acts. **2.** Management. — **con·duc′tion** n. —**con·duc′tive** adj.

**con·duc·tor** (kən-dŭk′tər) n. **1.** The person in charge of a train, bus, etc. **2.** The director of a musical ensemble. **3.** A substance that conducts electricity, etc.

**cone** (kōn) n. **1.** A circular-based figure tapering evenly to a point. **2.** A rounded seed-bearing structure. — **con′ic, con′i·cal** adj.

**con·fec·tion** (kən-fĕk′shən) n. A sweet food. — **con·fec′tion·er** n. — **con·fec′tion·er·y** n.

**con·fed·er·ate** (kən-fĕd′ər-ĭt) n. **1.** An ally. **2.** An accomplice. —adj. United; allied. —v. (-āt′) -**at·ed, -at·ing.** To unite. — **con·fed′er·a·cy** n. — **con·fed′er·a′tive** adj.

**con·fer** (kən-fûr′) v. **-ferred, -fer·ring. 1.** To bestow. **2.** To hold a conference.

**con·fer·ence** (kŏn′fə-rəns, -frəns) n. **1.** A meeting; consultation. **2.** A league.

**con·fess** (kən-fĕs′) v. **1.** To disclose a misdeed or fault. **2.** To concede the truth of. **3.** To make known (one's sins), esp. to a priest. — **con·fess′ed·ly** adv. — **con·fes′sion** n. — **con·fes′sor** n.

**con·fet·ti** (kən-fĕt′ē) n. Bits of colored paper scattered at celebrations.

**con·fi·dant** (kŏn′fə-dănt′, -dänt′, kŏn′fə-dănt′, -dänt′) n. One to whom secrets are confided.

**con·fide** (kən-fīd′) v. **-fid·ed, -fid·ing. 1.** To tell in confidence. **2.** To put into another's keeping. — **con·fid′er** n.

**con·fi·dence** (kŏn′fə-dəns) n. **1.** Trust. **2.** Secrecy; privacy. **3.** Something confided. **4.** A feeling of assurance or certainty. — **con′fi·dent** adj. — **con′fi·den′tial** adj. — **con′fi·dent·ly** adv.

**con·fig·u·ra·tion** (kən-fĭg′yə-rā′shən) n. The arrangement of the parts; form.

**con·fine** (kən-fīn′) v. **-fined, -fin·ing. 1.** To restrict. **2.** To imprison. — **con·fine′ment** n. — **con·fin′er** n.

**con·firm** (kən-fûrm′) v. **1.** To verify. **2.** To strengthen. **3.** To ratify. **4.** To admit as a church member. — **con·fir·ma′tion** n.

**con·fis·cate** (kŏn′fĭs-kāt′) v. **-cat·ed, -cat·ing.** To seize by authority. — **con·fis·ca′tion** n. — **con·fis·ca′tor** n.

**con·flict** (kŏn′flĭkt) n. **1.** A prolonged battle. **2.** A disagreement. —v. (kən-flĭkt′). To come into opposition; differ.

**con·form** (kən-fôrm′) v. **1.** To make or become similar. **2.** To be in agreement.

**3.** To act in accordance with customs or rules. — **con·form′ist** n. — **con·form′i·ty** n.

**con·found** (kən-found′, kŏn-) v. To confuse. — **con·found′er** n.

**con·front** (kən-frŭnt′) v. **1.** To come face to face with. **2.** To face; oppose. — **con′fron·ta′tion** n.

**con·fuse** (kən-fyōōz′) v. **-fused, -fus·ing. 1.** To perplex. **2.** To mix up. — **con·fus′ed·ly** adv. — **con·fus′ing·ly** adv. — **con·fu′sion** n.

**con·gen·ial** (kən-jēn′yəl) adj. Sympathetic; agreeable. — **con·ge′ni·al′i·ty** n. — **con·gen′ial·ly** adv.

**con·gen·i·tal** (kən-jĕn′ə-təl) adj. Existing at birth but not hereditary. — **con·gen′i·tal·ly** adv.

**con·glom·er·ate** (kən-glŏm′ə-rāt′) v. **-at·ed, -at·ing.** To form into a dense mass. —n. (-rĭt). **1.** A heterogeneous mass. **2.** A business corporation made up of diverse companies. — **con·glom′er·a′tion** n.

**con·grat·u·late** (kən-grăch′ōō-lāt′) v. **-lat·ed, -lat·ing.** To express pleasure at the achievement or good fortune of. — **con·grat′u·la′tion** n. — **con·grat′u·la·to′ry** adj.

**con·gre·gate** (kŏng′grə-gāt′) v. **-gat·ed, -gat·ing.** To come together in a crowd. — **con′gre·ga′tion** n.

**con·gress** (kŏng′grĭs) n. **1.** A formal assembly. **2.** A national legislature. — **con·gres′sion·al** adj. — **con′gress·man** n. — **con′gress·wom·an** n.

**con·ju·gate** (kŏn′jōō-gāt′, -jə-gāt′) v. **-gat·ed, -gat·ing.** To inflect (a verb). — **con′ju·ga′tion** n.

**con·junc·tion** (kən-jŭngk′shən) n. **1.** A connection. **2.** Simultaneous occurrence. **3.** A word connecting other words or word groups. — **con·junc′tive** adj.

**con·jure** (kŏn′jər, kən-jōōr′) v. **-jured, -jur·ing. 1.** To entreat. **2.** To summon or effect by or as if by magic. — **con′ju·ra′tion** n. — **con·jur′er** n.

**con·nect** (kə-nĕkt′) v. To join; link; unite. — **con·nect′ed·ly** adv. — **con·nec′tion** n. — **con·nec′tive** adj.

**con·nive** (kə-nīv′) v. **-nived, -niv·ing. 1.** To feign ignorance of a wrong. **2.** To cooperate secretly. — **con·niv′ance** n. — **con·niv′er** n.

**con·nois·seur** (kŏn′ə-sûr′) n. An informed judge in matters of taste.

**con·note** (kə-nōt′) v. **-not·ed, -not·ing.** To suggest in addition to literal meaning. — **con′no·ta′tion** n. — **con·no′ta·tive** adj.

**con·quer** (kŏng′kər) v. **1.** To defeat or subdue. **2.** To overcome. — **con′quer·a·ble**

*adj.* — con'quer·or *n.* — con'quest *n.*

**con·science** (kŏn'shəns) *n.* The faculty of recognizing right and wrong in one's own conduct.

**con·sci·en·tious** (kŏn'shē-ĕn'shəs) *adj.* 1. Scrupulous; honest. 2. Painstaking; careful. — con'sci·en'tious·ly *adv.* — con'sci·en'tious·ness *n.*

**con·scious** (kŏn'shəs) *adj.* 1. Not asleep; awake. 2. Aware; cognizant. 3. Intentional. — con'scious·ly *adv.* — con'scious·ness *n.*

**con·script** (kŏn'skrĭpt) *n.* One compulsorily enrolled for military service. — *v.* (kən-skrĭpt'). To draft for military service. — con·scrip'tion *n.*

**con·se·crate** (kŏn'sə-krāt') *v.* **-crated, -crating.** 1. To make or declare sacred. 2. To dedicate. — con'se·cra'tion *n.*

**con·sec·u·tive** (kən-sĕk'yə-tĭv) *adj.* Following successively without interruption. — con·sec'u·tive·ly *adv.*

**con·sen·sus** (kən-sĕn'səs) *n.* Collective opinion.

**con·sent** (kən-sĕnt') *v.* To agree. —*n.* Acceptance or approval. — con·sent'er *n.*

**con·se·quence** (kŏn'sə-kwĕns) *n.* 1. An effect. 2. Importance.

**con·se·quent** (kŏn'sə-kwĕnt, -kwənt) *adj.* Following as a result. — con'se·quent'ly *adv.*

**con·ser·va·tive** (kən-sûr'və-tĭv) *adj.* 1. Favoring preservation of the existing order. 2. Moderate; cautious. 3. Traditional. —*n.* A conservative person. — con·ser'va·tism *n.*

**con·ser·va·to·ry** (kən-sûr'və-tôr'ē, -tôr'ē) *n., pl.* **-ries.** A school of music or dramatic art.

**con·serve** (kən-sûrv') *v.* **-served, -serving.** 1. To protect; preserve. 2. To preserve (fruits). — con·serv'a·ble *adj.* — con'ser·va'tion *n.*

**con·sid·er** (kən-sĭd'ər) *v.* 1. To deliberate upon; examine. 2. To think or deem.

**con·sid·er·a·ble** (kən-sĭd'ər-ə-bəl) *adj.* Fairly large or significant. — con·sid'er·a·bly *adv.*

**con·sid·er·ate** (kən-sĭd'ər-ĭt) *adj.* Having regard for the needs or feelings of others. — con·sid'er·ate·ness *n.*

**con·sid·er·a·tion** (kən-sĭd'ə-rā'shən) *n.* 1. Deliberation. 2. A factor. 3. Thoughtfulness. — con·sid'er·ing *prep. & adv.*

**con·sign** (kən-sīn') *v.* 1. To entrust. 2. To deliver. 3. To allot. — con·sign'ment *n.* — con·sign'or *n.*

**con·sist** (kən-sĭst') *v.* 1. To be composed (with *of*). 2. To be inherent; lie.

**con·sis·ten·cy** (kən-sĭs'tən-sē) *n., pl.* **-cies.**

Also **con·sis·tence.** 1. Agreement or compatibility. 2. Steadiness; invariability. 3. Thickness. — con·sis'tent *adj.* — con·sis'tent·ly *adv.*

**con·sole** (kən-sōl') *v.* **-soled, -soling.** To comfort. — con·so·la'tion *n.* — con·sol'er *n.*

**con·sol·i·date** (kən-sŏl'ə-dāt') *v.* **-dated, -dating.** 1. To solidify. 2. To unite; combine. — con·sol'i·da'tion *n.* — con·sol'i·da'tor *n.*

**con·som·mé** (kŏn'sə-mā') *n.* A clear soup.

**con·so·nant** (kŏn'sə-nənt) *adj.* In agreement. —*n.* A letter representing a speech sound produced by obstructing the air flow.

**con·sort** (kŏn'sôrt) *n.* A husband or wife, esp. of a monarch. —*v.* (kən-sôrt'). To keep company; associate.

**con·spic·u·ous** (kən-spĭk'yōō-əs) *adj.* Easily seen; obvious. — con·spic'u·ous·ly *adv.* — con·spic'u·ous·ness *n.*

**con·spire** (kən-spīr') *v.* **-spired, -spiring.** To plan secretly; plot. — con·spir'a·cy *n.* — con·spir'a·tor *n.* — con·spir'a·to'ri·al *adj.* — con·spir'a·tor *n.*

**con·sta·ble** (kŏn'stə-bəl, kŭn'-) *n.* A policeman.

**con·stant** (kŏn'stənt) *adj.* 1. Persistent. 2. Unchanging. 3. Steadfast. —*n.* A thing that is unchanging. — con'stan·cy *n.* — con'stant·ly *adv.*

**con·stel·la·tion** (kŏn'stə-lā'shən) *n.* A group of stars.

**con·ster·na·tion** (kŏn'stər-nā'shən) *n.* Alarm.

**con·sti·pa·tion** (kŏn'stə-pā'shən) *n.* Difficult evacuation of the bowels. — con'sti·pate' *v.*

**con·stit·u·ent** (kən-stĭch'ōō-ənt) *adj.* Serving as part of a whole. —*n.* 1. One represented by an elected official. 2. A component. — con·stit'u·en·cy *n.*

**con·sti·tute** (kŏn'stə-t/y/ōōt') *v.* **-tuted, -tuting.** 1. To make up; compose. 2. To establish.

**con·sti·tu·tion** (kŏn'stə-t/y/ōō'shən) *n.* 1. Composition; make-up. 2. The basic law of a politically organized body. — con·sti·tu'tion·al *adj.* — con·sti·tu·tion·al'i·ty *n.*

**con·strain** (kən-strān') *v.* 1. To compel; oblige. 2. To confine. 3. To make uneasy. — con·strain'a·ble *adj.* — con·strain'er *n.* — con·straint' *n.*

**con·strict** (kən-strĭkt') *v.* To make narrower; squeeze. — con·stric'tion *n.* — con·stric'tive *adj.* — con·stric'tor *n.*

**con·struct** (kən-strŭkt') *v.* To build. — con·struc'tion *n.* — con·struc'tor *n.*

**con·struc·tive** (kən-strŭk'tĭv) *adj.* Useful;

helpful. — **con·struc'tive·ly** adv.

**con·sul** (kŏn'səl) n. An official appointed by a government to reside in a foreign city and represent its citizens there. — **con'su·lar** adj. — **con'su·late** n.

**con·sult** (kən-sŭlt') v. 1. To seek the advice of. 2. To confer. — **con·sult'ant** n. — **con·sul·ta'tion** n. — **con·sult'a·tive** adj.

**con·sume** (kən-s/y/ōōm') v. -sumed, -suming. 1. To eat up. 2. To expend. 3. To destroy. — **con·sum'a·ble** adj. — **con·sum'er** n.

**con·sum·mate** (kŏn'sə-māt') v. -mated, -mating. To complete; achieve. — adj. (kən-sŭm'ĭt). Perfect; complete. — **con·sum'mate·ly** adv.

**con·sump·tion** (kən-sŭmp'shən) n. 1. The act or process of consuming. 2. The amount consumed. 3. Tuberculosis.

**con·tact** (kŏn'tăkt') n. 1. A coming together or touching. 2. A relationship; association. 3. Connection. —v. 1. To come or put into contact. 2. To get in touch with.

**con·ta·gion** (kən-tā'jən) n. Disease transmission by contact. — **con·ta'gious** adj.

**con·tain** (kən-tān') v. 1. To enclose. 2. To have within; include. 3. To be able to hold. 4. To restrict. — **con·tain'er** n. — **con·tain'ment** n.

**con·tam·i·nate** (kən-tăm'ə-nāt') v. -nated, -nating. To make impure. — **con·tam'i·na'tion** n.

**con·tem·plate** (kŏn'təm-plāt') v. -plated, -plating. 1. To ponder or consider. 2. To intend; expect. — **con'tem·pla'tion** n. — **con'tem·pla·tive** adj.

**con·tem·po·rar·y** (kən-tĕm'pə-rĕr'ē) adj. 1. Belonging to the same period of time. 2. Current; modern. —n., pl. -ies. 1. One of the same period or age. 2. A person of the present time. — **con·tem·po·ra'ne·ous** adj.

**con·tempt** (kən-tĕmpt') n. 1. Bitter scorn; disdain. 2. Open disrespect to a court, legislature, etc. — **con·temp'tu·ous** adj. — **con·temp'tu·ous·ly** adv. — **con·temp'tu·ous·ness** n.

**con·tempt·i·ble** (kən-tĕmp'tə-bəl) adj. Deserving contempt.

**con·tend** (kən-tĕnd') v. 1. To compete; struggle. 2. To maintain. — **con·tend'er** n.

**con·tent¹** (kən-tĕnt') n. 1. Often contents. That which is contained in something. 2. Substance; meaning.

**con·tent²** (kən-tĕnt') adj. Satisfied. —v. To satisfy. — **con·tent'ed** adj. — **con·tent'ment** n.

**con·ten·tion** (kən-tĕn'shən) n. 1. Competition. 2. Dispute. — **con·ten'tious** adj. — **con·**

**ten'tious·ness** n.

**con·test** (kŏn'tĕst') n. 1. A struggle; fight. 2. A competition. —v. (kən-tĕst'). 1. To compete for. 2. To challenge. — **con·test'ant** n.

**con·text** (kŏn'tĕkst') n. 1. Situation; environment. 2. The surrounding words. — **con·tex'tu·al** adj.

**con·tig·u·ous** (kən-tĭg'yōō-əs) adj. 1. Touching. 2. Next to. — **con·ti·gu'i·ty** n.

**con·ti·nent** (kŏn'tə-nənt) n. One of the principal land masses of the earth. — **con'ti·nen'tal** adj.

**con·tin·gen·cy** (kən-tĭn'jən-sē) n., pl. -cies. A possible event.

**con·tin·gent** (kən-tĭn'jənt) adj. 1. Possible. 2. Conditional. —n. 1. A quota, as of troops. 2. A representative group.

**con·tin·ue** (kən-tĭn'yōō) v. -ued, -uing. 1. To persist. 2. To last. 3. To remain. 4. To resume. 5. To extend. 6. To postpone or adjourn. — **con·tin'u·al** adj. — **con·tin'u·al·ly** adv. — **con·tin'u·ance** n. — **con·tin'u·a'tion** n.

**con·ti·nu·i·ty** (kŏn'tə-n/y/ōō'ə-tē) n., pl. -ties. 1. Continuousness. 2. An uninterrupted succession.

**con·tin·u·ous** (kən-tĭn'yōō-əs) adj. Extending without interruption; unbroken. — **con·tin'u·ous·ly** adv.

**con·tort** (kən-tôrt') v. To twist out of shape. — **con·tor'tion** n.

**con·tour** (kŏn'tōŏr) n. 1. The outline of a figure, body, or mass. 2. A line joining points of equal elevation.

**con·tra·band** (kŏn'trə-bănd') n. Smuggled goods.

**con·tra·cep·tion** (kŏn'trə-sĕp'shən) n. Prevention of conception. — **con'tra·cep'tive** adj. & n.

**con·tract** (kŏn'trăkt') n. A legal agreement. —v. (kən-trăkt', kŏn'trăkt'). 1. To enter into or establish by contract. 2. To catch (a disease). 3. To shrink. 4. To shorten by omitting letters. — **con·trac'tion** n. — **con·trac'tor** n.

**con·tra·dict** (kŏn'trə-dĭkt') v. 1. To assert the opposite of. 2. To be inconsistent with. — **con·tra·dic'tion** n. — **con·tra·dic'to·ry** adj.

**con·tral·to** (kən-trăl'tō) n., pl. -tos. The lowest female voice.

**con·trap·tion** (kən-trăp'shən) n. An elaborate device.

**con·tra·ry** (kŏn'trĕr'ē) adj. 1. Opposite. 2. Adverse. 3. Perverse; willful. —n., pl. -ries. The opposite. —adv. In opposition. — **con'tra·ri·ly** adv. — **con'trar'i·wise'** adv.

**con·trast** (kən-trăst′) v. **1.** To set in opposition in order to show differences. **2.** To show differences when compared. —n. (kŏn′trăst). Dissimilarity.

**con·trib·ute** (kən-trĭb′yōōt) v. -uted, -uting. To give to or participate in a common fund or effort. — **con′tri·bu′tion** n. — **con·trib′u·tor** n. — **con·trib′u·to·ry** adj.

**con·trite** (kən-trīt′) adj. Repentant. — **con·trite′ly** adv. — **con·tri′tion** n.

**con·trive** (kən-trīv′) v. -trived, -triving. **1.** To devise. **2.** To make. **3.** To manage or effect. — **con·triv′er** n.

**con·trol** (kən-trōl′) v. -trolled, -trolling. To regulate; direct. —n. **1.** Power to regulate, direct, or dominate. **2.** Restraint; reserve. **3.** An instrument for regulating a machine. — **con·trol′la·ble** adj. — **con·trol′ler** n.

**con·tro·ver·sy** (kŏn′trə-vûr′sē) n. pl. -sies. A public dispute. — **con′tro·ver′sial** adj.

**con·va·lesce** (kŏn′və-lĕs′) v. -lesced, -lescing. To recuperate from an illness. — **con′va·les′cence** n. — **con′va·les′cent** adj. & n.

**con·vene** (kən-vēn′) v. -vened, -vening. To meet together; assemble.

**con·ven·ient** (kən-vēn′yənt) adj. **1.** Suited to one's comfort or needs. **2.** Easy to reach; accessible. — **con·ven′ience** n. — **con·ven′ient·ly** adv.

**con·vent** (kŏn′vənt, -vĕnt′) n. A monastic community, esp. of nuns.

**con·ven·tion** (kən-vĕn′shən) n. **1.** A formal assembly. **2.** An international agreement. **3.** An accepted or prescribed practice.

**con·ven·tion·al** (kən-vĕn′shən-əl) adj. **1.** Customary. **2.** Commonplace or ordinary. — **con·ven′tion·al·ism′** n. — **con·ven′tion·al′i·ty** n. — **con·ven′tion·al·ly** adv.

**con·verge** (kən-vûrj′) v. -verged, -verging. To tend toward a common point. — **con·ver′gence**, **con·ver′gen·cy** n. — **con·ver′gent** adj.

**con·ver·sa·tion** (kŏn′vər-sā′shən) n. A spoken exchange; talk. — **con′ver·sa′tion·al** adj.

**con·verse¹** (kən-vûrs′) v. -versed, -versing. To talk.

**con·verse²** (kən-vûrs′, kŏn′vûrs′) adj. Reversed. —n. The opposite. — **con·verse′ly** adv.

**con·vert** (kən-vûrt′) v. **1.** To change into another form; transform. **2.** To persuade or be persuaded to adopt a new religion. **3.** To adapt. —n. (kŏn′vûrt′). A converted person. — **con·vert′er**, **con·vert′or** n.

**con·vert·i·ble** (kən-vûr′tə-bəl) adj. Capable of being converted. —n. An automobile with a movable top.

**con·vex** (kŏn′vĕks, kən-vĕks′) adj. Curved outward. — **con·vex′i·ty** n.

**con·vey** (kən-vā′) v. **1.** To carry. **2.** To transmit. — **con·vey′er**, **con·vey′or** n.

**con·vey·ance** (kən-vā′əns) n. **1.** The act of transporting. **2.** A vehicle.

**con·vict** (kən-vĭkt′) v. To find or prove guilty. —n. (kŏn′vĭkt′). A person serving a prison sentence.

**con·vic·tion** (kən-vĭk′shən) n. **1.** The state of being convicted. **2.** A belief.

**con·vince** (kən-vĭns′) v. -vinced, -vincing. To bring to belief; persuade. — **con·vinc′er** n. — **con·vinc′ing·ly** adv.

**con·viv·i·al** (kən-vĭv′ē-əl) adj. Sociable; jovial. — **con·viv′i·al′i·ty** n.

**con·vo·lu·tion** (kŏn′və-lōō′shən) n. **1.** A coiling or twisting together. **2.** An intricacy. — **con′vo·lut′ed** adj.

**con·voy** (kŏn′voi, kən-voi′) v. To escort for protection. —n. An accompanying force.

**con·vulse** (kən-vŭls′) v. -vulsed, -vulsing. **1.** To shake violently. **2.** To cause involuntary muscular contractions. — **con·vul′sion** n. — **con·vul′sive** adj.

**cook** (kŏŏk) v. To heat (food) for eating. —n. One who prepares food for eating. — **cook′er·y** n.

**cook·y**, **cook·ie** (kŏŏk′ē) n. pl. -ies. A small, sweet cake.

**cool** (kōōl) adj. **1.** Moderately cold. **2.** Calm; controlled. **3.** Indifferent. —v. To make or become cool. —n. **1.** Moderate cold. **2.** Composure. — **cool′ly** adv. — **cool′ness** n.

**coop** (kōōp) n. A cage, as for poultry. —v. To confine.

**co·op·er·ate** (kō-ŏp′ər-āt′) v. -ated, -ating. To work together. — **co·op′er·a′tion** n.

**co·op·er·a·tive** (kō-ŏp′rə-tĭv, -ər-ā′tĭv) adj. **1.** Willing to cooperate. **2.** Engaged in joint economic activity. —n. An enterprise collectively owned and operated. — **co·op′er·a·tive·ly** adv.

**co·or·di·nate** (kō-ôr′də-nĭt) adj. Of equal rank or order. —v. (-nāt′) -nated, -nating. To harmonize in a common action. — **co·or′di·nate·ly** adv. — **co·or′di·na′tion** n. — **co·or′di·na′tor** n.

**cope** (kōp) v. coped, coping. To contend, esp. with success.

**co·pi·ous** (kō′pē-əs) adj. Abundant. — **co′pi·ous·ly** adv. — **co′pi·ous·ness** n.

**cop·per** (kŏp′ər) n. A reddish-brown metallic element.

**cop·y** (kŏp′ē) n. pl. -ies. **1.** A reproduction;

duplicate. **2.** A manuscript to be set in type. —v. **-led, -ying. 1.** To make a copy of. **2.** To imitate.

**cop·y·right** (kŏp′ē-rīt′) n. The exclusive right to publish, sell, or distribute a literary or artistic work. — **cop′y·right′** v.

**cor·al** (kôr′əl, kŏr′əl) n. **1.** A stony substance formed from the massed skeletons of minute marine organisms. **2.** Yellowish red or pink. — **cor′al** adj.

**cord** (kôrd) n. **1.** A thick string or small rope. **2.** An insulated electric wire. **3.** Fabric with raised ribs. **4.** A unit of cut fuel wood, equal to 128 cubic feet. —v. To fasten with a cord.

**cor·dial** (kôr′jəl) adj. Hearty; warm. —n. **1.** A stimulant. **2.** A liqueur. — **cor·dial′i·ty** n.

**cor·du·roy** (kôr′də-roi, kôr′də-roi′) n. A ribbed cotton fabric.

**core** (kôr, kōr) n. **1.** The central part of certain fruits. **2.** The center; essence. —v. **cored, coring.** To remove the core of. — **cor′er** n.

**cork** (kôrk) n. **1.** The light, porous bark of a tree. **2.** A bottle stopper. —v. To stop with a cork.

**cork·screw** (kôrk′skrōō′) n. A spiral-shaped device for drawing corks from bottles. —v. Spiral.

**corn¹** (kôrn) n. A cereal grass bearing seeds on large ears. —v. To preserve in brine. — **corn′y** adj.

**corn²** (kôrn) n. A horny thickening of the skin, usually on a toe.

**cor·ne·a** (kôr′nē-ə) n. A transparent, convex structure covering the lens of the eye. — **cor′ne·al** adj.

**cor·ner** (kôr′nər) n. **1.** The place where two streets or other lines meet. **2.** A region. **3.** Complete control of a stock or commodity. —v. **1.** To drive into a corner. **2.** To form a corner in (a stock or commodity).

**cor·nu·co·pi·a** (kôr′nə-kō′pē-ə) n. A cone-shaped horn overflowing with fruit and flowers.

**cor·ol·lar·y** (kôr′ə-lĕr′ē, kŏr′ə-) n., pl. **-ies. 1.** A proposition that follows from one already proven. **2.** A consequence; result.

**cor·o·nar·y** (kôr′ə-nĕr′ē, kŏr′ə-) adj. Of the heart or the arteries that supply it with blood.

**cor·o·na·tion** (kôr′ə-nā′shən, kŏr′-) n. The crowning of a sovereign.

**cor·o·ner** (kôr′ə-nər, kŏr′-) n. A public officer who investigates deaths.

**cor·o·net** (kôr′ə-nĕt′, -nĭt′, kŏr′-) n. A small crown.

**cor·po·ral¹** (kôr′pə-rəl) adj. Of the body.

**cor·po·ral²** (kôr′pə-rəl, -prəl) n. A noncommissioned officer of the lowest rank.

**cor·po·ra·tion** (kôr′pə-rā′shən) n. A body of persons legally recognized as a separate entity, usually to conduct a business enterprise. — **cor′po·rate** adj.

**cor·po·re·al** (kôr-pôr′ē-əl, -pōr′ē-əl) adj. **1.** Bodily. **2.** Material; tangible.

**corps** (kôr, kōr) n., pl. **corps. 1.** A branch of the armed forces. **2.** A body of persons.

**corpse** (kôrps) n. A dead body.

**cor·pu·lence** (kôr′pyə-ləns) n. Fatness; obesity. — **cor′pu·lent** adj.

**cor·pus·cle** (kôr′pəs-əl, -pŭs-əl) n. A cell capable of free movement in a fluid. — **cor·pus′cu·lar** adj.

**cor·ral** (kə-răl′) n. An enclosure for livestock. —v. **-ralled, -ralling. 1.** To drive into and hold in a corral. **2.** Informal. To seize.

**cor·rect** (kə-rĕkt′) v. **1.** To remove the mistakes from. **2.** To mark the errors in. **3.** To admonish or punish. **4.** To adjust. —adj. **1.** Accurate or true. **2.** Proper. — **cor·rec′tion** n. — **cor·rec′tive** adj. & n. — **cor·rect′ly** adv. — **cor·rect′ness** n.

**cor·re·la·tion** (kôr′ə-lā′shən, kŏr′-) n. A mutual relationship; correspondence. — **cor·re·late′** v.

**cor·re·spond** (kôr′ĭ-spŏnd′, kŏr′-) v. **1.** To be similar or equal (with to). **2.** To communicate by letter. — **cor′re·spon′dence** n. — **cor′re·spon′dent** n. & adj.

**cor·ri·dor** (kôr′ĭ-dər, -dôr, kŏr′-) n. A long passageway.

**cor·rob·o·rate** (kə-rŏb′ə-rāt′) v. **-rated, -rating.** To strengthen or support (other evidence). — **cor·rob′o·ra′tion** n.

**cor·rode** (kə-rōd′) v. **-roded, -roding.** To wear away gradually. — **cor·ro′sion** n. — **cor·ro′sive** adj.

**cor·ru·gate** (kôr′ə-gāt′, kŏr′ə-gāt, kŏr′-) v. **-gated, -gating.** To make folds or ridges in. — **cor′ru·gate′ — cor′ru·gat′ed** adj. — **cor·ru·ga′tion** n.

**cor·rupt** (kə-rŭpt′) adj. **1.** Immoral; perverted. **2.** Bribe-taking. **3.** Decaying. —v. To make or become corrupt. — **cor·rupt′i·ble** adj. — **cor·rup′tion** n. — **cor·rup′tive** adj. — **cor·rupt′ly** adv.

**cor·sage** (kôr-säzh′) n. A small bouquet worn by a woman.

**cor·set** (kôr′sĭt) n. A close-fitting, supportive undergarment.

**cor·tex** (kôr'těks') n. The outer layer of an organ or part.

**cos·met·ic** (kŏz-mět'ĭk) n. A preparation designed to beautify the body. —**cos·met·ic** adj.

**cos·mo·pol·i·tan** (kŏz'mə-pŏl'ə-tən) adj. 1. Common to the whole world. 2. At home in all places; broadened by travel. —n. A cosmopolitan person.

**cos·mos** (kŏz'məs, -mŏs) n. The universe regarded as an orderly whole. —**cos'mic** adj.

**cost** (kôst) n. 1. A price. 2. A loss or penalty. —v. **cost, costing.** To require a specified payment. —**cost·ly** adj.

**cos·tume** (kŏs't/y/ōom, kŏs-t/y/ōom') n. 1. A style of dress of a particular country or period. 2. A set of clothes.

**cot** (kŏt) n. A narrow bed.

**cot·tage** (kŏt'ĭj) n. A small country house.

**cottage cheese.** A soft, white cheese made of seasoned curds of skim milk.

**cot·ton** (kŏt'n) n. 1. The downy white fiber surrounding the seeds of a plant. 2. Thread or cloth made from cotton fiber. —**cot'ton·y** adj.

**couch** (kouch) n. An article of furniture on which one can lie.

**cough** (kôf, kŏf) v. To expel lung air violently. —**cough** n.

**could** (kŏod) p.t. of **can.**

**could·n't** (kŏod'ənt) Contraction of could not.

**coun·cil** (koun'səl) n. An administrative, legislative, or advisory body. —**coun'cil·man** n. —**coun'cil·or** n.

**coun·sel** (koun'səl) n. 1. Advice or guidance. 2. pl. **counsel.** A lawyer or group of lawyers. —v. **-seled** or **-selled, -seling** or **-selling.** To advise. —**coun'sel·or** n.

**count¹** (kount) v. 1. To name one by one for a total. 2. To recite numerals in order. 3. To include. 4. To matter. —**count on.** To rely. —n. 1. The act of counting. 2. A total. 3. Any of the charges in an indictment. —**count'a·ble** adj. —**count'less** adj.

**count²** (kount) n. A European nobleman. —**count'ess** fem.n.

**count·er¹** (koun'tər) adj. Contrary; opposing. —v. To oppose. —adv. In a contrary manner.

**count·er²** (koun'tər) n. 1. A table on which business is transacted or food served. 2. A piece for keeping a count or a place in games.

**coun·ter·feit** (koun'tər-fĭt) v. 1. To forge. 2. To pretend. —n. A fraudulent imitation.

—**coun'ter·feit** adj. —**coun'ter·feit·er** n.

**coun·ter·part** (koun'tər-pärt') n. A matching thing; mate.

**coun·try** (kŭn'trē) n., pl. **-tries.** 1. A large area; region. 2. A rural area. 3. A nation. —adj. Rural.

**coun·ty** (koun'tē) n., pl. **-ties.** An administrative subdivision of a state.

**coup** (kōo) n. 1. A bold, successful move. 2. A surprise overthrow of a government.

**cou·ple** (kŭp'əl) n. 1. A group of two; pair. 2. Two lovers or companions. 3. A few. —v. **-led, -ling.** To link together.

**cou·pon** (k/y/ōo'pŏn') n. A certificate entitling the owner to a payment, discount, or other benefit.

**cour·age** (kûr'ĭj) n. Resistance to fear; bravery. —**cou·ra'geous** adj. —**cou·ra'geous·ly** adv.

**cou·ri·er** (kŏor'ē-ər, kûr'-) n. A messenger.

**course** (kôrs, kōrs, kōors) n. 1. Onward movement in a particular direction. 2. A route; path. 3. Duration. 4. A mode of action. 5. A prescribed study or series of studies. 6. A part of a meal served separately. —**of course.** Certainly. —v. **coursed, coursing.** To move swiftly; run; race.

**court** (kôrt, kōrt) n. 1. An enclosed yard. 2. A short street. 3. A palace. 4. A sovereign's attendants and advisers. 5.a. A judge or panel of judges. A judicial session. 6. A marked playing area, as for tennis. —v. To attempt to gain the love of. —**court'ly** adj. —**court'ship** n. —**court'yard** n. —**court'i·er** n. —**court'li·ness** n.

**cour·te·ous** (kûr'tē-əs) adj. Considerate; polite. —**cour·te·ous·ly** adv. —**cour'te·sy** n.

**court-mar·tial** (kôrt'mär'shəl, kōrt'-) n., pl. **courts-martial.** A military trial or court. —v. **-tialed** or **-tialled, -tialing** or **-tialling.** To try by court-martial.

**cous·in** (kŭz'ən) n. A child of one's aunt or uncle.

**cove** (kōv) n. A small, sheltered bay.

**cov·e·nant** (kŭv'ə-nənt) n. A binding agreement.

**cov·er** (kŭv'ər) v. 1. To place something upon, over, or in front of. 2. To protect. 3. To deal with; treat of. 4. To include; encompass. —n. 1. Something that covers. 2. Shelter. 3. Concealment. —**cov'er·age** n.

**cov·ert** (kŭv'ərt, kōv'vərt) adj. Concealed; secret. —**cov'ert·ly** adv.

**cov·et** (kŭv'ĭt) v. To desire (that which is another's). —**cov'et·ous** adj. —**cov'et·ous·ly** adv.

**cow** (kou) *n.* The mature female of cattle or of other animals as the whale or elephant. —*v.* To intimidate.

**cow·ard** (kou'ərd) *n.* One who lacks courage. — **cow'ard·ice** *n.* — **cow'ard·ly** *adj. & adv.*

**cow·er** (kou'ər) *v.* To cringe in fear.

**cowl** (koul) *n.* A monk's hood.

**coy** (koi) *adj.* Affectedly shy or devious. — **coy'ly** *adv.* — **coy'ness** *n.*

**coy·o·te** (ki-ō'tē, kī'ō-tē') *n.* A small wolf-like animal.

**co·zy** (kō'zē) *adj.* **-zier, -ziest.** Snug and comfortable. — **co'zi·ly** *adv.* — **co'zi·ness** *n.*

**crab** (krăb) *n.* A broad-bodied crustacean with a shell-like covering.

**crack** (krăk) *v.* **1.** To break with a sharp sound; snap. **2.** To break without dividing into parts. **3.** To tell (a joke). —*n.* **1.** A sharp, snapping sound. **2.** A break; fissure. **3.** A narrow space. **4.** A chance. **5.** A sarcastic remark. —*adj.* Superior; first-rate. — **crack'le** *v. & n.*

**crack·er** (krăk'ər) *n.* A thin, crisp wafer or biscuit.

**cra·dle** (krād'l) *n.* An infant's low bed with rockers. —*v.* **-dled, -dling.** To place in a cradle.

**craft** (krăft, kräft) *n.* **1.** Skill; a trade. **2.** Guile; slyness. **3.** *pl.* **craft.** A boat, ship, or aircraft. — **crafts'man** *n.* — **crafts'man·ship** *n.* — **craft'y** *adj.* — **craft'i·ness** *n.*

**crag** (krăg) *n.* A steeply projecting rock mass. — **crag'gy** *adj.*

**cram** (krăm) *v.* **crammed, cramming.** **1.** To squeeze into an insufficient space; stuff. **2.** To study intensely.

**cramp** (krămp) *n.* A sudden painful muscular contraction. —*v.* To confine; hamper.

**cran·ber·ry** (krăn'běr'ē, -bər-ē) *n.* A red, tart, edible berry.

**crane** (krān) *n.* **1.** A long-legged wading bird. **2.** A machine for hoisting heavy objects. —*v.* **craned, craning.** To stretch one's neck.

**cra·ni·um** (krā'nē-əm) *n., pl.* **-ums** or **-nia.** The skull. — **cra'ni·al** *adj.*

**crank** (krăngk) *n.* **1.** A handle attached to a shaft, turned to start or run a machine. **2.** An eccentric person. —*v.* To operate (an engine) by a crank.

**crank·y** (krăng'kē) *adj.* **-ier, -iest.** **1.** Ill-tempered; peevish. **2.** Eccentric. — **crank'i·ly** *adv.* — **crank'i·ness** *n.*

**cran·ny** (krăn'ē) *n., pl.* **-nies.** A small crevice.

**craps** (krăps) *n.* A dice game.

**crash** (krăsh) *v.* **1.** To fall, break, or collide noisily. **2.** To fail suddenly. —*n.* **1.** A sudden loud noise. **2.** A collision. **3.** A sudden business failure.

**crass** (krăs) *adj.* Grossly ignorant; coarse. — **crass'ly** *adv.* — **crass'ness** *n.*

**crate** (krāt) *n.* A slatted wooden container for storing or shipping things. —*v.* **crated, crating.** To pack into a crate.

**cra·ter** (krā'tər) *n.* A bowl-shaped depression.

**crave** (krāv) *v.* **craved, craving.** **1.** To yearn for; desire intensely. **2.** To beg for. — **crav'er** *n.* — **crav'ing** *n.* — **crav'ing·ly** *adv.*

**crawl** (krôl) *v.* To move slowly by dragging the body along the ground; creep. —*n.* **1.** The act of crawling. **2.** A rapid swimming stroke.

**cra·zy** (krā'zē) *adj.* **-zier, -ziest.** **1.** Insane. **2.** Immoderately fond. — **craze** *v. & n.* — **cra'zi·ly** *adv.* — **cra'zi·ness** *n.*

**cream** (krēm) *n.* **1.** The fatty component of milk. **2.** Yellowish white. **3.** The choicest part. —*v.* **1.** To beat till smooth. **2.** To prepare in a cream sauce. — **cream** *adj.* — **cream'er** *n.* — **cream'y** *adj.*

**crease** (krēs) *n.* A line made by pressing, folding, or wrinkling. —*v.* **creased, creasing.** To make a crease in. — **creas'er** *n.*

**cre·ate** (krē-āt') *v.* **-ated, -ating.** To cause to exist; originate. — **cre·a'tion** *n.* — **cre·a'tive** *adj.* — **cre·a·tiv'i·ty** *n.* — **cre·a'tor** *n.*

**crea·ture** (krē'chər) *n.* A living being, esp. an animal.

**cre·dence** (krē'dəns) *n.* Belief.

**cre·den·tials** (krə-děn'shəlz) *pl.n.* Papers entitling one to credit or acceptance.

**cred·i·ble** (krěd'ə-bəl) *adj.* Believable. — **cred'i·bil'i·ty, cred'i·ble·ness** *n.* — **cred'i·bly** *adv.*

**cred·it** (krěd'ĭt) *n.* **1.** Belief; trust. **2.** A good reputation. **3.** A source of honor. **4.** Time allowed for payment. **5.** Entry in an account of payment received. —*v.* **1.** To believe; trust. **2.** To give credit to.

**cred·it·a·ble** (krěd'ĭ-tə-bəl) *adj.* Deserving commendation. — **cred'it·a·bly** *adv.*

**cred·i·tor** (krěd'ə-tər) *n.* One to whom money is owed.

**cred·u·lous** (krěj'ōō-ləs, krěd'yōō-) *adj.* Disposed to believe too readily; gullible. — **cre·du'li·ty** *n.* — **cred'u·lous·ly** *adv.*

**creed** (krēd) *n.* A statement of belief.

**creek** (krēk, krĭk) *n.* A small stream.

**creep** (krēp) *v.* **crept, creeping.** **1.** To move

furtively or slowly. **2.** To grow along the ground. — **creep'er** n.

**creep·y** (krē'pē) adj. **-ier, -iest.** Eerie. — **creep'i·ness** n.

**cre·mate** (krē'māt', krǐ-māt') v. **-mated, -mating.** To incinerate (a corpse). — **cre·ma'tion** n. — **cre'ma'tor** n.

**crept** (krĕpt). p.t. & p.p. of **creep.**

**cres·cen·do** (krə-shĕn'dō, -sĕn'dō) n., pl. **-dos.** A gradual increase in volume.

**cres·cent** (krĕs'ənt) n. The shape of the quarter moon.

**crest** (krĕst) n. **1.** A tuft on the head of a bird or other animal. **2.** The highest point; summit. — v. To reach a crest; peak.

**crew** (krōō) n. A team of workers.

**crib** (krǐb) n. **1.** A child's bed with high sides. **2.** A rack or trough for fodder.

**crime** (krīm) n. An act in violation of the law. — **crim'i·nal** n. — **crim'i·nal'i·ty** n. — **crim'i·nal·ly** adv. — **crim'i·nol'o·gy** n.

**crim·son** (krǐm'zən) n. A deep red. — v. To become crimson. — **crim'son** adj.

**cringe** (krǐnj) v. **cringed, cringing.** To shrink back, as with fear; cower.

**crin·kle** (krǐng'kəl) v. **-kled, -kling.** To wrinkle; rustle. — n. A rustle. — **crin'kly** adj.

**crip·ple** (krǐp'əl) n. A disabled or lame person. — v. **-pled, -pling.** To disable or damage.

**cri·sis** (krī'sǐs) n., pl. **-ses.** A crucial situation; turning point.

**crisp** (krǐsp) adj. **1.** Brittle. **2.** Firm and fresh. **3.** Brisk; invigorating. — **crisp'i·ness** .n. — **crisp'ly** adv. — **crisp'y** adj.

**cri·te·ri·on** (krī-tîr'ē-ən) n., pl. **-teria.** A standard of judgment.

**crit·ic** (krǐt'ǐk) n. **1.** A judge or reviewer of artistic works. **2.** One who finds fault.

**crit·i·cal** (krǐt'ǐ-kəl) adj. **1.** Tending to criticize. **2.** Characterized by careful evaluation. **3.** Of critics or criticism. **4.** Crucial. — **crit'i·cal·ly** adv. — **crit'i·cal·ness** n.

**crit·i·cize** (krǐt'ǐ-sīz') v. **-cized, -cizing.** **1.** To judge the merits and faults of; evaluate. **2.** To find fault with. — **crit'i·cism'** n. — **cri·tique'** n.

**cro·chet** (krō-shā') v. To make needlework by looping thread with a hooked needle.

**croc·o·dile** (krŏk'ə-dīl') n. A large tropical aquatic reptile.

**cro·ny** (krō'nē) n., pl. **-nies.** A close friend.

**crook** (krōōk) n. **1.** A bend or angle. **2.** A swindler; thief. — v. To curve; bend. — **crook'ed** adj. — **crook'ed·ly** adv.

**croon** (krōōn) v. To sing softly. — n. A

crooning sound. — **croon'er** n.

**crop** (krŏp) n. **1. a.** A food grown on a farm. **b.** A harvest; yield. **2.** A short riding whip. **3.** A pouchlike enlargement of a bird's esophagus. — v. **cropped, cropping. 1.** To cut off the ends of. **2.** To cut short.

**cross** (krôs, krŏs) n. **1.** An upright post with a transverse piece near the top. **2.** A trial or affliction. **3.** A pattern formed by two intersecting lines. **4.** A hybrid. — v. **1.** To go or extend across. **2.** To intersect. **3.** To go crosswise. **4.** To obstruct. **5.** To breed. — adj. **1.** Lying crosswise. **2.** Contrary. **3.** Irritable. — **cross'ing** n.

**crotch** (krŏch) n. The fork formed by the junction of parts. — **crotched** adj.

**crouch** (krouch) v. To stoop with the limbs close to the body. — **crouch** n.

**croup** (krōōp) n. A children's larynx disease marked by a harsh cough.

**crowd** (kroud) n. A large number of persons or things gathered together. — v. **1.** To gather in numbers. **2.** To press or shove.

**crown** (kroun) n. **1.** A head covering worn by a monarch. **2.** A top or covering part. — v. **1.** To put a crown upon. **2.** To honor. **3.** To surmount; top.

**cru·cial** (krōō'shəl) adj. Decisive. — **cru'cial·ly** adv.

**cru·ci·ble** (krōō'sə-bəl) n. A vessel for melting materials.

**cru·ci·fix** (krōō'sə-fǐks') n. An image of Christ on the cross.

**cru·ci·fy** (krōō'sə-fī') v. **-fied, -fying.** To put to death by nailing or binding to a cross. — **cru'ci·fix'ion** n.

**crude** (krōōd) adj. **cruder, crudest. 1.** Unrefined; raw. **2.** Lacking finish, tact, or taste. — **crude'ly** adv. — **cru'di·ty, crude'ness** n.

**cru·el** (krōō'əl) adj. Causing pain or suffering; merciless. — **cru'el·ly** adv. — **cru'el·ty** n.

**cruise** (krōōz) v. **cruised, cruising.** To sail or travel over or about. — n. A sea voyage for pleasure.

**cruis·er** (krōō'zər) n. **1.** A fast warship of medium tonnage. **2.** A police squad car.

**crum·ble** (krŭm'bəl) v. **-bled, -bling.** To break into small parts. — **crumb** n.

**crunch** (krŭnch) v. **1.** To chew or crush noisily. — **crunch** n.

**cru·sade** (krōō-sād') n. A zealous movement for a cause. — v. **-saded, -sading.** To engage in a crusade. — **cru·sad'er** n.

**crush** (krŭsh) v. **1.** To mash or squeeze so as to injure. **2.** To pound or grind. **3.** To overwhelm; subdue. — n. **1.** The act of crushing. **2.** A crowd. **3.** An infatuation.

**crust** (krŭst) *n.* A hard outer covering. —*v.* To cover or become covered with a crust. —**crust′y** *adj.*

**crus·ta·cean** (krū-stā′shən) *n.* A segmented, hard-shelled arthropod, as a lobster.

**crutch** (krŭch) *n.* A supporting stick fitted under the armpit in walking.

**crux** (krŭks, krōōks) *n.* A critical or crucial point.

**cry** (krī) *v.* **cried, cry·ing. 1.** To make sobbing sounds; weep. **2.** To utter loudly. —*n., pl.* **cries. 1.** A loud utterance. **2.** A fit of weeping. **3.** An urgent appeal. —**cri′er** *n.*

**crypt** (krĭpt) *n.* An underground chamber, esp. for burial.

**cryp·tic** (krĭp′tĭk) *adj.* Veiled; mystifying. —**cryp′ti·cal·ly** *adv.*

**crys·tal** (krĭs′təl) *n.* **1.** Solid matter with a highly regular, periodically repeated structure and plane faces. **2.** Clear quartz. **3.** Fine glass. —**crys′tal·line** *adj.* —**crys′tal·li·za′tion** *n.* —**crys′tal·lize′** *v.*

**cub** (kŭb) *n.* A young bear, wolf, lion, etc.

**cube** (kyōōb) *n.* **1.** A solid having six congruent faces. **2.** The third power of a number. —*v.* **cubed, cub·ing. 1.** To raise to the third power. **2.** To cut into cubes. —**cu′bic, cu′bi·cal** *adj.*

**cu·bi·cle** (kyōō′bĭ-kəl) *n.* A small room.

**cu·cum·ber** (kyōō′kŭm′bər) *n.* A long, green-skinned vegetable.

**cud** (kŭd) *n.* Food regurgitated from the first stomach of a ruminant and chewed again.

**cud·dle** (kŭd′l) *v.* **-dled, -dling.** To fondle; hug.

**cudg·el** (kŭj′əl) *n.* A short, heavy club. —*v.* To beat with a cudgel.

**cue¹** (kyōō) *n.* The long, tapered rod used to propel a billiard ball.

**cue²** (kyōō) *n.* A signal, esp. to begin or enter. —**cue** *v.*

**cuff** (kŭf) *n.* **1.** A fold at the bottom of a sleeve or trouser leg. **2.** A light blow; slap. —*v.* To slap.

**cu·li·nar·y** (kyōō′lə-nĕr′ē, kŭl′ə-) *adj.* Of kitchens or cookery.

**cull** (kŭl) *v.* To pick out; select. —**cull′er** *n.*

**cul·mi·nate** (kŭl′mə-nāt′) *v.* **-nated, -nating.** To reach the highest point; climax. —**cul′mi·na′tion** *n.*

**cul·pa·ble** (kŭl′pə-bəl) *adj.* Guilty; blameworthy. —**cul′pa·bil′i·ty** *n.* —**cul′pa·bly** *adv.*

**cul·prit** (kŭl′prĭt) *n.* A person charged with or found guilty of a crime.

**cult** (kŭlt) *n.* **1.** A system or community of worship. **2.** Obsessive devotion.

**cul·ti·vate** (kŭl′tə-vāt′) *v.* **-vated, -vating. 1.** To prepare (land) for raising crops. **2.** To grow or tend. **3.** To form and refine, as by education. —**cul′ti·va′tion** *n.* —**cul′ti·va′tor** *n.*

**cul·ture** (kŭl′chər) *n.* **1.** The raising of animals or growing of plants. **2.** A growth or colony of microorganisms. **3.** Socially transmitted behavior patterns. **4.** Social and artistic expression and activity. —*v.* **-tured, -turing.** To cultivate. —**cul′tur·al** *adj.* —**cul′tur·al·ly** *adv.*

**cum·ber·some** (kŭm′bər-səm) *adj.* Unwieldy. —**cum′ber·some·ness** *n.*

**cu·mu·la·tive** (kyōōm′yə-lā′tĭv, -yə-lə-tĭv) *adj.* Increasing by successive addition. —**cu′mu·la·tive·ly** *adv.*

**cun·ning** (kŭn′ĭng) *adj.* Shrewd; crafty. —*n.* Craftiness; skill. —**cun′ning·ly** *adv.*

**cup** (kŭp) *n.* A small, open container for drinking. —*v.* **cupped, cupping.** To shape like a cup.

**cup·board** (kŭb′ərd) *n.* A shelved cabinet for storing food or dishes.

**cu·ra·tor** (kyōō-rā′tər, kyōōr′ə-tər) *n.* The director of a museum or similar institution.

**curb** (kûrb) *n.* **1.** Anything that checks or restrains. **2.** A concrete edging along a sidewalk. —*v.* To check or restrain. —**curb′er** *n.*

**curd** (kûrd) *n.* Often **curds.** The coagulated part of sour milk. —**cur′dle** *v.*

**cure** (kyōōr) *n.* **1.** Restoration of health. **2.** A medical remedy. —*v.* **cured, curing. 1.** To restore to health. **2.** To rid of (disease). **3.** To preserve. —**cur′a·ble** *adj.* —**cur′a·tive** *adj.*

**cur·few** (kûr′fyōō) *n.* An order to retire from the streets at a prescribed hour.

**cu·ri·ous** (kyōōr′ē-əs) *adj.* **1.** Eager to know. **2.** Singular; odd. —**cu′ri·os′i·ty** *n.* —**cu′ri·ous·ly** *adv.*

**curl** (kûrl) *v.* **1.** To twist into ringlets. **2.** To curve; wind. —*n.* **1.** A spiral or coil. **2.** A ringlet. —**curl′i·ness** *n.* —**curl′y** *adj.*

**cur·ren·cy** (kûr′ən-sē) *n., pl.* **-cies. 1.** Money in circulation. **2.** Common acceptance.

**cur·rent** (kûr′ənt) *adj.* **1.** Belonging to the present time. **2.** Commonly accepted; prevalent. —*n.* A steady and smooth onward movement, as of water or electricity. —**cur′rent·ly** *adv.*

**cur·ric·u·lum** (kə-rĭk′yə-ləm) *n., pl.* **-la** or **-lums.** A course of study. —**cur·ric′u·lar** *adj.*

**curse** (kûrs) *n.* **1.** A call for evil to afflict someone or something. **2.** A scourge; evil.

**3.** Any profane oath. —*v.* **cursed** or **curst, cursing. 1.** To invoke evil upon; damn. **2.** To afflict. **3.** To utter curses. —**curs'ed** *adj.* —**curs'er** *n.*

**curt** (kûrt) *adj.* Rudely brief or abrupt. —**curt'ly** *adv.* —**curt'ness** *n.*

**cur-tail** (kər-tāl´) *v.* To cut short. —**cur-tail'ment** *n.*

**cur-tain** (kûrt'n) *n.* A piece of material hanging in a window or other opening. —*v.* To provide or shut off with a curtain.

**curve** (kûrv) *n.* A line or surface that deviates from straightness in a smooth, continuous fashion. —*v.* **curved, curving.** To move in, form, or cause to form a curve. —**curv'a-ture** *n.*

**cush-ion** (kŏosh'ən) *n.* **1.** A pad or pillow. **2.** Anything that absorbs shock. —*v.* To provide with a cushion. —**cush'ion-y** *adj.*

**cus-to-dy** (kŭs'tə-dē) *n., pl.* **-dies. 1.** The act or right of guarding or maintaining. **2.** Detainment. —**cus-to'di-al** *adj.* —**cus-to'di-an** *n.*

**cus-tom** (kŭs'təm) *n.* **1.** A usual practice; convention. **2.** A habit. **3. customs.** A tax on imported goods. —*adj.* Made to order. —**cus'tom-ar'y** *adj.* —**cus'tom-ar'i-ly** *adv.*

**cus-tom-er** (kŭs'təm-ər) *n.* One who buys goods or services.

**cut** (kŭt) *v.* **cut, cutting. 1.** To penetrate with a sharp edge. **2.** To sever. **3.** To harvest. **4.** To reduce; shorten. **5.** To omit; drop. —*n.* **1.** The act or result of cutting. **2.** A dug passage. **3.** A reduction. **4.** A share. —**cut'ter** *n.*

**cute** (kyōōt) *adj.* **cuter, cutest.** Pretty or dainty. —**cute'ly** *adv.* —**cute'ness** *n.*

**cu-ti-cle** (kyōō'ti-kəl) *n.* The hardened skin at the base of a nail.

**cut-ler-y** (kŭt'lēr-ē) *n.* **1.** Cutting instruments. **2.** Tableware.

**cy-cle** (sī'kəl) *n.* **1. a.** A regularly repeated sequence of events. **b.** The period of such a sequence. **2.** A related series of artistic works. **3.** A bicycle or motorcycle. —*v.* **-cled, -cling.** To ride a bicycle or motorcycle. —**cy'clic, cy'cli-cal** *adj.* —**cy'cli-cal-ly** *adv.* —**cy'clist** *n.*

**cy-clone** (sī'klōn´) *n.* A violent rotating windstorm. —**cy-clon'ic** *adj.*

**cyl-in-der** (sĭl'ən-dər) *n.* A figure with a rounded surface bounded by flat, parallel ends. —**cy-lin'dri-cal** *adj.*

**cym-bal** (sĭm'bəl) *n.* One of a pair of brass plates struck together as percussion instruments.

**cyn-ic** (sĭn'ĭk) *n.* One who believes all men are motivated by selfishness. —**cyn'i-cal** *adj.* —**cyn'i-cal-ly** *adv.* —**cyn'i-cism'** *n.*

**czar** (zär) *n.* Also **tsar, tzar. 1.** A Russian emperor. **2.** A powerful ruler.

# D

**d, D** (dē) *n.* The 4th letter of the English alphabet.

**dab** (dăb) *v.* **dabbed, dabbing.** To touch or apply with short, light strokes. —*n.* **1.** A small amount. **2.** A pat.

**dab-ble** (dăb'əl) *v.* **-bled, -bling. 1.** To splash gently. **2.** To undertake something superficially. —**dab'bler** *n.*

**dag-ger** (dăg'ər) *n.* A short, pointed weapon.

**dai-ly** (dā'lē) *adj.* Occurring or published every day. —*n., pl.* **-lies.** A daily publication. —**dai'ly** *adv.*

**dain-ty** (dān'tē) *adj.* **-tier, -tiest. 1.** Delicately beautiful. **2.** Refined; fastidious. —*n., pl.* **-ties.** A delicacy. —**dain'ti-ly** *adv.*

**dair-y** (dâr'ē) *n., pl.* **-ies.** An establishment that processes or sells milk and milk products. —**dair'y** *adj.*

**da-is** (dā'ĭs, dās) *n., pl.* **-ises.** A raised platform.

**dam** (dăm) *n.* A barrier, esp. one across a waterway. —*v.* **dammed, damming. 1.** To construct a dam across. **2.** To obstruct.

**dam-age** (dăm'ĭj) *n.* **1.** Impairment of usefulness or value; harm. **2. damages.** Money paid for injury or loss. —*v.* **-aged, -aging.** To cause injury to.

**damn** (dăm) *v.* To condemn. —**dam'na-ble** *adj.* —**dam-na'tion** *n.* —**damned** *adj.*

**damp** (dămp) *adj.* Slightly wet. —*n.* Moisture. —*v.* **1.** To make damp. **2.** To restrain or check. —**damp'en** *v.* —**damp'er** *n.* —**damp'ness** *n.*

**dance** (dăns, däns) *v.* **danced, dancing.** To move rhythmically to music. —*n.* **1.** A series of rhythmical motions and steps. **2.** A gathering or piece of music for dancing. —**danc'er** *n.*

**dan-der** (dăn'dər) *n.* Temper.

**dan-druff** (dăn'drəf) *n.* A scaly scurf from the scalp.

**dan-dy** (dăn'dē) *n., pl.* **-dies.** A man who

affects extreme elegance. —*adj.* **-dier, -diest.**
Fine; good.

**dan·ger** (dān'jər) *n.* **1.** Chance of harm or evil. **2.** A source of peril. —**dan'ger·ous** *adj.* —**dan'ger·ous·ly** *adv.*

**dan·gle** (dăng'gəl) *v.* **-gled, -gling.** To hang loosely.

**dare** (dâr) *v.* **dared, daring. 1.** To have the courage for. **2.** To challenge (someone) to do something bold. —*n.* A challenge. —**dar'ing** *adj.* —**dar'ing·ly** *adv.*

**dark** (därk) *adj.* **1.** Lacking light. **2.** Somber in color. **3.** Gloomy. **4.** Obscure. —*n.* Absence of light. —**dark'en** *v.* —**dark'ly** *adv.* —**dark'ness** *n.*

**darn** (därn) *v.* To mend by weaving thread across a hole. —**darn'er** *n.*

**dart** (därt) *n.* **1.** A slender, pointed missile to be thrown or shot. **2.** A sudden movement. —*v.* To move suddenly. —**dart'er** *n.*

**dash** (dăsh) *v.* **1.** To smash; destroy. **2.** To knock or thrust violently. **3.** To perform hastily (with *off*). **4.** To rush. —*n.* **1.** A small amount. **2.** A rush. **3.** A short foot race. **4.** Verve. **5.** A punctuation mark (-).

**da·ta** (dā'tə, dăt'ə, dä'tə) *pl.n.* Information.

**date** (dāt) *n.* **1.** The time at which something happens. **2.** The day of the month. **3. a.** An appointment to meet socially. **b.** A person so met. —*v.* **dated, dating. 1.** To mark with a date. **2.** To determine the date of. **3.** To originate (with *from*). **4.** To make or have social engagements with.

**daub** (dôb) *v.* **1.** To smear. **2.** To paint crudely. —**daub'er** *n.*

**daugh·ter** (dô'tər) *n.* One's female child. —**daugh'ter·ly** *adj.*

**daugh·ter-in-law** (dô'tər-ĭn-lô') *n., pl.* **daughters-in-law.** The wife of one's son.

**daw·dle** (dôd'l) *v.* **-dled, -dling.** To waste time. —**daw'dler** *n.*

**dawn** (dôn) *n.* **1.** The first appearance of daylight. **2.** A beginning. —*v.* **1.** To begin to become light in the morning. **2.** To begin to appear or be understood. —**dawn'ing** *adj.*

**day** (dā) *n.* **1.** The period between dawn and nightfall. **2.** A 24-hour period, esp. one starting at midnight.

**daze** (dāz) *v.* **dazed, dazing. 1.** To stun or dazzle. —*n.* A stunned condition.

**daz·zle** (dăz'əl) *v.* **-zled, -zling.** To overpower, as with intense light. —**daz'zle** *n.*

**dead** (dĕd) *adj.* **1.** No longer alive. **2.** No longer in existence or use. **3.** Weary and worn-out.

**dead·en** (dĕd'n) *v.* To render less intense; dull.

**dead·ly** (dĕd'lē) *adj.* **-lier, -liest. 1.** Causing or tending to cause death. **2.** Implacable; mortal. —*adv.* To an extreme. —**dead'li·ness** *n.*

**deaf** (dĕf) *adj.* **1.** Unable to hear. **2.** Heedless. —**deaf·en** *v.* —**deaf'ness** *n.*

**deaf-mute** (dĕf'myōōt') *n.* Also **deaf mute.** One who can neither speak nor hear.

**deal** (dēl) *v.* **dealt** (dĕlt), **dealing. 1.** To distribute. **2.** To be concerned; treat. **3.** To do business; trade. —*n.* **1.** The act of dealing. **2.** An amount. **3.** An agreement or business transaction. —**deal'er** *n.*

**dean** (dēn) *n.* **1.** An administrative officer in a college or school. **2.** The senior member.

**dear** (dĭr) *adj.* **1.** Beloved. **2.** High-priced. —*n.* A greatly loved person. —**dear'ly** *adv.*

**death** (dĕth) *n.* The act of dying or state of being dead. —**death'less** *adj.* —**death'less·ness** *n.* —**death'ly** *adj. & adv.*

**de·bate** (dĭ-bāt') *v.* **-bated, -bating.** To discuss or argue formally. —*n.* A formal argument. —**de·bat'a·ble** *adj.* —**de·bat'er** *n.*

**de·bil·i·tate** (dĭ-bĭl'ə-tāt') *v.* **-tated, -tating.** To make feeble; weaken. —**de·bil'i·ta'tion** *n.*

**deb·it** (dĕb'ĭt) *n.* An item of debt. —*v.* To enter a debit in an account.

**deb·o·nair** (dĕb'ə-nâr') *adj.* Suave; affable. —**deb'o·nair'ly** *adv.*

**de·bris** (də-brē', dā'brē') *n.* Also **dé·bris.** Scattered remains.

**debt** (dĕt) *n.* Something owed. —**debt'or** *n.*

**de·but** (dĭ-byōō', dā-, dā'byōō') *n.* Also **dé·but.** A first public appearance.

**de·cade** (dĕk'ād, dĕ-kād') *n.* A period of 10 years.

**dec·a·dence** (dĕk'ə-dəns, dĭ-kā'dəns) *n.* A decay, esp. in morality. —**dec'a·dent** *adj.* —**dec'a·dent·ly** *adv.*

**de·cay** (dĭ-kā') *v.* **1.** To decompose; rot. **2.** To decline. —*n.* **1.** Decomposition. **2.** Deterioration.

**de·cease** (dĭ-sēs') *v.* **-ceased, -ceasing.** To die. —*n.* Death. —**de·ceased'** *adj.*

**de·ceit** (dĭ-sēt') *n.* **1.** Deception. **2.** A trick. —**de·ceit'ful** *adj.* —**de·ceit'ful·ly** *adv.*

**de·ceive** (dĭ-sēv') *v.* **-ceived, -ceiving.** To delude; mislead. —**de·ceiv'er** *n.*

**De·cem·ber** (dĭ-sĕm'bər) *n.* The 12th month of the year.

**de·cent** (dē'sənt) *adj.* **1.** Proper. **2.** Modest. **3.** Adequate. **4.** Kind. —**de'cen·cy** *n.* —**de'cent·ly** *adv.*

**de·cep·tion** (dĭ-sĕp'shən) *n.* **1.** The use of deceit. **2.** The fact or state of being deceived. —**de·cep'tive** *adj.* —**de·cep'tive·ly** *adv.*

**de·cide** (dĭ-sīd′) v. -cided, -ciding. 1. To conclude, settle, or announce a verdict. 2. To determine the outcome of. 3. To make up one's mind. —de·cid′er n. —de·ci′sion n.

**dec·i·mal** (dĕs′ə-məl) adj. Of or based on 10.

**de·ci·pher** (dĭ-sī′fər) v. To decode; interpret.

**de·ci·sive** (dĭ-sī′sĭv) adj. 1. Conclusive. 2. Resolute. —de·ci′sive·ly adv. —de·ci′sive·ness n.

**deck**[1] (dĕk) n. 1. An exposed floor on a ship. 2. A pack of playing cards.

**deck**[2] (dĕk) v. To adorn.

**de·clare** (dĭ-klâr′) v. -clared, -claring. To state officially or formally. —dec′la·ra′tion n. —de·clar′a·tive adj. —de·clar′er n.

**de·cline** (dĭ-klīn′) v. -clined, -clining. 1. To refuse to do or accept (something). 2. To slope downward. 3. To wane. —de·cline′ n.

**de·com·pose** (dē′kəm-pōz′) v. -posed, -posing. To rot. —de·com′po·si′tion n.

**dec·o·rate** (dĕk′ə-rāt′) v. -rated, -rating. 1. To furnish or adorn. 2. To confer a medal upon. —dec′o·ra′tion n. —dec′o·ra·tive adj. —dec′o·ra′tor n.

**de·coy** (dē′koi′, dĭ-koi′) n. 1. A living or artificial animal used to entice game. 2. A lure.

**de·crease** (dĭ-krēs′) v. -creased, -creasing. To diminish gradually; reduce. —n. (dē′krēs). Reduction; decline.

**de·cree** (dĭ-krē′) n. An authoritative order; edict. —de·cree′ v.

**de·crep·it** (dĭ-krĕp′ĭt) adj. Worn-out; broken down. —de·crep′i·tude′ n.

**ded·i·cate** (dĕd′ĭ-kāt′) v. -cated, -cating. 1. To set apart for special purposes. 2. To inscribe. 3. To devote. —ded′i·ca′tion n.

**de·duce** (dĭ-d/y/ōōs′) v. -duced, -ducing. To reach (a conclusion) by reasoning. —de·duc′i·ble adj.

**de·duct** (dĭ-dŭkt′) v. To subtract. —de·duct′i·ble adj. —de·duc′tion n.

**deed** (dēd) n. 1. An act. 2. A legal document, esp. one certifying ownership. —v. To transfer by deed.

**deem** (dēm) v. To judge; consider.

**deep** (dēp) adj. 1. Extending far down, back, or inward. 2. Learned; profound. 3. Intense; extreme. 4. Dark. 5. Absorbed. 6. Low. —n. Any deep place. —adv. 1. Profoundly. 2. Late. —deep′en v. —deep′ly adv. —deep′ness n.

**de·fame** (dĭ-fām′) v. -famed, -faming. To slander or libel. —def′a·ma′tion n. —de·fam′er n.

**de·fault** (dĭ-fôlt′) n. A failure to fulfill an obligation. —de·fault′ v. —de·fault′er n.

**de·feat** (dĭ-fēt′) v. 1. To win victory over. 2. To thwart. —n. The act of defeating or state of being defeated. —de·feat′er n.

**de·fect** (dē′fĕkt′, dĭ-fĕkt′) n. An imperfection; fault. —v. (dĭ-fĕkt′). To abandon an allegiance. —de·fec′tion n. —de·fec′tive adj. —de·fec′tive·ly adv. —de·fec′tive·ness n. —de·fec′tor n.

**de·fend** (dĭ-fĕnd′) v. 1. To protect from danger. 2. To represent (a legal defendant). —de·fend′er n.

**de·fen·dant** (dĭ-fĕn′dənt) n. A person accused or sued.

**de·fense** (dĭ-fĕns′) n. 1. The act of defending. 2. One that defends or protects. —de·fense′less adj. —de·fense′less·ly adv. —de·fen′si·ble adj. —de·fen′sive adj.

**de·fer**[1] (dĭ-fûr′) v. -ferred, -ferring. To postpone. —de·fer′ment, de·fer′ral n.

**de·fer**[2] (dĭ-fûr′) v. -ferred, -ferring. To yield or submit respectfully. —def′er·ence n. —def′er·en′tial adj. —def′er·en′tial·ly adv.

**de·fi·ant** (dĭ-fī′ənt) adj. Marked by resistance to authority. —de·fi′ance n. —de·fi′ant·ly adv.

**de·fi·cient** (dĭ-fĭsh′ənt) adj. 1. Lacking; incomplete. 2. Inadequate. —de·fi′cien·cy n. —de·fi′cient·ly adv.

**def·i·cit** (dĕf′ə-sĭt) n. The amount by which a sum falls short.

**de·file** (dĭ-fīl′) v. -filed, -filing. 1. To make filthy or dirty. 2. To corrupt. —de·file′ment n. —de·fil′er n.

**de·fine** (dĭ-fīn′) v. -fined, -fining. 1. To state the meaning of. 2. To delineate. 3. To specify distinctly. —de·fin′a·ble adj. —de·fin′a·bly adv. —de·fin′er n. —def′i·ni′tion n.

**def·i·nite** (dĕf′ə-nĭt) adj. 1. Having distinct limits. 2. Known positively. 3. Clearly defined. —def′i·nite·ly adv.

**de·fin·i·tive** (dĭ-fĭn′ə-tĭv) adj. Determining finally; decisive. —de·fin′i·tive·ly adv. —de·fin′i·tive·ness n.

**de·flate** (dĭ-flāt′) v. -flated, -flating. 1. To release contained air or gas from. 2. To lessen the confidence, pride, or certainty of. —de·fla′tion n. —de·fla′tor n.

**de·flect** (dĭ-flĕkt′) v. To turn aside. —de·flec′tion n.

**de·form** (dĭ-fôrm′) v. To misshape; disfigure. —de·for·ma′tion n. —de·formed′ adj. —de·form′i·ty n.

**de·fray** (dĭ-frā′) v. To pay. —de·fray′a·ble

*adj.* — **de·tray′al** *n.*

**deft** (dĕft) *adj.* Skillful; adroit. — **deft′ly** *adv.*

**de·funct** (dĭ-fŭngkt′) *adj.* Having ceased to exist.

**de·fy** (dĭ-fī′) *v.* **-fied, -fying.** **1.** To oppose boldly. **2.** To resist successfully; withstand. **3.** To dare; challenge.

**de·gen·er·ate** (dĭ-jĕn′ə-rāt′) *v.* **-ated, -ating.** To deteriorate or decay. — *adj.* (-ər-ĭt). Morally degraded. — *n.* (-ĭt). A degenerate person. — **de·gen′er·a·cy** *n.* — **de·gen′er·a′tion** *n.* — **de·gen′er·a·tive** *adj.*

**de·grade** (dĭ-grād′) *v.* **-graded, -grading.** To debase; corrupt. — **deg′ra·da′tion** *n.* — **de·grad′ed·ly** *adv.* — **de·grad′er** *n.*

**de·gree** (dĭ-grē′) *n.* **1.** A step or stage in a series. **2.** Extent; intensity. **3.** A unit on a subdivided scale or range, as of temperature. **4.** An academic title or rank.

**de·hy·drate** (dē-hī′drāt′) *v.* **-drated, -drating.** To remove water from. — **de′hy·dra′tion** *n.*

**deign** (dān) *v.* To condescend.

**de·i·ty** (dē′ə-tē) *n., pl.* **-ties.** **1.** A god. **2.** Divinity.

**de·ject·ed** (dĭ-jĕk′tĭd) *adj.* Depressed; disheartened. — **de·ject′ed·ly** *adv.* — **de·jec′tion** *n.*

**de·lay** (dĭ-lā′) *v.* **1.** To cause to be late. **2.** To postpone. — *n.* The act of delaying or condition of being delayed. — **de·lay′er** *n.*

**de·lec·ta·ble** (dĭ-lĕk′tə-bəl) *adj.* **1.** Delightful. **2.** Delicious. — **de·lec′ta·bly** *adv.*

**del·e·gate** (dĕl′ə-gāt′, -gĭt) *n.* One authorized to act for another. — *v.* (-gāt′) **-gated, -gating.** **1.** To send (a person) as one's representative. **2.** To commit to a subordinate. — **del′e·ga′tion** *n.*

**de·lete** (dĭ-lēt′) *v.* **-leted, -leting.** To strike out; omit. — **de·le′tion** *n.*

**de·lib·er·ate** (dĭ-lĭb′ə-rāt′) *v.* **-ated, -ating.** To consider carefully. — *adj.* (-ər-ĭt). **1.** Intentional. **2.** Careful in deciding. **3.** Unhurried. — **de·lib′er·ate·ly** *adv.* — **de·lib′er·ate·ness** *n.* — **de·lib′er·a′tion** *n.* — **de·lib′er·a′tive** *adj.*

**del·i·cate** (dĕl′ĭ-kĭt) *adj.* **1.** Pleasingly small. **2.** Frail and fine. **3.** Easily damaged. **4.** Requiring or marked by careful skill. — **del′i·ca·cy** *n.* — **del′i·cate·ly** *adv.*

**del·i·ca·tes·sen** (dĕl′ĭ-kə-tĕs′ən) *n.* A shop that sells cooked or prepared foods.

**de·li·cious** (dĭ-lĭsh′əs) *adj.* Highly pleasing to the taste. — **de·li′cious·ly** *adv.*

**de·light** (dĭ-līt′) *n.* Great pleasure; joy. — *v.* To give or take great pleasure or joy. — **de·light′ful** *adj.* — **de·light′ful·ly** *adv.*

**de·lin·quent** (dĭ-lĭng′kwənt) *adj.* Failing to do what is required. — *n.* A delinquent person. — **de·lin′quen·cy** *n.*

**de·lir·i·um** (dĭ-lĭr′ē-əm) *n., pl.* **-ums** or **-ia.** **1.** Temporary mental confusion and clouded consciousness. **2.** Ecstasy; rapture. — **de·lir′i·ous** *adj.* — **de·lir′i·ous·ly** *adv.*

**de·liv·er** (dĭ-lĭv′ər) *v.* **1.** To set free. **2.** To assist in birth. **3.** To take to an intended recipient. **4.** To utter. — **de·liv′er·ance** *n.* — **de·liv′er·er** *n.* — **de·liv′er·y** *n.*

**de·lude** (dĭ-lōōd′) *v.* **-luded, -luding.** To mislead into error. — **de·lu′sion** *n.* — **de·lu′sive** *adj.*

**del·uge** (dĕl′yōōj) *v.* **-uged, -uging.** To flood. — *n.* A flood.

**delve** (dĕlv) *v.* **delved, delving.** To search deeply. — **delv′er** *n.*

**dem·a·gogue** (dĕm′ə-gôg′, -gŏg′) *n.* A leader who appeals to popular emotions and prejudices. — **dem′a·gog′ic** *adj.* — **dem′a·gogu′er·y** *n.*

**de·mand** (dĭ-mănd′, -mänd′) *v.* **1.** To ask for insistently. **2.** To claim as just or due. — *n.* **1.** The act of demanding. **2.** Something demanded. **3.** The state of being sought after. — **de·mand′er** *n.* — **de·mand′ing** *adj.*

**de·mean·or** (dĭ-mē′nər) *n.* Behavior.

**de·ment·ed** (dĭ-mĕn′tĭd) *adj.* Insane.

**de·mise** (dĭ-mīz′) *n.* Death.

**de·moc·ra·cy** (dĭ-mŏk′rə-sē) *n., pl.* **-cies.** **1.** Government by the people. **2.** Social equality. — **dem′o·crat′** *n.* — **dem′o·crat′ic** *adj.* — **dem′o·crat′i·cal·ly** *adv.*

**de·mol·ish** (dĭ-mŏl′ĭsh) *v.* To destroy. — **dem′o·li′tion** *n.*

**de·mon** (dē′mən) *n.* A devil or evil spirit. — **de′mo·ni′a·cal, de·mon′ic** *adj.*

**dem·on·strate** (dĕm′ən-strāt′) *v.* **-strated, -strating.** **1.** To prove. **2.** To show. — **de·mon′stra·ble** *adj.* — **dem′on·stra′tion** *n.* — **de·mon′stra·tive** *adj.* — **dem′on·stra′tor** *n.*

**de·mor·al·ize** (dĭ-môr′əl-īz′, dĭ-mŏr′-) *v.* **-ized, -izing.** **1.** To corrupt the morals of. **2.** To dishearten. — **de·mor′al·i·za′tion** *n.* — **de·mor′al·iz′er** *n.*

**de·mote** (dĭ-mōt′) *v.* **-moted, -moting.** To lower in rank. — **de·mo′tion** *n.*

**den** (dĕn) *n.* **1.** The shelter of a wild animal; lair. **2.** A refuge, esp. if hidden. **3.** A small room for study or relaxation.

**den·im** (dĕn′əm) *n.* A coarse twilled cloth.

**de·nom·i·na·tion** (dĭ-nŏm′ə-nā′shən) *n.* **1.** A name. **2.** A unit in a system of currency or weights. **3.** A religious group or sect. — **de·nom′i·na′tion·al** *adj.*

**de·nom·i·na·tor** (dĭ-nŏm′ə-nā′tər) *n.* The

quantity below the line in a fraction.

**de·note** (dǐ-nōt') v. -noted, -noting. 1. To indicate plainly. 2. To mean. — **de·no·ta·tion** n.

**de·nounce** (dǐ-nouns') v. -nounced, -nouncing. 1. To speak out against; condemn. 2. To accuse formally. — **de·nounce'·ment** n. — **de·nounc'er** n. — **de·nun·ci·a'·tion** n.

**dense** (dĕns) adj. **denser, densest.** 1. Compact. 2. Thick. 3. Stupid. — **dense'ly** adv. — **den'si·ty** n.

**dent** (dĕnt) n. A depression or hollow. — **dent** v.

**den·tal** (dĕnt'l) adj. Of the teeth.

**den·tist·ry** (dĕn'tǐ-strē) n. The diagnosis and treatment of diseases of the teeth. — **den'tist** n.

**de·ny** (dǐ-nī') v. -nied, -nying. 1. To declare untrue. 2. To refuse to recognize or acknowledge. 3. To refuse to grant. — **de·ni'al** n. — **de·ni'er** n.

**de·part** (dǐ-pärt') v. 1. To leave. 2. To deviate. — **de·par'ture** n.

**de·part·ment** (dǐ-pärt'mənt) n. A division, as of a government, having a specialized function. — **de·part·men'tal** adj.

**de·pend** (dǐ-pĕnd') v. 1. To rely, as for support. 2. To place trust. 3. To be determined. — **de·pend·a·bil'i·ty** n. — **de·pend'a·ble** adj. — **de·pend'a·bly** adv. — **de·pen'dence** n. — **de·pen'dent** adj.

**de·pict** (dǐ-pǐkt') v. 1. To represent in a picture. 2. To describe. — **de·pic'tion** n.

**de·plete** (dǐ-plēt') v. -pleted, -pleting. To use up or exhaust. — **de·ple'tion** n.

**de·plore** (dǐ-plôr', -plōr') v. -plored, -ploring. To regard as unfortunate or wrong. — **de·plor'a·ble** adj. — **de·plor'a·bly** adv.

**de·port** (dǐ-pôrt', -pōrt') v. 1. To expel from a country. 2. To conduct (oneself). — **de·por·ta'tion** n. — **de·port'ment** n.

**de·pose** (dǐ-pōz') v. -posed, -posing. 1. To remove from office. 2. To testify under oath. — **dep·o·si'tion** n.

**de·pos·it** (dǐ-pŏz'ĭt) v. 1. To place for safe-keeping. 2. To put down in layers. 3. To give as partial payment. — n. Something deposited. — **de·pos'i·tor** n. — **de·pos'i·to·ry** n.

**de·pot** (dē'pō) n. 1. A railroad or bus station. 2. A warehouse.

**de·prave** (dǐ-prāv') v. -praved, -praving. To corrupt. — **de·praved'** adj. — **de·prav'i·ty** n.

**de·pre·ci·ate** (dǐ-prē'shē-āt') v. -ated, -ating. 1. To make or become less in value. 2. To belittle. — **de·pre·ci·a'tion** n. — **de·pre'ci·a'tor** n.

**de·press** (dǐ-prĕs') v. 1. To sadden. 2. To press down. 3. To lower in value, price, etc. — **de·pres'sion** n. — **de·pres'sor** n.

**de·prive** (dǐ-prīv') v. -prived, -priving. 1. To take something away from; divest. 2. To keep something from. — **dep'ri·va'tion** n.

**depth** (dĕpth) n. 1. The condition of being deep. 2. The distance downward.

**dep·u·ty** (dĕp'yə-tē) n., pl. -ties. A person empowered to act for another. — **dep'u·ta'tion** n. — **dep'u·tize'** v. — **dep'u·ty** adj.

**de·range** (dǐ-rānj') v. -ranged, -ranging. 1. To disturb. 2. To make insane. — **de·range'ment** n.

**der·e·lict** (dĕr'ə-lĭkt) adj. 1. Neglectful. 2. Abandoned. — n. A vagrant. — **der'e·lic'tion** n.

**de·ride** (dǐ-rīd') v. -rided, -riding. To scoff at. — **de·ri'sion** n. — **de·ri'sive** adj. — **de·ri'sive·ly** adv.

**de·rive** (dǐ-rīv') v. -rived, -riving. 1. To obtain or issue from a source. 2. To deduce. — **der·i·va'tion** n. — **de·riv'a·tive** adj. n.

**de·rog·a·to·ry** (dǐ-rŏg'ə-tôr'ē, -tōr'ē) adj. Detracting; disparaging. — **de·rog·a'tion** n.

**der·rick** (dĕr'ĭk) n. A large hoisting crane.

**de·scend** (dǐ-sĕnd') v. 1. To move or go down. 2. To slope downward. — **de·scen'dant** adj. — **de·scent'** n.

**de·scen·dant** (dǐ-sĕn'dənt) n. An immediate or remote offspring.

**de·scribe** (dǐ-skrīb') v. -scribed, -scribing. 1. To tell about. 2. To trace the figure of. — **de·scrib'er** n. — **de·scrip'tion** n. — **de·scrip'tive** adj.

**des·ert'** (dĕz'ərt) n. A dry and barren region. — **des'ert** adj.

**de·sert²** (dǐ-zûrt') v. To abandon. — **de·sert'er** n. — **de·ser'tion** n.

**de·serve** (dǐ-zûrv') v. -served, -serving. To be worthy of; merit. — **de·served'** adj. — **de·serv'ing** adj.

**de·sign** (dǐ-zīn') v. 1. To conceive; invent. 2. To form a plan for. 3. To intend; scheme. — n. 1. A plan. 2. A pattern. 3. An intention. — **de·sign'er** n. — **de·sign'ing** adj.

**des·ig·nate** (dĕz'ĭg-nāt') v. -nated, -nating. 1. To indicate or specify. 2. To give a name to. 3. To appoint. — adj. (-nĭt). Appointed. — **des'ig·na'tion** n.

**de·sire** (dǐ-zīr') v. -sired, -siring. To wish or long for; crave. — n. 1. A wish. 2. A request. 3. Something longed for. 4. Sexual appetite. — **de·sir'a·ble** adj. — **de·sir·a·bil'i·ty** n. — **de·sir'ous** adj.

**de·sist** (dǐ-zǐst') v. To cease; stop.

**desk** (dĕsk) n. A writing table.

**des·o·late** (dĕs'ə-lĭt) adj. **1.** Deserted. **2.** Dismal. **3.** Forlorn. —v. (-lāt') **-lated, -lating.** To make desolate. —**des·o·la'tion** n.

**de·spair** (dĭ-spâr') v. To lose all hope. —n. Utter loss of hope. —**de·spair'ing·ly** adv.

**des·per·ate** (dĕs'pər-ĭt) adj. **1.** Reckless because of despair. **2.** Nearly hopeless. **3.** Extreme. —**des'per·ate·ly** adv. —**des'per·ate·ness, des'per·a'tion** n.

**des·pi·ca·ble** (dĕs'pĭ-kə-bəl, dĭ-spĭk'-) adj. Contemptible. —**des'pi·ca·bly** adv.

**de·spise** (dĭ-spīz') v. **-spised, -spising.** To regard with contempt. —**de·spis'er** n.

**de·spite** (dĭ-spīt') prep. In spite of.

**de·spon·den·cy** (dĭ-spŏn'dən-sē) n., pl. **-cies.** Also **de·spon·dence.** Depression; dejection. —**de·spon'dent** adj.

**des·pot** (dĕs'pət) n. An autocratic ruler. —**des·pot'ic** adj. —**des'pot·ism** n.

**des·sert** (dĭ-zûrt') n. A usually sweet food served at the end of a meal.

**des·ti·na·tion** (dĕs'tə-nā'shən) n. The place to which one is going; goal.

**des·tine** (dĕs'tĭn) v. **-tined, -tining. 1.** To preordain. **2.** To intend or direct.

**des·ti·ny** (dĕs'tə-nē) n., pl. **-nies.** Fate.

**des·ti·tute** (dĕs'tə-t/y̅oȯt') adj. **1.** Altogether lacking; devoid. **2.** Very poor; penniless. —**des'ti·tu'tion** n.

**de·stroy** (dĭ-stroi') v. **1.** To ruin. **2.** To demolish. **3.** To kill. —**de·stroy'er** n.

**de·struc·tion** (dĭ-strŭk'shən) n. The act of destroying or state of being destroyed. —**de·struc'tive** adj. —**de·struc'tive·ly** adv. —**de·struc'tive·ness** n.

**de·tach** (dĭ-tăch') v. To separate; remove. —**de·tach'a·ble** adj.

**de·tail** (dĭ-tāl', dē'tāl) n. **1.** An individual part or item. **2.** Itemized treatment of particulars. —v. To relate item by item.

**de·tain** (dĭ-tān') v. **1.** To keep from proceeding; delay. **2.** To confine. —**de·tain'ment, de·ten'tion** n.

**de·tect** (dĭ-tĕkt') v. To discover the existence, presence, or fact of. —**de·tect'a·ble** adj. —**de·tec'tion** n. —**de·tec'tive** n. —**de·tec'tor** n.

**de·ter** (dĭ-tûr') v. **-terred, -terring.** To prevent or discourage from acting. —**de·ter'rent** adj. & n.

**de·ter·gent** (dĭ-tûr'jənt) n. A cleansing substance.

**de·te·ri·o·rate** (dĭ-tîr'ē-ə-rāt') v. **-rated, -rating.** To become or make worse. —**de·te'ri·o·ra'tion** n.

**de·ter·mine** (dĭ-tûr'mĭn) v. **-mined, -mining. 1.** To decide conclusively. **2.** To limit or regulate. **3.** To be the cause of. —**de·ter'mi·na·ble** adj. —**de·ter'mi·na·bly** adv. —**de·ter'mi·na'tion** n.

**de·test** (dĭ-tĕst') v. To dislike intensely; loathe. —**de·test'a·ble** adj. —**de·tes·ta'tion** n.

**de·tour** (dē'tŏŏr', dĭ-tŏŏr') n. A roundabout way. —v. To go by a detour.

**de·tract** (dĭ-trăkt') v. To be a drawback; diminish. —**de·trac'tion** n. —**de·trac'tive** adj. —**de·trac'tor** n.

**det·ri·ment** (dĕt'rə-mənt) n. Harm; disadvantage. —**det'ri·men'tal** adj.

**de·val·u·ate** (dē-văl'yŏŏ-āt') v. **-ated, -ating.** Also **de·val·ue, -ued, -uing.** To lower the value of. —**de·val'u·a'tion** n.

**dev·as·tate** (dĕv'ə-stāt') v. **-tated, -tating. 1.** To lay waste. **2.** To overwhelm. —**dev'as·ta'tion** n.

**de·vel·op** (dĭ-vĕl'əp) v. **1.** To bring, grow, or evolve to a more complete state. **2.** To appear or disclose graphically. **3.** To elaborate; expand. —**de·vel'op·er** n. —**de·vel'op·ment** n.

**de·vi·ate** (dē'vē-āt') v. **-ated, -ating.** To turn away from an accepted course or standard. —n. (-ĭt). A sexual pervert. —**de'vi·ance** n. —**de'vi·ant** adj. & n. —**de'vi·a'tion** n.

**de·vice** (dĭ-vīs') n. **1.** Something, as a mechanical contrivance, made for a particular purpose. **2.** A scheme; trick.

**dev·il** (dĕv'əl) n. **1.** The major spirit of evil. **2.** A wicked or mischievous person. —**dev'il·ish** adj.

**de·vi·ous** (dē'vē-əs) adj. **1.** Roundabout. **2.** Deceitful. —**de'vi·ous·ly** adv. —**de'vi·ous·ness** n.

**de·vise** (dĭ-vīz') v. **-vised, -vising.** To plan; invent. —**de·vis'er** n.

**de·void** (dĭ-void') adj. Completely lacking.

**de·vote** (dĭ-vōt') v. **-voted, -voting. 1.** To give or apply entirely. **2.** To dedicate.

**de·vo·tion** (dĭ-vō'shən) n. **1.** Ardent attachment or affection. **2.** Religious zeal. **3.** devotions. Prayers. —**de·vo'tion·al** adj.

**de·vour** (dĭ-vour') v. To eat up or consume greedily. —**de·vour'er** n.

**de·vout** (dĭ-vout') adj. **1.** Deeply religious; pious. **2.** Earnest. —**de·vout'ly** adv. —**de·vout'ness** n.

**dew** (d/y̅oȯ) n. Water droplets condensed onto cool surfaces. —**dew'i·ness** n. —**dew'y** adj.

**dex·ter·ous** (dĕk'strəs) adj. Also **dex·trous.** Skillful; adroit. —**dex·ter'i·ty** n. —**dex'ter·ous·**

ly *adv.*

**di·a·bol·ic** (dī'ə-bŏl'ĭk) *adj.* Also **di·a·bol·i·cal.** Devilish; wicked. —**di'a·bol'i·cal·ly** *adv.*

**di·ag·no·sis** (dī'əg-nō'sĭs) *n., pl.* **-ses** (-sēz'). Identification, esp. of a disease. —**di'ag·nose'** *v.* —**di'ag·nos'tic** *adj.* —**di'ag·nos'ti·cal·ly** *adv.* —**di'ag·nos·ti'cian** *n.*

**di·ag·o·nal** (dī-ăg'ə-nəl) *adj.* Slanted or oblique in direction. —*n.* A diagonal line. —**di·ag'o·nal·ly** *adv.*

**di·a·gram** (dī'ə-grăm') *n.* A simplified explanatory drawing or plan. —*v.* To represent by a diagram. —**di'a·gram·mat'ic, di'a·gram·mat'i·cal** *adj.*

**di·al** (dī'əl) *n.* **1.** A marked disk or plate on which a measurement is indicated. **2.** A rotatable disk, as of a telephone. —*v.* **1.** To indicate or select by means of a dial. **2.** To call on a telephone with a dial.

**di·a·lect** (dī'ə-lěkt') *n.* **1.** A regional variety of a spoken language. **2.** A jargon. —**di'a·lec'tal** *adj.*

**di·a·logue** (dī'ə-lôg', -lŏg') *n.* Also **di·a·log.** A conversation, esp. in a play or narrative.

**di·am·e·ter** (dī-ăm'ə-tər) *n.* **1.** A straight line through the center of a circle or other figure. **2.** Its length. —**di'a·met'ric, di'a·met'ri·cal** *adj.* —**di'a·met'ri·cal·ly** *adv.*

**dia·mond** (dī'mənd, dī'ə-) *n.* **1.** An extremely hard, brilliant gemstone. **2.** A rhombus or lozenge. **3.** A baseball field.

**di·a·per** (dī'ə-pər, dī'pər) *n.* A folded cloth used to cover a baby's genital and anal areas. —*v.* To put a diaper on.

**di·a·phragm** (dī'ə-frăm') *n.* **1.** A muscular membrane separating the abdomen and chest. **2.** Any similar muscular partition.

**di·ar·rhe·a** (dī'ə-rē'ə) *n.* Also **di·ar·rhoe·a.** Frequent and watery bowel movements.

**di·a·ry** (dī'ə-rē) *n., pl.* **-ries.** A daily record, esp. of personal experiences. —**di'a·rist** *n.*

**dice** (dīs) *pl.n. Sing.* **die.** Small cubes used in gambling games. —*v.* **diced, dicing.** To cut into small cubes. —**dic'er** *n.*

**dic·tate** (dĭk'tāt', dĭk-tāt') *v.* **-tated, -tating.** **1.** To speak for recording or transcription. **2.** To issue (a command, order, etc.) authoritatively. —**dic·ta'tion** *n.*

**dic·ta·tor** (dĭk'tā-tər) *n.* An absolute or tyrannical ruler. —**dic'ta·to'ri·al** *adj.* —**dic·ta'tor·ship'** *n.*

**dic·tion·ar·y** (dĭk'shə-něr'ē) *n., pl.* **-ies.** A book containing an alphabetical list of words with definitions or translations.

**did** (dĭd). *p.t.* of **do.**

**did·n't** (dĭd'ənt). Contraction of *did not.*

**die**[1] (dī) *v.* **died, dying.** **1.** To cease living. **2.** To pass out of existence.

**die**[2] (dī) *n.* **1.** A device used for cutting out, forming, or stamping material. **2.** *Sing.* of **dice.**

**di·et** (dī'ət) *n.* **1.** One's usual food and drink. **2.** A restricted selection of food. —*v.* To eat according to a diet. —**di'e·tar'y** *adj.* —**di'et·er** *n.* —**di'e·tet'ic** *adj.* —**di'e·ti'tian** *n.*

**dif·fer** (dĭf'ər) *v.* **1.** To be unlike. **2.** To disagree; dissent. —**dif'fer·ence** *n.* —**dif'fer·ent** *adj.*

**dif·fi·cult** (dĭf'ĭ-kŭlt', -kəlt) *adj.* Hard; not easy. —**dif'fi·cul'ty** *n.*

**dig** (dĭg) *v.* **dug, digging.** **1.** To turn over or remove (soil) with a tool. **2.** To make or extract by removing soil. **3.** To search; probe.

**di·gest** (dĭ-jĕst', dī-) *v.* **1.** To transform food into an assimilable condition. **2.** To absorb mentally. —*n.* (dī'jĕst'). A summary; condensation. —**di·gest'i·ble** *adj.* —**di·ges'tion** *n.* —**di·ges'tive** *adj.*

**dig·it** (dĭj'ĭt) *n.* **1.** A finger or toe. **2.** Any of the Arabic number symbols, 0 through 9. —**dig'i·tal** *adj.*

**dig·ni·ty** (dĭg'nə-tē) *n., pl.* **-ties.** **1.** Nobility; honor; worth. **2.** A high rank. **3.** Calm assurance; composure.

**dike** (dīk) *n.* Also **dyke.** An embankment to contain a body of water.

**di·late** (dī-lāt', dī'lāt', dī-lāt') *v.* **-lated, -lating.** To expand. —**di·la'tion, dil'a·ta'tion** *n.*

**di·lem·ma** (dĭ-lĕm'ə) *n.* A perplexing choice or predicament.

**dil·i·gence** (dĭl'ə-jəns) *n.* Persistent and energetic application to a task. —**dil'i·gent** *adj.* —**dil'i·gent·ly** *adv.*

**di·lute** (dī-lōōt', dĭ-) *v.* **-luted, -luting.** To reduce the concentration of. —**di·lut'er** *n.* —**di·lu'tion** *n.*

**dim** (dĭm) *adj.* **dimmer, dimmest.** **1.** Not bright; faint. **2.** Indistinct; obscure. —*v.* **dimmed, dimming.** To make or become dim. —**dim'ly** *adv.* —**dim'ness** *n.*

**dime** (dīm) *n.* A coin worth ten cents.

**di·men·sion** (dĭ-mĕn'shən) *n.* **1.** A measure of spatial extent. **2.** Often **dimensions.** Extent; size; scope. —**di·men'sion·al** *adj.*

**di·min·ish** (dĭ-mĭn'ĭsh) *v.* To make or become smaller. —**di·min'ish·ment, dim'i·nu'tion** *n.*

**di·min·u·tive** (dĭ-mĭn'yə-tĭv) *adj.* Small.

**din** (dĭn) *n.* Discordant noise. —*v.* **dinned, dinning.** To impress by wearying repetition.

**dine** (dīn) *v.* **dined, dining.** To eat dinner.

— din'er n.

**din·gy** (dǐn'jē) adj. **-gier, -giest.** Drab; shabby. — **din'gi·ness** n.

**din·ner** (dǐn'ər) n. The chief meal of the day.

**di·o·cese** (dī'ə-sĭs, -sēs, -sēz') n. The district of churches under a bishop. — **di·oc'e·san** n.

**dip** (dǐp) v. **dipped, dipping. 1.** To plunge briefly into a liquid. **2.** To scoop up (liquid). **3.** To drop or sink. — **dip'per** n.

**di·plo·ma** (dǐ-plō'mə) n. A document certifying completion of a course of study.

**di·plo·ma·cy** (dǐ-plō'mə-sē) n., pl. **-cies. 1.** The art or profession of conducting international relations. **2.** Tact. — **dip'lo·mat'** n. — **dip'lo·mat'ic** adj. — **dip'lo·mat'i·cal·ly** adv.

**dire** (dīr) adj. **direr, direst.** Dreadful. — **dire'ly** adv.

**di·rect** (dǐ-rĕkt', dī-) v. **1.** To conduct; manage. **2.** To instruct; order. **3.** To aim. — adj. **1.** Straight. **2.** Straightforward. — **rect'ly** adv. — **di·rec'tor** n.

**di·rec·tion** (dǐ-rĕk'shən, dī-) n. **1.** The act or function of directing. **2.** Often **directions.** Instructions. **3.** A command. **4.** The line or course along which a person or thing moves. — **di·rec'tion·al** adj.

**dirge** (dûrj) n. A funeral hymn.

**dirt** (dûrt) n. **1.** Earth or soil. **2.** A soiling substance. — **dirt'y** adj.

**dis·a·ble** (dǐs-ā'bəl) v. **-bled, -bling.** To weaken or cripple. — **dis'a·bil'i·ty** n.

**dis·ad·van·tage** (dǐs'əd-văn'tǐj, -vän'tǐj) n. A handicap; detriment. — **dis'ad·van'taged** adj. — **dis·ad'van·ta'geous** adj.

**dis·a·gree** (dǐs'ə-grē') v. **-greed, -greeing. 1.** To be different. **2.** To have a different opinion. — **dis'a·gree'ment** n.

**dis·a·gree·a·ble** (dǐs'ə-grē'ə-bəl) adj. Unpleasant; offensive. — **dis'a·gree'a·bly** adv.

**dis·ap·pear** (dǐs'ə-pîr') v. To pass out of sight; vanish. — **dis'ap·pear'ance** n.

**dis·ap·point** (dǐs'ə-point') v. To fail to satisfy the hopes of. — **dis'ap·point'ing·ly** adv. — **dis'ap·point'ment** n.

**dis·ap·prove** (dǐs'ə-prōōv') v. **-proved, -proving.** To have an unfavorable opinion. — **dis'ap·prov'al** n.

**dis·arm** (dǐs-ärm') v. **1.** To deprive of weapons. **2.** To overcome the hostility of. — **dis·ar'ma·ment** n. — **dis·arm'ing** adj. — **dis·arm'ing·ly** adv.

**dis·ar·ray** (dǐs'ə-rā') n. Disorder.

**dis·as·ter** (dǐ-zăs'tər, -zäs'tər) n. **1.** An occurrence inflicting widespread destruction

and distress. **2.** A total failure. — **dis·as'trous** adj. — **dis·as'trous·ly** adv.

**dis·bar** (dǐs-bär') v. **-barred, -barring.** To expel from the legal profession. — **dis·bar'ment** n.

**dis·burse** (dǐs-bûrs') v. **-bursed, -bursing.** To pay out. — **dis·burse'ment** n.

**disc** (dǐsk) n. A phonograph record.

**dis·card** (dǐs-kärd') v. To throw away; reject.

**dis·charge** (dǐs-chärj') v. **-charged, -charging. 1.** To unload. **2.** To release or dismiss. **3.** To emit. **4.** To shoot. **5.** To perform (a duty). — n. (dǐs'chärj'). **1.** The act of discharging. **2.** Something discharged.

**dis·ci·ple** (dǐ-sī'pəl) n. A follower; adherent.

**dis·ci·pline** (dǐs'ə-plǐn) n. **1.** Training, esp. to instill good behavior. **2.** Controlled behavior. **3.** Corrective punishment. — v. **-plined, -plining. 1.** To train. **2.** To punish. — **dis·ci·pli·nar'i·an** n. — **dis·ci·pli·nar'y** adj.

**dis·claim** (dǐs-klām') v. To deny; disown. — **dis·claim'er** n.

**dis·close** (dǐs-klōz') v. **-closed, -closing.** To expose to view; reveal. — **dis·clo'sure** n.

**dis·com·fort** (dǐs-kŭm'fərt) n. **1.** The condition of being uncomfortable. **2.** Something that disturbs one's comfort.

**dis·con·nect** (dǐs'kə-nĕkt') v. To sever the connection of. — **dis·con·nect'ed** adj. — **dis'con·nec'tion** n.

**dis·con·so·late** (dǐs-kŏn'sə-lǐt) adj. Hopelessly sad. — **dis·con'so·late·ly** adv. — **dis·con'so·late·ness** n.

**dis·con·tent** (dǐs'kən-tĕnt') n. Dissatisfaction. — **dis'con·tent'ed** adj.

**dis·con·tin·ue** (dǐs'kən-tǐn'yōō) v. **-ued, -uing.** To cease; stop. — **dis'con·tin'u·ance,** **dis'con·tin'u·a'tion** n.

**dis·cord** (dǐs'kôrd') n. **1.** Dissension. **2.** Dissonance. — **dis·cor'dant** adj. — **dis·cor'dant·ly** adv.

**dis·count** (dǐs'kount', dǐs-kount') v. **1.** To deduct, as from a cost. **2.** To disregard. — n. (dǐs'kount'). A reduction from the full amount.

**dis·cour·age** (dǐs-kûr'ǐj) v. **-aged, -aging. 1.** To deprive of confidence, hope, or spirit. **2.** To dissuade. — **dis·cour'age·ment** n.

**dis·cour·te·ous** (dǐs-kûr'tē-əs) adj. Impolite. — **dis·cour'te·sy** n.

**dis·cov·er** (dǐs-kŭv'ər) v. **1.** To arrive at through search or study. **2.** To be the first to find, learn of, or observe. — **dis·cov'er·a·ble** adj. — **dis·cov'er·er** n. — **dis·cov'er·y** n.

**discredit**

**dis·cred·it** (dĭs-krĕd′ĭt) v. **1.** To disgrace; dishonor. **2.** To cast doubt on. —n. **1.** Damage to one's reputation. **2.** Loss of trust or belief. —**dis·cred′it·a·ble** adj.

**dis·creet** (dĭs-krēt′) adj. Tactful; prudent. —**dis·creet′ly** adv. —**dis·cre′tion** n.

**dis·crep·an·cy** (dĭs-krĕp′ən-sē) n. pl. -cies. Disagreement, as between facts. —**dis·crep′ant** adj.

**dis·crim·i·nate** (dĭs-krĭm′ə-nāt) v. -nated, -nating. **1.** To distinguish. **2.** To act on the basis of prejudice. —**dis·crim′i·na′tion** n. —**dis·crim′i·na′tive, dis·crim′i·na·to′ry** adj.

**dis·cuss** (dĭs-kŭs′) v. **1.** To speak or write about. **2.** To talk over. —**dis·cus′sion** n.

**dis·dain** (dĭs-dān′) v. To regard with contempt. —n. Scornful superiority. —**dis·dain′ful** adj.

**dis·ease** (dĭ-zēz′) n. An abnormal condition that impairs normal functioning; illness. —**dis·eased′** adj.

**dis·fa·vor** (dĭs-fā′vər) n. Disapproval.

**dis·fig·ure** (dĭs-fĭg′yər) v. -ured, -uring. To deform. —**dis·fig′ure·ment** n.

**dis·grace** (dĭs-grās′) n. Loss of honor; shame. —v. -graced, -gracing. To bring shame or dishonor upon. —**dis·grace′ful** adj. —**dis·grace′ful·ly** adv.

**dis·guise** (dĭs-gīz′) v. -guised, -guising. To modify the appearance of to prevent recognition. —n. **1.** The condition of being disguised. **2.** Something that serves to disguise.

**dis·gust** (dĭs-gŭst′) v. To excite nausea or loathing in; sicken. —n. Profound repugnance. —**dis·gust′ed** adj. —**dis·gust′ing** adj.

**dish** (dĭsh) n. **1.** An open, shallow container for food. **2.** A particular preparation of food.

**dis·heart·en** (dĭs-härt′n) v. To discourage. —**dis·heart′en·ing·ly** adv.

**dis·hon·est** (dĭs-ŏn′ĭst) adj. Not honest. —**dis·hon′est·ly** adv. —**dis·hon′es·ty** n.

**dis·hon·or** (dĭs-ŏn′ər) n. Loss of honor; disgrace. —v. To deprive of honor; disgrace. —**dis·hon′or·a·ble** adj. —**dis·hon′or·a·bly** adv.

**dis·il·lu·sion** (dĭs′ĭ-lōō′zhən) v. To free of illusion. —**dis′il·lu′sion·ment** n.

**dis·in·fect** (dĭs′ĭn-fĕkt′) v. To cleanse of germs. —**dis′in·fec′tant** n.

**dis·in·her·it** (dĭs′ĭn-hĕr′ĭt) v. To prevent from inheriting.

**dis·in·te·grate** (dĭs-ĭn′tə-grāt′) v. -grated, -grating. To separate into fragments. —**dis·in′te·gra′tion** n.

**dis·in·ter·est·ed** (dĭs-ĭn′trĭ-stĭd, -ĭn′tə-rĕs′- tĭd) adj. Impartial. —**dis·in′ter·est·ed·ly** adv.

**disk** (dĭsk) n. Any thin, flat, circular plate.

**dis·like** (dĭs-līk′) n. Distaste or aversion. —**dis·like′** v.

**dis·lo·cate** (dĭs′lō-kāt, dĭs-lō′kāt′) v. -cated, -cating. **1.** To displace from the normal position. **2.** To upset; disturb. —**dis′lo·ca′tion** n.

**dis·mal** (dĭz′məl) adj. Causing gloom. —**dis′mal·ly** adv.

**dis·man·tle** (dĭs-mănt′l) v. -tled, -tling. To take apart. —**dis·man′tle·ment** n.

**dis·may** (dĭs-mā′) v. **1.** To make anxious or afraid. **2.** To discourage. —n. Consternation.

**dis·miss** (dĭs-mĭs′) v. **1.** To discharge, as from employment. **2.** To direct to leave. **3.** To reject. —**dis·miss′al** n.

**dis·o·bey** (dĭs′ə-bā′) v. To fail or refuse to obey. —**dis′o·be′di·ence** n. —**dis′o·be′di·ent** adj.

**dis·or·der** (dĭs-ôr′dər) n. **1.** Lack of order. **2.** A public disturbance. **3.** An illness. —**dis·or′der·ly** adj.

**dis·own** (dĭs-ōn′) v. To repudiate.

**dis·par·age** (dĭs-păr′ĭj) v. -aged, -aging. To belittle. —**dis·par′age·ment** n. —**dis·par′ag·ing·ly** adv.

**dis·pa·rate** (dĭs′pər-ĭt, dĭs-păr′ĭt) adj. Distinct; dissimilar. —**dis′pa·rate·ly** adv. —**dis·par′i·ty** n.

**dis·patch** (dĭs-păch′) v. **1.** To send. **2.** To perform promptly. —n. **1.** The act of dispatching. **2.** Efficient performance. **3.** A message. **4.** A shipment. —**dis·patch′er** n.

**dis·pel** (dĭs-pĕl′) v. -pelled, -pelling. To drive away.

**dis·pense** (dĭs-pĕns′) v. -pensed, -pensing. **1.** To distribute; give out. **2.** To exempt. —**dis′pen·sa′tion** n. —**dis·pens′er** n.

**dis·perse** (dĭs-pûrs′) v. -persed, -persing. **1.** To scatter. **2.** To distribute. —**dis·per′sal, dis·per′sion** n.

**dis·place** (dĭs-plās′) v. -placed, -placing. **1.** To remove from a place or position. **2.** To take the place of. —**dis·place′ment** n.

**dis·play** (dĭs-plā′) v. To place in view; show. —n. **1.** An act of displaying. **2.** Something displayed.

**dis·please** (dĭs-plēz′) v. -pleased, -pleasing. To annoy or irritate. —**dis·pleas′ure** n.

**dis·pose** (dĭs-pōz′) v. -posed, -posing. **1.** To arrange. **2.** To settle; conclude. **3.** To incline. —**dis·pos′a·ble** adj. —**dis·pos′al** n. —**dis′po·si′tion** n.

**dis·prove** (dĭs-prōōv′) v. -proved, -proving. To prove false; refute. —**dis·proof′** n.

**dis·pute** (dĭs-pyōōt′) v. **-puted, -puting. 1.** To argue; debate. **2.** To question. —n. **1.** An argument; debate. **2.** A quarrel. — **dis·put′a·ble** adj. — **dis·put′ant** adj. & n. — **dis′pu·ta′tion** n.

**dis·qual·i·fy** (dĭs-kwŏl′ə-fī′) v. **-fied, -fying.** To declare or render unqualified. — **dis·qual′i·fi·ca′tion** n.

**dis·re·gard** (dĭs′rĭ-gärd′) v. To ignore. —n. Willful lack of regard.

**dis·re·spect** (dĭs′rĭ-spĕkt′) n. Lack of respect; rudeness. — **dis·re·spect′ful** adj.

**dis·rupt** (dĭs-rŭpt′) v. To throw into confusion. — **dis·rup′tion** n. — **dis·rup′tive** adj.

**dis·sat·is·fy** (dĭs-săt′ĭs-fī′) v. **-fied, -fying.** To make discontented. — **dis·sat′is·fac′tion** n.

**dis·sect** (dĭ-sĕkt′, dī-, dī′sĕkt′) v. **1.** To cut apart for study. **2.** To analyze. — **dis·sec′tion** n.

**dis·sent** (dĭ-sĕnt′) v. To disagree. —n. **1.** Disagreement. **2.** Political or religious nonconformity. — **dis·sen′sion** n. — **dis·sent′er** n.

**dis·sim·i·lar** (dĭ-sĭm′ə-lər) adj. Unlike. — **dis·sim′i·lar′i·ty** n.

**dis·si·pate** (dĭs′ə-pāt′) v. **-pated, -pating. 1.** To dispel or scatter. **2.** To waste. **3.** To indulge oneself intemperately. — **dis′si·pa′tion** n.

**dis·solve** (dĭ-zŏlv′) v. **-solved, -solving. 1.** To enter or cause to enter into solution. **2.** To melt. **3.** To dispel. **4.** To terminate or dismiss.

**dis·so·nance** (dĭs′ə-nəns) n. Discord. — **dis′so·nant** adj. — **dis′so·nant·ly** adv.

**dis·suade** (dĭ-swād′) v. **-suaded, -suading.** To discourage by persuasion. — **dis·sua′sion** n. — **dis·sua′sive** adj.

**dis·tance** (dĭs′təns) n. **1.** Separation in space or time. **2.** The length of a line joining two points. **3.** Coldness; aloofness. — **dis′tant** adj. — **dis′tant·ly** adv.

**dis·taste** (dĭs-tāst′) n. Dislike. — **dis·taste′ful** adj. — **dis·taste′ful·ly** adv.

**dis·till** (dĭs-tĭl′) v. To extract, purify, or produce by vaporizing and condensing. — **dis′til·la′tion** n. — **dis·till′er** n. — **dis·till′er·y** n.

**dis·tinct** (dĭs-tĭngkt′) adj. **1.** Individual. **2.** Different; unlike. — **dis·tinct′ly** adv.

**dis·tinc·tion** (dĭs-tĭngk′shən) n. **1.** A difference. **2.** A distinguishing factor or characteristic. **3.** Personal excellence. **4.** Honor.

**dis·tinc·tive** (dĭs-tĭngk′tĭv) adj. **1.** Serving to identify. **2.** Characteristic. — **dis·tinc′tive·ly** adv.

**dis·tin·guish** (dĭs-tĭng′gwĭsh) v. **1.** To recognize as distinct. **2.** To perceive distinctly; discern. **3.** To set apart. — **dis·tin′guish·a·ble** adj. — **dis·tin′guished** adj.

**dis·tort** (dĭs-tôrt′) v. **1.** To twist out of proper shape. **2.** To misrepresent. — **dis·tor′tion** n.

**dis·tract** (dĭs-trăkt′) v. **1.** To divert. **2.** To unsettle emotionally. — **dis·trac′tion** n. — **dis·trac′tive** adj.

**dis·tress** (dĭs-trĕs′) v. To cause anxiety or suffering to. —n. **1.** Anxiety or suffering. **2.** Misfortune.

**dis·trib·ute** (dĭs-trĭb′yōōt) v. **-uted, -uting. 1.** To divide and dispense in portions. **2.** To pass or send out. **3.** To spread through an area. — **dis·tri·bu′tion** n. — **dis·trib′u·tive** adj. — **dis·trib′u·tor, dis·trib′ut·er** n.

**dis·trict** (dĭs′trĭkt) n. **1.** A territorial division, esp. for administrative purposes. **2.** An area; region.

**dis·trust** (dĭs-trŭst′) n. Lack of trust; suspicion. —v. To lack confidence in. — **dis·trust′ful** adj. — **dis·trust′ful·ly** adv.

**dis·turb** (dĭs-tûrb′) v. **1.** To upset or disarrange. **2.** To intrude upon. — **dis·tur′bance** n. — **dis·turb′ing·ly** adv.

**ditch** (dĭch) n. A trench dug in the ground. —v. To discard.

**dive** (dīv) v. **dived** or **dove, dived, diving. 1.** To plunge headfirst into water. **2.** To submerge. **3.** To drop sharply. —n. An act or instance of diving. — **div′er** n.

**di·verge** (dĭ-vûrj′, dī-) v. **-verged, -verging. 1.** To tend in different directions from a common point. **2.** To differ; deviate. — **di·ver′gence** n. — **di·ver′gent** adj.

**di·verse** (dĭ-vûrs′, dī-, dī′vûrs′) adj. **1.** Unlike. **2.** Varied. — **di·verse′ly** adv. — **di·verse′ness** n. — **di·ver′si·fy** v. — **di·ver·si·fi·ca′tion** n. — **di·ver′si·ty** n.

**di·vert** (dĭ-vûrt′, dī-) v. **1.** To turn aside; deflect. **2.** To distract. **3.** To entertain. — **di·ver′sion** n. — **di·vert′er** n.

**di·vide** (dĭ-vīd′) v. **-vided, -viding. 1.** To separate or become separated into parts. **2.** To disunite. **3.** To apportion or share. **4.** To determine how many times one quantity is contained in another. — **di·vid′a·ble** adj. — **di·vid′er** n. — **di·vis′i·ble** adj. — **di·vi′sion** n. — **di·vi′sor** n.

**div·i·dend** (dĭv′ə-dĕnd′) n. **1.** A quantity to be divided. **2.** A share of profits received by a stockholder.

**di·vine¹** (dĭ-vīn′) adj. **-viner, -vinest. 1.** Of God or a god. **2.** Supremely good. — **di·vine′ly** adv. — **di·vin′i·ty** n.

**divine** 66

di·vine[2] (dĭ-vīn′) v. -vined, -vining. 1. To foretell or prophesy. 2. To guess. —di′i·na′tion n. —di·vin′er n.

di·vorce (dĭ-vôrs′, -vōrs′) n. The dissolution of a marriage by law. —di·vorce′ v.

di·vulge (dĭ-vŭlj′) v. -vulged, -vulging. To reveal. —di·vulg′er n.

diz·zy (dĭz′ē) adj. -zier, -ziest. Giddy. —diz′zi·ly adv. —diz′zi·ness n. —diz′zy v.

do (dōō) v. did, done, doing, does. 1. To perform. 2. To fulfill; complete. 3. To create, compose, or make. 4. To effect. 5. To exert. 6. To deal with. 7. To work at. 8. To be adequate. 9. To get along; fare. —do′er n.

doc·ile (dŏs′əl) adj. Tractable; submissive. —do·cil′i·ty n.

dock[1] (dŏk) n. 1. A pier or wharf. 2. The place for the defendant in a courtroom. —v. To maneuver into a dock.

dock[2] (dŏk) v. 1. To clip or cut off. 2. To withhold a part of (salary).

doc·tor (dŏk′tər) n. 1. One who holds the highest academic degree of a university. 2. A physician, surgeon, dentist, or veterinarian. —doc′tor·al adj. —doc′tor·ate n.

doc·trine (dŏk′trĭn) n. A tenet; teaching. —doc′tri·nal adj.

doc·u·ment (dŏk′yə-mənt) n. A paper bearing evidence, proof, or information. —v. To support by a document. —doc′u·men′ta·ry adj. & n. —doc′u·men·ta′tion n.

dodge (dŏj) v. dodged, dodging. 1. To avoid by moving aside. 2. To evade. —n. 1. A quick move or shift. 2. A trick; stratagem. —dodg′er n.

does (dŭz). 3rd person sing. present tense of do.

does·n't (dŭz′ənt). Contraction of does not.

dog (dôg, dŏg) n. A domesticated mammal related to wolves and foxes. —v. dogged, dogging. To track or trail persistently.

dog·ged (dô′gĭd, dŏg′ĭd) adj. Stubborn. —dog′ged·ly adv. —dog′ged·ness n.

dog·ma (dôg′mə, dŏg′-) n. A strict doctrine or system of beliefs. —dog·mat′ic adj. —dog·mat′i·cal·ly adv. —dog′ma·tism′ n.

dole (dōl) n. Relief payments to the needy or unemployed. —v. doled, doling. To distribute in small portions.

doll (dŏl) n. A child's toy shaped like a person.

dol·lar (dŏl′ər) n. The basic U.S. monetary unit.

do·main (dō-mān′) n. A sphere; field.

dome (dōm) n. A hemispheric roof.

do·mes·tic (də-mĕs′tĭk) adj. 1. Of the family or household. 2. Tame. 3. Of a country's internal affairs. 4. Indigenous. —n. A household servant. —do·mes′ti·cal·ly adv. —do·mes′ti·cate′ v. —do·mes′tic′i·ty n.

dom·i·nate (dŏm′ə-nāt′) v. -nated, -nating. 1. To control or rule. 2. To be most prominent among. 3. To overlook from a height. —dom′i·nance n. —dom′i·nant adj. —dom′i·na′tion n. —dom′i·na′tor n.

dom·i·neer (dŏm′ə-nîr′) v. To tyrannize.

do·min·ion (də-mĭn′yən) n. 1. Control; sovereignty. 2. A realm; domain.

do·nate (dō′nāt′, dō-nāt′) v. -nated, -nating. To contribute. —do·na′tion n. —do′nor n.

done (dŭn). p.p. of do.

don't (dōnt). Contraction of do not.

doom (dōōm) n. 1. Condemnation to a severe penalty. 2. A terrible fate. —v. To condemn.

door (dôr, dōr) n. A movable panel used to close an entranceway. 2. An entranceway.

dope (dōp) n. 1. A narcotic. 2. A stupid person. 3. Factual information. —v. doped, doping. To drug. —dop′er n.

dor·mant (dôr′mənt) adj. 1. Sleeping. 2. Inactive. —dor′man·cy n.

dor·mi·to·ry (dôr′mə-tôr′ē, -tōr′ē) n. pl. -ries. A large bedroom or building for a number of people.

dose (dōs) n. An amount of medicine to be taken at one time. —dos′age n. —dose v. —dos′er n.

dot (dŏt) n. A spot; point. —v. dotted, dotting. To mark with a dot or dots.

dou·ble (dŭb′əl) adj. 1. Twice as much. 2. Of or for two. 3. Something increased twofold. 2. A duplicate. —v. -bled, -bling. 1. To make twice as great. 2. To be twice as much. 3. To duplicate or fold in two. 4. To serve in an additional capacity. —adv. 1. Twice. 2. In two. —doub′ly adv.

doubt (dout) v. 1. To be uncertain about. 2. To consider unlikely. —n. 1. Uncertainty. 2. doubts. Suspicion. —doubt′er n. —doubt′ful adj. —doubt′ful·ly adv. —doubt′less adj.

dough (dō) n. 1. A mixture of flour and other ingredients baked as bread, pastry, etc. 2. Money. —dough′y adj.

douse (dous) v. doused, dousing. 1. To plunge into liquid. 2. To drench; soak. 3. To extinguish.

dove (dŭv) n. Alternate p.t. of dive.

dow·a·ger (dou′ə-jər) n. A titled or rich widow.

down[1] (doun) adv. From a higher to a lower place, position, condition, etc. —adj. 1.

Moving or directed downward. **2.** In a low position. —*prep.* In a descending direction along, upon, or through. —*v.* To put, strike, or throw down. —**down′ward** *adv. & adj.*

**down²** (doun) *n.* Fine, soft feathers. —**down′y** *adj.*

**down·fall** (doun′fôl′) *n.* A sudden loss of wealth, reputation, etc.; ruin.

**down·grade** (doun′grād′) *n.* A descending slope. —*v.* To lower the importance of.

**doze** (dōz) *v.* **dozed, dozing.** To sleep lightly. —**doze** *n.* —**doz′er** *n.*

**doz·en** (dŭz′ən) *n.* **1.** *pl.* **-en.** A set of 12. **2.** *pl.* **-ens.** A great many. —**doz′enth** *adj.*

**drab** (drăb) *adj.* **drabber, drabbest.** Dull; dreary. —**drab′ly** *adv.* —**drab′ness** *n.*

**draft** (drăft, dräft) *n.* **1.** A current of air. **2.** The depth of a vessel's keel below the water line. **3.** A document for transferring money. **4.** A gulp, swallow, or drink. **5.** Conscription for military service. **6.** A preliminary outline, version, or design. —*v.* **1.** To select for an assignment, as military service. **2.** To draw up a plan or rough outline for. —**draft′y** *adj.*

**drag** (drăg) *v.* **dragged, dragging.** **1.** To pull or draw along the ground. **2.** To search the bottom of (a body of water), as with a hook. **3.** To prolong tediously (with *out*). —*n.* **1.** The act of dragging. **2.** Something that retards motion or progress.

**drag·net** (drăg′nĕt′) *n.* **1.** A net, esp. one for trawling. **2.** A large-scale search for a criminal.

**drain** (drān) *v.* **1.** To draw or flow off gradually. **2.** To empty. **3.** To exhaust. —*n.* A pipe or channel. —**drain′age** *n.*

**dra·ma** (drä′mə, drăm′ə) *n.* **1. a.** A play. **b.** Works for the theater. **2.** A situation of interesting conflict or emotion. —**dra·mat′ic** *adj.* —**dram′a·tist** *n.* —**dram′a·tize′** *v.* —**dram′a·ti·za′tion** *n.*

**drank** (drăngk) *p.t.* of **drink.**

**drape** (drāp) *v.* **draped, draping.** **1.** To dress or hang with cloth in loose folds. **2.** To arrange in loose folds. —*n.* Often **drapes.** A long curtain. —**drap′er·y** *n.*

**dras·tic** (drăs′tĭk) *adj.* Severe; extreme. —**dras′ti·cal·ly** *adv.*

**draw** (drô) *v.* **drew, drawn, drawing.** **1.** To pull. **2.** To take or pull out. **3.** To suck or take in (air). **4.** To attract. **5.** To formulate. **6.** To withdraw (money). **7.** To evoke; elicit. **8.** To make (pictures or lines), as with a pencil; sketch. —*n.* A contest ending in a tie. —**draw′ing** *n.*

**draw·back** (drô′băk′) *n.* A disadvantage.

**draw·er** (drôr) *n.* A boxlike compartment in furniture.

**drawl** (drôl) *v.* To speak with lengthened or drawn-out vowels. —**drawl** *n.*

**drawn** (drôn) *p.p.* of **draw.** —*adj.* Haggard.

**dread** (drĕd) *v.* **1.** To fear greatly. **2.** To anticipate with anxiety. —*n.* **1.** Profound fear. **2.** Anxious or fearful anticipation. —**dread′ful** *adj.* —**dread′ful·ly** *adv.*

**dream** (drēm) *n.* **1.** A series of images, ideas, etc., occurring in sleep. **2.** A reverie. **3.** A wild fancy or hope. —*v.* **dreamed** or **dreamt, dreaming.** **1.** To experience a dream. **2.** To aspire or hope (with *of*). **3.** To imagine. —**dream′er** *n.* —**dream′y** *adj.*

**drear·y** (drîr′ē) *adj.* **-ier, -iest.** Also *poetic* **drear.** Gloomy; dismal. —**drear′i·ly** *adv.*

**dredge** (drĕj) *n.* A machine used to scoop or remove dirt, sand, etc., from under water. —*v.* **dredged, dredging.** To deepen or scoop with a dredge.

**dregs** (drĕgz) *pl.n.* The sediment of a liquid.

**drench** (drĕnch) *v.* To wet thoroughly. —**drench′er** *n.*

**dress** (drĕs) *v.* **1.** To put on clothing. **2.** To adorn or arrange. **3.** To treat (a wound). —*n.* **1.** Clothing. **2.** A one-piece skirted outer garment for women.

**dress·er** (drĕs′ər) *n.* A chest of drawers.

**drew** (drōō) *p.t.* of **draw.**

**drib·ble** (drĭb′əl) *v.* **-bled, -bling.** **1.** To flow unsteadily; trickle. **2.** To drool. —*n.* A trickle.

**dri·er** *compar.* of **dry.**

**drift** (drĭft) *v.* **1.** To carry or be carried along by a current. **2.** To wander aimlessly. **3.** To pile up. —*n.* **1.** Drifting material. **2.** A bank or pile, as of snow. **3.** A trend or general meaning. —**drift′er** *n.* —**drift′y** *adj.*

**drill** (drĭl) *n.* **1.** An implement with a pointed end for boring holes. **2.** Disciplined, repetitious training. **3.** A training exercise. —*v.* **1.** To make a hole in with a drill. **2.** To train by repetition. —**drill′er** *n.*

**drink** (drĭngk) *v.* **drank, drunk, drinking.** **1.** To swallow (a liquid). **2.** To absorb. **3.** To imbibe alcoholic liquors, esp. to excess. —*n.* **1.** A beverage. **2.** Alcoholic liquor. —**drink′a·ble** *adj.* —**drink′er** *n.*

**drip** (drĭp) *v.* **dripped, dripping.** To fall or allow to fall in drops. —*n.* The process or sound of dripping.

**drive** (drīv) *v.* **drove, driven, driving.** **1.** To push, propel, or press forcibly. **2.** To force to act or work. **3.** To operate (a vehicle). —*n.*

**1.** A trip in a vehicle. **2.** A campaign. **3.** A strong tendency or instinct. —**driv'er** n.

**driv·el** (drĭv'əl) v. **-eled** or **-elled, -eling** or **-elling.** To slobber; drool. —n. **1.** Saliva flowing from the mouth. **2.** Senseless talk. —**driv'el·er** n.

**driz·zle** (drĭz'əl) v. **-zled, -zling.** To rain gently in fine drops. —**driz'zle** n. —**driz'zly** adj.

**drone** (drōn) n. **1.** A male bee. **2.** A loafer. **3.** A humming sound. —v. **droned, droning. 1.** To hum. **2.** To speak monotonously.

**drool** (drōōl) v. To let saliva run from the mouth. —n. Saliva; drivel.

**droop** (drōōp) v. To hang downward. —**droop** n. —**droop'y** adj.

**drop** (drŏp) n. **1.** A small, rounded mass of liquid. **2.** A minute quantity. **3.** A sudden fall or decline. **4.** Vertical distance downward. —v. **dropped, dropping. 1.** To descend, fall, or let fall. **2.** —**drop'per** n.

**drought** (drout) n. A long period with no rain.

**drove** (drōv) p.t. of **drive.** —n. A flock or herd.

**drown** (droun) v. **1.** To kill or die by suffocation in water. **2.** To overwhelm or muffle.

**drowse** (drouz) v. **drowsed, drowsing.** To be half asleep; doze. —**drow'si·ly** adv. —**drow'si·ness** n. —**drow'sy** adj.

**drug** (drŭg) n. **1.** A medicine. **2.** A narcotic, esp. one that is addictive. —v. **drugged, drugging.** To administer or add a drug to. —**drug'gist** n.

**drum** (drŭm) n. **1.** A percussion instrument consisting of a hollow cylinder with a membrane stretched tightly over it. **2.** A cylindrical metal container. —v. **drummed, drumming.** To beat or thump rhythmically. —**drum'mer** n.

**drunk** (drŭngk) p.p. & p.t. of **drink.** —adj. Intoxicated with alcoholic liquor. —n. An intoxicated person. —**drunk'ard** n. —**drunk'en** adj. —**drunk'en·ly** adv. —**drunk'en·ness** n.

**dry** (drī) adj. **drier** or **dryer, driest** or **dryest. 1.** Free from liquid or moisture. **2.** Having little or no rain. **3.** Needing drink. **4.** Not sweet. **5.** Dull; boring. —v. **dried, drying.** To make or become dry. —**dry'ly** adv. —**dry'ness** n.

**dry·er** (drī'ər) n. An appliance for removing moisture, esp. by heating.

**dub** (dŭb) v. **dubbed, dubbing. 1.** To name or rename. **2.** To provide (a film) with a new sound track.

**du·bi·ous** (d/y/ōō'bē-əs) adj. **1.** Undecided. **2.** Doubtful. —**du'bi·ous·ly** adv. —**du'bi·ous·ness** n.

**duch·ess** (dŭch'ĭs) n. A duke's wife.

**duck** (dŭk) n. A web-footed water bird. —v. **1.** To lower quickly, esp. so as to avoid something. **2.** To evade; dodge. **3.** To submerge briefly.

**duct** (dŭkt) n. A tubular passage for fluid.

**dude** (d/y/ōōd) n. A dandy.

**due** (d/y/ōō) adj. **1.** Payable immediately or on demand. **2.** Owed. **3.** Fitting or appropriate. —n. **1.** Something owed or deserved. **2. dues.** A charge or fee for membership. —adv. Straight.

**du·el** (d/y/ōō'əl) n. A prearranged combat between two persons. —v. To fight in a duel. —**du'el·er, du'el·ist** n.

**du·et** (d/y/ōō-ĕt') n. A musical composition for two performers.

**dug** (dŭg) p.t. & p.p. of **dig.**

**duke** (d/y/ōōk) n. A nobleman with the highest rank. —**duke'dom** n.

**dull** (dŭl) adj. **1.** Lacking mental agility. **2.** Sluggish. **3.** Blunt. **4.** Not keenly felt. **5.** Boring. **6.** Not bright. **7.** Muffled. —v. To make or become dull. —**dull'y** adv. —**dull'ness** n.

**dumb** (dŭm) adj. **1.** Unable to speak; mute. **2.** Speechless. **3.** Stupid. —**dumb'ly** adv. —**dumb'ness** n.

**dum·my** (dŭm'ē) n., pl. **-mies. 1.** An imitation of a real object, used as a substitute. **2.** A figure imitating the human form.

**dump** (dŭmp) v. **1.** To drop in a large mass. **2.** To discard. —n. **1.** A place where refuse is dumped. **2.** A storage place.

**dunce** (dŭns) n. A stupid person.

**dune** (d/y/ōōn) n. A ridge of wind-blown sand.

**dun·ga·ree** (dŭng'gə-rē') n. **1.** A sturdy denim fabric. **2. dungarees.** Trousers of this fabric.

**dun·geon** (dŭn'jən) n. A dark cell for prisoners.

**du·pli·cate** (d/y/ōō'plĭ-kĭt) n. An identical copy; facsimile. —v. (-kāt') **-cated, -cating. 1.** To make a duplicate of. **2.** To make or perform again. —**du'pli·ca'tion** n.

**du·plic·i·ty** (d/y/ōō-plĭs'ə-tē) n., pl. **-ties.** Deliberate deceptiveness.

**du·ra·ble** (d/y/ōōr'ə-bəl) adj. Able to withstand wear and tear; lasting. —**du'ra·bil'i·ty** n.

**du·ra·tion** (d/y/ōō-rā'shən) n. **1.** Continuance in time. **2.** The time during which something exists.

**du·ress** (d/y/ŏŏ-rĕs′, d/y/ŏŏr′ĭs) n. Compulsion by threat; coercion.

**dur·ing** (d/y/ŏŏr′ĭng) prep. **1.** Throughout the course or duration of. **2.** Within the time of.

**dusk** (dŭsk) n. The darker stage of twilight. —**dusk′y** adj.

**dust** (dŭst) n. **1.** Fine particulate matter. **2.** A cloud of such matter. —v. **1.** To remove dust. **2.** To sprinkle with a powdery substance. —**dust′er** n. —**dust′y** adj.

**du·ty** (d/y/ŏŏ′tē) n., pl. -ties. **1.** Moral obligation. **2.** A task or assignment. **3.** A tax charged by a government, esp. on imports. —**du′te·ous** adj. —**du′ti·ful** adj.

**dwarf** (dwôrf) n., pl. dwarfs or dwarves. An abnormally small person, animal, or plant. —v. To cause to appear small by comparison.

**dwell** (dwĕl) v. dwelt or dwelled, dwelling. **1.** To live; reside. **2.** To linger over; emphasize (with on or upon). —**dwell′ing** n.

**dwin·dle** (dwĭnd′l) v. -dled, -dling. To waste away; diminish.

**dye** (dī) n. **1.** A substance used to color materials, hair, etc. **2.** A color imparted by dyeing. —v. dyed, dyeing. To color with or become colored by a dye.

**dyke** (dīk) n. A dike.

**dy·nam·ic** (dī-năm′ĭk) adj. Also **dy·nam·i·cal. 1.** Energetic; vigorous. **2.** Of energy, force, or motion in relation to force. —**dy·nam′i·cal·ly** adv.

**dy·na·mite** (dī′nə-mīt′) n. A powerful explosive.

**dy·na·mo** (dī′nə-mō′) n., pl. -mos. **1.** A generator, esp. one for producing direct current. **2.** An energetic person.

**dy·nas·ty** (dī′nə-stē) n., pl. -ties. A succession of rulers from the same family or line. —**dy·nas′tic** adj.

# E

**e, E** (ē) n. The 5th letter of the English alphabet.

**each** (ēch) adj. One of two or more considered individually; every. —pron. Every individual one of a group; each one. —adv. Apiece.

**ea·ger** (ē′gər) adj. Impatiently desirous. —**ea′ger·ly** adv. —**ea′ger·ness** n.

**ea·gle** (ē′gəl) n. A large bird of prey.

**ear**[1] (îr) n. **1.** The organ of hearing in vertebrates. **2.** Attention; heed. —**ear′ache** n.

**ear**[2] (îr) n. The seed-bearing spike of a cereal plant.

**ear·drum** (îr′drŭm′) n. The tympanic membrane.

**earl** (ûrl) n. A British peer ranking below a marquis. —**earl′dom** n.

**ear·ly** (ûr′lē) adj. -lier, -liest. **1.** Near the beginning of a given period of time. **2.** Occurring before the usual time. —adv. **1.** Near the beginning of a given period of time. **2.** Before the expected time.

**earn** (ûrn) v. To gain or deserve for one's labor or as a result of one's behavior. —**earn′er** n. —**earn′ings** pl.n.

**ear·nest**[1] (ûr′nĭst) adj. **1.** Serious. **2.** Sincere. —in earnest. With serious intent. —**ear′nest·ly** adv. —**ear′nest·ness** n.

**ear·nest**[2] (ûr′nĭst) n. A token or assurance of something to come.

**ear·ring** (îr′rĭng, -ĭng) n. An ear ornament.

**earth** (ûrth) n. **1.** The land surface of the world. **2.** Soil; dirt. **3.** Earth. The 3rd planet from the sun. —**earth′en** adj. —**earth′ly** adj.

**earth·quake** (ûrth′kwāk′) n. A trembling movement of the earth's surface.

**ease** (ēz) n. **1.** Freedom from pain, worry, or agitation. **2.** Freedom from awkwardness; naturalness. **3.** Freedom from difficulty; facility. —v. eased, easing. **1.** To comfort; relieve. **2.** To alleviate or lighten (discomfort); mitigate; lessen. **3.** To slacken; loosen.

**ea·sel** (ē′zəl) n. An upright frame used to support an artist's canvas.

**east** (ēst) n. **1.** The direction of the earth's rotation. **2.** Often East. The E part of any country or region. **3.** East. Asia; the Orient. —adj. & adv. To, from, or in the east. —**east′er·ly** adj. & adv. —**east′ern, East′ern** adj. —**east′ern·er, East′ern·er** n. —**east′ward** adj. & adv.

**eas·y** (ē′zē) adj. -ier, -iest. **1.** Capable of being accomplished without difficulty. **2.** Free from worry, anxiety, or pain. —adv. In a cautious, restrained manner. —take it easy. **1.** To relax. **2.** To remain calm. —**eas′i·ly** adv.

**eat** (ēt) v. ate, eaten, eating. **1.** To consume (food). **2.** To erode or corrode. —**eat′er** n.

**eaves** (ēvz) pl.n. The overhang at the edge of a roof.

**ebb** (ĕb) n. A period of declining or diminishing. —v. To fall back or recede.

**eb·on·y** (ĕb′ə-nē) n. A hard, dark wood of a tropical Asian tree. —adj. 1. Made of ebony. 2. Black.

**ec·cen·tric** (ĕk-sĕn′trĭk, ĭk-) adj. 1. Deviating from a conventional pattern. 2. Not having the same center as a circle or sphere. —n. An odd person. —**ec′cen·tric′i·ty** n.

**ec·cle·si·as·ti·cal** (ĭ-klē′zē-ăs′tĭ-kəl) adj. Of a church. —**ec·cle′si·as′tic** adj. & n.

**ech·e·lon** (ĕsh′ə-lŏn′) n. A level of authority in a hierarchy.

**ech·o** (ĕk′ō) n., pl. -oes. 1. Repetition of a sound by reflection of sound waves. 2. A sound so produced. 3. Any repetition or imitation. —v. 1. To resound with an echo; reverberate. 2. To imitate.

**ec·lec·tic** (ĭ-klĕk′tĭk) adj. Choosing or consisting of the best from diverse sources. —**ec·lec′ti·cal·ly** adv.

**e·clipse** (ĭ-klĭps′) n. 1. The obscuring of one celestial body by another. 2. A falling into obscurity; decline. —v. eclipsed, eclipsing. To obscure.

**e·clip·tic** (ĭ-klĭp′tĭk) n. The apparent path of the sun among the stars.

**e·col·o·gy** (ĭ-kŏl′ə-jē) n. The science of the relationships between organisms and their environments. —**ec′o·log′i·cal** adj. —**ec′o·log′i·cal·ly** adv. —**e·col′o·gist** n.

**e·co·nom·ic** (ĕk′ə-nŏm′ĭk, ē′kə-) adj. 1. Of the production, development, and management of material wealth. 2. Of the necessities of life. —n. **economics.** The science of the production, distribution, and consumption of commodities. —**ec′o·nom′i·cal** adj. —**ec′o·nom′i·cal·ly** adv. —**e·con′o·mist** n.

**e·con·o·my** (ĭ-kŏn′ə-mē) n., pl. -mies. 1. The careful or thrifty management of resources. 2. A system for the management of resources. —**e·con′o·mize′** v.

**ec·sta·sy** (ĕk′stə-sē) n., pl. -sies. Overwhelming delight; rapture. —**ec·stat′ic** adj.

**ec·u·men·i·cal** (ĕk′yōō-mĕn′ĭ-kəl) adj. Of the general unity of all Christian sects. —**ec′u·men′ism′** n.

**edge** (ĕj) n. 1. The sharp side of a cutting blade. 2. A rim or brink. 3. A margin; border. 4. An advantage. —**on edge.** Highly tense; irritable; impatient. —v. edged, edging. 1. To give an edge to. 2. To move gradually. —**edg′i·ness** n. —**edg′ing** n. —**edg′y** adj.

**ed·i·ble** (ĕd′ə-bəl) adj. Fit to be eaten.

**ed·it** (ĕd′ĭt) v. To prepare something for publication. —**ed′i·tor** n.

**e·di·tion** (ĭ-dĭsh′ən) n. 1. The form in which a book is published. 2. The entire number of

copies of a publication printed at one time.

**ed·i·to·ri·al** (ĕd′ə-tôr′ē-əl, -tōr′ē-əl) n. An article in a publication expressing the opinion of its editors or publishers. —adj. Of an editor. —**ed′i·to′ri·al·ize′** v. —**ed′i·to′ri·al·ly** adv.

**ed·u·cate** (ĕj′ōō-kāt′) v. -cated, -cating. To provide with knowledge, esp. through formal schooling; teach. —**ed′u·ca·ble** adj. —**ed′u·ca′tion** n. —**ed′u·ca′tion·al** adj. —**ed′u·ca′tion·al·ly** adv. —**ed′u·ca′tor** n.

**eel** (ēl) n. A long, snakelike fish.

**ef·fect** (ĭ-fĕkt′) n. 1. A result. 2. Influence. 3. Basic meaning; purport. 4. **effects.** Possessions; belongings. —**in effect.** Actually; virtually. —v. To bring about. —**ef·fec′tive** adj. —**ef·fec′tive·ly** adv. —**ef·fec′tive·ness** n.

**ef·fem·i·nate** (ĭ-fĕm′ə-nĭt) adj. Having qualities associated with women; unmanly.

**ef·fi·cient** (ĭ-fĭsh′ənt) adj. 1. Acting effectively with little waste or effort. 2. Exhibiting a high ratio of output to input. —**ef·fi′cien·cy** n. —**ef·fi′cient·ly** adv.

**ef·fort** (ĕf′ərt) n. 1. The use of physical or mental energy; exertion. 2. An attempt. 3. An achievement.

**egg¹** (ĕg) n. 1. A female reproductive cell; ovum. 2. The thin-shelled ovum of a bird, used as food.

**egg²** (ĕg) v. —**egg on.** To urge or incite.

**egg·plant** (ĕg′plănt′, -plănt′) n. A plant with large, purple-skinned fruit.

**e·go** (ē′gō, ĕg′ō) n. 1. The self. 2. Conceit; egotism. —**e·go·cen′tric** adj.

**e·go·ism** (ē′gō-ĭz′əm, ĕg′ō-) n. 1. The belief that self-interest is the most important motive force. 2. Egotism. —**e′go·ist** n. —**e′go·is′tic, e′go·is′ti·cal** adj.

**e·go·tism** (ē′gə-tĭz′əm, ĕg′ə-) n. 1. The tendency to speak excessively about oneself. 2. An exaggerated sense of self-importance; conceit. —**e′go·tist** n. —**e′go·tis′tic, e′go·tis′ti·cal** adj. —**e′go·tis′ti·cal·ly** adv.

**eight** (āt) n. The cardinal number written 8. —**eight** n. & adj. —**eighth** n. & adj.

**eight·een** (ā-tēn′) n. The cardinal number written 18. —**eight·een′** adj. & pron. —**eight·eenth′** n. & adj.

**eight·y** (ā′tē) n. The cardinal number written 80. —**eight′i·eth** n. & adj. —**eight′y** adj. & adv.

**ei·ther** (ē′thər, ī′thər) pron. One or the other. —conj. —Used before the first of two or more stated alternatives, the following one signaled by or. —adj. Any one (of two). —adv. Likewise; also.

**eke** (ēk) v. eked, eking. To make with great

effort (with *out*).

**e·lab·o·rate** (ĭ-lăb′ər-ĭt) *adj.* Planned with attention to detail; complicated. —*v.* (-ə-rāt′) **-rated, -rating.** To work out in detail; develop thoroughly.

**e·lapse** (ĭ-lăps′) *v.* **elapsed, elapsing.** To pass; slip by, as time.

**e·las·tic** (ĭ-lăs′tĭk) *adj.* **1.** Capable of returning to an initial shape after deformation; springy. **2.** Adaptable to change; flexible. —*n.* **1.** An elastic fabric. **2.** A rubber band. — **e·las·tic′i·ty** *n.*

**e·late** (ĭ-lāt′) *v.* **elated, elating.** To raise the spirits of; make happy. — **e·la′tion** *n.*

**el·bow** (ĕl′bō) *n.* **1.** The joint of the arm between the forearm and upper arm. **2.** Something having a bend similar to an elbow. —*v.* To push or shove.

**eld·er** (ĕl′dər) *n.* Alternate *compar.* of **old.** —*n.* **1.** An older person. **2.** An older, influential man of a family, tribe, etc. — **el·der·ly** *adj.*

**e·lect** (ĭ-lĕkt′) *v.* To select, esp. by vote. —*adj.* Chosen. — **e·lec′tion** *n.* — **e·lec′tion·eer** *v.* — **e·lec′tive** *adj.*

**e·lec·tor·ate** (ĭ-lĕk′tər-ĭt) *n.* The body of qualified voters. — **e·lec′tor** *n.* — **e·lec′tor·al** *adj.*

**e·lec·tric** (ĭ-lĕk′trĭk) *adj.* Also **e·lec·tri·cal.** Of, producing, derived from, produced, powered, or operated by electricity. — **e·lec′tri·cal·ly** *adv.*

**e·lec·tric·i·ty** (ĭ-lĕk′trĭs′ə-tē, ē′lĕk-) *n.* **1.** The class of physical phenomena arising from the existence and interactions of electric charge. **2.** Electric current. — **e·lec′tri′cian** *n.* — **e·lec′tri·fy** *v.*

**e·lec·tro·cute** (ĭ-lĕk′trə-kyōōt′) *v.* **-cuted, -cuting.** To kill or execute with electricity. — **e·lec′tro·cu′tion** *n.*

**e·lec·tron** (ĭ-lĕk′trŏn′) *n.* A subatomic particle having a negative electric charge.

**e·lec·tron·ic** (ĭ-lĕk′trŏn′ĭk, ē′lĕk-) *adj.* Of electrons or electronics. —*n.* **electronics.** The commercial industry of electronic devices and systems.

**el·e·gance** (ĕl′ə-gəns) *n.* **1.** Refinement and grace. **2.** Tasteful opulence. — **el′e·gant** *adj.*

**el·e·ment** (ĕl′ə-mənt) *n.* **1.** A fundamental constituent or principle of something. **2.** In chemistry and physics, a substance composed of atoms having an identical number of protons in each nucleus. **3.** elements. The forces that collectively constitute the weather. — **el′e·men′tal** *adj.*

**el·e·men·ta·ry** (ĕl′ə-mĕn′tə-rē, -trē) *adj.* **1.** Fundamental, essential, or irreducible. **2.** Of the basic aspects of a subject.

**el·e·phant** (ĕl′ə-fənt) *n.* A large mammal with tusks and a long, flexible trunk.

**el·e·vate** (ĕl′ə-vāt′) *v.* **-vated, -vating. 1.** To raise to a higher place; lift up. **2.** To raise to a higher moral level. — **el·e·va′tion** *n.*

**el·e·va·tor** (ĕl′ə-vā′tər) *n.* **1.** An enclosure raised and lowered to transport freight or people. **2.** A granary with devices for hoisting and discharging grain.

**e·lev·en** (ĭ-lĕv′ən) *n.* The cardinal number written 11. — **e·lev′en** *adj. & pron.* — **e·lev′enth** *n. & adj.*

**el·i·gi·ble** (ĕl′ə-jə-bəl) *adj.* Qualified; worthy of choice. — **el′i·gi·bil′i·ty** *n.*

**e·lim·i·nate** (ĭ-lĭm′ə-nāt′) *v.* **-nated, -nating. 1.** To get rid of; remove. **2.** To omit from consideration. — **e·lim′i·na′tion** *n.*

**el·lipse** (ĭ-lĭps′) *n.* An oval figure formed around two foci, the sum of the distances from the foci to any point on the perimeter being a constant. — **el·lip′tic** *adj.*

**elm** (ĕlm) *n.* A shade tree with arching branches.

**e·lon·gate** (ĭ-lông′gāt′, ĭ-lŏng′-) *v.* **-gated, -gating.** To lengthen; grow in length. — **e′·lon·ga′tion** *n.*

**e·lope** (ĭ-lōp′) *v.* **eloped, eloping.** To run away with a lover, esp. to get married. — **e·lope′ment** *n.*

**e·lo·quent** (ĕl′ə-kwənt) *adj.* Persuasive and fluent in speech. — **el′o·quence** *n.*

**else** (ĕls) *adj.* **1.** Other; different. **2.** In addition; more. —*adv.* **1.** In a different time, place, or manner. **2.** If not; otherwise.

**else·where** (ĕls′hwâr′) *adv.* Somewhere else.

**e·man·ci·pate** (ĭ-măn′sə-pāt′) *v.* **-pated, -pating.** To free from oppression or bondage. — **e·man′ci·pa′tion** *n.* — **e·man′ci·pa′tor** *n.*

**em·balm** (ĕm-bäm′, ĭm-) *v.* To prevent the decay of (a corpse) by treatment with preservatives. — **em·balm′er** *n.*

**em·bark** (ĕm-bärk′, ĭm-) *v.* **1.** To board or cause to board a vessel. **2.** To set out on a venture; commence. — **em′bar·ka′tion** *n.*

**em·bar·rass** (ĕm-băr′əs, ĭm-) *v.* **1.** To cause to feel ill at ease. **2.** To impede. — **em·bar′rass·ing** *adj.* — **em·bar′rass·ment** *n.*

**em·bas·sy** (ĕm′bə-sē) *n., pl.* **-sies. 1.** A mission to a foreign government. **2.** An ambassador and his staff. **3.** The headquarters of an ambassador.

**em·bel·lish** (ĕm-bĕl′ĭsh, ĭm-) *v.* To make more beautiful; adorn; add details to. — **em·bel′lish·ment** *n.*

**em·ber** (ĕm′bər) *n.* A piece of live coal or

wood.

**em·bez·zle** (ĕm-bĕz'əl, ĭm-) v. **-zled, -zling.** To take (money or property) by fraud. —**em·bez'zle·ment** n.—**em·bez'zler** n.

**em·blem** (ĕm'bləm) n. **1.** A symbol. **2.** A distinctive badge, design, etc.

**em·bod·y** (ĕm-bŏd'ē, ĭm-) v. **-ied, -ying. 1.** To invest with bodily form; make corporeal. **2.** To personify. —**em·bod'i·ment** n.

**em·boss** (ĕm-bôs', -bŏs', ĭm-) v. To cover with a raised design.

**em·brace** (ĕm-brās', ĭm-) v. **-braced, -bracing. 1.** To hug. **2.** To include. **3.** To adopt, as a cause. **4.** To accept eagerly. —n. An affectionate hug.

**em·broi·der** (ĕm-broi'dər, ĭm-) v. **1.** To ornament (fabric) with needlework. **2.** To embellish (a narrative). —**em·broi'der·y** n.

**em·bry·o** (ĕm'brē-ō') n., pl. **-os.** An organism in its earliest stages of development. —**em'bry·on'ic** adj.

**em·er·ald** (ĕm'ər-əld, ĕm'rəld) n. **1.** A brilliant, transparent green gemstone. **2.** Strong yellowish green. —**em'er·ald** adj.

**e·merge** (ĭ-mûrj') v. **emerged, emerging. 1.** To rise up or come into sight. **2.** To come into existence. —**e·mer'gence** n.

**e·mer·gen·cy** (ĭ-mûr'jən-sē) n., pl. **-cies.** A sudden, unexpected occurrence demanding immediate action.

**em·i·grate** (ĕm'ĭ-grāt') v. **-grated, -grating.** To leave one country to settle in another. —**em'i·grant** n.—**em'i·gra'tion** n.

**em·i·nence** (ĕm'ə-nəns) n. A position of superiority or distinction. —**em'i·nent** adj.

**e·mit** (ĭ-mĭt') v. **emitted, emitting. 1.** To release or send forth. **2.** To utter.

**e·mo·tion** (ĭ-mō'shən) n. **1.** A feeling, passion, or sensibility. **2.** Any strong subjective feeling. —**e·mo'tion·al** adj.

**em·per·or** (ĕm'pər-ər) n. The ruler of an empire. —**em'press** fem.n.

**em·pha·sis** (ĕm'fə-sĭs) n., pl. **-ses.** Special importance placed upon something; stress. —**em'pha·size'** v.—**em·phat'ic** adj.

**em·pire** (ĕm'pīr') n. A political unit of territories or nations ruled by a single authority.

**em·pir·i·cal** (ĕm-pĭr'ĭ-kəl, ĭm-) adj. **1.** Relying on observation or experiment. **2.** Guided by experience rather than theory.

**em·ploy** (ĕm-ploi', ĭm-) v. **1.** To use. **2.** To apply (one's time or energies) to some activity. **3.** To provide with a job. —**em·ploy'ee** n.—**em·ploy'er** n.—**em·ploy'ment** n.

**emp·ty** (ĕmp'tē) adj. **1.** Containing nothing.

**2.** Having no occupants; vacant. **3.** Lacking purpose or substance; meaningless. —v. **-tied, -tying.** To remove the contents of. —**emp'ti·ness** n.

**en·a·ble** (ĕn-ā'bəl) v. **-bled, -bling.** To supply with the means to do something.

**en·am·el** (ĭ-năm'əl) n. **1.** A glassy, opaque coating baked on metal, ceramic ware, etc. **2.** A paint that dries to a hard, glossy surface. —v. To coat with enamel.

**en·chant** (ĕn-chănt', ĭn-) v. **1.** To bewitch. **2.** To delight completely; charm. —**en·chant'er** n.—**en·chant'ment** n.

**en·cir·cle** (ĕn-sûr'kəl, ĭn-) v. **-cled, -cling.** To surround. —**en·cir'cle·ment** n.

**en·close** (ĕn-klōz', ĭn-) v. **-closed, -closing.** Also **in·close. 1.** To surround; fence in. **2.** To insert in the same container with a letter or package. —**en·clo'sure** n.

**en·com·pass** (ĕn-kŭm'pəs, ĭn-) v. **1.** To surround. **2.** To include; contain.

**en·coun·ter** (ĕn-koun'tər, ĭn-) n. **1.** A meeting, esp. when unplanned. **2.** A hostile confrontation. —v. **1.** To meet esp. unexpectedly. **2.** To confront in battle.

**en·cour·age** (ĕn-kûr'ĭj, ĭn-) v. **-aged, -aging. 1.** To impart courage or confidence to. **2.** To give support to; foster. —**en·cour'age·ment** n.

**en·croach** (ĕn-krōch', ĭn-) v. To intrude on the possessions or rights of another; trespass. —**en·croach'ment** n.

**en·cy·clo·pe·di·a** (ĕn-sī'klə-pē'dē-ə, ĭn-) n. Also **en·cy·clo·pae·di·a.** A reference work with articles on many subjects. —**en·cy·clo·pe'dic, en·cy·clo·pae'dic** adj.

**end** (ĕnd) n. **1.** An extremity; tip. **2.** A boundary; limit. **3.** The point at which something is completed; conclusion. **4.** A result; outcome. **5.** A purpose; goal. —v. To bring or come to an end. —**end'less** adj. —**end'less·ly** adv.

**en·deav·or** (ĕn-dĕv'ər, ĭn-) v. To make an attempt; strive. —**en·deav'or** n.

**en·dorse** (ĕn-dôrs', ĭn-) v. **-dorsed, -dorsing.** Also **in·dorse. 1.** To write one's signature on the back of (a check, stock certificate, etc.). **2.** To approve; sanction. —**en·dorse'ment** n.

**en·dow** (ĕn-dou', ĭn-) v. **1.** To provide with property or income. **2.** To equip with a talent or quality. —**en·dow'ment** n.

**en·dure** (ĕn-d/y/ŏŏr', ĭn-) v. **-dured, -during. 1.** To put up with; withstand. **2.** To continue in existence; last. —**en·dur'a·ble** adj.—**en·dur'ance** n.—**en·dur'ing** adj.

**en·e·my** (ĕn'ə-mē) n., pl. **-mies.** A foe.

**en·er·gy** (ĕn'ər-jē) n., pl. **-gies. 1.** Vigor or

power. **2.** Capacity for action or accomplishment. — **en·er·get·ic** *adj.*

**en·force** (ĕn-fôrs′, -fōrs′, ĭn-) *v.* -forced, -forcing. To compel obedience to. — **en·force·a·ble** *adj.* — **en·force′ment** *n.*

**en·gage** (ĕn-gāj′, ĭn-) *v.* -gaged, -gaging. **1.** To employ; hire. **2.** To attract and hold the attention of. **3.** To pledge, esp. by a promise to marry. **4.** To enter into conflict with. **5.** To interlock or cause to interlock. **6.** To become occupied. — **en·gage′ment** *n.*

**en·gine** (ĕn′jən) *n.* **1.** A machine that converts energy into mechanical motion. **2.** A locomotive.

**en·gi·neer** (ĕn′jə-nîr′) *n.* **1.** One skilled at engineering. **2.** One who operates an engine. — *v.* **1.** To act as engineer. **2.** To plan or accomplish by skillful acts or contrivance.

**en·gi·neer·ing** (ĕn′jə-nîr′ĭng) *n.* The application of scientific principles to practical ends.

**en·grave** (ĕn-grāv′, ĭn-) *v.* -graved, -graving. To carve, cut, or etch into a material. — **en·grav′er** *n.* — **en·grav′ing** *n.*

**en·gross** (ĕn-grōs′, ĭn-) *v.* To occupy the complete attention of. — **en·gross′ing** *adj.*

**en·hance** (ĕn-hăns′, -häns′, ĭn-) *v.* -hanced, -hancing. To increase, as in value or beauty. — **en·hance′ment** *n.*

**e·nig·ma** (ĭ-nĭg′mə) *n.* **1.** An obscure riddle. **2.** A person or thing that is puzzling. — **en′ig·mat′ic** *adj.* — **en′ig·mat′i·cal·ly** *adv.*

**en·joy** (ĕn-joi′, ĭn-) *v.* **1.** To experience joy in. **2.** To have as one's lot. — **en·joy′a·ble** *adj.* — **en·joy′ment** *n.*

**en·large** (ĕn-lärj′, ĭn-) *v.* -larged, -larging. To make or become larger. — **en·large′ment** *n.*

**en·list** (ĕn-lĭst′, ĭn-) *v.* **1.** To engage the assistance of. **2.** To enter the armed forces voluntarily. — **en·list′ment** *n.*

**e·nor·mous** (ĭ-nôr′məs) *adj.* Huge; immense. — **e·nor′mous·ly** *adv.*

**e·nough** (ĭ-nŭf′) *adj.* Sufficient to meet a need. — *n.* An adequate quantity. — *adv.* **1.** To a satisfactory degree. **2.** Very; quite.

**en·rich** (ĕn-rĭch′, ĭn-) *v.* To make rich or richer; add to the quality or enjoyment of. — **en·rich′ment** *n.*

**en·roll** (ĕn-rōl′, ĭn-) *v.* Also **en·rol,** -rolled, -rolling. To enter one's name or the name of another in a register, record, or roll. — **en·roll′ment** *n.*

**en·sem·ble** (än-säm′bəl) *n.* A group of parts that contribute to a single effect, as a coordinated costume or a group of musicians.

**en·tan·gle** (ĕn-tăng′gəl, ĭn-) *v.* -gled, -gling.

**1.** To twist together; snarl. **2.** To complicate; confuse. **3.** To involve inextricably. — **en·tan′gle·ment** *n.*

**en·ter** (ĕn′tər) *v.* **1.** To come or go into. **2.** To penetrate; pierce. **3.** To enroll. **4.** To become a participant in; join. **5.** To place on record.

**en·ter·prise** (ĕn′tər-prīz′) *n.* **1.** An undertaking; project. **2.** Readiness to venture; initiative. — **en′ter·pris′ing** *adj.*

**en·ter·tain** (ĕn′tər-tān′) *v.* **1.** To hold the attention of; amuse. **2.** To extend hospitality toward. **3.** To hold in mind. — **en·ter·tain′er** *n.* — **en′ter·tain′ing** *adj.* — **en′ter·tain′ment** *n.*

**en·thu·si·asm** (ĕn-thōō′zē-ăz′əm, ĭn-) *n.* **1.** Great interest or excitement. **2.** Something that inspires a lively interest. — **en·thuse′** *v.* — **en·thu′si·ast** *n.* — **en·thu′si·as′tic** *adj.*

**en·tire** (ĕn-tîr′, ĭn-) *adj.* Whole; complete. — **en·tire′ly** *adv.* — **en·tire′ty** *n.*

**en·ti·tle** (ĕn-tīt′l, ĭn-) *v.* -tled, -tling. **1.** To give a name to. **2.** To give (one) a right.

**en·ti·ty** (ĕn′tə-tē) *n., pl.* -ties. **1.** The fact of existence. **2.** Something that exists independently.

**en·trance** (ĕn′trəns) *n.* **1.** The act of entering. **2.** A passage or opening. **3.** Admission.

**en·trée** (än′trā) *n.* Also **en·tree.** The main course of a meal.

**en·tre·pre·neur** (än′trə-prə-nûr′) *n.* A person who organizes, operates, and assumes the risk for business ventures.

**en·try** (ĕn′trē) *n., pl.* -tries. **1.** An entrance. **2.** An item included in a list. **3.** A participant in a competition.

**en·vel·op** (ĕn-vĕl′əp, ĭn-) *v.* -oped, -oping. **1.** To enclose. **2.** To surround.

**en·ve·lope** (ĕn′və-lōp′, än′-) *n.* **1.** Something that envelops; cover. **2.** A paper container for a letter.

**en·vi·a·ble** (ĕn′vē-ə-bəl) *adj.* Highly desirable. — **en′vi·a·ble·ness** *n.* — **en′vi·a·bly** *adv.*

**en·vi·ron·ment** (ĕn-vī′rən-mənt, ĭn-) *n.* **1.** Surroundings. **2.** The external conditions that affect the growth and development of organisms. — **en·vi′ron·men′tal** *adj.*

**en·voy** (ĕn′voi, än′-) *n.* **1.** A messenger. **2.** A diplomatic representative.

**en·vy** (ĕn′vē) *n.* Discontent aroused by another's possessions or qualities, with a strong desire to have them for oneself. — *v.* -vied, -vying. To feel envy for. — **en′vi·ous** *adj.* — **en′vi·ous·ly** *adv.*

**ep·ic** (ĕp′ĭk) *n.* A long narrative poem about heroic characters and deeds. — *adj.* Grand; heroic.

**ep·i·dem·ic** (ĕp'ə-dĕm'ĭk) adj. Spreading rapidly among many in an area. —n. A contagious disease that spreads rapidly.

**ep·i·lep·sy** (ĕp'ə-lĕp'sē) n. A nervous disorder characterized by convulsions. —**ep'i·lep'tic** adj. & n.

**ep·i·logue** (ĕp'ə-lôg', -lŏg') n. Also **ep·i·log**. A short concluding section at the end of any literary work.

**ep·i·neph·rine** (ĕp'ə-nĕf'rĭn) n. 1. A hormone that stimulates involuntary nerve action. 2. A compound used as a heart stimulant and asthma medication.

**e·pis·co·pal** (ĭ-pĭs'kə-pəl) adj. Of a bishop.

**ep·i·sode** (ĕp'ə-sōd') n. 1. An incident in a continuous experience. 2. A portion of a narrative that relates an event.

**ep·och** (ĕp'ək) n. A particular period of history, esp. one that is memorable.

**e·qual** (ē'kwəl) adj. 1. Having the same capability. 2. Alike; identical. 3. Having the same status, rights, etc. 4. Qualified; fit. —n. One that is equal to another. —v. 1. To be equal to, esp. in value. 2. To do or produce something equal to. —**e·qual'i·ty** n. —**e'qual·ly** adv.

**e·qua·tion** (ĭ-kwā'zhən, -shən) n. A mathematical statement that two quantities are equal.

**e·qua·tor** (ĭ-kwā'tər) n. The imaginary circle dividing the earth's surface between the N and S hemispheres. —**e'qua·to'ri·al** adj.

**e·qui·lib·ri·um** (ē'kwə-lĭb'rē-əm) n. Any condition in which all acting influences are stable; balance.

**e·qui·nox** (ē'kwə-nŏks', ĕk'wə-) n. Either of the two times during a year when the length of day and night are approximately equal.

**e·quip** (ĭ-kwĭp') v. **equipped, equipping**. To supply with what is needed or wanted. —**equip'ment** n.

**e·quiv·a·lent** (ĭ-kwĭv'ə-lənt) adj. Equal; similar in effect. —n. That which is equivalent. —**e·quiv'a·lence** n.

**e·ra** (ĭr'ə, ĕr'ə) n. A period of time.

**e·rase** (ĭ-rās') v. **erased, erasing**. 1. To rub, scrape, or blot out. 2. To remove all traces of. —**e·ras'er** n. —**e·ra'sure** n.

**e·rect** (ĭ-rĕkt') adj. Standing upright; vertical. —v. 1. To construct; build. 2. To raise upright; set on end. —**e·rec'tion** n.

**e·ro·sion** (ĭ-rō'zhən) n. A natural process by which earth or rock is gradually worn away and removed by wind, water, etc. —**e·rode'** v.

**e·rot·ic** (ĭ-rŏt'ĭk) adj. Of sexual love.

**er·rand** (ĕr'ənd) n. A short trip taken for a specific purpose.

**er·rat·ic** (ĭ-răt'ĭk) adj. Irregular; inconsistent. —**er·rat'i·cal·ly** adv.

**er·ror** (ĕr'ər) n. 1. A mistake. 2. A transgression; wrongdoing.

**er·u·dite** (ĕr'y/ōō-dīt') adj. Deeply learned. —**er·u·di'tion** n.

**e·rupt** (ĭ-rŭpt') v. To emerge or eject violently. —**e·rup'tion** n.

**es·ca·late** (ĕs'kə-lāt') v. **-lated, -lating**. To increase or intensify. —**es'ca·la'tion** n.

**es·cape** (ĕs-kāp', ĭ-skāp') v. **-caped, -caping**. 1. To break from confinement; get free. 2. To avoid; elude. —n. 1. The act of escaping. 2. Temporary freedom from trouble. —**es'cap·ee'** n.

**es·cort** (ĕs'kôrt') n. 1. A person or vehicle accompanying another to give guidance or protection or to pay honor. 2. A male companion of a woman in public. —v. (ĕs-kôrt'). To accompany as an escort.

**e·soph·a·gus** (ĭ-sŏf'ə-gəs) n. A tube for the passage of food from the pharynx to the stomach.

**es·pe·cial** (ĕ-spĕsh'əl, ĭ-spĕsh'-) adj. Special; exceptional. —**es·pe'cial·ly** adv.

**es·say** (ĕs'ā, ĕ-sā') v. To try. —n. 1. An attempt. 2. A short literary composition on a single subject. —**es'say'ist** n.

**es·sence** (ĕs'əns) n. 1. The intrinsic properties of a thing. 2. A concentrated extract of a substance.

**es·sen·tial** (ĭ-sĕn'shəl) adj. 1. Constituting the essence of something; basic. 2. Indispensable; necessary. —n. An essential thing.

**es·tab·lish** (ĕ-stăb'lĭsh, ĭ-stăb'-) v. 1. To settle securely in a position. 2. To found or create. 3. To prove. —**es·tab'lish·ment** n.

**es·tate** (ĕ-stāt', ĭ-stāt') n. 1. A sizable piece of land with a large house. 2. All of one's possessions.

**es·teem** (ĕ-stēm', ĭ-stēm') v. To regard favorably; respect. —n. Favorable regard; respect.

**es·ti·mate** (ĕs'tə-māt') v. **-mated, -mating**. 1. To calculate approximately the likely cost, quantity, or extent of. 2. To evaluate. —n. (-mĭt). 1. A rough or preliminary calculation, as of the cost of work to be undertaken. 2. An opinion. —**es·ti·ma'tion** n.

**es·trange** (ĕs-trānj') v. **-tranged, -tranging**. To alienate the affections of.

**etch** (ĕch) v. To make (a pattern) on a surface with acid. —**etch'er** n. —**etch'ing** n.

**e·ter·nal** (ĭ-tûr'nəl) adj. 1. Without beginning or end. 2. Lasting; timeless. —**e·ter'nal·ly**

ly *adv.* —**e·ter'ni·ty** *n.*

**e·ther** (ē'thər) *n.* Also **ae·ther.** **1.** A liquid used as an anesthetic. **2.** The heavens.

**e·the·re·al** (ĭ-thîr'ē-əl) *adj.* **1.** Highly refined; delicate. **2.** Heavenly; spiritual.

**eth·ic** (ĕth'ĭk) *n.* A principle of right or good conduct or a body of such principles. —*n.* **ethics.** **1.** *(takes sing. v.).* The study of the nature of morals and moral choices. **2.** Any set of moral principles or values. —**eth'i·cal** *adj.* —**eth'i·cal·ly** *adv.*

**eth·nic** (ĕth'nĭk) *adj.* Of a specific race or social group. —**eth'ni·cal·ly** *adv.*

**et·i·quette** (ĕt'ə-kĕt', -kĭt) *n.* Prescribed social behavior and manners.

**et·y·mol·o·gy** (ĕt'ə-mŏl'ə-jē) *n., pl.* **-gies.** The origin and historical development of a word. —**et'y·mo·log'i·cal** *adj.* —**et'y·mol'o·gist** *n.*

**e·vac·u·ate** (ĭ-văk'yōō-āt') *v.* **-ated, -ating. 1.** To remove the contents of. **2.** To withdraw. —**e·vac'u·a'tion** *n.* —**e·vac'u·ee'** *n.*

**e·vade** (ĭ-vād') *v.* **evaded, evading.** To escape or avoid by cleverness. —**e·va'sion** *n.* —**e·va'sive** *adj.* —**e·va'sive·ness** *n.*

**e·val·u·ate** (ĭ-văl'yōō-āt') *v.* **-ated, -ating.** To ascertain or judge. —**e·val'u·a'tion** *n.*

**e·van·gel·i·cal** (ē'văn-jĕl'ĭ-kəl) *adj.* Also **e·van·gel·ic.** Of the Christian Gospel.

**e·van·gel·ism** (ĭ-văn'jə-lĭz'əm) *n.* The preaching of the Gospel. —**e·van'gel·ist** *n.*

**e·vap·o·rate** (ĭ-văp'ə-rāt') *v.* **-rated, -rating. 1.** To change into a vapor. **2.** To vanish. —**e·vap'o·ra'tion** *n.*

**eve** (ēv) *n.* The evening or day preceding a holiday or a certain event.

**e·ven** (ē'vən) *adj.* **1.** Flat; smooth; level. **2.** Uniform; steady; regular. **3.** Tranquil; calm. **4.** Equal; balanced. **5.** Exactly divisible by 2. —*v.* To make or become even. —**e'ven·ly** *adv.* —**e'ven·ness** *n.*

**eve·ning** (ēv'nĭng) *n.* Late afternoon and early night.

**e·vent** (ĭ-vĕnt') *n.* **1.** An occurrence, esp. a significant one. **2.** One of the items in a sports program. —**e·vent'ful** *adj.*

**ev·er** (ĕv'ər) *adv.* **1.** At any time. **2.** In any way.

**ev·er·green** (ĕv'ər-grēn') *adj.* Having foliage that remains green all year. —*n.* An evergreen tree or plant.

**ev·er·y** (ĕv'rē, -ə-rē) *adj.* **1.** Each without exception. **2.** Not lacking anything necessary; complete. —**eve'ry·bod'y, eve'ry·one', eve'ry·place', eve'ry·where'** *adv.*

**e·vict** (ĭ-vĭkt') *v.* To expel (a tenant) by legal

process; force out. —**e·vic'tion** *n.*

**ev·i·dence** (ĕv'ə-dəns) *n.* The data on which a judgment or proof can be based. —*v.* **-denced, -dencing.** To indicate clearly.

**ev·i·dent** (ĕv'ə-dənt) *adj.* Easily recognized; obvious. —**ev'i·dent·ly** *adv.*

**e·vil** (ē'vəl) *adj.* **1.** Wicked. **2.** Injurious; harmful. —*n.* Wickedness.

**e·vo·lu·tion** (ĕv'ə-lōō'shən) *n.* A gradual process in which something changes, esp. into a more complex form.

**ewe** (yōō) *n.* A female sheep.

**ex·act** (ĕg-zăkt') *adj.* Strictly accurate. —**ex·act'ly** *adv.*

**ex·ag·ger·ate** (ĕg-zăj'ə-rāt', ĭg-) *v.* **-ated, -ating.** To enlarge (something) disproportionately; overstate. —**ex·ag·ger·a'tion** *n.*

**ex·am·ine** (ĕg-zăm'ĭn, ĭg-) *v.* **-ined, -ining. 1.** To inspect or analyze in detail. **2.** To test knowledge or skills. **3.** To interrogate formally. —**ex·am·i·na'tion** *n.* —**ex·am'in·er** *n.*

**ex·am·ple** (ĕg-zăm'pəl, -zăm'pəl, ĭg-) *n.* **1.** One representative of a group; a sample. **2.** A model. **3.** One that serves as a warning.

**ex·ceed** (ĕk-sēd', ĭk-) *v.* **1.** To be greater than; surpass. **2.** To go or be beyond the limits of. —**ex·ceed'ing** *adj.*

**ex·cel·lent** (ĕk'sə-lənt) *adj.* Exceptionally good; superb. —**ex'cel·lence** *n.* —**ex'cel·lent·ly** *adv.*

**ex·cept** (ĕk-sĕpt', ĭk-) *prep.* With the exclusion of; but. —*conj.* Were it not for the fact that; only. —*v.* To leave out; exclude.

**ex·cep·tion** (ĕk-sĕp'shən, ĭk-) *n.* **1.** An exclusion or omission. **2.** A case that does not conform to normal rules.

**ex·cep·tion·al** (ĕk-sĕp'shən-əl, ĭk-) *adj.* Uncommon; extraordinary.

**ex·cerpt** (ĕk'sûrpt') *n.* A passage selected from a speech, book, etc.

**ex·cess** (ĕk-sĕs', ĭk-, ĕk'sĕs') *n.* **1.** An amount beyond what is required; superfluity. **2.** Overindulgence. —*adj.* Being more than is required. —**ex·ces'sive** *adj.*

**ex·change** (ĕks-chānj', ĭks-) *v.* **-changed, -changing. 1.** To give and receive reciprocally; trade. **2.** To replace (one thing by another). —*n.* **1.** An act of exchanging. **2.** A place where things are exchanged.

**ex·cise** (ĕk'sīz', ĕk-sīz', ĭk-) *n.* A tax on certain commodities within a country.

**ex·cite** (ĕk-sīt', ĭk-) *v.* **-cited, -citing. 1.** To stimulate; stir to activity. **2.** To arouse strong feeling in (a person); provoke. —**ex·cit'ed·ly** *adv.* —**ex·cite'ment** *n.*

**ex·claim** (ĕks-klām', ĭks-) *v.* To cry out or speak suddenly. —**ex'cla·ma'tion** *n.*

**ex·clude** (ĕks-klōōd', ĭks-) v. -cluded, -cluding. 1. To prevent from entering a place, group, etc.; bar. 2. To force out; expel. — **ex·clu·sion** n.

**ex·clu·sive** (ĕks-klōō'sĭv, ĭks-) adj. 1. Not divided or shared with others. 2. Admitting only certain people; select. — **ex·clu·sive·ly** adv. — **ex·clu·siv·i·ty** n.

**ex·crete** (ĕk-skrēt', ĭk-) v. -creted, -creting. To eliminate (waste matter) from the body. — **ex·cre·tion** n. — **ex·cre·to·ry** adj.

**ex·cru·ci·at·ing** (ĕk-skrōō'shē-ā'tĭng, ĭk-) adj. Intensely painful.

**ex·cur·sion** (ĕk-skûr'zhən, ĭk-) n. A short journey or pleasure trip; outing.

**ex·cuse** (ĕk-skyōōz', ĭk-) v. -cused, -cusing. 1. To forgive. 2. To overlook; condone. 3. To free, as from an obligation. —n. (-skyōōs'). An explanation.

**ex·e·cute** (ĕk'sĭ-kyōōt') v. -cuted, -cuting. 1. To carry out; perform. 2. To subject to capital punishment. — **ex·e·cu·tion** n. — **ex·e·cu·tion·er** n.

**ex·ec·u·tive** (ĕg-zĕk'yə-tĭv, ĭg-) n. One having administrative authority in an organization.

**ex·empt** (ĕg-zĕmpt', ĭg-) v. To free from an obligation or duty. — **ex·empt'** adj. — **ex·emp·tion** n.

**ex·er·cise** (ĕk'sər-sīz') n. 1. An act of employing. 2. Physical activity to develop fitness. 3. A lesson, problem, etc., designed to increase some skill. 4. Often exercises. A public ceremony. —v. -cised, -cising. 1. To put into operation; employ. 2. To subject to or engage in exercises for physical fitness.

**ex·ert** (ĕg-zûrt', ĭg-) v. To put into vigorous action. — **ex·er·tion** n.

**ex·hale** (ĕks-hāl', ĕk-sāl', ĭk-sāl') v. -haled, -haling. 1. To breathe out. 2. To emit (vapor, smoke, etc.). — **ex·ha·la·tion** n.

**ex·haust** (ĕg-zôst', ĭg-) v. 1. To let out (air or fumes). 2. To use up; expend. 3. To wear out completely; tire. —n. Vapor or fumes exhausted. — **ex·haus·tion** n.

**ex·haus·tive** (ĕg-zôs'tĭv, ĭg-) adj. Comprehensive; thorough.

**ex·hib·it** (ĕg-zĭb'ĭt, ĭg-) v. To show; display. —n. That which is exhibited. — **ex·hi·bi·tion** n.

**ex·hort** (ĕg-zôrt', ĭg-) v. To urge by strong appeal. — **ex·hor·ta·tion** n.

**ex·ile** (ĕg'zīl', ĕk'sīl') n. 1. Banishment. 2. One who has been banished from his country. —v. -iled, -iling. To send (someone) into exile.

**ex·ist** (ĕg-zĭst', ĭg-) v. 1. To be or live. 2. To occur. — **ex·is·tence** n. — **ex·is·tent** adj.

**ex·it** (ĕg'zĭt, ĕk'sĭt) n. 1. The act of going out; departure. 2. A way out.

**ex·o·dus** (ĕk'sə-dəs) n. A departure, usually of a large number of people.

**ex·or·bi·tant** (ĕg-zôr'bə-tənt, ĭg-) adj. Excessive; immoderate. — **ex·or·bi·tance** n.

**ex·or·cise** (ĕk'sôr-sīz', ĕk'sər-) v. -cised, -cising. To expel (an evil spirit) by incantation. — **ex·or·cism** n. — **ex·or·cist** n.

**ex·ot·ic** (ĕg-zŏt'ĭk, ĭg-) adj. 1. Not indigenous; foreign. 2. Having the charm of the unfamiliar; unusual.

**ex·pand** (ĕk-spănd', ĭk-) v. 1. To unfold; spread out. 2. To increase in size, extent, etc. — **ex·pan·sion** n.

**ex·panse** (ĕk-spăns', ĭk-) n. A wide and open extent, as of land.

**ex·pect** (ĕk-spĕkt', ĭk-) v. 1. To look forward to; anticipate. 2. To consider reasonable or due. — **ex·pec·tan·cy** n. — **ex·pec·tant·ly** adv. — **ex·pec·ta·tion** n.

**ex·pe·di·ent** (ĕk-spē'dē-ənt) adj. 1. Appropriate; suitable. 2. Serving to promote one's interest without regard for principle. —n. Something expedient. — **ex·pe·di·en·cy, ex·pe·di·ence** n. — **ex·pe·di·ent·ly** adv.

**ex·pe·dite** (ĕk'spə-dīt') v. -dited, -diting. To speed the progress of; facilitate. — **ex·pe·dit·er** n.

**ex·pe·di·tion** (ĕk'spə-dĭsh'ən) n. A trip or march made by a group, as for military action. — **ex·pe·di·tion·ar·y** n. — **ex·pe·di·tious** adj.

**ex·pel** (ĕk-spĕl', ĭk-) v. -pelled, -pelling. 1. To drive out; eject forcefully. 2. To dismiss by official decision.

**ex·pend** (ĕk-spĕnd', ĭk-) v. To pay out; use up; consume. — **ex·pend·a·ble** adj. — **ex·pen·di·ture** n.

**ex·pense** (ĕk-spĕns', ĭk-) n. 1. Often expenses. Money needed for a purpose. 2. Cost; sacrifice. — **ex·pen·sive** adj. — **ex·pen·sive·ly** adv.

**ex·pe·ri·ence** (ĕk-spîr'ē-əns, ĭk-) n. 1. An event or events participated in or lived through. 2. a. Activity through which knowledge or skill is gained. b. Knowledge or skill gained through activity. —v. -enced, -encing. To have as an experience; undergo. — **ex·pe·ri·enced** adj.

**ex·per·i·ment** (ĕk-spĕr'ə-mənt, -mĕnt', ĭk-) n. A test made to demonstrate a known truth, examine a hypothesis, etc. —v. To conduct an experiment; try or test. — **ex·per·i·men·tal** adj. — **ex·per·i·men·ta·tion** n.

**ex·pert** (ĕk'spûrt) *n.* A person with skill or specialized knowledge. —*adj.* Highly skilled or knowledgeable. — **ex'per·tise'** *n.* — **ex·pert'ly** *adv.* — **ex·pert'ness** *n.*

**ex·pire** (ĕk-spīr', ĭk-) *v.* -**pired, -piring. 1.** To die. **2.** To come to an end. **3.** To exhale. — **ex'pi·ra'tion** *n.*

**ex·plain** (ĕk-splān', ĭk-) *v.* **1.** To make plain or comprehensible. **2.** To offer reasons for; account for. — **ex'pla·na'tion** *n.*

**ex·plic·it** (ĕk-splĭs'ĭt, ĭk-) *adj.* Precisely expressed; clear and specific.

**ex·plode** (ĕk-splōd', ĭk-) *v.* -**ploded, -ploding.** To burst or cause to burst suddenly and violently. — **ex·plo'sion** *n.*

**ex·ploit** (ĕk'sploit') *n.* A noteworthy act or deed; feat. —*v.* (ĕk-sploit'). **1.** To utilize fully or advantageously. **2.** To make selfish or unethical use of. — **ex·ploit'a·tive** *n.* — **ex'ploi·ta'tion** *n.*

**ex·plore** (ĕk-splôr', -splōr', ĭk-) *v.* -**plored, -ploring. 1.** To investigate systematically. **2.** To travel into (an area) for the purpose of discovery. — **ex'plo·ra'tion** *n.* — **ex·plor'a·to'ry** *adj.* — **ex·plor'er** *n.*

**ex·plo·sive** (ĕk-splō'sĭv, ĭk-) *adj.* **1.** Of an explosion. **2.** Tending to explode. —*n.* A substance that explodes or causes explosion. — **ex·plo'sive·ly** *adv.*

**ex·port** (ĕk-spôrt', -spōrt', ĭk-, ĕks'pôrt', -pōrt') *v.* To send abroad, esp. for sale. —*n.* (ĕks'pôrt', -pōrt'). Something exported. — **ex·port'er** *n.*

**ex·pose** (ĕk-spōz', ĭk-) *v.* -**posed, -posing. 1.** To reveal. **2.** To lay open; to an influence or danger. — **ex·po'sure** *n.*

**ex·press** (ĕk-sprĕs', ĭk-) *v.* To make known or indicate, as by words, facial aspect, or symbols. —*adj.* **1.** Clearly stated; explicit. **2.** Used for speedy, direct transportation. —*adv.* By express transportation. —*n.* An express train, bus, etc.

**ex·pres·sion** (ĕk-sprĕsh'ən, ĭk-) *n.* **1.** Communication of an idea, emotion, etc. **2.** A facial aspect or tone of voice conveying feeling. **3.** A word or phrase. — **ex·pres'sive** *adj.* — **ex·pres'sive·ly** *adv.*

**ex·pul·sion** (ĕk-spŭl'shən, ĭk-) *n.* The act of expelling or state of being expelled.

**ex·qui·site** (ĕks'kwĭ-zĭt) *adj.* **1.** Delicately beautiful. **2.** Sensitive; discriminating. **3.** Keen; intense. — **ex'qui·site·ly** *adv.*

**ex·tant** (ĕk'stənt, ĕk-stănt') *adj.* Still in existence.

**ex·tend** (ĕk-stĕnd', ĭk-) *v.* **1.** To spread, stretch, or enlarge. **2.** To exert to full capac-

ity. **3.** To offer; tender. — **ex·tend'i·ble, ex·ten'si·ble** *adj.*

**ex·ten·sion** (ĕk-stĕn'shən, ĭk-) *n.* **1.** The act of extending or condition of being extended. **2.** An extended or added part.

**ex·ten·sive** (ĕk-stĕn'sĭv, ĭk-) *adj.* Great in extent, range, etc. — **ex·ten'sive·ly** *adv.*

**ex·tent** (ĕk-stĕnt', ĭk-) *n.* **1.** The distance over which something extends; size. **2.** Degree to which something extends; scope.

**ex·te·ri·or** (ĕk-stîr'ē-ər, ĭk-) *adj.* Outer; external. —*n.* An outer part or surface.

**ex·ter·mi·nate** (ĕk-stûr'mə-nāt', ĭk-) *v.* -**nated, -nating.** To destroy completely; wipe out. — **ex·ter'mi·na'tion** *n.* — **ex·ter'mi·na'tor** *n.*

**ex·ter·nal** (ĕk-stûr'nəl, ĭk-) *adj.* Of the outside or an outer part.

**ex·tinct** (ĕk-stĭngkt', ĭk-) *adj.* No longer existing; having died out. — **ex·tinc'tion** *n.*

**ex·tin·guish** (ĕk-stĭng'gwĭsh, ĭk-) *v.* To put out (a fire, light, etc.).

**ex·tol** (ĕk-stōl', ĭk-) *v.* -**tolled, -tolling.** To praise highly.

**ex·tort** (ĕk-stôrt', ĭk-) *v.* To obtain (money, information, etc.) by coercion or intimidation. — **ex·tor'tion** *n.* — **ex·tor'tion·ist** *n.*

**ex·tra** (ĕk'strə) *adj.* Additional. —*n.* **1.** Something additional. **2.** A special edition of a newspaper. —*adv.* Very; unusually.

**ex·tract** (ĕk-străkt', ĭk-) *v.* **1.** To draw forth or pull out by force. **2.** To pick out for separate mention; excerpt. —*n.* (ĕk'străkt'). An extracted substance or concentrated preparation. — **ex·trac'tion** *n.*

**ex·traor·di·nar·y** (ĕk-strôr'də-nĕr'ē, ĭk-, ĕk'strə-ôr'-) *adj.* Unusual; exceptional.

**ex·trav·a·gant** (ĕk-străv'ə-gənt, ĭk-) *adj.* **1.** Spending too much; wasteful. **2.** Immoderate; excessive. — **ex·trav'a·gance** *n.* — **ex·trav'a·gant·ly** *adv.*

**ex·treme** (ĕk-strēm', ĭk-) *adj.* **1.** Farthest; most remote. **2.** Final; last. **3.** Very great; intense. **4.** To the utmost degree; radical. **5.** Drastic; severe. —*n.* **1.** The greatest or utmost degree. **2.** Either of the two ends of a scale, series, etc. — **ex·treme'ly** *adv.*

**ex·trem·i·ty** (ĕk-strĕm'ə-tē, ĭk-) *n., pl.* -**ties.** **1.** The outermost point or part. **2.** A bodily limb or appendage.

**ex·tro·vert** (ĕk'strə-vûrt') *n.* One interested in others or in outside activities as opposed to self. — **ex'tro·vert'ed** *adj.*

**ex·u·ber·ant** (ĕg-zōō'bər-ənt, ĭg-) *adj.* Full of high spirits. — **ex·u'ber·ance** *n.*

**eye** (ī) *n.* **1.** An organ of vision. **2.** Ability to perceive or discern. —*v.* **eyed, eyeing** or **eying.**

To look at; regard.

**eye·ball** (ī'bôl') n. The ball-shaped portion of the eye.

**eye·brow** (ī'brou') n. The hairs covering the ridge over the eye.

**eye·glass** (ī'glăs', -gläs') n. 1. A lens used to aid vision. 2. **eyeglasses.** A pair of mounted lenses worn to correct faulty vision.

**eye·lash** (ī'lăsh') n. A hair fringing the edge of an eyelid.

**eye·let** (ī'lĭt) n. A small, often rimmed hole used for fastening with a cord or for decoration.

**eye·lid** (ī'lĭd') n. A fold of skin that can be closed over an eye.

**eye·sight** (ī'sīt') n. The faculty of sight; vision.

# F

**f, F** (ĕf) n. The 6th letter of the English alphabet.

**fa·ble** (fā'bəl) n. A brief moral story.

**fab·ric** (făb'rĭk) n. Cloth.

**fab·ri·cate** (făb'rĭ-kāt') v. -cated, -cating. 1. To make or fashion. 2. To make up (a deception). — **fab·ri·ca'tion** n.

**fab·u·lous** (făb'yə-ləs) adj. 1. Legendary. 2. Excellent or wonderful.

**fa·cade** (fə-säd') n. Also **fa·cade.** The front of a building.

**face** (fās) n. 1. The front of the head. 2. A facial expression. 3. Dignity; prestige. —v. **faced, facing.** 1. To turn or be turned in the direction of. 2. To meet; encounter. 3. To meet boldly; confront. — **fa'cial** adj.

**fac·et** (făs'ĭt) n. 1. One of the flat surfaces cut on a gemstone. 2. An aspect; phase.

**fa·ce·tious** (fə-sē'shəs) adj. Joking; humorous. — **fa·ce'tious·ly** adv. — **fa·ce'tious·ness** n.

**fac·ile** (făs'əl, -īl) adj. 1. Superficial. 2. Easy.

**fa·cil·i·tate** (fə-sĭl'ə-tāt') v. -tated, -tating. To make easier. — **fa·cil'i·ta'tion** n.

**fa·cil·i·ty** (fə-sĭl'ə-tē) n., pl. -ties. 1. An aptitude or skill. 2. Something that provides a service or assistance.

**fac·sim·i·le** (făk-sĭm'ə-lē) n. An exact copy or reproduction.

**fact** (făkt) n. 1. Something actually happening; a certainty. 2. Truth; reality. — **fac'tu·al** adj. — **fac'tu·al·ly** adv.

**fac·tion** (făk'shən) n. A group forming a usually contentious minority. — **fac'tion·al** adj. — **fac'tion·al·ism'** n.

**fac·tor** (făk'tər) n. One that actively contributes to a result or process.

**fac·to·ry** (făk'tə-rē) n., pl. -ries. A building in which goods are manufactured.

**fac·ul·ty** (făk'əl-tē) n., pl. -ties. 1. An inherent power or ability. 2. The teachers in a school.

**fade** (fād) v. **faded, fading.** 1. To lose color or brightness; dim. 2. To wither.

**Fahr·en·heit** (făr'ən-hīt') adj. Of a temperature scale that registers the freezing point of water as 32°F and the boiling point as 212°F.

**fail** (fāl) v. 1. To be deficient or unsuccessful. 2. To decline, weaken, or cease. 3. To disappoint. 4. To omit or neglect. — **fail'ure** n.

**faint** (fānt) adj. 1. Lacking strength. 2. Indistinct; dim. 3. Suddenly dizzy. —n. A brief loss of consciousness. — **faint** v. — **faint'ly** adv. — **faint'ness** n.

**fair¹** (fâr) adj. 1. Beautiful; lovely. 2. Sunny. 3. Light in color, as hair. 4. Just; equitable. 5. Moderately good. — **fair'ly** adv. — **fair'ness** n.

**fair²** (fâr) n. A gathering for buying and selling goods.

**fair·y** (fâr'ē) n., pl. -ies. A supernatural being of folklore.

**faith** (fāth) n. 1. a. Confident belief; trust. b. Religious conviction. 2. Loyalty; allegiance. — **faith'ful** adj. — **faith'ful·ly** adv. — **faith'ful·ness** n. — **faith'less** adj.

**fake** (fāk) adj. False; fraudulent. —n. 1. A counterfeit. 2. An impostor. — **fake** v. — **fak'er** n. — **fak'er·y** n.

**fall** (fôl) v. **fell, fallen, falling.** 1. To drop without restraint. 2. To come down from an erect position; collapse. 3. To be killed or wounded. 4. To be conquered. 5. To diminish. 6. To occur at a specified time or place. —n. 1. The act of falling. 2. That which has fallen. 3. Often **Fall.** Autumn. 4. An overthrow, as of a government.

**fal·la·cy** (făl'ə-sē) n., pl. -cies. An erroneous idea or opinion. — **fal·la'cious** adj. — **fal·la'cious·ly** adv.

**fal·li·ble** (făl'ə-bəl) adj. Capable of erring. — **fal'li·bil'i·ty** n.

**false** (fôls) adj. **falser, falsest.** 1. Contrary to fact or truth. 2. Insincere. 3. Artificial. — **false'hood'** n. — **false'ly** adv. — **false'ness** n. — **fal'si·fi·ca'tion** n. — **fal'si·fy'** v.

**fal·ter** (fôl'tər) v. 1. To waver or weaken. 2. To stammer. 3. To stumble. — **fal'ter·ing·ly**

**fame** (fām) n. Public esteem; renown.
—**famed** adj.

**fa·mil·iar** (fə-mĭl′yər) adj. 1. Well-known; often encountered; common. 2. Having knowledge of. 3. Friendly; intimate. —**fa·mil′i·ar′i·ty** n. —**fa·mil′iar·ize′** v. —**fa·mil′iar·ly** adv.

**fam·i·ly** (făm′ə-lē, făm′lē) n., pl. -**lies**. 1. Parents and their children. 2. Relatives. 3. A group or category of like things. —**fa·mil′ial** adj.

**fam·ine** (făm′ĭn) n. A drastic shortage of food.

**fa·mous** (fā′məs) adj. Widely known. —**fa·mous·ly** adv.

**fan¹** (făn) n. An implement for creating a cooling breeze. —v. **fanned, fan·ning**. 1. To direct a current of air upon. 2. To stir up. 3. To spread out.

**fan²** (făn) n. An ardent admirer.

**fa·nat·ic** (fə-năt′ĭk) n. A person possessed by an excessive or irrational zeal. —**fa·nat′ic**, **fa·nat′i·cal** adj. —**fa·nat′i·cal·ly** adv. —**fa·nat′i·cism′** n.

**fan·cy** (făn′sē) n., pl. -**cies**. 1. Imagination. 2. An unfounded opinion; notion. 3. A capricious idea; whim. 4. Taste or preference. —adj. -**cier, -ciest**. 1. Elegant. 2. Illusory. 3. Executed with whim. —v. -**cied, -cy·ing**. 1. To imagine. 2. To like. 3. To suppose; guess. —**fan′ci·ful** adj. —**fan′ci·ful·ly** adv. —**fan′ci·ly** adv. —**fan′ci·ness** n.

**fang** (făng) n. A long, pointed tooth. —**fanged** adj.

**fan·tas·tic** (făn-tăs′tĭk) adj. 1. Grotesque. 2. Unreal; imaginary. 3. Wonderful; superb. —**fan·tas′ti·cal·ly** adv.

**fan·ta·sy** (făn′tə-sē, -zē) n., pl. -**sies**. 1. Imagination. 2. An illusion or delusion. 3. A story based on fantastic elements.

**far** (fär) adv. **farther, farthest**. 1. To, from, or at a considerable distance. 2. To a considerable degree; much. 3. Not at all. —adj. **farther, farthest**. 1. Distant. 2. More distant; opposite.

**fare** (fâr) v. **fared, far·ing**. To get along. —n. 1. A transportation charge. 2. A passenger transported. 3. Food and drink.

**farm** (färm) n. A tract of land for producing crops or raising livestock. —v. To cultivate land or raise livestock. —**farm′er** n. —**farm′house′** n. —**farm′ing** n. —**farm′yard′** n.

**fas·ci·nate** (făs′ə-nāt′) v. -**nated, -nating**. To attract irresistibly. —**fas′ci·nat′ing·ly** adv. —**fas′ci·na′tion** n.

**fas·cism** (făsh′ĭz′əm) n. A dictatorship of the extreme right. —**fas′cist** n. & adj.

**fash·ion** (făsh′ən) n. 1. Kind; sort. 2. Manner. 3. The current style. —v. To make. —**fash′ion·a·ble** adj. —**fash′ion·a·bly** adv. —**fash′ion·er** n.

**fast¹** (făst, fäst) adj. 1. Rapid. 2. Firmly attached or fastened. 3. Loyal. 4. Proof against fading. —adv. 1. Firmly. 2. Deeply. 3. Quickly. —**fast′ness** n.

**fast²** (făst, fäst) v. To abstain from food. —**fast** n.

**fas·ten** (făs′ən, fäs′-) v. 1. To attach. 2. To make secure. —**fas′ten·er** n.

**fas·tid·i·ous** (fă-stĭd′ē-əs, fə-) adj. 1. Exacting; meticulous. 2. Difficult to please. —**fas·tid′i·ous·ness** n.

**fat** (făt) n. 1. A compound in animal and plant tissue. 2. Solidified animal or vegetable oil. 3. Plumpness. —adj. 1. Plump. 2. Oily; greasy. —**fat′ness** n. —**fat′ten** v. —**fat′ty** adj.

**fa·tal** (fāt′l) adj. 1. Deadly. 2. Ruinous; disastrous. —**fa·tal′i·ty** n. —**fa′tal·ly** adv.

**fate** (fāt) n. 1. The supposed force that predetermines events. 2. Fortune. 3. Outcome. 4. Doom or ruin. —**fat′ed** adj. —**fate′ful** adj. —**fate′ful·ly** adv.

**fa·ther** (fä′thər) n. 1. A male parent. 2. A male ancestor. 3. An originator. 4. **Father.** God. —v. To beget. —**fa′ther·hood′** n. —**fa′ther·less** adj. —**fa′ther·ly** adj. & adv.

**fa·tigue** (fə-tēg′) n. 1. Weakness or weariness. 2. **fatigues.** Military work dress. —v. -**tigued, -tiguing**. To tire out; weary.

**fat·u·ous** (făch′ōō-əs) adj. Stupid; foolish; inane. —**fa·tu′i·ty** n. —**fat′u·ous·ly** adv.

**fau·cet** (fô′sĭt) n. A device for regulating the flow of a liquid, as from a pipe.

**fault** (fôlt) n. 1. A defect. 2. A mistake. 3. Responsibility for something wrong. 4. A break in the continuity of a rock formation. —**to a fault.** Excessively. —v. To find a fault in. —**fault′less** adj. —**fault′less·ly** adv. —**fault′y** adj.

**fa·vor** (fā′vər) n. 1. High esteem. 2. An act of kindness. 3. Approval or support. —v. 1. To show favor toward. 2. To resemble. —**fa′vor·a·ble** adj. —**fa′vor·a·ble·ness** n. —**fa′vor·a·bly** adv. —**fa′vor·ite** n. & adj. —**fa′vor·it·ism′** n.

**fawn** (fôn) n. A young deer.

**fear** (fîr) n. 1. A feeling of alarm caused by expectation of danger. 2. A state of dread or awe. —v. To be afraid of. —**fear′ful** adj. —**fear′ful·ly** adv. —**fear′ful·ness** n. —**fear′less**

*adj.* — **fear′less·ly** *adv.* — **fear′less·ness** *n.*
— **fear′some** *adj.*

**fea·si·ble** (fē′zə-bəl) *adj.* Capable of being accomplished; practicable. — **fea′si·bil′i·ty, fea′si·ble·ness** *n.* — **fea′si·bly** *adv.*

**feast** (fēst) *n.* **1.** A large meal; banquet. **2.** A religious festival. —*v.* To have a feast. — **feast′er** *n.*

**feat** (fēt) *n.* A remarkable achievement.

**feath·er** (fĕth′ər) *n.* One of the structures forming the covering of birds. — **feath′er** *v.* — **feath′er·i·ness** *n.* — **feath′er·y** *adj.*

**fea·ture** (fē′chər) *n.* **1.** The shape or aspect of the face. **2.** Any distinctive characteristic. **3.** The main presentation at a motion-picture theater. **4.** An article in a newspaper or periodical. —*v.* **-tured, -turing.** To make prominent.

**Feb·ru·ar·y** (fĕb′rōō-ĕr′ē, fĕb′yōō-) *n., pl.* **-ies** or **-ys.** The 2nd month of the year.

**fe·ces** (fē′sēz) *pl.n.* Excrement. — **fe′cal** *adj.*

**fed** (fĕd). *p.t. & p.p.* of **feed.**

**fed·er·al** (fĕd′ər-əl) *adj.* **1.** Of a league or a union of states recognizing a central government. **2.** Federal. Of the central government of the U.S. — **fed′er·al·ism** *n.* — **fed′er·al·ist** *n.* — **fed′er·ate′** *v.* — **fed′er·a′tion** *n.*

**fe·do·ra** (fĭ-dôr′ə, -dōr′ə) *n.* A soft felt hat.

**fee** (fē) *n.* **1.** A fixed charge. **2.** A payment for professional services.

**fee·ble** (fē′bəl) *adj.* **-bler, -blest.** Frail; weak. — **fee′ble·ness** *n.* — **fee′bly** *adv.*

**feed** (fēd) *v.* **fed, feeding. 1.** To give food to. **2.** To eat. —*n.* Food for animals.

**feel** (fēl) *v.* **felt, feeling. 1.** To perceive by touch. **2.** To touch. **3.** To experience (an emotion). **4.** To believe in. —*n.* **1.** The sense of touch. **2.** The way something feels. — **feel′ing** *n. & adj.* — **feel′ing·ly** *adv.*

**feet** (fēt). *pl.* of **foot.**

**feign** (fān) *v.* To pretend. — **feign′er** *n.*

**fe·lic·i·ty** (fĭ-lĭs′ə-tē) *n., pl.* **-ties.** Great happiness. — **fe·lic′i·tous** *adj.*

**fe·line** (fē′līn′) *adj.* **1.** Of cats or related animals. **2.** Catlike. —*n.* A feline animal.

**fell** (fĕl). *p.t.* of **fall.**

**fel·low** (fĕl′ō) *n.* **1.** A man or boy. **2.** A comrade; associate. **3.** An equal; peer. **4.** A member of a learned society. — **fel′low·ship′** *n.*

**fel·on** (fĕl′ən) *n.* A criminal.

**fel·o·ny** (fĕl′ə-nē) *n., pl.* **-nies.** A serious crime, such as murder or rape. — **fe·lo′ni·ous** *adj.* — **fe·lo′ni·ous·ly** *adv.*

**felt¹** (fĕlt) *n.* A fabric of matted, compressed fibers of wool, fur, etc.

**felt²** (fĕlt). *p.t. & p.p.* of **feel.**

**fe·male** (fē′māl′) *adj.* **1.** Of the sex that produces ova or bears young. **2.** Feminine. —*n.* A female person, plant, or animal. — **te′male′ness** *n.*

**fem·i·nine** (fĕm′ə-nĭn) *adj.* **1.** Of the female sex. **2.** Characterized by qualities attributed to women. — **fem′i·nin′i·ty** *n.*

**fen** (fĕn) *n.* Swampy land; marsh.

**fence** (fĕns) *n.* **1.** An enclosure made of posts, boards, wire, etc. **2.** A receiver of stolen goods. —*v.* **fenced, fencing. 1.** To close in or off by a fence. **2.** To act as a fence for stolen goods. — **fenc′er** *n.* — **fenc′ing** *n.*

**fend·er** (fĕn′dər) *n.* **1.** A metal guard over the wheel of an automobile. **2.** A fireplace screen.

**fer·ment** (fûr′mĕnt′) *n.* **1.** Something that causes fermentation, as a yeast or enzyme. **2.** Unrest. —*v.* (fər-mĕnt′). **1.** To produce by fermentation. **2.** To undergo or cause to undergo fermentation. — **fer·ment′a·ble** *adj.*

**fer·men·ta·tion** (fûr′mĕn-tā′shən) *n.* Chemical conversion of compounds, esp. the conversion of sugar to carbon dioxide and alcohol by yeast.

**fern** (fûrn) *n.* A flowerless plant having divided leaves.

**fe·ro·cious** (fə-rō′shəs) *adj.* Extremely savage; fierce. — **fe·ro′cious·ly** *adv.* — **fe·roc′i·ty** *n.*

**fer·ry·boat** (fĕr′ē-bōt′) *n.* A boat used to transport passengers or goods. — **fer′ry** *v. & n.*

**fer·tile** (fûr′tl) *adj.* **1.** Capable of reproduction. **2.** Rich in material for plant growth. **3.** Highly productive; inventive. — **fer′tile·ly** *adv.* — **fer·til′i·ty** *n.* — **fer′til·i·za′tion** *n.* — **fer′til·ize′** *v.* — **fer′til·iz′er** *n.*

**fer·vent** (fûr′vənt) *adj.* Showing deep feeling; earnest. — **fer′ven·cy, fer′vor** *n.* — **fer′vent·ly** *adv.*

**fes·ter** (fĕs′tər) *v.* **1.** To generate pus. **2.** To rankle.

**fes·ti·val** (fĕs′tə-vəl) *n.* **1.** A day of feasting or special observances. **2.** A program of cultural events. — **fes′tive** *adj.* — **fes′tive·ly** *adv.* — **fes·tiv′i·ty** *n.*

**fetch** (fĕch) *v.* To go after and return with. — **fetch′er** *n.*

**fete** (fāt) *n.* Also **fête. 1.** A festival. **2.** An elaborate party. —*v.* **feted, feting.** To honor with a fete.

**fet·id** (fĕt′ĭd, fē′tĭd) *adj.* Foul-smelling.

**fet·ish** (fĕt′ĭsh) *n.* **1.** An object believed to have magical power. **2.** An object of obsessive attention. — **fet′ish·ism** *n.* — **fet′ish·ist** *n.*

**fet·ter** (fĕt′ər) *n.* **1.** A chain attached to the

**fe·tus** (fē'təs) *n., pl.* **-tuses.** The unborn young of a mammal. — **fe'tal** *adj.*

**feud** (fyōōd) *n.* A protracted quarrel. — **feud** *v.*

**fe·ver** (fē'vər) *n.* **1.** A sickness characterized by high body temperature. **2.** Heightened activity or excitement. — **fe'ver·ish** *adj.* — **fe'ver·ish·ly** *adv.* — **fe'ver·ish·ness** *n.*

**few** (fyōō) *adj.* **fewer, fewest.** Consisting of a small number. — *n.* A small number. — *pron.* A small number. — **few'ness** *n.*

**fi·as·co** (fē·ăs'kō) *n., pl.* **-coes** or **-cos.** A complete failure.

**fi·ber** (fī'bər) *n.* A slender, elongated structure; a filament or strand. — **fi'brous** *adj.*

**fick·le** (fĭk'əl) *adj.* Changeable; capricious. — **fick'le·ness** *n.*

**fic·tion** (fĭk'shən) *n.* **1.** Something invented or imagined. **2.** Literature that includes novels, short stories, etc. — **fic'tion·al** *adj.* — **fic'tion·al·ly** *adv.* — **fic·ti'tious** *adj.*

**fid·dle** (fĭd'l) *n.* A violin. — *v.* **-dled, -dling. 1.** To play a violin. **2.** To fidget. — **fid'dler** *n.*

**fi·del·i·ty** (fĭ-dĕl'ə-tē, fī-) *n., pl.* **-ties. 1.** Faithfulness; loyalty. **2.** Accuracy.

**fidg·et** (fĭj'ĭt) *v.* To move nervously or restlessly. — *n.* Often **fidgets.** Restlessness. — **fidg'et·i·ness** *n.* — **fidg'et·y** *adj.*

**field** (fēld) *n.* **1.** A broad, level expanse of open land, esp. one devoted to a particular crop. **2.** An area of activity or knowledge. — **field'er** *n.*

**fiend** (fēnd) *n.* **1.** A demon. **2.** A wicked person. — **fiend'ish** *adj.* — **fiend'ish·ly** *adv.* — **fiend'ish·ness** *n.*

**fierce** (fîrs) *adj.* **fiercer, fiercest.** Violent; ferocious. — **fierce'ly** *adv.* — **fierce'ness** *n.*

**fif·teen** (fĭf-tēn') *n.* The cardinal number written 15. — **fif·teen'** *adj. & pron.* — **fif·teenth'** *n. & adj.*

**fif·ty** (fĭf'tē) *n.* The cardinal number written 50. — **fif'ty** *adj. & pron.* — **fif'ti·eth** *n. & adj.*

**fight** (fīt) *v.* **fought, fighting. 1.** To participate in combat. **2.** To quarrel; argue. **3.** To oppose. — *n.* **1.** A battle; combat. **2.** A quarrel. — **fight'er** *n.*

**fig·ure** (fĭg'yər) *n.* **1.** A written symbol other than a letter, esp. a number. **2.** An amount. **3.** An outline or shape. **4.** A well-known person. **5.** An expression, as a simile. — *v.* **-ured, -uring. 1.** To compute. **2.** To make a likeness of. — **fig'ur·a·tive** *adj.*

**fil·a·ment** (fĭl'ə-mənt) *n.* A thin threadlike structure.

**file**[1] (fīl) *n.* **1.** A receptacle for keeping papers, cards, etc. **2.** A line of animals, or things. — **file** *v.* — **fil'er** *n.*

**file**[2] (fīl) *n.* A tool with ridged surfaces, used in smoothing. — *v.* **filed, filing.** To work with a file. — **fil'er** *n.* — **fil'ing** *n.*

**fil·i·bus·ter** (fĭl'ə-bŭs'tər) *n.* A prolonged speech made to obstruct legislative action. — **fil'i·bus'ter** *v.*

**fill** (fĭl) *v.* **1.** To make or become full. **2.** To supply the materials for. **3.** To pervade. — *n.* **1.** A full supply. **2.** A built-up piece of land. — **fill'ing** *n.*

**fil·ly** (fĭl'ē) *n., pl.* **-lies.** A young female horse.

**film** (fĭlm) *n.* **1.** Any thin layer, covering, or coating. **2.** A thin sheet with a photosensitive coating used to make photographic negatives or transparencies. **3.** A motion picture. — **film** *v.* — **film'i·ly** *adv.* — **film'i·ness** *n.* — **film'y** *adj.*

**fil·ter** (fĭl'tər) *n.* A porous substance or device through which a liquid is strained. — *v.* **1.** To pass through a filter. **2.** To remove by filtering. — **fil'ter·a·ble** *adj.* — **fil·tra'tion** *n.*

**filth** (fĭlth) *n.* **1.** Dirty matter. **2.** A dirty condition. — **filth'i·ness** *n.* — **filth'y** *adj.*

**fin** (fĭn) *n.* One of the swimming and balancing appendages of a fish, whale, etc.

**fi·nal** (fī'nəl) *adj.* Concluding; last. — *n.* The last of a series of athletic contests, school examinations, etc. — **fi'nal·ist** *n.* — **fi·nal'i·ty** *n.* — **fi'nal·ize** *v.* — **fi'nal·ly** *adv.*

**fi·nance** (fĭ-nǎns', fī'nǎns', fī'nǎns') *n.* **1.** The management of money. **2. finances.** Monetary resources. — *v.* **-nanced, -nancing.** To supply the capital for. — **fi·nan'cial** *adj.* — **fi·nan'cial·ly** *adv.* — **fin'an·cier** *n.*

**find** (fīnd) *v.* **found, finding. 1.** To come upon. **2.** To determine. **3.** To consider; regard. — *n.* What is found, esp. a rare discovery. — **find'er** *n.* — **find'ing** *n.*

**fine**[1] (fīn) *adj.* **finer, finest. 1.** Of superior quality; excellent. **2.** Enjoyable; pleasant. **3.** Sharp. **4.** Consisting of extremely small particles. **5.** Subtle or precise. — *adv.* Very well. — **fine'ly** *adv.* — **fine'ness** *n.*

**fine**[2] (fīn) *n.* A sum of money imposed as a penalty. — *v.* **fined, fining.** To impose a fine on.

**fi·nesse** (fĭ-nĕs') *n.* Artful performance or behavior.

**fin·ger** (fĭng'gər) *n.* One of the five digits of the hand. — *v.* To touch with the fingers; handle. — **fin'ger·print** *n. & v.*

**fin·ick·y** (fĭn'ĭ-kē) *adj.* Very fussy.

**fin·ish** (fĭn'ĭsh) *v.* **1.** To terminate. **2.** To complete a task. **3.** To use up. — *n.* The

conclusion of something; end. — **fin′ish·er** n.
**fi·nite** (fī′nīt′) adj. Having boundaries; limited. — **fi′nite′ly** adv. — **fi′nite′ness** n.

**fir** (fûr) n. An evergreen tree or its wood.

**fire** (fīr) n. **1.** A burning. **2.** Enthusiasm. —v. **fired, firing. 1.** To ignite. **2.** To stimulate. **3.** To shoot (a weapon). **4.** To discharge from a position. — **fier′y** adj.

**fire·arm** (fīr′ärm′) n. A pistol, rifle, etc.

**fire·place** (fīr′plās′) n. An open recess for a fire; hearth.

**firm¹** (fûrm) adj. **1.** Unyielding to pressure; solid. **2.** Fixed in place. **3.** Indicating resolution. —v. To make or become firm. —adv. Resolutely; unwaveringly. — **firm′ly** adv. — **firm′ness** n.

**firm²** (fûrm) n. A commercial partnership.

**fir·ma·ment** (fûr′mə·mənt) n. The sky.

**first** (fûrst) adj. **1.** Located before all others. **2.** Earliest. **3.** Foremost in importance or quality. —adv. **1.** Before or above all others in time or rank. **2.** For the first time. —n. **1.** The ordinal number one in a series. **2.** The one occurring or ranking first. **3.** The beginning. **4.** The lowest forward gear in a vehicle. — **first′ly** adv.

**fis·cal** (fis′kəl) adj. Of finances. — **fis′cal·ly** adv.

**fish** (fish) n., pl. **fish** or **fishes**. **1.** An aquatic vertebrate having fins and gills. **2.** Its edible flesh. —v. To catch or try to catch fish. — **fish′er·man** n. — **fish′er·y** n. — **fish′i·ness** n. — **fish′ing** n. — **fish′y** adj.

**fis·sion** (fish′ən) n. The act or process of splitting into parts. — **fis′sion·a·ble** adj.

**fis·sure** (fish′ər) n. A narrow groove, crack, or split.

**fist** (fist) n. The hand closed tightly.

**fit** (fit) v. **fitted** or **fit, fitted, fitting. 1.** To be or make the proper size and shape (for). **2.** To be suitable. **3.** To equip. —adj. **fitter, fittest. 1.** Appropriate; proper. **2.** Healthy. —n. The manner in which clothing fits. — **fit′ly** adv. — **fit′ness** n. — **fit′ting** adj. & n. — **fit′ting·ly** adv. — **fit′ting·ness** n.

**fit·ful** (fit′fəl) adj. Intermittent; irregular. — **fit′ful·ly** adv. — **fit′ful·ness** n.

**five** (fīv) n. The cardinal number written 5. — **fifth** n. & adj. — **five** adj. & pron.

**fix** (fiks) v. **1.** To place or fasten securely. **2.** To repair. **3.** To direct steadily, as a stare. **4.** To put together; prepare. —n. **1.** A predicament; dilemma. **2.** A position, as of a ship or aircraft, as determined by observations or radio. — **fix′a·tive** adj. — **fixed** adj. — **fix′ed·ly** adv. — **fix′er** n.

**fix·a·tion** (fik·sā′shən) n. A strong attachment to a person or thing.

**fix·ture** (fiks′chər) n. Something attached as a permanent appendage, apparatus, or appliance.

**flab·by** (flăb′ē) adj. **-bier, -biest.** Lacking firmness. — **flab′bi·ly** adv. — **flab′bi·ness** n.

**flag¹** (flăg) n. A piece of fabric used as a symbol, signal, etc. —v. **flagged, flagging. 1.** To mark with a flag. **2.** To signal with or as with a flag.

**flag²** (flăg) v. **flagged, flagging. 1.** To hang limply; droop. **2.** To become languid; tire. **3.** To grow dull.

**fla·grant** (flā′grənt) adj. Extremely conspicuous; shocking. — **fla′grance, fla′gran·cy** n. — **fla′grant·ly** adv.

**flair** (flâr) n. A natural aptitude.

**flake** (flāk) n. A thin piece or fragment. —v. **flaked, flaking.** To come off in flakes. — **flak′y** adj.

**flam·boy·ant** (flăm-boi′ənt) adj. Highly elaborate; showy. — **flam·boy′ance** n. — **flam·boy′ant·ly** adv.

**flame** (flām) n. **1.** Active, blazing combustion. **2.** A violent or intense passion. —v. **flamed, flaming. 1.** To burn brightly. **2.** To burst into or as into flame.

**flam·ma·ble** (flăm′ə·bəl) adj. Easily ignitable.

**flank** (flăngk) n. A side or lateral part. —v. **1.** To be at the side of. **2.** To go around the flank of.

**flan·nel** (flăn′əl) n. A soft woven cloth of wool or a wool blend.

**flap** (flăp) v. **flapped, flapping. 1.** To wave up and down, as wings; beat. **2.** To swing loosely. —n. **1.** An appendage attached on one side, as of an envelope. **2.** The action or sound of flapping. **3.** A control on an aircraft wing.

**flare** (flâr) v. **flared, flaring. 1.** To flame up with a bright, wavering light. **2.** To expand outward, as a bell. —n. **1.** A brief blaze. **2.** A device that produces a bright light, as for signaling. **3.** An expanding contour.

**flash** (flăsh) v. **1.** To occur suddenly in or as in flame. **2.** To be or cause to be lighted intermittently. **3.** To move rapidly. **4.** To signal with light. —n. **1.** A brief, intense light. **2.** An instant. **3.** A brief news dispatch.

**flash·y** (flăsh′ē) adj. **-ier, -iest.** Showy; gaudy.

**flask** (flăsk, fläsk) n. A small bottle-shaped container.

**flat¹** (flăt) adj. **flatter, flattest. 1.** Having a

smooth, even, level surface. **2.** Lying prone; prostrate. **3.** Unequivocal. **4.** Fixed, as a rate. **5.** Flavorless. **6.** Deflated, as a tire. **7.** In music, being below the intended pitch. —*adv.* **1.** Horizontally. **2.** Prostrate. **3.** In music, below the intended pitch. —*n.* **1.** A flat object, surface, or part. **2.** A deflated tire. — **flat'ly** *adv.* — **flat'ness** *n.* — **flat'ten** *v.*

**flat²** (flăt) *n.* An apartment.

**flat·ter** (flăt'ər) *v.* To compliment, often insincerely. — **flat'ter·er** *n.* — **flat'ter·ing** *adj.* — **flat'ter·y** *n.*

**flaunt** (flônt) *v.* To exhibit ostentatiously; show off. — **flaunt'er** *n.*

**fla·vor** (flā'vər) *n.* A distinctive taste. —*v.* To give flavor to. — **fla'vor·ing** *n.*

**flaw** (flô) *n.* An imperfection; defect. — **flaw'less** *adj.*

**flay** (flā) *v.* To strip off the skin of. — **flay'er** *n.*

**flea** (flē) *n.* A bloodsucking, parasitic insect.

**fleck** (flĕk) *n.* A tiny mark or spot. —*v.* To spot or streak.

**flee** (flē) *v.* **fled, fleeing.** To run away, as from danger. — **fle'er** *n.*

**fleece** (flēs) *n.* The coat of wool of a sheep. —*v.* **fleeced, fleecing.** **1.** To shear the fleece from. **2.** To swindle. — **fleec'i·ness** *n.* — **fleec'y** *adj.*

**fleet¹** (flēt) *n.* A number of ships, esp. warships.

**fleet²** (flēt) *adj.* Moving swiftly; rapid. — **fleet'ing** *adj.* — **fleet'ing·ly** *adv.* — **fleet'ness** *n.*

**flesh** (flĕsh) *n.* **1.** The soft tissue of the body. **2.** Meat. **3.** The pulpy part of a fruit or vegetable. — **flesh'i·ness** *n.* — **flesh'y** *adj.*

**flew** (floō). *p.t.* of **fly¹**.

**flex** (flĕks) *v.* **1.** To bend. **2.** To contract (a muscle). — **flex'i·bil'i·ty** *n.* — **flex'i·ble** *adj.* — **flex'i·bly** *adv.*

**flick** (flĭk) *n.* A light, quick motion or touch. — **flick** *v.*

**flick·er** (flĭk'ər) *v.* To yield irregular light. —*n.* **1.** A brief or wavering light. **2.** A brief sensation.

**flight¹** (flīt) *n.* **1.** Motion through the earth's atmosphere. **2.** A group flying together, as of birds or aircraft. **3.** A scheduled airline run. **4.** A soaring, as of the imagination. **5.** A series of stairs.

**flight²** (flīt) *n.* A running away.

**flight·y** (flī'tē) *adj.* **-ier, -iest.** Capricious. — **flight'i·ness** *n.*

**flim·sy** (flĭm'zē) *adj.* **-sier, -siest.** Not strong or substantial. — **flim'si·ly** *adv.* — **flim'si·ness** *n.*

**flinch** (flĭnch) *v.* To shrink or wince, as from pain or fear.

**fling** (flĭng) *v.* **flung, flinging.** To throw or move forcefully. —*n.* A toss; a throw.

**flint** (flĭnt) *n.* Quartz that sparks when struck with steel.

**flip** (flĭp) *v.* **flipped, flipping.** To toss or turn with a light quick motion. —*n.* A nimble turn or motion. —*adj.* Pert.

**flirt** (flûrt) *v.* **1.** To amuse oneself in playful courtship. **2.** To move jerkily; dart. —*n.* A person who flirts. — **flir·ta'tion** *n.* — **flir·ta'tious** *adj.* — **flir·ta'tious·ly** *adv.*

**float** (flōt) *v.* **1.** To drift or be suspended on water, in space, etc. **2.** To move easily and lightly. —*n.* **1.** Something that floats. **2.** A vehicle bearing an exhibit in a parade. — **float'er** *n.*

**flock** (flŏk) *n.* A group of animals. —*v.* To congregate or travel in a flock.

**flog** (flŏg, flôg) *v.* **flogged, flogging.** To beat, esp. with a whip. — **flog'ger** *n.*

**flood** (flŭd) *n.* **1.** An overflowing of water onto land. **2.** Any abundant flow. —*v.* **1.** To cover with a flood; inundate. **2.** To fill abundantly.

**floor** (flôr, flōr) *n.* **1.** The surface of a room on which one stands. **2.** The lowermost surface, as of a forest or ocean. **3.** The right to address an assembly. **4.** A story of a building. —*v.* **1.** To provide with a floor. **2.** To knock down.

**flop** (flŏp) *v.* **flopped, flopping.** **1.** To fall down heavily. **2.** To move about clumsily. **3.** To fail. —*n.* **1.** The action of flopping. **2.** A failure.

**flo·ral** (flôr'əl, flōr'-) *adj.* Of flowers.

**flor·id** (flôr'ĭd, flŏr'-) *adj.* **1.** Ruddy. **2.** Heavily embellished.

**flo·rist** (flôr'ĭst, flōr'-, flŏr'-) *n.* One who sells flowers.

**floss** (flôs, flŏs) *n.* **1.** Silk from the cocoon of a silkworm. **2.** Any soft, fibrous substance. — **floss'y** *adj.*

**flounce** (flouns) *n.* Gathered or pleated material used for trimming, as on a garment.

**floun·der** (floun'dər) *v.* To move clumsily or in confusion. — **floun'der** *n.*

**flour** (flour) *n.* A powdery substance obtained by grinding grain. —*v.* To coat with flour. — **flour'y** *adj.*

**flour·ish** (flûr'ĭsh) *v.* **1.** To grow well; thrive. **2.** To make bold, sweeping movements. —*n.* A dramatic action or gesture.

**flout** (flout) *v.* To show contempt for.

**flow** (flō) v. **1.** To move in or as in a stream. **2.** To be plentiful. **3.** To hang gracefully. —n. **1.** The act of flowing. **2.** A continuous movement or circulation.

**flow·er** (flou'ər) n. **1.** A plant blossom. **2.** Highest development; peak. —v. **1.** To bloom. **2.** To develop fully. —**flow'er·y** adj.

**flown** (flōn) p.p. of **fly.**

**fluc·tu·ate** (flŭk'chōō-āt') v. **-ated, -ating.** To vary irregularly. —**fluc'tu·a'tion** n.

**flu·ent** (flōō'ənt) adj. Having facility in the use of a language. —**flu'en·cy** n. —**flu'ent·ly** adv.

**fluff** (flŭf) n. Something having a soft or frothy consistency, as down or nap. —v. To make light and puffy by shaking or patting. —**fluffy** adj.

**flu·id** (flōō'ĭd) n. A substance that flows readily; liquid. —**flu·id'i·ty** n. —**flu'id·ly** adv.

**flung** (flŭng) p.t. & p.p. of **fling.**

**flu·o·res·cence** (flōō-ə-rĕs'əns, flôr-ĕs'-) n. The emission of electromagnetic radiation, esp. of visible light. —**flu·o·res'cent** adj.

**flu·o·rine** (flōō'ə-rēn') n. A pale-yellow chemical element.

**flur·ry** (flûr'ē) n., pl. **-ries. 1.** A gust of wind. **2.** A light snowfall. **3.** A burst of activity.

**flush** (flŭsh) v. **1.** To redden; blush. **2.** To wash out by a gush of water. —n. **1.** A brief flow or gushing. **2.** A reddish tinge; a blush. —adj. **1.** Blushing. **2.** Prosperous. **3.** Having surfaces in the same plane; even. —adv. **1.** So as to be even. **2.** Squarely; solidly.

**flus·ter** (flŭs'tər) v. To upset. —n. A state of agitation.

**flute** (flōōt) n. **1.** A musical woodwind instrument. **2.** A groove. —v. **fluted, fluting.** To make a groove in the.

**flut·ter** (flŭt'ər) v. **1.** To wave or flap rapidly, esp. in the air. **2.** To behave in a restless manner. —n. **1.** An act of fluttering. **2.** A condition of excitement or agitation. —**flut'ter·er** n. —**flut'ter·y** adj.

**flux** (flŭks) n. **1.** Continual change or flow. **2.** A substance used, as in soldering, to facilitate melting and fusing.

**fly¹** (flī) v. **flew, flown, flying. 1.** To move or cause to move through the air with the aid of wings or winglike parts. **2.** To hasten; rush. —**fli'er** n.

**fly²** (flī) n., pl. **flies.** A winged insect.

**foal** (fōl) n. The young offspring of a horse. —v. To give birth to (a foal).

**foam** (fōm) n. A mass of gas bubbles trapped in a film of liquid. —v. To form foam; froth. —**foam'i·ness** n. —**foam'y** adj.

**fo·cus** (fō'kəs) n. **1.** A point in an optical system at which rays of light come together or from which they appear to spread. **2.** The condition or adjustment in which an eye or optical instrument gives its best image. **3.** A center of interest or activity. —v. **to·cus** v.

**fod·der** (fŏd'ər) n. Feed for livestock.

**foe** (fō) n. An enemy; adversary; opponent.

**fog** (fŏg, fôg) n. Cloudlike masses of condensed water vapor limiting visibility. —v. **fogged, fogging.** To cover or be obscured by or as by fog. —**fog'gi·ly** adv. —**fog'gi·ness** n. —**fog'gy** adj.

**foi·ble** (foi'bəl) n. A minor personal peculiarity.

**foil¹** (foil) v. To thwart.

**foil²** (foil) n. A fencing sword with a blunt point.

**foist** (foist) v. **1.** To pass off (something inferior) as genuine, etc. **2.** To impose, as by coercion.

**fold** (fōld) v. **1.** To bend over so that one part lies on another. **2.** To bring to a closed position. **3.** To wrap; envelop. —n. **1.** The act of folding. **2.** The junction of two folded parts.

**fo·li·age** (fō'lē-ĭj) n. Plant leaves.

**folk** (fōk) n. People.

**folk·lore** (fōk'lôr', -lōr') n. Traditions, tales, etc., of a people. —**folk'lor'ist** n.

**fol·low** (fŏl'ō) v. **1.** To come or go after. **2.** To pursue. **3.** To move along the course of. **4.** To engage in. **5.** To result. **6.** To be attentive to. **7.** To understand. —**fol'low·er** n. —**fol'low·ing** n.

**fol·ly** (fŏl'ē) n., pl. **-lies.** An act of foolishness.

**fond** (fŏnd) adj. **1.** Affectionate. **2.** Cherished. —**fond'ly** adv. —**fond'ness** n.

**fon·dle** (fŏn'dl) v. **-dled, -dling.** To caress.

**food** (fōōd) n. Any material that is taken in to maintain life and growth.

**fool** (fōōl) n. **1.** One lacking judgment, sense, etc. —v. **1.** To trick. **2.** To play; joke. —**fool'ish** adj. —**fool'ish·ly** adv. —**fool'ish·ness** n.

**foot** (fŏŏt) n., pl. **feet. 1.** The part of the leg that rests on or touches the ground. **2.** Something resembling a foot in position or function. **3.** A unit of length equal to 12 inches." —v. To walk. —**foot'less** adj. —**foot'print'** n.

**foot·ball** (fŏŏt'bôl') n. A game played with an inflated oblong ball on a rectangular field.

**foot·ing** (fŏŏt'ĭng) n. **1.** A secure place. **2.** A basis; foundation.

**for** (fôr, unstressed fər) prep. **1.** Directed to.

**2.** As a result of. **3.** Through the duration of. **4.** On behalf of. **5.** In place of. **6.** In favor or support of. —*conj.* Because; since.

**for·age** (fôr'ij) *n.* Food for animals. —*v.* -aged, -aging. To search for food or supplies.

**for·ay** (fôr'ā') *n.* A raid. —**for·ay'** *v.*

**for·bear** (fôr-bâr') *v.* -bore, -borne, -bearing. **1.** To refrain from. **2.** To be tolerant or patient. —**for·bear'ance** *n.*

**for·bid** (fər-bid') *v.* -bade or -bad, -bidden or -bid, -bidding. To prohibit.

**force** (fôrs, fōrs) *n.* **1.** Strength; power. **2.** Coercion. —*v.* forced, forcing. **1.** To compel to perform an action. **2.** To extort. —**force'ful** *adj.* —**force'ful·ly** *adv.* —**for'ci·ble** *adj.* —**for'ci·ble·ness** *n.* —**for'ci·bly** *adv.*

**ford** (fôrd, fōrd) *n.* A shallow place in a body of water where a crossing can be made on foot. —*v.* To cross at such a place.

**fore·bear** (fôr'bâr') *n.* An ancestor; forefather.

**fore·bode** (fôr-bōd', fōr-) *v.* -boded, -boding. To portend. —**fore·bod'ing** *n. & adj.*

**fore·cast** (fôr'kăst', -käst', fōr'-) *v.* -cast or -casted, -casting. To predict; foreshadow. —*n.* A prediction. —**fore'cast'er** *n.*

**fore·close** (fôr-klōz', fōr-) *v.* -closed, -closing. To reclaim mortgaged property, esp. for nonpayment. —**fore·clo'sure** *n.*

**fore·fa·ther** (fôr'fä'thər, fōr'-) *n.* An ancestor.

**fore·front** (fôr'frŭnt', fōr'-) *n.* The foremost part of something.

**fore·go** (fôr-gō') *v.* To precede. —**fore·go'ing** *adj. & n.*

**fore·head** (fôr'ĭd, fōr'-, fôr'hĕd', fōr'-) *n.* The part of the face between eyebrows and hairline.

**for·eign** (fôr'ĭn, fōr'-) *adj.* **1.** Of or from a country other than one's own. **2.** Situated in an abnormal place. —**for'eign·er** *n.* —**for'eign·ness** *n.*

**fore·man** (fôr'mən, fōr'-) *n.* One in charge of a group of workers.

**fore·most** (fôr'mōst', fōr'-) *adj.* Ahead of all others; first. —**fore'most** *adv.*

**fo·ren·sic** (fə-rĕn'sĭk) *adj.* **1.** Of legal proceedings. **2.** Of debate or argument.

**fore·see** (fôr-sē', fōr-) *v.* To know beforehand. —**fore·see'a·ble** *adj.* —**fore'sight** *n.* —**fore'sight·ed** *adj.*

**for·est** (fôr'ĭst, fōr'-) *n.* A growth of trees covering a large area. —**for'est·er** *n.* —**for'est·ry** *n.*

**fore·tell** (fôr-tĕl', fōr-) *v.* To predict.

**fore·thought** (fôr'thôt', fōr'-) *n.* Planning beforehand.

**for·ev·er** (fôr-ĕv'ər, fər-) *adv.* **1.** Eternally. **2.** Incessantly.

**fore·word** (fôr'wûrd', -wərd, fōr'-) *n.* An introductory note; preface.

**for·feit** (fôr'fĭt) *n.* A penalty or fine. —*v.* To surrender as a forfeit. —**for'fei·ture** *n.*

**for·gave** (fər-gāv', fōr-). *p.t.* of **forgive**.

**forge¹** (fôrj, fōrj) *n.* A place where metals are heated and hammered. —*v.* forged, forging. **1.** To form (metal) in a forge. **2.** To reproduce for fraudulent purposes. —**forge'a·ble** *adj.* —**for'ger·y** *n.*

**forge²** (fôrj, fōrj) *v.* forged, forging. To advance gradually but firmly.

**for·get** (fər-gĕt', fōr-) *v.* -got (-gŏt'), -gotten (-gŏt'n) or -got, -getting. **1.** To be unable to remember. **2.** To neglect. —**for·get'ful** *adj.* —**for·get'ful·ness** *n.*

**for·give** (fər-gĭv', fōr-) *v.* -gave, -given, -giving. To excuse for a fault or offense. —**for·giv'a·ble** *adj.* —**for·giv'er** *n.* —**for·give'ness** *n.*

**fork** (fôrk) *n.* **1.** A pronged implement used for raising, eating, etc. **2.** A separation into branches. —**fork** *v.* —**forked** *adj.*

**for·lorn** (fôr-lôrn', fər-) *adj.* **1.** Deserted. **2.** Pitiful. —**for·lorn'ly** *adv.*

**form** (fôrm) *n.* **1.** The contour of something. **2.** A mold. **3.** Kind; variety. **4.** A document for the collection of information. —**form** *v.* —**for·ma'tion** *n.* —**for'ma·tive** *adj.*

**for·mal** (fôr'məl) *adj.* **1.** Following accepted conventions or rules. **2.** Calling for elegant clothes. **3.** Ceremonious. —*n.* An occasion requiring formal attire. —**for·mal'i·ty** *n.* —**for'mal·ly** *adv.*

**for·mat** (fôr'măt') *n.* The organization and arrangement of something.

**for·mer** (fôr'mər) *adj.* Earlier. —**for'mer·ly** *adv.*

**for·mi·da·ble** (fôr'mə-də-bəl) *adj.* Arousing dread or awe. —**for'mi·da·bly** *adv.*

**for·mu·la** (fôr'myə-lə) *n.*, *pl.* -las or -lae (-lē'). A set form of words or symbols.

**for·mu·late** (fôr'myə-lāt') *v.* -lated, -lating. To state in systematic terms. —**for·mu·la'tion** *n.*

**for·ni·cate** (fôr'nĭ-kāt') *v.* -cated, -cating. To have illicit sexual intercourse. —**for·ni·ca'tion** *n.*

**for·sake** (fôr-sāk', fər-) *v.* -sook (-sŏŏk'), -saken (-sā'kən), -saking. **1.** To give up. **2.** To abandon. —**for·sak'er** *n.*

**for·swear** (fôr-swâr') *v.* -swore (-swôr', -swōr'), -sworn (-swôrn', -swōrn'), -swearing. **1.** To renounce. **2.** To commit perjury.

**fort** 86

**fort** (fôrt, fōrt) n. A fortified place, esp. a permanent post. — **for'tress** n.

**forth** (fôrth, fōrth) adv. 1. Forward; onward. 2. Out into view.

**forth-right** (fôrth'rīt', fōrth'-) adj. Straightforward; frank.

**forth-with** (fôrth'wĭth', -wĭth', fōrth'-) adv. Immediately.

**for-ti-fy** (fôr'tə-fī') v. -fied, -fying. To strengthen. — **for'ti-fi-ca'tion** n. — **for'ti-fi'er** n.

**for-ti-tude** (fôr'tə-t/y/ōōd') n. Strength of mind; courage.

**fort-night** (fôrt'nīt', -nĭt) n. Two weeks. — **fort'night'ly** adj. & adv.

**for-tu-i-tous** (fôr-t/y/ōō'ə-təs) adj. 1. Accidental. 2. Fortunate. — **for-tu'i-tous-ly** adv. — **for-tu'i-ty** n.

**for-tune** (fôr'chən) n. 1. Good or bad luck. 2. Wealth or riches. — **for'tu-nate** adj. — **for'tu-nate-ly** adv.

**for-ty** (fôr'tē) n. The cardinal number written 40. — **for'ti-eth** n. & adj. — **for'ty** adj. & pron.

**fo-rum** (fôr'əm) n. Any public place or medium used for discussion.

**for-ward** (fôr'wərd) adj. 1. At or toward the front. 2. Bold. 3. Progressive; advanced. — adv. 1. Toward the front. 2. In the future. — v. To send on.

**fos-sil** (fŏs'əl) n. A remnant of an organism of a past age embedded in the earth's crust. — adj. Of fossils.

**fos-ter** (fôs'tər, fŏs'-) v. 1. To bring up; rear. 2. To cultivate. — adj. Receiving parental care although not related.

**fought** (fôt). p.t. & p.p. of **fight**.

**foul** (foul) adj. 1. Offensive. 2. Dirty; filthy. 3. Immoral; wicked. 4. Unfair. — n. An infraction of the rules in sports. — adv. In a foul manner. — v. 1. To make or become foul. 2. To entangle or become entangled, as a rope. 3. To commit a foul in sports. — **foul'ly** adv. — **foul'ness** n.

**found¹** (found) v. To originate or establish. — **foun-da'tion** n. — **foun-da'tion-al** adj. — **found'er** n.

**found²** (found). p.t. & p.p. of **find**.

**found-ling** (found'lĭng) n. A child abandoned by unknown parents.

**foun-tain** (foun'tən) n. 1. A spring, esp. the source of a stream. 2. An artificial jet of water. — **foun't** n.

**four** (fôr, fōr) n. The cardinal number written 4. — **four** adj. & pron. — **fourth** n. & adj.

**four-teen** (fôr-tēn', fōr-) n. The cardinal number written 14. — **four-teen'** adj. & pron. — **four-teenth'** n. & adj.

**fowl** (foul) n. 1. Any bird used as food or hunted as game. 2. The common domesticated chicken.

**fox** (fŏks) n. An animal related to the dogs and wolves.

**fox-hole** (fŏks'hōl') n. A pit dug for refuge against enemy fire.

**fox-y** (fŏk'sē) adj. -ier, -iest. Sly; clever. — **fox'i-ness** n.

**foy-er** (foi'ər, foi'ā') n. A lobby or entrance hall.

**fra-cas** (frā'kəs) n. A brawl.

**frac-tion** (frăk'shən) n. A part of something. — **frac'tion-al** adj.

**frac-ture** (frăk'chər) n. A break or crack. — v. -tured, -turing. To break; crack.

**frag-ile** (frăj'əl, -ĭl') adj. 1. Easily broken. 2. Physically weak; frail. 3. Tenuous; flimsy. — **tra-gil'i-ty, frag'ile-ness** n.

**frag-ment** (frăg'mənt) n. 1. A part broken off. 2. Something incomplete. — **frag-ment'** v. — **frag'men-tar'y** adj. — **frag-men-ta'tion** n.

**fra-grance** (frā'grəns) n. A pleasing odor. — **fra'grant** adj. — **fra'grant-ly** adv.

**frail** (frāl) adj. Weak. — **frail'ty** n.

**frame** (frām) v. framed, framing. 1. To construct; build. 2. To design. 3. To enclose. — n. Something composed of parts fitted and joined together; a structure. — **fram'er** n. — **frame'work'** n.

**fran-chise** (frăn'chīz') n. 1. A privilege or authorization. 2. A constitutional or statutory right.

**frank** (frăngk) adj. Straightforward; direct. — v. To send (mail free of charge. — **frank'ly** adv. — **frank'ness** n.

**fran-tic** (frăn'tĭk) adj. Emotionally distraught; frenzied. — **fran'ti-cal-ly** adv.

**fra-ter-ni-ty** (frə-tûr'nə-tē) n., pl. -ties. 1. Brotherhood; brotherliness. 2. A social club of male college students. — **fra-ter'nal** adj. — **frat'er-nize'** v.

**fraud** (frôd) n. 1. Deception for unlawful gain. 2. A swindle; trick. — **fraud'u-lence** n. — **fraud'u-lent** adj. — **fraud'u-lent-ly** adv.

**fraught** (frôt) adj. Attended; full of.

**fray¹** (frā) n. A brawl.

**fray²** (frā) v. To unravel or tatter.

**freak** (frēk) n. An abnormal person or thing. — **freak'ish** adj.

**freck-le** (frĕk'əl) n. A small spot of dark pigment on the skin. — v. -led, -ling. To mark or become marked with freckles. — **freck'ly** adj.

**free** (frē) adj. **freer, freest.** 1. At liberty; not imprisoned or enslaved. 2. Not under obfrustrate **F-6**

ligation. **3.** Costing nothing. **4.** Unoccupied. —*adv.* **1.** In a free manner. **2.** Without charge. —*v.* **treed, freeing. 1.** To set free. **2.** To disengage; untangle. — **free'dom** *n.* — **free'ly** *adv.*

**freeze** (frēz) *v.* **troze, frozen, freezing. 1.** To form ice. **2.** To preserve (food) by cooling. **3.** To fix (prices or wages) at a current level. —*n.* An act of freezing. — **freez'er** *n.*

**freight** (frāt) *n.* **1.** Goods carried by a vehicle; cargo. **2.** The transportation of goods. **3.** The charge for transporting such goods. — **freight'er** *n.*

**fre-net-ic** (frə-nĕt'ĭk) *adj.* Frantic; frenzied. — **fre-net'i-cal-ly** *adv.*

**fren-zy** (frĕn'zē) *n., pl.* **-zies.** Violent agitation. — **fren'zied** *adj.*

**fre-quent** (frē'kwənt) *adj.* Occurring often or at close intervals. —*v.* (frē-kwĕnt') To pay frequent visits to. — **fre'quen-cy** *n.* — **fre-quent'er** *n.* — **fre'quent-ly** *adv.* — **fre'quent-ness** *n.*

**fres-co** (frĕs'kō) *n., pl.* **-coes** or **-cos.** The art of painting on wet plaster.

**fresh** (frĕsh) *adj.* **1.** New; original. **2.** Recently made or harvested. **3.** Not saline. **4.** Impudent. —*adv.* Recently; newly. — **fresh'en** *v.* — **fresh'en-er** *n.* — **fresh'ly** *adv.* — **fresh'ness** *n.*

**fresh-man** (frĕsh'mən) *n.* A first-year student.

**fret**[1] (frĕt) *v.* **tretted, tretting.** To worry. —*n.* Irritation; annoyance. — **fret'ful** *adj.* — **fret'ful-ly** *adv.* — **fret'ful-ness** *n.*

**fret**[2] (frĕt) *n.* A design within a band or border. — **tret** —*v.* — **fret'work** *n.*

**fri-ar** (frī'ər) *n.* A member of a Roman Catholic order.

**fric-tion** (frĭk'shən) *n.* **1.** The rubbing of one object against another. **2.** A conflict. — **fric'tion-al** *adj.*

**Fri-day** (frī'dē, -dā') *n.* The 6th day of the week.

**fried** (frīd) *p.t.* & *p.p.* of **try.**

**friend** (frĕnd) *n.* **1.** A person one knows, likes, and trusts. **2. Friend.** A member of the Society of Friends; Quaker. — **friend'less** *adj.* — **friend'li-ness** *n.* — **friend'ly** *adj.* — **friend'ship** *n.*

**frieze** (frēz) *n.* A decorative band, as along a wall.

**frig-ate** (frĭg'ĭt) *n.* A fast-sailing warship.

**fright** (frīt) *n.* **1.** Sudden fear. **2.** Something very ugly or alarming. — **fright'en** *v.* — **fright'ful** *adj.* — **fright'ful-ly** *adv.*

**frig-id** (frĭj'ĭd) *adj.* Extremely cold. — **frig'id-ness, fri-gid'i-ty** *n.*

**frill** (frĭl) *n.* A ruffle. — **frill'y** *adj.*

**fringe** (frĭnj) *n.* A decorative border of hanging threads, etc. —*v.* **tringed, fringing.** To decorate with a fringe. — **fringe'less** *adj.*

**frisk** (frĭsk) *v.* To move about briskly and playfully. — **frisk'er** *n.* — **frisk'i-ly** *adv.* — **frisk'i-ness** *n.* — **frisk'y** *adj.*

**friv-o-lous** (frĭv'ə-ləs) *adj.* Unworthy of serious attention. — **fri-vol'i-ty** *n.*

**frizz** (frĭz) *v.* To form or be formed into tight curls. — **trizz** —*n.* — **friz'zi-ly** *adv.* — **friz'zi-ness** *n.* — **friz'zy** *adj.*

**fro** (frō) *adv.* Away; back.

**frock** (frŏk) *n.* A dress.

**frog** (frŏg, frôg) *n.* **1.** A tailless amphibian with hind legs adapted for leaping. **2.** Hoarseness.

**frol-ic** (frŏl'ĭk) *n.* Gaiety; merriment. —*v.* **-icked, -icking.** To engage in merrymaking. — **frol'ick-er** *n.* — **frol'ic-some** *adj.*

**from** (frŭm, frŏm) *prep.* **1.** Beginning at. **2.** With a specified point as the first of two limits. **3.** Because of. **4.** Out of.

**front** (frŭnt) *n.* **1.** The forward part or surface. **2.** Demeanor or bearing. **3.** A false appearance or manner. **4.** The most forward line of combat force. —*adj.* Of or in the front. —*v.* **1.** To face. **2.** To serve as a front for. — **front'age** *n.* — **front'al** *adj.*

**fron-tier** (frŭn-tîr') *n.* **1.** A boundary between countries. **2.** A region beyond a settled area. — **fron-tiers'man** *n.*

**frost** (frŏst, frôst) *n.* **1.** A covering of ice crystals. **2.** Weather conditions when this covering forms. —*v.* **1.** To cover or become covered with frost. **2.** To decorate with icing. — **frost'i-ness** *n.* — **frost'y** *adj.*

**frost-ing** (frôs'tĭng, frŏs'-) *n.* **1.** Icing. **2.** A speckled surface on glass or metal.

**froth** (frŏth, frôth) *n.* Foam. —*v.* To foam. — **froth'i-ly** *adv.* — **froth'i-ness** *n.* — **froth'y** *adj.*

**frown** (froun) *v.* To wrinkle the brow, as in displeasure. — **frown'er** *n.*

**froze** (frōz) *p.t.* of **freeze.**

**fro-zen** (frō'zən) *p.p.* of **freeze.**

**fru-gal** (frōo'gəl) *adj.* Thrifty. — **fru-gal'i-ty** *n.* — **fru'gal-ly** *adv.*

**fruit** (frōot) *n.* **1.** An edible plant crop or product. **2.** Result; outcome. —*v.* To produce fruit. — **fruit'ful** *adj.* — **fruit'i-ness** *n.* — **fruit'less** *adj.* — **fruit'y** *adj.*

**fru-i-tion** (frōo-ĭsh'ən) *n.* **1.** The bearing of fruit. **2.** Achievement.

**frus-trate** (frŭs'trāt') *v.* **-trated, -trating.** To prevent from accomplishing something.

— **frus·tra'tion** *n.*

**fry** (frī) *v.* **fried, frying.** To cook over direct heat in oil or fat. — **try'er** *n.*

**fu·el** (fyoo'əl) *n.* Anything burned to produce energy or heat. —*v.* To provide with or take in fuel.

**fu·gi·tive** (fyoo'jə-tĭv) *adj.* **1.** Running or having run away. **2.** Passing quickly; fleeting. —*n.* One who flees. — **fu'gi·tive·ly** *adv.*

**ful·crum** (fool'krəm) *n.* The point or support on which a lever turns.

**ful·fill** (fool-fĭl') *v.* **1.** To effect. **2.** To satisfy. **3.** To complete. — **ful·fill'er** *n.* — **ful·fill'ment** *n.*

**full** (fool) *adj.* **1.** Containing all that is possible; filled. **2.** Having a great deal or many. —*adv.* **1.** To a complete extent; entirely. **2.** Very. — **fully** *adv.* — **full'ness** *n.*

**ful·mi·nate** (fŭl'mə-nāt', fool'-) *v.* **-nated, -nating. 1.** To denounce severely. **2.** To explode. — **ful·mi·na'tion** *n.*

**ful·some** (fool'səm) *adj.* Excessive or insincere. — **ful'some·ly** *adv.* — **ful'some·ness** *n.*

**fum·ble** (fŭm'bəl) *v.* **-bled, -bling. 1.** To grope awkwardly and uncertainly; blunder. **2.** To drop. — **fum'ble** *n.* — **fum'bler** *n.*

**fume** (fyoom) *n.* **1.** An exhalation of smoke, gas, etc. **2.** A strong or acrid odor. —*v.* **fumed, fuming. 1.** To give off or treat with fumes. **2.** To show anger.

**fu·mi·gate** (fyoo'mĭ-gāt') *v.* **-gated, -gating.** To subject to fumes, esp. to exterminate vermin or insects. — **fu'mi·ga'tion** *n.* — **fu'mi·ga'tor** *n.*

**fun** (fŭn) *n.* Enjoyment; amusement.

**func·tion** (fŭngk'shən) *n.* **1.** The proper action for which a person or thing is fitted. **2.** An official ceremony or elaborate social occasion. —*v.* To have or perform a function; serve. — **func'tion·al** *adj.*

**fund** (fŭnd) *n.* A source of supply, esp. of money.

**fun·da·men·tal** (fŭn'də-mĕnt'l) *adj.* Elemental; basic. —*n.* — **fun'da·men'tal** *n.* — **fun'da·men'tal·ly** *adv.*

**fu·ner·al** (fyoo'nər-əl) *n.* Burial ceremonies. — **fu·ne're·al** *adj.*

**fun·gus** (fŭng'gəs) *n., pl.* **-gi** or **-guses.** A group of plants that includes the yeasts, molds, and mushrooms. — **fun'gal, fun'gous** *adj.*

**fun·nel** (fŭn'əl) *n.* **1.** A conical utensil used to channel a substance into a small-mouthed container. **2.** A smokestack. — **fun'nel** *v.*

**fun·ny** (fŭn'ē) *adj.* **-nier, -niest. 1.** Causing laughter or amusement. **2.** Strange; odd.

**fur** (fûr) *n.* **1.** The thick hair covering the body of various animals. **2.** The pelt of an animal, used for garments. — **furred** *adj.* — **fur'ry** *adj.*

**fu·ri·ous** (fyoor'ē-əs) *adj.* **1.** Extremely angry. **2.** Fierce; violent. — **fu'ri·ous·ly** *adv.* — **fu'ri·y** *n.*

**fur·long** (fûr'lông', -lŏng') *n.* A unit of length, equal to $1/8$ mile.

**fur·lough** (fûr'lō) *n.* A leave of absence. — **fur'lough** *v.*

**fur·nace** (fûr'nĭs) *n.* An enclosed chamber in which heating fuel is burned.

**fur·nish** (fûr'nĭsh) *v.* **1.** To provide furniture for. **2.** To supply; give.

**fur·ni·ture** (fûr'nə-chər) *n.* Movable articles in a room or establishment.

**fu·ror** (fyoor'ôr', -ōr') *n.* A state of intense excitement.

**fur·row** (fûr'ō) *n.* **1.** A trench made by a plow. **2.** A deep wrinkle, as on the forehead. — **fur'row** *v.* — **fur'row·y** *adj.*

**fur·ther** (fûr'thər) *adj.* **1.** More distant in time or degree. **2.** Additional. —*adv.* **1.** To a greater extent; more. **2.** In addition; also. —*v.* To help the progress of; advance. — **fur'ther·ance** *n.*

**fur·tive** (fûr'tĭv) *adj.* Stealthy; sly. — **fur'tive·ly** *adv.* — **fur'tive·ness** *n.*

**fuse¹** (fyooz) *n.* A length of combustible material that is lighted at one end to detonate an explosive at the other.

**fuse²** (fyooz) *v.* **fused, fusing.** To mix together by melting; blend. —*n.* A device containing an element that protects an electric circuit by melting when overloaded. — **fu'si·ble** *adj.* — **fu'sion** *n.*

**fu·se·lage** (fyoo'sə-läzh', fyoo'zə-) *n.* The central body of an airplane.

**fuss** (fŭs) *n.* Needlessly nervous or useless activity. —*v.* To trouble or worry over trifles. — **fuss'y** *adj.*

**fu·tile** (fyoot'l, fyoo'tīl') *adj.* Having no useful result; ineffectual. — **fu'tile·ly** *adv.* — **fu·til'i·ty** *n.*

**fu·ture** (fyoo'chər) *n.* **1.** The period of time yet to be. **2.** That which will happen in time to come. — **fu'ture** *adj.* — **fu·tu'ri·ty** *n.*

**fuzz** (fŭz) *n.* A mass of fine particles, hairs, etc.

**gang**

# G

**g, G** (jē) *n.* The 7th letter of the English alphabet.

**gab** (găb) *v.* **gabbed, gabbing.** To chatter. —*n.* Chatter; prattle. —**gab′by** *adj.*

**gab·ar·dine** (găb′ər-dēn′, găb′ər-dēn′) *n.* A worsted fabric.

**ga·ble** (gā′bəl) *n.* A triangular wall section at the ends of a pitched roof. —**ga′bled** *adj.*

**gad** (găd) *v.* **gadded, gadding.** To roam about restlessly; rove. —**gad′a·bout** *n.*

**gad·fly** (găd′flī′) *n.* **1.** A large, stinging fly. **2.** An annoying person.

**gadg·et** (găj′ĭt) *n.* A small mechanical device. —**gadg′et·ry** *n.*

**gaff** (găf) *n.* An iron hook used to land large fish.

**gaffe** (găf) *n.* A social error.

**gag** (găg) *n.* **1.** Something forced into the mouth to prevent speech. **2.** A joke. —*v.* **gagged, gagging. 1.** To prevent from uttering sounds by using a gag. **2.** To choke or retch.

**gage** (gāj) *n.* **1.** A pledge. **2.** Something thrown down as a challenge to fight.

**gai·e·ty** (gā′ə-tē) *n.* Merriment.

**gai·ly** (gā′lē) *adv.* **1.** Cheerfully. **2.** Colorfully.

**gain** (gān) *v.* **1.** To acquire. **2.** To win. **3.** To earn. **4.** To increase. **5.** To progress. —*n.* A profit; advantage; increase.

**gain·ful** (gān′fəl) *adj.* Profitable; lucrative. —**gain′ful·ly** *adv.*

**gain·say** (gān-sā′) *v.* **-said** (-sĕd′), **-saying.** To deny or contradict.

**gait** (gāt) *n.* A manner of walking or running.

**gai·ter** (gā′tər) *n.* **1.** A leather or cloth covering for the legs. **2.** An ankle-high shoe.

**ga·la** (gā′lə, găl′ə, gä′lə) *n.* A festive occasion. —*adj.* Festive.

**gal·ax·y** (găl′ək-sē) *n., pl.* **-ies. 1.** A large cluster of stars. **2. the Galaxy.** The galaxy of which the earth's sun is a part. **3.** An assembly of distinguished persons. —**ga·lac′tic** *adj.*

**gale** (gāl) *n.* **1.** A very strong wind. **2.** An outburst, as of laughter.

**gall¹** (gôl) *n.* **1.** Bile. **2.** Bitterness. **3.** Impudence; effrontery.

**gall²** (gôl) *n.* **1.** A skin sore. **2.** Exasperation; irritation. —*v.* **1.** To chafe. **2.** To irritate.

**gal·lant** (găl′ənt) *adj.* **1.** Dashing. **2.** Courageous; daring. **3.** Chivalrous; courteous. —**gal′lant·ly** *adv.* —**gal′lant·ry** *n.*

**gall·blad·der** (gôl′blăd′ər) *n.* Also **gall bladder.** A small, pear-shaped muscular sac located under the liver.

**gal·le·on** (găl′ē-ən) *n.* A large, three-masted old Spanish ship.

**gal·ler·y** (găl′ə-rē) *n., pl.* **-ies. 1.** A long balcony. **2.** Any enclosed narrow passageway. **3.** The balcony of a theater. **4.** A place in which artwork is displayed or sold.

**gal·ley** (găl′ē) *n.* **1.** An ancient ship propelled by sails and oars. **2.** The kitchen of a ship or airliner.

**gal·li·vant** (găl′ə-vănt′, găl′ə-vănt′) *v.* To roam about frivolously.

**gal·lon** (găl′ən) *n.* A unit of measure equal to 4 quarts.

**gal·lop** (găl′əp) *n.* A fast gait of a horse. —*v.* To move or ride at a gallop.

**gal·lows** (găl′ōz) *n., pl.* **-lowses** or **-lows.** A frame from which condemned prisoners are hanged.

**gall·stone** (gôl′stōn′) *n.* A small, hard mass formed in the gallbladder.

**ga·lore** (gə-lôr′, -lōr′) *adj.* In abundance.

**ga·losh·es** (gə-lŏsh′ĭz) *pl.n.* Waterproof overshoes.

**gal·va·nize** (găl′və-nīz′) *v.* **-nized, -nizing. 1.** To stimulate with an electric current. **2.** To spur; startle. **3.** To coat (metal) with zinc. —**gal·van′ic** *adj.* —**gal′va·ni·za′tion** *n.*

**gam·bit** (găm′bĭt) *n.* **1.** An opening move in chess in which one or more pieces are sacrificed. **2.** A stratagem.

**gam·ble** (găm′bəl) *v.* **-bled, -bling. 1.** To bet money on a game of chance. **2.** To play a game of chance. **3.** To risk. —*n.* **1.** A bet. **2.** A risk. —**gam′bler** *n.*

**gam·bol** (găm′bəl) *v.* To frolic.

**game¹** (gām) *n.* **1.** A pastime; diversion. **2.** A sport or contest. **3.** Wildlife hunted for food or sport. —*adj.* **gamer, gamest. 1.** Plucky; resolute. **2.** Ready and willing.

**game²** (gām) *adj.* Lame.

**gam·ete** (găm′ēt, gə-mēt′) *n.* A reproductive cell, as a mature sperm or egg.

**gam·in** (găm′ĭn) *n.* A street urchin.

**gam·ut** (găm′ət) *n.* The complete range of anything.

**gam·y** (gā′mē) *adj.* **-ier, -iest. 1.** Having the flavor or odor of game. **2.** Plucky; hardy.

**gang** (găng) *n.* A group of people. —**gang up**

**gan·gling** (găng'glĭng) *adj.* Also **gan·gly, -lier, -liest.** Tall, thin, and ungraceful.

**gan·gli·on** (găng'glē-ən) *n., pl.* **-glia** or **-ons.** A bundle of nerve cells.

**gang·plank** (găng'plăngk') *n.* A removable bridge between a ship and a pier.

**gan·grene** (găng'grēn', găng-grēn') *n.* Death and decay of bodily tissue. —**gan'gre·nous** *adj.*

**gang·ster** (găng'stər) *n.* A member of a criminal group.

**gang·way** (găng'wā') *n.* **1.** A passageway. **2.** A gangplank.

**gap** (găp) *n.* **1.** An opening; fissure; cleft. **2.** A blank space; an interval.

**gape** (gāp, găp) *v.* **gaped, gaping. 1.** To open the mouth wide; yawn. **2.** To stare, as with the mouth open. —**gap'ing** *adj.*

**ga·rage** (gə-räzh', -räj') *n.* **1.** A structure for housing cars. **2.** A commercial establishment where cars are repaired. —**ga·rage'** *v.*

**garb** (gärb) *n.* Clothing. —*v.* To clothe; array.

**gar·bage** (gär'bĭj) *n.* **1.** Food wastes. **2.** Refuse; rubbish.

**gar·ble** (gär'bəl) *v.* **-bled, -bling.** To distort (an account or message) so as to be unintelligible; jumble.

**gar·den** (gärd'n) *n.* **1.** A plot of land used for growing flowers, vegetables, or fruit. **2.** A public park. —*adj.* Of a garden. —*v.* To work in a garden. —**gar'den·er** *n.*

**gar·de·ni·a** (gär-dēn'yə) *n.* **1.** A shrub with glossy leaves and fragrant white flowers. **2.** Its flower.

**gar·gan·tu·an** (gär-găn'chōō-ən) *adj.* Of immense size.

**gar·gle** (gär'gəl) *v.* **-gled, -gling.** To rinse the throat, as with a medicated liquid. —*n.* A medicated solution for gargling.

**gar·goyle** (gär'goil') *n.* A roof spout carved to represent a grotesque creature.

**gar·ish** (gâr'ĭsh) *adj.* Gaudy. —**gar'ish·ly** *adv.*

**gar·land** (gär'lənd) *n.* A wreath of flowers, leaves, etc. —*v.* To adorn with a garland.

**gar·lic** (gär'lĭk) *n.* A plant bulb with a strong, distinctive odor and flavor, used as a seasoning.

**gar·ment** (gär'mənt) *n.* An article of clothing.

**gar·ner** (gär'nər) *v.* To amass; acquire.

**gar·net** (gär'nĭt) *n.* A deep-red gem.

**gar·nish** (gär'nĭsh) *v.* To decorate or adorn. —*n.* A decoration for food.

**gar·nish·ment** (gär'nĭsh-mənt) *n.* A proceeding whereby money or property of a debtor is attached and applied to the payment of the debt. —**gar·nish·ee'** *v.*

**gar·ret** (găr'ĭt) *n.* An attic.

**gar·ri·son** (găr'ĭ-sən) *n.* **1.** A military post. **2.** The troops stationed at such a post.

**gar·ru·lous** (găr'y/ə-ləs) *adj.* Talking much. —**gar·ru'li·ty, gar'ru·lous·ness** *n.*

**gar·ter** (gär'tər) *n.* An elastic band to hold up hose.

**gas** (găs) *n., pl.* **gases** or **gasses. 1.** The state of matter distinguished from the solid and liquid states by low density, the ability to diffuse readily, and the tendency to expand. **2.** A substance in this state. **3.** Gasoline. —*v.* **gassed, gassing. 1.** To supply with gas. **2.** To poison with gas. —**gas'e·ous** *adj.*

**gash** (găsh) *n.* A long, deep cut. —**gash** *v.*

**gas·ket** (găs'kĭt) *n.* A seal used between machine parts or joints to prevent the escape of a gas or fluid.

**gas·o·line** (găs'ə-lēn', găs'ə-lēn') *n.* A flammable liquid derived from petroleum and used as a motor fuel.

**gasp** (găsp, gäsp) *v.* **1.** To draw in the breath sharply. **2.** To breathe with difficulty. —**gasp** *n.*

**gas·tric** (găs'trĭk) *adj.* Of the stomach.

**gas·tron·o·my** (găs-trŏn'ə-mē) *n.* The art of good eating. —**gas'tro·nom'ic** *adj.*

**gate** (gāt) *n.* **1.** A hinged door in a wall or fence. **2.** The total admission at a public spectacle. —**gate'way** *n.*

**gath·er** (găth'ər) *v.* **1.** To bring or come together. **2.** To accumulate; collect. **3.** To harvest. **4.** To infer. —**gath'er·ing** *n.*

**gaud·y** (gô'dē) *adj.* **-ier, -iest.** Tasteless and showy. —**gaud'i·ly** *adv.*

**gauge** (gāj) *n.* **1.** A standard of measurement. **2.** A standard dimension, quantity, or capacity. —*v.* **gauged, gauging. 1.** To measure. **2.** To estimate. —**gaug'er** *n.*

**gaunt** (gônt) *adj.* Very thin and bony; emaciated. —**gaunt'ly** *adv.*

**gaunt·let[1]** (gônt'lĭt, gänt'-) *n.* A protective glove.

**gaunt·let[2]** (gônt'lĭt, gänt'-) *n.* A double line of men armed with clubs with which to beat a person forced to run between them.

**gauze** (gôz) *n.* A thin, transparent fabric. —**gauz'y** *adj.*

**gave** (gāv) *p.t.* of **give.**

**gav·el** (găv'əl) *n.* A mallet used by a presiding officer or auctioneer.

**gawk** (gôk) *n.* An awkward, stupid person. —*v.* To stare stupidly. —**gawk'y** *adj.*

**gay** (gā) adj. 1. Merry; lively. 2. Given to social pleasures. 3. Homosexual.

**gaze** (gāz) v. gazed, gazing. To stare. —**gaze** n.

**ga·zelle** (gə-zĕl') n. A slender, swift-running antelope.

**ga·zette** (gə-zĕt') n. A newspaper.

**gaz·et·teer** (găz'ə-tîr') n. A geographic dictionary.

**gear** (gîr) n. 1. A toothed wheel that meshes with another in a machinery. 2. Equipment. —v. 1. To connect by gears. 2. To adjust.

**Gei·ger counter** (gī'gər). An electronic instrument used to measure radioactivity.

**gei·sha** (gā'shə, gē'-) n., pl. **-sha** or **-shas**. A Japanese female entertainer.

**gel·a·tin** (jĕl'ə-tən) n. Also **gel·a·tine**. A transparent, sticky protein formed from animal tissue, used in foods, drugs, and photographic film. —**ge·lat'i·nous** adj.

**geld·ing** (gĕl'dĭng) n. A castrated animal, esp. a horse. —**geld** v.

**gel·id** (jĕl'ĭd) adj. Very cold; icy.

**gem** (jĕm) n. A precious stone.

**gen·der** (jĕn'dər) n. A grammatical category, as masculine, feminine, and neuter, into which words are divided.

**gene** (jēn) n. A functional hereditary unit on a chromosome.

**ge·ne·al·o·gy** (jē'nē-ăl'ə-jē) n., pl. **-gies**. 1. A record of ancestry. 2. The study of ancestry. —**ge'ne·a·log'i·cal** adj. —**ge'ne·al'o·gist** n.

**gen·er·a** (jĕn'ər-ə). pl. of **genus**.

**gen·er·al** (jĕn'ər-əl) adj. 1. Of the whole or every member of a group. 2. Widespread. 3. Being usually the case. 4. Diversified. 5. Lacking detail. —n. A high-ranking military officer. —**in general**. For the most part. —**gen'er·al·ly** adv.

**gen·er·al·i·ty** (jĕn'ə-răl'ə-tē) n., pl. **-ties**. 1. A general principle. 2. A vague statement.

**gen·er·al·ize** (jĕn'ər-ə-līz') v. **-ized, -izing**. 1. To render general. 2. To infer. 3. To speak or think in generalities. —**gen'er·al·i·za'tion** n.

**gen·er·ate** (jĕn'ə-rāt') v. **-ated, -ating**. To produce. —**gen'er·a'tive** adj.

**gen·er·a·tion** (jĕn'ə-rā'shən) n. 1. A group of contemporaneous individuals. 2. The average time interval between the birth of parents and the birth of their offspring.

**gen·er·a·tor** (jĕn'ə-rā'tər) n. A machine that converts mechanical energy into electrical energy.

**ge·ner·ic** (jĭ-nĕr'ĭk) adj. 1. Of an entire group or class. 2. Of a genus. —**ge·ner'i·cal·ly** adv.

**gen·er·ous** (jĕn'ər-əs) adj. 1. Liberal in giving; unselfish. 2. Abundant. —**gen·er·os'i·ty** n. —**gen'er·ous·ly** adv.

**gen·e·sis** (jĕn'ə-sĭs) n., pl. **-ses**. An origin.

**ge·net·ics** (jə-nĕt'ĭks) n. The biology of heredity. —**ge·net'ic** adj. —**ge·net'i·cist** n.

**gen·ial** (jēn'yəl, jē'nē-əl) adj. Cheerful and friendly; kindly. —**ge·ni·al'i·ty** n. —**gen'ial·ly** adv.

**gen·i·ta·li·a** (jĕn'ə-tā'lē-ə, -tāl'yə) pl.n. The external sex organs. —**gen'i·tal** adj.

**gen·i·tals** (jĕn'ə-təlz) pl.n. Genitalia.

**gen·ius** (jēn'yəs) n., pl. **-iuses**. 1. Great intellectual and creative power. 2. A person having this power.

**gen·o·cide** (jĕn'ə-sīd') n. The systematic killing of a racial, political, or cultural group.

**gen·teel** (jĕn-tēl') adj. 1. Refined in manner; polite. 2. Fashionable. —**gen·til'i·ty** n.

**gen·tian** (jĕn'shən) n. A plant with showy blue flowers.

**Gen·tile** (jĕn'tīl) n. A Christian as distinguished from a Jew.

**gen·tle** (jĕn'tl) adj. **-tler, -tlest**. 1. Considerate or kindly. 2. Not harsh; moderate; mild. 3. Easily managed. —**gen'tle·ness** n. —**gen'tly** adv.

**gen·tle·man** (jĕnt'l-mən) n. 1. A polite or considerate man. 2. A polite term for any man.

**gen·try** (jĕn'trē) n. People of good birth and social position.

**gen·u·flect** (jĕn'yə-flĕkt') v. To bend the knee, as in worship. —**gen'u·flec'tion** n.

**gen·u·ine** (jĕn'yōō-ĭn) adj. 1. Not artificial; real. 2. Sincere; frank.

**ge·nus** (jē'nəs) n., pl. **genera**. A category of related organisms usually including several species.

**ge·og·ra·phy** (jē-ŏg'rə-fē) n., pl. **-phies**. The study of the earth and its features, including human life. —**ge·og'ra·pher** n. —**ge'o·graph'ic, ge'o·graph'i·cal** adj.

**ge·ol·o·gy** (jē-ŏl'ə-jē) n., pl. **-gies**. The scientific study of the origin, history, and structure of the earth. —**ge·o·log'ic, ge'o·log'i·cal** adj. —**ge·ol'o·gist** n.

**ge·om·e·try** (jē-ŏm'ə-trē) n., pl. **-tries**. The branch of mathematics dealing with points, lines, angles, surfaces, and solids. —**ge'o·met'ric** adj.

**ge·ra·ni·um** (jĭ-rā'nē-əm) n. A plant with showy clusters of flowers.

**ger·i·at·rics** (jĕr'ē-ăt'rĭks) n. The medical study of old age. —**ger'i·at'ric** adj. & n.

**germ** (jûrm) n. 1. A microscopic organism that causes disease. 2. Something that may serve as the basis of further development. — ger'mi·nal adj.

**ger·mi·cide** (jûr'mə-sīd') n. Anything that kills germs.

**ger·mi·nate** (jûr'mə-nāt') v. -nated, -nating. To begin to grow; sprout. — ger'mi·na'tion n.

**ger·und** (jĕr'ənd) n. A verbal form that can be used as a noun, in English ending in -ing.

**ges·ta·tion** (jĕ-stā'shən) n. The carrying of offspring in the uterus.

**ges·tic·u·late** (jĕ-stĭk'yə-lāt') v. -lated, -lating. To make gestures. — ges·tic'u·la'tion n.

**ges·ture** (jĕs'chər) n. A movement of the limbs or body, to express feelings, ideas, etc. —v. -tured, -turing. To make or signal by gestures.

**get** (gĕt) v. got, got or gotten, getting. 1. To obtain or acquire. 2. To cause to move, come, or go. 3. To arrive. 4. To go after; fetch. 5. To bring or take. 6. To cause to become or to be in a specific condition. 7. To become or grow. 8. To understand. 9. To have the obligation. — get along. To manage. — get around. To avoid doing; circumvent. — get away. To escape. — get by. To manage. — get over. To recover from.

**gew·gaw** (gyōō'gô') n. A trinket; bauble.

**gey·ser** (gī'zər) n. A hot spring that ejects a column of water.

**ghast·ly** (găst'lē, gäst'-) adj. -lier, -liest. 1. Dreadful; horrible. 2. Deathly pale.

**ghet·to** (gĕt'ō) n., pl. -tos or -toes. A section of a city to which an ethnic or economically depressed minority group is restricted.

**ghost** (gōst) n. 1. The disembodied spirit of a dead person. 2. A slight trace. — ghost'ly adj.

**GI** (jē'ī') n., pl. GIs or GI's. An enlisted man in the U.S. army.

**gi·ant** (jī'ənt) n. A being of enormous size and strength. —adj. Huge.

**gib·ber·ish** (jĭb'ər-ĭsh, gĭb'-) n. Rapid, meaningless talk.

**gib·bet** (jĭb'ĭt) n. A gallows.

**gib·bon** (gĭb'ən) n. An ape with a slender body and long arms.

**gibe** (jīb) v. gibed, gibing. Also jibe. To mock; taunt.

**gib·let** (jĭb'lĭt) n. The edible heart, liver, or gizzard of a fowl.

**gid·dy** (gĭd'ē) adj. -dier, -diest. 1. Light-headed; dizzy. 2. Frivolous; flighty. — gid'di·ness n.

**gift** (gĭft) n. 1. A present. 2. The act of giving. 3. A natural ability; talent.

**gift·ed** (gĭf'tĭd) adj. Talented.

**gi·gan·tic** (jī-găn'tĭk) adj. Enormous; huge.

**gig·gle** (gĭg'əl) v. -gled, -gling. To laugh in a nervous, high-pitched manner. —n. A nervous, high-pitched laugh. — gig'gly adj.

**gild** (gĭld) v. gilded or gilt, gilding. To cover with a thin layer of gold.

**gill** (gĭl) n. The respiratory organ of fishes.

**gilt** (gĭlt) Alternate p.t. & p.p. of gild. —n. A thin layer of gold.

**gim·let** (gĭm'lĭt) n. A small tool for boring holes.

**gim·mick** (gĭm'ĭk) n. A deceptive, often dishonest, device.

**gin**[1] (jĭn) n. An alcoholic liquor flavored with juniper berries.

**gin**[2] (jĭn) n. A mechanical device used to remove seeds from cotton fibers. —v. ginned, ginning. To remove seeds from (cotton) with such a gin.

**gin·ger** (jĭn'jər) n. The root of a tropical plant, used as flavoring.

**gin·ger·ly** (jĭn'jər-lē) adj. Cautiously careful; timid. —adv. Carefully; timidly.

**ging·ham** (gĭng'əm) n. A cotton fabric with a checked pattern.

**gi·raffe** (jī-răf', -räf') n. An African mammal with a long neck.

**gird** (gûrd) v. girded or girt, girding. 1. To encircle. 2. To prepare for action.

**gird·er** (gûr'dər) n. A beam used as a main support in building.

**gir·dle** (gûrd'l) n. 1. An encircling band, as a belt. 2. A light corset.

**girl** (gûrl) n. A female child or young woman. — girl'hood n. — girl'ish adj.

**girth** (gûrth) n. 1. Circumference. 2. A strap encircling an animal's body.

**gist** (jĭst) n. The central idea.

**give** (gĭv) v. gave, given, giving. 1. To make a present of. 2. To hand over; deliver. 3. To place in the hands of. 4. To produce. 5. To provide (something required or expected). 6. To relinquish. 7. To emit or issue. 8. To allot; assign. 9. To bend or yield. — give back. To return. — give in. To concede. — give out. To break down; fail. — give up. 1. To surrender. 2. To stop. — give way. 1. To make room for. 2. To collapse. 3. To relinquish. —n. Resilient springiness.

**giv·en** (gĭv'ən) adj. 1. Specified. 2. Bestowed. 3. Acknowledged. 4. Habitually inclined.

**giz·zard** (gĭz'ərd) n. A part of the digestive

tract in birds.

**gla·cier** (glā′shər) *n.* A huge mass of moving ice originating from compacted snow. —**gla′cial** *adj.*

**glad** (glăd) *adj.* **gladder, gladdest. 1.** Feeling, showing, or giving joy; happy. **2.** Pleased. —**glad′den** *v.* —**glad′ly** *adv.* —**glad′ness** *n.*

**glade** (glād) *n.* An open space in a forest.

**glad·i·a·tor** (glăd′ē-ā′tər) *n.* A professional combatant fighting for public entertainment in ancient Rome.

**glad·i·o·lus** (glăd′ē-ō′ləs) *n., pl.* -**li** *or* -**luses.** A plant with a spike of showy, variously colored flowers.

**glam·our** (glăm′ər) *n.* Also **glam·or.** Alluring charm and excitement. —**glam′or·ize′** *v.* —**glam′or·ous** *adj.*

**glance** (glăns, gläns) *v.* **glanced, glancing. 1.** To strike and be deflected. **2.** To look briefly. —*n.* A quick look.

**gland** (glănd) *n.* A body organ or structure that secretes a substance. —**glan′du·lar** *adj.*

**glare** (glâr) *v.* **glared, glaring. 1.** To stare fixedly. **2.** To shine blindingly. —*n.* **1.** An angry stare. **2.** A blinding light.

**glass** (glăs, gläs) *n.* **1.** Transparent or translucent materials that solidify from the molten state without crystallization. **2.** Something made of glass. **3.** Often **glasses.** A device containing lenses and used as an aid to vision. —**glass′y** *adj.*

**glaze** (glāz) *n.* A thin, smooth, glassy coating. —*v.* **glazed, glazing. 1.** To furnish with glass. **2.** To apply a glaze to.

**gla·zier** (glā′zhər) *n.* One who cuts and fits window glass.

**gleam** (glēm) *n.* **1.** A brief flash or glow of light. **2.** A brief indication. —*v.* To send out a gleam.

**glean** (glēn) *v.* To collect bit by bit, as grain left behind by reapers.

**glee** (glē) *n.* Joy. —**glee′ful** *adj.*

**glen** (glĕn) *n.* A narrow valley.

**glib** (glĭb) *adj.* **glibber, glibbest.** Fluent and often superficial. —**glib′ly** *adv.* —**glib′ness** *n.*

**glide** (glīd) *v.* **glided, gliding. 1.** To move smoothly and easily. **2.** To fly without propulsion. —*n.* A smooth, effortless movement or descent.

**glid·er** (glī′dər) *n.* A light, engineless aircraft.

**glim·mer** (glĭm′ər) *v.* To emit a dim, flickering light. —*n.* **1.** A dim, flickering light. **2.** A brief indication.

**glimpse** (glĭmps) *n.* A brief look. —*v.* **glimpsed, glimpsing.** To catch a brief view

of.

**glint** (glĭnt) *n.* A gleam. —*v.* To gleam.

**glis·ten** (glĭs′ən) *v.* To shine; gleam.

**glit·ter** (glĭt′ər) *v.* To sparkle. —*n.* **1.** Brightness. **2.** Showy splendor.

**gloam·ing** (glō′mĭng) *n.* Twilight.

**gloat** (glōt) *v.* To show malicious pleasure or satisfaction.

**globe** (glōb) *n.* **1.** A spherical object. **2.** The earth. —**glob′al** *adj.* —**glob′al·ly** *adv.*

**glob·ule** (glŏb′yōōl) *n.* A small spherical mass. —**glob′u·lar** *adj.*

**gloom** (glōōm) *n.* **1.** Darkness. **2.** Melancholy; depression. —**gloom′i·ly** *adv.* —**gloom′y** *adj.*

**glo·ry** (glôr′ē, glōr′ē) *n., pl.* -**ries. 1.** Great honor; renown. **2.** Adoration; praise. **3.** Magnificent splendor. —**glo′ri·fy′** *v.* —**glo′ri·ous** *adj.*

**gloss**[1] (glôs, glŏs) *n.* Surface shine; luster. —**gloss′y** *adj.*

**gloss**[2] (glôs, glŏs) *n.* A commentary or footnote.

**glos·sa·ry** (glôs′ə-rē, glŏs′-) *n., pl.* -**ries.** A list of specialized terms with definitions.

**glot·tis** (glŏt′ĭs) *n., pl.* -**tises.** The space between the vocal cords. —**glot′tal** *adj.*

**glove** (glŭv) *n.* **1.** A covering for the hand with separate sheaths for the fingers. **2.** A padded mitt, as for boxing, baseball, etc.

**glow** (glō) *v.* **1.** To shine brightly. **2.** To have a bright or ruddy color. **3.** To be elated. —*n.* **1.** A bright, steady light. **2.** Brightness. **3.** A warm feeling. —**glow′ing** *adj.*

**glow·er** (glou′ər) *v.* To stare angrily or sullenly. —*n.* An angry or sullen stare.

**glu·cose** (glōō′kōs′) *n.* A sugar, dextrose.

**glue** (glōō) *n.* An adhesive substance or solution. —*v.* **glued, gluing.** To fasten with glue.

**glum** (glŭm) *adj.* **glummer, glummest.** Dejected; gloomy. —**glum′ly** *adv.*

**glut** (glŭt) *v.* **glutted, glutting.** To eat or fill to excess. —*n.* An oversupply.

**glut·ton** (glŭt′n) *n.* One that eats to excess. —**glut′ton·ous** *adj.* —**glut′ton·y** *n.*

**gnarl** (närl) *n.* A knot on a tree.

**gnash** (năsh) *v.* To grind (the teeth) together.

**gnat** (năt) *n.* A small, winged, biting insect.

**gnaw** (nô) *v.* **gnawed, gnawed** *or* **gnawn, gnawing.** To wear away by nibbling.

**gnu** (n/y/ōō) *n.* A large, bearded antelope.

**go** (gō) *v.* **went, gone, going. 1.** To move or start to move. **2.** To move to or from a given place. **3.** To function. **4.** To belong (somewhere). **5.** To fail. **6.** To be used up. **7.** To become. **8.** To fit; harmonize.

**goad** (gōd) n. **1.** A stick used for prodding animals. **2.** A stimulus; spur. — **goad** v.

**goal** (gōl) n. **1.** An objective. **2.** The finish line of a race. **3.** The place where a ball or puck scores.

**goat** (gōt) n. A horned, bearded mammal.

**goat-ee** (gō-tē') n. A small pointed beard.

**gob** (gŏb) n. A lump or mass.

**gob-ble¹** (gŏb'əl) v. **-bled, -bling.** To devour greedily.

**gob-ble²** (gŏb'əl) v. **-bled, -bling.** To make the guttural sound of a male turkey. — **gob'-bler** n.

**gob-ble-dy-gook** (gŏb'əl-dē-gŏŏk') n. Also **gob-ble-de-gook.** Unintelligible jargon.

**go-be-tween** (gō'bĭ-twēn') n. An intermediary.

**gob-let** (gŏb'lĭt) n. A drinking glass with a stem.

**gob-lin** (gŏb'lən) n. A grotesque, mischievous elf or sprite.

**god** (gŏd) n. **1.** A supernatural being worshiped by a people. **2. God.** The creator and ruler of the universe in monotheistic religions.

**god-child** (gŏd'chīld') n. One for whom another serves as sponsor at baptism. — **god'-daugh'ter** n. — **god'son'** n.

**god-head** (gŏd'hĕd') n. **1.** Divinity. **2. God-head.** The essential nature of God.

**god-ly** (gŏd'lē) adj. **-lier, -liest. 1.** Pious; devout. **2.** Divine. — **god'less** adj. — **god'li-ness** n.

**god-par-ent** (gŏd'pâr'ənt) n. A person who sponsors a child at its baptism. — **god'fa'ther** n. — **god'moth'er** n.

**god-send** (gŏd'sĕnd') n. A stroke of luck.

**gog-gle** (gŏg'əl) v. **-gled, -gling.** To stare. —n., pl. **goggles.** Large, protective eyeglasses.

**goi-ter** (goi'tər) n. Also **goi-tre.** An enlargement of the thyroid gland. — **goi'trous** adj.

**gold** (gōld) n. **1.** A soft, yellow metallic element that is used as an international monetary standard. **2.** Money; riches. **3.** Yellow color. — **gold'en** adj.

**gold-en-rod** (gōl'dən-rŏd') n. A plant with small yellow flowers.

**gold-finch** (gōld'fĭnch') n. A small bird with yellow and black plumage.

**gold-fish** (gōld'fĭsh') n. A small freshwater fish.

**golf** (gŏlf, gôlf) n. A game played on an outdoor course, the object being to propel a small ball with the use of a club into various holes. — **golf** v. — **golf'er** n.

**gon-do-la** (gŏnd'l-ə, gŏn-dō'lə) n. A narrow barge used on the canals of Venice. — **gon'-do-lier'** n.

**gone** (gôn, gŏn). p.p. of **go.**

**gong** (gông, gŏng) n. A metal disk that produces a sonorous tone when struck.

**gon-or-rhe-a** (gŏn'ə-rē'ə) n. An infectious venereal disease.

**good** (gŏŏd) adj. **better, best. 1.** Having positive or desirable qualities. **2.** Suitable; serviceable. **3.** Not spoiled; whole or sound. **4.** Of high quality. **5.** Beneficial. **6.** Competent; skilled. **7.** Pleasant; enjoyable. **8.** Virtuous; upright. **9.** Well-behaved; obedient. —n. **1.** That which is good. **2.** Welfare; benefit. **3.** Virtue; merit. — **good'ness** n.

**good-by, good-bye** (gŏŏd'bī') interj. Farewell. — **good-by', good-bye'** n.

**goods** (gŏŏdz) pl.n. Merchandise.

**go-pher** (gō'fər) n. Any of various burrowing rodents.

**gore¹** (gôr) v. **gored, goring.** To stab with a horn or tusk.

**gore²** (gôr) n. Blood, esp. from a wound. — **gor'y** adj.

**gorge** (gôrj) n. A deep, narrow ravine. —v. **gorged, gorging. 1.** To stuff; glut. **2.** To eat greedily.

**gor-geous** (gôr'jəs) adj. **1.** Resplendent; magnificent. **2.** Strikingly beautiful. — **gor'-geous-ly** adv.

**go-ril-la** (gə-rĭl'ə) n. A large African ape.

**gos-pel** (gŏs'pəl) n. **1.** Often **Gospel.** The teachings of Christ and the Apostles. **2. Gospel.** Any of the first four books of the New Testament. **3.** Something accepted as unquestionably true.

**gos-sa-mer** (gŏs'ə-mər) n. **1.** A fine film of floating cobwebs. **2.** A sheer gauzy fabric. — **gos'sa-mer** adj.

**gos-sip** (gŏs'əp) n. **1.** Rumor of a personal nature. **2.** One who engages in such talk. —v. To engage in gossip.

**got** (gŏt). p.t. & p.p. of **get.**

**got-ten** (gŏt'n). Alternate p.p. of **get.**

**gouge** (gouj) n. **1.** A chisel with a troughlike blade. **2.** A groove or hole. —v. **gouged, gouging.** To cut or scoop out with a gouge.

**gourd** (gôrd, gŏŏrd, gōŏrd) n. **1.** A vine related to the pumpkin. **2.** The dried shell of a fruit from this vine.

**gour-met** (gŏŏr-mā') n. A person who likes fine food.

**gout** (gout) n. A disease marked by painful swelling of the joints. — **gout'y** adj.

**gov·ern** (gŭv′ərn) v. **1.** To control; guide. **2.** To rule by exercise of sovereign authority. **3.** To regulate or determine. — **gov′ern·a·bil′i·ty** n. — **gov′ern·a·ble** adj. — **gov′er·nance** n.

**gov·ern·ess** (gŭv′ər-nĭs) n. A woman who supervises the children of a private household.

**gov·ern·ment** (gŭv′ərn-mənt) n. **1.** The administration of policy by a ruling body. **2.** The office or authority whereby political power is exercised. **3.** A prevailing political system or policy. **4.** A governing body. — **gov′ern·men′tal** adj.

**gov·er·nor** (gŭv′ər-nər) n. The chief executive of a state. — **gov′er·nor·ship′** n.

**gown** (goun) n. **1.** A loose, flowing garment, esp. a nightgown. **2.** A woman's formal dress.

**grab** (grăb) v. **grabbed, grabbing.** To grasp suddenly; snatch; seize. — **grab** n. — **grab′ber** n.

**grace** (grās) n. **1.** Beauty of movement or form. **2.** Mercy; clemency. **3.** Temporary immunity. **4.** Divine love and protection. —v. **graced, gracing.** To honor or favor. — **grace′ful** adj. — **grace′ful·ly** adv. — **grace′less** n.

**gra·cious** (grā′shəs) adj. **1.** Tactful and courteous. **2.** Merciful; compassionate. **3.** Tasteful. — **gra′cious·ly** adv. — **gra′cious·ness** n.

**gra·da·tion** (grā-dā′shən) n. A progression of successive stages.

**grade** (grād) n. **1.** A stage in a process; position in a scale. **2.** A school class. **3.** A mark indicating a student's level of achievement. **4.** A military rank. —v. **graded, grading. 1.** To arrange in degrees; rank. **2.** To assign an academic grade to. **3.** To level or smooth.

**grad·u·al** (grăj′ōō-əl) adj. Occurring by stages or degrees. — **grad′u·al·ly** adv.

**grad·u·ate** (grăj′ōō-āt′) v. **-ated, -ating. 1.** To grant or be granted an academic degree. **2.** To divide into intervals. —n. (-ĭt) A recipient of an academic degree. — **grad′u·a′tion** n.

**graft¹** (grăft, gräft) v. **1.** To unite (a shoot, bud, or plant) with a growing plant. **2.** To transplant (tissue) into a bodily part. —n. A detached shoot grafted onto a growing plant.

**graft²** (grăft, gräft) n. **1.** The unscrupulous use of one's position or knowledge to derive profit or advantages. **2.** Money thus obtained.

**grain** (grān) n. **1.** A small, hard seed. **2.** A mass of particles. **3.** Cereal grasses collectively. **4.** A tiny quantity. **5.** Texture, esp. of wood. — **grain′i·ness** n. — **grain′y** adj.

**gram** (grăm) n. A metric unit of mass and weight.

**gram·mar** (grăm′ər) n. **1.** The study of syntax and word inflection. **2.** A system of usage rules for language. — **gram·mar′i·an** n. — **gram·mat′i·cal** adj. — **gram·mat′i·cal·ly** adv.

**gran·a·ry** (grăn′ə-rē, grā′nə-) n., pl. **-ries.** A building for storing grain.

**grand** (grănd) adj. **1.** Large and impressive. **2.** Magnificent; sumptuous. **3.** Illustrious. **4.** Dignified; stately. **5.** Inclusive; complete. — **grand′ly** adv.

**grand·child** (grănd′chīld′) n. A child of one's son or daughter. — **grand′daugh′ter** n. — **grand′son′** n.

**gran·deur** (grăn′jər, -jōōr) n. Greatness; splendor.

**grand·par·ent** (grănd′pâr′ənt, grăn′-) n. A parent of one's mother or father. — **grand′fa′ther** n. — **grand′moth′er** n.

**grand·stand** (grănd′stănd′, grăn′-) n. A stand for spectators at a stadium.

**gran·ite** (grăn′ĭt) n. A common, hard rock, used for building.

**grant** (grănt, gränt) v. **1.** To allow; consent to. **2.** To accord, as a favor. **3.** To bestow; confer. **4.** To acknowledge. —n. Something granted.

**gran·u·late** (grăn′yə-lāt′) v. **-lated, -lating.** To form into granules.

**gran·ule** (grăn′yōōl) n. A small grain.

**grape** (grāp) n. A juicy, smooth-skinned, edible fruit.

**grape·fruit** (grāp′frōōt′) n. A large, yellow-skinned citrus fruit.

**grape·vine** (grāp′vīn′) n. A vine on which grapes grow.

**graph** (grăf, gräf) n. A drawing that exhibits a relationship between two sets of numbers. —v. To represent by or plot on a graph.

**graph·ic** (grăf′ĭk) adj. Also **graph·i·cal. 1.** Written, printed, drawn, or engraved. **2.** Vividly outlined; lifelike. — **graph′i·cal·ly** adv.

**graph·ite** (grăf′īt′) n. The soft, crystallized form of carbon, used in lead pencils.

**grap·nel** (grăp′nəl) n. A small anchor.

**grap·ple** (grăp′əl) n. A clawed implement, formerly used to secure enemy ships while boarding. —v. **-pled, -pling. 1.** To seize firmly. **2.** To attempt to cope.

**grasp** (grăsp) v. **1.** To take hold of; seize. **2.** To comprehend. —n. **1.** Hold; grip. **2.** Comprehension.

**grass** (grăs, gräs) n. **1.** Any of numerous plants with narrow leaves. **2.** Ground, as a

**grasshopper**

lawn, covered with such plants. — **grass'y** adj.

**grass·hop·per** (grás'hŏp'ər, grás'-) n. An insect with long legs for jumping.

**grate**[1] (grāt) v. **grated, grating. 1.** To shred by rubbing. **2.** To make a rasping sound. **3.** To irritate. — **grat'er** n. — **grat'ing** adj.

**grate**[2] (grāt) n. A framework of parallel bars over an opening.

**grate·ful** (grāt'fəl) adj. Appreciative; thankful. — **grate'ful·ly** adv. — **grate'ful·ness** n.

**grat·i·fy** (grāt'ə-fī') v. -**fied, -fying.** To please, favor, or indulge. — **grat'i·fi·ca'tion** n.

**gra·tis** (grā'tĭs, grăt'ĭs) adv. Without charge; free. — **gra'tis** adj.

**grat·i·tude** (grăt'ə-t/y/ōōd') n. Thankfulness.

**gra·tu·i·tous** (grə-t/y/ōō'ə-təs) adj. **1.** Free; gratis. **2.** Unnecessary or unwarranted. — **gra·tu'i·tous·ly** adv.

**gra·tu·i·ty** (grə-t/y/ōō'ə-tē) n., pl. -**ties.** A tip for service.

**grave**[1] (grāv) n. A burial excavation. — **grave'stone'** n. — **grave'yard'** n.

**grave**[2] (grāv) adj. **graver, gravest. 1.** Extremely serious; important; weighty. **2.** Fraught with danger. — **grave'ly** adv.

**grav·el** (grăv'əl) n. A mixture of rock fragments.

**grav·i·ta·tion** (grăv'ə-tā'shən) n. **1.** The natural attraction between massive bodies. **2.** A movement toward a source of attraction. — **grav'i·tate'** v. — **grav'i·ta'tion·al** adj.

**grav·i·ty** (grăv'ə-tē) n. **1.** The force of gravitation, esp. the attractive central force exerted by a celestial body such as the earth. **2.** Seriousness; importance.

**gra·vy** (grā'vē) n., pl. -**vies.** The juices that drip from cooking meat.

**gray** (grā). Also **grey.** adj. **1.** Of a color between black and white. **2.** Dull or dark; gloomy. —n. A neutral color. — **gray'ish** adj.

**gray matter.** The nerve tissue of the brain and spinal cord.

**graze**[1] (grāz) v. **grazed, grazing.** To feed on growing grass.

**graze**[2] (grāz) v. **grazed, grazing.** To touch lightly in passing.

**grease** (grēs) n. **1.** Melted animal fat. **2.** Any thick oil or viscous lubricant. —v. **greased, greasing.** To coat, lubricate, or soil with grease. — **greas'y** adj.

**great** (grāt) adj. **1.** Extremely large; bulky; big. **2.** Remarkable; outstanding. **3.** Eminent; distinguished. — **great'ly** adv. — **great'ness** n.

**greed** (grēd) n. Rapacious desire; avarice.

— **greed'i·ly** adv. — **greed'y** adj.

**green** (grēn) n. **1.** A color whose hue is that of the emerald or grass. **2.** Leafy plants. **3.** A grassy lawn. —adj. **1.** Of the color green. **2.** Not ripe; immature. **3.** Lacking experience. — **green'er·y** n. — **green'ish** adj.

**green·house** (grēn'hous') n. A structure in which plants are grown.

**greet** (grēt) v. To address in a friendly way; welcome. — **greet'ing** n.

**gre·gar·i·ous** (grĭ-gâr'ē-əs) adj. **1.** Tending to live or move in herds. **2.** Enjoying the company of others; sociable.

**gre·nade** (grə-nād') n. An explosive missile thrown by hand.

**grew** (grōō). p.t. of **grow.**

**grey·hound** (grā'hound') n. A large, slender, swift-running dog.

**grid** (grĭd) n. **1.** A grating. **2.** A pattern of lines forming squares on a map.

**grid·dle** (grĭd'l) n. A flat pan used for cooking.

**grid·i·ron** (grĭd'ī'ərn) n. **1.** A grill framework for broiling. **2.** A football field.

**grief** (grēf) n. Acute sorrow or anguish.

**griev·ance** (grē'vəns) n. A complaint or protest.

**grieve** (grēv) v. **grieved, grieving. 1.** To cause grief to; distress. **2.** To lament; mourn. — **griev'ous** adj. — **griev'ous·ly** adv.

**grill** (grĭl) n. A cooking utensil composed of thin metal bars. —v. To broil on a grill.

**grille** (grĭl) n. Also **grill.** A metal grate used as a screen.

**grim** (grĭm) adj. **grimmer, grimmest. 1.** Stern; forbidding. **2.** Ghastly; sinister. — **grim'ly** adv.

**gri·mace** (grĭ-mās', grĭm'ĭs) n. A facial contortion expressing pain, contempt, or disgust. — **gri·mace'** v.

**grime** (grīm) n. Black dirt or soot. — **grim'y** adj.

**grin** (grĭn) v. **grinned, grinning.** To smile broadly. —n. The expression produced by grinning.

**grind** (grīnd) v. **ground, grinding. 1.** To crush into fine particles. **2.** To shape, sharpen, or refine with friction. **3.** To rub together; gnash. **4.** To turn a crank. — **grind'er** n. — **grind'stone'** n.

**grip** (grĭp) n. **1.** A tight hold. **2.** A handle. — **come to grips.** To confront and resolve a problem. —v. **gripped, gripping.** To grasp and keep a tight hold on.

**gripe** (grīp) v. **griped, griping. 1.** To cause or suffer sharp pain in the bowels. **2.** To complain; grumble.

**grippe** (grĭp) *n.* Also **grip.** Influenza. — **grip′-py** *adj.*

**gris·ly** (grĭz′lē) *adj.* **-lier, -liest.** Horrifying; gruesome.

**grist** (grĭst) *n.* Grain to be or already ground.

**gris·tle** (grĭs′əl) *n.* Cartilage, esp. in meat.

**grit** (grĭt) *n.* **1.** Minute rough granules. **2.** Spirit; pluck. — *v.* **gritted, gritting.** To clamp (the teeth) together. — **grit′ty** *adj.*

**grits** (grĭts) *pl.n.* Coarsely ground grain.

**griz·zly** (grĭz′lē) *adj.* **-zlier, -zliest.** Grayish. — *n., pl.* **-zlies.** Also **grizzly bear.** A large grayish bear.

**groan** (grōn) *v.* To moan in pain, annoyance, or disapproval. — *n.* Such a moan.

**gro·cer** (grō′sər) *n.* A storekeeper who sells foodstuffs and household supplies. — **gro′cer·y** *n.*

**grog·gy** (grŏg′ē) *adj.* **-gier, -giest.** Unsteady and dazed; shaky.

**groin** (groin) *n.* The crease at the juncture of the thigh and abdomen.

**grom·met** (grŏm′ĭt) *n.* A reinforced eyelet in cloth, leather, etc.

**groom** (grōōm) *n.* **1.** A man employed to take care of horses. **2.** A bridegroom. — *v.* **1.** To make neat and trim; brush. **2.** To train.

**groove** (grōōv) *n.* **1.** A long, narrow channel. **2.** A settled routine. — *v.* **grooved, grooving.** To cut a groove in.

**grope** (grōp) *v.* **groped, groping. 1.** To feel one's way uncertainly. **2.** To search blindly. — **grop′ing·ly** *adv.*

**gross** (grōs) *adj.* **1.** Exclusive of deductions. **2.** Glaringly obvious; flagrant. **3.** Coarse; vulgar. — *n., pl.* **gross.** Twelve dozen. — *v.* To earn a total before deductions. — **gross′ly** *adv.* — **gross′ness** *n.*

**gro·tesque** (grō-tĕsk′) *adj.* **1.** Extravagant; outlandish. **2.** Bizarre; distorted. — **gro·tesque′ly** *adv.* — **gro·tesque′ness** *n.*

**grot·to** (grŏt′ō) *n., pl.* **-toes** or **-tos.** A small cave.

**grouch** (grouch) *v.* To sulk. — *n.* **1.** A grumbling or sulky mood. **2.** An irritable person. — **grouch′y** *adj.*

**ground¹** (ground) *n.* **1.** The solid surface of the earth. **2.** Often **grounds.** An area of land designated for a particular purpose. **3.** Often **grounds.** The basis for an argument, belief, or action. **4. grounds.** The sediment at the bottom of a liquid. — *v.* **1.** To prevent from flying. **2.** To instruct in fundamentals. — **ground′less** *adj.*

**ground²** (ground). *p.t. & p.p.* of **grind.**

**ground·work** (ground′wûrk′) *n.* Basis; preliminary work.

**group** (grōōp) *n.* A number of individuals or things with certain similarities. — *v.* To place in or form a group.

**grouse** (grous) *n., pl.* **grouse.** A chickenlike bird.

**grove** (grōv) *n.* A small group of trees.

**grov·el** (grŭv′əl, grŏv′-) *v.* To humble oneself; cringe. — **grov′el·er** *n.*

**grow** (grō) *v.* **grew, grown** (grōn), **growing. 1.** To increase in size. **2.** To develop and reach maturity. **3.** To become. — **grown** *adj.* — **grown′-up′** *n. & adj.*

**growl** (groul) *n.* A low, menacing sound. — *v.* To utter such a sound.

**growth** (grōth) *n.* **1.** The process of growing. **2.** Something that has grown. **3.** An abnormal tissue formation.

**grub** (grŭb) *v.* **grubbed, grubbing. 1.** To dig up by the roots. **2.** To toil arduously; drudge. — *n.* The larva of certain insects.

**grub·by** (grŭb′ē) *adj.* **-bier, -biest.** Dirty; unkempt. — **grub′bi·ness** *n.*

**grudge** (grŭj) *v.* **grudged, grudging.** To be reluctant to give. — *n.* Resentment or rancor. — **grudg′ing·ly** *adv.*

**gru·el** (grōō′əl) *n.* A watery porridge. — *v.* To exhaust. — **gru′el·ing** *adj.*

**grue·some** (grōō′səm) *adj.* Causing horror and repugnance; frightful. — **grue′some·ly** *adv.* — **grue′some·ness** *n.*

**gruff** (grŭf) *adj.* **1.** Brusk and stern. **2.** Hoarse. — **gruff′ly** *adv.* — **gruff′ness** *n.*

**grum·ble** (grŭm′bəl) *v.* **-bled, -bling.** To mumble in discontent. — *n.* A grumbling utterance.

**grump·y** (grŭm′pē) *adj.* **-ier, -iest.** Irritable; cranky. — **grump′i·ness** *n.*

**grunt** (grŭnt) *v.* To utter (with) a low, guttural sound. — *n.* A low, guttural sound.

**guar·an·tee** (găr′ən-tē′) *n.* A formal assurance that something is as represented or that a specified act will be performed. — *v.* **-teed, -teeing. 1.** To assume responsibility for the debt of. **2.** To furnish security for. — **guar′an·tor** *n.*

**guard** (gärd) *v.* **1.** To protect from harm. **2.** To watch over to prevent escape. **3.** To take precautions. — *n.* One that guards.

**guard·ed** (gär′dĭd) *adj.* **1.** Protected. **2.** Cautious; restrained. — **guard′ed·ly** *adv.*

**guard·i·an** (gär′dē-ən) *n.* **1.** A custodian. **2.** A person legally responsible for the care of one incompetent to manage his own affairs.

—**guard'i·an·ship**′ n.

**gu·ber·na·to·ri·al** (g/y/ōō′bər-nə-tôr′ē-əl, -tōr′ē-) adj. Of a governor.

**guer·ril·la, gue·ril·la** (gə-rĭl′ə) n. A member of an irregular military force. —adj. Of or by guerrillas.

**guess** (gĕs) v. **1.** To predict (a result or event) or assume (a fact) without sufficient information. **2.** To estimate correctly. —n. **1.** An instance of guessing. **2.** A conjecture arrived at by guessing. —**guess′work**′ n.

**guest** (gĕst) n. **1.** A visitor. **2.** A patron; customer.

**guf·faw** (gə-fô′) n. A hearty laugh. —**guf·faw**′ v.

**guide** (gīd) n. **1.** One who shows the way. **2.** An example or model. **3.** A sign or indicator. —v. **guided, guiding. 1.** To show the way to; conduct. **2.** To manage the affairs of others; govern. **3.** To counsel. —**guid'ance** n.

**guided missile.** Any missile capable of being guided while in flight.

**guild** (gĭld) n. An association of persons of the same trade.

**guile** (gīl) n. Insidious cunning; craftiness. —**guile'ful** adj.

**guil·lo·tine** (gĭl′ə-tēn′, gē′ə-) n. A machine to behead a condemned prisoner. —v. **-tined, -tining.** To behead with a guillotine.

**guilt** (gĭlt) n. **1.** The fact of being responsible for a wrongdoing. **2.** Remorseful awareness of having done something wrong. —**guilt'i·ly** adv. —**guilt'less** adj. —**guilt'y** adj.

**guinea pig. 1.** A variously colored rodent. **2.** A subject for experimentation.

**guise** (gīz) n. **1.** Outward appearance. **2.** False appearance; pretense.

**gui·tar** (gĭ-tär′) n. A stringed musical instrument. —**gui·tar'ist** n.

**gulch** (gŭlch) n. A shallow canyon or ravine.

**gulf** (gŭlf) n. **1.** A large area of a sea partially enclosed by land. **2.** A deep, wide chasm; abyss.

**gull¹** (gŭl) n. A coastal water bird.

**gull²** (gŭl) n. An easily deceived person; dupe. —v. To deceive; dupe. —**gull'i·ble** adj.

**gul·let** (gŭl′ĭt) n. The esophagus.

**gul·ly** (gŭl′ē) n., pl. **-lies.** A channel cut in the earth by water.

**gulp** (gŭlp) v. **1.** To gasp, as in nervousness. **2.** To swallow in large amounts. —n. **1.** The act of gulping. **2.** A large mouthful.

**gum¹** (gŭm) n. A viscous plant substance. —v. **gummed, gumming.** To seal or fill with gum. —**gum'my** adj.

**gum²** (gŭm) n. The firm connective tissue at the base of the teeth.

**gun** (gŭn) n. A weapon consisting of a metal tube from which a projectile is fired. —v. **gunned, gunning.** To shoot (with down). —**gun'ner** n.

**gun·ny** (gŭn′ē) n. A coarse fabric; burlap.

**gun·pow·der** (gŭn′pou′dər) n. An explosive powder used in firearms.

**gup·py** (gŭp′ē) n., pl. **-pies.** A small tropical freshwater fish.

**gur·gle** (gûr′gəl) v. **-gled, -gling. 1.** To flow making intermittent, bubbling sounds. **2.** To make such sounds. —**gur'gle** n.

**gush** (gŭsh) v. **1.** To flow forth suddenly. **2.** To display sentiment effusively. —n. A sudden, copious outflow. —**gush'er** n.

**gust** (gŭst) n. An abrupt rush of wind. —**gust'y** adj.

**gus·ta·to·ry** (gŭs′tə-tôr′ē, -tōr′ē) adj. Of the sense of taste.

**gus·to** (gŭs′tō) n. Vigorous enjoyment; relish.

**gut** (gŭt) n. **1.** The intestine or stomach. **2.** guts. Courage; fortitude. —v. **gutted, gutting.** To destroy the interior of.

**gut·ter** (gŭt′ər) n. A channel for draining off water.

**gut·tur·al** (gŭt′ər-əl) adj. **1.** Of the throat. **2.** Produced in the throat. —**gut'tur·al·ly** adv.

**guy¹** (gī) n. A rope or cable used to steady or guide something.

**guy²** (gī) n. A man.

**guz·zle** (gŭz′əl) v. **-zled, -zling.** To drink greedily.

**gym·na·si·um** (jĭm-nā′zē-əm) n. A building equipped for gymnastics and sports.

**gym·nas·tics** (jĭm-năs′tĭks) pl.n. Body-building exercises. —**gym'nast**′ n. —**gym·nas'tic** adj.

**gy·ne·col·o·gy** (gī′nə-kŏl′ə-jē, jī′-, jĭn′ə-) n. The medical science of the diseases and functions of women. —**gy·ne·co·log'i·cal** adj. —**gy·ne·col'o·gist** n.

**gy·rate** (jī′rāt′) v. **-rated, -rating.** To revolve; circle; spiral. —**gy·ra'tion** n.

**gy·ro·scope** (jī′rə-skōp′) n. A spinning disk, suspended to rotate freely around an axis, used to maintain equilibrium.

# H

**h, H** (āch) n. The 8th letter of the English alphabet.

**hab·er·dash·er** (hăb′ər-dăsh′ər) n. A dealer in men's furnishings. **—hab′er·dash′er·y** n.

**hab·it** (hăb′ĭt) n. **1.** An activity repeated so frequently it is done without thinking. **2.** A customary manner or practice. **3.** An addiction. **4.** A distinctive dress or costume. **—hab·it′u·al** adj. **—ha·bit′u·ate** v.

**hab·i·tat** (hăb′ə-tăt′) n. The area or environment in which a plant or animal normally lives or occurs.

**hack¹** (hăk) v. **1.** To cut or chop roughly; mangle. **2.** To cough in short spasms.

**hack²** (hăk) n. **1.** A worn-out horse. **2.** A vehicle for hire; taxicab. **3.** One hired to do routine writing. **—adj.** Banal; trite.

**hack·ney** (hăk′nē) n., pl. **-neys. 1.** A horse for riding. **2.** A carriage for hire.

**hack·neyed** (hăk′nēd) adj. Overused; trite.

**hack·saw** (hăk′sô′) n. A saw for cutting metal.

**had** (hăd). p.t. & p.p. of **have.**

**had·n't** (hăd′ənt). Contraction of **had not.**

**hag** (hăg) n. An ugly old woman.

**hag·gard** (hăg′ərd) adj. Appearing worn and exhausted; gaunt.

**hag·gle** (hăg′əl) v. **-gled, -gling.** To urge or dispute in an attempt to bargain. **—hag′gler** n.

**hail¹** (hāl) n. Pellets of ice and hard snow. **—v.** To precipitate hail. **—hail′stone′** n.

**hail²** (hāl) v. **1.** To salute or greet. **2.** To call out to. **—n.** A greeting or expression of acclaim.

**hair** (hâr) n. **1.** A fine, threadlike outgrowth, esp. from the skin of a mammal. **2.** A minute distance or narrow margin. **—hair′i·ness** n. **—hair′y** adj.

**hale¹** (hāl) adj. **haler, halest.** Healthy; robust.

**hale²** (hāl) v. **haled, haling.** To compel to go; force.

**half** (hăf, häf) n., pl. **halves.** One of two equal parts. **—adj. 1.** Being a half. **2.** Partial; incomplete. **—adv. 1.** To the extent of 50%. **2.** Not completely; partly.

**half-heart·ed** (hăf′här′tĭd, häf′-) adj. Lacking interest or enthusiasm; uninspired.

**—half′heart′ed·ly** adv.

**hall** (hôl) n. **1.** A corridor; lobby. **2.** A large public building. **3.** A large room. **—hall′way** n.

**hal·le·lu·jah** (hăl′ə-lōō′yə) interj. Expressive of praise or joy.

**hal·low** (hăl′ō) v. To consecrate. **—hal′lowed** adj.

**hal·lu·ci·na·tion** (hə-lōō′sə-nā′shən) n. False perception; delusion. **—hal·lu′ci·nate′** v. **—hal·lu′ci·na·to′ry** adj.

**ha·lo** (hā′lō) n., pl. **-los** or **-loes. 1.** A ring of light around the head, as in a picture of a holy person. **2.** A circular band of light around a light source, as the sun or moon.

**halt¹** (hôlt) n. A suspension of movement; a stop.

**halt²** (hôlt) v. To limp or hobble. **—adj.** Lame.

**hal·ter** (hôl′tər) n. **1.** A strap that fits around the head of an animal. **2.** A noose used for execution by hanging. **3.** A backless bodice for women. **—v.** To put a halter on; control with a halter.

**halve** (hăv, häv) v. **halved, halving. 1.** To divide into two equal parts. **2.** To reduce by half.

**halves.** pl. of **half.**

**hal·yard** (hăl′yərd) n. A rope used to raise a sail, flag, etc.

**ham** (hăm) n. **1.** The thigh of the hind leg of a hog. **2.** An actor who exaggerates excessively. **3.** A licensed amateur radio operator.

**ham·burg·er** (hăm′bûr′gər) n. **1.** Ground beef. **2.** A cooked patty of such meat.

**ham·let** (hăm′lĭt) n. A small village.

**ham·mer** (hăm′ər) n. A hand tool with an iron head, used for pounding, driving nails, etc. **—v.** To strike, pound, or drive with or as with a hammer.

**ham·mock** (hăm′ək) n. A hanging bed suspended by cords.

**ham·per¹** (hăm′pər) v. To restrain movement, action, etc.; impede.

**ham·per²** (hăm′pər) n. A large basket.

**ham·ster** (hăm′stər) n. A rodent often used in laboratory research.

**hand** (hănd) n. **1.** The terminal part of the arm below the wrist. **2.** A lateral direction; side. **3.** Handwriting. **4.** A round of applause. **5.** Help. **6.** The cards held by or dealt to a player. **7.** A laborer. **—v.** To pass with the hands. **—hand′ful** n.

**hand·book** (hănd′bŏŏk′) n. A manual or small reference book.

**hand·cuff** (hănd′kŭf′) n. Often **handcuffs.** A

restraining device that can be locked about the wrist. —v. To restrain with handcuffs.

**hand·i·cap** (hăn'dē-kăp') n. 1. An advantage or penalty given different contestants in a race to equalize their chances of winning. 2. A deficiency that prevents or restricts normal achievement. —v. **-capped, -capping.** 1. To assign a handicap or handicaps to (a contestant). 2. To hinder.

**hand·i·work** (hăn'dē-wûrk') n. 1. Work performed by hand. 2. The results of one's efforts.

**hand·ker·chief** (hăng'kər-chĭf) n. A small cloth used in wiping the nose, mouth, etc.

**han·dle** (hănd'l) v. **-dled, -dling.** 1. To touch, lift, or turn with the hands. 2. To manipulate. 3. To manage; deal with or in. —n. A part that is held with the hand.

**hand·some** (hăn'səm) adj. 1. Pleasing and dignified in appearance. 2. Generous; liberal. —**hand'some·ly** adv.

**hand·y** (hăn'dē) adj. **-ier, -iest.** 1. Manually adroit. 2. Readily accessible. 3. Easy to use. —**hand'i·ly** adv.

**hang** (hăng) v. hung or hanged, hanging. 1. To fasten or be fastened from above. 2. To suspend or be suspended so as to allow free movement. 3. To execute or be executed by suspending by the neck.

**han·gar** (hăng'ər) n. A shed, esp. for aircraft.

**hang·man** (hăng'mən) n. One employed to execute prisoners by hanging.

**hank** (hăngk) n. A coil or loop.

**han·ker** (hăng'kər) v. To crave.

**hap·haz·ard** (hăp-hăz'ərd) adj. Dependent on or characterized by mere chance. —**hap·haz'ard·ly** adv.

**hap·less** (hăp'lĭs) adj. Luckless; unfortunate.

**hap·pen** (hăp'ən) v. 1. To take place. 2. To come upon or appear by chance; turn up.

**hap·pen·ing** (hăp'ə-nĭng) n. An event.

**hap·py** (hăp'ē) adj. **-pier, -piest.** 1. Characterized by good fortune; prosperous. 2. Having pleasure; gratified. —**hap'pi·ly** adv. —**hap'pi·ness** n.

**ha·rangue** (hə-răng') n. A speech characterized by vehement expression. —**ha·rangue'** v.

**har·ass** (hăr'əs, hə-răs') v. To disturb or irritate persistently. —**har·ass·ment** n.

**har·bin·ger** (här'bĭn-jər) n. A forerunner.

**har·bor** (här'bər) n. 1. A shelter for ships; port. 2. A refuge. —v. 1. To give shelter to; protect. 2. To hold a thought or feeling

about.

**hard** (härd) adj. 1. Not easily penetrated; rigid. 2. Difficult. 3. Severe; harsh. 4. Callous; unfeeling. 5. Real.

**hard·ly** (härd'lē) adv. 1. Barely; just. 2. Probably or almost surely not.

**hard·ship** (härd'shĭp') n. Extreme privation; suffering.

**hard·ware** (härd'wâr') n. Metal goods and utensils.

**har·dy** (här'dē) adj. **-dier, -diest.** 1. Rugged; strong. 2. Capable of surviving severe cold, drought; etc., as a plant. 3. Courageous. —**har'di·ness** n.

**hare** (hâr) n. A mammal related to and resembling the rabbits.

**har·em** (hâr'əm, hăr'-) n. 1. A section of a house reserved for women in a Moslem household. 2. The women occupying a harem.

**hark** (härk) v. To listen attentively.

**har·lot** (här'lət) n. A prostitute.

**harm** (härm) n. 1. Injury or damage. 2. Wrong; evil. —v. To damage; injure; impair. —**harm'ful** adj. —**harm'less** adj.

**har·mon·i·ca** (här-mŏn'ĭ-kə) n. A small wind instrument.

**har·mo·ny** (här'mə-nē) n., pl. **-nies.** 1. Agreement or accord, as of feeling. 2. A pleasing combination of parts or elements. 3. Combination and progression of chords in musical structure. —**har·mon'ic** adj. —**har·mo'ni·ous** adj. —**har'mo·nize'** v.

**har·ness** (här'nĭs) n. Gear by which a draft animal pulls a vehicle or implement. —v. 1. To put a harness on. 2. To control and direct the force of.

**harp** (härp) n. A musical instrument with strings played by plucking. —**harp'ist** n.

**har·poon** (här-pōōn') n. A spearlike weapon used esp. in whaling. —v. To strike with a harpoon.

**har·ri·dan** (hăr'ə-dən) n. A disagreeable old woman.

**har·row** (hăr'ō) n. An implement used to break up plowed ground. —v. 1. To break up (soil) with a harrow. 2. To distress greatly; torment.

**har·ry** (hăr'ē) v. **-ried, -rying.** To distress by constant attacks; harass.

**harsh** (härsh) adj. 1. Severe; stern. 2. Unpleasant; irritating. —**harsh'ly** adv. —**harsh'ness** n.

**hart** (härt) n. An adult male deer.

**har·vest** (här'vĭst) n. 1. The gathering in of a crop. 2. A gathered crop. —v. 1. To gather (a crop). **2.** To gain, win, or acquire; reap.

**has** (hăz). 3rd person sing. present indicative of **have.**

**hash** (hăsh) n. **1.** Chopped meat and potatoes. **2.** A jumble; hodgepodge. —v. **1.** To chop up; mince. **2.** To discuss.

**has·n't** (hăz'ənt). Contraction of *has not.*

**hasp** (hăsp, häsp) n. A hinged metal fastener that fits over a staple.

**has·sle** (hăs'əl) n. **1.** An argument or fight. **2.** Trouble; bother.

**has·sock** (hăs'ək) n. A cushion used as a footstool.

**haste** (hāst) n. **1.** Swiftness. **2.** Eagerness; urgency. **3.** Careless or headlong hurrying. —**hast'i·ly** adv. —**hast'i·ness** n.—**hast'y** adj.

**has·ten** (hā'sən) v. To move or cause to move swiftly; hurry.

**hat** (hăt) n. A covering for the head, esp. one with a brim.

**hatch¹** (hăch) n. A small door or trap door, esp. one on board a ship. —**hatch'way** n.

**hatch²** (hăch) v. **1.** To emerge or cause to emerge from an egg. **2.** To cause (an egg or eggs) to produce young. —**hatch'er·y** n.

**hatch·et** (hăch'ĭt) n. A short-handled ax.

**hate** (hāt) v. **hated, hating.** **1.** To loathe; detest. **2.** To dislike. —n. Strong dislike; animosity. —**hate'ful** adj. —**ha'tred** n.

**haugh·ty** (hô'tē) adj. **-tier, -tiest.** Proud and vain to the point of arrogance. —**haugh'ti·ly** adv.—**haugh'ti·ness** n.

**haul** (hôl) v. To pull or drag. —n. **1.** The act of hauling. **2.** The distance over which a load is carted or the load carted. **3.** An amount collected; a take.

**haunch** (hônch, hänch) n. The hip, buttock, and upper thigh.

**haunt** (hônt, hänt) v. **1.** To visit or appear to in the form of a ghost. **2.** To frequent. —n. A place much frequented.

**hau·teur** (hō-tûr') n. Haughtiness; arrogance.

**have** (hăv) v. **had, having, has.** —Used as an auxiliary before a past participle to form the past, present, and future perfect tenses. **1.** To possess; own. **2.** To be obliged to. **3.** To keep. **4.** To accept or take. **5.** To be made of or contain. **6.** To experience. **7.** To give birth to. **8.** To hold in one's mind.

**ha·ven** (hā'vən) n. **1.** A harbor. **2.** A place of sanctuary.

**have·n't** (hăv'ənt). Contraction of *have not.*

**hav·er·sack** (hăv'ər-săk') n. A canvas bag to transport supplies on a hike.

**hav·oc** (hăv'ək) n. Widespread destruction

or confusion.

**hawk¹** (hôk) n. A bird of prey.

**hawk²** (hôk) v. To peddle (wares). —**hawk'er** n.

**haw·ser** (hô'zər) n. A cable used in mooring or towing a ship.

**hay** (hā) n. Grass and other plants cut and dried for fodder. —v. To cut and process grass and other plants to make hay. —**hay'stack'** n.

**haz·ard** (hăz'ərd) n. **1.** A chance or accident. **2.** A danger; risk. —v. To run the risk of; venture. —**haz'ard·ous** adj. —**haz'ard·ous·ly** adv.

**haze¹** (hāz) n. **1.** A foglike mixture of dust, smoke, and vapor suspended in the air. **2.** A vague state of mind. —**haz'i·ness** n. —**haz'y** adj.

**haze²** (hāz) v. **hazed, hazing.** To harass with humiliating tasks or practical jokes.

**ha·zel** (hā'zəl) n. **1.** A small tree bearing edible nuts. **2.** Light yellowish brown. —**ha'zel** adj.

**he** (hē) pron. The 3rd person sing. pronoun in the nominative case, masculine gender. **1.** The male person last mentioned. **2.** Anyone. —n. A male.

**head** (hĕd) n. **1.** The upper or anterior bodily extremity. **2.** Intellect; mind. **3.** A leader. **4.** The foremost position. **5.** The upper or higher end of something. —adj. Foremost in importance. —v. **1.** To be chief of. **2.** To proceed or set out.

**head·ing** (hĕd'ĭng) n. A word or words at the beginning of a chapter, paragraph, etc.

**head·light** (hĕd'lĭt') n. A lamp on the front of a vehicle.

**head·line** (hĕd'lĭn') n. The title of a newspaper article.

**head·long** (hĕd'lông', -lŏng') adv. **1.** With the head leading. **2.** Impetuously. **3.** At breakneck speed.

**head·quar·ters** (hĕd'kwôr'tərz) pl.n. A command center or center of operations.

**head·strong** (hĕd'strông', -strŏng') adj. Willful; obstinate.

**head·way** (hĕd'wā') n. Progress.

**head·y** (hĕd'ē) adj. **-ier, -iest.** **1.** Intoxicating. **2.** Headstrong; obstinate.

**heal** (hēl) v. To restore or return to health.

**health** (hĕlth) n. **1.** The condition or functioning of an organism at any given time. **2.** Freedom from disease and abnormality. —**health'ful** adj. —**health'y** adj.

**heap** (hēp) n. A pile. —v. **1.** To put in a heap. **2.** To fill to overflowing.

**hear** (hîr) v. **heard, hearing. 1.** To perceive by the ear. **2.** To listen attentively. **3.** To learn.

**hear·ing** (hîr'ing) n. **1.** The capacity to hear. **2.** An opportunity to be heard.

**hear·say** (hîr'sā') n. Information or a rumor heard from another.

**hearse** (hûrs) n. A vehicle for conveying a dead body to a cemetery.

**heart** (härt) n. **1.** The organ that pumps blood into the arteries. **2.** The seat of emotions, as affection, compassion, courage, etc. **3.** The innermost area; essence.

**heart·ache** (härt'āk') n. Emotional anguish; deep sorrow. —**heart'break'** n. —**heart'break'ing** adj.

**heart·en** (härt'n) v. To encourage.

**heart·felt** (härt'fĕlt') adj. Deeply or sincerely felt.

**hearth** (härth) n. **1.** The floor of a fireplace. **2.** Family life; the home.

**heart·less** (härt'lĭs) adj. Pitiless; cruel. —**heart'less·ly** adv.

**heart·y** (här'tē) adj. **-ier, -iest. 1.** Exuberant. **2.** Complete or thorough. **3.** Vigorous. **4.** Nourishing. —**heart'i·ly** adv.

**heat** (hēt) n. **1.** Hotness. **2.** The sensation of being hot. **3.** A height of feeling or energy. **4.** A time in which a female animal is ready to mate. **5.** A single course in a race or competition. —v. To make or become warm or hot. —**heat'er** n.

**heath** (hēth) n. An uncultivated tract of land covered with low-growing shrubs.

**hea·then** (hē'thən) n., pl. **-thens** or **-then.** One whose religion does not acknowledge the God of Judaism, Christianity, or Islam. —**hea'then·ish** adj.

**heave** (hēv) v. **heaved** or **hove, heaving. 1.** To raise or lift. **2.** To throw, esp. with great effort. **3.** To rise and fall. **4.** To utter with effort. **5.** To vomit. —n. The act or effort of heaving.

**heav·en** (hĕv'ən) n. **1.** Often **heavens.** The sky or universe as seen from the earth. **2.** The abode of God. **3.** A place or thing that affords supreme happiness. —**heav'en·ly** adj. —**heav'en·ward** adv. & adj.

**heav·y** (hĕv'ē) adj. **-ier, -iest. 1.** Having relatively great weight. **2.** Large in number, amount, etc.; substantial. **3.** Dense or thick. **4.** Rough; violent. **5.** Difficult or oppressive. **6.** Deeply concerned or sad. —**heav'i·ly** adv. —**heav'i·ness** n.

**heck·le** (hĕk'əl) v. **-led, -ling.** To harass, as with questions or objections. —**heck'ler** n.

**hec·tic** (hĕk'tĭk) adj. Marked by feverish activity, confusion, or haste.

**he'd** (hēd). **1.** Contraction of *he had.* **2.** Contraction of *he would.*

**hedge** (hĕj) n. A row of closely planted shrubs forming a boundary. —v. **hedged, hedging. 1.** To enclose with hedges. **2.** To avoid committing oneself.

**hedge·hog** (hĕj'hŏg', -hôg') n. A small mammal covered with dense spines.

**heed** (hēd) v. To pay attention (to). —n. Close attention or consideration. —**heed'ful** adj. —**heed'ful·ly** adv. —**heed'less** adj. —**heed'less·ly** adv.

**heel**[1] (hēl) n. **1.** The rounded rear portion of the human foot. **2.** The part of footwear that covers the heel. —v. To furnish with a heel.

**heel**[2] (hēl) v. To tip or cause to tip to one side.

**heft·y** (hĕf'tē) adj. **-ier, -iest. 1.** Heavy. **2.** Large and powerful. —**heft** n.

**heif·er** (hĕf'ər) n. A young cow.

**height** (hīt) n. **1.** The highest or uppermost point; summit. **2.** The highest or most advanced degree; zenith; climax. **3.** The distance from the base to the top; altitude. **4.** Measurement from head to foot; stature. **5.** Often **heights.** A high place.

**height·en** (hīt'n) v. **1.** To intensify. **2.** To become or make higher.

**hei·nous** (hā'nəs) adj. Reprehensible.

**heir** (âr) n. A person who inherits the property of another. —**heir·ess** fem.n.

**heir·loom** (âr'lōōm') n. A possession passed down in a family.

**held** (hĕld). p.t. & p.p. of **hold.**

**hel·i·cop·ter** (hĕl'ĭ-kŏp'tər) n. An aircraft with blades that rotate horizontally about a vertical central axis.

**he·li·um** (hē'lē-əm) n. A colorless, odorless gaseous element used to provide lift for balloons.

**hell** (hĕl) n. **1.** The place of punishment for the wicked after death. **2.** Torment; anguish. —**hell'ish** adj.

**he'll** (hĕl). **1.** Contraction of *he will.* **2.** Contraction of *he shall.*

**hel·lo** (hĕ-lō', hə-) interj. Expressive of greeting.

**helm** (hĕlm) n. The steering gear of a ship. —**helms'man** n.

**hel·met** (hĕl'mĭt) n. A protective head covering.

**help** (hĕlp) v. **1.** To aid. **2.** To contribute to; further. **3.** To give relief to. **4.** To avoid. —n. **1.** Aid; assistance. **2.** Relief; remedy. **3.** A person employed to assist. —**help'er** n.

—**help′ful** *adj.* —**help′ful·ly** *adv.* —**help′ful·ness** *n.*

**help·ing** (hĕl′pĭng) *n.* A portion of food for one person.

**help·less** (hĕlp′lĭs) *adj.* **1.** Defenseless; dependent. **2.** Powerless. —**help′less·ly** *adv.* —**help′less·ness** *n.*

**hem** (hĕm) *n.* An edge or border of a piece of cloth. —*v.* **hemmed, hemming. 1.** To fold back and stitch down the edge of. **2.** To encircle; enclose.

**hem·i·sphere** (hĕm′ĭ-sfîr′) *n.* **1.** A half of a sphere. **2.** Either the N or S half of the earth or the E or W half. —**hem′i·spher′ic, hem′i·spher′i·cal** *adj.*

**hem·or·rhage** (hĕm′ər-ĭj) *n.* Bleeding, esp. heavy bleeding. —*v.* **-rhaged, -rhaging.** To bleed heavily.

**hemp** (hĕmp) *n.* A plant with a coarse fiber used to make rope, cord, etc.

**hen** (hĕn) *n.* A female bird, esp. of the domestic fowl.

**hence** (hĕns) *adv.* **1.** Therefore. **2.** From now. **3.** Forth from this place.

**hence·forth** (hĕns′fôrth′) *adv.* Also **hence·for·ward.** From now on.

**hench·man** (hĕnch′mən) *n.* A trusted follower.

**hen·na** (hĕn′ə) *n.* A reddish-brown dye obtained from a shrub.

**hep·a·ti·tis** (hĕp′ə-tī′tĭs) *n.* Inflammation of the liver.

**her** (hûr) *pron.* **1.** The objective case of *she.* **2.** The possessive form of *she.*

**her·ald** (hĕr′əld) *n.* One who proclaims important news or gives indication of something to come. —*v.* To proclaim; foretell. —**he·ral′dic** *adj.*

**herb** (ûrb, hûrb) *n.* **1.** A plant with a fleshy rather than woody stem. **2.** A plant used in medicine or as seasoning. —**her·ba′ceous** *adj.* —**herb′age** *n.* —**herb′al** *adj.*

**herd** (hûrd) *n.* A group of animals that remain or are kept together. —*v.* To congregate, gather, or drive in a herd. —**herd′er** *n.* —**herds′man** *n.*

**here** (hîr) *adv.* **1.** At, in, or to this place. **2.** At this time.

**here·af·ter** (hîr-ăf′tər, -äf′tər) *adv.* After this. —*n.* Life after death.

**here·by** (hîr-bī′) *adv.* By this means.

**he·red·i·tar·y** (hə-rĕd′ĭ-tĕr′ē) *adj.* **1.** Passing down by inheritance. **2.** Genetically transmitted.

**he·red·i·ty** (hə-rĕd′ĭ-tē) *n., pl.* **-ties.** The genetic transmission of characteristics from parents to offspring.

**here·in** (hîr-ĭn′) *adv.* In this.

**her·e·sy** (hĕr′ĭ-sē) *n., pl.* **-sies.** An opinion or doctrine at variance with established beliefs, esp. religious beliefs. —**her·e·tic** *n.* —**he·ret′i·cal** *adj.*

**here·to·fore** (hîr′tə-fôr′, -fōr′) *adv.* Up to the present time.

**her·i·tage** (hĕr′ĭ-tĭj) *n.* **1.** Property inherited. **2.** Tradition passed down from preceding generations.

**her·met·ic** (hər-mĕt′ĭk) *adj.* Also **her·met·i·cal.** Completely sealed; airtight. —**her·met′i·cal·ly** *adv.*

**her·mit** (hûr′mĭt) *n.* One who lives in solitude and seclusion.

**he·ro** (hîr′ō) *n., pl.* **-roes. 1.** A man noted for his special achievements. **2.** The principal male character in a novel, poem, or dramatic work. —**he·ro′ic** *adj.* —**her′o·ine** *fem.n.* —**her′o·ism′** *n.*

**her·o·in** (hĕr′ō-ən) *n.* A narcotic derived from morphine.

**her·ring** (hĕr′ĭng) *n., pl.* **-ring** or **-rings.** A food fish of Atlantic waters.

**hers** (hûrz) The possessive form of *she.*

**her·self** (hûr-sĕlf′) *pron.* The reflexive form of *she.*

**he's** (hēz). **1.** Contraction of *he is.* **2.** Contraction of *he has.*

**hes·i·tate** (hĕz′ə-tāt′) *v.* **1.** To be slow to act or decide; waver. **2.** To pause briefly, as in uncertainty. —**hes′i·tan·cy** *n.* —**hes′i·tant** *adj.* —**hes′i·ta′tion** *n.*

**het·er·o·dox** (hĕt′ər-ə-dŏks′) *adj.* Holding unorthodox opinions. —**het′er·o·dox′y** *n.*

**het·er·o·ge·ne·ous** (hĕt′ər-ə-jē′nē-əs, -jēn′-yəs) *adj.* Also **het·er·og·e·nous.** Having dissimilar elements; not homogeneous. —**het′er·o·ge·ne′i·ty** *n.*

**hew** (hyōō) *v.* **hewed, hewn** or **hewed, hewing.** To shape or cut down with an ax.

**hex** (hĕks) *n.* An evil spell; curse. —*v.* To bring bad luck to.

**hex·a·gon** (hĕk′sə-gŏn′) *n.* A polygon having six sides. —**hex·ag′o·nal** *adj.*

**hey** (hā) *interj.* **1.** Expressive of surprise. **2.** Used to attract attention.

**hey·day** (hā′dā′) *n.* The period of greatest popularity, success, etc.

**hi** (hī) *interj.* Expressive of greeting.

**hi·a·tus** (hī-ā′təs) *n., pl.* **-tuses** or **-tus. 1.** A gap. **2.** An interruption in time.

**hi·ber·nate** (hī′bər-nāt′) *v.* **-nated, -nating.** To pass the winter in a dormant or torpid state. —**hi′ber·na′tion** *n.*

**hic-cup** (hĭk′ŭp) *n.* A spasm of the diaphragm resulting in a sudden inhalation quickly cut off by a spasm in the glottis. —*v.* -**cupped,** -**cupping.** To have such a spasm or spasms.

**hide**[1] (hīd) *v.* **hid, hidden** or **hid, hiding.** **1.** To put or keep out of sight; conceal. **2.** To seek refuge.

**hide**[2] (hīd) *n.* The skin of an animal.

**hid-e-ous** (hĭd′ē-əs) *adj.* **1.** Physically repulsive; ugly. **2.** Despicable.

**hier-ar-chy** (hī′ə-rär′kē, hī′rär′-) *n., pl.* -**chies.** A body of persons, esp. clergy, classified according to rank or authority. —**hi·er·ar·chi·cal,** **hi·er·ar·chic** *adj.*

**hi·er·o·glyph·ic** (hī′ər-ə-glĭf′ĭk, hī′rə-) *n.* A picture or symbol used in writing, esp. in the writing system of ancient Egypt.

**high** (hī) *adj.* **1.** Tall; elevated. **2.** Above average, as in degree, amount, etc. **3.** Piercing in tone or sound. **4.** Costly; expensive. **5.** Excited; elated. **6.** Being at or near its peak. **7.** Of great importance. —*adv.* At, in, or to a high position, price, or level. —*n.* **1.** A high degree, level, point, etc. **2.** The transmission gear giving the greatest output speed. —**high·ly** *adv.*

**high-flown** (hī′flōn′) *adj.* **1.** Lofty; exalted. **2.** Pretentious.

**high-hand·ed** (hī′hăn′dĭd) *adj.* In an arrogant or arbitrary manner.

**high·light** (hī′līt′) *n.* An outstanding event or prominent detail. —*v.* **1.** To give prominence to. **2.** To be the highlight of.

**high-strung** (hī′strŭng′) *adj.* Acutely nervous.

**high·way** (hī′wā′) *n.* A main public road.

**hi·jack** (hī′jăk′) *v.* **1.** To rob (a vehicle) by stopping it in transit. **2.** To seize or commandeer (a moving vehicle). —**hi′jack′er** *n.*

**hike** (hīk) *v.* **hiked, hiking.** **1.** To go on an extended walk. **2.** To raise or go up. —*n.* **1.** A walk. **2.** A rise, as in prices. —**hik′er** *n.*

**hi·lar·i·ous** (hĭ-lâr′ē-əs, hī-) *adj.* Boisterously funny. —**hi·lar·i·ty** *n.*

**hill** (hĭl) *n.* A naturally elevated area of land smaller than a mountain. —**hill′side**′ *n.* —**hill′top**′ *n.* —**hill′y** *adj.*

**hilt** (hĭlt) *n.* The handle of a weapon or tool.

**him** (hĭm) *pron.* The objective case of *he.*

**him·self** (hĭm-sĕlf′) *pron.* The reflexive form of *he.*

**hind**[1] (hīnd) *adj.* Located at the rear; posterior.

**hind**[2] (hīnd) *n.* A female deer.

**hin·der** (hĭn′dər) *v.* **1.** To hamper. **2.** To

prevent. —**hin′drance** *n.*

**hind·most** (hīnd′mōst′) *adj.* Farthest to the rear.

**Hin·du·ism** (hĭn′dōō-ĭz′əm) *n.* The major religion of India. —**Hin′du** *n. & adj.*

**hinge** (hĭnj) *n.* A jointed device on which a door, gate, etc., turns or swings. —*v.* **hinged, hinging.** **1.** To attach by a hinge. **2.** To depend.

**hint** (hĭnt) *n.* A subtle suggestion; clue. —*v.* To give a hint.

**hip** (hĭp) *n.* The laterally projecting prominence of the pelvis from the waist to the thigh.

**hip·po·drome** (hĭp′ə-drōm′) *n.* An arena.

**hip·po·pot·a·mus** (hĭp′ə-pŏt′ə-məs) *n., pl.* -**muses** or -**mi.** A large African river mammal.

**hire** (hīr) *v.* **hired, hiring.** **1.** To engage the services of (a person) for a fee; employ. **2.** To rent or rent out. —*n.* The payment for services or use of something.

**hir·sute** (hûr′sōōt′, hûr′sōōt′) *adj.* Hairy.

**his** (hĭz) The possessive form of *he.*

**hiss** (hĭs) *n.* A sharp, sibilant sound similar to a sustained *s.* —*v.* **1.** To make a hiss. **2.** To direct hisses at in disapproval.

**his·to·ry** (hĭs′tə-rē) *n., pl.* -**ries.** **1.** A chronological record of events. **2.** The branch of knowledge that analyzes past events. —**his·to′ri·an** *n.* —**his·tor′ic, his·tor′i·cal** *adj.* —**his·tor′i·cal·ly** *adv.*

**his·tri·on·ic** (hĭs′trē-ŏn′ĭk) *adj.* Theatrical; affected. —*n.* **histrionics.** Showy, exaggerated emotional behavior.

**hit** (hĭt) *v.* **hit, hitting.** **1.** To come or cause to come in contact with; strike. **2.** To affect adversely. **3.** To propel with a blow. **4.** To get to; reach. —*n.* **1.** A collision or impact. **2.** A shot, blow, or throw. **3.** A successful or popular venture. —**hit′ter** *n.*

**hitch** (hĭch) *v.* **1.** To fasten with a loop, hook, or noose. **2.** To connect or attach. **3.** To raise with a tug or jerk. —*n.* **1.** A short jerking motion. **2.** An impediment or delay. **3.** A term of military service.

**hith·er** (hĭth′ər) *adv.* To or toward this place.

**hith·er·to** (hĭth′ər-tōō′) *adv.* Until this time.

**hive** (hīv) *n.* **1.** A structure for housing bees, esp. honeybees. **2.** A colony of bees.

**hoard** (hôrd, hōrd) *n.* A supply for future use; cache. —*v.* To save, keep, or store away. —**hoard′er** *n.*

**hoarse** (hôrs, hōrs) *adj.* **hoarser, hoarsest.** Grating in sound; husky; croaking.

**hoar·y** (hôr′ē, hōr′ē) *adj.* -**ier,** -**iest.** White

or grayish. **2.** Very old; aged.

**hoax** (hōks) *n.* A trick or action intended to deceive. —*v.* To deceive or cheat by a hoax.

**hob·ble** (hŏb'əl) *v.* **-bled, -bling. 1.** To limp. **2.** To fetter; restrain.

**hob·by** (hŏb'ē) *n., pl.* **-bies.** A pastime.

**hob·nob** (hŏb'nŏb') *v.* **-nobbed, -nobbing.** To associate familiarly (with *with*).

**ho·bo** (hō'bō) *n., pl.* **-boes** or **-bos.** A tramp; vagrant.

**hock**[1] (hŏk) *n.* The joint of the hind leg of a horse or other four-footed animal.

**hock**[2] (hŏk) *v.* To pawn.

**hock·ey** (hŏk'ē) *n.* A game played on ice with curved sticks and a puck.

**hod** (hŏd) *n.* **1.** A trough for transporting loads, as of bricks. **2.** A coal scuttle.

**hoe** (hō) *n.* A tool used for weeding, cultivating, and gardening. — **hoe** *v.*

**hog** (hŏg, hôg) *n.* **1.** A pig. **2.** A greedy or selfish person. —*v.* **hogged, hogging.** To take more than one's share of.

**hogs·head** (hŏgz'hĕd', hôgz'-) *n.* A large barrel or cask.

**hoist** (hoist) *v.* To raise or haul up. —*n.* **1.** A device for hoisting. **2.** A pull; lift.

**hold**[1] (hōld) *v.* **held, holding. 1.** To have and keep in possession; grasp; clasp. **2.** To bear; support. **3.** To contain. **4.** To restrain. **5.** To believe; assert; affirm. **6.** To stand up under stress; last. —*n.* **1.** A grip; clasp. **2.** A strong influence. — **hold'er** *n.*

**hold**[2] (hōld) *n.* The interior of a ship where cargo is stored.

**hold·ing** (hōl'dĭng) *n.* **1.** Land rented or leased. **2.** Often **holdings.** Legally possessed property.

**hole** (hōl) *n.* **1.** A cavity. **2.** An opening; gap. **3.** An animal's burrow.

**hol·i·day** (hŏl'ə-dā') *n.* A day on which a particular event is celebrated. — **hol'i·day** *adj.*

**hol·ler** (hŏl'ər) *v.* To yell or shout.

**hol·low** (hŏl'ō) *adj.* **1.** Having a cavity within. **2.** Concave; sunken. **3.** Without substance or validity. —*n.* **1.** A cavity. **2.** A valley. —*v.* To make or become hollow.

**hol·ly** (hŏl'ē) *n., pl.* **-lies.** A shrub bearing bright-red berries.

**hol·o·caust** (hŏl'ə-kôst', hō'lə-) *n.* Great or total destruction, esp. by fire.

**hol·ster** (hōl'stər) *n.* A leather case for a pistol.

**ho·ly** (hō'lē) *adj.* **-lier, -liest. 1.** Associated with a divine power; sacred. **2.** Blessed. **3.** Saintly. **4.** Regarded with special respect. — **ho'li·ness** *n.*

**hom·age** (hŏm'ĭj, ŏm'-) *n.* Honor or respect publicly expressed.

**home** (hōm) *n.* **1.** The place where one resides. **2.** A family living in a dwelling; household. **3.** A customary environment; habitat. **4.** A place of origin. —*adj.* Of a household or house. —*adv.* **1.** At or to one's home. **2.** To the center or heart of something. — **home'ward** *adv. & adj.* — **home'y** *adj.*

**home·ly** (hōm'lē) *adj.* **-lier, -liest. 1.** Familiar. **2.** Not pretty; plain.

**home·spun** (hōm'spŭn') *adj.* **1.** Spun or woven at home. **2.** Simple; unpretentious. —*n.* A coarse woolen cloth.

**hom·i·cide** (hŏm'ə-sīd', hō'mə-) *n.* **1.** The killing of one person by another. **2.** A person who kills another. — **hom'i·ci'dal** *adj.*

**hom·i·ly** (hŏm'ə-lē) *n., pl.* **-lies.** A sermon.

**ho·mo·ge·ne·ous** (hō'mə-jē'nē-əs, -jēn'yəs, hŏm'ə-) *adj.* Uniform in composition throughout. — **ho'mo·ge·ne'i·ty** *n.* — **ho'mo·ge'ne·ous·ly** *adv.* — **ho·mog'e·nize'** *v.*

**ho·mo·sex·u·al·i·ty** (hō'mə-sĕk'shōō-ăl'ə-tē, hŏm'ə-) *n.* Sexual desire for or activity with another or others of one's own sex. — **ho·mo·sex'u·al** *adj. & n.*

**hone** (hōn) *n.* A fine-grained whetstone. —*v.* **honed, honing.** To sharpen on a hone.

**hon·est** (ŏn'ĭst) *adj.* **1.** Truthful and trustworthy. **2.** Not deceptive; genuine. **3.** Frank; sincere. — **hon'est·ly** *adv.* — **hon'es·ty** *n.*

**hon·ey** (hŭn'ē) *n., pl.* **-eys.** A sweet fluid produced by bees.

**hon·ey·comb** (hŭn'ē-kōm') *n.* A wax structure made by honeybees to hold honey. —*v.* To fill with holes; riddle.

**hon·ey·moon** (hŭn'ē-mōōn') *n.* A trip taken by a newly married couple. —*v.* To spend a honeymoon.

**hon·or** (ŏn'ər) *n.* **1.** Esteem; respect. **2.** Glory; distinction. **3.** Great privilege. **4.** Personal integrity. —*v.* **1.** To esteem; show respect for. **2.** To confer distinction upon. **3.** To accept or pay as valid, as a check. — **hon'or·a·ble** *adj.* — **hon'or·a·bly** *adv.*

**hon·or·ar·y** (ŏn'ə-rĕr'ē) *adj.* Conferred as an honor without the usual duties, privileges, etc.

**hood** (hŏod) *n.* **1.** A loose covering for the head. **2.** The metal lid over an automobile engine. — **hood'ed** *adj.*

**hood·lum** (hōod'ləm, hŏod'-) *n.* A thug.

**hood·wink** (hŏod'wĭngk') *v.* To deceive; trick.

**hoof** (hŏof, hōof) *n., pl.* **hoofs** or **hooves.** The

**horny** covering of the foot of horses, cattle, etc.

**hook** (hŏŏk) n. A curved device, usually of metal, used to catch, drag, or fasten something. —v. To get hold of with a hook.

**hoop** (hōōp, hŏŏp) n. A circular band.

**hoot** (hōōt) v. 1. To utter the cry of an owl. 2. To make a derisive cry. —n. 1. The cry of an owl. 2. A cry of derision.

**hooves.** Alternate pl. of **hoof.**

**hop** (hŏp) v. **hopped, hopping.** To jump, esp. on one foot. —n. A light, springy jump, on one foot.

**hope** (hōp) v. **hoped, hoping.** To desire (something) with confidence of fulfillment. —n. 1. A desire supported by confidence of its fulfillment. 2. That which is desired. 3. Expectation; confidence. —**hope'ful** adj. —**hope'ful·ly** adv. —**hope'less** adj. —**hope'less·ly** adv. —**hope'less·ness** n.

**hop·per** (hŏp'ər) n. A receptacle in which materials are stored.

**horde** (hôrd, hōrd) n. A throng or swarm.

**ho·ri·zon** (hə-rī'zən) n. The apparent intersection of the earth and sky.

**hor·i·zon·tal** (hôr'ə-zŏnt'l, hōr'-) adj. 1. Parallel to the plane of the horizon. 2. Flat.

**hor·mone** (hôr'mōn') n. A substance formed by one organ that stimulates another to function. —**hor·mo'nal** adj.

**horn** (hôrn) n. 1. One of the hard structures projecting from the head of cattle, sheep, etc. 2. A wind instrument made of brass. —**horned** adj. —**horn'y** adj.

**hor·net** (hôr'nĭt) n. A large wasp.

**ho·ro·scope** (hôr'ə-skōp', hōr'-) n. An astrological forecast of a person's future.

**hor·ren·dous** (hô-rĕn'dəs, hŏ-) adj. Hideous; dreadful.

**hor·ri·ble** (hôr'ə-bəl, hŏr'-) adj. 1. Causing horror. 2. Unpleasant. —**hor'ri·bly** adv.

**hor·rid** (hôr'ĭd, hŏr'-) adj. 1. Causing horror. 2. Unpleasant, disagreeable, etc. —**hor'rid·ly** adv.

**hor·ror** (hôr'ər, hŏr'-) n. 1. An intense feeling of repugnance and fear; terror. 2. Intense dislike; abhorrence. —**hor'ri·fy** v.

**horse** (hôrs) n. 1. A large hoofed mammal used for riding, carrying loads, etc. 2. A supportive device.

**horse·back** (hôrs'băk') adv. On the back of a horse.

**horse·pow·er** (hôrs'pou'ər) n. A unit of power equal to 745.7 watts.

**horse·shoe** (hôrs'shōō', hôrsh'-) n. A U-shaped iron plate nailed to a horse's hoof.

**hor·ti·cul·ture** (hôr'tə-kŭl'chər) n. The science of cultivating plants. —**hor'ti·cul'tur·al** adj. —**hor'ti·cul'tur·ist** n.

**hose** (hōz) n. 1. pl. **hose.** Stockings or socks. 2. pl. **hoses.** A flexible tube for spraying water. —v. **hosed, hosing.** To water with a hose.

**ho·sier·y** (hō'zhə-rē) n. Hose.

**hos·pi·ta·ble** (hŏs'pə-tə-bəl, hŏs·pĭt'ə-bəl) adj. Cordial and generous to guests. —**hos'pi·ta'bly** adv.

**hos·pi·tal** (hŏs'pə-təl) n. An institution providing treatment for the sick and injured. —**hos'pi·tal·i·za'tion** n. —**hos'pi·tal·ize'** v.

**host¹** (hōst) n. One who entertains guests. —**hostess** fem.n.

**host²** (hōst) n. A great number.

**host³** (hōst) n. Also **Host.** The consecrated bread of the Eucharist.

**hos·tage** (hŏs'tĭj) n. A person held as a security.

**hos·tile** (hŏs'təl, -tīl') adj. 1. Of an enemy. 2. Feeling or showing enmity.

**hos·til·i·ty** (hŏ-stĭl'ə-tē) n. pl. **-ties.** 1. Antagonism; enmity. 2. **hostilities.** Open warfare.

**hot** (hŏt) adj. **hotter, hottest.** 1. Being at a high temperature. 2. Warmer than is normal or desirable. 3. Spicy. 4. Angry. 5. Currently popular. —**hot'ly** adv.

**ho·tel** (hō-tĕl') n. A public house that provides lodging and board.

**hot·head·ed** (hŏt'hĕd'ĭd) adj. 1. Having a fiery temper. 2. Impetuous; rash. —**hot'head'** n.

**hot·house** (hŏt'hous') n. A greenhouse.

**hound** (hound) n. A dog originally bred and used for hunting. —v. To pursue relentlessly.

**hour** (our) n. 1. The 24th part of a day. 2. The time of day. 3. A customary or specified time. —**hour'ly** adj. & adv.

**house** (hous) n., pl. **houses.** 1. A building used as a dwelling. 2. A household. 3. A commercial firm. 4. A legislative assembly. —v. **housed, housing.** 1. To provide living quarters for. 2. To contain.

**house·hold** (hous'hōld') n. The members of a family and others living under the same roof. —**house'hold'** adj.

**house·keep·er** (hous'kē'pər) n. One who has charge of domestic tasks in a house. —**house'keep'ing** n.

**house·wife** (hous'wīf') n. A woman who manages her own house.

**hous·ing** (hou'zĭng) n. 1. A dwelling, or

dwellings collectively. **2.** A protective covering, as for a mechanical part.

**hov·el** (hŭv'əl, hŏv'-) *n.* A small, miserable dwelling.

**hov·er** (hŭv'ər, hŏv'-) *v.* **1.** To fly or float as if suspended. **2.** To linger close to a place.

**how** (hou) *adv.* **1.** In what manner or way. **2.** In what state or condition. **3.** To what extent, amount, or degree. **4.** For what purpose.

**how·ev·er** (hou-ĕv'ər) *adv.* **1.** By whatever manner or means. **2.** To whatever degree or extent. —*conj.* Nevertheless; yet.

**howl** (houl) *v.* **1.** To utter a long, wailing cry. **2.** To laugh heartily. —*n.* A long, wailing cry.

**hub** (hŭb) *n.* **1.** The center portion of a wheel. **2.** A center of activity.

**hub·bub** (hŭb'ŭb') *n.* A confused din.

**hu·bris** (hyōō'brĭs) *n.* Overbearing pride.

**huck·le·ber·ry** (hŭk'əl-bĕr'ē) *n.* A blackish, edible berry.

**huck·ster** (hŭk'stər) *n.* A peddler.

**hud·dle** (hŭd'əl) *v.* **-dled, -dling. 1.** To crowd in a close group. **2.** To hunch up; crouch.

**hue** (hyōō) *n.* Color; tint; shade.

**huff** (hŭf) *n.* A fit of anger. —*v.* To blow; breathe heavily. —**huff'y** *adj.*

**hug** (hŭg) *v.* **hugged, hugging. 1.** To clasp; embrace. **2.** To keep close to. —*n.* A close embrace.

**huge** (hyōōj) *adj.* **huger, hugest.** Very large; enormous. —**huge'ness** *n.*

**hulk** (hŭlk) *n.* **1.** The hull of a ship, esp. an old or wrecked ship. **2.** A large, clumsy person or object. —**hulk'ing** *adj.*

**hull** (hŭl) *n.* **1.** The outer covering of a fruit, seed, or nut. **2.** The main body of a ship. —*v.* To remove the hulls of (fruit or seeds).

**hum** (hŭm) *v.* **hummed, humming. 1.** To produce a continuous droning sound. **2.** To sing with closed lips. —*n.* A continuous droning sound.

**hu·man** (hyōō'mən) *adj.* **1.** Of mankind or of persons. **2.** Having the form or qualities of man. —*n.* Also **human being.** A person. —**hu'man·ly** *adv.*

**hu·mane** (hyōō-mān') *adj.* Compassionate; kind. —**hu·mane'ly** *adv.*

**hu·man·i·tar·i·an** (hyōō-măn'ə-târ'ē-ən) *n.* One devoted to the promotion of human welfare. —*adj.* Concerned with human welfare. —**hu·man'i·tar'i·an·ism'** *n.*

**hu·man·i·ty** (hyōō-măn'ə-tē) *n.* **1.** Mankind. **2.** The condition of being human. **3.** Kindness; mercy.

**hum·ble** (hŭm'bəl) *adj.* **-bler, -blest. 1.** Mod-

est; meek. **2.** Deeply respectful. **3.** Lowly. —*v.* **-bled, -bling.** To abase. —**hum'bly** *adv.*

**hum·bug** (hŭm'bŭg') *n.* **1.** A hoax. **2.** Nonsense.

**hum·drum** (hŭm'drŭm') *adj.* Monotonous; uneventful.

**hu·mid** (hyōō'mĭd) *adj.* Having a high concentration of moisture. —**hu·mid'i·fy'** *v.* —**hu·mid'i·ty** *n.*

**hu·mil·i·ate** (hyōō-mĭl'ē-āt') *v.* **-ated, -ating.** To destroy the dignity or pride of; shame; disgrace. —**hu·mil'i·a'tion** *n.*

**hu·mil·i·ty** (hyōō-mĭl'ə-tē) *n.* The quality of being humble.

**hu·mor** (hyōō'mər) *n.* **1.** The quality of being comical. **2.** The ability to perceive, enjoy, etc., what is comical. **3.** State of mind; mood. —*v.* To indulge. —**hu'mor·ist** *n.* —**hu'mor·ous** *adj.*

**hump** (hŭmp) *n.* A rounded protuberance. —*v.* To make into a hump; round.

**hunch** (hŭnch) *v.* To arch into a hump. —*n.* A strong feeling or guess; premonition.

**hunch·back** (hŭnch'băk') *n.* One having an abnormally humped back.

**hun·dred** (hŭn'drĭd) *n. pl.* **-dreds** or **-dred.** The cardinal number written 100. —**hun'dred** *adj. & pron.* —**hun'dredth** *n.*

**hung** (hŭng) Alternate *p.t.* & *p.p.* of **hang.**

**hun·ger** (hŭng'gər) *n.* **1.** A strong desire or need for food. **2.** A strong desire; craving. —*v.* **1.** To be hungry. **2.** To desire; yearn. —**hun'gri·ly** *adv.* —**hun'gry** *adj.*

**hunk** (hŭngk) *n.* A large piece; chunk.

**hunt** (hŭnt) *v.* **1.** To pursue (animals) for food, sport, etc. **2.** To search for; seek. —*n.* **1.** The act or sport of hunting. **2.** A search or pursuit. —**hunt'er** *n.* —**hunt'ress** *fem.n.*

**hur·dle** (hûrd'l) *n.* **1.** A barrier in obstacle races. **2.** Any obstacle or problem that must be overcome. —*v.* **-dled, -dling.** To jump over (a barrier). —**hur'dler** *n.*

**hurl** (hûrl) *v.* To throw forcefully; fling.

**hur·rah** (hōo-rä', -rô') *interj.* Also **hoo-ray, hur·ray.** Expressive of elation, approval, etc. —**hur·rah'** *n.*

**hur·ri·cane** (hûr'ĭ-kān') *n.* A severe tropical cyclone.

**hur·ry** (hûr'ē) *v.* **-ried, -rying.** To move or cause to move with speed or haste; rush. —*n., pl.* **-ries.** Haste; a rush. —**hur'ried·ly** *adv.*

**hurt** (hûrt) *v.* **hurt, hurting. 1.** To cause to feel physical pain. **2.** To offend or distress. **3.** To damage; harm. —*n.* Something that hurts; a pain, injury, or wound. —**hurt'ful** *adj.*

**hur·tle** (hûrt'l) v. -tled, -tling. 1. To move with forceful speed. 2. To collide violently; crash.

**hus·band** (hŭz'bənd) n. A male spouse. —v. To spend or use wisely.

**hus·band·ry** (hŭz'bən-drē) n. 1. Farming; agriculture. 2. Careful management.

**hush** (hŭsh) v. To make or become silent. —n. A silence; stillness.

**husk** (hŭsk) n. A dry or leaflike outer covering, as of an ear of corn. —v. To remove the husk from.

**husk·y¹** (hŭs'kē) adj. -ier, -iest. Hoarse.

**husk·y²** (hŭs'kē) adj. -ier, -iest. Large and strong.

**hus·sy** (hŭz'ē, hŭs'ē) n, pl. -sies. A saucy girl.

**hus·tle** (hŭs'əl) v. -tled, -tling. 1. To jostle; shove. 2. To hurry along. 3. To work busily and quickly. —n. Energetic activity.

**hut** (hŭt) n. A makeshift or crude dwelling; shack.

**hutch** (hŭch) n. 1. A coop for small animals. 2. A cupboard with open shelves above it.

**hy·a·cinth** (hī'ə-sĭnth) n. A plant with fragrant flowers.

**hy·brid** (hī'brĭd) n. The offspring of genetically dissimilar parents or stock. —**hy'brid** adj.

**hy·drant** (hī'drənt) n. An upright pipe serving as an outlet from a water main.

**hy·drau·lic** (hī-drô'lĭk) adj. 1. Of or operated by a fluid, esp. water, under pressure. 2. Of hydraulics. —n. **hydraulics** (takes sing. v.). The physical science and technology of the behavior of fluids.

**hy·dro·e·lec·tric** (hī'drō-ĭ-lĕk'trĭk) adj. Generating electricity from the energy of running or falling water.

**hy·dro·gen** (hī'drə-jən) n. A colorless, highly flammable gaseous element used in rocket fuels.

**hy·dro·pho·bi·a** (hī'drə-fō'bē-ə) n. Rabies.

**hy·dro·plane** (hī'drə-plān') n. 1. A seaplane. 2. A high-speed motorboat that skims the water.

**hy·e·na** (hī-ē'nə) n. A carnivorous African or Asian mammal.

**hy·giene** (hī'jēn') n. The science of health and the prevention of disease. —**hy'gien'ic** adj.

**hymn** (hĭm) n. A song of praise, esp. to God.

**hym·nal** (hĭm'nəl) n. A book of hymns.

**hy·per·bo·le** (hī-pûr'bə-lē) n. Exaggeration used as a figure of speech.

**hy·per·ten·sion** (hī'pər-tĕn'shən) n. Abnormally high blood pressure.

**hy·phen** (hī'fən) n. A punctuation mark ( - ) used between parts of a compound word or between syllables of a divided word.

**hyp·no·sis** (hĭp-nō'sĭs) n. An artificially induced sleeplike condition. —**hyp·not'ic** adj. —**hyp'no·tism** n. —**hyp'no·tize'** v.

**hy·po·chon·dri·a** (hī'pə-kŏn'drē-ə) n. The persistent conviction that one is or is likely to become ill. —**hy'po·chon'dri·ac'** n. & adj.

**hy·poc·ri·sy** (hĭ-pŏk'rə-sē) n. The feigning of beliefs, feelings, or virtues one does not hold. —**hyp'o·crite'** n. —**hyp'o·crit'i·cal** adj.

**hy·po·der·mic** (hī'pə-dûr'mĭk) adj. Injected beneath the skin. —n. A hypodermic injection.

**hy·pot·e·nuse** (hī-pŏt'n/y/ōōs') n. The side of a right triangle opposite the right angle.

**hy·poth·e·sis** (hī-pŏth'ə-sĭs) n, pl. -ses. An assumption subject to verification or proof. —**hy·poth'e·size'** v. —**hy'po·thet'i·cal** adj.

**hys·te·ri·a** (hĭ-stĕr'ē-ə) n. Uncontrollable fear or other strong emotion. —**hys·ter'i·cal·ly** adv.

**hys·ter·ics** (hĭ-stĕr'ĭks) n. A fit of uncontrollable laughing and crying.

**I**

**i, I** (ī) n. The 9th letter of the English alphabet.

**I** (ī) pron. The first person sing. pronoun in the nominative case.

**ice** (īs) n. 1. Frozen water. 2. A dessert of flavored crushed ice. —v. **iced, icing.** 1. To chill. 2. To cover with ice or icing. —**i'ci·ly** adv. —**i'cy** adj.

**i·ci·cle** (ī'sĭ-kəl) n. A tapering spike of ice.

**I'd** (īd). Contraction of I had, I would, and I should.

**i·de·a** (ī-dē'ə) n. 1. A mental conception; thought. 2. An opinion. 3. A plan or method. —**i·de·a'tion·al** n.

**i·de·al** (ī-dē'əl, ī-dēl') n. 1. A standard or model of absolute perfection. 2. An honorable principle. —adj. 1. Perfect or near-perfect. 2. Existing only in the mind. —**i·de·al·ly** adv.

**i·de·al·ism** (ī-dē'ə-lĭz'əm) n. Seeing things in ideal forms rather than as they actually are. —**i·de·al·ist** n. —**i·de·al·is'tic** adj. —**i·de·**

**al·ize′** v.

**i·den·ti·cal** (ī-děn′tǐ-kəl) adj. The same; equal. — **i·den′ti·cal·ly** adv.

**i·den·ti·fy** (ī-děn′tə-fī′) v. **-fied, -fying. 1.** To establish the identity of. **2.** To consider as identical; equate. **3.** To associate (oneself) with. — **i·den′ti·fi′a·ble** adj. — **i·den′ti·fi·ca′tion** n.

**i·den·ti·ty** (ī-děn′tə-tē) n., pl. **-ties. 1.** The set of characteristics by which a person or thing is known. **2.** Individuality.

**i·de·ol·o·gy** (ī′dē-ŏl′ə-jē, ĭd′ē-) n., pl. **-gies.** The body of ideas forming the basis of an individual, group, or culture. — **i′de·o·log′i·cal** adj.

**id·i·ot** (ĭd′ē-ət) n. **1.** A mentally deficient person. **2.** An imbecile; blockhead. — **id′i·o·cy** n. — **id′i·ot′ic** adj.

**i·dle** (īd′l) adj. **idler, idlest. 1.** Inactive. **2.** Lazy. **3.** Useless or groundless. —v. **idled, idling.** To pass time without working. — **i′dly** adv.

**i·dol** (īd′l) n. **1.** An image of a deity; false god. **2.** One that is adored. — **i′dol·a·try** n. — **i′dol·ize′** v.

**if** (ĭf) conj. **1.** In the event that. **2.** Even though. **3.** Whether.

**ig·nite** (ĭg-nīt′) v. **-nited, -niting.** To cause or begin to burn. — **ig·ni′tion** n.

**ig·no·min·i·ous** (ĭg′nō-mĭn′ē-əs) adj. **1.** Dishonorable; despicable. **2.** Humiliating; degrading. — **ig′no·min′i·ous·ly** adv. — **ig′no·min′y** n.

**ig·no·rant** (ĭg′nər-ənt) adj. **1.** Without education or knowledge. **2.** Unaware or uninformed. — **ig′no·rance** n. — **ig′no·rant·ly** adv.

**ig·nore** (ĭg-nôr′, -nōr′) v. **-nored, -noring.** To disregard.

**ill** (ĭl) adj. **worse, worst. 1.** Not healthy; sick. **2.** Unfavorable. **3.** Hostile. —adv. **worse, worst. 1.** Not well. **2.** With difficulty. —n. **1.** Evil. **2.** Disaster or harm.

**I′ll** (īl). Contraction of *I will* and *I shall.*

**il·le·gal** (ĭ-lē′gəl) adj. Prohibited by law. — **il′le·gal′i·ty** n. — **il·le′gal·ly** adv.

**il·le·git·i·mate** (ĭl′ĭ-jĭt′ə-mĭt) adj. **1.** Illegal. **2.** Born out of wedlock. — **il′le·git′i·ma·cy** n. — **il′le·git′i·mate·ly** adv.

**il·lic·it** (ĭ-lĭs′ĭt) adj. Unlawful. — **il·lic′it·ly** adv.

**il·lit·er·ate** (ĭ-lĭt′ər-ĭt) adj. Unable to read and write. — **il·lit′er·a·cy** n. — **il·lit′er·ate·ly** adv.

**ill·ness** (ĭl′nĭs) n. Sickness.

**il·log·i·cal** (ĭ-lŏj′ĭ-kəl) adj. Contradicting logic; irrational. — **il·log′i·cal·ly** adv.

**il·lu·mi·nate** (ĭ-lōō′mə-nāt′) v. **-nated, -nating. 1.** To provide with light. **2.** To clar-ify. — **il·lu′mi·na′tion** n. — **il·lu′mi·na′tor** n.

**il·lu·sion** (ĭ-lōō′zhən) n. **1.** A false appearance or perception. **2.** Delusion; misconception. — **il·lu′sive, il·lu′so·ry** adj.

**il·lus·trate** (ĭl′ə-strāt′, ĭ-lŭs′trāt′) v. **-trated, -trating. 1.** To explain by example. **2.** To provide (a text) with pictures, photographs, etc. — **il′lus·tra′tion** n. — **il·lus′tra·tive** adj. — **il′lus·tra′tor** n.

**il·lus·tri·ous** (ĭ-lŭs′trē-əs) adj. Eminent; famous. — **il·lus′tri·ous·ly** adv. — **il·lus′tri·ous·ness** n.

**I′m** (īm). Contraction of *I am.*

**im·age** (ĭm′ĭj) n. **1.** A likeness; resemblance. **2.** A figure of speech. **3.** A mental picture. —v. **-aged, -aging.** To mirror; reflect. — **im′age·ry** n.

**im·ag·i·na·tion** (ĭ-măj′ə-nā′shən) n. **1.** The power of forming a mental image of something that is not present, has not been experienced, or is not real. **2.** Creativity; inventiveness; resourcefulness. — **im·ag′i·na·ble** adj. — **im·ag′i·nar′y** adj. — **im·ag′i·na·tive** adj. — **im·ag′i·na·tive·ly** adv. — **im·ag′ine** v.

**im·i·tate** (ĭm′ə-tāt′) v. **-tated, -tating. 1.** To copy or emulate. **2.** To mimic or counterfeit. — **im′i·ta′tion** n. — **im′i·ta·tive** adj. — **im′i·ta·tor** n.

**im·mac·u·late** (ĭ-măk′yə-lĭt) adj. **1.** Pure. **2.** Impeccably clean. — **im·mac′u·late·ly** adv. — **im·mac′u·late·ness** n.

**im·ma·ture** (ĭm′ə-tyŏŏr′, -chŏŏr′) adj. **1.** Not fully developed; unripe. **2.** Exhibiting less than normal maturity. — **im′ma·tur′i·ty** n.

**im·me·di·ate** (ĭ-mē′dē-ĭt) adj. **1.** Next in line. **2.** Without delay. **3.** Near to the present. — **im·me′di·a·cy** n. — **im·me′di·ate·ly** adv. & conj. — **im·me′di·ate·ness** n.

**im·mense** (ĭ-měns′) adj. Vast; huge. — **im·mense′ly** adv. — **im·men′si·ty** n.

**im·merse** (ĭ-mûrs′) v. **-mersed, -mersing. 1.** To plunge into liquid. **2.** To absorb; engross. — **im·mer′sion** n.

**im·mi·grate** (ĭm′ĭ-grāt′) v. **-grated, -grating.** To settle in a foreign country. — **im′mi·grant** n. — **im′mi·gra′tion** n.

**im·mi·nent** (ĭm′ə-nənt) adj. About to occur; impending. — **im′mi·nence** n. — **im′mi·nent·ly** adv.

**im·mor·tal** (ĭ-môr′tl) adj. **1.** Not subject to death. **2.** Having eternal fame; everlasting. **3.** Of eternal life. —n. **1.** One exempt from death. **2.** One whose fame is enduring. — **im′mor·tal′i·ty** n. — **im·mor′tal·ize′** v. — **im·mor′tal·ly** adv.

**im·mune** (ĭ-myōōn′) adj. **1.** Exempt. **2.**

Resistant to a disease. —**im·mu·ni·ty** n. —**im'-mu·ni·za'tion** n. —**im'mu·nize'** v.

**im·pact** (im'păkt') n. **1.** A collision. **2.** A strong impression; effect.

**im·pair** (im-pâr') v. To diminish in strength, value, etc.; weaken. —**im·pair'ment** n.

**im·pal·pa·ble** (im-păl'pə-bəl) adj. **1.** Intangible. **2.** Imperceptible. —**im·pal'pa·bly** adv.

**im·part** (im-pärt') v. **1.** To transmit or give. **2.** To disclose.

**im·par·tial** (im-pär'shəl) adj. Unbiased; unprejudiced. —**im'par·ti·al'i·ty** n. —**im·par'tial·ly** adv.

**im·pas·sive** (im-păs'ĭv) adj. Revealing no emotion; calm. —**im·pas'sive·ly** adv. —**im'·pas·siv'i·ty** n.

**im·pa·tience** (im-pā'shəns) n. **1.** Lack of patience. **2.** Eagerness, desire, or anticipation. —**im·pa'tient** adj. —**im·pa'tient·ly** adv.

**im·peach** (im-pēch') v. **1.** To charge with misconduct in office before a proper tribunal. **2.** To discredit. —**im·peach'a·ble** adj. —**im·peach'ment** n.

**im·pec·ca·ble** (im-pěk'ə-bəl) adj. Faultless; flawless. —**im·pec'ca·bly** adv. —**im·pec'ca·bil'-i·ty** n.

**im·pede** (im-pēd') v. **-peded, -peding.** To obstruct; block. —**im·ped'i·ment** n.

**im·pel** (im-pěl') v. **-pelled, -pelling.** To urge; compel.

**im·pen·e·tra·ble** (im-pĕn'ə-trə-bəl) adj. **1.** Not capable of being entered. **2.** Incomprehensible. —**im·pen'e·tra·bil'i·ty** n. —**im·pen'e·tra·bly** adv.

**im·per·a·tive** (im-pĕr'ə-tĭv) adj. **1.** Expressing a command. **2.** Urgent or obligatory. —**im·per'a·tive** n. —**im·per'a·tive·ly** adv.

**im·per·fect** (im-pûr'fĭkt) adj. **1.** Defective; flawed. **2.** Of a verb tense expressing continuous or incomplete action. —n. The imperfect tense. —**im·per·fec'tion** n. —**im·per'fect·ly** adv.

**im·pe·ri·al·ism** (im-pîr'ē-ə-lĭz'əm) n. The policy of extending rule over other nations. —**im·pe'ri·al·ist** n. & adj. —**im·pe'ri·al·is'tic** adj.

**im·per·son·al** (im-pûr'sə-nəl) adj. **1.** Not referring to a particular person. **2.** Emotionless; aloof; heartless. —**im·per'son·al'i·ty** n. —**im·per'son·al·ly** adv.

**im·per·son·ate** (im-pûr'sə-nāt') v. **-ated, -ating.** To act the part of. —**im·per'son·a'tion** n. —**im·per'son·a'tor** n.

**im·per·ti·nent** (im-pûrt'n-ənt) adj. **1.** Impudent; insolent. **2.** Not pertinent. —**im·per'·ti·nence** n. —**im·per'ti·nent·ly** adv.

**im·per·turb·a·ble** (im'pər-tûr'bə-bəl) adj.

Calm and collected. —**im'per·turb'a·bil'i·ty** n. —**im'per·turb'a·bly** adv.

**im·per·vi·ous** (im-pûr'vē-əs) adj. **1.** Not allowing penetration. **2.** Unfeeling. —**im·per'vi·ous·ly** adv.

**im·pet·u·ous** (im-pĕch'ōō-əs) adj. **1.** Impulsive; hasty. **2.** Rushing with violence. —**im·pet'u·os'i·ty, im·pet'u·ous·ness** n. —**im·pet'u·ous·ly** adv.

**im·pe·tus** (im'pə-təs) n., pl. **-tuses. 1.** An impelling force; stimulus. **2.** Force associated with a moving body.

**im·pinge** (im-pĭnj') v. **-pinged, -pinging.** To encroach; infringe.

**im·pla·ca·ble** (im-plā'kə-bəl, -plăk'ə-bəl) adj. Inexorable; relentless. —**im·pla'ca·bly** adv.

**im·plant** (im-plănt', -plänt') v. **1.** To fix firmly. **2.** To instill.

**im·ple·ment** (im'plə-mənt) n. A tool or utensil. —v. To carry into effect. —**im'ple·men·ta'tion** n.

**im·pli·cate** (im'plĭ-kāt') v. **-cated, -cating. 1.** To involve; entangle. **2.** To imply. —**im'·pli·ca'tion** n.

**im·plic·it** (im-plĭs'ĭt) adj. **1.** Implied or understood. **2.** Inherent in the nature of something. **3.** Unquestioning. —**im·plic'it·ly** adv.

**im·plore** (im-plôr', -plōr') v. **-plored, -ploring.** To beseech.

**im·ply** (im-plī') v. **-plied, -plying. 1.** To entail. **2.** To express indirectly; suggest.

**im·port** (im-pôrt', -pōrt', im'pôrt', -pōrt') v. **1.** To bring in from a foreign country. **2.** To signify. —n. (im'pôrt') **1.** Something imported. **2.** Significance. —**im·port'a·ble** adj. —**im·por·ta'tion** n.

**im·por·tant** (im-pôr'tənt) adj. **1.** Significant; essential; weighty. **2.** Prominent; noteworthy. —**im·por'tance** n. —**im·por'tant·ly** adv.

**im·pose** (im-pōz') v. **-posed, -posing. 1.** To set or establish (a tax, etc.). **2.** To apply or force upon by authority. **3.** To take unfair advantage of. —**im·pos'er** n. —**im'po·si'tion** n.

**im·pos·si·ble** (im-pŏs'ə-bəl) adj. **1.** Not capable of existing or happening. **2.** Intolerable. —**im·pos'si·bil'i·ty** n. —**im·pos'si·bly** adv.

**im·pos·tor** (im-pŏs'tər) n. A person who deceives under an assumed identity.

**im·po·tent** (im'pə-tənt) adj. **1.** Lacking physical strength. **2.** Ineffectual. **3.** Incapable of sexual intercourse. —**im'po·tence** n. —**im'po·tent·ly** adv.

**im·pound** (im-pound') v. To seize, esp. legally.

**im·preg·nate** (im-prĕg'nāt') v. **-nated,**

-nating. **1.** To make pregnant. **2.** To fill throughout. — im'preg·na'tion n.

im·press (ĭm-prĕs') v. **1.** To stamp. **2.** To fix in the mind. **3.** To affect deeply. — im·pres'·sion n. — im·pres'sion·a·ble adj. — im·pres'sive adj. — im·pres'sive·ly adv.

im·prop·er (ĭm-prŏp'ər) adj. **1.** Not suitable; unseemly. **2.** Incorrect; wrong. — im·prop'er·ly adv. — im'pro·pri'e·ty n.

im·prove (ĭm-prōōv') v. -proved, -proving. To make or become better. — im·prove'ment n.

im·pu·dent (ĭm'pyə-dənt) adj. Impertinent; rude. — im'pu·dence n.

im·pulse (ĭm'pŭls') n. **1.** An impelling force or the motion it produces. **2.** A sudden urge. **3.** A stimulus. — im·pul'sive adj. — im·pul'sive·ly adv. — im·pul'sive·ness n.

in (ĭn) prep. **1.** Within; inside. **2.** During. **3.** Into. **4.** Out of. — adv. **1.** To or toward the inside. **2.** Into a given place, state, etc. **3.** Indoors. **4.** Inward.

in·ane (ĭn-ān') adj. Lacking substance; silly. — in·an'i·ty n.

in·au·gu·rate (ĭn-ô'gyə-rāt') v. -rated, -rating. **1.** To induct into office. **2.** To begin officially. — in·au'gu·ral adj. & n. — in·au'gu·ra'tion n.

in·can·des·cent (ĭn'kən-dĕs'ənt) adj. **1.** Emitting visible light from being heated. **2.** Shining brilliantly. — in'can·des'cence n. — in'can·des'cent·ly adv.

in·ca·pac·i·tate (ĭn'kə-pǎs'ĭ-tāt') v. -tated, -tating. **1.** To deprive of strength; disable. **2.** To disqualify. — in'ca·pac'i·ta'tion n.

in·car·nate (ĭn-kär'nĭt) adj. **1.** Embodied in human form. **2.** Personified. — v. -nated, -nating. **1.** To give bodily form to. **2.** To personify. — in'car·na'tion n.

in·cen·tive (ĭn-sĕn'tĭv) n. Something motivating action; stimulus.

in·cep·tion (ĭn-sĕp'shən) n. The beginning of something.

in·ces·sant (ĭn-sĕs'ənt) adj. Constant; unceasing. — in·ces'sant·ly adv.

in·cest (ĭn'sĕst') n. Sexual union between close relatives. — in·ces'tu·ous adj.

inch (ĭnch) n. A unit of length equal to $\frac{1}{12}$ of a foot. — v. To move by small degrees.

in·ci·dence (ĭn'sə-dəns) n. The extent or frequency of occurrence.

in·ci·dent (ĭn'sə-dənt) n. An occurrence. — adj. Tending to arise in connection with. — in'ci·den'tal adj.

in·cin·er·ate (ĭn-sĭn'ə-rāt') v. -ated, -ating. To consume by burning. — in·cin'er·a'tor n.

in·ci·sion (ĭn-sĭzh'ən) n. **1.** A surgical cut into tissue. **2.** The scar from such a cut.

in·ci·sive (ĭn-sī'sĭv) adj. **1.** Cutting; penetrating. **2.** Trenchant. — in·ci'sive·ly adv.

in·cite (ĭn-sīt') v. -cited, -citing. To provoke to action; stir up.

in·cline (ĭn-klīn') v. -clined, -clining. **1.** To lean; slant. **2.** To influence. **3.** To tend. — n. An inclined surface; a slope. — in'cli·na'tion n.

in·clude (ĭn-klōōd') v. -cluded, -cluding. **1.** To contain. **2.** To regard as part of a general category. — in·clu'sion n. — in·clu'sive adj. — in·clu'sive·ly adv. — in·clu'sive·ness n.

in·come (ĭn'kŭm') n. Money received from investments, salary, etc.

in·cor·po·rate (ĭn-kôr'pə-rāt') v. -rated, -rating. **1.** To form a legal corporation. **2.** To combine together into a whole. — in·cor'po·ra'tion n.

in·cor·ri·gi·ble (ĭn-kôr'ə-jə-bəl, ĭn-kŏr'-) adj. Incapable of being corrected or reformed. — in·cor'ri·gi·bly adv.

in·crease (ĭn-krēs') v. -creased, -creasing. To make or become greater. — n. (ĭn'krēs'). **1.** Addition; enlargement. **2.** The amount of such increase. — in·creas'ing·ly adv.

in·cred·i·ble (ĭn-krĕd'ə-bəl) adj. Unbelievable; remarkable. — in·cred'i·ble·ness n. — in·cred'i·bly adv.

in·cum·bent (ĭn-kŭm'bənt) adj. Required; obligatory. — n. A person who holds an office. — in·cum'ben·cy n.

in·cur (ĭn-kûr') v. -curred, -curring. To bring upon oneself.

in·deed (ĭn-dēd') adv. **1.** Certainly. **2.** In fact. **3.** Admittedly.

in·dem·ni·ty (ĭn-dĕm'nə-tē) n., pl. -ties. **1.** Insurance against loss. **2.** Compensation for loss incurred. — in·dem'ni·fy' v. — in·dem'ni·fi·ca'tion n.

in·dent (ĭn-dĕnt') — v. **1.** To notch; make jagged. **2.** To set in from the margin. — in'den·ta'tion n.

in·de·pend·ent (ĭn'dĭ-pĕn'dənt) adj. **1.** Politically autonomous. **2.** Free from the control of others. **3.** Not affiliated with. — n. A voter not committed to any one political party. — in'de·pen'dence n. — in'de·pend'ent·ly adv.

in·dex (ĭn'dĕks') n., pl. -dexes or -dices **1.** An alphabetized list of the names and subjects in a printed work, with page references. **2.** An indicator; a sign. — v. **1.** To furnish with an index. **2.** To enter in an index.

in·di·cate (ĭn'dĭ-kāt') v. -cated, -cating. **1.** To point out. **2.** To serve as a sign of. **3.** To state. — in'di·ca'tion n. — in·dic'a·tive adj. — in'di·ca'tor n.

**in·dict** (ĭn-dīt′) v. To accuse formally of a crime. —**in·dict′ment** n.

**in·dif·fer·ent** (ĭn-dĭf′ər-ənt) adj. **1.** Impartial. **2.** Callous; unfeeling. **3.** Having no interest in; apathetic. **4.** Mediocre. —**in·dif′fer·ence** n. —**in·dif′fer·ent·ly** adv.

**in·dig·e·nous** (ĭn-dĭj′ə-nəs) adj. Natural to; native.

**in·di·gent** (ĭn′də-jənt) adj. Impoverished, needy. —n. A destitute person. —**in′di·gence** n. —**in′di·gent·ly** adv.

**in·dig·na·tion** (ĭn′dĭg-nā′shən) n. Anger aroused by something unjust. —**in·dig′nant** adj. —**in·dig′nant·ly** adv.

**in·di·vid·u·al** (ĭn′də-vĭj′ōō-əl) adj. **1.** Of, by, or for one person. **2.** Single; separate. **3.** Distinctive. —n. **1.** A single person, organism, or thing. **2.** A particular person. —**in′di·vid′u·al′i·ty** n. —**in′di·vid′u·al·ly** adv.

**in·di·vid·u·al·ist** (ĭn′də-vĭj′ōō-ə-lĭst) n. A person of independent thought and action. —**in′di·vid′u·al·ism′** n. —**in′di·vid′u·al·is′tic** adj.

**in·dom·i·ta·ble** (ĭn-dŏm′ə-tə-bəl) adj. Unyielding; unconquerable.

**in·duce** (ĭn-d/y/ōōs′) v. **-duced, -ducing. 1.** To persuade. **2.** To cause. **3.** To infer by logic. —**in·duce′ment** n.

**in·duct** (ĭn-dŭkt′) v. To install formally, esp. in office or into military service. —**in′duc·tee′** n. —**in·duc′tion** n.

**in·dulge** (ĭn-dŭlj′) v. **-dulged, -dulging. 1.** To yield to desires of. **2.** To gratify. —**in·dul′gence** n. —**in·dul′gent** adj.

**in·dus·tri·ous** (ĭn-dŭs′trē-əs) adj. Diligent; hardworking. —**in·dus′tri·ous·ly** adv. —**in·dus′tri·ous·ness** n.

**in·dus·try** (ĭn′də-strē) n., pl. **-tries. 1.** The production of goods. **2.** A specific branch of manufacture and trade. **3.** Diligence. —**in·dus′tri·al** adj. —**in·dus′tri·al·ist** n. —**in·dus′tri·al·ize′** v.

**in·ept** (ĭn-ĕpt′) adj. **1.** Clumsy. **2.** Incompetent. —**in·ep′ti·tude′** n.

**in·ert** (ĭn-ûrt′) adj. **1.** Not able to move or act. **2.** Sluggish or inactive. —**in·er′tia** n.

**in·ev·i·ta·ble** (ĭn-ĕv′ə-tə-bəl) adj. Not able to be avoided or prevented. —**in·ev′i·ta·bil′i·ty** n. —**in·ev′i·ta·bly** adv.

**in·ex·o·ra·ble** (ĭn-ĕk′sər-ə-bəl) adj. Relentless. —**in·ex′o·ra·bly** adv.

**in·fa·mous** (ĭn′fə-məs) adj. **1.** Having a bad reputation. **2.** Loathsome; disgraceful. —**in′fa·my** n.

**in·fant** (ĭn′fənt) n. A baby. —**in′fan·cy** n. —**in′fan·tile′** adj.

**in·fan·try** (ĭn′fən-trē) n., pl. **-tries.** Army units trained to fight on foot. —**in′fan·try·man** n.

**in·fat·u·ate** (ĭn-făch′ōō-āt′) v. **-ated, -ating.** To inspire with foolish passion. —**in·fat′u·a′tion** n.

**in·fect** (ĭn-fĕkt′) v. **1.** To contaminate with germs; pollute. **2.** To communicate a disease to. **3.** To affect as if by contagion; catch on. —**in·fec′tion** n. —**in·fec′tious** adj.

**in·fer** (ĭn-fûr′) v. **-ferred, -ferring.** To conclude from evidence; deduce. —**in′fer·ence** n. —**in′fer·en′tial·ly** adv.

**in·fe·ri·or** (ĭn-fîr′ē-ər) adj. **1.** Lower. **2.** Lower in degree or rank. **3.** Lower in quality. —**in·fe′ri·or′i·ty** n.

**in·fin·i·tive** (ĭn-fĭn′ə-tĭv) n. An uninflected verb form.

**in·fin·i·ty** (ĭn-fĭn′ə-tē) n., pl. **-ties.** Unbounded space, time, or quantity. —**in·fi′nite** adj. —**in′fi·nite·ly** adv.

**in·flam·ma·tion** (ĭn′flə-mā′shən) n. Localized redness, swelling, and pain. —**in·flame′** v. —**in·flam′ma·to′ry** adj.

**in·flate** (ĭn-flāt′) v. **-flated, -flating. 1.** To fill and swell with a gas. **2.** To raise abnormally, as prices. —**in·fla′tion** n. —**in·fla′tion·ar′y** adj.

**in·flict** (ĭn-flĭkt′) v. To impose.

**in·flu·ence** (ĭn′flōō-əns) n. **1.** A power affecting a person or events. **2.** A person or thing exercising such power. —v. **-enced, -encing.** To have power over; affect. —**in′flu·en′tial** adj.

**in·form** (ĭn-fôrm′) v. To impart information to. —**in·form′ant, in·form′er** n.

**in·for·mal** (ĭn-fôr′məl) adj. **1.** Performed without ceremony. **2.** Of or for ordinary use; casual. —**in′for·mal′i·ty** n. —**in·for′mal·ly** adv.

**in·for·ma·tion** (ĭn′fər-mā′shən) n. **1.** Knowledge. **2.** News. —**in·for′ma·tion·al** adj. —**in·form′a·tive** adj.

**in·gen·ious** (ĭn-jēn′yəs) adj. **1.** Inventive. **2.** Resourceful; clever. —**in·ge·nu′i·ty** n.

**in·gra·ti·ate** (ĭn-grā′shē-āt′) v. **-ated, -ating.** To work (oneself) into another's good graces.

**in·gre·di·ent** (ĭn-grē′dē-ənt) n. A component; a part of a mixture.

**in·hab·it** (ĭn-hăb′ĭt) v. To reside in. —**in·hab′it·a·ble** adj. —**in·hab′i·tant** n.

**in·hale** (ĭn-hāl′) v. **-haled, -haling.** To breathe in. —**in′ha·la′tion** n.

**in·her·ent** (ĭn-hîr′ənt, -hĕr′ənt) adj. Existing as an essential part. —**in·her′ent·ly** adv.

**in·her·it** (ĭn-hĕr′ĭt) v. **1.** To receive, esp. as an heir. **2.** To receive genetically from an ancestor. —**in·her′i·tance** n.

**in·hib·it** (ĭn-hĭb′ĭt) v. To restrain; repress.

—in'hi·bi'tion n.

**in·i·tial** (ĭ-nĭsh'əl) adj. Occurring first. —n. 1. Often **initials.** The first letters of a person's name. 2. The first letter of a word. —v. **-tialed, -tialing.** To sign with one's initials. —in·i'tial·ly adv.

**in·i·ti·ate** (ĭ-nĭsh'ē-āt') v. **-ated, -ating.** 1. To begin. 2. To admit into membership, as with ceremonies. —n. (-ĭt). One who has been initiated. —in·i'ti·a'tion n.

**in·i·ti·a·tive** (ĭ-nĭsh'ē-ə-tĭv, -ē·ā'tĭv, -nĭsh'ə·tĭv) n. 1. The ability to follow through with a plan; enterprise. 2. The first step.

**in·ject** (ĭn-jĕkt') v. To force (a fluid) into. —in·jec'tion n.

**in·junc·tion** (ĭn-jŭngk'shən) n. 1. A directive or order. 2. A court order prohibiting a specific course of action.

**in·jure** (ĭn'jər) v. **-jured, -juring.** 1. To harm; hurt. 2. To commit an offense against. —in·ju'ri·ous adj. —in'ju·ry n.

**in·jus·tice** (ĭn-jŭs'tĭs) n. 1. Lack of justice. 2. An unjust act.

**ink** (ĭngk) n. A pigmented liquid for writing.

**in·lay** (ĭn-lā', ĭn'lā') v. To set into a surface to form a design. —n. (ĭn'lā'). 1. An inlaid object or design. 2. A solid filling fitted to a cavity in a tooth. —in'laid' adj.

**inn** (ĭn) n. 1. A hotel. 2. A tavern.

**in·nate** (ĭ-nāt', ĭn'āt') adj. 1. Inborn. 2. Inherent. —in·nate'ly adv.

**in·ner** (ĭn'ər) adj. 1. Located farther inside. 2. Of the soul, emotions, or mind. —in'ner·most' adj.

**in·no·cent** (ĭn'ə-sənt) adj. 1. Without guile. 2. Not guilty of a crime. 3. Not experienced; naive. —in'no·cence n. —in'no·cent n. —in'no·cent·ly adv.

**in·noc·u·ous** (ĭ-nŏk'yōō-əs) adj. 1. Harmless. 2. Insignificant.

**in·no·vate** (ĭn'ə-vāt') v. **-vated, -vating.** To begin or introduce (something new). —in'no·va'tion n. —in'no·va'tive adj.

**in·nu·en·do** (ĭn'yōō-ĕn'dō) n., pl. **-does.** An indirect, often derogatory implication.

**in·oc·u·late** (ĭ-nŏk'yə-lāt') v. **-lated, -lating.** To introduce the virus of a disease into (the body) in order to immunize. —in·oc'u·la'tion n.

**in·quest** (ĭn'kwĕst') n. A legal or judicial inquiry.

**in·quire** (ĭn-kwīr') v. **-quired, -quiring.** 1. To ask. 2. To investigate. —in·quir'er n. —in·quir'ing·ly adv. —in·quir'y n.

**in·quis·i·tive** (ĭn-kwĭz'ə-tĭv) adj. 1. Unduly

curious. 2. Eager to learn.

**in·sane** (ĭn-sān') adj. 1. Of or afflicted with mental disorder. 2. Mad. —in·san'i·ty n.

**in·scribe** (ĭn-skrīb') v. **-scribed, -scribing.** 1. To write or engrave. 2. To dedicate to another. —in·scrip'tion n.

**in·sect** (ĭn'sĕkt') n. A small animal with a three-segmented body.

**in·se·cure** (ĭn'sĭ-kyŏŏr') adj. 1. Not safe. 2. Unstable; shaky. 3. Lacking self-confidence. —in'se·cure'ly adv. —in'se·cu'ri·ty n.

**in·sert** (ĭn-sûrt') v. 1. To put or thrust into. 2. To put in between other parts. —n. (ĭn'sûrt'). Something inserted. —in·ser'tion n.

**in·side** (ĭn-sīd', ĭn'sīd') n. 1. The inner part. 2. An inner surface. —adj. Inner. —adv. (ĭn-sīd'). Within. —prep. (ĭn-sīd'). 1. Within. 2. Into.

**in·sid·i·ous** (ĭn-sĭd'ē-əs) adj. 1. Cunning. 2. Treacherous. 3. Sly; beguiling.

**in·sight** (ĭn'sīt') n. 1. Discernment. 2. An elucidating glimpse.

**in·sig·ni·a** (ĭn-sĭg'nē-ə) n., pl. **-nia** or **-as.** A badge of office, rank, etc.

**in·sin·u·ate** (ĭn-sĭn'yōō-āt') v. **-ated, -ating.** 1. To introduce insidiously. 2. To worm (oneself) in by subtle means. 3. To hint covertly. —in·sin'u·a'tion n.

**in·sip·id** (ĭn-sĭp'ĭd) adj. Dull; vapid. —in·sip'id·ly adv.

**in·sist** (ĭn-sĭst') v. 1. To emphasize an assertion, demand, or course. 2. To assert or demand persistently. —in·sis'tence n. —in·sis'tent adj.

**in·so·lent** (ĭn'sə-lənt) adj. 1. Insulting in manner; arrogant. 2. Impudent. —in'so·lence n. —in'so·lent·ly adv.

**in·som·ni·a** (ĭn-sŏm'nē-ə) n. Chronic inability to sleep. —in·som'ni·ac' n.

**in·spect** (ĭn-spĕkt') v. To examine carefully and critically. —in·spec'tion n. —in·spec'tor n.

**in·spire** (ĭn-spīr') v. **-spired, -spiring.** 1. To arouse the mind or emotions of. 2. To stimulate; impel. 3. To inhale. —in'spi·ra'tion n. —in'spi·ra'tion·al adj.

**in·stall** (ĭn-stôl') v. Also **in·stal, -stalled, -stalling.** 1. To set in position for use. 2. To put in an office. 3. To establish. —in'stal·la'tion n.

**in·stall·ment** (ĭn-stôl'mənt) n. Also **in·stal·ment.** 1. One of several payments of a debt. 2. A portion of anything issued at intervals.

**in·stance** (ĭn'stəns) n. 1. A case or example. 2. A prompting; request.

**in·stant** (ĭn'stənt) n. 1. A very brief time.

2. A particular point in time. —*adj.* 1. Immediate. 2. Urgent. 3. Prepared for rapid completion with minimal effort. — **in·stan·ta·ne·ous** *adj.* — **in·stan·ta·ne·ous·ly** *adv.* — **in·stant·ly** *adv.*

**in·sti·gate** (ĭn'stĭ-gāt') *v.* -gated, -gating. To incite. — **in·sti·ga·tion** *n.* — **in·sti·ga·tor** *n.*

**in·stinct** (ĭn'stĭngkt') *n.* 1. A powerful and natural impulse. 2. An innate aptitude. — **in·stinc·tive** *adj.* — **in·stinc·tive·ly** *adv.* — **in·stinc·tu·al** *adj.*

**in·sti·tute** (ĭn'stə-t/y/ōōt') *v.* -tuted, -tuting. 1. To establish. 2. To initiate. —*n.* 1. An organization founded to promote some cause. 2. An educational institution.

**in·sti·tu·tion** (ĭn'stə-t/y/ōō'shən) *n.* 1. An established custom or practice. 2. An organization, esp. one dedicated to public service. 3. A place of confinement. — **in·sti·tu·tion·al** *adj.*

**in·struct** (ĭn-strŭkt') *v.* 1. To teach. 2. To direct. — **in·struc·tion** *n.* — **in·struc·tion·al** *adj.* — **in·struc·tive** *adj.* — **in·struc·tor** *n.*

**in·stru·ment** (ĭn'strə-mənt) *n.* 1. A means. 2. A tool. 3. A device for producing music. — **in·stru·men·tal** *adj.* — **in·stru·men·tal·ly** *adv.*

**in·su·late** (ĭn'sə-lāt', ĭns'yə-) *v.* -lated, -lating. 1. To detach; isolate. 2. To prevent the passage of heat, electricity, or sound into or out of by interposition of a nonconducting material. — **in·su·la·tion** *n.* — **in·su·la·tor** *n.*

**in·sult** (ĭn-sŭlt') *v.* To treat in a contemptuous way. —*n.* (ĭn'sŭlt') An offensive remark or act.

**in·sure** (ĭn-shŏŏr') *v.* -sured, -suring. 1. To protect against loss, damage, etc. 2. To guarantee. — **in·sur·ance** *n.* — **in·sur·er** *n.*

**in·tact** (ĭn-tăkt') *adj.* 1. Not impaired. 2. Whole.

**in·te·ger** (ĭn'tə-jər) *n.* 1. A whole number. 2. An intact unit.

**in·te·gral** (ĭn'tə-grəl) *adj.* 1. Essential for completion. 2. Whole; entire. — **in·te·gral·ly** *adv.*

**in·te·grate** (ĭn'tə-grāt') *v.* -grated, -grating. 1. To make into a whole. 2. To unite. 3. To open to all ethnic groups. — **in·te·gra·tion** *n.* — **in·te·gra·tive** *adj.*

**in·teg·ri·ty** (ĭn-tĕg'rə-tē) *n.* 1. Adherence to a code of values. 2. Soundness; completeness.

**in·tel·lect** (ĭn'tə-lĕkt') *n.* 1. The ability to learn, reason, and understand. 2. A person of great intellectual ability. — **in·tel·lec·tu·al** *adj. & n.*

**in·tel·li·gence** (ĭn-tĕl'ə-jəns) *n.* 1. The capacity to acquire and apply knowledge; intellect. 2. News, esp. secret information. — **in·tel·li·gent** *adj.* — **in·tel·li·gent·ly** *adv.*

**in·tend** (ĭn-tĕnd') *v.* 1. To have in mind; plan. 2. To mean.

**in·tense** (ĭn-tĕns') *adj.* 1. Of great concentration or force. 2. Extreme in degree, strength, or size. 3. Deeply felt; emotional. — **in·tense·ly** *adv.* — **in·tense·ness** *n.* — **in·ten·si·fy** *v.* — **in·ten·si·ty** *n.* — **in·ten·sive** *adj.*

**in·tent** (ĭn-tĕnt') *n.* 1. Aim; purpose. 2. Volition. 3. Meaning. —*adj.* 1. Firmly fixed; determined. 2. Engrossed. — **in·ten·tion** *n.* — **in·ten·tion·al** *adj.* — **in·ten·tion·al·ly** *adv.*

**in·ter·cede** (ĭn'tər-sēd') *v.* -ceded, -ceding. 1. To plead on another's behalf. 2. To mediate.

**in·ter·cept** (ĭn'tər-sĕpt') *v.* To stop or interrupt the progress of. — **in·ter·cep·tion** *n.*

**in·ter·course** (ĭn'tər-kôrs', -kōrs') *n.* 1. Social communication. 2. Sexual relations.

**in·ter·est** (ĭn'trĭst, -tər-ĭst) *n.* 1. A feeling of curiosity, fascination, etc. 2. Advantage; benefit. 3. A right or legal share in something. 4. A charge for a financial loan. —*v.* To arouse or hold the attention of.

**in·ter·fere** (ĭn'tər-fîr') *v.* -fered, -fering. 1. To hinder; impede. 2. To intrude; meddle. — **in·ter·fer·ence** *n.*

**in·ter·im** (ĭn'tər-ĭm) *n.* An intervening period of time. —*adj.* Temporary.

**in·te·ri·or** (ĭn-tîr'ē-ər) *adj.* 1. Situated inside; inner. 2. Inland. —*n.* 1. The inner area of something. 2. The inland part.

**in·ter·jec·tion** (ĭn'tər-jĕk'shən) *n.* 1. An exclamation. 2. A part of speech consisting of exclamatory words. 3. An interruption. — **in·ter·ject'** *v.*

**in·ter·me·di·ar·y** (ĭn'tər-mē'dē-ĕr'ē) *n., pl.* -ies. A mediator or agent. —*adj.* 1. Acting as a mediator. 2. In between.

**in·ter·me·di·ate** (ĭn'tər-mē'dē-ĭt) *adj.* In between; in the middle.

**in·ter·mis·sion** (ĭn'tər-mĭsh'ən) *n.* An interval as the period between the acts of a drama, etc.

**in·ter·mit·tent** (ĭn'tər-mĭt'ənt) *adj.* Stopping and starting at intervals. — **in·ter·mit'tent·ly** *adv.*

**in·ter·nal** (ĭn-tûr'nəl) *adj.* 1. Inner; interior. 2. Intrinsic; inherent. 3. Of the domestic affairs of a country. — **in·ter·nal·ly** *adv.*

**in·ter·na·tion·al** (ĭn'tər-năsh'ən-əl) *adj.* Of, or involving two or more nations or nationalities. — **in·ter·na·tion·al·ly** *adv.*

**in·ter·pret** (ĭn-tûr'prĭt) *v.* 1. To clarify. 2. To

explain and expound the significance of. **3.** To translate. — **in·ter'pret·a·ble** *adj.* — **in·ter'pre·ta'tion** *n.* — **in·ter'pret·er** *n.*

**in·ter·ro·gate** (ĭn-tĕr'ə-gāt') *v.* -gated, -gating. To question, esp. formally. — **in·ter'ro·ga'tion** *n.* — **in·ter·rog'a·tive** *adj.* & *n.* — **in·ter'ro·ga'tor** *n.*

**in·ter·rupt** (ĭn'tə-rŭpt') *v.* **1.** To break the continuity of. **2.** To hinder by breaking in upon. — **in'ter·rup'tion** *n.*

**in·ter·sect** (ĭn'tər-sĕkt') *v.* To cut through. — **in'ter·sec'tion** *n.*

**in·ter·val** (ĭn'tər-vəl) *n.* **1.** An intervening space or time period. **2.** A difference in pitch.

**in·ter·vene** (ĭn'tər-vēn') *v.* -vened, -vening. **1.** To occur between two things or periods of time. **2.** To mediate. **3.** To interfere in the affairs of another. — **in'ter·ven'tion** *n.*

**in·ter·view** (ĭn'tər-vyōō') *n.* **1.** A formal discussion. **2.** A conversation between a reporter and one from whom he seeks information. — **in'ter·view'** *v.*

**in·tes·tine** (ĭn-tĕs'tən) *n.* The lower portion of the digestive tract. — **in·tes'ti·nal** *adj.* — **in·tes'ti·nal·ly** *adv.*

**in·ti·mate** (ĭn'tə-mĭt) *adj.* **1.** Close or familiar. **2.** Of love or sexual relations. **3.** Very personal; private. — **in'ti·ma·cy** *n.* — **in'ti·mate·ly** *adv.*

**in·tim·i·date** (ĭn-tĭm'ə-dāt') *v.* -dated, -dating. **1.** To make timid; frighten. **2.** To discourage as by threats. — **in·tim'i·da'tion** *n.*

**in·to** (ĭn'tōō) *prep.* **1.** To the inside of. **2.** To the condition or form of. **3.** To a time or place. **4.** Against.

**in·tox·i·cate** (ĭn-tŏk'sĭ-kāt') *v.* -cated, -cating. **1.** To induce drunkenness. **2.** To stimulate or excite. — **in·tox'i·cant** *n.* — **in·tox'i·ca'tion** *n.*

**in·tran·si·tive** (ĭn-trăn'sə-tĭv) *adj.* Designating a verb that does not require a direct object.

**in·trep·id** (ĭn-trĕp'ĭd) *adj.* Resolutely courageous; fearless. — **in·trep'id·ly** *adv.*

**in·tri·cate** (ĭn'trĭ-kĭt) *adj.* **1.** Having many complex elements. **2.** Puzzling; confusing. — **in'tri·ca·cy** *n.* — **in'tri·cate·ly** *adv.*

**in·trigue** (ĭn'trēg', ĭn-trēg') *n.* **1.** A secret scheme. **2.** A clandestine love affair. **3.** Mystery; suspense. —*v.* (ĭn-trēg') -trigued, -triguing. **1.** To engage in covert schemes. **2.** To arouse the curiosity of.

**in·trin·sic** (ĭn-trĭn'sĭk) *adj.* Of the essential nature of a thing. — **in·trin'si·cal·ly** *adv.*

**in·tro·duce** (ĭn'trə-d/y/ōōs') *v.* -duced, -ducing. **1.** To make acquainted. **2.** To bring

into use, notice, etc. **3.** To insert. **4.** To preface. — **in'tro·duc'tion** *n.* — **in'tro·duc'to·ry** *adj.*

**in·tro·spec·tion** (ĭn'trə-spĕk'shən) *n.* Contemplation of one's own thoughts and sensations. — **in'tro·spec'tive** *adj.*

**in·tro·vert** (ĭn'trə-vûrt') *n.* One whose thoughts and interests are directed inward. — **in'tro·ver'sion** *n.*

**in·trude** (ĭn-trōōd') *v.* -truded, -truding. To come in rudely or inappropriately. — **in·trud'er** *n.* — **in·tru'sion** *n.* — **in·tru'sive** *adj.* — **in·tru'sive·ly** *adv.*

**in·tu·i·tion** (ĭn't/y/ōō-ĭsh'ən) *n.* The knowing of something without reasoning; instinctive understanding. — **in·tu'it** *v.* — **in·tu'i·tive** *adj.*

**in·un·date** (ĭn'ŭn-dāt') *v.* -dated, -dating. To flood; overwhelm. — **in'un·da'tion** *n.*

**in·vade** (ĭn-vād') *v.* -vaded, -vading. **1.** To enter by force in order to conquer. **2.** To encroach. — **in·vad'er** *n.* — **in·va'sion** *n.*

**in·val·id** (ĭn'və-lĭd) *n.* A chronically ill or disabled person. —*adj.* Physically disabled.

**in·vent** (ĭn-vĕnt') *v.* **1.** To devise first; originate. **2.** To fabricate. — **in·ven'tion** *n.* — **in·ven'tive** *adj.* — **in·ven'tor** *n.*

**in·ven·to·ry** (ĭn'vən-tôr'ē, -tōr'ē) *n.*, *pl.* -ries. A detailed list of things, esp. goods in stock. — **in'ven·to'ry** *v.*

**in·vert** (ĭn-vûrt') *v.* **1.** To turn inside out or upside down. **2.** To reverse. — **in·ver'sion** *n.*

**in·ver·te·brate** (ĭn-vûr'tə-brĭt, -brāt') *adj.* Having no backbone. — **in·ver'te·brate** *n.*

**in·vest** (ĭn-vĕst') *v.* **1.** To commit (money) in order to gain profit. **2.** To endow with authority or power. — **in·vest'ment** *n.* — **in·ves'tor** *n.*

**in·ves·ti·gate** (ĭn-vĕs'tĭ-gāt') *v.* -gated, -gating. To examine systematically. — **in·ves'ti·ga'tion** *n.* — **in·ves'ti·ga'tive** *adj.* — **in·ves'ti·ga'tor** *n.*

**in·vin·ci·ble** (ĭn-vĭn'sə-bəl) *adj.* Unconquerable. — **in·vin'ci·bil'i·ty** *n.* — **in·vin'ci·bly** *adv.*

**in·vi·o·la·ble** (ĭn-vī'ə-lə-bəl) *adj.* **1.** That cannot or must not be violated. **2.** Impregnable. — **in·vi'o·la·bil'i·ty** *n.* — **in·vi'o·la·bly** *adv.* — **in·vi'o·late** *adj.*

**in·vite** (ĭn-vīt') *v.* -vited, -viting. **1.** To request the presence of. **2.** To request formally. **3.** To provoke. **4.** To attract. — **in'vi·ta'tion** *n.*

**in·voice** (ĭn'vois') *n.* A list of goods shipped; a bill.

**in·voke** (ĭn-vōk') *v.* -voked, -voking. **1.** To call upon (a higher power) for assistance. **2.** To appeal to.

**in·volve** (ĭn-vŏlv') *v.* -volved, -volving. **1.** To

include. **2.** To have as a necessary feature. **3.** To engross. **—in·volve·ment** *n.*

**in·ward** (ĭn'wərd) *adj.* **1.** Inner. **2.** Toward the interior. *—adv.* Also **in·wards.** **1.** Toward the inside or center. **2.** Toward the self. **—in'ward·ly** *adv.*

**i·o·dine** (ī'ə-dīn', -dĭn, -dĕn') *n.* A nonmetallic element used in medicine.

**i·on** (ī'ən, ī'ŏn') *n.* An electrically charged atom. **—i·on·i·za·tion** *n.* **—i'on·ize'** *v.*

**i·rate** (ī'rāt, ī-rāt') *adj.* Angry; enraged. **—i'rate·ly** *adv.*

**ire** (īr) *n.* Wrath; anger. **—ire'ful** *adj.*

**i·ris** (ī'rĭs) *n.* **1.** The colored part of the eye. **2.** A plant with variously colored flowers.

**irk** (ûrk) *v.* To vex; irritate. **—irk'some** *adj.*

**i·ron** (ī'ərn) *n.* **1.** A silvery-white metallic element. **2.** An appliance used to press fabric. *—adj.* Of or like iron. *—v.* To press (fabric) with a heated iron.

**i·ro·ny** (ī'rə-nē) *n., pl.* **-nies.** The use of words to convey the opposite of their literal meaning. **—i·ron'ic, i·ron'i·cal** *adj.* **—i·ron'i·cal·ly** *adv.*

**ir·ri·gate** (ĭr'ĭ-gāt') *v.* **-gated, -gating.** To supply with water. **—ir'ri·ga'tion** *n.*

**ir·ri·ta·ble** (ĭr'ə-tə-bəl) *adj.* Easily annoyed. **—ir'ri·ta·bil'i·ty** *n.* **—ir'ri·ta·bly** *adv.*

**ir·ri·tate** (ĭr'ə-tāt') *v.* **-tated, -tating.** **1.** To exasperate. **2.** To chafe. **—ir'ri·tant** *adj. & n.* **—ir'ri·tat'ing·ly** *adv.* **—ir'ri·ta'tion** *n.*

**is** (ĭz). 3rd person sing. present indicative of **be.**

**Is·lam** (ĭs'ləm, ĭz'-, ĭs-läm') *n.* A monotheistic religion based upon the teachings of Mohammed; the Moslem religion. **—Is·lam'ic** *adj.*

**is·land** (ī'lənd) *n.* A land mass surrounded by water. **—is'land·er** *n.* **—isle** *n.*

**is·n't** (ĭz'ənt). Contraction of *is not.*

**i·so·late** (ī'sə-lāt', ĭs'ə-) *v.* **-lated, -lating.** To separate and set apart. **—i'so·la'tion** *n.*

**i·sos·ce·les** (ī-sŏs'ə-lēz') *adj.* Having two equal sides.

**is·sue** (ĭsh'ōō) *n.* **1.** An act of flowing. **2.** Something produced or published. **3.** The result of an action. **4.** Offspring. **5.** A point of discussion. *—v.* **-sued, -suing.** **1.** To go or come out. **2.** To distribute, as supplies. **3.** To be descended. **4.** To result from. **5.** To publish or be published. **—is'su·er** *n.*

**isth·mus** (ĭs'məs) *n., pl.* **-muses** or **-mi.** A strip of land connecting two larger masses of land.

**it** (ĭt) *pron.* The 3rd person sing. pronoun, neuter gender.

**i·tal·ic** (ĭ-tăl'ĭk, ī-tăl'-) *adj.* Being a type with the letters slanting to the right. **—i·tal'ic·ize'** *v.*

**itch** (ĭch) *n.* **1.** An irritating sensation of the skin. **2.** A restless craving. **—itch** *v.* **—itch'i·ness** *n.* **—itch'y** *adj.*

**i·tem** (ī'təm) *n.* **1.** A single unit. **2.** A bit of information. **—i'tem·ize'** *v.*

**i·tin·er·ar·y** (ī-tĭn'ə-rĕr'ē, ĭ-tĭn'-) *n., pl.* **-ies. 1.** A route. **2.** A record of a journey. **3.** A traveler's guidebook.

**its** (ĭts). The possessive form of the pronoun *it.*

**it's** (ĭts). **1.** Contraction of *it is.* **2.** Contraction of *it has.*

**it·self** (ĭt-sĕlf') *pron.* A form of the 3rd person sing. neuter pronoun.

**I've** (īv). Contraction of *I have.*

**i·vo·ry** (ī'və-rē, ī'vrē) *n., pl.* **-ries. 1.** The hard, white substance forming the tusks of certain animals. **2.** Creamy white. **—i'vo·ry** *adj.*

# J

**j, J** (jā) *n.* The 10th letter of the English alphabet.

**jack** (jăk) *n.* **1.** A device for raising heavy objects. **2.** A kind of socket that accepts a plug at one end to make an electrical connection. **3.** A playing card showing a knave.

**jack·al** (jăk'əl, -ôl') *n.* A doglike mammal of Africa and Asia.

**jack·ass** (jăk'ăs') *n.* **1.** A male ass. **2.** A foolish person.

**jack·et** (jăk'ĭt) *n.* **1.** A short coat. **2.** An outer covering.

**jack·pot** (jăk'pŏt') *n.* A top prize or reward.

**jade** (jād) *n.* A hard gemstone that is usually pale green or white.

**jag·uar** (jăg'wär', -yōō-är') *n.* A large tropical American wildcat.

**jail** (jāl) *n.* A prison. *—v.* To detain in custody; imprison. **—jail'er** *n.*

**jam** (jăm) *v.* **jammed, jamming. 1.** To squeeze; cram. **2.** To become or cause to become locked, stuck, or unworkable. *—n.* A predicament.

**jamb** (jăm) *n.* The side posts of a door or window frame.

**jan·i·tor** (jăn'ə-tər) *n.* A caretaker of a

building.

**Jan·u·ar·y** (jăn′yŏŏ-ĕr′ē) n., pl. **-ies.** The 1st month of the year.

**jar¹** (jär) n. A wide-mouthed bottle.

**jar²** (jär) v. **jarred, jarring. 1.** To make a harsh sound. **2.** To shake from impact. **3.** To clash. —n. **1.** A jolt. **2.** A harsh, grating sound.

**jar·gon** (jär′gən) n. The specialized language of a group, profession, etc.

**jas·mine** (jăz′mən) n. A fragrant flowering shrub.

**jaun·dice** (jôn′dĭs, jän′-) n. Yellowish discoloration of tissues and bodily fluids caused by a malfunction of the liver.

**jaun·diced** (jôn′dĭst, jän′-) adj. Affected by envy, jealousy, etc.

**jaun·ty** (jôn′tē, jän′-) adj. **-tier, -tiest. 1.** Dapper. **2.** Carefree; self-confident. —**jaun′ti·ly** adv.

**jave·lin** (jăv′lən, jăv′ə-) n. A light spear for throwing.

**jaw** (jô) n. **1.** Either of two bony structures holding the teeth. **2. jaws.** Anything resembling a pair of jaws.

**jay** (jā) n. A noisy, crowlike bird.

**jay·walk** (jā′wôk′) v. To cross a street carelessly. —**jay′walk′er** n.

**jazz** (jăz) n. A kind of American music, evolved from African origins, featuring solo and ensemble improvisations.

**jeal·ous** (jĕl′əs) adj. **1.** Fearful of losing another's affection. **2.** Envious. —**jeal′ous·ly** adv. —**jeal′ous·y** n.

**jeans** (jēnz) pl.n. Pants made of heavy, usually blue cotton cloth.

**jeep** (jēp) n. A small, rugged motor vehicle.

**jeer** (jĭr) v. To shout derisively; taunt. —**jeer** n.

**jell** (jĕl) v. To pass from a liquid to a semisolid state; congeal.

**jel·ly** (jĕl′ē) n., pl. **-ies.** A soft food made by using gelatin to cause a liquid to set. —v. **-lied, -lying.** To make into jelly.

**jel·ly·fish** (jĕl′ē-fĭsh′) n. A gelatinous, umbrella-shaped sea animal.

**jeop·ard·ize** (jĕp′ər-dīz′) v. **-ized, -izing.** To endanger; risk. —**jeop′ard·y** n.

**jerk** (jûrk) v. To move with a sharp, abrupt motion. —n. **1.** A sudden, abrupt motion. **2.** A stupid person. —**jerk′i·ly** adv. —**jerk′i·ness** n. —**jerk′y** adj.

**jer·sey** (jûr′zē) n., pl. **-seys. 1.** A plain-knitted fabric. **2.** A knitted pullover shirt, jacket, or sweater.

**jest** (jĕst) n. A joke. —v. To joke. —**jest′er** n.

**jet¹** (jĕt) n. **1.** A dense black coal used for jewelry. **2.** A deep black.

**jet²** (jĕt) n. **1.** A stream forced from a small-diameter opening. **2.** A jet-propelled aircraft. —v. **jetted, jetting. 1.** To gush out; squirt. **2.** To travel by jet aircraft.

**jet·sam** (jĕt′səm) n. Cargo thrown overboard to lighten a ship in distress.

**jet·ty** (jĕt′ē) n., pl. **-ties.** A wharf; pier.

**Jew** (jōō) n. **1.** An adherent of Judaism. **2.** A descendant of the Hebrew people. —**Jew′ish** adj. —**Jew′ry** n.

**jew·el** (jōō′əl) n. **1.** An ornament of gems. **2.** A precious stone; a gem. **3.** A treasured person or thing. —**jew′el·er** n. —**jew′el·ry** n.

**jig** (jĭg) n. A lively dance. —v. **jigged, jigging.** To dance a jig.

**jig·saw** (jĭg′sô′) n. A saw used to cut sharp curves.

**jilt** (jĭlt) v. To discard (a lover) unexpectedly.

**jin·gle** (jĭng′gəl) v. **-gled, -gling.** To make a tinkling sound. —n. **1.** A tinkling sound. **2.** A simple, catchy rhyme.

**jinx** (jĭngks) n. A cause of bad luck. —v. To bring bad luck to.

**jit·ter** (jĭt′ər) v. To be nervous; fidget. —**jit′ter·y** adj.

**job** (jŏb) n. **1.** An activity performed for payment. **2. a.** A piece of work. **b.** The object to be worked on. —v. **jobbed, jobbing. 1.** To work by the piece. **2.** To sell wholesale.

**jock·ey** (jŏk′ē) n., pl. **-eys.** One who rides racehorses. —v. To maneuver for position.

**jo·cose** (jō-kōs′) adj. Merry; humorous. —**jo·cose′ly** adv. —**jo·cos′i·ty** n.

**joc·u·lar** (jŏk′yə-lər) adj. Humorous; facetious. —**joc′u·lar′i·ty** n. —**joc′u·lar·ly** adv.

**jog** (jŏg) v. To jolt or nudge. **2.** To run at a steady slow trot. —n. **1.** A jolt or nudge. **2.** A trot.

**join** (join) v. **1.** To put together or into close association. **2.** To connect. **3.** To take part; participate.

**joint** (joint) n. **1.** A point or position at which two or more things are joined. **2.** A connection between movable bodily parts. **3.** A marijuana cigarette. —adj. Shared by or common to two or more.

**joke** (jōk) n. **1.** An amusing remark or story. **2.** A mischievous trick. —v. **joked, joking. 1.** To tell or play jokes. **2.** To be facetious.

**jok·er** (jō′kər) n. **1.** One who tells or plays jokes. **2.** A playing card typically used as a wild card.

**jol·ly** (jŏl′ē) adj. **-lier, -liest.** Merry; festive. —**jol′li·ty** n.

**jolt** (jōlt) v. **1.** To shake. **2.** To jar with a sudden blow. —n. A sudden jerking.

**josh** (jŏsh) v. To tease; joke.

**jos·tle** (jŏs′əl) v. **-tled, -tling. 1.** To collide. **2.** To push or elbow. —n. A shove.

**jot** (jŏt) v. **jotted, jotting.** To write down briefly. The smallest bit. —v.

**jour·nal** (jûr′nəl) n. **1.** A daily record. **2.** A newspaper or periodical.

**jour·nal·ism** (jûr′nə-lĭz′əm) n. The collecting, writing, editing, and publishing of news in periodicals. —**jour′nal·ist** n. —**jour′nal·is′tic** adj.

**jour·ney** (jûr′nē) n., pl. **-neys.** Travel; a trip. —v. To travel.

**jo·vi·al** (jō′vē-əl) adj. Cheery; convivial; festive. —**jo′vi·al′i·ty** n.

**jowl**[1] (joul) n. **1.** The jaw. **2.** The cheek.

**jowl**[2] (joul) n. The flesh under the lower jaw.

**joy** (joi) n. **1.** Delight; happiness; gladness. **2.** A source of pleasure. —**joy′ful** adj. —**joy′ful·ly** adv. —**joy′ous** adj. —**joy′ous·ly** adv.

**ju·bi·la·tion** (jōō′bə-lā′shən) n. Rejoicing; joy; exultation. —**ju′bi·lant** adj.

**ju·bi·lee** (jōō′bə-lē′) n. A 50th anniversary.

**Ju·da·ism** (jōō′dē-ĭz′əm) n. The monotheistic religion of the Hebrew people. —**Ju·da′ic** adj.

**judge** (jŭj) v. **judged, judging. 1.** To pass judgment upon in a court of law. **2.** To determine after deliberation; decide. **3.** To form an opinion about. **4.** To criticize; censure. —n. **1.** A public official who decides cases in a court of law; justice. **2.** A connoisseur.

**judg·ment** (jŭj′mənt) n. Also **judge·ment. 1.** The capacity to make reasonable decisions; discernment. **2.** An idea; opinion; estimation. **3.** Criticism. **4.** A judicial decision. —**judg·men′tal** adj.

**ju·di·cial** (jōō-dĭsh′əl) adj. Of courts of law or the administration of justice.

**ju·di·ci·ar·y** (jōō-dĭsh′ē-ĕr′ē) adj. Of courts, judges, or their decisions. —n., pl. **-ies.** The judicial branch of government.

**ju·di·cious** (jōō-dĭsh′əs) adj. Exhibiting sound judgment; wise. —**ju·di′cious·ly** adv. —**ju·di′cious·ness** n.

**ju·do** (jōō′dō) n. A modern form of jujitsu.

**jug** (jŭg) n. A pitcher or rounded vessel for holding liquids.

**jug·gle** (jŭg′əl) v. **-gled, -gling. 1.** To keep (two or more objects) in the air at one time by alternately tossing and catching them. **2.** To manipulate in order to deceive. —**jug′gler** n.

**jug·u·lar** (jŭg′yə-lər) adj. Of the neck or throat.

**juice** (jōōs) n. **1.** Fluid contained in plant or animal tissue. **2.** Electric current. —v. **juiced, juicing.** To extract the juice from. —**juice′less** adj. —**juic′y** adj.

**ju·jit·su** (jōō-jĭt′sōō) n. A Japanese art of hand-to-hand combat.

**Ju·ly** (jōō-lī′, jŏō-) n., pl. **-lys.** The 7th month of the year.

**jum·ble** (jŭm′bəl) v. **-bled, -bling. 1.** To move or mix in a confused manner. **2.** To confuse. —**jum′ble** n.

**jump** (jŭmp) v. **1.** To spring up; leap; bound. **2.** To throw oneself down, off, out, etc. **3.** To spring at in attack. **4.** To start; jerk. **5.** To skip over; omit. —n. **1.** A leap. **2.** A sudden rise. **3.** A level or stage. —**jump′er** n.

**junc·tion** (jŭngk′shən) n. **1.** The act or process of joining. **2.** A place where two things join.

**junc·ture** (jŭngk′chər) n. **1.** Junction. **2.** A point in time.

**June** (jōōn) n. The 6th month of the year.

**jun·gle** (jŭng′gəl) n. Densely overgrown land.

**jun·ior** (jōōn′yər) adj. **1.** Younger. **2.** Designed for youthful persons. **3.** Of lower standing. **4.** Designating the 3rd year of a high school or college. —n. **1.** A younger person. **2.** A subordinate. **3.** A third-year student.

**ju·ni·per** (jōō′nə-pər) n. An evergreen tree or shrub with berrylike fruit.

**junk**[1] (jŭngk) n. **1.** Scrapped materials; rubbish. —v. To throw away.

**junk**[2] (jŭngk) n. A Chinese flat-bottomed ship.

**jun·ket** (jŭng′kĭt) n. **1.** A sweet, custardlike food. **2.** An outing. **3.** A trip taken by an official.

**Ju·pi·ter** (jōō′pə-tər) n. The 5th planet from the sun.

**ju·ris·dic·tion** (jōōr-əs-dĭk′shən) n. **1.** The authority to apply the law. **2.** The extent of such authority. —**ju′ris·dic′tion·al** adj.

**ju·ris·pru·dence** (jōōr′əs-prōō′dəns) n. The science of law.

**ju·rist** (jōōr′əst) n. One skilled in law.

**ju·ror** (jōōr′ər, -ôr′) n. One who serves on a jury.

**ju·ry** (jōōr′ē) n., pl. **-ries.** A group of persons chosen to judge and give a decision, esp. in a court of law.

**just** (jŭst) adj. **1.** Honorable and fair; equitable. **2.** Merited. **3.** Legitimate. **4.** Suitable; fitting. **5.** Sound; accurate. —*adv.* **1.** Exactly. **2.** Only a moment ago. **3.** Barely; merely. —**just'ly** *adv.* —**just'ness** *n.*

**jus·tice** (jŭs'tĭs) *n.* **1.** Moral rightness; equity. **2.** Fairness. **3.** The administration and procedure of law. **4.** A judge.

**jus·ti·fy** (jŭs'tə-fī') *v.* **-fied, -fying. 1.** To demonstrate to be just, right, or valid. **2.** To warrant or defend. —**jus'ti·fi'a·ble** *adj.* —**jus'-ti·fi'a·bly** *adv.* —**jus'ti·fi·ca'tion** *n.*

**jut** (jŭt) *v.* **jutted, jutting.** To project; protrude.

**ju·ve·nile** (jōō'və-nəl, -nīl') *adj.* **1.** Young. **2.** Immature. —*n.* A young person.

**jux·ta·pose** (jŭk'stə-pōz') *v.* **-posed, -posing.** To put side by side. —**jux'ta·po·si'tion** *n.*

# K

**k, K** (kā) *n.* The 11th letter of the English alphabet.

**kale** (kāl) *n.* A type of cabbage.

**ka·lei·do·scope** (kə-lī'də-skōp') *n.* **1.** A small tube in which light shines through loose bits of colored glass that form designs when the tube is rotated. **2.** A series of changing events. —**ka·lei'do·scop'ic** *adj.*

**kan·ga·roo** (kăng'gə-rōō') *n.* An Australian marsupial with large hind limbs adapted for leaping.

**ka·pok** (kā'pŏk') *n.* A silky fiber from the fruit of a tropical tree, used in pillows, etc.

**kar·at** (kăr'ət) *n.* Also **car·at.** A measure comprising 24 units used to specify the proportion of pure gold in an alloy.

**ka·ra·te** (kə-rä'tē, kä-rä'tā) *n.* A Japanese system of unarmed self-defense.

**kar·ma** (kär'mə) *n.* **1.** In Hinduism and Buddhism, the sum and consequences of a person's actions during the successive phases of his existence. **2.** Fate; destiny. —**kar'mic** *adj.*

**ka·ty·did** (kā'tē-dĭd') *n.* A green insect related to the grasshoppers.

**kay·ak** (kī'ăk') *n.* An Eskimo canoe with a covering that closes around the paddler's waist.

**keel** (kēl) *n.* The principal structural member of a ship, extending from bow to stern and forming the backbone of the vessel.

—*v.* —**keel over. 1.** To capsize. **2.** To faint.

**keen** (kēn) *adj.* **1.** Having a sharp cutting edge. **2.** Intellectually acute. **3.** Acutely sensitive. **4.** Eager; enthusiastic. —**keen'ly** *adv.* —**keen'ness** *n.*

**keep** (kēp) *v.* **kept, keeping. 1.** To retain possession of. **2.** To support. **3.** To manage; maintain. **4.** To remain or cause to continue in some condition. **5.** To preserve and protect. **6.** To detain. **7.** To refrain from divulging. **8.** To celebrate; observe. **9.** To remain fresh or unspoiled. —*n.* **1.** Care; charge. **2.** Means of support. —**keep'er** *n.*

**keep·sake** (kēp'sāk') *n.* A memento.

**keg** (kĕg) *n.* A small cask.

**kelp** (kĕlp) *n.* Brown, often very large seaweed.

**ken·nel** (kĕn'əl) *n.* **1.** A dog shelter. **2.** An establishment where dogs are bred or boarded.

**kept** (kĕpt) *p.t. & p.p.* of **keep.**

**ker·chief** (kûr'chĭf) *n.* **1.** A scarf, worn as a head covering. **2.** A handkerchief.

**ker·nel** (kûr'nəl) *n.* **1.** A grain or seed. **2.** The inner, often edible part of a nut. **3.** The core; essence.

**ker·o·sene** (kĕr'ə-sēn', kĕr'ə-sēn') *n.* A thin oil used as a fuel.

**ketch** (kĕch) *n.* A two-masted sailing vessel.

**ketch·up** (kĕch'əp, kăch'-) *n.* A thick, spicy tomato sauce.

**ket·tle** (kĕt'l) *n.* A metal pot for boiling.

**ket·tle·drum** (kĕt'l-drŭm') *n.* A large drum with a parchment head.

**key¹** (kē) *n.* **1.** A metal implement to open or close a lock. **2.** A crucial fact; clue; explanation. **3.** A button or lever on a musical instrument, typewriter, etc. **4.** In music, a tonal system of seven tones in fixed relationship to a tonic. **5.** A general tone or level of intensity. —*v.* To tune up; adjust. —*adj.* Crucial; essential.

**key²** (kē) *n.* A small offshore island or reef.

**key·board** (kē'bôrd', -bōrd') *n.* A set of keys, as on a piano, typewriter, etc.

**key·note** (kē'nōt') *n.* A central element.

**key·stone** (kē'stōn') *n.* The central wedge-shaped stone of an arch.

**khak·i** (kăk'ē, kä'kē) *n., pl.* **-is. 1.** Light olive or yellowish brown. **2.** A cloth of this color. —**khak'i** *adj.*

**kib·butz** (kĭ-bōōts') *n., pl.* **-butzim** (-bōōt'sēm'). A collective farm in Israel.

**kick** (kĭk) *v.* **1.** To strike with the foot. **2.** To recoil, as a gun. —*n.* **1.** The act of kicking. **2.** A temporary interest.

**kickback**

**kick-back** (kĭk'băk') *n.* A payment to a person able to influence or control a source of income.

**kid** (kĭd) *n.* **1.** A young goat. **2.** Leather from the skin of a young goat. **3.** A child. —*v.* **kidded, kidding.** To tease or deceive playfully. — **kid'der** *n.*

**kid-nap** (kĭd'năp') *v.* **-naped** or **-napped, -naping** or **-napping.** To abduct and detain (a person), often for ransom. — **kid'nap'er, kid'nap'per** *n.*

**kid-ney** (kĭd'nē) *n., pl.* **-neys.** Either of a pair of glands that maintain proper water balance and excrete urine.

**kill** (kĭl) *v.* **1.** To put to death; slay. **2.** To thwart; veto. —*n.* That which is killed or destroyed, as an animal in hunting. — **kill'er** *n.*

**kill-ing** (kĭl'ĭng) *n.* **1.** A murder. **2.** A sudden large profit.

**kiln** (kĭl, kĭln) *n.* An oven for hardening or drying, esp. ceramics.

**ki-lo-cy-cle** (kĭl'ə-sī'kəl) *n.* One thousand cycles per second.

**kil-o-gram** (kĭl'ə-grăm') *n.* The fundamental unit of mass in the metric system, about 2.2046 pounds.

**kil-o-me-ter** (kĭl'ə-mē'tər, kĭ-lŏm'ə-tər) *n.* One thousand meters.

**kil-o-watt** (kĭl'ə-wŏt') *n.* One thousand watts.

**kilt** (kĭlt) *n.* A man's skirt worn in the Scottish Highlands.

**ki-mo-no** (kə-mō'nə, -nō) *n., pl.* **-nos. 1.** A wide-sleeved Japanese robe. **2.** A type of dressing gown.

**kin** (kĭn) *n.* One's relatives collectively. — **kins'folk'** *n.*

**kind**[1] (kīnd) *adj.* Showing sympathy or understanding; helpful or giving. — **kind'ness** *n.*

**kind**[2] (kīnd) *n.* A class or category; sort; type.

**kin-dle** (kĭnd'l) *v.* **-dled, -dling. 1.** To start (a fire). **2.** To arouse; inspire.

**kin-dling** (kĭnd'lĭng) *n.* Material used to start a fire.

**kind-ly** (kīnd'lē) *adj.* **-lier, -liest.** Sympathetic; considerate; helpful. —*adv.* **1.** In a kind manner. **2.** Please; accommodatingly. — **kind'li-ness** *n.*

**kin-dred** (kĭn'drĭd) *n.* A person's relatives. —*adj.* Similar or related.

**kin-e-scope** (kĭn'ə-skōp') *n.* A cathode-ray tube that translates received TV signals into a visible picture.

**king** (kĭng) *n.* **1.** A male monarch. **2.** A playing card bearing a picture of a king. — **king'li-ness** *n.* — **king'ly** *adj.*

**king-dom** (kĭng'dəm) *n.* **1.** A country ruled by a king or queen. **2.** A broad category of living or natural forms.

**king-fish-er** (kĭng'fĭsh'ər) *n.* A large-billed bird that feeds on fish.

**kink** (kĭngk) *n.* **1.** A curl or twist. **2.** A painful muscle spasm. —*v.* To form kinks (in). — **kink'y** *adj.*

**kin-ship** (kĭn'shĭp') *n.* **1.** Blood relations. **2.** A close connection.

**ki-osk** (kē-ŏsk', kē'ŏsk') *n.* A small structure used as a newsstand, etc.

**kip-per** (kĭp'ər) *n.* A salted, smoked herring.

**kis-met** (kĭz'mĭt, kĭs'-) *n.* Fate; fortune.

**kiss** (kĭs) *v.* To touch with the lips in affection, greeting, etc. —*n.* **1.** A touching with the lips. **2.** A small piece of candy.

**kit** (kĭt) *n.* **1.** A set of instruments or equipment. **2.** A set of parts to be assembled.

**kitch-en** (kĭch'ən) *n.* A room in which food is cooked. — **kitch'en-ette'** *n.*

**kite** (kīt) *n.* **1.** A light framework covered with paper and designed to hover in the wind. **2.** A predatory bird with a long tail.

**kit-ten** (kĭt'n) *n.* A young cat.

**kit-ty** (kĭt'ē) *n., pl.* **-ties.** A pool or fund of money.

**klep-to-ma-ni-a** (klĕp'tə-mā'nē-ə) *n.* An obsessive impulse to steal. — **klep'to-ma'ni-ac'** *n.*

**knack** (năk) *n.* A specific ability.

**knap-sack** (năp'săk') *n.* A supply bag worn on the back.

**knave** (nāv) *n.* An unprincipled, crafty person. — **knav'ish** *adj.*

**knead** (nēd) *v.* **1.** To mix and work (a substance). **2.** To massage.

**knee** (nē) *n.* The joint between the upper and lower parts of the leg.

**knee-cap** (nē'kăp') *n.* The patella.

**kneel** (nēl) *v.* **knelt** (nĕlt) or **kneeled, kneeling.** To rest on bent knees.

**knell** (nĕl) *v.* **1.** To ring a bell; toll. **2.** To signal by tolling. —*n.* **1.** The slow sounding of a bell. **2.** An omen of sorrow.

**knew** (n/y/ōō). *p.t.* of **know.**

**knick-ers** (nĭk'ərz) *pl.n.* Full breeches gathered below the knee.

**knick-knack** (nĭk'năk') *n.* A decorative trinket.

**knife** (nīf) *n., pl.* **knives** (nīvz) A cutting blade with a handle. —*v.* **knifed, knifing.** To cut, stab, or wound.

**knight** (nīt) *n.* **1.** A medieval gentleman-soldier. **2.** The holder of a nonhereditary dignity conferred by a sovereign. —*v.* To raise (a person) to knighthood. —**knight′hood**′ *n.* —**knight′ly** *adj.*

**knit** (nĭt) *v.* **knit** or **knitted, knitting. 1.** To make by intertwining yarn in a series of loops. **2.** To join closely. —*n.* A knitted fabric or garment.

**knob** (nŏb) *n.* A rounded protuberance or a rounded handle. —**knob′by** *adj.*

**knock** (nŏk) *v.* **1.** To strike hard. **2.** To criticize adversely. **3.** To collide; bump. —**knock** *n.*

**knoll** (nōl) *n.* A small hill.

**knot** (nŏt) *n.* **1.** A tightly tied intersection, as of string. **2.** Any bond. **3.** A cluster of persons or things. **4.** A hard lump from which a tree branch grows. **5.** A unit of speed, one nautical mile per hour. —*v.* **knotted, knotting. 1.** To snarl or tangle. **2.** To form a knot (in).

**knot·ty** (nŏt′ē) *adj.* **-tier, -tiest. 1.** Covered with or having knots; gnarled. **2.** Difficult; intricate.

**know** (nō) *v.* **knew, known, knowing. 1.** To perceive directly; be aware of. **2.** To be capable of. **3.** To understand. **4.** To be acquainted with.

**know·ing** (nō′ĭng) *adj.* **1.** Possessing knowledge or understanding. **2.** Clever; shrewd. —**know′ing·ly** *adv.* —**know′ing·ness** *n.*

**knowl·edge** (nŏl′ĭj) *n.* **1.** Familiarity, awareness, or understanding. **2.** That which is known. **3.** Learning. —**knowl′edge·a·ble** *adj.*

**knuck·le** (nŭk′əl) *n.* Any joint of a finger. —*v.* **-led, -ling. —knuckle down.** To apply oneself. —**knuckle under.** To yield to pressure.

**ko·a·la** (kō-ä′lə) *n.* A furry, tree-dwelling Australian marsupial.

**ko·sher** (kō′shər) *adj.* **1.** Conforming to Jewish dietary laws. **2.** Proper; legitimate.

**ku·dos** (k/y/ōō′dŏz′, -dōs′) *n.* Acclaim or prestige.

**kum·quat** (kŭm′kwŏt′) *n.* A small, edible orangelike fruit.

# L

**l, L** (ĕl) *n.* The 12th letter of the English alphabet.

**la·bel** (lā′bəl) *n.* A tag attached to an article to designate its owner, contents, etc. —*v.* **1.** To attach a label to. **2.** To classify.

**la·bor** (lā′bər) *n.* **1.** Physical or mental work. **2.** Work for wages. **3.** Workers collectively. —*v.* **1.** To work. **2.** To proceed slowly; plod. —**la′bor·er** *n.* —**la·bo′ri·ous** *adj.*

**lab·o·ra·to·ry** (lăb′rə-tôr′ē, -tōr′ē) *n., pl.* **-ries.** A place for scientific research or experiment.

**lab·y·rinth** (lăb′ə-rĭnth′) *n.* A network of interconnecting passages. —**lab′y·rin′thine**′ *adj.*

**lace** (lās) *n.* **1.** A cord. **2.** A delicate fabric in a weblike pattern. —*v.* **laced, lacing.** To fasten with a lace.

**lac·er·ate** (lăs′ə-rāt′) *v.* **-ated, -ating.** To tear; mangle. —**lac′er·a′tion** *n.*

**lack** (lăk) *n.* A deficiency or absence. —*v.* To be without or be wanting.

**lack·ey** (lăk′ē) *n., pl.* **-eys. 1.** A footman. **2.** A servile follower.

**la·con·ic** (lə-kŏn′ĭk) *adj.* Terse; concise.

**lac·quer** (lăk′ər) *n.* A coating used to give surfaces a high gloss. —**lac′quer** *v.*

**lac·tic** (lăk′tĭk) *adj.* Of or derived from milk.

**lad** (lăd) *n.* A young man.

**lad·der** (lăd′ər) *n.* A device consisting of two long poles crossed by parallel rungs, used to climb.

**la·dle** (lād′l) *n.* A long-handled spoon with a deep bowl. —*v.* **-dled, -dling.** To lift out with a ladle.

**la·dy** (lā′dē) *n., pl.* **-dies. 1.** A woman of refinement. **2.** The female head of a household. **3.** A feminine title of rank.

**lag** (lăg) *v.* **lagged, lagging. 1.** To fail to keep up a pace. **2.** To slacken. —*n.* **1.** A falling behind. **2.** A gap. —**lag′gard** *n.*

**la·goon** (lə-gōōn′) *n.* A body of brackish water, esp. one separated from the sea by sandbars or reefs.

**laid** (lād) *p.t. & p.p.* of **lay¹.**

**lain** (lān) *p.p.* of **lie¹.**

**lair** (lâr) *n.* The den of a wild animal.

**lake** (lāk) *n.* A large inland body of water.

**lamb** (lăm) *n.* A young sheep.

**lame** (lām) *adj.* **lamer, lamest. 1.** Crippled, esp. in a leg or foot. **2.** Ineffectual. —*v.* **lamed, laming.** To cause to become lame. —**lame'ness** *n.*

**la·ment** (lə-mĕnt') *v.* **1.** To mourn. **2.** To wail; complain. —*n.* **1.** An expression of mourning. **2.** A dirge. —**lam'en·ta·ble** *adj.* —**lam·en·ta'tion** *n.*

**lam·i·nate** (lăm'ə-nāt') *v.* **-nated, -nating. 1.** To bond together in thin layers. **2.** To divide into thin layers. —**lam'i·na'tion** *n.*

**lamp** (lămp) *n.* A device for providing light.

**lam·poon** (lăm-pōōn') *n.* Satire, esp. that intended to ridicule. —*v.* To ridicule in a lampoon.

**lance** (lăns, läns) *n.* A spear with a long shaft. —*v.* **lanced, lancing.** To cut into with a surgical knife.

**land** (lănd) *n.* **1.** The solid part of the earth's surface. **2.** A portion or region of this. —*v.* To arrive or cause to arrive on land or at a certain place.

**land·lord** (lănd'lôrd') *n.* One who owns and leases property. —**land'la·dy** *fem.n.*

**land·scape** (lănd'skāp') *n.* **1.** A view of rural scenery. **2.** A pictorial representation of this.

**lane** (lān) *n.* A narrow way or road.

**lan·guage** (lăng'gwĭj) *n.* **1.** Speech. **2.** Any system of signs, symbols, etc., used for communication.

**lan·guish** (lăng'gwĭsh) *v.* **1.** To lose strength or vigor. **2.** To become listless or disconsolate. —**lan'guid** *adj.* —**lan'guor** *n.* —**lan'guor·ous** *adj.*

**lank** (lăngk) *adj.* Long and lean; gaunt. —**lank'y** *adj.*

**lan·tern** (lăn'tərn) *n.* A case for holding and protecting a light.

**lap¹** (lăp) *n.* The front part of a seated person from the lower trunk to the knees.

**lap²** (lăp) *v.* **lapped, lapping. 1.** To fold or wrap over or around. —*n.* **1.** An overlapping part. **2.** A complete circuit of a racecourse.

**lap³** (lăp) *v.* **lapped, lapping.** To lift and take in (a liquid or food) with the tongue. —**lap** *n.*

**la·pel** (lə-pĕl') *n.* A front of a coat, jacket, etc., folded back against the chest.

**lapse** (lăps) *v.* **lapsed, lapsing. 1.** To fall away gradually. **2.** To become invalid. —*n.* **1.** A slipping into a lower state. **2.** A minor slip or failure. **3.** A passing or interval of time.

**lar·ce·ny** (lär'sə-nē) *n., pl.* **-nies.** Theft. —**lar'ce·nous** *adj.*

**large** (lärj) *adj.* **larger, largest.** Of considerable size, capacity, etc.; big. —**at large. 1.** At liberty. **2.** Not representing or assigned to a specific country, district, etc. —**large'ly** *adv.*

**lar·i·at** (lăr'ē-ət) *n.* A lasso.

**lark** (lärk) *n.* A carefree romp or prank.

**lar·ynx** (lăr'ĭngks) *n.* The upper part of the respiratory tract, containing the vocal cords. —**la·ryn'ge·al** *adj.*

**las·civ·i·ous** (lə-sĭv'ē-əs) *adj.* Lewd; lecherous.

**lash¹** (lăsh) *n.* **1.** A whip or thong of a whip. **2.** A blow with a whip. **3.** An eyelash. —*v.* To strike with or as with a whip.

**lash²** (lăsh) *v.* To secure, as with a rope.

**lass** (lăs) *n.* A girl or young woman.

**las·si·tude** (lăs'ə-t/y/ōōd') *n.* Listless weakness or exhaustion.

**las·so** (lăs'ō) *n., pl.* **-sos** or **-soes.** A long rope with a running noose, used esp. to catch horses. —**las'so** *v.*

**last¹** (lăst, läst) *adj.* **1.** Being, coming, or remaining after all others. **2.** Most recent; latest. **3.** Conclusive and authoritative. —*adv.* **1.** Most recently. **2.** In conclusion. —*n.* One that is last. —**last'ly** *adv.*

**last²** (lăst, läst) *v.* To endure.

**latch** (lăch) *n.* A fastening or lock, as for a gate.

**late** (lāt) *adj.* **later, latest. 1.** Coming or occurring after the expected time. **2.** Recent. **3.** Recently deceased. —*adv.* **1.** After the expected time. **2.** Recently. —**late'ly** *adv.*

**la·tent** (lā'tənt) *adj.* Present or potential but not manifest. —**la'ten·cy** *n.*

**lat·er·al** (lăt'ər·əl) *adj.* Of, at, on, or toward the side.

**la·tex** (lā'tĕks') *n.* The viscous sap of certain plants and trees. —**la'tex'** *adj.*

**lathe** (lāth) *n.* A machine on which a piece is spun and shaped by a cutting tool.

**lath·er** (lăth'ər) *n.* **1.** Foam, esp. that formed by soap and water. **2.** Frothy sweat. —*v.* **1.** To produce lather. **2.** To apply lather to.

**lat·i·tude** (lăt'ə-t/y/ōōd') *n.* **1.** Extent; range. **2.** Freedom from limitations. **3.** The angular distance N or S of the equator.

**lat·ter** (lăt'ər) *adj.* **1.** Second of two. **2.** Further advanced; later.

**lat·tice** (lăt'ĭs) *n.* An open framework made of interwoven strips. —**lat'tice·work** *n.*

**laud** (lôd) *v.* To praise; commend. —**laud'a·ble** *adj.*

**laugh** (lăf, läf) *v.* To produce sounds expressive of mirth or derision. —*n.* The sound or act of laughing. —**laugh'a·ble** *adj.*

**launch¹** (lônch, länch) v. **1.** To set in motion. **2.** To move (a boat) into the water. —n. An act of launching.

**launch²** (lônch, länch) n. An open motorboat.

**laun·der** (lôn′dər, län′-) v. To wash and iron (clothes or linens). — **laun′dress** *fem.n.* — **laun′dry** n.

**la·va** (lä′və, lăv′ə) n. Molten rock from a volcano.

**lav·a·to·ry** (lăv′ə-tôr′ē) n., pl. **-ries.** A room with a toilet and sink.

**lav·en·der** (lăv′ən-dər) n. **1.** An aromatic plant having fragrant purplish flowers. **2.** Pale to light purple. — **lav·en·der** adj.

**lav·ish** (lăv′ĭsh) adj. Extravagant. —v. To give, spend, etc., unstintingly.

**law** (lô) n. **1.** A rule established by authority, society, or custom. **2.** A body of such rules. **3.** The profession relating to such rules. **4.** A generalization based on observed phenomena. — **law′ful** adj. — **law′less** adj. — **law′mak·er** n.

**lawn** (lôn) n. A closely mown area planted with grass.

**law·suit** (lô′sōōt′) n. A case brought before a law court.

**law·yer** (lô′yər) n. A professional who practices law.

**lax** (lăks) adj. **1.** Negligent; remiss. **2.** Not strict. — **lax′i·ty, lax′ness** n.

**lay¹** (lā) v. **laid, laying. 1.** To place on a surface. **2.** To produce and deposit (eggs). **3.** To set or place in a desired position. **4.** To prepare; contrive. —n. The relative position of something.

**lay²** (lā). p.t. of **lie¹.**

**lay·er** (lā′ər) n. A single thickness.

**lay·out** (lā′out′) n. A arrangement or plan.

**la·zy** (lā′zē) adj. **-zier, -ziest. 1.** Indolent; slothful. **2.** Slow-moving; sluggish. — **la′zi·ness** n.

**lea** (lē, lā) n. A meadow.

**lead¹** (lēd) v. **led, leading. 1.** To guide, conduct, escort, or direct. **2.** To influence. **3.** To be ahead or at the head of. **4.** To pursue; live. —n. **1.** The first place. **2.** A clue. **3.** The amount by which one is ahead. **4.** The main part in a play, movie, etc. — **lead′er** n. — **lead′er·ship** n.

**lead²** (lĕd) n. **1.** A soft, dense, dull-gray metallic element. **2.** Graphite used as a marking substance in a pencil. — **lead** adj.

**leaf** (lēf) n., pl. **leaves. 1.** A usually green, flattened plant structure attached to a stem.

**2.** A thin sheet of paper, as a page of a book. **3.** A thin sheet of gold. —v. To turn or glance at pages rapidly. — **leaf′y** adj.

**league** (lēg) n. An association or alliance.

**leak** (lēk) n. **1.a.** A flaw, crack, or hole permitting escape of fluid or light. **b.** Such escape. **2.** A disclosure of confidential information. —v. **1.** To escape through a leak. **2.** To disclose or become known through a breach of secrecy. — **leak′age** n. — **leak′y** adj.

**lean¹** (lēn) v. **leaned** or **leant, leaning. 1.** To bend; incline. **2.** To rely on for assistance.

**lean²** (lēn) adj. **1.** Thin. **2.** Containing little or no fat. — **lean′ness** n.

**leap** (lēp) v. **leaped** or **leapt, leaping. 1.** To jump off the ground. **2.** To jump forward; bound. —v. A jump.

**learn** (lûrn) v. **learned** or **learnt, learning. 1.** To gain knowledge or mastery. **2.** To become informed. — **learn′ed** adj. — **learn′er** n. — **learn′ing** n.

**lease** (lēs) n. A contract granting use of land or holdings in exchange for rent. —v. **leased, leasing.** To grant by or hold under lease.

**leash** (lēsh) n. A restraining chain, strap, etc., for an animal. — **leash** v.

**least** (lēst) Alternate *superl.* of **little.** —adj. **1.** Lowest in importance or rank. **2.** Smallest in magnitude. —adv. In the smallest degree. —n. The smallest; slightest.

**leath·er** (lĕth′ər) n. The tanned hide of an animal. — **leath′er** adj. — **leath′er·y** adj.

**leave¹** (lēv) v. **left, leaving. 1.** To go away from; depart. **2.** To let or cause to remain. **3.** To bequeath.

**leave²** (lēv) n. **1.** Permission, esp. to be absent from duty. **2.** Farewell.

**leaves** (lēvz). pl. of **leaf.**

**lech·er** (lĕch′ər) n. A person given to excessive sexual indulgence. — **lech′er·ous** adj.

**lec·ture** (lĕk′chər) n. **1.** An instructional speech. **2.** A solemn scolding. — **lec′ture** v. — **lec′tur·er** n.

**led** (lĕd). p.t. & p.p. of **lead¹.**

**ledge** (lĕj) n. A shelflike projection.

**ledg·er** (lĕj′ər) n. A book in which monetary transactions are posted.

**lee** (lē) n. **1.** The side away from the wind. **2.** Cover; shelter. — **lee** adj.

**leer** (lîr) n. A suggestive or cunning look. — **leer** v.

**lee·way** (lē′wā′) n. A margin of freedom; latitude.

**left¹** (lĕft) adj. Of, at, or on the side of the

body that faces north when the subject is facing east. —n. **1.** The left side or hand. **2.** Often **the Left.** The persons and groups pursuing egalitarian political goals by reform or revolution. —adv. Toward or on the left.

**left²** (lĕft). p.t. & p.p. of **leave¹**.

**leg** (lĕg) n. **1.** A limb of an animal, used for locomotion or support. **2.** Something resembling a leg.

**leg·a·cy** (lĕg'ə-sē) n., pl. **-cies. 1.** A bequest. **2.** Something handed down; heritage. — **leg'a·tee'** n.

**le·gal** (lē'gəl) adj. **1.** Of law or lawyers. **2.** Authorized by law. — **le·gal'i·ty** n. — **le·gal·i·za'tion** n. — **le'gal·ize'** v. — **le'gal·ly** adv.

**le·ga·tion** (lə-gā'shən) n. **1.** A diplomatic mission headed by a minister. **2.** The premises occupied by the mission.

**leg·end** (lĕj'ənd) n. **1.** A story handed down from the past. **2.** An inscription. — **leg'en·dar'y** adj.

**leg·i·ble** (lĕj'ə-bəl) adj. Capable of being read. — **leg'i·bil'i·ty** n. — **leg'i·bly** adv.

**le·gion** (lē'jən) n. **1.** A large military division. **2.** A multitude.

**leg·is·late** (lĕj'ĭs-lāt') v. **-lated, -lating.** To pass a law. — **leg'is·la'tion** n. — **leg'is·la'tive** adj. — **leg'is·la'tor** n.

**leg·is·la·ture** (lĕj'ĭs-lā'chər) n. A body of persons vested with the power to legislate.

**le·git·i·mate** (lə-jĭt'ə-mĭt) adj. **1.** Lawful. **2.** Reasonable. **3.** Authentic; genuine. **4.** Born in wedlock. — **le·git'i·ma·cy** n.

**lei·sure** (lē'zhər, lĕzh'ər) n. Freedom from work; time not spent in compulsory activity. — **lei'sure·ly** adj. & adv.

**lem·on** (lĕm'ən) n. A yellow citrus fruit with sour, juicy pulp.

**lend** (lĕnd) v. **lent, lending. 1.** To give out or allow for temporary use. **2.** To impart. — **lend'er** n.

**length** (lĕngkth, lĕngth) n. **1.** The measure of something along its greatest dimension. **2.** Duration or extent. — **length'en** v. — **length'wise'** adv. & adj. — **length'y** adj.

**le·ni·ent** (lē'nē-ənt, lēn'yənt) adj. Merciful; generous. — **le'ni·en·cy, le'ni·ence** n.

**lens** (lĕnz) n. **1.** A piece of glass or other transparent material used to make light rays converge or diverge to form an image. **2.** A transparent part of the eye that focuses light entering the eye on the retina.

**lent** (lĕnt). p.t. & p.p. of **lend.**

**leop·ard** (lĕp'ərd) n. A large wild cat, usually having a spotted coat.

**lep·ro·sy** (lĕp'rə-sē) n. A chronic disease

causing ulcers and sores on the body. — **lep'er** n. — **lep'rous** adj.

**le·sion** (lē'zhən) n. A wound, injury, or mass of diseased tissue.

**less** (lĕs). Alternate compar. of **little.** —adj. **1.** Smaller. **2.** Lower in importance. —adv. To a smaller extent. —n. A smaller amount. —prep. Minus. — **less'en** v.

**les·son** (lĕs'ən) n. **1.** Something learned or to be learned. **2.** A period of instruction. **3.** An instructive example or experience.

**let** (lĕt) v. **let, letting. 1.** To allow. **2.** To rent or lease.

**le·thal** (lē'thəl) adj. Deadly.

**leth·ar·gy** (lĕth'ər-jē) n., pl. **-gies.** Sluggishness and indifference; drowsiness. — **le·thar'gic** adj.

**let·ter** (lĕt'ər) n. **1.** A written symbol representing a speech sound. **2.** A written communication. **3.** **letters.** Literature or learning. —v. To mark or write with letters.

**lev·ee** (lĕv'ē) n. **1.** An embankment to prevent a river from flooding. **2.** A landing place on a river.

**lev·el** (lĕv'əl) n. **1.** Relative position or rank. **2.** A flat, horizontal surface. **3.** Elevation; height. **4.** An instrument for ascertaining whether a surface is horizontal. —adj. **1.** Having a flat, smooth surface. **2.** Horizontal. **3.** Even. **4.** Uniform; consistent. —v. **1.** To make or become horizontal, flat, or even. **2.** To raze. **3.** To aim. — **lev'el·er** n.

**le·ver** (lĕv'ər, lē'vər) n. A simple machine consisting of a rigid bar that turns on a fixed fulcrum.

**le·ver·age** (lĕv'ər-ĭj, lē'vər-) n. **1.** The mechanical advantage of a lever. **2.** Positional advantage.

**lev·i·ty** (lĕv'ə-tē) n., pl. **-ties.** Frivolity.

**lev·y** (lĕv'ē) v. **-ied, -ying. 1.** To impose or collect (a tax). **2.** To wage (a war). —n. **1.** The act or process of levying. **2.** Money or property levied.

**lewd** (lood) adj. **1.** Licentious; lustful. **2.** Obscene.

**lex·i·con** (lĕk'sĭ-kŏn') n. **1.** A dictionary. **2.** A vocabulary used in a particular subject.

**li·a·bil·i·ty** (lī'ə-bĭl'ə-tē) n., pl. **-ties. 1.** The state of being liable. **2. liabilities.** Debts. **3.** A drawback.

**li·a·ble** (lī'ə-bəl) adj. **1.** Legally obligated; responsible. **2.** Likely; apt.

**li·ai·son** (lē-ā'zŏn', lē-ā'zŏn', lē'ə-) n. **1.** Communication between groups or units. **2.** An illicit relationship.

**li·bel** (lī'bəl) n. A written, printed, or

**limp**

pictorial statement that unjustly damages a person's reputation. —v. To defame or malign. —li'bel·ous adj.

lib·er·al (lib'ər·əl, lib'rəl) adj. 1. Favoring individual freedom and nonrevolutionary reform. 2. Broad-minded or tolerant. 3. Generous; bountiful. —n. One holding liberal political views. —lib'er·al·ism' n. —lib'er·al'i·ty n. —lib'er·al·ize' v.

lib·er·ate (lib'ə·rāt') v. -ated, -ating. To set free. —lib'er·a'tion n. —lib'er·a'tor n.

lib·er·ty (lib'ər·tē) n., pl. -ties. 1. Freedom from restriction or control; independence. 2. Freedom from confinement. 3. Often liberties. Unwarranted familiarity.

li·brar·y (lī'brĕr'ē) n., pl. -ies. 1. A repository for books, records, prints, etc. 2. A permanent collection of such materials. —li·brar'i·an n.

li·bret·to (li·brĕt'ō) n., pl. -tos or -bretti. The dialogue of an opera or other dramatic musical work. —li·bret'tist n.

lice (līs). pl. of louse.

li·cense (lī'səns) n. 1. Legal permission to do or own something. 2. Excessive or undisciplined freedom. —v. licensed, licensing. To grant a license to or for.

li·cen·tious (lī·sĕn'shəs) adj. Unrestrained; immoral.

lick (lĭk) v. 1. To pass the tongue over. 2. To defeat. —n. The act of licking.

lid (lĭd) n. 1. A cover for any hollow receptacle. 2. An eyelid.

lie¹ (lī) v. lay, lain, lying. 1. To assume a recumbent position; recline. 2. To be or remain in a specific location.

lie² (lī) n. A deliberate falsehood. —v. lied, lying. To tell a lie. —li'ar n.

lieu·ten·ant (lōō·tĕn'ənt) n. 1. A commissioned officer in the armed forces. 2. A chief assistant; deputy.

life (līf) n., pl. lives. 1. The quality by which living organisms are distinguished from dead organisms or inanimate matter. 2. Living organisms collectively. 3. The interval between birth and death. 4. A manner of living. 5. Liveliness. —life'less adj. —life'time' n.

lift (lĭft) v. 1. To raise; elevate. 2. To ascend; rise. —n. 1. The act of raising or rising. 2. A rising of spirits. 3. A short ride in a vehicle.

lig·a·ment (lĭg'ə·mənt) n. A band of tough, fibrous tissue that connects bones or supports an organ.

light¹ (līt) n. 1. Electromagnetic radiation. 2. Illumination or a source of illumination.

3. Daylight or visible light. 4. A means for igniting a fire. 5. An aspect. —v. lighted or lit, lighting. 1. To ignite. 2. To illuminate. —adj. 1. Radiant; bright. 2. Not dark; pale.

light² (līt) adj. 1. Not heavy. 2. Not serious. 3. Frivolous; silly. 4. Small in intensity or amount. —adv. With little baggage. —v. lighted or lit, lighting. 1. To dismount. 2. To land. —light'ly adv.

light·en¹ (līt'n) v. To make or become light or lighter; brighten.

light·en² (līt'n) v. 1. To make or become less heavy. 2. To make or become less oppressive.

light·house (līt'hous') n. A tower topped by a powerful light for guiding ships.

light·ning (līt'nĭng) n. A large natural electric discharge in the atmosphere. —adj. Very fast or sudden.

light-year (līt'yĭr') n. Also light year. The distance that light travels in one year, approx. 6 trillion miles.

like¹ (līk) v. liked, liking. 1. To enjoy. 2. To want or wish. 3. To be fond of. —lik'a·ble, like'a·ble adj. —lik'ing n.

like² (līk) prep. 1. Similar to. 2. Typical of. 3. Disposed to. 4. Indicative of. —adj. 1. Similar. 2. Equivalent. —n. Similar or related persons or things.

like·ly (līk'lē) adj. -lier, -liest. 1. Probable; apt. 2. Suitable. 3. Seemingly true; credible. —adv. Probably. —like'li·hood' n.

like·ness (līk'nĭs) n. 1. A resemblance. 2. An image.

like·wise (līk'wīz') adv. 1. In the same way; similarly. 2. Also; too.

li·lac (lī'lăk, -lŏk') n. 1. A shrub bearing fragrant purplish or white flowers. 2. Pale purple. —li'lac adj.

lilt (lĭlt) n. A cheerful, rhythmic manner of speaking.

limb (lĭm) n. 1. One of the jointed appendages of an animal, as an arm, leg, or wing. 2. A tree branch.

lim·ber (lĭm'bər) adj. 1. Bending easily; pliable. 2. Agile.

lime (lĭm) n. A green citrus fruit.

lim·er·ick (lĭm'ər·ĭk) n. A humorous five-line poem.

lim·it (lĭm'ĭt) n. 1. The point, edge, or line where something ends. 2. The greatest amount or number allowed. —v. To place a limit on. —lim·i·ta'tion n. —lim'it·less adj.

limp (lĭmp) v. To walk lamely. —n. An irregular or awkward gait. —adj. Lacking rigidity; flabby.

**lim·pid** (lim'pid) *adj.* Crystal clear; transparent.

**line¹** (lin) *n.* 1. A thin, continuous mark. 2. A border or boundary. 3. A cable, rope, wire, etc. 4. A course of progress or movement. 5. Often **lines.** Outline or styling. 6. One's occupation. 7. A group of persons or things arranged in a row. 8. A system of transportation. 9. Merchandise of a similar nature. —*v.* **lined, lining.** 1. To mark with lines. 2. To place in a series or row. 3. To form a bordering line along.

**line²** (lin) *v.* **lined, lining.** To sew or fit a covering to the inside surface of. —**lin'ing** *n.*

**lin·e·age** (lin'ē-ij) *n.* Ancestry.

**lin·en** (lin'ən) *n.* 1. Cloth made of flax. 2. Articles made from this cloth. —**lin'en** *adj.*

**lin·ger** (ling'gər) *v.* 1. To remain; tarry. 2. To persist. 3. To procrastinate.

**lin·ge·rie** (län'zhə-rā', län'zhə-rē) *n.* Women's underwear.

**lin·guis·tics** (ling-gwis'tiks) *n.* The science of language. —**lin'guist** *n.* —**lin·guis'tic** *adj.*

**lin·i·ment** (lin'ə-mənt) *n.* A soothing medicinal fluid applied to the skin.

**link** (lingk) *n.* 1. One of the rings forming a chain. 2. A bond or tie. —*v.* To connect or become connected. —**link'age** *n.*

**li·no·le·um** (li-nō'lē-əm) *n.* A durable, washable material used as a floor covering.

**lint** (lint) *n.* Bits of fiber and fluff; fuzz.

**li·on** (li'ən) *n.* A very large carnivorous cat. —**li'on·ess** *fem.n.*

**lip** (lip) *n.* 1. Either of two fleshy, muscular folds that together surround the opening of the mouth. 2. The rim of a container, wound, etc.

**liq·uid** (lik'wid) *n.* A substance capable of flowing. —*adj.* 1. Of a liquid. 2. Readily converted into cash. —**liq'ue·fy** *v.*

**liq·ui·date** (lik'wə-dāt') *v.* **-dated, -dating.** 1. To pay off or settle. 2. To wind up the affairs of (a business firm). 3. To convert (assets) into cash. —**liq'ui·da'tion** *n.*

**liq·uor** (lik'ər) *n.* An alcoholic beverage.

**lisp** (lisp) *n.* A speech defect in which *s* and *z* are pronounced *th.* —**lisp** *v.*

**list¹** (list) *n.* A printed or written series of persons or things. —*v.* To make a list of or enter in a list. —**list** *v.*

**list²** (list) *n.* A tilt. —*v.* To lean or tilt.

**lis·ten** (lis'ən) *v.* 1. To make an effort to hear something. 2. To pay attention. —**lis'ten·er** *n.*

**list·less** (list'lis) *adj.* Indifferent; languid. —**list'less·ly** *adv.* —**list'less·ness** *n.*

**lit** (lit). 1. Alternate *p.t.* & *p.p.* of **light¹.** 2. Alternate *p.t.* & *p.p.* of **light².**

**li·ter** (lē'tər) *n.* A metric unit of volume.

**lit·er·a·cy** (lit'ər-ə-sē) *n.* The ability to read and write. —**lit'er·ate** *adj.*

**lit·er·al** (lit'ər-əl) *adj.* Exact; word for word. —**lit'er·al·ly** *adv.*

**lit·er·a·ture** (lit'ər-ə-chŏŏr') *n.* 1. Imaginative or creative writing. 2. A body of writing on a given subject. —**lit'er·ar·y** *adj.*

**lit·i·gate** (lit'i-gāt') *v.* **-gated, -gating.** To engage in or subject to legal proceedings. —**lit'i·gant** *n.* —**lit'i·ga'tion** *n.* —**lit'i·ga'tor** *n.*

**lit·ter** (lit'ər) *n.* 1. A stretcher. 2. The young produced at one birth by mammals. 3. Discarded waste. —*v.* To discard rubbish carelessly.

**lit·tle** (lit'l) *adj.* **-tler, -tlest.** 1. Small in size, quantity, or degree. 2. Also *compar.* **less,** *superl.* **least.** a. Brief. b. Insignificant. —*adv.* **less, least.** Not much. —*n.* A small quantity.

**live¹** (liv) *v.* **lived, living.** 1. To have life. 2. To reside. 3. To pass; spend.

**live²** (liv) *adj.* 1. Alive. 2. Glowing. 3. Carrying electric current. 4. Not exploded. 5. Of current interest.

**live·li·hood** (liv'lē-hŏŏd') *n.* Means of support.

**live·ly** (liv'lē) *adj.* **-lier, -liest.** 1. Full of life; vigorous. 2. Intense; keen. 3. Cheerful. —**live'li·ness** *n.*

**liv·en** (li'vən) *v.* To make or become lively.

**liv·er** (liv'ər) *n.* A glandular organ that secretes bile.

**lives** (livz). *pl.* of **life.**

**live·stock** (liv'stŏk') *n.* Domestic animals, as cattle, horses, or sheep.

**liv·id** (liv'id) *adj.* 1. Discolored, as from a bruise. 2. Ashen, as with anger.

**liv·ing** (liv'ing) *adj.* 1. Alive. 2. Of persons who are alive. 3. Of or characteristic of daily life. 4. Currently in use. —*n.* 1. The state of being alive. 2. Livelihood.

**liz·ard** (liz'ərd) *n.* A reptile having a long, scaly body.

**load** (lōd) *n.* 1. A supported weight or mass. 2. Material or an amount of material transported by a vehicle or animal. —*v.* 1. To place (a load) in or on a structure, device, or conveyance. 2. To charge (a firearm) with ammunition.

**loaf¹** (lōf) *n., pl.* **loaves.** A shaped mass of bread or other baked food.

**loaf²** (lōf) *v.* To spend time lazily or aimlessly. —**loaf'er** *n.*

**loan** (lōn) *n.* 1. A sum of money lent at

interest. **2.** Anything lent for temporary use.
—v. To lend.

**loathe** (lōth) v. loathed, loathing. To detest;
abhor. —**loath'some** adj.

**loaves** (lōvz) pl. of **loaf'**.

**lob·by** (lŏb'ē) n., pl. -bies. **1.** A hall or waiting
room. **2.** Persons engaged in influencing
legislation. —v. -bied, -bying. To seek to
influence legislators. —**lob'by·ist** n.

**lobe** (lōb) n. A rounded projection. —**lo'bar**
adj.

**lob·ster** (lŏb'stər) n. A large, edible marine
crustacean.

**lo·cal** (lō'kəl) adj. **1.** Of a limited place.
**2.** Affecting a limited part of the body.
**3.** Making many stops. —n. **1.** A local branch
of an organization. **2.** A local train, bus,
etc. —**lo·cal·ize'** v.

**lo·cal·i·ty** (lō-kăl'ə-tē) n., pl. -ties. A neigh-
borhood, place, or region.

**lo·cate** (lō'kāt, lō-kāt') v. -cated, -cating.
**1.** To find or determine the position of. **2.** To
situate or place. —**lo·ca'tion** n.

**lock¹** (lŏk) n. **1.** A mechanism used to secure
a door, lid, etc. **2.** A section of a canal closed
off with gates. **3.** A mechanism in a firearm.
—v. **1.** To fasten or become fastened with a
lock. **2.** To become entangled; interlock.
**3.** To jam or force together so as to make
unmovable. —**lock'er** n.

**lock²** (lŏk) n. A curl of hair.

**lo·co·mo·tion** (lō'kə-mō'shən) n. The act of
moving or ability to move from place to
place.

**lo·co·mo·tive** (lō'kə-mō'tĭv) n. An engine
that moves railroad cars. —adj. Of locomotion.

**lode** (lōd) n. A vein of mineral ore.

**lodge** (lŏj) n. **1.** A cottage, cabin, or inn.
**2.** A local chapter of a fraternal society. —v.
lodged, lodging. **1.** To quarters temporarily. **2.** To live in a rented room. **3.** To be
or become embedded. —**lodg'er** n. —**lodg'ing**
n.

**loft** (lôft, lŏft) n. **1.** An attic. **2.** A gallery or
balcony.

**loft·y** (lôf'tē, lŏf'-) adj. -ier, -iest. **1.** Towering.
**2.** Noble.

**log** (lôg, lŏg) n. **1.** A section of a felled tree.
**2.** Any record of performance, as of a ship's
progress. —v. logged, logging. **1.** To cut
(trees) into logs. **2.** To enter (something) in a
ship's or aircraft's log. —**log'ger** n.

**log·ic** (lŏj'ĭk) n. **1.** The study of reasoning.
**2.** Valid reasoning. —**log'i·cal** adj. —**lo·gi'cian** n.

**loin** (loin) n. The part of the sides and back
of the body between the ribs and hipbones.

**loi·ter** (loi'tər) v. **1.** To stand idly about;
loaf. **2.** To proceed slowly. —**loi'ter·er** n.

**loll** (lŏl) v. **1.** To recline indolently. **2.** To
hang laxly.

**lone** (lōn) adj. Solitary; isolated.

**lone·ly** (lōn'lē) adj. -lier, -liest. **1.** Solitary.
**2.** Desolate. **3.** Dejected by the awareness of
being alone. —**lone'li·ness** n.

**lone·some** (lōn'səm) adj. Feeling or producing a feeling of loneliness.

**long¹** (lông, lŏng) adj. **1.** Having great
length. **2.** Of great duration. **3.** Far-reach-
ing. **4.** Having an abundance of. —adv. For
an extended period of time.

**long²** (lông, lŏng) v. To yearn. —**long'ing** n.

**lon·gev·i·ty** (lŏn-jĕv'ə-tē) n. Long duration
of life.

**lon·gi·tude** (lŏn'jə-t/y/ood') n. Angular
distance E or W. —**lon'gi·tu'di·nal** adj.

**look** (lŏok) v. **1.** To use one's eyes to see.
**2.** To turn one's eyes on. **3.** To seem or seem
to be. **4.** To face in a specified direction.
—**look for.** **1.** To search for. **2.** To expect.
—n. **1.** The action of looking; a gaze or
glance. **2.** Appearance. **3.** looks. Personal
appearance.

**loom¹** (lŏom) v. **1.** To come into view as a
massive, distorted, or indistinct image. **2.** To
seem imminent.

**loom²** (lŏom) n. A weaving machine on
which cloth is produced.

**loop** (lŏop) n. **1.** A length of line, thread,
etc., that is folded over and joined at the
ends. **2.** Any roughly oval turn or figure. —v.
To form or form into a loop.

**loop·hole** (lŏop'hōl') n. **1.** A small hole in a
wall. **2.** A means of evasion.

**loose** (lŏos) adj. looser, loosest. **1.** Slack.
**2.** Not tightly fitted. **3.** Immoral. **4.** Not
literal or exact. —v. loosed, loosing. **1.** To set
free. **2.** To make less tight or firm. **3.** To let
fly (a missile). —**loose'ly** adv.

**loos·en** (lŏo'sən) v. **1.** To make or become
loose. **2.** To free from restraint, strictness,
etc.

**loot** (lŏot) n. Spoils. —v. To pillage. —**loot'er**
n.

**lop** (lŏp) v. lopped, lopping. To cut off from;
trim.

**lope** (lōp) v. loped, loping. To run or ride
with a steady, easy gait. —n. A steady, easy
gait.

**lop·sid·ed** (lŏp'sī'dĭd) adj. Not symmetrical.

**lo·qua·cious** (lō-kwā'shəs) adj. Very talkative. — **lo·qua'cious·ness**, **lo·quac'i·ty** n.

**lord** (lôrd) n. **1.** A ruler or master. **2. Lord.** The general masculine title of nobility and other rank in Britain. **3. Lord.** God. —v. To domineer. — **lord'ly** adj.

**lore** (lôr, lōr) n. Tradition or belief.

**lose** (lōōz) v. **lost, losing. 1.** To mislay. **2.** To be unable to maintain or keep. **3.** To be deprived of. **4.** To fail to win.

**loss** (lôs, lŏs) n. **1.** The act or fact of losing. **2.** Someone or something lost.

**lost** (lôst, lŏst) adj. **1.** Strayed or missing. **2.** Ruined. **3.** No longer possessed. **4.** Uncertain; bewildered. **5.** Not used; wasted.

**lot** (lŏt) n. **1.** An object used in making a determination by chance. **2.** Fate. **3.** Often **lots.** A large amount or number. **4.** A piece of land. — adv. Very much.

**lo·tion** (lō'shən) n. A liquid for external application.

**lot·ter·y** (lŏt'ə-rē) n., pl. **-ies.** A contest in which the winner is chosen in a drawing of lots.

**loud** (loud) adj. **1.** Characterized by high volume and intensity of sound. **2.** Having offensively bright colors. — **loud, loud'ly** adv. — **loud'ness** n.

**lounge** (lounj) v. **lounged, lounging.** To stand, sit, lie, or pass time in a relaxed way. —n. A waiting room.

**louse** (lous) n., pl. **lice.** A small insect that lives as a parasite on various animals.

**lou·ver** (lōō'vər) n. **1.** An opening fitted with slanted slats. **2.** A slat in such an opening. — **lou'vered** adj.

**love** (lŭv) n. **1.** An intense affectionate concern for or passionate attraction to another person. **2.** A beloved person. **3.** A strong liking for something. —v. **loved, loving.** To feel love for. — **lov'a·ble, love'a·ble** adj. — **lov'er** n.

**love·ly** (lŭv'lē) adj. **-lier, -liest. 1.** Beautiful. **2.** Enjoyable; delightful. — **love'li·ness** n.

**low¹** (lō) adj. **1.** Having little height. **2.** Of less than usual depth; shallow. **3.** Of inferior quality or character. **4.** Dejected. **5.** Below average, as in degree, intensity, etc. **6.** Not loud. — adv. **1.** In a low position, level, etc. **2.** At or to a low volume, intensity, etc. —n. **1.** A low level, position, etc. **2.** The transmission gear giving the smallest output speed.

**low²** (lō) v. To moo. — **low** n.

**low·er¹** (lou'ər) v. **1.** To scowl. **2.** To appear dark and threatening.

**low·er²** (lō'ər) adj. Below someone or some-

thing. —v. **1.** To move down to a lower level. **2.** To reduce.

**low·ly** (lō'lē) adj. **-lier, -liest.** Low in rank, position, etc.

**loy·al** (loi'əl) adj. Faithful to a person, ideal, etc. — **loy'al·ty** n.

**lu·bri·cate** (lōō'brĭ-kāt') v. **-cated, -cating.** To apply oil or grease to. — **lu'bri·cant** n. — **lu'bri·ca'tion** n.

**lu·cid** (lōō'sĭd) adj. **1.** Easily understood. **2.** Rational. — **lu·cid'i·ty, lu'cid·ness** n.

**luck** (lŭk) n. **1.** Chance; fortune. **2.** Good fortune. — **luck'y** adj.

**lu·cra·tive** (lōō'krə-tĭv) adj. Profitable.

**lu·di·crous** (lōō'dĭ-krəs) adj. Laughable; ridiculous.

**lug** (lŭg) v. **lugged, lugging.** To drag or carry (something) laboriously.

**lug·gage** (lŭg'ĭj) n. Baggage.

**luke·warm** (lōōk'wôrm') adj. **1.** Mildly warm. **2.** Halfhearted.

**lull** (lŭl) v. **1.** To cause to sleep; soothe. **2.** To deceive into trustfulness. —n. A calm or inactive period.

**lull·a·by** (lŭl'ə-bī') n., pl. **-bies.** A song with which to lull a child to sleep.

**lum·ber¹** (lŭm'bər) n. Timber sawed into boards.

**lum·ber²** (lŭm'bər) v. To move heavily.

**lu·mi·nous** (lōō'mə-nəs) adj. **1.** Emitting light, esp. self-generated light. **2.** Full of light. — **lu'mi·nos'i·ty** n.

**lump** (lŭmp) n. **1.** An irregularly shaped mass. **2.** An abnormal swelling in the body. **3.** An aggregate; collection. —v. To put together in a single group or pile. — **lump'y** adj.

**lu·nar** (lōō'nər) adj. Of the moon.

**lu·na·tic** (lōō'nə-tĭk) adj. **1.** Of or for the insane. **2.** Wildly foolish. — **lu'na·tic** n.

**lunch** (lŭnch) n. A meal eaten at midday. — **lunch** v. — **lunch'eon** n.

**lung** (lŭng) n. A spongy, saclike organ in most vertebrates that functions in respiration.

**lunge** (lŭnj) n. Any sudden forward movement. —v. **lunged, lunging.** To move with a lunge.

**lurch** (lûrch) v. **1.** To stagger. **2.** To roll or tip abruptly. —n. **1.** A staggering movement. **2.** An abrupt rolling or tipping.

**lure** (lōōr) n. **1.** Anything that attracts. **2.** An artificial bait for fish. —v. **lured, luring.** To entice.

**lu·rid** (lōōr'ĭd) adj. Shocking; sensational.

**lurk** (lûrk) v. **1.** To lie in wait. **2.** To move

furtively.

**lus·cious** (lŭsh′əs) *adj.* **1.** Delicious. **2.** Sensually appealing.

**lush** (lŭsh) *adj.* Luxurious; opulent.

**lust** (lŭst) *n.* **1.** Sexual craving. **2.** Any overwhelming craving. —*v.* To have an inordinate desire. —**lust′ful** *adj.*

**lus·ter** (lŭs′tər) *n.* **1.** Sheen; gloss. **2.** Brilliance or radiance. —**lus′trous** *adj.*

**lux·u·ri·ant** (lŭg-zhŏŏr′ē-ənt, lŭk-shŏŏr′-) *adj.* **1.** Growing abundantly. **2.** Elaborate; ornate. —**lux·u′ri·ance** *n.*

**lux·u·ry** (lŭg′zhə-rē, lŭk′shə-) *n., pl.* -ries. **1.** Something not necessary that provides comfort or enjoyment. **2.** A sumptuous environment or lifestyle. —**lux·u′ri·ous** *adj.*

**ly·ing** (lī′ĭng) **1.** *pres.p.* of **lie¹. 2.** *pres.p.* of **lie².**

**lymph** (lĭmf) *n.* A clear bodily liquid. —**lym·phat′ic** *adj.*

**lynch** (lĭnch) *v.* To execute without due process of law.

**lyr·ic** (lĭr′ĭk) *adj.* **1.** Of poetry that is a direct, often songlike expression of feelings. **2.** Exuberant; unrestrained. —*n.* **1.** A lyric poem. **2. lyrics.** The words of a song. —**lyr′i·cal** *adj.* —**lyr′i·cist** *n.*

# M

**m, M** (ĕm) *n.* The 13th letter of the English alaphabet.

**ma·ca·bre** (mə-kä′brə, -bər) *adj.* Gruesome; ghastly.

**mac·a·ro·ni** (măk′ə-rō′nē) *pl.n.* Also **mac·ca·ro·ni.** Dried pasta, usually tube-shaped.

**mace** (mās) *n.* **1.** A medieval spiked war club. **2.** A ceremonial staff of authority.

**ma·chet·e** (mə-shĕt′ē, -chĕt′ē) *n.* A large knife used esp. for chopping.

**mach·i·na·tion** (măk′ĭ-nā′shən, măsh′ĭ-) *n.* A hostile or evil scheme or plot.

**ma·chine** (mə-shēn′) *n.* **1.** A mechanical system or device that assists in the performance of work. **2.** A powerful political group under the control of one or more leaders. —*v.* -chined, -chining. To cut, shape, or finish by machine. —**ma·chin′er·y** *n.* —**ma·chin′ist** *n.*

**mad** (măd) *adj.* madder, maddest. **1.** Insane. **2.** Frantic. **3.** Angry; resentful. **4.** Affected

by rabies. —**mad′den** *v.* —**mad′ly** *adv.* —**mad′man′** *n.* —**mad′ness** *n.*

**Mad·am** (măd′əm) *n.* A courteous form of address to a woman.

**made** (mād). *p.t. & p.p.* of **make.**

**Ma·don·na** (mə-dŏn′ə) *n.* **1.** The Virgin Mary. **2.** An artistic representation of the Virgin Mary.

**mael·strom** (māl′strəm) *n.* **1.** A large whirlpool. **2.** Turmoil; confusion.

**mag·a·zine** (măg′ə-zēn′, măg′ə-zēn′) *n.* **1.** A storehouse for ammunition. **2.** A periodical containing articles, stories, etc. **3.** A compartment in some types of firearms for holding cartridges.

**mag·ic** (măj′ĭk) *n.* **1.** The production of seemingly supernatural effects. **2.** Any mysterious quality that lends enchantment. **3.** Sleight of hand, as for entertainment. —**mag′ic, mag′i·cal** *adj.* —**ma·gi′cian** *n.*

**mag·is·trate** (măj′ĭs-trāt′, -trĭt) *n.* A civil officer who administers the law.

**mag·nan·i·mous** (măg-năn′ə-məs) *adj.* Generous and noble; above revenge or resentment. —**mag′na·nim′i·ty** *n.*

**mag·nate** (măg′nāt′) *n.* A powerful or influential man.

**mag·ne·si·um** (măg-nē′zē-əm) *n.* A light, silvery metallic element.

**mag·net** (măg′nĭt) *n.* **1.** A metal body that attracts iron. **2.** Anything that attracts. —**mag·net′ic** *adj.* —**mag′net·ism′** *n.* —**mag′net·ize′** *v.*

**mag·nif·i·cent** (măg-nĭf′ĭ-sənt) *adj.* **1.** Splendid; lavish; sumptuous. **2.** Outstanding; impressive. —**mag·nif′i·cence** *n.*

**mag·ni·fy** (măg′nĭ-fī′) *v.* -fied, -fying. **1.** To make greater in size; enlarge. **2.** To exaggerate. **3.** To increase the apparent size of, esp. by means of a lens. —**mag′ni·fi·ca′tion** *n.* —**mag′ni·fi′er** *n.*

**mag·ni·tude** (măg′nĭ-t/y/ōōd′) *n.* **1.** Greatness in size, extent, or significance. **2.** The relative brightness of a celestial body.

**ma·hog·a·ny** (mə-hŏg′ə-nē) *n., pl.* -nies. A tropical American tree with hard, reddish-brown wood.

**maid** (mād) *n.* **1.** A young girl. **2.** A female servant.

**maid·en** (mād′n) *n.* An unmarried girl. —*adj.* First or earliest. —**mald′en·ly** *adj.*

**mail¹** (māl) *n.* **1.** Letters, packages, etc., handled by a postal system. **2.** A postal system. —*v.* To send by mail. —**mail′box′** *n.* —**mail′man′** *n.*

**mail²** (māl) *n.* Armor made of small overlapping metal rings.

**maim** (mām) v. 1. To mutilate; disable; cripple. 2. To impair.

**main** (mān) adj. Most important; principal; major. —n. 1. The principal pipe or conduit in a utility system. 2. Physical strength. —**main'ly** adv.

**main-stay** (mān'stā') n. A principal support.

**main-tain** (mān-tān') v. 1. To continue; carry on. 2. To preserve. 3. To keep in repair. 4. To support. 5. To assert or declare. —**main-te-nance** n.

**maj-es-ty** (măj'ĭs-tē) n., pl. **-ties.** 1. **Majesty.** A title used in speaking of or to a monarch. 2. Dignity, splendor, and grandeur. —**ma-jes'tic** adj.

**ma-jor** (mā'jər) adj. 1. Greater in importance or extent. —n. 1. A military officer ranking next above a captain. 2. The principal field of specialization of a college student. —v. To pursue academic studies in a major field.

**ma-jor-i-ty** (mə-jôr'ĭ-tē, mə-jŏr'-) n., pl. **-ties.** 1. The greater number or part of something. 2. The excess of a greater number over a smaller. 3. The status of legal age.

**make** (māk) v. made, making. 1. To create; construct. 2. To compel. 3. To appoint. 4. To do; execute. 5. To achieve; attain. 6. To prepare. 7. To constitute. —n. 1. The style in which a thing is made. 2. A specific line of manufactured goods. —**mak'er** n.

**make-shift** (māk'shĭft') n. A temporary substitute. —**make'shift** adj.

**make-up** (māk'ŭp') n. Also **make-up.** 1. The way in which something is arranged or constructed. 2. Cosmetics.

**mal-ad-just-ment** (măl'ə-jŭst'mənt) n. 1. Faulty adjustment, as in a machine. 2. Inability to adjust to one's environment or circumstances. —**mal-ad-just'ed** adj.

**mal-a-dy** (măl'ə-dē) n., pl. **-dies.** A disease, disorder, or ailment.

**mal-con-tent** (măl'kən-tĕnt') adj. Discontented. —n. A discontented person.

**male** (māl) adj. 1. Of the sex capable of fertilizing ova. 2. Masculine. —n. One that is male.

**ma-lev-o-lent** (mə-lĕv'ə-lənt) adj. Exhibiting ill will or malice. —**ma-lev'o-lence** n.

**mal-fea-sance** (măl-fē'zəns) n. Wrongdoing, esp. by a public official.

**mal-func-tion** (măl-fŭngk'shən) v. To fail to function normally. —**mal-func'tion** n.

**mal-ice** (măl'ĭs) n. Ill will; spite. —**ma-li'cious** adj.

**ma-lign** (mə-līn') v. To speak evil of; de-

fame. —adj. Evil.

**ma-lig-nant** (mə-lĭg'nənt) adj. 1. Malevolent. 2. Designating a pathological growth that tends to spread. —**ma-lig'nan-cy** n.

**ma-lin-ger** (mə-lĭng'gər) v. To feign sickness to avoid duty or work. —**ma-lin'ger-er** n.

**mall** (môl, măl) n. 1. A shady public walk. 2. A shop-lined street closed to vehicles.

**mal-le-a-ble** (măl'ē-ə-bəl) adj. 1. Capable of being shaped, as by hammering. 2. Amenable; pliable. —**mal'le-a-bil'i-ty** n.

**mal-nu-tri-tion** (măl'n/yŏŏ-trĭsh'ən) n. Poor nutrition, esp. because of a poorly balanced diet.

**mal-o-dor-ous** (măl-ō'dər-əs) adj. Ill-smelling.

**mal-prac-tice** (măl-prăk'tĭs) n. Improper conduct or treatment, esp. by a physician.

**malt** (môlt) n. Sprouted and dried grain, usually barley, used in brewing.

**mal-treat** (măl-trēt') v. To treat cruelly; abuse. —**mal-treat'ment** n.

**mam-mal** (măm'əl) n. A vertebrate animal the female of which suckles its young. —**mam-ma'li-an** adj. & n.

**mam-ma-ry** (măm'ə-rē) adj. Of a breast.

**mam-moth** (măm'əth) n. An extinct elephant. —adj. Huge; gigantic.

**man** (măn) n., pl. **men.** 1. An adult male human being. 2. A human being; a person. 3. Mankind. 4. A piece used in board games. —v. **manned, manning.** 1. To supply with men. 2. To take one's place for work at. —**man'hood'** n. —**man'li-ness** n. —**man'ly** adj.

**man-a-cle** (măn'ə-kəl) n. Often **manacles.** Handcuffs. —v. **-cled, -cling.** To restrain with manacles.

**man-age** (măn'ĭj) v. **-aged, -aging.** 1. To direct; control. 2. To administer or regulate. 3. To contrive or arrange. 4. To get along. —**man-age-a-ble** adj. —**man'age-ment** n. —**man'ag-er** n. —**man'a-ge'ri-al** adj.

**man-date** (măn'dāt') n. 1. The wishes of a political electorate, expressed to its representatives. 2. a. A commission authorizing a nation to administer a territory. b. A territory under such administration.

**man-da-to-ry** (măn'də-tôr'ē, -tōr'ē) adj. Required; obligatory.

**man-do-lin** (măn'də-lĭn', măn'də-lĭn') n. A stringed instrument with a pear-shaped body.

**mane** (mān) n. The long hair on the neck of a horse, male lion, etc.

**ma-neu-ver** (mə-n/yŏŏ'vər) n. 1. a. A strategic military movement. b. Often **maneu-**

**vers.** A large-scale military training exercise. **2.** A stratagem. —*v.* **1.** To perform a military maneuver. **2.** To scheme; manipulate.

**man·ger** (mān'jər) *n.* A feeding trough for horses or cattle.

**man·gle** (mǎng'gəl) *v.* **-gled, -gling. 1.** To mutilate by battering, hacking, etc. **2.** To ruin through ineptitude. —**man'gler** *n.*

**man·han·dle** (mǎn'hǎn'dəl) *v.* To handle roughly. —**man'han'dler** *n.*

**man·hole** (mǎn'hōl') *n.* An entrance hole to a sewer, boiler, etc.

**ma·ni·a** (mā'nē-ə, mān'yə) *n.* An intense enthusiasm; craze; obsession. —**man'ic** *adj.*

**ma·ni·ac** (mā'nē-ǎk') *n.* An insane person; lunatic. —**ma'ni·ac', ma·ni'a·cal** *adj.*

**man·i·cure** (mǎn'ǐ-kyǒor') *n.* Treatment of the hands and fingernails. —*v.* **-cured, -curing.** To care for (the fingernails). —**man'i·cur'ist** *n.*

**man·i·fest** (mǎn'ə-fěst') *adj.* Clearly apparent; obvious. —*v.* To show plainly; reveal. —*n.* A list of cargo or passengers. —**man'i·fes·ta'tion** *n.*

**man·i·fes·to** (mǎn'ə-fěs'tō) *n., pl.* **-toes** or **-tos.** A public declaration of principles or intentions.

**man·i·fold** (mǎn'ə-fōld) *adj.* Of many kinds; varied; numerous. —*n.* A pipe having apertures for multiple connections.

**man·i·kin, man·ni·kin** (mǎn'ǐ-kǐn) *n.* **1.** A model of the human body. **2.** A mannequin.

**ma·nip·u·late** (mə-nǐp'yə-lāt') *v.* **-lated, -lating. 1.** To control skillfully. **2.** To manage shrewdly or deviously. —**ma·nip'u·la'tion** *n.* —**ma·nip'u·la'tor** *n.*

**man·kind** (mǎn'kīnd', -kīnd') *n.* The human race.

**man·ne·quin** (mǎn'ǐ-kǐn) *n.* **1.** A model used for displaying clothes. **2.** A woman who models clothes.

**man·ner** (mǎn'ər) *n.* **1.** A way of doing something; custom. **2.** One's natural bearing. **3. manners.** Polite social behavior. **4.** Kind or sort.

**man·ner·ism** (mǎn'ər-ǐz'əm) *n.* **1.** A distinctive trait; idiosyncrasy. **2.** An exaggerated or affected habit.

**man·ner·ly** (mǎn'ər-lē) *adj.* Polite.

**man·or** (mǎn'ər) *n.* A landed estate. —**ma·no'ri·al** *adj.*

**man·sion** (mǎn'shən) *n.* A large, stately house.

**man·slaugh·ter** (mǎn'slô'tər) *n.* An unintentional homicide.

**man·tel** (mǎn'təl) *n.* **1.** A facing around a fireplace. **2.** A mantelpiece.

**man·tel·piece** (mǎn'təl-pēs') *n.* The shelf over a fireplace.

**man·til·la** (mǎn-tē'yə, -tǐl'ə) *n.* A shawl worn by women in Spain and Latin America.

**man·tle** (mǎn'təl) *n.* **1.** A loose, sleeveless cloak. **2.** Anything that covers or conceals. —*v.* **-tled, -tling.** To cover with or as with a mantle; cloak.

**man·u·al** (mǎn'yōō-əl) *adj.* **1.** Of or operated by the hands. **2.** Employing human rather than mechanical energy. —*n.* **1.** A handbook. **2.** An organ keyboard. —**man'u·al·ly** *adv.*

**man·u·fac·ture** (mǎn'yə-fǎk'chər) *v.* **-tured, -turing. 1.** To make into a finished product, esp. through a large-scale industrial operation. **2.** To concoct or fabricate. —*n.* The process of manufacturing. —**man'u·fac'tur·er** *n.*

**ma·nure** (mə-n'y/ǒor') *n.* Animal dung or other material used to fertilize soil. —*v.* **-nured, -nuring.** To apply manure to.

**man·u·script** (mǎn'yə-skrǐpt') *n.* **1.** A document written by hand. **2.** A typewritten or handwritten version of a book, article, etc., submitted for publication.

**man·y** (měn'ē) *adj.* **more, most.** Consisting of a large number; numerous. —*n.* (takes pl. v.) A large number. —*pron.* (takes pl. v.) A large number of persons or things.

**map** (mǎp) *n.* A representation of a region of the earth. —*v.* **mapped, mapping. 1.** To make a map of. **2.** To plan, esp. in detail.

**ma·ple** (mā'pəl) *n.* **1.** A North American tree with sap that is boiled to produce a sweet syrup or sugar. **2.** The hard wood of such a tree.

**mar** (mär) *v.* **marred, marring.** To damage, deface, or spoil.

**mar·a·thon** (mǎr'ə-thŏn') *n.* **1.** A long-distance race. **2.** A contest of endurance. —**mar'a·thon'** *adj.*

**ma·raud** (mə-rôd') *v.* To raid for plunder. —**ma·raud'er** *n.*

**mar·ble** (mär'bəl) *n.* **1.** A metamorphic rock often irregularly colored by impurities. **2.** A small ball used in children's games.

**march** (märch) *v.* To walk or cause to walk in a military manner with measured steps. —*n.* **1.** The act of marching. **2.** The distance covered. **3.** A musical composition to accompany marching.

**March** (märch) *n.* The 3rd month of the year.

**mare** (mâr) *n.* A female horse.

**mar·ga·rine** (mär'jə-rĭn) n. A butter substitute made with vegetable oils.

**mar·gin** (mär'jən) n. 1. An edge; border. 2. The blank border on a printed page. 3. A surplus measure or amount. 4. A measure or degree of difference. — **mar'gin·al** adj.

**mar·i·jua·na, mar·i·hua·na** (măr'ə-wä'nə) n. The dried flowers and leaves of the hemp plant, smoked to induce euphoria.

**ma·rine** (mə-rēn') adj. Of the sea, sea life, or maritime activities. —n. **Marine.** A member of the U. S. Marine Corps.

**Marine Corps.** A branch of the U.S. Armed Forces.

**mar·i·o·nette** (măr'ē-ə-nĕt') n. A puppet manipulated by strings.

**mar·i·tal** (măr'ə-təl) adj. Of marriage.

**mar·i·time** (măr'ə-tīm') adj. 1. Located on or near the sea. 2. Of shipping or navigation.

**mark** (märk) n. 1. A visible impression on something, as a spot, dent, or line. 2. A written or printed symbol. 3. A grade, as in school. 4. A target; goal. 5. An indication of some quality. 6. A label, seal, etc., placed on an article. —v. 1. To make a mark on. 2. To pay attention to: 3. To characterize; set off. 4. To grade (school papers). — **marked** adj. — **mark'ed·ly** adv. — **mark'er** n.

**mar·ket** (mär'kĭt) n. 1. A place where merchandise is offered for sale. 2. A store selling a particular type of merchandise. 3. The process of buying and selling. 4. Demand for goods. —v. 1. To offer for sale; sell. 2. To buy household supplies. — **mar'ket·a·ble** adj.

**marks·man** (märks'mən) n. A sharpshooter. — **marks'man·ship** n.

**mar·ma·lade** (mär'mə-lād') n. A jellylike preserve made of fruits.

**ma·roon¹** (mə-rōōn') v. To abandon (a person), as on a deserted island, with little hope of rescue or escape.

**ma·roon²** (mə-rōōn') n. Dark red.

**mar·quee** (mär-kē') n. A rooflike structure projecting over an entrance.

**mar·row** (măr'ō) n. The soft material that fills bone cavities.

**mar·ry** (măr'ē) v. **-ried, -rying.** 1. To take as a husband or wife. 2. To unite as husband and wife. — **mar'riage** n. — **mar'riage·a·ble** adj.

**Mars** (märz) n. The 4th planet from the sun. — **Mar'tian** adj. & n.

**marsh** (märsh) n. Low-lying, wet land; a swamp. — **marsh'y** adj.

**mar·shal** (mär'shəl) n. A federal or city officer who carries out court orders. —v. To arrange or place in order.

**mar·su·pi·al** (mär-sōō'pē-əl) n. A mammal of which the female carries its young in an external pouch. — **mar·su'pi·al** adj.

**mar·tial** (mär'shəl) adj. Of war or warriors; warlike; military.

**mar·ti·net** (mär'tə-nĕt') n. A rigid disciplinarian.

**mar·tyr** (mär'tər) n. One who chooses to suffer or die rather than renounce religious principles. — **mar'tyr** v. — **mar'tyr·dom** n.

**mar·vel** (mär'vəl) n. Something that evokes surprise, admiration, or wonder. —v. To feel wonder or astonishment. — **mar'vel·ous** adj.

**mas·car·a** (măs-kăr'ə) n. A cosmetic used to darken the eyelashes.

**mas·cot** (măs'kŏt, -kət) n. A person, animal, or object believed to bring good luck.

**mas·cu·line** (măs'kyə-lĭn) adj. 1. Of men or boys; male. 2. Mannish. 3. Of the gender of words referring normally to males. — **mas'cu·lin'i·ty** n.

**mash** (măsh) n. 1. A fermentable starchy mixture from which alcohol can be distilled. 2. A soft, pulpy mixture, esp. one fed to livestock. —v. To convert (something) into a soft, pulpy mixture.

**mask** (măsk, mäsk) n. 1. A cover worn on the face. 2. Anything that disguises or conceals. —v. To cover, disguise, or protect with a mask.

**mas·o·chism** (măs'ə-kĭz'əm) n. The deriving of pleasure from being mistreated in some way. — **mas'o·chist** n. — **mas·o·chis'tic** adj.

**ma·son** (mā'sən) n. 1. One who builds with stone or brick. 2. **Mason.** A Freemason. — **ma'son·ry** n.

**mas·quer·ade** (măs'kə-rād') n. 1. A costume ball at which masks are worn. 2. A disguise. —v. **-aded, -ading.** To wear a disguise. — **mas'quer·ad'er** n.

**mass** (măs) n. 1. A unified body of matter with no specific shape. 2. A large amount or number. 3. The major part of something. 4. The physical bulk of a solid body. —v. To gather, form, or assemble into a mass.

**Mass** (măs) n. In Roman Catholic and some Protestant churches, the celebration of the Eucharist.

**mas·sa·cre** (măs'ə-kər) n. Savage and indiscriminate killing; slaughter. — **mas'sa·cre** v.

**mas·sage** (mə-säzh') n. The rubbing or kneading of the body to aid circulation or relax the muscles. — **mas'sage** v.

**mas·sive** (măs'ĭv) adj. Large; bulky.

**mast** (măst, mäst) n. **1.** A tall vertical pole to support a ship's sails and rigging. **2.** Any vertical pole.

**mas·ter** (măs'tər, mäs'-) n. **1.** A person having control over others; an employer or owner. **2.** The captain of a merchant ship. **3.** One highly skilled, in a trade. —v. **1.** To make oneself a master of (an art, craft, or science). **2.** To overcome or subdue. —**mas'ter·ful** adj. —**mas'ter·ly** adj. —**mas'ter·y** n.

**mas·ter·piece** (măs'tər-pēs', mäs'-) n. **1.** An outstanding work of art. **2.** Anything superlative.

**mas·ti·cate** (măs'tə-kāt') v. **-cated, -cating.** To chew. —**mas'ti·ca'tion** n.

**mas·tur·ba·tion** (măs'tər-bā'shən) n. Excitation of the genitals by means other than sexual intercourse. —**mas'tur·bate'** v.

**mat¹** (măt) n. **1.** A flat piece of material used as a floor covering, table pad, etc. **2.** A dense or tangled mass. —v. matted, matting. **1.** To cover, protect, or decorate with a mat. **2.** To form into a mat.

**mat²** (măt) n. A border placed around a picture.

**match¹** (măch) n. **1.** One equal or similar to another. **2.** A game or contest. **3.** A marriage. —v. **1.** To be or make similar or equal to. **2.** To harmonize with; fit together. **3.** To place in competition with. —**match'less** adj.

**match²** (măch) n. A narrow strip of wood or cardboard coated on one end with a compound that ignites easily by friction. —**match'book'** n.

**mate** (māt) n. **1.** One of a matched pair. **2.** A spouse. **3.** A deck officer on a merchant ship. —v. mated, mating. **1.** To join closely; couple. **2.** To unite in marriage or for breeding.

**ma·te·ri·al** (mə-tîr'ē-əl) n. **1.** The substance out of which a thing is constructed. **2.** materials. Tools or apparatus for a certain task. —adj. **1.** Of the physical as distinct from the spiritual. **2.** Of importance to an argument; relevant.

**ma·te·ri·al·ism** (mə-tîr'ē-əl-ĭz'əm) n. Preoccupation with money and possessions. —**ma·te'ri·al·ist** adj. & n. —**ma·te'ri·al·is'tic** adj.

**ma·te·ri·al·ize** (mə-tîr'ē-əl-īz') v. -ized, -izing. To assume or cause to assume material or effective form.

**ma·te·ri·el, ma·té·ri·el** (mə-tîr'ē-ĕl') n. The equipment and apparatus of an organization, esp. of an army.

**ma·ter·ni·ty** (mə-tûr'nə-tē) n. Motherhood. —**ma·ter'nal** adj.

**math·e·mat·ics** (măth'ə-măt'ĭks) n. The study of numbers, forms, sets, etc., and their associated relationships. —**math·e·mat'i·cal** adj. —**math·e·ma·ti'cian** n.

**mat·i·nee, mat·i·née** (măt'n-ā') n. An afternoon dramatic or musical performance.

**ma·tri·arch** (mā'trē-ärk') n. A woman who rules a family, clan, or tribe. —**ma'tri·ar'chal** adj. —**ma'tri·ar'chy** n.

**ma·tric·u·late** (mə-trĭk'yə-lāt') v. -lated, -lating. To enroll in a college or university. —**ma·tric'u·la'tion** n.

**mat·ri·mo·ny** (măt'rə-mō'nē) n. Marriage. —**mat'ri·mo'ni·al** adj.

**ma·tron** (mā'trən) n. **1.** A married woman. **2.** A woman who supervises a public institution. —**ma'tron·ly** adj. & adv.

**mat·ter** (măt'ər) n. **1.** That which constitutes any physical body or the universe as a whole; substance. **2.** The substance of thought or expression. **3.** Any subject of concern or action. —v. To be of importance.

**mat·tress** (măt'rĭs) n. A pad filled with soft material, used as or on a bed.

**ma·ture** (mə-t/y/ōor', -chōor') adj. -turer, -turest. **1.** Fully grown or developed. **2.** Fully aged or ripened. **3.** Payable; due. —v. -tured, -turing. To bring or come to full development. —**ma·tur'i·ty** n.

**maud·lin** (môd'lĭn) adj. Effusively sentimental.

**maul** (môl) v. To handle roughly; bruise or tear. —**maul'er** n.

**mau·so·le·um** (mô'sə-lē'əm, mô'zə-) n., pl. **-leums** or **-lea** A large, stately tomb.

**mav·er·ick** (măv'ər-ĭk, măv'rĭk) n. **1.** An unbranded calf. **2.** An independent, as in politics.

**maw** (mô) n. The stomach, mouth, or gullet of a voracious animal.

**mawk·ish** (mô'kĭsh) adj. Excessively and objectionably sentimental.

**max·im** (măk'sĭm) n. A principle or rule of conduct; a saying.

**max·i·mum** (măk'sə-məm) n., pl. -mums or -ma. The greatest or greatest possible quantity, degree, or number. —adj. Of or having the greatest quantity or highest degree that can be attained.

**may** (mā) v. —Used as an auxiliary to indicate: **1.** A requesting or granting of permission. **2.** Possibility. **3.** Ability or capacity. **4.** Desire or fervent wish.

**May** (mā) n. The 5th month of the year.

**may·be** (mā'bē) adv. Perhaps; possibly.

**may·hem** (mā'hĕm', mā'əm) n. The offense

of willfully maiming a person.

**may·or** (māʹər, mâr) n. The chief magistrate of a city. —**may·or·al** adj. —**may·or·al·ty** n.

**maze** (māz) n. An intricate network of pathways; a labyrinth.

**me** (mē) pron. The objective case of I.

**mead·ow** (mĕdʹō) n. A tract of grassland.

**mea·ger** (mēʹgər) adj. **1.** Thin; lean. **2.** Lacking in quantity; scant.

**meal¹** (mēl) n. Coarsely ground grain. —**meal·y** adj.

**meal²** (mēl) n. The food served in one sitting.

**mean¹** (mēn) v. **meant, meaning. 1.** To be defined as; denote; represent. **2.** To intend. **3.** To have as a purpose. **4.** To be of a specific importance; matter.

**mean²** (mēn) adj. **1.** Low in quality; inferior. **2.** Ignoble; base. **3.** Miserly. **4.** Lacking kindness and good will; cruel. —**mean·ness** n.

**mean³** (mēn) n. **1.** The middle point between two extremes. **2.** An average. **3. means.** A course of action or instrument by which some act can be accomplished. **4. means.** Money, property, or other wealth. —adj. Occupying a middle or intermediate position.

**me·an·der** (mē-ănʹdər) v. **1.** To follow a winding course. **2.** To wander aimlessly.

**mean·ing** (mēʹnĭng) n. That which is signified by something; sense. —**mean·ing·ful** adj. —**mean·ing·less** adj.

**meant** (mĕnt). p.t. & p.p. of mean.

**mean·time** (mēnʹtīmʹ) n. The time between one occurrence and another. —adv. In the intervening time. —**mean·while** n. & adv.

**meas·ure** (mĕzhʹər) n. **1.** The dimensions, quantity, or capacity of anything. **2.** A unit specified by a scale, as an inch, or by variable conditions, as a day's march. **3.** A device used for measuring. **4.** The extent, amount, or degree of something. **5.** Limit; bounds. **6.** An action taken for a specified purpose. —v. **-ured, -uring. 1.** To ascertain or mark off the dimensions, quantity, or capacity of. **2.** To have a specified measure. —**meas·ur·a·ble** adj. —**meas·ure·ment** n.

**meat** (mēt) n. **1.** The edible flesh of animals. **2.** The essence or principal part of something. —**meat·y** adj.

**me·chan·ic** (mĭ-kănʹĭk) n. One who works with machines and tools.

**me·chan·i·cal** (mĭ-kănʹĭ-kəl) adj. **1.** Of, operated by, or produced by a machine or machines. **2.** Like a machine.

**me·chan·ics** (mĭ-kănʹĭks) n. **1.** The analysis of the action of forces on matter or material systems. **2.** The technical aspect of an activity.

**mech·a·nism** (mĕkʹə-nĭzʹəm) n. **1.** A machine or the arrangement of its parts. **2.** Any system of interacting parts. **3.** An instrument or process by which something is done.

**med·al** (mĕdʹl) n. A flat piece of metal having a special shape and design, often given as an award.

**me·dal·lion** (mə-dălʹyən) n. A large medal.

**med·dle** (mĕdʹl) v. **-dled, -dling.** To interfere in other people's business. —**med·dler** n.

**me·di·a.** Alternate pl. of medium.

**me·di·an** (mēʹdē-ən) adj. Of the middle. —n. A median point, plane, line, or part. —**me·di·al** adj.

**me·di·ate** (mēʹdē-ātʹ) v. **-ated, -ating.** To act as an intermediary, esp. to seek to resolve (differences). —**me·di·a·tion** n. —**me·di·a·tor** n.

**med·i·cate** (mĕdʹə-kātʹ) v. **-cated, -cating.** To treat with medicine. —**med·i·ca·tion** n.

**med·i·cine** (mĕdʹə-sən) n. **1.** The science of diagnosing, treating, or preventing disease. **2.** A drug or other agent used to treat disease. —**me·dicʹi·nal** adj.

**me·di·e·val** (mēʹdē-ēʹvəl, mĕdʹē-vəl) adj. Also **me·di·ae·val.** Of the Middle Ages.

**me·di·o·cre** (mēʹdē-ōʹkər) adj. Of medium and unimpressive quality. —**me·di·ocʹri·ty** n.

**me·di·um** (mēʹdē-əm) n., pl. **-dia** (-dē-ə) or **-ums. 1.** Something midway between extremes. **2.** An intervening substance. **3.** A means; agency. **4.** A means of mass communication. **5.** pl. **-ums** only. One thought to have powers of communicating with the dead. **6.** An environment. —adj. Intermediate in degree, amount, quantity, or quality.

**med·ley** (mĕdʹlē) n., pl. **-leys.** **1.** A jumbled assortment; mixture. **2.** A musical arrangement of various melodies.

**meek** (mēk) adj. **1.** Humble and patient. **2.** Submissive. —**meekʹly** adv. —**meekʹness** n.

**meet¹** (mēt) v. **met, meeting. 1.** To come upon; encounter. **2.** To connect with; join. **3.** To assemble; get together. **4.** To satisfy (a demand, need, etc.). **5.** To be introduced to. —n. A meeting or contest.

**meet²** (mēt) adj. Fitting; proper.

**meet·ing** (mēʹtĭng) n. A coming together; assembly.

**meg·a·phone** (mĕgʹə-fōnʹ) n. A horn-shaped device used to project the voice.

**mel·an·chol·y** (mĕlʹən-kŏlʹē) n. Sadness; gloom. —adj. Sad; gloomy. —**melʹan·cholʹic** adj.

**adj.**

**me·lee** (mā′lā′, mā-lā′) *n.* Also **mê·lée** A confused fight or brawl.

**mel·low** (mĕl′ō) *adj.* 1. Sweet, juicy, and full-flavored because of ripeness. 2. Rich and soft in quality. 3. Relaxed and at ease. —*v.* To make or become mellow.

**mel·o·dra·ma** (mĕl′ə-drä′mə, -drăm′ə) *n.* 1. A sentimental and sensational drama. 2. Exaggeratedly emotional or sentimental behavior. —**mel′o·dra·mat′ic** *adj.*

**mel·o·dy** (mĕl′ə-dē) *n., pl.* **-dies.** A pleasing arrangement of musical sounds; tune. —**me·lod′ic** *adj.* —**me·lo′di·ous** *adj.*

**mel·on** (mĕl′ən) *n.* Any of several edible fruits.

**melt** (mĕlt) *v.* 1. To change or be changed from a solid to a liquid by heat. 2. To dissolve. 3. To blend gradually. 4. To soften. 5. To disappear.

**mem·ber** (mĕm′bər) *n.* 1. A distinct part of a whole. 2. One who belongs to a group. —**mem′ber·ship** *n.*

**mem·brane** (mĕm′brān′) *n.* A thin, pliable layer of animal or plant tissue. —**mem′bra·nous** *adj.*

**me·men·to** (mə-mĕn′tō) *n., pl.* **-tos** or **-toes.** A reminder; souvenir.

**mem·oir** (mĕm′wär′, -wôr′) *n.* 1. **memoirs.** An autobiography; biography. 2. A written reminder; memorandum.

**mem·o·ra·ble** (mĕm′ər-ə-bəl) *adj.* Worth being remembered; remarkable.

**mem·o·ran·dum** (mĕm′ə-răn′dəm) *n., pl.* **-dums** or **-da.** 1. A written reminder. 2. A written record or communication.

**me·mo·ri·al** (mə-môr′ē-əl, mə-mōr′-) *n.* An established remembrance of a person or event; monument. —*adj.* Commemorative. —**me·mo′ri·al·ize′** *v.*

**mem·o·rize** (mĕm′ə-rīz′) *v.* **-rized, -rizing.** To commit to memory; learn by heart. —**mem′o·ri·za′tion** *n.*

**mem·o·ry** (mĕm′ər-ē) *n., pl.* **-ries.** 1. The ability to remember. 2. A remembrance; recollection. 3. All that a person can remember. 4. The period of time covered by recollection.

**men.** *pl. of* **man.**

**men·ace** (mĕn′ĭs) *n.* A threat. —*v.* **-aced, -acing.** To threaten.

**me·nag·er·ie** (mə-năj′ə-rē, mə-năzh′-) *n.* A collection of live wild animals.

**mend** (mĕnd) *v.* 1. To correct; repair. 2. To heal. 3. To correct errors. —*n.* A mended place.

**men·da·cious** (mĕn-dā′shəs) *adj.* Lying; untruthful. —**men·dac′i·ty** *n.*

**men·di·cant** (mĕn′dĭ-kənt) *adj.* Begging. —*n.* A beggar.

**me·ni·al** (mē′nē-əl, mēn′yəl) *adj.* Of or appropriate to a servant. —*n.* A servant.

**men·o·pause** (mĕn′ə-pôz′) *n.* The cessation of menstruation.

**men·stru·ate** (mĕn′strōō-āt′) *v.* **-ated, -ating.** To discharge blood from the uterus monthly. —**men′stru·al** *adj.* —**men′stru·a′tion** *n.*

**men·tal** (mĕn′təl) *adj.* Of the mind; intellectual. —**men′tal·ly** *adv.*

**men·tal·i·ty** (mĕn-tăl′ə-tē) *n., pl.* **-ties.** 1. Intellectual capability; intelligence. 2. A habitual frame of mind.

**men·tion** (mĕn′shən) *v.* To cite or refer to; speak of. —*n.* An act of mentioning.

**men·u** (mĕn′yōō, mān′yōō) *n.* A list of dishes available for a meal.

**me·ow** (mē-ou′) *n.* Also **mi·aow, mi·aou.** The cry of a cat. —**me·ow′** *v.*

**mer·ce·nar·y** (mûr′sə-nĕr′ē) *adj.* 1. Motivated solely by a desire for money. 2. Hired for service in a foreign army. —**mer′ce·nar′y** *n.*

**mer·chan·dise** (mûr′chən-dīz′, -dīs′) Also **mer·chan·dize.** *n.* Goods that can be bought or sold. —*v.* **-dised, -dising.** To buy and sell.

**mer·chant** (mûr′chənt) *n.* 1. One whose occupation is the retail sale of goods for profit. 2. A shopkeeper.

**merchant marine.** A nation's ships that are engaged in commerce.

**mer·cu·ry** (mûr′kyə-rē) *n.* 1. A silvery-white, poisonous metallic element, liquid at room temperature, used in thermometers, barometers, vapor lamps, and batteries. 2. **Mercury.** The planet nearest the sun. —**mer·cu′ri·al** *adj.*

**mer·cy** (mûr′sē) *n., pl.* **-cies.** 1. Kindness; clemency. 2. A fortunate act or occurrence. —**mer′ci·ful** *adj.* —**mer′ci·less** *adj.*

**mere** (mîr) *adj.* Being nothing more than; only. —**mere′ly** *adv.*

**mer·e·tri·cious** (mĕr′ə-trĭsh′əs) *adj.* Attractive in a vulgar manner; showy; gaudy.

**merge** (mûrj) *v.* **-merged, -merging.** To blend together so as to lose identity; unite. —**merg′er** *n.*

**me·rid·i·an** (mə-rĭd′ē-ən) *n.* 1. A great circle on the earth's surface passing through both geophysical poles. 2. The highest stage of development; zenith. —**me·rid′i·an** *adj.*

**mer·it** (mĕr′ĭt) *n.* 1. Superior value; excellence. 2. **merits.** The actual facts of a legal case or other issue. 3. A praiseworthy feature or quality. —*v.* To earn; deserve; warrant. —**mer′i·to′ri·ous** *adj.*

**mer·ry** (mĕr′ē) *adj.* **-ri·er, -ri·est. 1.** Gay; jolly. **2.** Festive; lively. —**mer′ri·ly** *adv.* —**mer′ri·ment** *n.* —**mer′ry·mak′ing** *n.*

**me·sa** (mā′sə) *n.* A flat-topped elevation with clifflike sides.

**mesh** (mĕsh) *n.* **1.** Any of the open spaces in a net, sieve, etc. **2.** A net or network. **3.** The engagement of gear teeth. —*v.* **1.** To entangle or ensnare. **2.** To engage or become engaged, as gear teeth. **3.** To coordinate; harmonize.

**mess** (mĕs) *n.* **1.** A disorderly accumulation; jumble. **2.** A muddle; chaos. **3.** A group who regularly eat meals together. —*v.* **1.** To make disorderly; clutter. **2.** To bungle or mismanage. —**mess′i·ness** *n.* —**mess′y** *adj.*

**mes·sage** (mĕs′ĭj) *n.* A communication transmitted from one person or place to another.

**mes·sen·ger** (mĕs′ən-jər) *n.* One who transmits messages or performs errands.

**met** (mĕt). *p.t.* & *p.p.* of **meet.**

**me·tab·o·lism** (mə-tăb′ə-lĭz′əm) *n.* The physical and chemical processes involved in the maintenance of life. —**met′a·bol′ic** *adj.* —**me·tab′o·lize′** *v.*

**met·al** (mĕt′l) *n.* Any of the usually lustrous elements that are often ductile and malleable, with high tensile strength. —**me·tal′lic** *adj.*

**met·al·lur·gy** (mĕt′l-ûr′jē) *n.* The study and technology of metals. —**met′al·lur′gic, met′al·lur′gi·cal** *adj.* —**met′al·lur′gist** *n.* —**met′al·lur′gi·cal·ly** *adv.*

**met·a·mor·pho·sis** (mĕt′ə-môr′fə-sĭs) *n., pl.* **-ses. 1.** A complete, often sudden change in appearance, character, etc. **2.** Changes in form and life function during natural development. —**met′a·mor′phose′** *v.*

**met·a·phor** (mĕt′ə-fôr′, -fər) *n.* A figure of speech in which a term is used to describe an object by implicit comparison or analogy, as in the phrase *evening of life.* —**met′a·phor′ic, met′a·phor′i·cal** *adj.*

**met·a·phys·ics** (mĕt′ə-fĭz′ĭks) *n.* The philosophical investigation of the ultimate nature or first causes of things. —**met′a·phys′i·cal** *adj.*

**mete** (mēt) *v.* **met·ed, met·ing.** To deal out; allot.

**me·te·or** (mē′tē-ər, -ôr′) *n.* **1.** The bright trail or streak seen in the sky when a meteoroid falls into the earth's atmosphere and burns. **2.** A meteoroid. —**me′te·or′ic** *adj.*

**me·te·or·ite** (mē′tē-ə-rīt′) *n.* The stony or metallic material of a meteoroid that passes through the atmosphere and reaches the earth.

**me·te·or·oid** (mē′tē-ə-roid′) *n.* A celestial body that appears as a meteor when entering the earth's atmosphere.

**me·te·or·ol·o·gy** (mē′tē-ə-rŏl′ə-jē) *n.* The science of the earth's atmosphere, esp. weather conditions. —**me′te·o·ro·log′i·cal** *adj.* —**me′te·or·ol′o·gist** *n.*

**me·ter¹** (mē′tər) *n.* The measured rhythm of verse. —**me′tri·cal** *adj.*

**me·ter²** (mē′tər) *n.* The fundamental metric unit of length, approx. 39.37 inches.

**me·ter³** (mē′tər) *n.* A device designed to measure and indicate, record, or control. —*v.* To measure or control with a meter.

**meth·od** (mĕth′əd) *n.* A systematic means or manner of procedure. —**me·thod′i·cal** *adj.*

**me·tic·u·lous** (mə-tĭk′yə-ləs) *adj.* Extremely careful and precise; scrupulous.

**met·ro·nome** (mĕt′rə-nōm′) *n.* An adjustable device that marks time at a steady beat. —**met′ro·nom′ic** *adj.*

**me·trop·o·lis** (mə-trŏp′ə-lĭs) *n., pl.* **-lises. 1.** A major city or large urban center. —**met′ro·pol′i·tan** *adj.*

**met·tle** (mĕt′l) *n.* **1.** Character and temperament. **2.** Courage and fortitude; spirit.

**mez·za·nine** (mĕz′ə-nēn′, mĕz′ə-nēn′) *n.* **1.** A partial story between two main stories of a building. **2.** The lowest balcony in a theater.

**mice.** *pl.* of **mouse.**

**mi·crobe** (mī′krōb′) *n.* A minute life form; a microorganism, esp. one that causes disease. —**mi·cro′bi·al, mi·cro′bic** *adj.*

**mi·cro·or·gan·ism** (mī′krō-ôr′gən-ĭz′əm) *n.* An organism that can be seen only with a microscope.

**mi·cro·phone** (mī′krə-fōn′) *n.* An instrument that converts sound waves into electric signals, as in broadcasting.

**mi·cro·scope** (mī′krə-skōp′) *n.* An instrument that uses lenses to produce magnified images of small objects. —**mi′cro·scop′ic** *adj.*

**mid** (mĭd) *adj.* Middle; central.

**mid·day** (mĭd′dā′) *n.* Noon. —**mid′day′** *adj.*

**mid·dle** (mĭd′l) *adj.* **1.** Equally distant from extremes; central. **2.** Medium; moderate. —*n.* A middle area or point.

**middle class.** The members of society occupying an intermediate social and economic position. —**mid′dle-class′** *adj.*

**mid·dle·man** (mĭd′l-măn′) *n.* An intermediary, esp. one who buys from producers and sells to retailers or consumers.

**midg·et** (mĭj'ĭt) *n.* An extremely small person. — **midg'et** *adj.*

**mid·night** (mĭd'nīt') *n.* Twelve o'clock at night.

**mid·riff** (mĭd'rĭf') *n.* **1.** The diaphragm. **2.** The part of the body extending from the chest to the waistline. — **mid'riff** *adj.*

**mid·ship·man** (mĭd'shĭp'mər, mĭd·shĭp'-mən) *n.* A student training to be an officer in the U.S. Navy or Coast Guard.

**midst** (mĭdst, mĭtst) *n.* The middle part; center. —*prep.* Among.

**mid·way** (mĭd'wā') *n.* The area of a fair, carnival, etc., where side shows are located. —*adv. & adj.* In the middle; halfway.

**mid·wife** (mĭd'wīf') *n.* A woman who assists women in childbirth. — **mid'wife'ry** *n.*

**mien** (mēn) *n.* Manner; appearance; aspect.

**miff** (mĭf) *v.* To offend; upset.

**might**[1] (mīt) *n.* **1.** Great or supreme power. **2.** Great physical strength. — **might'y** *adj.*

**might**[2] (mīt). *p.t.* of **may.**

**mi·grant** (mī'grənt) *n.* **1.** One that migrates. **2.** One who travels from place to place in search of work. —*adj.*

**mi·grate** (mī'grāt') *v.* **-grated, -grating.** To move from one country or region and settle in another, esp. seasonally. — **mi·gra'tion** *n.* — **mi'gra·to·ry** *adj.*

**mild** (mīld) *adj.* **1.** Gentle or meek; kind. **2.** Not extreme; moderate; temperate. **3.** Not sharp or strong in taste. — **mild'ly** *adv.* — **mild'ness** *n.*

**mil·dew** (mĭl'd/y/ōō') *n.* A white or grayish coating formed by fungi. — **mil'dew'** *v.*

**mile** (mīl) *n.* A unit of length equal to 5,280 feet.

**mile·age** (mī'lĭj) *n.* Also **mil·age. 1.** Distance measured or expressed in miles. **2.** An allowance for each mile for travel expenses.

**mile·stone** (mīl'stōn') *n.* An important event or turning point.

**mi·lieu** (mē-lyœ') *n.* Environment or surroundings.

**mil·i·tant** (mĭl'ə-tənt) *adj.* Warlike; combative; aggressive. —*n.* One who is militant. — **mil'i·tan·cy** *n.*

**mil·i·ta·rism** (mĭl'ə-tə-rĭz'əm) *n.* The glorification of the military or its predominance in state affairs. — **mil'i·ta·rist** *n.* — **mil'i·ta·ris'tic** *adj.*

**mil·i·tar·y** (mĭl'ə-tĕr'ē) *adj.* Of soldiers, the armed forces, or warfare. —*n.* **the military.** The armed forces; soldiers collectively.

**mil·i·tate** (mĭl'ə-tāt') *v.* **-tated, -tating.** To operate or work.

**mi·li·tia** (mə-lĭsh'ə) *n.* Those who are called to military service in an emergency. — **mi·li'tia·man** *n.*

**milk** (mĭlk) *n.* **1.** A whitish liquid produced by the mammary glands of female mammals for feeding their young. **2.** A milklike liquid. —*v.* To draw milk from (a female mammal). — **milk'y** *adj.*

**mill** (mĭl) *n.* **1.** A building with machinery for grinding grain. **2.** A machine for grinding, crushing, etc. **3.** A factory. —*v.* **1.** To grind or crush in a mill. **2.** To move around in a confused or disorderly manner. — **mill'er** *n.*

**mil·len·ni·um** (mə-lĕn'ē-əm) *n., pl.* **-ums** or **-lennia. 1.** A span of a thousand years. **2.** A thousand-year reign of Christ on earth, expected by early Christians. **3.** A hoped-for period of prosperity and justice. — **mil·len'ni·al** *adj.*

**mil·li·ner** (mĭl'ə-nər) *n.* One who makes or sells women's hats. — **mil'li·ner'y** *n.*

**mil·lion** (mĭl'yən) *n., pl.* **-lion** or **-lions. 1.** The cardinal number written 1,000,000. **2.** Often **millions.** An indefinitely large number. — **mil'lion** *adj.* — **mil'lionth** *n. & adj.*

**mil·lion·aire** (mĭl'yə-nâr') *n.* One whose wealth amounts to a million or more dollars, pounds, etc.

**mill·stone** (mĭl'stōn') *n.* **1.** A cylindrical stone for grinding grain. **2.** A heavy burden.

**mime** (mīm) *n.* **1.** The art of pantomime. **2.** A performer in pantomime. **3.** A mimic. —*v.* **mimed, miming. 1.** To mimic. **2.** To portray in pantomime.

**mim·ic** (mĭm'ĭk) *v.* **-icked, -icking.** To imitate another's speech, gestures, etc., as in mockery; ape. —*n.* One who mimics others. — **mim'ick·er** *n.* — **mim'ic·ry** *n.*

**min·a·ret** (mĭn'ə-rĕt') *n.* A tall, slender tower on a mosque.

**mince** (mĭns) *v.* **minced, mincing. 1.** To cut into very small pieces. **2.** To moderate or restrain (words). **3.** To walk in a prim way.

**mind** (mīnd) *n.* **1.** The consciousness that directs mental and physical behavior. **2.** Memory. **3.** Conscious thoughts; attention. **4.** Opinion or intentions. **5.** Intellect; intelligence. —*v.* **1.** To pay attention to; obey. **2.** To take care of; tend. — **mind'ful** *adj.* — **mind'less** *adj.*

**mine**[1] (mīn) *n.* **1.** An excavation in the earth to extract metals or other minerals. **2.** An abundant supply. **3.** An explosive device detonated by contact or a time fuse. —v. **mined, mining. 1.** To dig from a mine. **2.** To lay explosive mines in or under. — **min'er** n.

**mine²** (mīn). The possessive form of *I.*

**min·er·al** (mĭn'ər-əl) n. **1.** A natural, inorganic, crystalline substance such as stone, coal, salt, etc. **2.** Any substance that is neither animal nor vegetable; inorganic matter. **3.** An ore. —adj. Of minerals.

**min·er·al·o·gy** (mĭn'ə-rŏl'ə-jē, -răl'ə-jē) n. The scientific study of minerals. — **min'er·al'o·gist** n.

**min·gle** (mĭng'gəl) v. **-gled, -gling.** To mix together; associate.

**min·i·a·ture** (mĭn'ē-ə-choŏr', mĭn'ə-choŏr', -chər) n. **1.** A greatly reduced copy or model. **2.** A small painting. —adj. On a small or greatly reduced scale.

**min·i·mum** (mĭn'ə-məm) n., pl. **-mums** or **-ma. 1.** The smallest possible or allowable quantity or degree. **2.** The lowest amount or degree reached or recorded. — **min'i·mal** adj. — **min'i·mize'** v. — **min'i·mum** adj.

**min·is·ter** (mĭn'ĭ-stər) n. **1.** A clergyman; pastor. **2.** A head of a governmental department. **3.** A diplomat ranking next below an ambassador. —v. To attend to the needs of others. — **min'is·te'ri·al** adj. — **min'is·tra'tion** n.

**min·is·try** (mĭn'ĭ-strē) n., pl. **-tries. 1.** The act of ministering or serving. **2. a.** The profession of a minister of religion. **b.** The clergy. **3.** A governmental department presided over by a minister.

**mi·nor** (mī'nər) adj. **1.** Lesser in amount, size, or importance. **2.** Not yet of full legal age. —n. One under full legal age.

**mi·nor·i·ty** (mə-nôr'ə-tē, -nŏr'ə-tē, mī-) n., pl. **-ties. 1.** A group numbering less than half of a total. **2.** A racial, religious, or other group regarded as being different from the larger group of which it is part. **3.** The state or period of being under legal age.

**mint** (mĭnt) n. A place where coins are manufactured. —v. To produce (money) by stamping metal. —adj. In original condition; unused.

**min·u·end** (mĭn'yoŏ-ĕnd') n. The quantity from which another is to be subtracted.

**mi·nus** (mī'nəs) prep. **1.** Less. **2.** Lacking; without. —adj. **1.** Less than zero; negative. **2.** Slightly lower or less than. —n. A loss, deficiency, or disadvantage.

**min·us·cule** (mĭn'ə-skyoŏl', mĭ-nŭs'kyoŏl) adj. Very small; tiny; minute.

**min·ute¹** (mĭn'ĭt) n. **1.** A unit of time equal to 60 seconds. **2.** A moment. **3. minutes.** An official record of proceedings at a meeting.

**mi·nute²** (mī-n/yoŏt', mī-) adj. **1.** Exceptionally small; tiny. **2.** Characterized by close examination.

**mir·a·cle** (mĭr'ə-kəl) n. **1.** An event that is held to be supernatural because it appears unexplainable. **2.** Something that causes great admiration, wonder, etc. — **mi·rac'u·lous** adj.

**mi·rage** (mĭ-räzh') n. An optical illusion of water, often with inverted reflections of distant objects.

**mire** (mīr) n. **1.** A bog. **2.** Swampy, slimy soil or mud. —v. **mired, miring.** To sink or become stuck in mire.

**mir·ror** (mĭr'ər) n. **1.** A polished surface that reflects a virtual image. **2.** Anything that gives a true picture of something else. —v. To reflect in or as in a mirror.

**mirth** (mûrth) n. Gaiety or merriment. — **mirth'ful** adj.

**mis·ad·ven·ture** (mĭs'əd-vĕn'chər) n. A mishap; misfortune.

**mis·an·thrope** (mĭs'ən-thrōp', mĭz'-) n. A hater of mankind. — **mis·an'thro·py** n.

**mis·ap·pre·hend** (mĭs'ăp-rĭ-hĕnd') v. To interpret incorrectly; misunderstand. — **mis·ap·pre·hen'sion** n.

**mis·ap·pro·pri·ate** (mĭs'ə-prō'prē-āt') v. To take dishonestly for one's own use. — **mis·ap·pro'pri·a'tion** n.

**mis·be·have** (mĭs'bĭ-hāv') v. To behave badly. — **mis'be·hav'ior** n.

**mis·cal·cu·late** (mĭs-kăl'kyə-lāt') v. To calculate incorrectly. — **mis·cal'cu·la'tion** n.

**mis·car·ry** (mĭs-kăr'ē) v. **1.** To fail; go wrong. **2.** To bring forth a fetus too early; abort. — **mis·car'riage** n.

**mis·ce·ge·na·tion** (mĭs'ĭ-jə-nā'shən, mĭ-sĕj'ə-nā'shən) n. The interbreeding of different human races.

**mis·cel·la·ne·ous** (mĭs'ə-lā'nē-əs) adj. Made up of a variety of different elements; mixed. — **mis'cel·la'ny** n.

**mis·chance** (mĭs-chăns', -chäns') n. A mishap; bad luck.

**mis·chief** (mĭs'chĭf) n. **1.** An inclination to misbehave or cause trouble. **2.** Harm or damage. — **mis'chie·vous** adj.

**mis·con·ceive** (mĭs'kən-sēv') v. To interpret incorrectly; misunderstand. — **mis'con·cep'tion** n.

**mis·con·duct** (mĭs-kŏn'dŭkt) n. **1.** Improper behavior; impropriety. **2.** Malfeasance.

**mis·con·strue** (mĭs′kən-strōō′) v. To misinterpret.

**mis·count** (mĭs-kount′) v. To count incorrectly; miscalculate.

**mis·cre·ant** (mĭs′krē-ənt) n. An evil person; villain. — **mis′cre·ant** adj.

**mis·de·mean·or** (mĭs′dĭ-mē′nər) n. An offense less serious than a felony.

**mi·ser** (mī′zər) n. A stingy person, esp. one who hoards money. — **mi′ser·ly** adj.

**mis·er·a·ble** (mĭz′ər-ə-bəl, mĭz′rə-bəl) adj. 1. Very unhappy; wretched. 2. Wretchedly inadequate or inferior; deplorable.

**mis·er·y** (mĭz′ər-ē) n., pl. -ies. Extreme suffering; wretchedness.

**mis·fire** (mĭs-fīr′) v. 1. To fail to explode. 2. To fail to achieve an anticipated result. — **mis′fire** n.

**mis·fit** (mĭs′fĭt, mĭs-fĭt′) n. 1. A poor fit. 2. A maladjusted person.

**mis·for·tune** (mĭs-fôr′chən) n. 1. Bad fortune. 2. An unfortunate occurrence.

**mis·giv·ing** (mĭs-gĭv′ĭng) n. Often **misgivings.** A feeling of uncertainty or doubt; fear.

**mis·guide** (mĭs-gīd′) v. To give misleading direction to; lead astray.

**mis·hap** (mĭs′hăp′, mĭs-hăp′) n. An unfortunate accident.

**mis·in·form** (mĭs′ĭn-fôrm′) v. To give false or inaccurate information to. — **mis·in·for·ma′tion** n.

**mis·in·ter·pret** (mĭs′ĭn-tûr′prĭt) v. 1. To explain inaccurately. 2. To err in understanding. — **mis·in·ter·pre·ta′tion** n.

**mis·judge** (mĭs-jŭj′) v. To judge or estimate wrongly. — **mis·judg′ment** n.

**mis·lay** (mĭs-lā′) v. 1. To lose. 2. To put in a place that is afterward forgotten.

**mis·lead** (mĭs-lēd′) v. 1. To deceive. 2. To lead into error of action or belief. — **mis·lead′ing** adj.

**mis·man·age** (mĭs-măn′ĭj) v. To manage badly or carelessly. — **mis·man′age·ment** n.

**mis·no·mer** (mĭs-nō′mər) n. A name that is wrongly applied.

**mi·sog·y·ny** (mĭ-sŏj′ə-nē) n. Hatred of women. — **mi·sog′y·nist** n.

**mis·place** (mĭs-plās′) v. 1. To put in a wrong place. 2. To mislay. 3. To place unwisely.

**mis·print** (mĭs′prĭnt′) n. An error in printing.

**mis·pro·nounce** (mĭs′prə-nouns′) v. To pronounce incorrectly.

**mis·quote** (mĭs-kwōt′) v. To quote incorrectly.

**mis·read** (mĭs-rēd′) v. 1. To read incorrectly. 2. To misinterpret.

**mis·rep·re·sent** (mĭs′rĕp-rĭ-zĕnt′) v. To give a false or misleading representation of. — **mis·rep·re·sen·ta′tion** n.

**miss¹** (mĭs) v. 1. To fail to hit, reach, etc. 2. To fail to attend. 3. To omit. 4. To avoid. 5. To discover or feel the absence of. —n. A failure to hit, reach, etc.

**miss²** (mĭs) n., pl. misses. 1. Miss. A title preceding the name of an unmarried woman or girl. 2. An unmarried woman or girl.

**mis·sile** (mĭs′əl) n. Any object or weapon fired, thrown, or dropped.

**miss·ing** (mĭs′ĭng) adj. Absent; lost; lacking.

**mis·sion** (mĭsh′ən) n. 1. A body of envoys to a foreign country, esp. a permanent diplomatic staff and office. 2. A body of missionaries, their ministry, or the place of its exercise. 3. A combat assignment. 4. A function or task.

**mis·sion·ar·y** (mĭsh′ə-nĕr′ē) n., pl. -ies. One sent to do religious work in some territory or foreign country. —adj. Of church missions or missionaries.

**mis·sive** (mĭs′ĭv) n. A letter or message.

**mis·spell** (mĭs-spĕl′) v. To spell incorrectly. — **mis·spell′ing** n.

**mis·state** (mĭs-stāt′) v. To state wrongly or falsely. — **mis·state′ment** n.

**mis·step** (mĭs-stĕp′) n. 1. A wrong step. 2. A mistake in conduct.

**mist** (mĭst) n. 1. A mass of fine droplets of water in the atmosphere. 2. Fine drops of any liquid sprayed into the air. — **mist′y** adj.

**mis·take** (mĭ-stāk′) n. 1. An error or blunder. 2. A misconception or misunderstanding. — **mis·take′** v. — **mis·tak′en** adj.

**Mis·ter** (mĭs′tər) n. A title preceding a man's surname.

**mis·treat** (mĭs-trēt′) v. To treat roughly or wrongly; abuse. — **mis·treat′ment** n.

**mis·tress** (mĭs′trĭs) n. 1. A woman in a position of authority, control, or ownership. 2. A man's female lover.

**mis·tri·al** (mĭs-trī′əl, -trīl′) n. A trial that becomes invalid because of basic error in procedure.

**mis·trust** (mĭs-trŭst′) n. Lack of trust; suspicion. —v. To regard without confidence. — **mis·trust′ful** adj.

**mis·un·der·stand** (mĭs′ŭn-dər-stănd′) v. To fail to understand or understand incorrectly. — **mis·un·der·stand′ing** n.

**mis·use** (mĭs-yōōs′) n. Improper use; misapplication. —v. (-yŏoz'). **1.** To misapply. **2.** To abuse.

**mit·i·gate** (mĭt'ə-gāt') v. -gated, -gating. To make or become less severe; alleviate. — **mit'i·ga'tion** n.

**mitt** (mĭt) n. A large baseball glove.

**mit·ten** (mĭt'n) n. A hand covering that encases the thumb separately and the four fingers together.

**mix** (mĭks) v. **1.** To blend into a single mass. **2.** To combine or join. **3.** To associate socially; mingle. — **mix'ture** n.

**mne·mon·ic** (nĭ-mŏn'ĭk) adj. Assisting the memory.

**moan** (mōn) n. A low, sustained, mournful sound. — **moan** v.

**mob** (mŏb) n. **1.** A large, disorderly crowd. **2.** An organized gang of hoodlums. —v. **mobbed, mobbing. 1.** To crowd around and jostle or attack. **2.** To crowd into (a place).

**mo·bile** (mō'bəl, -bēl', -bīl') adj. **1.** Movable. **2.** Moving quickly from one condition to another. — **mo·bil'i·ty** n.

**mo·bi·lize** (mō'bə-līz') v. -lized, -lizing. To assemble or prepare for war or a similar emergency. — **mo'bi·li·za'tion** n.

**mob·ster** (mŏb'stər) n. A member of a criminal gang.

**moc·ca·sin** (mŏk'ə-sĭn) n. A soft leather slipper or shoe.

**mock** (mŏk) v. **1.** To treat with scorn or contempt; deride. **2.** To mimic in derision. —adj. Simulated; sham. — **mock'er·y** n.

**mode** (mōd) n. **1.** A way, manner, or style of doing or acting. **2.** The current fashion or style.

**mod·el** (mŏd'l) n. **1.** A miniature reproduction of something. **2.** A type or design. **3.** A preliminary pattern. **4.** An example to be emulated. **5.** One who poses for an artist, photographer, etc. —v. **1.** To plan or construct. **2.** To display (clothes) by wearing. **3.** To work as a model. — **mod'el** n.

**mod·er·ate** (mŏd'ər-ĭt) adj. **1.** Not excessive or extreme. **2.** Temperate. **3.** Average; mediocre. **4.** Avoiding political extremes. —n. One who holds moderate political views. —v. (-āt') -ated, -ating. **1.** To make or become less severe or extreme. **2.** To preside over (a meeting, discussion, etc.). — **mod·er·a'tor** n.

**mod·ern** (mŏd'ərn) adj. Of or characteristic of recent times or the present. — **mod'ern·is'tic** adj. — **mod·ern'i·ty** n. — **mod'ern·i·za'tion** n. — **mod'ern·ize'** v.

**mod·est** (mŏd'ĭst) adj. **1.** Having a moderate

estimation of oneself. **2.** Shy; reserved. **3.** Unpretentious. **4.** Moderate in size or amount. — **mod'es·ty** n.

**mod·i·cum** (mŏd'ĭ-kəm) n. A small amount.

**mod·i·fy** (mŏd'ə-fī') v. -fied, -fying. **1.** To change; alter. **2.** To make or become less extreme or severe. — **mod'i·fi·ca'tion** n. — **mod'i·fi'er** n.

**mod·u·late** (mŏj'ŏo-lāt', mŏd'yə-) v. -lated, -lating. **1.** To regulate; temper. **2.** To change or vary the pitch, intensity, or tone of. — **mod'u·la'tion** n.

**moist** (moist) adj. Slightly wet or damp; humid. — **mois'ten** v. — **mois'ture** n.

**mo·las·ses** (mə-lăs'ĭz) n. A thick syrup produced in refining sugar.

**mold¹** (mōld) n. **1.** A form for shaping a fluid or plastic substance. **2.** Something made or shaped from a mold. **3.** General shape or form. —v. To shape in a mold.

**mold²** (mōld) n. A fungous growth formed on organic matter. —v. To become covered with mold. — **mold'y** adj.

**mold·ing** (mōl'dĭng) n. A decorative strip, esp. on a wall.

**mole** (mōl) n. A small growth on the human skin.

**mol·e·cule** (mŏl'ə-kyōol') n. The simplest structural unit that displays the characteristic physical and chemical properties of a compound. — **mo·lec'u·lar** adj.

**mo·lest** (mə-lĕst') v. **1.** To interfere with or annoy. **2.** To accost sexually. — **mo'les·ta'tion** n. — **mo·lest'er** n.

**mol·li·fy** (mŏl'ə-fī') v. -fied, -fying. **1.** To placate; calm. **2.** To soften or ease. — **mol'li·fi·ca'tion** n.

**mol·lusk** (mŏl'əsk) n. Also **mol·lusc.** A soft-bodied, usually shell-bearing invertebrate.

**molt** (mōlt) v. To shed an outer covering, as feathers, for replacement by a new growth.

**mol·ten** (mōlt'n) adj. Melted.

**mo·ment** (mō'mənt) n. **1.** A brief interval of time. **2.** A specific point in time. **3.** Importance.

**mo·men·tar·y** (mō'mən-tĕr'ē) adj. Brief; short-lived. — **mo'men·tar'i·ly** adv.

**mo·men·tous** (mō-mĕn'təs) adj. Of utmost importance or significance.

**mo·men·tum** (mō-mĕn'təm) n. Force or speed of motion; impetus.

**mon·arch** (mŏn'ərk) n. **1.** A sovereign, as a king. **2.** A large orange and black butterfly. — **mon·ar'chic, mon·ar'chi·cal** adj.

**mon·ar·chy** (mŏn'ər-kē) n., pl. -chies. **1.**

Government by a monarch. **2.** A state ruled by a monarch. — **mon'ar·chism** n. — **mon'ar·chist** n. & adj.

**mon·as·ter·y** (mŏn'ə-stĕr'ē) n., pl. **-ies.** The dwelling place of a community of monks. — **mo·nas'tic** adj.

**Mon·day** (mŭn'dē, -dā') n. The 2nd day of the week.

**mon·e·tar·y** (mŏn'ĭ-tĕr'ē, mŭn'-) adj. **1.** Of money. **2.** Of a nation's currency or coinage.

**mon·ey** (mŭn'ē) n., pl. **-eys** or **-ies. 1.** Something, as gold, that is legally established as an exchangeable equivalent of all other commodities. **2.** Currency. **3.** Wealth.

**Mon·gol·oid** (mŏng'gə-loid', mŏn'-) adj. Of a major ethnic division of the human species having yellowish-brown to white skin color. — **Mon'gol·oid'** n.

**mon·grel** (mŭng'grəl, mŏng'-) n. A plant or animal of mixed breed.

**mon·i·tor** (mŏn'ĭ-tər) n. **1.** A student who assists a teacher. **2.** Any device used to record or control a process. — v. To check, watch, or keep track of, often by means of an electronic device.

**monk** (mŭngk) n. A member of a religious brotherhood living in a monastery.

**mon·key** (mŭng'kē) n., pl. **-keys.** Any member of the primates except man, esp. one of the long-tailed small- to medium-sized species. — v. To play or tamper with something.

**mo·nog·a·my** (mə-nŏg'ə-mē) n. The custom of being married to only one person at a time. — **mo·nog'a·mist** n. — **mo·nog'a·mous** adj.

**mon·o·gram** (mŏn'ə-grăm') n. A design composed of two or more initials of a name. — **mon'o·gram'** v.

**mon·o·lith** (mŏn'ə-lĭth') n. A large, single block of stone. — **mon·o·lith'ic** adj.

**mon·o·logue** (mŏn'ə-lŏg', -lôg') n. A long speech by a single actor, character in a story, or person in a group.

**mo·nop·o·ly** (mə-nŏp'ə-lē) n., pl. **-ies. 1.** Exclusive ownership or control. **2.** A company or group having such control. **3.** A commodity or service thus controlled. — **mo·nop'o·lis'tic** adj. — **mo·nop'o·lize'** v.

**mon·o·syl·la·ble** (mŏn'ə-sĭl'ə-bəl) n. A word of one syllable. — **mon'o·syl·lab'ic** adj.

**mon·o·the·ism** (mŏn'ə-thē-ĭz'əm) n. The belief that there is only one God. — **mon'o·the·is'tic** adj.

**mo·not·o·nous** (mə-nŏt'n-əs) adj. **1.** Unvarying in pitch. **2.** Repetitiously dull. — **mo·not'o·ny** n.

**mon·soon** (mŏn-sōōn') n. A seasonal wind system, esp. the system that produces dry and wet seasons in S Asia.

**mon·ster** (mŏn'stər) n. **1.** An animal or plant of abnormal or grotesque form. **2.** Any very large animal, plant, or object. **3.** One who inspires horror or disgust. — adj. Gigantic; huge. — **mon·stros'i·ty** n. — **mon'strous** adj.

**month** (mŭnth) n. One of the 12 divisions of the year.

**month·ly** (mŭnth'lē) adj. **1.** Of, occurring, coming due, or published every month. **2.** Lasting for a month. — n., pl. **-ies.** A monthly publication. — **month'ly** adv.

**mon·u·ment** (mŏn'yə-mənt) n. **1.** A structure erected as a memorial. **2.** A tombstone. **3.** An exceptional example of something. — **mon'u·men'tal** adj.

**moo** (mōō) v. To emit the deep, bellowing sound made by a cow. — **moo** n.

**mood** (mōōd) n. A state of mind or feeling.

**mood·y** (mōō'dē) adj. **-ier, -iest. 1.** Given to changeable emotional states. **2.** Gloomy; uneasy.

**moon** (mōōn) n. **1.** The natural satellite of the earth. **2.** Any natural satellite of a planet. **3.** A month. — v. **1.** To mope aimlessly. **2.** To exhibit infatuation. — **moon'light'** n.

**moon·shine** (mōōn'shīn') n. **1.** The light of the moon. **2.** Illegally distilled whiskey.

**moor¹** (mŏor) v. To secure or make fast, as with cables or anchors.

**moor²** (mŏor) n. A broad tract of open, often boggy land.

**moose** (mōōs) n., pl. **moose.** A very large deer of N North America.

**moot** (mōōt) adj. Subject to debate; arguable.

**mop** (mŏp) n. A device made of absorbent material attached to a handle, used for cleaning floors. — **mop** v.

**mope** (mōp) v. **moped, moping.** To be gloomy or dejected.

**mor·al** (môr'əl, mŏr'-) adj. **1.** Of or concerned with the discernment of what is good and evil. **2.** Virtuous; upright. **3.** Arising from conscience. — n. **1.** The principle taught by a story. **2.** morals. Rules or habits of conduct. — **mor'al·ist** n. — **mor·a·lis'tic** adj. — **mo·ral'i·ty** n. — **mor'al·ize'** v.

**mo·rale** (mə-răl') n. The attitude of a person or group with respect to confidence, cheerfulness, discipline, etc.

**mo·rass** (mə-răs', mô'-) n. **1.** A bog or marsh. **2.** Any perplexing situation.

**mor·a·to·ri·um** (môr'ə-tôr'ē-əm, -tōr'ē-əm, mōr'-) n., pl. **-ums** or **-toria** 1. An authorization to a debtor permitting temporary suspension of payments. 2. A delay of any action.

**mor·bid** (môr'bĭd) adj. 1. Of or caused by disease. 2. Characterized by preoccupation with unwholesome matters. — **mor·bid'i·ty** n.

**mor·dant** (môr'dənt) adj. 1. Bitingly sarcastic. 2. Incisive and trenchant.

**more** (môr, mōr) adj. superl. most. 1. a. compar. of many. Greater in number. b. compar. of much. Greater in size, amount, extent, or degree. 2. Additional; extra. — n. A greater or additional degree or amount. — adv. 1. To a greater degree. 2. In addition; further; again; longer.

**more·o·ver** (môr-ō'vər, mōr-, môr'ō'vər, mōr'-) adv. Further; besides.

**mo·res** (môr'āz, mōr'-, -ēz) pl.n. The traditional customs of a social group, often having the force of law.

**morgue** (môrg) n. A place in which the bodies of persons found dead are temporarily kept.

**mor·i·bund** (môr'ə-bŭnd', mōr'-) adj. At the point of death; dying.

**Mor·mon** (môr'mən) n. A member of the Church of Jesus Christ of Latter-day Saints.

**morn** (môrn) n. The morning.

**morn·ing** (môr'nĭng) n. The first or early part of the day, esp. from sunrise to noon.

**mo·ron** (môr'ŏn', mōr'-) n. A mentally retarded person. — **mo·ron'ic** adj.

**mo·rose** (mə-rōs', mō-) adj. Sullenly melancholy; gloomy.

**mor·phine** (môr'fēn') n. A drug extracted from opium, used as an anesthetic and sedative.

**mor·sel** (môr'səl) n. A small piece, esp. of food.

**mor·tal** (môrt'l) adj. 1. Subject to death. 2. Causing death; fatal. 3. Unrelenting; implacable. 4. Extreme; dire. — n. A human being. — **mor'tal·ly** adv.

**mor·tal·i·ty** (môr-tăl'ə-tē) n., pl. **-ties.** 1. The condition of being subject to death. 2. Death rate.

**mor·tar** (môr'tər) n. 1. A receptacle in which substances are crushed or ground. 2. A muzzle-loading cannon. 3. A mixture of cement or lime with sand and water, used in building.

**mort·gage** (môr'gĭj) n. A pledge of property to a creditor as security against a debt. — v. **-gaged, -gaging.** To pledge (property) by

mortgage. — **mort'ga·gee'** n. — **mort'ga·gor** n.

**mor·ti·cian** (môr-tĭsh'ən) n. A funeral director.

**mor·ti·fy** (môr'tə-fī') v. **-fied, -fying.** 1. To shame; humiliate. 2. To discipline (one's body and appetites) by self-denial. 3. To become gangrenous. — **mor'ti·fi·ca'tion** n.

**mor·tu·ar·y** (môr'chōō-ĕr'ē) n., pl. **-ies.** A place where dead bodies are prepared for burial.

**Mos·lem** (mŏz'ləm, mŏs'-) n. A believer in Islam. — **Mos'lem** adj.

**mosque** (mŏsk) n. A Moslem house of worship.

**mos·qui·to** (mə-skē'tō) n., pl. **-toes** or **-tos.** A winged insect of which the females bite and suck blood.

**moss** (môs, mŏs) n. A small, green plant often forming a matlike growth. — **moss'y** adj.

**most** (mōst) adj. 1. a. superl. of many. Greatest in number. b. superl. of much. Greatest in amount, size, or degree. 2. In the greatest number of instances. — n. 1. The greatest amount, quantity, or degree. 2. (takes pl. v.). The majority. — adv. 1. In the highest degree, quantity, or extent. 2. Very. — **most'ly** adv.

**mote** (mōt) n. A speck, esp. of dust.

**mo·tel** (mō-tĕl') n. A hotel for motorists.

**moth** (môth, mŏth) n. An insect related to the butterfly but generally night-flying.

**moth·er** (mŭth'ər) n. A female parent. — adj. 1. Being or characteristic of a mother. 2. Native. — v. To care for; nourish and protect. — **moth'er·hood** n. — **moth'er·ly** adj.

**moth·er-in-law** (mŭth'ər-ĭn-lô') n., pl. **mothers-in-law.** The mother of one's spouse.

**mo·tion** (mō'shən) n. 1. The action or process of change of position. 2. A gesture. 3. A formal proposal to put vote under parliamentary procedures. — v. To direct or signal by making a gesture. — **mo'tion·less** adj.

**motion picture.** A series of filmed images projected so rapidly as to create the illusion of motion. — **mo'tion-pic'ture** adj.

**mo·ti·vate** (mō'tə-vāt') v. **-vated, -vating.** To provide with an incentive; impel. — **mo'ti·va'tion** n.

**mo·tive** (mō'tĭv) n. An impulse acting as an incitement to action; incentive; cause. — adj. Producing motion.

**mot·ley** (mŏt'lē) adj. 1. Having components of great variety; heterogeneous; varied. 2. Multicolored.

**multiple**

**mo·tor** (mō′tər) n. 1. Anything that imparts or produces motion. 2. A device that converts any form of energy into mechanical energy; engine. —adj. 1. Causing or producing motion. 2. Relating to movements of the muscles. —v. To drive a motor vehicle. —mo′tor·ist n.

**mo·tor·cy·cle** (mō′tər-sī′kəl) n. A two-wheeled vehicle propelled by an engine. —mo′tor·cy′clist n.

**mot·tle** (mŏt′l) v. -tled, -tling. To cover (a surface) with colored spots or streaks. —mot′tled adj.

**mot·to** (mŏt′ō) n., pl. -toes or -tos. A brief phrase used to express a principle, goal, or ideal.

**mound** (mound) n. 1. A pile or bank of earth. 2. A natural elevation, as a small hill.

**mount** (mount) v. 1. To climb or ascend. 2. To get up on. 3. To settle in an appropriate setting. 4. a. To set (guns) in position. b. To launch and carry out. —n. 1. A horse on which to ride. 2. An object to which another is affixed for accessibility, display, or use.

**moun·tain** (moun′tən) n. A large natural elevation of the earth's surface. —moun′tain·ous adj.

**mourn** (môrn, mōrn) v. To feel or express sorrow for; grieve. —mourn′er n. —mourn′ful adj. —mourn′ing n.

**mouse** (mous) n., pl. mice A small, usually long-tailed rodent.

**mous·tache** (mŭs′tăsh′, mə-stăsh′) n. A mustache.

**mouth** (mouth) n., pl. mouths. 1. The body opening with which food is taken in. 2. A natural opening, as a harbor entrance. —v. (mouthz). To utter mechanically, without conviction.

**mouth·piece** (mouth′pēs′) n. 1. A part of an instrument that functions in the mouth. 2. A spokesman.

**move** (mōōv) v. moved, moving. 1. To change position. 2. To settle in a new place. 3. To affect deeply. 4. To take some action. 5. To make a formal motion in parliamentary procedure. —n. 1. An act of moving. 2. A change of residence. 3. A player's turn to move a piece in a board game. 4. One of a series of actions undertaken to achieve some end. —mov′a·ble adj. —mov′er n.

**move·ment** (mōōv′mənt) n. 1. An act of moving. 2. The activities of a group toward a specific goal. 3. Activity, esp. in business or commerce. 4. A primary section of a

musical composition. 5. A mechanism that produces or transmits motion.

**mov·ie** (mōō′vē) n. 1. A motion picture. 2. the movies. A showing of a motion picture.

**mow¹** (mō) v. mowed, mowed or mown, mowing. To cut down (grain, grass, etc.). —mow down. To fell in great numbers, as in battle. —mow′er n.

**mow²** (mou) n. A place for storing hay or grain.

**much** (mŭch) adj. more, most. Great in quantity, degree, or extent. —n. 1. A large quantity or amount. 2. Anything impressive or important. —adv. more, most. 1. To a great degree. 2. Just about; almost.

**muck** (mŭk) n. 1. A moist mixture of mud and filth. 2. Moist animal dung.

**muck·rake** (mŭk′rāk′) v. -raked, -raking. To expose political or commercial corruption. —muck′rak′er n.

**mu·cous** (myōō′kəs) adj. Also mu·cose. Producing or secreting mucus.

**mu·cus** (myōō′kəs) n. A viscous bodily secretion.

**mud** (mŭd) n. Wet, sticky, soft earth. —mud′dy adj.

**mud·dle** (mŭd′l) v. -dled, -dling. 1. To mix up; confuse. 2. To mismanage or bungle. —n. A confusion, jumble, or mess.

**muff¹** (mŭf) v. To perform (an act) clumsily; bungle.

**muff²** (mŭf) n. A small, tubelike cover for keeping the hands warm.

**muf·fin** (mŭf′in) n. A small, cup-shaped bread.

**muf·fle** (mŭf′əl) v. -fled, -fling. 1. To wrap up snugly. 2. To deaden (a sound). —muf′fler n.

**mug¹** (mŭg) n. A drinking vessel.

**mug²** (mŭg) v. mugged, mugging. To waylay and beat severely. —mug′ger n.

**mug·gy** (mŭg′ē) adj. -gier, -giest. Warm and humid.

**mu·lat·to** (m/y/ōō-lăt′ō, -lă′tō) n., pl. -tos or -toes. A person having one white and one black parent.

**mule¹** (myōōl) n. The sterile offspring of an ass and a mare.

**mule²** (myōōl) n. A slipper with no heel strap.

**mul·ish** (myōō′lish) adj. Stubborn.

**mull** (mŭl) v. To ponder or ruminate on (with over).

**mul·ti·far·i·ous** (mŭl′tə-fâr′ē-əs) adj. Having great variety; of many kinds.

**mul·ti·ple** (mŭl′tə-pəl) adj. Of or having more than one element, component, etc. —n.

A quantity into which another can be divided with zero remainder.

**mul·ti·pli·cand** (mŭl'tə-plĭ-kănd') *n.* A number to be multiplied by another.

**mul·ti·plic·i·ty** (mŭl'tə-plĭs'ə-tē) *n.* A large number or variety.

**mul·ti·ply** (mŭl'tə-plī') *v.* -plied, -plying. 1. To increase in number, amount, or degree. 2. To add (a pair of numbers) a given number of times to find their product. — **mul'ti·pli·ca'tion** *n.* — **mul'ti·pli'er** *n.*

**mul·ti·tude** (mŭl'tə-t/yōōd') *n.* A great, indefinite number. — **mul'ti·tu'di·nous** *adj.*

**mum·ble** (mŭm'bəl) *v.* -bled, -bling. To speak or utter indistinctly. — **mum'ble** *n.*

**mum·my** (mŭm'ē) *n., pl.* -ies. A body embalmed after death, as by the ancient Egyptians.

**munch** (mŭnch) *v.* To chew steadily and noisily.

**mun·dane** (mŭn'dān', mŭn'dān') *adj.* 1. Not spiritual; worldly. 2. Typical of the ordinary.

**mu·nic·i·pal** (myōō-nĭs'ə-pəl) *adj.* 1. Of a city or its government. 2. Having local self-government. — **mu·nic'i·pal'i·ty** *n.*

**mu·nif·i·cent** (myōō-nĭf'ə-sənt) *adj.* Extremely generous. — **mu·nif'i·cence** *n.*

**mu·ni·tions** (myōō-nĭsh'ənz) *pl.n.* War materiel.

**mu·ral** (myŏŏr'əl) *n.* A large picture or decoration applied directly to a wall.

**mur·der** (mûr'dər) *n.* The deliberate killing of one human being by another. — *v.* 1. To kill (a human being). 2. To ruin. — **mur'der·er** *n.* — **mur'der·ess** *fem.n.* — **mur'der·ous** *adj.*

**murk·y** (mûr'kē) *adj.* -ier, -iest. 1. Dark; gloomy. 2. Cloudy and dark with smoke, mist, etc.

**mur·mur** (mûr'mər) *n.* 1. A low, indistinct, and continuous sound. 2. An indistinct complaint. — *v.* To make or utter in a murmur.

**mus·cle** (mŭs'əl) *n.* 1. **a.** A tissue composed of fibers capable of contracting and relaxing to effect bodily movement. **b.** A part made of such tissue. 2. Strength. — *v.* -cled, -cling. To force one's way. — **mus'cu·lar** *adj.*

**muse** (myōōz) *v.* mused, musing. To ponder; consider reflectively or at length.

**mu·se·um** (myōō-zē'əm) *n.* A building in which works of artistic, historical, and scientific interest are exhibited.

**mush** (mŭsh) *n.* 1. Boiled cornmeal. 2. Anything thick, soft, and pulpy. 3. Maudlin sentimentality. — **mush'y** *adj.*

**mush·room** (mŭsh'rōōm', -rŏŏm') *n.* A fleshy fungus having an umbrella-shaped

cap, esp. one that is edible. — *v.* To multiply or grow rapidly.

**mu·sic** (myōō'zĭk) *n.* The art of organizing sounds so as to create an aesthetic combination of rhythm, melody, and harmony. — **mu'si·cal** *adj.* — **mu·si'cian** *n.*

**musk** (mŭsk) *n.* An odorous animal secretion used in perfume. — **musk'y** *adj.*

**mus·ket** (mŭs'kĭt) *n.* A 17th- and 18th-century rifle. — **mus'ket·eer'** *n.*

**mus·lin** (mŭz'lĭn) *n.* A sturdy cotton fabric.

**muss** (mŭs) *v.* To make untidy; rumple. — *n.* Disorder; mess. — **muss'y** *adj.*

**mus·sel** (mŭs'əl) *n.* A bivalve mollusk often edible.

**must** (mŭst) *v.* —Used as an auxiliary to indicate: 1. Necessity or obligation. 2. Probability. 3. Inevitability or certainty. — *n.* An absolute requirement.

**mus·tache** (mŭs'tăsh', mə-stăsh') *n.* The hair growing on the upper lip.

**mus·tard** (mŭs'tərd) *n.* 1. A plant with yellow flowers and pungent seeds. 2. A condiment made from mustard seeds.

**mus·ter** (mŭs'tər) *v.* 1. To summon (troops). 2. To gather up. — *n.* A gathering, esp. of troops, for inspection.

**must·y** (mŭs'tē) *adj.* -ier, -iest. Having a stale odor.

**mu·ta·tion** (myōō-tā'shən) *n.* 1. An alteration or change, as in nature or form. 2. In biology, any heritable alteration of an organism. — **mu'tant** *n. & adj.*

**mute** (myōōt) *adj.* 1. Incapable of producing speech. 2. Not speaking or spoken; silent. — *n.* 1. A person incapable of speech. 2. A device used to muffle the tone of a musical instrument. — *v.* muted, muting. To soften the sound, color, or shade of.

**mu·ti·late** (myōōt'l-āt') *v.* -lated, -lating. To injure or disfigure by seriously damaging a limb, part, etc. — **mu'ti·la'tion** *n.*

**mu·ti·ny** (myōōt'n-ē) *n., pl.* -nies. Open rebellion against constituted authority, esp. by sailors or soldiers. — **mu'ti·neer'** *v.* — **mu'ti·nous** *adj.* — **mu'ti·ny** *n.*

**mut·ter** (mŭt'ər) *v.* 1. To speak in low, indistinct tones. 2. To complain or grumble. — *n.* A muttering utterance.

**mu·tu·al** (myōō'chōō-əl) *adj.* 1. Having the same feelings each for the other. 2. Given and received in equal amounts. 3. Possessed in common. — **mu'tu·al'i·ty** *n.*

**muz·zle** (mŭz'əl) *n.* 1. The projecting jaws and nose of certain animals. 2. A protective device fitted over an animal's snout. 3. The

front end of the barrel of a firearm. —v. **-zled,
-zling. 1.** To put a muzzle on (an animal).
**2.** To prevent (someone) from expressing
opinions.

**my** (mī). The possessive form of *I.*

**myr·i·ad** (mĭr'ē-əd) *adj.* Amounting to a
very large, indefinite number. —n. A vast
number.

**my·self** (mī-sĕlf') *pron.* The reflexive form of
*I.*

**mys·ter·y** (mĭs'tər-ē) *n., pl.* **-ies. 1.** Anything
that arouses curiosity because it is unex-
plained, inexplicable, or secret. **2.** The quality of being inexplicable or secret. — **mys·
te'ri·ous** *adj.*

**mys·tic** (mĭs'tĭk) *adj.* **1.** Of mystics or mysticism. **2.** Inspiring a quality of mystery. —n.
One who believes in mysticism. — **mys'ti·cal**
*adj.*

**mys·ti·cism** (mĭs'tə-sĭz'əm) *n.* A spiritual
discipline aiming at union with the divine
through deep meditation or contemplation.

**mys·ti·fy** (mĭs'tə-fī') *v.* **-fied, -fying.** To
perplex; bewilder. — **mys'ti·fi·ca'tion** *n.*

**myth** (mĭth) *n.* **1.** A traditional story about
ancestors, heroes, or supernatural beings.
**2.** A fictitious or imaginary story, person,
thing, explanation, etc. — **myth'ic** *adj.*

**my·thol·o·gy** (mĭ-thŏl'ə-jē) *n., pl.* **-gies. 1.** A
body of myths about the origin and history
of a people. **2.** The study of myths. — **myth'·
o·log'i·cal** *adj.*

# N

**n, N** (ĕn) *n.* The 14th letter of the English
alphabet.

**na·dir** (nā'dər, nā'dîr') *n.* **1.** A celestial point
opposite the zenith. **2.** The lowest point.

**nag¹** (năg) *v.* **gged, -gging. 1.** To annoy
by constant complaining. **2.** To complain or
find fault constantly. —n. One who nags.
— **nag'ging·ly** *adv.*

**nag²** (năg) *n.* A horse.

**nail** (nāl) *n.* **1.** A thin, pointed piece of metal
used as a fastener. **2.** A fingernail or toenail.
—v. To fasten with nails.

**na·ive, na·ïve** (nä-ēv') *adj.* Lacking so-
phistication; ingenuous. — **na·ïve'te, na·ïve·té**
*n.*

**na·ked** (nā'kĭd) *adj.* Without clothing on the

body; nude. — **na'ked·ness** *n.*

**name** (nām) *n.* **1.** A word or words by which
any entity is designated. **2.** Reputation; renown. —v. **named, naming. 1.** To give a name
to. **2.** To call by the name of. **3.** To appoint.
— **name'less** *adj.* — **name'ly** *adv.*

**name·sake** (nām'sāk') *n.* One named after
another.

**nap¹** (năp) *n.* A brief sleep. —v. **napped,
napping.** To sleep for a brief period.

**nap²** (năp) *n.* A fuzzy surface on certain
textiles.

**nape** (nāp) *n.* The back of the neck.

**nap·kin** (năp'kĭn) *n.* A piece of fabric or
paper used at table to protect the clothes or
wipe the lips.

**nar·cot·ic** (när-kŏt'ĭk) *n.* An often addictive
drug that dulls the senses and induces sleep.
— **nar·cot'ic** *adj.*

**nar·rate** (năr'āt', nă-rāt') *v.* **-rated, -rating.
1.** To tell (a story). **2.** To give an account or
commentary. — **nar·ra'tion** *n.* — **nar'ra·tive** *n.*
— **nar'ra·tor** *n.*

**nar·row** (năr'ō) *adj.* **1.** Of small or limited
width. **2.** Limited in area or scope. **3.** Rigid
in views or ideas; limited in outlook. —v. To
make or become narrow or narrower. —n.
**narrows.** A narrow body of water connecting
two larger ones. — **nar'row·ly** *adv.*

**na·sal** (nā'zəl) *adj.* Of the nose.

**nas·ty** (năs'tē) *adj.* **-tier, -tiest. 1.** Disgusting
to see, smell, or touch; filthy. **2.** Malicious;
spiteful. **3.** Unpleasant; disagreeable. — **nas'·
ti·ly** *adv.* — **nas'ti·ness** *n.*

**na·tal** (nāt'l) *adj.* Of birth.

**na·tion** (nā'shən) *n.* **1.** A group of people
under a single government. **2.** A people
having common origins or traditions; federation or tribe. — **na'tion·al** *adj.* & *n.* — **na'·
tion·al·ism'** *n.* — **na'tion·al·ist** *n.* — **na'tion·al·
is'tic** *adj.* — **na'tion·al·i·ty** *n.* — **na'tion·al·ly** *adv.*

**na·tive** (nā'tĭv) *adj.* **1.** Inborn; innate. **2.**
Originating in a certain place; indigenous.
—n. **1.** One born in a place. **2.** An original
inhabitant of a place.

**na·tiv·i·ty** (nə-tĭv'ə-tē, nā-) *n., pl.* **-ties.** Birth.

**nat·u·ral** (năch'ər-əl, năch'rəl) *adj.* **1.**
Present in or produced by nature; not
artificial. **2.** Of nature. **3.** Free from affectation. **4.** Consonant with particular circumstances; expected and accepted. —n.
One with talent for a particular endeavor.
— **nat'u·ral·ly** *adv.* — **nat'u·ral·ness** *n.*

**nat·u·ral·ist** (năch'ər-ə-lĭst, năch'rə-) *n.* One
who studies plants and animals.

**nat·u·ral·ize** (năch'ər-ə-līz', năch'rə-) —

**nature** 146

-ized, -izing. To grant full citizenship to. —nat'u·ral·i·za'tion n.

**na·ture** (nā'chər) n. 1. The fundamental character of a person or thing. 2. The order, disposition, and behavior of all entities composing the physical universe. 3. The physical world, including living things, natural phenomena, etc.

**naught** (nôt) n. Nothing; zero.

**naugh·ty** (nô'tē) adj. -tier, -tiest. Disobedient; mischievous. —naugh'ti·ly adv. —naugh'ti·ness n.

**nau·se·a** (nô'zē-ə, -zhə, -sē-ə, -shə) n. 1. A stomach disturbance. 2. Strong disgust. —nau'se·ate' v. —nau'seous adj.

**nau·ti·cal** (nô'tĭ-kəl) adj. Of ships, seamen, or navigation.

**na·vel** (nā'vəl) n. The mark on the abdomen of mammals where the umbilical cord was attached before birth.

**nav·i·gate** (năv'ə-gāt') v. -gated, -gating. 1. To control the course of a ship or aircraft. 2. To voyage over water; sail. —nav'i·ga·ble adj. —nav'i·ga'tion n. —nav'i·ga'tor n.

**na·vy** (nā'vē) n., pl. -vies. All of a nation's warships. —v.

**nay** (nā) adv. No. —n. A negative vote.

**near** (nîr) adv. To, at, or within a short distance or interval in space or time. —adj. 1. Close. 2. Closely related; intimate. —prep. Close to. —v. To come close or closer to; draw near. —near'by' adj. & adv. —near'ly adv. —near'ness n.

**near·sight·ed** (nîr'sī'tĭd) adj. Unable to see distant objects clearly. —near'sight'ed·ness n.

**neat** (nēt) adj. 1. Tidy. 2. Orderly in appearance or procedure. —neat'ly adv. —neat'ness n.

**neb·u·lous** (nĕb'yə-ləs) adj. Lacking definite form; vague; unclear. —neb'u·lous·ly adv.

**nec·es·sar·y** (nĕs'ə-sĕr'ē) adj. 1. Needed for the continuing existence or functioning of something; essential; requisite. 2. Inevitable. —n., pl. -ies. Often necessaries. Something that is essential. —nec'es·sar'i·ly adv.

**ne·ces·si·ty** (nĭ-sĕs'ə-tē) n., pl. -ties. 1. Something necessary. 2. Pressing or urgent need. —ne·ces'si·tate' v.

**neck** (nĕk) n. 1. The part of the body joining the head to the trunk. 2. A narrow projecting or connecting part of anything, as of a bottle.

**neck·lace** (nĕk'lĭs) n. An ornament worn around the neck.

**neck·tie** (nĕk'tī') n. A narrow band of fabric knotted or tied and worn around the neck of a shirt.

**nec·tar** (nĕk'tər) n. 1. The drink of the gods. 2. A sweet liquid secreted by flowers.

**nec·tar·ine** (nĕk'tə-rēn') n. A smooth-skinned variety of peach.

**need** (nēd) n. 1. A state in which something necessary is required. 2. Something required or wanted. 3. Poverty. 4. Necessity; obligation. —v. To require or want. —need'ful adj. —need'i·ness n. —need'less adj. —need'less·ly adv. —need'y adj.

**nee·dle** (nēd'l) n. 1. A slender implement for knitting, sewing, etc. 2. A pointer or indicator, as on a magnet. 3. A stiff, narrow leaf, as of a pine. —v. -dled, -dling. To goad, provoke, or tease.

**need·n't** (nēd'ənt). Contraction of need not.

**ne·far·i·ous** (nĭ-fâr'ē-əs) adj. Evil; wicked. —ne·far'i·ous·ness n.

**ne·gate** (nĭ-gāt') v. -gated, -gating. 1. To render ineffective; nullify. 2. To rule out; deny. —ne·ga'tion n.

**neg·a·tive** (nĕg'ə-tĭv) adj. 1. Expressing negation, refusal, or denial. 2. Lacking the quality of being positive or affirmative. 3. Of an electric charge that tends to repel electrons. —n. 1. A negative word or statement. 2. An image in which the light areas appear dark and the dark areas appear light. —neg'a·tive·ly adv.

**ne·glect** (nĭ-glĕkt') v. 1. To disregard; ignore. 2. To fail to give proper attention to. —n. 1. The act of neglecting something. 2. The state of being neglected. —ne·glect'ful adj.

**neg·li·gee** (nĕg'lĭ-zhā') n. A woman's dressing gown.

**neg·li·gent** (nĕg'lĭ-jənt) adj. Habitually guilty of neglect. —neg'li·gence n.

**neg·li·gi·ble** (nĕg'lĭ-jə-bəl) adj. Not worth considering; trifling.

**ne·go·ti·ate** (nĭ-gō'shē-āt') v. -ated, -ating. 1. To confer with another or others in order to come to terms; bargain. 2. To transfer ownership of (financial documents) in return for value received. —ne·go'tia·ble adj. —ne·go'ti·a'tion n. —ne·go'ti·a'tor n.

**Ne·gro** (nē'grō) n., pl. -groes. A member of the division of the human species having brown to black skin color; a black. —adj. Of a Negro. —Ne'groid' adj. & n.

**neigh** (nā) v. To utter the cry of a horse! —neigh n.

**neigh·bor** (nā'bər) n. One living near an-

other. —v. To live or be situated nearby.
—**neigh'bor·hood'** n. —**neigh'bor·ing** adj.
—**neigh'bor·ly** adj.

**nei·ther** (nē'thər, nī'-) adj. Not one or the other. —pron. Not the one nor the other. —conj. Not either.

**nem·e·sis** (nĕm'ə-sĭs) n., pl. -ses 1. An inflicter of retribution; avenger. 2. An unbeatable rival, as in sports.

**ne·on** (nē'ŏn') n. A gaseous chemical element, used in display and television tubes.

**ne·o·phyte** (nē'ə-fīt') n. A beginner.

**neph·ew** (nĕf'yōo) n. The son of one's sister or brother.

**nep·o·tism** (nĕp'ə-tĭz'əm) n. Favoritism shown to relatives, esp. in politics.

**Nep·tune** (nĕp't/yōon') n. The 8th planet from the sun.

**nerve** (nûrv) n. 1. A bundle of fibers capable of transmitting sensory stimuli and motor impulses through the body. 2. Courage. 3. Impudence.

**nerv·ous** (nûr'vəs) adj. 1. High-strung; excitable. 2. Of the nerves. 3. Uneasy; anxious. —**ner'vous·ly** adv. —**ner'vous·ness** n.

**nest** (nĕst) n. 1. The structure made by a bird or other creature for holding its eggs and young. 2. A snug place. 3. A set of objects that can be stacked together. —v. 1. To build or occupy a nest. 2. To fit or place snugly together.

**nes·tle** (nĕs'əl) v. -tled, -tling. To settle snugly and comfortably.

**net¹** (nĕt) n. 1. An openwork meshed fabric. 2. Something made of net. —v. netted, netting. To catch in a net. —**net'ting** n. —**net'work'** n.

**net²** (nĕt) adj. Remaining after all costs have been deducted. —n. Total gain, as of profit. —v. netted, netting. To bring in as profit.

**net·tle** (nĕt'l) n. A plant with stinging hairs. —v. -tled, -tling. To irritate; vex. —**net'tler** n.

**neu·ral** (n/y/ōōr'əl) adj. Of the nerves.

**neu·rol·o·gy** (n/y/ōō-rŏl'ə-jē) n. The medical science of the nervous system and its disorders. —**neu'ro·log'i·cal** adj. —**neu·rol'o·gist** n.

**neu·ro·sis** (n/y/ōō-rō'sĭs) n., pl. -ses. A disorder of the mind or emotions, involving anxiety, phobia, etc. —**neu·rot'ic** adj. & n.

**neu·ter** (n/y/ōō'tər) adj. Neither masculine nor feminine.

**neu·tral** (n/y/ōō'trəl) adj. 1. Not favoring or belonging to either side in a dispute. 2. Indifferent. 3. Designating a color with no hue. —n. One that is neutral. —**neu·tral'i·ty** n. —**neu'tral·ize'** v. —**neu'tral·ly** adv.

**nev·er** (nĕv'ər) adv. Not ever. —**nev'er·more'** adv.

**nev·er·the·less** (nĕv'ər·thə-lĕs') adv. None the less; however.

**new** (n/y/ōō) adj. 1. Not old; recent. 2. Unfamiliar. 3. Different and distinct from what was before. 4. Modern; current. —adv. Freshly; recently. —**new'ly** adv. —**new'ness** n.

**news** (n/y/ōōz) n. (takes sing. v.) A report about recent events.

**news·cast** (n/y/ōōz'kăst', -kăst') n. A broadcast of news events.

**news·pa·per** (n/y/ōōz'pā'pər) n. A daily or weekly publication containing news, advertising, etc. —**news'pa'per·man'** n.

**news·reel** (n/y/ōōz'rēl') n. A short film of current events.

**next** (nĕkst) adj. 1. Nearest; adjacent. 2. Immediately succeeding. —adv. 1. In the time, order, or place immediately following. 2. On the first subsequent occasion. —prep. Close to; nearest.

**nib·ble** (nĭb'əl) v. -bled, -bling. To eat with small, quick bites. —n. A small bite.

**nice** (nīs) adj. nicer, nicest. 1. Pleasing; appealing. 2. Considerate; well-mannered. 3. Respectable; virtuous. 4. Fastidious; exacting. —**nice'ly** adv. —**nice'ness** n. —**ni'ce·ty** n.

**niche** (nĭch) n. A recess in a wall, as for a statue.

**nick** (nĭk) n. A notch or indentation on a surface. —v. To cut a nick in.

**nick·el** (nĭk'əl) n. 1. A silvery, metallic chemical element. 2. A U.S. coin worth five cents.

**nick·name** (nĭk'nām') n. A descriptive, informal, or affectionate name used instead of a real name. —v. -named, -naming. To call by a nickname.

**nic·o·tine** (nĭk'ə-tēn') n. A poisonous substance derived from tobacco.

**niece** (nēs) n. A daughter of one's brother or sister.

**nig·gard·ly** (nĭg'ərd-lē) adj. -lier, -liest. 1. Stingy. 2. Meager. —**nig'gard·ly** adv.

**nigh** (nī) adj. nigher, nighest or next. Close; near. —adv. 1. Near. 2. Nearly; almost. —prep. Not far from; near to.

**night** (nīt) n. The period of darkness between sunset and sunrise. —**night'fall'** n. —**night'ly** adj. & adv. —**night'time'** n.

**night·gown** (nīt'goun') n. A loose gown worn in bed.

**night·mare** (nīt'mâr') n. A frightening dream or event.

**night·shirt** (nīt′shûrt′) *n.* A long shirt worn in bed.

**night·stick** (nīt′stĭk′) *n.* A club carried by a policeman.

**nil** (nĭl) *n.* Nothing; naught.

**nim·ble** (nĭm′bəl) *adj.* **-bler, -blest. 1.** Quick and agile; deft. **2.** Clever in thinking, responding, etc. — **nim′bly** *adv.*

**nine** (nīn) *n.* The cardinal number written 9. — **nine** *adj. & pron.* — **ninth** *n. & adj.*

**nine·teen** (nīn′tēn′) *n.* The cardinal number written 19. — **nine′teen′** *adj. & pron.* — **nine′teenth′** *n. & adj.*

**nine·ty** (nīn′tē) *n.* The cardinal number written 90. — **nine′ty** *adj. & pron.* — **nine′ti·eth** *n. & adj.*

**nip¹** (nĭp) *v.* **nipped, nipping. 1.** To squeeze, pinch, or bite. **2.** To sting, as cold. **3.** To check growth or development. — *n.* **1.** A bite or pinch. **2.** A stinging quality, as of frosty air. — **nip′py** *adj.*

**nip²** (nĭp) *n.* A small drink or sip of liquor. — *v.* **nipped, nipping.** To drink (liquor) in small portions.

**nip·ple** (nĭp′əl) *n.* **1.** A small projection near the center of the mammary gland. **2.** The rubber cap on a nursing bottle. **3.** Anything resembling a nipple.

**nir·va·na** (nîr-vä′nə, nər-) *n.* **1.** Nirvana. The Buddhist state of perfect bliss. **2.** An ideal condition of rest, joy, etc.

**nit** (nĭt) *n.* The egg of a parasitic insect, as a louse.

**ni·tro·gen** (nī′trə-jən) *n.* One of the elements, a colorless, odorless gas.

**ni·tro·glyc·er·in** (nī′trō-glĭs′ər-ĭn) *n.* Also **ni·tro·glyc·er·ine.** A dangerously explosive pale-yellow liquid.

**nit·wit** (nĭt′wĭt′) *n.* A stupid or silly person.

**no** (nō) *adv.* **1.** Not so. Used to express refusal. **2.** Not at all. Used with the comparative. — *adj.* **1.** Not any. **2.** Not at all. — *n., pl.* **noes. 1.** A negative response; denial; refusal. **2.** A negative vote.

**no·ble** (nō′bəl) *adj.* **-bler, -blest. 1.** Of high hereditary rank. **2.** Showing greatness of character; illustrious. **3.** Grand; stately; magnificent. — *n.* A person of noble rank. — **no·bil′i·ty** *n.* — **no′ble·man** *n.* — **no′ble·ness** *n.* — **no′bly** *adv.*

**no·bod·y** (nō′bŏd′ē, -bə-dē) *pron.* No person; no one. — *n., pl.* **-bodies.** One without fame or influence.

**noc·tur·nal** (nŏk-tûr′nəl) *adj.* **1.** Of the night. **2.** Active or functioning at night.

**nod** (nŏd) *v.* **nodded, nodding. 1.** To bow the head briefly. **2.** To express (greeting, approval, etc.) by bowing the head. **3.** To let the head fall forward as if sleepy. — *n.* A nodding motion.

**node** (nōd) *n.* **1.** A knob, knot, protuberance, or swelling. **2.** The point on a plant stem where a leaf is attached. — **nod′al** *adj.*

**nod·ule** (nŏj′ool) *n.* A small node. — **nod′u·lar** *adj.*

**noise** (noiz) *n.* A sound or sounds, esp. when loud or disagreeable. — **nois′y** *adj.*

**noi·some** (noi′səm) *adj.* **1.** Offensive, disgusting, or foul. **2.** Harmful or injurious.

**no·mad** (nō′măd′) *n.* **1.** One of a people having no permanent home and moving from place to place. **2.** A wanderer. — **no·mad′ic** *adj.*

**no·men·cla·ture** (nō′mən-klā′chər, nō-mĕn′klə-chər) *n.* A system of names, esp. in an art or science.

**nom·i·nal** (nŏm′ə-nəl) *adj.* **1.** In name only. **2.** Insignificant. — **nom′i·nal·ly** *adv.*

**nom·i·nate** (nŏm′ə-nāt′) *v.* **-nated, -nating. 1.** To propose as a candidate. **2.** To appoint to an office, honor, etc. — **nom′i·na′tion** *n.* — **nom′i·nee′** *n.*

**nom·i·na·tive** (nŏm′ə-nə-tĭv, nŏm′nə-tĭv) *adj.* Of the grammatical case that indicates the subject of a verb. — *n.* The nominative case.

**non·cha·lant** (nŏn′shə-länt′) *adj.* Appearing casually unconcerned. — **non′cha·lance′** *n.* — **non′cha·lant·ly** *adv.*

**non·com·mit·tal** (nŏn′kə-mĭt′l) *adj.* Revealing no preference or purpose.

**non·de·script** (nŏn′dĭ-skrĭpt′) *adj.* Lacking in distinctive qualities; hard to describe.

**none** (nŭn) *pron.* **1.** No one; nobody. **2.** No part; not any. — *adv.* Not one; no. — **1.** In no way; not at all.

**non·en·ti·ty** (nŏn-ĕn′tə-tē) *n., pl.* **-ties.** An insignificant person or thing.

**none·the·less** (nŭn′thə-lĕs′) *adv.* Nevertheless.

**non·pa·reil** (nŏn′pə-rĕl′) *adj.* Without rival; matchless. — **non′pa·reil′** *n.*

**non·plus** (nŏn-plŭs′) *v.* To perplex; baffle.

**non·sense** (nŏn′sĕns′, -səns) *n.* Foolish or absurd behavior or language. — **non·sen′si·cal** *adj.*

**noo·dle** (nood′l) *n.* A thin strip of dried dough.

**nook** (nook) *n.* **1.** A corner, esp. in a room. **2.** A quiet or secluded spot.

**noon** (noon) *n.* Twelve o'clock in the daytime; midday. — **noon′day′** *n.* — **noon′tide′** *n.*

**noose** (noos) n. A loop in a rope formed by a knot that tightens when pulled.

**nor** (nôr; *unstressed* nər) conj. And not; or not; not either.

**norm** (nôrm) n. A standard regarded as typical.

**nor·mal** (nôr′məl) adj. Conforming to a usual or typical pattern. —n. Anything normal; the standard. —**nor·mal′i·ty, nor′mal·cy** n. —**nor′mal·ly** adv.

**north** (nôrth) n. **1.** The direction along a meridian 90° counterclockwise from east. **2.** Often **North.** The N part of any country or region. —adj. & adv. & adv. —**north′er·ly** adj. & adv. —**north′ern, North′ern** adj. —**north′ern·er, North′ern·er** n. —**north′ward** adj. & adv.

**north·east** (nôrth-ēst′) n. The direction or area halfway between north and east. —adj. & adv. To, from, or in the northeast. —**north·east′ern** adj. —**north·east′er·ly** adj. & adv.

**north·west** (nôrth-wĕst′) n. The direction or area halfway between north and west. —adj. & adv. To, from, or in the northwest. —**north·west′ern** adj. —**north·west′er·ly** adj. & adv.

**nose** (nōz) n. **1.** The facial structure containing the nostrils and organs of smell. **2.** The sense of smell. **3.** Anything like a nose in shape or position. —v. **nosed, nosing. 1.** To find out by or as by smell. **2.** To pry curiously. —**nos′i·ness** n. —**nos′y, nos′ey** adj.

**nose·gay** (nōz′gā′) n. A small bunch of flowers.

**nos·tal·gia** (nŏ-stăl′jə, nə-) n. **1.** A longing for things of the past. **2.** Homesickness. —**nos·tal′gic** adj.

**nos·tril** (nŏs′trəl) n. Either of the external openings of the nose.

**not** (nŏt) adv. In no way; to no degree.

**no·ta·ble** (nō′tə-bəl) adj. Worthy of notice; remarkable. —n. A person of note or distinction. —**no′ta·bil′i·ty** n. —**no′ta·bly** adv.

**no·ta·rize** (nō′tə-rīz′) v. **-rized, -rizing.** To witness and authenticate (a document).

**no·ta·tion** (nō-tā′shən) n. **1.** A system of symbols used to represent numbers, quantities, etc. **2.** The use of such a system.

**notch** (nŏch) n. A V-shaped cut. —v. To cut notches in.

**note** (nōt) n. **1.** A brief written record or communication. **2.** A commentary to a passage in a text. **3.** A promissory note. **4.** A tone of definite pitch or the symbol of such a tone in musical notation. **5.** Importance; consequence. **6.** Notice; observation. —v.

**noted, noting. 1.** To observe carefully; notice. **2.** To write down; make a note of. **3.** To make mention of; remark. —**note′wor′thy** adj.

**note·book** (nōt′bŏŏk′) n. A book of blank pages for notes.

**not·ed** (nō′tĭd) adj. Distinguished by reputation; eminent.

**noth·ing** (nŭth′ĭng) n. **1.** No thing; not anything. **2.** A person or thing of no consequence. **3.** Zero; naught. —adv. Not at all. —**noth′ing·ness** n.

**no·tice** (nō′tĭs) n. **1.** The act of observing; attention. **2.** An announcement or indication of some event. **3.** A critical review, as of a play. —v. **-ticed, -ticing. 1.** To observe; be aware of. **2.** To take note of; remark on. —**no′tice·a·ble** adj. —**no′tice·a·bly** adv.

**no·ti·fy** (nō′tə-fī′) v. **-fied, -fying. 1.** To let (someone) know; inform. **2.** To tell by a notice; proclaim. —**no′ti·fi·ca′tion** n.

**no·tion** (nō′shən) n. **1.** A general impression or feeling. **2.** A view or theory. **3.** Intention or inclination. **4. notions.** Small items for household and clothing use.

**no·to·ri·ous** (nō-tôr′ē-əs, -tōr′ē-əs) adj. Known widely and regarded unfavorably; infamous. —**no·to·ri′e·ty** n. —**no·to′ri·ous·ly** adv.

**not·with·stand·ing** (nŏt′wĭth-stăn′dĭng, nŏt′wĭth-) prep. In spite of. —adv. All the same; nevertheless.

**noun** (noun) n. A word used to name a person, place, thing, quality, or act.

**nour·ish** (nûr′ĭsh) v. To provide (a living thing) with food that it needs to grow and live. —**nour′ish·ment** n.

**nov·el¹** (nŏv′əl) n. A long fictional prose narrative. —**nov′el·ist** n.

**nov·el²** (nŏv′əl) adj. Strikingly new, unusual, or different. —**nov′el·ty** n.

**No·vem·ber** (nō-vĕm′bər) n. The 11th month of the year.

**nov·ice** (nŏv′ĭs) n. **1.** A beginner. **2.** One who has entered a religious order but has not yet taken final vows.

**now** (nou) adv. **1.** At the present time. **2.** At once; immediately. —conj. Since; seeing that. —n. The present time.

**now·a·days** (nou′ə-dāz′) adv. In or during the present time.

**no·where** (nō′hwâr′) adv. Not anywhere.

**nox·ious** (nŏk′shəs) adj. Injurious to health.

**noz·zle** (nŏz′əl) n. A projecting spout.

**nu·ance** (n/y/ōō-äns′, n/y/ōō′äns′) n. A slight variation, as in meaning, color, or tone.

**nub** (nŭb) *n.* **1.** A lump or knob. **2.** The gist or point. — **nub'by** *adj.*

**nu·cle·us** (n/y/ōō'klē·əs) *n., pl.* **-clei** (-klē·ī'). **1.** A central part around which other parts are grouped; core. **2.** A complex structure within a living cell, controlling its metabolism, reproduction, etc. **3.** The positively charged central region of an atom. — **nu'cle·ar** *adj.*

**nude** (n/y/ōōd) *adj.* Without clothing; naked. — *n.* The nude human figure or a representation of it. — **nud'ism'** *n.* — **nud'ist** *n. & adj.* — **nu'di·ty** *n.*

**nudge** (nŭj) *v.* **nudged, nudging.** To push gently. — **nudge** *n.*

**nug·get** (nŭg'ĭt) *n.* A small lump, esp. of natural gold.

**nui·sance** (n/y/ōō'səns) *n.* A source of inconvenience or annoyance; a bother.

**null** (nŭl) *adj.* Having no legal force; invalid. — **nul'li·fi·ca'tion** *n.* — **nul'li·fy'** *v.* — **nul'li·ty** *n.*

**numb** (nŭm) *adj.* **1.** Insensible, as from excessive chill. **2.** Stunned, as from shock. — **numb** *v.* — **numb'ly** *adv.* — **numb'ness** *n.*

**num·ber** (nŭm'bər) *n.* **1.** A member of the set of integers. **2.** A sum or quantity of units. **3.** One item in a sequence or series. — *v.* **1.** To add up to. **2.** To count. **3.** To include in. **4.** To assign a number to. — **num'ber·less** *adj.*

**nu·mer·al** (n/y/ōō'mər·əl) *n.* A symbol used to represent a number. — **nu'mer·al** *adj.* — **nu·mer'i·cal** *adj.* — **nu·mer'i·cal·ly** *adv.*

**nu·mer·a·tor** (n/y/ōō'mə·rā'tər) *n.* The number written above the line in a fraction.

**nu·mer·ous** (n/y/ōō'mər·əs) *adj.* Many. — **nu'mer·ous·ly** *adv.*

**nun** (nŭn) *n.* A woman who belongs to a religious order. — **nun'ner·y** *n.*

**nup·tial** (nŭp'shəl, -chəl) *adj.* Of marriage or the wedding ceremony. — *n.* Often **nuptials.** A wedding ceremony.

**nurse** (nûrs) *n.* **1.** A person trained to care for the sick. **2.** A woman employed to take care of children. — *v.* **nursed, nursing. 1.** To suckle. **2.** To care for or tend (a child or invalid).

**nurs·er·y** (nûr'sə·rē, nûrs'rē) *n.,pl.* **-ies. 1.** A room for children. **2.** A place where plants are grown.

**nur·ture** (nûr'chər) *n.* **1.** Anything that nourishes; food. **2.** Upbringing; rearing. — *v.* **-tured, -turing.** To nourish.

**nut** (nŭt) *n.* **1.** A fruit or seed with a hard shell. **2.** An eccentric person. **3.** A small metal block that holds a bolt or screw. — **nut'crack'er** *n.* — **nut'shell'** *n.* — **nut'ty** *adj.*

**nu·tri·ent** (n/y/ōō'trē·ənt) *n.* A nourishing substance. — **nu'tri·ent** *adj.*

**nu·tri·ment** (n/y/ōō'trə·mənt) *n.* Food.

**nu·tri·tion** (n/y/ōō·trĭsh'ən) *n.* The process of nourishing or being nourished. — **nu·tri'tion·al** *adj.* — **nu·tri'tion·al·ly** *adv.* — **nu·tri'tious** *adj.* — **nu'tri·tive** *adj.*

**nuz·zle** (nŭz'əl) *v.* **-zled, -zling. 1.** To rub or push against gently with the nose or snout. **2.** To nestle or cuddle together.

**ny·lon** (nī'lŏn') *n.* **1.** A high-strength, resilient synthetic material. **2. nylons.** Stockings made of nylon.

**nymph** (nĭmf) *n.* **1.** A female spirit representing a feature of nature. **2.** A young stage of an insect.

# O

**o, O** (ō) *n.* The 15th letter of the English alphabet.

**oak** (ōk) *n.* An acorn-bearing tree with hard, durable wood. — **oak'en** *adj.*

**oar** (ôr, ōr) *n.* A long pole with a blade at one end, used to row a boat. — **oar'lock'** *n.* — **oars'man** *n.*

**o·a·sis** (ō·ā'sĭs) *n., pl.* **-ses.** A fertile spot in a desert.

**oat** (ōt) *n.* A cereal grass having edible seeds. — **oat'meal'** *n.*

**oath** (ōth) *n., pl.* **oaths. 1.** A formal promise to do something. **2.** A curse; profanity.

**ob·du·rate** (ŏb'd/y/ōō-rĭt) *adj.* Stubborn; unyielding. — **ob'du·ra·cy** *n.*

**o·be·lisk** (ŏb'ə·lĭsk) *n.* A four-sided column tapering and ending in a pyramid.

**o·bese** (ō·bēs') *adj.* Extremely fat. — **o·be'si·ty** *n.*

**o·bey** (ō·bā') *v.* To do what one is ordered to do. — **o·be'di·ence** *n.* — **o·be'di·ent** *adj.* — **o·be'di·ent·ly** *adv.*

**ob·fus·cate** (ŏb'fə·skāt', ŏb·fŭs'kāt') *v.* **-cated, -cating.** To confuse; obscure. — **ob'fus·ca'tion** *n.*

**o·bit·u·ar·y** (ō·bĭch'ōō·ĕr'ē) *n., pl.* **-ies.** A notice of death.

**ob·ject'** (əb·jĕkt') *v.* **1.** To present a dissenting or opposing argument. **2.** To disapprove of something. — **ob·jec'tion** *n.* — **ob·jec'tion·a·ble** *adj.*

**ob·ject²** (ŏb´jĭkt, -jĕkt´) *n*. **1.** A material thing. **2.** An aim or purpose. **3.** A noun that receives or is affected by the action of a verb or that follows and is governed by a preposition.

**ob·jec·tive** (ăb-jĕk´tĭv) *adj*. **1.** Of a material object as distinguished from a mental concept, idea, or belief. **2.** Uninfluenced by emotion or personal prejudice. **3.** Denoting the grammatical case of a noun or pronoun serving as the object of a verb or preposition. **4.** Serving as the goal of a course of action. —*n*. **1.** An aim or purpose; a goal. **2.** In grammar, the objective case. —**ob·jec´tive·ly** *adv*. —**ob´jec·tiv·i·ty** *n*.

**ob·li·ga·tion** (ŏb´lə-gā´shən) *n*. **1.** The act of binding oneself by a social, legal, or moral tie. **2.** A binding contract, promise, etc. —**ob·li·gate´** *v*. —**o·blig´a·to·ry** *adj*.

**o·blige** (ə-blīj´) *v*. **obliged, obliging. 1.** To constrain by physical, legal, or moral means. **2.** To make grateful or thankful. **3.** To do a favor for.

**o·blique** (ō-blēk´, ə-) *adj*. **1.** Slanting or sloping. **2.** Indirect or evasive. —**o·blique´ly** *adv*. —**o·bliq´ui·ty** *n*.

**o·blit·er·ate** (ə-blĭt´ə-rāt´) *v*. **-ated, -ating.** To destroy completely; wipe out; erase. —**o·blit´er·a´tion** *n*.

**o·bliv·i·on** (ə-blĭv´ē-ən) *n*. The state of being completely forgotten. —**o·bliv´i·ous** *adj*.

**ob·long** (ŏb´lông´, -lŏng´) *adj*. Shaped like or resembling a rectangle or ellipse. —**ob´long´** *n*.

**ob·lo·quy** (ŏb´lə-kwē) *n*., *pl*. **-quies. 1.** Abusively detractive language; calumny. **2.** Discredit; disgrace.

**ob·nox·ious** (ŏb-nŏk´shəs, əb-) *adj*. Offensive; odious. —**ob·nox´ious·ly** *adv*. —**ob·nox´ious·ness** *n*.

**o·boe** (ō´bō) *n*. A woodwind instrument with a double-reed mouthpiece. —**o´bo·ist** *n*.

**ob·scene** (ŏb-sēn´, əb-) *adj*. **1.** Offensive to decency. **2.** Inciting lustful feelings; lewd. **3.** Disgusting. —**ob·scene´ly** *adv*. —**ob·scen´i·ty** *n*.

**ob·scure** (ŏb-skyoor´, əb-) *adj*. **-scurer, scurest. 1.** Dark; gloomy. **2.** Indistinctly heard or perceived. **3.** Out of sight; hidden. **4.** Difficult to understand. —*v*. **-scured, -scuring. 1.** To make indistinct or unclear. **2.** To conceal; hide. —**ob·scure´ly** *adv*. —**ob·scu´ri·ty** *n*.

**ob·se·qui·ous** (ŏb-sē´kwē-əs, əb-) *adj*. Servile and fawning. —**ob·se´qui·ous·ly** *adv*. —**ob·se´qui·ous·ness** *n*.

**ob·ser·vance** (əb-zûr´vəns) *n*. **1.** Compliance with a law, custom, etc. **2.** The celebration of a holiday or religious festival.

**ob·ser·va·to·ry** (əb-zûr´və-tôr´ē, -tōr´ē) *n*., *pl*. **-ries.** A building equipped for making observations, as in astronomy or meteorology.

**ob·serve** (əb-zûrv´) *v*. **-served, -serving. 1.** To perceive, notice, or watch attentively. **2.** To make a comment. **3.** To abide by. **4.** To celebrate (a holiday, rite, etc.). —**ob·serv´a·ble** *adj*. —**ob·serv´ant** *adj*. —**ob´ser·va´tion** *n*. —**ob·serv´er** *n*.

**ob·ses·sion** (əb-sĕsh´ən, ŏb-) *n*. Compulsive preoccupation with a fixed idea or unwanted feeling. —**ob·sess´** *v*. —**ob·ses´sive** *adj*.

**ob·so·lete** (ŏb´sə-lēt´, ŏb´sə-lēt´) *adj*. No longer in use. —**ob·sess´** *v*. —**ob´so·les´cence** *n*. —**ob´so·les´cent** *adj*.

**ob·sta·cle** (ŏb´stə-kəl) *n*. One that opposes or stands in the way of progress toward some goal.

**ob·stet·rics** (ŏb-stĕt´rĭks, əb-) *n*. The branch of medicine concerned with pregnancy and childbirth. —**ob·stet´ric** *adj*. —**ob´ste·tri´cian** *n*.

**ob·sti·nate** (ŏb´stə-nĭt) *adj*. Stubborn; inflexible. —**ob´sti·na·cy** *n*. —**ob´sti·nate·ly** *adv*.

**ob·strep·er·ous** (ŏb-strĕp´ər-əs, əb-) *adj*. Unruly.

**ob·struct** (əb-strŭkt´, ŏb-) *v*. **1.** To block (a passage) with obstacles. **2.** To impede or retard. **3.** To get in the way of so as to hide. —**ob·struc´tion** *n*. —**ob·struc´tive** *adj*.

**ob·tain** (əb-tān´, ŏb-) *v*. To get or acquire. —**ob·tain´a·ble** *adj*.

**ob·trude** (ŏb-trōōd´, əb-) *v*. **-truded, -truding.** To force (oneself or one's ideas) upon others; intrude. —**ob·tru´sion** *n*. —**ob·tru´sive** *adj*.

**ob·tuse** (ŏb-t/yōōs´, əb-) *adj*. **1.** Not sharp or pointed; blunt. **2.** Slow to understand. —**ob·tuse´ness** *n*.

**obtuse angle.** An angle greater than 90° and less than 180°.

**ob·verse** (ŏb-vûrs´, ŏb´vûrs´) *adj*. Facing the observer. —*n*. The side of a coin that bears the principal design.

**ob·vi·ate** (ŏb´vē-āt´) *v*. **-ated, -ating.** To prevent by making unnecessary.

**ob·vi·ous** (ŏb´vē-əs) *adj*. Easily perceived or understood. —**ob´vi·ous·ly** *adv*. —**ob´vi·ous·ness** *n*.

**oc·ca·sion** (ə-kā´zhən) *n*. **1.** A significant event. **2.** The time of an occurrence. **3.** A favorable time; opportunity. **4.** Ground; reason. —v. To provide occasion for. —**oc·ca'sion·al** adj. —**oc·ca'sion·al·ly** adv.

**Oc·ci·dent** (ŏk'sə-dənt, -dĕnt') n. Europe and the W Hemisphere. —**Oc·ci·den'tal** adj. & n.

**oc·clude** (ə-klōōd') v. **-cluded, -cluding.** To close off; obstruct. —**oc·clu'sion** n.

**oc·cult** (ə-kŭlt', ŏ-kŭlt', ŏk'ŭlt') adj. **1.** Of or dealing with magic, astrology, supernatural powers, etc. **2.** Not readily explained; mysterious.

**oc·cu·pa·tion** (ŏk'yə-pā'shən) n. **1.** A means of making a living; a profession or job. **2.** The act of occupying or state of being occupied. **3.** The invasion and seizure of a nation by a foreign military force. —**oc·cu·pa'tion·al** adj.

**oc·cu·py** (ŏk'yə-pī') v. **-pied, -pying. 1.** To seize possession of (a place or region). **2.** To reside in. **3.** To engage or busy (oneself). —**oc'cu·pan·cy** n. —**oc'cu·pant** n.

**oc·cur** (ə-kûr') v. **-curred, -curring. 1.** To take place. **2.** To exist or appear. **3.** To come to mind. —**oc·cur'rence** n.

**o·cean** (ō'shən) n. **1.** The entire body of salt water that covers about 72% of the earth's surface. **2.** Often **Ocean.** Any of the principal divisions of this body of water. —**o'ce·an'ic** adj. —**o'cean·og·ra·phy** n.

**oc·e·lot** (ŏs'ə-lŏt', ō'sə-) n. A spotted American wild cat.

**oc·ta·gon** (ŏk'tə-gŏn') n. A polygon with eight sides. —**oc·tag'o·nal** adj.

**oc·tane** (ŏk'tān') n. A hydrocarbon occurring in petroleum and used in gasoline to prevent knocking.

**oc·tave** (ŏk'tĭv, -tāv') n. The interval of eight degrees between two musical tones.

**oc·tet** (ŏk-tĕt') n. Also **oc·tette. 1.** A musical composition written for eight voices or instruments. **2.** Any group of eight.

**Oc·to·ber** (ŏk-tō'bər) n. The 10th month of the year.

**oc·to·ge·nar·i·an** (ŏk'tə-jə-nâr'ē-ən) n. Someone between eighty and ninety years of age.

**oc·to·pus** (ŏk'tə-pəs) n., pl. **-puses** or **-pi.** A sea animal with eight sucker-bearing tentacles.

**oc·u·lar** (ŏk'yə-lər) adj. Of the eye.

**oc·u·list** (ŏk'yə-lĭst) n. A physician who treats diseases of the eyes.

**odd** (ŏd) adj. **1. a.** Strange; unusual. **b.** Eccentric in conduct. **2.** In addition to what is usual or approximated. **3.** Being one of an

incomplete pair or set; extra. **4.** Not divisible by two. —**odd'i·ty** n. —**odd'ly** adv.

**odds** (ŏdz) pl.n. **1.** An advantage given to a weaker side. **2.** A ratio expressing the probability of an outcome.

**ode** (ōd) n. A lyric poem characterized by noble style.

**o·di·ous** (ō'dē-əs) adj. Hateful; repugnant. —**o'di·um** n.

**o·dor** (ō'dər) n. Scent; smell. —**o'dor·if·er·ous** adj. —**o'dor·less** adj. —**o'dor·ous** adj.

**od·ys·sey** (ŏd'ə-sē) n. An extended adventurous journey.

**of** (ŭv; unstressed əv) prep. **1.** From. **2.** Owing to. **3.** Away from. **4.** From the total or group comprising. **5.** Composed or made from. **6.** Belonging or connected to. **7.** Possessing; having. **8.** Specified as; named or called. **9.** Before; until.

**off** (ôf, ŏf) adv. **1.** At a distance from. **2.** Distant in time. **3.** So as to be unattached, disconnected, or removed. **4.** So as to be away from work. —adj. **1.** More distant or removed. **2.** Not on, attached, or connected. **3.** Away from work. —prep. **1.** Away from. **2.** Extending or branching out from. **3.** Below the usual level of.

**of·fal** (ô'fəl, ŏf'əl) n. **1.** Waste parts, esp. of a butchered animal. **2.** Refuse; rubbish.

**of·fend** (ə-fĕnd') v. To anger or annoy; affront; displease. —**of·fend'er** n.

**of·fense** (ə-fĕns') n. **1. a.** A violation of a moral or social code. **b.** A crime. **2.** The act of attacking. —**of·fen'sive** adj. & n. —**of·fen'sive·ly** adv.

**of·fer** (ô'fər, ŏf'ər) v. **1.** To present for acceptance or rejection; suggest. **2.** To present for sale. **3.** To propose as payment; bid. **4.** To volunteer. —**of'fer** n. —**of'fer·ing** n.

**of·fice** (ô'fĭs, ŏf'ĭs) n. **1.** A place of business. **2.** A duty or function. **3.** A position of authority. **4.** A public position, esp. an elective one.

**of·fi·cer** (ô'fĭ-sər, ŏf'ĭ-) n. **1.** One who holds an office of authority or trust. **2.** One holding a commission in the armed forces.

**of·fi·cial** (ə-fĭsh'əl) adj. **1.** Of or authorized by a proper authority; authoritative. **2.** Formal or ceremonious. —n. One who holds an office. —**of·fi'cial·dom** n. —**of·fi'cial·ly** adv.

**of·fi·ci·ate** (ə-fĭsh'ē-āt') v. **-ated, -ating.** To perform official duties and functions, esp. as a priest or minister.

**of·fi·cious** (ə-fĭsh'əs) adj. Excessively forward in offering one's services or advice to others. —**of·fi'cious·ly** adv. —**of·fi'cious·ness**

*n.*

**off·set** (ôf'sĕt', ŏf'-) *n.* **1.** Something that balances, counteracts, or compensates. **2.** Printing by indirect image transfer. —*v.* **-set, -setting. 1.** To counterbalance, counteract, or compensate for. **2.** To print by offset. —**off'set'** *adj.*

**off·spring** (ôf'sprĭng', ŏf'-) *n., pl.* **-spring.** Progeny; young.

**of·ten** (ô'fən, ŏf'ən) *adv.* Frequently; repeatedly.

**o·gle** (ō'gəl, ō'-) *v.* **ogled, ogling.** To stare in an impertinent or amorous manner. —**o'gle** *n.*

**o·gre** (ō'gər) *n.* **1.** A fabled man-eating giant. **2.** A cruel or coarse person.

**oh** (ō) *interj.* Expressive of surprise, fear, etc.

**oil** (oil) *n.* A natural or synthetic combustible liquid or liquefiable substance, used in a great variety of products, esp. lubricants and fuels. —*v.* **1.** To lubricate with oil. **2.** To take on fuel oil. —**oil'y** *adj.*

**oint·ment** (oint'mənt) *n.* A viscous salve used for cosmetic or medical purposes.

**o.k.** (ō-kā') *n., pl.* **o.k.'s.** Approval; agreement. —*v.* **o.k.'d, o.k.'ing.** To approve; agree to. —*interj.* Expressive of approval or agreement. —**o.k.** *adj. & adv.*

**old** (ōld) *adj.* **older** or **elder, oldest** or **eldest. 1.** Far advanced in years or life. **2.** Ancient; antique. **3.** Of age. **4.** Mature; experienced. **5.** Of an earlier time. **6.** Worn-out. —*n.* Former times; yore. —**old'en** *adj.*

**old-fash·ioned** (ōld'făsh'ənd) *adj.* Having the beliefs, style, etc., of an earlier era.

**Old World.** The E Hemisphere, esp. Europe. —**old'-world', Old'-World'** *adj.*

**ol·fac·to·ry** (ŏl-făk'tər-ē, -trē, ōl-) *adj.* Of the sense of smell.

**ol·i·gar·chy** (ŏl'ə-gär'kē) *n., pl.* **-chies.** Government by the few, esp. by a small faction. —**ol'i·garch'** *n.* —**ol'i·gar'chic** *adj.*

**ol·ive** (ŏl'ĭv) *n.* **1.** The edible fruit of an Old World tree, pressed to extract a yellowish oil. **2.** Dull yellowish green. —**ol'ive** *adj.*

**om·e·let** (ŏm'lĭt, ŏm'ə-lĭt) *n.* Also **om·e·lette.** A dish consisting of beaten eggs cooked and often folded around a filling.

**o·men** (ō'mən) *n.* A prophetic sign.

**om·i·nous** (ŏm'ə-nəs) *adj.* Of an evil omen; foreboding; threatening. —**om'i·nous·ly** *adv.*

**o·mit** (ō-mĭt') *v.* **omitted, omitting. 1.** To leave out. **2.** To neglect; fail (to do). —**o·mis'sion** *n.*

**om·nip·o·tent** (ŏm-nĭp'ə-tənt) *adj.* All-powerful. —**om·nip'o·tence** *n.*

**om·niv·o·rous** (ŏm-nĭv'ər-əs) *adj.* Eating all kinds of food. —**om·niv'o·rous·ly** *adv.* —**om·niv'o·rous·ness** *n.*

**on** (ŏn, ôn) *prep.* **1.** Atop; in contact with. **2.** Toward or against. **3.** During. **4.** In the state, condition, or process of. **5.** Concerning; about. —*adv.* **1. a.** In the direction of. **b.** Forward. **2.** In or into operation. **3.** In or into a position of being attached to or covering.

**once** (wŭns) *adv.* **1.** One time only. **2.** Formerly. **3.** At any time; ever. —**at once. 1.** Simultaneously. **2.** Immediately. —*conj.* As soon as; when.

**one** (wŭn) *adj.* **1.** Being a single thing. **2.** Of a single kind; undivided. **3.** Designating an unspecified person or thing; a certain. **4.** Single in kind; alike or the same. —*n.* **1.** The cardinal number written 1. **2.** A single person or thing; unit. —*pron.* A person or thing. —**one'ness** *n.*

**on·er·ous** (ŏn'ər-əs, ō'nər-) *adj.* Troublesome; burdensome.

**one·self** (wŭn-sĕlf') *pron.* The reflexive form of the pronoun *one.*

**on·ion** (ŭn'yən) *n.* A plant with an edible bulb of pungent flavor.

**on·ly** (ōn'lē) *adj.* Alone in kind; sole. —*adv.* **1.** Alone. **2. a.** No more than; at least. **b.** Merely. **3.** Exclusively; solely. —*conj.* But.

**on·set** (ŏn'sĕt', ôn'-) *n.* **1.** An attack. **2.** A beginning.

**on·slaught** (ŏn'slôt', ôn'-) *n.* A violent attack.

**on·to** (ŏn'tōō', ôn'-, ŏn'tə, ôn'-) *prep.* On top of; upon.

**o·nus** (ō'nəs) *n.* A burden, esp. a disagreeable responsibility.

**on·ward** (ŏn'wərd, ôn'-) *adv.* Also **on·wards.** Forward; in advance; ahead. —*adj.* Moving forward.

**on·yx** (ŏn'ĭks) *n.* A kind of quartz that occurs in bands of different colors.

**ooze**[1] *v.* **oozed, oozing.** To leak out slowly; exude. —**ooze** *n.*

**ooze**[2] (ōōz) *n.* Soft, thin mud. —**ooz'y** *adj.*

**o·pal** (ō'pəl) *n.* A translucent mineral having iridescent colors and often used as a gem.

**o·paque** (ō-pāk') *adj.* **1. a.** Impenetrable by light. **b.** Not reflecting light. **2.** Obtuse; dense. —**o·pac'i·ty, o·paque'ness** *n.*

**o·pen** (ō'pən) *adj.* **1.** Affording unobstructed passage; not shut or closed. **2.** Having no cover; exposed. **3.** Not sealed. **4.** Accessible to all; unrestricted. **5.** Candid; receptive. —*v.* **1.** To become or cause to become open.

**2.** To spread out or apart. **3.** To remove wrapping from. **4.** To begin. **5.** To become more responsive or understanding. —*n.* The outdoors. —**o'pen-er** *n.* —**o'pen-ing** *n.* —**o'pen-ly** *adv.* —**o'pen-ness** *n.*

**op·er·a** (ŏp'ə-rə, ŏp'rə) *n.* A dramatic presentation set to music. —**op'er·at'ic** *adj.*

**op·er·ate** (ŏp'ə-rāt') *v.* **-ated, -ating. 1.** To function effectively; work. **2.** To perform surgery. **3.** To manage; run. —**op'er·a·ble** *adj.* —**op'er·a'tion** *n.* —**op'er·a'tion·al** *adj.* —**op'er·a'tor** *n.*

**op·er·a·tive** (ŏp'ər-ə-tĭv, ŏp'rə-, ŏp'ə-rā'tĭv) *adj.* **1.** Exerting influence or force. **2.** Functioning; working. —*n.* **1.** A skilled worker. **2.** A secret agent.

**oph·thal·mol·o·gy** (ŏf'thăl-mŏl'ə-jē, ŏf'-thăl-, ŏp'-) *n.* The medical specialty encompassing the eye. —**oph·thal'mic** *adj.* —**oph'thal·mol'o·gist** *n.*

**o·pi·ate** (ō'pē-ĭt, -āt') *n.* **1.** A narcotic containing opium. **2.** Any sedative or narcotic drug.

**o·pin·ion** (ə-pĭn'yən) *n.* **1.** A belief, conclusion, or judgment not substantiated by proof. **2.** An evaluation based on special knowledge.

**o·pin·ion·at·ed** (ə-pĭn'yə-nā'tĭd) *adj.* Holding stubbornly to one's own opinions.

**o·pi·um** (ō'pē-əm) *n.* A narcotic drug made from the dried juice of a certain poppy.

**o·pos·sum** (ə-pŏs'əm, pŏs'əm) *n.* Also **pos·sum.** A furry, tree-dwelling marsupial.

**op·po·nent** (ə-pō'nənt) *n.* One that opposes, as in a fight; adversary.

**op·por·tune** (ŏp'ər-t/y'ōōn') *adj.* **1.** Suitable; appropriate. **2.** Timely.

**op·por·tun·ist** (ŏp'ər-t/y'ōō'nĭst) *n.* One who takes advantage of any opportunity, usually unethically. —**op'por·tun'ism'** *n.* —**op'por·tun·is'tic** *adj.*

**op·por·tu·ni·ty** (ŏp'ər-t/y'ōō'nə-tē) *n., pl.* **-ties.** A favorable combination of circumstances.

**op·pose** (ə-pōz') *v.* **-posed, -posing. 1.** To resist; fight. **2.** To contrast. —**op'po·si'tion** *n.*

**op·po·site** (ŏp'ə-zĭt) *adj.* **1.** Located directly across from. **2.** Facing the other way. **3.** Diametrically opposed; altogether different. —*n.* One that is contrary to another. —**op'po·site·ly** *adv.*

**op·press** (ə-prĕs') *v.* **1.** To govern in a cruel or arbitrary way. **2.** To weigh heavily upon. —**op·pres'sion** *n.* —**op·pres'sive** *adj.* —**op·pres'sor** *n.*

**op·pro·bri·um** (ə-prō'brē-əm) *n.* **1.** Disgrace; ignominy. **2.** Reproach or contempt. —**op·pro'bri·ous** *adj.*

**op·ti·cian** (ŏp-tĭsh'ən) *n.* One who makes or sells lenses and eyeglasses.

**op·tics** (ŏp'tĭks) *n.* The scientific study of light and vision. —**op'tic, op'ti·cal** *adj.*

**op·ti·mism** (ŏp'tə-mĭz'əm) *n.* A tendency to expect the best possible outcome. —**op'ti·mist** *n.* —**op'ti·mis'tic** *adj.*

**op·ti·mum** (ŏp'tə-məm) *n., pl.* **-ma** (-mə) or **-mums.** The best or most favorable condition. —**op'ti·mal** *adj.* —**op'ti·mal·ly** *adv.*

**op·tion** (ŏp'shən) *n.* **1.** The act of choosing; choice. **2.** The freedom to choose. **3.** The right to buy or sell within a specified time and at a specified price. —**op'tion·al** *adj.* —**op'tion·al·ly** *adv.*

**op·tom·e·try** (ŏp-tŏm'ə-trē) *n.* The profession of treating visual defects with corrective lenses. —**op·tom'e·trist** *n.*

**op·u·lent** (ŏp'yə-lənt) *adj.* **1.** Wealthy; rich. **2.** Abundant; copious. —**op'u·lence** *n.*

**or** (ôr; *unstressed* ər) *conj.* —Used to indicate: **1.** An alternative. **2.** An equivalent expression. **3.** Uncertainty or indefiniteness.

**or·a·cle** (ôr'ə-kəl, ŏr'-) *n.* **1. a.** A shrine consecrated to a prophetic god. **b.** A priest or priestess at such a shrine. **2.** A wise adviser.

**o·ral** (ôr'əl, ōr'-) *adj.* **1.** Spoken. **2.** Of the mouth. —**o'ral·ly** *adv.*

**or·ange** (ôr'ĭnj, ŏr'-) *n.* **1.** A round, reddish-yellow citrus fruit. **2.** Reddish yellow. —**or'ange** *adj.*

**o·rang-u·tan** (ō-răng'ə-tăn', ə-răng'-) *n.* A shaggy-haired, long-armed ape.

**o·ra·tion** (ô-rā'shən, ō-rā'-) *n.* A formal speech. —**o·rate'** *v.* —**or'a·tor** *n.*

**or·a·to·ry** (ôr'ə-tôr'ē, -tōr'ē, ŏr'-) *n.* Eloquent public speaking; rhetoric.

**orb** (ôrb) *n.* A sphere; globe.

**or·bit** (ôr'bĭt) *n.* **1.** The path of a celestial body, man-made satellite, etc., as it revolves around another body. **2.** A cavity in the skull for the eye. —*v.* To put into an orbit or move in orbit. —**or'bit·al** *adj.*

**or·chard** (ôr'chərd) *n.* A tract of land where fruit trees are cultivated.

**or·ches·tra** (ôr'kĭ-strə, ôr'kĕs'trə) *n.* **1.** A large ensemble of musicians. **2.** The main floor of a theater. —**or·ches'tral** *adj.*

**or·chid** (ôr'kĭd) *n.* **1.** A tropical plant with irregularly shaped flowers. **2.** The flower of such a plant.

**or·dain** (ôr-dān') *v.* **1.** To invest as a minister, priest, etc. **2.** To decree; order. —**or·**

**dain·ment** *n.* — **or′di·na′tion** *n.*

**or·deal** (ôr-dēl′) *n.* A severely difficult experience.

**or·der** (ôr′dər) *n.* **1.** A logical arrangement among the separate elements of a group. **2.** A sequence of things. **3.** Customary procedure. **4.** A command or direction. **5.** A portion of food in a restaurant. **6.** A monastic institution. **7.** A group of people bound by some common bond or social aim. — *v.* **1.** To issue a command or instruction to. **2.** To request to be supplied with (something). **3.** To put in a systematic arrangement.

**or·der·ly** (ôr′dər-lē) *adj.* **1.** Tidy; neat. **2.** Peaceful; well-behaved. — *n.*, *pl.* **-lies. 1.** A hospital attendant. **2.** A soldier who attends an officer.

**or·di·nal** (ôrd′n-əl) *adj.* Of a specified position in a series.

**or·di·nance** (ôrd′n-əns) *n.* A statute or regulation.

**or·di·nar·y** (ôrd′n-ĕr′ē) *adj.* **1.** Usual; normal. **2.** Average; commonplace. — **or·di·nar′i·ness** *n.* — **or′di·nar′i·ly** *adv.*

**ord·nance** (ôrd′nəns) *n.* Military supplies, esp. weapons and ammunition.

**ore** (ôr, ōr) *n.* A metal-yielding mineral.

**or·gan** (ôr′gən) *n.* **1.** A musical keyboard instrument played by forcing air through pipes. **2.** A part of an organism, adapted for a specific function. **3.** An instrument of communication, esp. a periodical publication. — **or′gan·ist** *n.*

**or·gan·ic** (ôr-găn′ĭk) *adj.* **1.** Of a bodily organ. **2.** Of a living organism. **3.** In chemistry, of carbon compounds. — **or·gan′i·cal·ly** *adv.*

**or·gan·ism** (ôr′gə-nĭz′əm) *n.* Any living being; a plant or animal.

**or·gan·ize** (ôr′gə-nīz′) *v.* **-ized, -izing. 1.** To form a functional, structured whole. **2.** To arrange; systematize. **3.** To induce employees to form or join a union. — **or′gan·i·za′tion** *n.* — **or′gan·i·za′tion·al** *adj.* — **or′gan·iz′er** *n.*

**or·gasm** (ôr′găz′əm) *n.* A sexual climax. — **or·gas′mic** *adj.*

**or·gy** (ôr′jē) *n.*, *pl.* **-gies. 1.** Unrestrained drinking or sexual activity. **2.** Excessive indulgence in any activity. — **or′gi·as′tic** *adj.*

**o·ri·ent** (ôr′ē-ənt, -ĕnt′, ōr′-) *n.* Orient. The countries of Asia, esp. E Asia. — *v.* **1.** To align or position. **2.** To adjust to a situation. — **O′ri·en′tal** *adj. & n.* — **o′ri·en·ta′tion** *n.*

**or·i·fice** (ôr′ə-fĭs, ŏr′-) *n.* An opening; mouth.

**or·i·gin** (ôr′ə-jĭn, ŏr′-) *n.* **1.** A source. **2.** Ancestry. **3.** A coming into being.

**o·rig·i·nal** (ə-rĭj′ə-nəl) *adj.* **1.** First in order or existence. **2.** Fresh and novel. **3.** Creative; inventive. — *n.* **1.** The first form of anything. **2.** An authentic work of art. — **o·rig′i·nal′i·ty** *n.* — **o·rig′i·nal·ly** *adv.*

**o·rig·i·nate** (ə-rĭj′ə-nāt′) *v.* **-nated, -nating. 1.** To come or bring into being; begin. — **o·rig′i·na′tion** *n.*

**o·ri·ole** (ôr′ē-ōl′, ōr′-) *n.* An orange and black songbird.

**or·na·ment** (ôr′nə-mənt) *n.* A decoration or adornment. — *v.* (-mĕnt′). To decorate; adorn. — **or′na·men′tal** *adj.* — **or′na·men·ta′tion** *n.*

**or·nate** (ôr-nāt′) *adj.* **1.** Elaborately ornamented. **2.** Showy in style; florid. — **or·nate′ly** *adv.*

**or·ni·thol·o·gy** (ôr′nə-thŏl′ə-jē) *n.* The study of birds. — **or′ni·tho·log′i·cal** *adj.* — **or′ni·thol′o·gist** *n.*

**or·phan** (ôr′fən) *n.* A child whose parents are dead. — **or′phan·age** *n.*

**or·tho·dox** (ôr′thə-dŏks′) *adj.* Adhering to traditional and established beliefs. — **or′tho·dox′y** *n.*

**or·tho·pe·dics** (ôr′thə-pē′dĭks) *n.* The medical treatment of skeletal-system disorders. — **or′tho·pe′dic** *adj.* — **or′tho·pe′dist** *n.*

**os·cil·late** (ŏs′ə-lāt′) *v.* **-lated, -lating.** To swing back and forth. — **os′cil·la′tion** *n.* — **os′cil·la·to′ry** *adj.*

**os·cu·late** (ŏs′kyə-lāt′) *v.* **-lated, -lating.** To kiss. — **os′cu·la′tion** *n.*

**os·mo·sis** (ŏz-mō′sĭs, ŏs-) *n.* The diffusion of fluid through a porous membrane. — **os·mot′ic** *adj.*

**os·prey** (ŏs′prē, -prā′) *n.*, *pl.* **-preys.** A large fish-eating hawk.

**os·si·fy** (ŏs′ə-fī′) *v.* **-fied, -fying.** To change into bone. — **os′si·fi·ca′tion** *n.*

**os·ten·si·ble** (ŏ-stĕn′sə-bəl) *adj.* Apparent; pretended. — **os·ten′si·bly** *adv.*

**os·ten·ta·tion** (ŏs′tĕn-tā′shən, ŏs′tən-) *n.* Pretentious showiness. — **os′ten·ta′tious** *adj.* — **os′ten·ta′tious·ly** *adv.*

**os·te·op·a·thy** (ŏs′tē-ŏp′ə-thē) *n.* A medical therapy that treats disease through manipulative techniques. — **os′te·o·path′** *n.* — **os′te·o·path′ic** *adj.*

**os·tra·cize** (ŏs′trə-sīz′) *v.* **-cized, -cizing.** To banish or exclude from a group. — **os′tra·cism′** *n.*

**os·trich** (ŏs′trĭch, ôs′-) *n.* A large, long-legged, flightless African bird.

**oth·er** (ŭth'ər) *adj.* **1.** Being or designating the remaining one. **2.** Different. **3.** Additional; extra. —*pron.* **1.** The remaining one. **2.** A different or additional person or thing. —*adv.* Differently.

**oth·er·wise** (ŭth'ər-wīz') *adv.* **1.** In another way; differently. **2.** Under other circumstances. —*adj.* Other than supposed.

**ot·ter** (ŏt'ər) *n.* A weasellike aquatic mammal with dark-brown fur.

**ought** (ôt) *v.* —Used as an auxiliary verb to indicate: **1.** Obligation. **2.** Expediency. **3.** Desirability. **4.** Probability.

**ounce** (ouns) *n.* **1.** A unit of weight equal to 16 drams. **2.** A unit of liquid measure equal to 8 fluid drams or 1.804 cubic inches. **3.** A tiny bit.

**our** (our) *A possessive form of* we.

**ours** (ourz) *A possessive form of* we.

**our·selves** (our-sĕlvz', är-) *pron.* The reflexive form of *we.*

**oust** (oust) *v.* To eject; force out. —**oust'er** *n.*

**out** (out) *adv.* **1.** Away from inside. **2.** Away from the center. **3.** Away from a usual place. **4.** To depletion or extinction. —*adj.* **1.** Exterior; external. **2.** Unable to be used. —*prep.* **1.** Through; forth from. **2.** Beyond or outside of. —*n.* A means of escape.

**out·cast** (out'kăst', -käst') *n.* One that has been excluded. —**out'cast'** *adj.*

**out·come** (out'kŭm') *n.* A result; consequence.

**out·door** (out'dōr', -dôr') *adj.* Located or done in the open air. —**out·doors'** *adv. & n.*

**out·fit** (out'fĭt') *n.* A set of equipment or clothing, esp. for a special purpose. —*v.* To provide with an outfit.

**out·go·ing** (out'gō'ĭng) *adj.* **1.** Departing. **2.** Friendly; sociable.

**out·ing** (ou'tĭng) *n.* A pleasure trip.

**out·land·ish** (out-lăn'dĭsh) *adj.* Conspicuously odd; bizarre. —**out·land'ish·ly** *adv.* —**out·land'ish·ness** *n.*

**out·law** (out'lô') *n.* **1.** A person excluded from normal legal protection. **2.** One who lives lawlessly. —*v.* **1.** To ban. **2.** To deprive of the protection of the law.

**out·lay** (out'lā') *n.* An expenditure.

**out·let** (out'lĕt', -lĭt) *n.* **1.** A passage for escape or exit. **2.** A means of releasing emotions, energies, etc. **3.** A market for commercial goods. **4.** An electric receptacle with a socket for a plug.

**out·line** (out'līn') *n.* **1.** A line forming the boundary of an object. **2.** Drawing in which

objects are depicted only in lines. **3.** A general description or summary. —*v.* **1.** To draw the outline of. **2.** To give the main points of. —**lined, ·lining.**

**out·look** (out'lŏok') *n.* **1.** The view seen from a place. **2.** A point of view; attitude. **3.** An expectation.

**out·ly·ing** (out'lī'ĭng) *adj.* Distant or remote.

**out·put** (out'pŏot') *n.* An amount of something produced, esp. during a given period of time.

**out·rage** (out'rāj') *n.* **1.** An extremely vicious or wicked act. **2.** Great anger aroused by such an act. —*v.* **1.** To give offense to. **2.** To make extremely angry. —**out·ra'geous** *adj.*

**out·right** (out'rīt', -rīt') *adj.* **1.** Wholly; openly. **2.** Without delay. —*adj.* **1.** Unqualified. **2.** Complete.

**out·side** (out-sīd', out'sīd') *n.* **1.** The outer surface; exterior. **2.** The external aspect. **3.** The space beyond a boundary or limit. —*adj.* **1.** Coming from without. **2.** External. **3.** Slight; remote. —*adv.* On or to the outside. —*prep.* **1.** On or to the outer side of. **2.** Except. —**out·sid'er** *n.*

**out·skirts** (out'skŭrts') *pl.n.* The surrounding areas.

**out·spo·ken** (out-spō'kən) *adj.* Frank and direct. —**out·spo'ken·ly** *adv.*

**out·stand·ing** (out'stăn'dĭng, out-stăn'dĭng) *adj.* **1.** Prominent; distinguished. **2.** Not paid or settled.

**out·ward** (out'wərd) *adj.* **1.** Toward the outside. **2.** Outer. —*adv.* Also **out·wards.** Toward the outside. —**out'ward·ly** *adv.*

**o·va.** *pl. of* ovum.

**o·val** (ō'vəl) *adj.* Egg-shaped; elliptical. —**o'val** *n.*

**o·va·ry** (ō'və-rē) *n., pl.* **-ries.** A female reproductive gland. —**o·var'i·an, o·var'i·al** *adj.*

**o·va·tion** (ō-vā'shən) *n.* Enthusiastic applause.

**ov·en** (ŭv'ən) *n.* A compartment for baking, heating, or drying.

**o·ver** (ō'vər) *prep.* **1.** Above. **2.** Above and across. **3.** On the other side of. **4.** Upon. **5.** Throughout or during. **6.** Concerning. —*adv.* **1.** Above. **2.** Across an intervening distance. **3.** So as to be completely covered. **4.** From an upward to an inverted or reversed position. **5.** Again. **6.** In addition or excess. —*adj.* **1.** Finished. **2.** a. Upper. b. Outer. **3.** In excess. —**o'ver·ly** *adv.*

**o·ver·alls** (ō'vər-ôlz') *pl.n.* Loose-fitting trousers with shoulder straps.

**o·ver·bear·ing** (ō′vər-bâr′ĭng) adj. Domineering; arrogant. —**o′ver·bear′ing·ly** adv.

**o·ver·cast** (ō′vər-kăst′, -kăst′, ō′vər-kăst′, -kăst′) adj. Clouded; gloomy.

**o·ver·coat** (ō′vər-kōt′) n. A heavy outdoor coat.

**o·ver·come** (ō′vər-kŭm′) v. 1. To defeat 2. To surmount. 3. To overpower or exhaust.

**o·ver·do** (ō′vər-dōō′) v. 1. To exaggerate. 2. To do too much.

**o·ver·flow** (ō′vər-flō′) v. 1. To flow over the top or banks (of). 2. To flood. —n. (ō′vər-flō′). 1. A flood. 2. An excess.

**o·ver·hang** (ō′vər-hăng′) v. To project over, out, or beyond. —**o′ver·hang′** n.

**o·ver·haul** (ō′vər-hôl′, ō′vər-hôl′) v. To dismantle for needed repairs. —**o′ver·haul′** n.

**o·ver·head** (ō′vər-hĕd′) adj. Above the level of the head. —n. The operating expenses of a business. —adv. Over or above the level of the head.

**o·ver·lap** (ō′vər-lăp′) v. -lapped, -lapping. 1. To extend over. 2. To coincide partly. —**o′ver·lap′** n.

**o·ver·look** (ō′vər-lŏŏk′) v. 1. To afford a view over. 2. To miss or disregard. 3. To supervise.

**o·ver·night** (ō′vər-nīt′) adj. Lasting for a night. —adv. (ō′vər-nīt′). 1. During the night. 2. Suddenly.

**o·ver·rule** (ō′vər-rōōl′) v. To disallow; invalidate.

**o·ver·seas** (ō′vər-sēz′, ō′vər-sēz′) adv. Beyond the sea; abroad. —**o′ver·seas′** adj.

**o·ver·see** (ō′vər-sē′) v. To supervise. —**o′ver·se′er** n.

**o·ver·sight** (ō′vər-sīt′) n. An unintentional mistake.

**o·vert** (ō-vûrt′, ō′vûrt′) adj. Not concealed; open. —**o·vert′ly** adv.

**o·ver·take** (ō′vər-tāk′) v. To catch up with.

**o·ver·throw** (ō′vər-thrō′) v. 1. To bring about the downfall of. 2. To throw something over and beyond. —**o′ver·throw′** n.

**o·ver·time** (ō′vər-tīm′) n. Time, esp. working hours, beyond an established limit. —**o′ver·time′** adv. & adj.

**o·ver·ture** (ō′vər-chŏŏr′) n. 1. An instrumental introduction to an extended musica′ work. 2. An offer or proposal.

**o·ver·ween·ing** (ō′vər-wē′nĭng) adj. Arrogant.

**o·ver·whelm** (ō′vər-hwĕlm′) v. 1. To engulf. 2. To overpower. —**o′ver·whelm′ing** adj.

**o·void** (ō′void′) adj. Egg-shaped.

**o·vu·late** (ō′vyə-lāt′) v. -lated, -lating. To produce ova. —**o′vu·la′tion** n.

**o·vum** (ō′vəm) n., pl. **ova**. A female reproductive cell; an egg.

**owe** (ō) v. **owed, owing**. 1. To be in debt to. 2. To be obliged for. —**owing to**. Because of.

**owl** (oul) n. A night-flying bird of prey. —**owl′et** n. —**owl′ish** adj.

**own** (ōn) adj. Of or belonging to. —v. 1. To possess. 2. To acknowledge or confess. —**own′er** n. —**own′er·ship′** n.

**ox** (ŏks) n., pl. **oxen** An adult castrated bull.

**ox·ide** (ŏk′sīd′) n. A compound of an element or radical with oxygen.

**ox·i·dize** (ŏk′sə-dīz′) v. -dized, -dizing. 1. To combine with oxygen. 2. To rust. —**ox′i·di·za′tion** n. —**ox′i·diz′er** n.

**ox·y·gen** (ŏk′sĭ-jən) n. A colorless, tasteless, odorless gaseous element, constituting 21% of the atmosphere by volume, required for nearly all combustion and combustive processes.

**oys·ter** (oi′stər) n. An edible bivalve mollusk.

**o·zone** (ō′zōn′) n. A blue, gaseous form of oxygen found in the atmosphere.

# P

**p, P** (pē) n. The 16th letter of the English alphabet.

**pace** (pās) n. 1. A step made in walking. 2. Rate of progress. 3. A horse's gait. —v. **paced, pacing**. 1. To go at a pace. 2. To measure by paces. 3. To set the speed for. —**pac′er** n.

**pach·y·derm** (păk′ĭ-dûrm′) n. A large, thick-skinned animal, as the elephant or rhinoceros.

**pac·i·fism** (păs′ə-fĭz′əm) n. Opposition to war or violence as a means of resolving disputes. —**pac′i·fist** n. & adj.

**pac·i·fy** (păs′ə-fī′) v. -fied, -fying. 1. To calm; appease. 2. To establish peace in; subdue. —**pac′i·fi·ca′tion** n. —**pac′i·fi′er** n.

**pack** (păk) n. 1. A bundle. 2. A package containing a standard number of similar items. —v. 1. To combine into a bundle. 2. To cover. 3. To fill up tight; cram. 4. To

**pact** 158

compact firmly. —**pack'age** n. & v. —**pack'er** n. —**pack'et** n.

**pact** (păkt) n. 1. A treaty. 2. A compact; bargain.

**pad** (păd) n. 1. A cushion or something functioning as a cushion. 2. Sheets of paper, stacked and glued together at one end. —v. **padded, padding.** To line or fill with padding.

**pad·dle** (păd'l) n. An oar for a canoe. —v. **-dled, -dling.** 1. To row with a paddle. 2. To play in shallow water. —**pad'dler** n.

**pad·lock** (păd'lŏk') n. A detachable lock. —**pad'lock'** v.

**pa·gan** (pā'gən) n. One who is not a Christian, Moslem, or Jew. —**pa'gan** adj. —**pa'gan·ism'** n.

**page** (pāj) n. A leaf of a book. —v. **paged, paging.** To number the pages of.

**pag·eant** (păj'ənt) n. An elaborate public spectacle. —**pag'eant·ry** n.

**paid** (pād) p.t. & p.p. of **pay.**

**pail** (pāl) n. A bucket.

**pain** (pān) n. 1. An unpleasant feeling or hurting arising from injury, disease, etc. 2. Suffering or distress. 3. **pains.** Trouble; effort. —v. To cause or suffer pain. —**pain'ful** adj. —**pain'ful·ly** adv. —**pain'less** adj. —**pain'less·ly** adv. —**pains'tak'ing** adj. —**pains'tak'ing·ly** adv.

**paint** (pānt) n. A mixture of a pigment in a liquid. —v. 1. To coat with paint. 2. To paint pictures. —**paint'er** n. —**paint'ing** n.

**pair** (pâr) n., pl. **pairs** or **pair.** 1. Two persons or items, similar in form or function. 2. Something composed of two corresponding parts. —v. To arrange in or form a pair or pairs.

**pa·ja·mas** (pə-jä'məz, -jăm'əz) pl.n. An outfit of jacket and trousers, for sleeping or lounging.

**pal·ace** (păl'ĭs) n. The official residence of a royal person. —**pa·la'tial** adj.

**pal·ate** (păl'ĭt) n. 1. The roof of the mouth. 2. The sense of taste. —**pal'at·a·ble** adj. —**pal'a·tal** adj.

**pale**[1] (pāl) n. 1. A stake or picket. 2. The area enclosed by a fence or boundary. —**pal'ing** n.

**pale**[2] (pāl) adj. **paler, palest.** 1. Pallid. 2. Of a low intensity of color; light. 3. Dim. —v. **paled, paling.** To make or become pale. —**pale'ness** n.

**pall** (pôl) v. 1. To make or become boring or wearisome. 2. To cloy.

**pal·li·ate** (păl'ē-āt') v. **-ated, -ating.** 1. To

excuse. 2. To alleviate. —**pal'li·a'tion** n. —**pal'li·a'tive** adj. & n.

**pal·lid** (păl'ĭd) adj. Pale; wan.

**pal·lor** (păl'ər) n. Extreme or unnatural paleness.

**palm**[1] (päm) n. The inner surface of the hand. —v. To conceal in the palm.

**palm**[2] (päm) n. A tropical tree usually having an unbranched trunk with fanlike leaves.

**pal·pa·ble** (păl'pə-bəl) adj. 1. Capable of being felt; tangible. 2. Easily perceived; obvious. —**pal'pa·bil'i·ty** n. —**pal'pa·bly** adv.

**pal·pi·tate** (păl'pə-tāt') v. **-tated, -tating.** 1. To shake. 2. To beat rapidly; throb. —**pal'pi·ta'tion** n.

**pal·try** (pôl'trē) adj. **-trier, -triest.** Petty; trifling.

**pam·per** (păm'pər) v. To coddle; cater to. —**pam'per·er** n.

**pam·phlet** (păm'flĭt) n. A booklet with a paper cover and no binding. —**pam'phlet·eer'** n.

**pan** (păn) n. A shallow, wide, open container used for holding liquids, for cooking, etc. —v. **panned, panning.** To wash (gravel, sand, etc.) in a pan to separate precious metal.

**pan·a·ce·a** (păn'ə-sē'ə) n. A cure-all.

**pan·cake** (păn'kāk') n. A batter cake cooked on a skillet.

**pan·cre·as** (păng'krē-əs, păn'-) n. A gland that secretes juice that aids digestion. —**pan'cre·at'ic** adj.

**pan·de·mo·ni·um** (păn'də-mō'nē-əm) n. Wild uproar.

**pane** (pān) n. A sheet of glass in a window or door.

**pan·el** (păn'əl) n. 1. A flat piece, as a board, forming part of a surface or overlaying it. 2. A group of people selected to make a judgment, etc. —v. To cover with panels. —**pan'el·ing** n. —**pan'el·ist** n.

**pang** (păng) n. A sudden feeling of pain or distress.

**pan·han·dle** (păn'hănd'l) v. **-dled, -dling.** To beg. —**pan'han'dler** n.

**pan·ic** (păn'ĭk) n. An overpowering terror. —v. **-icked, -icking.** To affect or be affected with panic. —**pan'ick·y** adj.

**pan·o·ram·a** (păn'ə-răm'ə, -rä'mə) n. 1. A view over a wide area. 2. A view or picture of a long series of events. —**pan'o·ram'ic** adj. —**pan'o·ram'i·cal·ly** adv.

**pant** (pănt) v. 1. To breathe in short gasps. 2. To yearn desperately. —n. A short, quick gasp. —**pant'ing·ly** adv.

**pan·to·mime** (păn'tə-mīm') n. A theatrical performance in which the actors use motions and gestures rather than speech. —v. **-mimed, -miming.** To act in pantomime.

**pan·try** (păn'trē) n., pl. **-tries.** A small room off a kitchen for storage.

**pants** (pănts) pl.n. A pair of trousers.

**pap** (păp) n. Soft or semiliquid food.

**pa·pal** (pā'pəl) adj. Of the pope. —**pa'pal·ly** adv. —**pa'pa·cy** n.

**pa·per** (pā'pər) n. **1.** A thin material derived mainly from wood and rags. **2.** An official document. **3.** An essay, report, etc. **4.** A newspaper. —v. To cover with wallpaper. —adj. Made of paper. —**pa'per·y** adj.

**pa·pier·mâ·ché** (pā'pər-mə-shā') n. Paper pulp mixed with glue or paste, that can be molded when wet.

**par** (pär) n. **1.** An accepted average. **2.** An equal status. **3.** The face value of a stock, bond, etc.

**par·a·ble** (păr'ə-bəl) n. A simple story illustrating a moral.

**par·a·chute** (păr'ə-shōōt') n. An umbrella-shaped apparatus used to slow the fall of persons or things from great heights. —v. **-chuted, -chuting.** To drop or descend by parachute. —**par'a·chut'ist** n.

**pa·rade** (pə-rād') n. A public procession held on a ceremonial occasion. —v. **-raded, -rading. 1.** To march in or as in a parade. **2.** To flaunt. —**pa·rad'er** n.

**par·a·dise** (păr'ə-dīs', -dīz') n. **1.** Heaven. **2.** A place of perfect happiness or beauty.

**par·a·dox** (păr'ə-dŏks') n. A seemingly contradictory statement that may nonetheless be true. —**par·a·dox'i·cal** adj. —**par'a·dox'i·cal·ly** adv.

**par·af·fin** (păr'ə-fĭn) n. A waxy mixture used to make candles, sealing materials, etc.

**par·a·gon** (păr'ə-gŏn', -gən) n. A model of excellence.

**par·a·graph** (păr'ə-grăf', -grăf') n. A distinct division of a written work or composition, begun on a new line. —v. To arrange in paragraphs.

**par·a·keet** (păr'ə-kēt') n. A small parrot.

**par·al·lel** (păr'ə-lĕl') adj. **1.** Being an equal distance at every point so as never to intersect. **2.** Corresponding. —n. **1.** A surface or line that is parallel. **2.** A set of parallel lines. **3.** Anything that closely resembles something else. —v. **1.** To extend parallel to. **2.** To correspond to.

**par·al·lel·o·gram** (păr'ə-lĕl'ə-grăm') n. A four-sided plane figure with opposite sides parallel.

**pa·ral·y·sis** (pə-răl'ə-sĭs) n., pl. **-ses.** Loss of movement or sensation in a bodily part. —**par'a·lyt'ic** adj. & n. —**par'a·lyze'** v.

**par·a·mount** (păr'ə-mount') adj. Primary; foremost.

**par·a·noi·a** (păr'ə-noi'ə) n. A mental disorder characterized by delusions of persecution or grandeur. —**par'a·noi'ac** n. —**par'a·noid'** adj.

**par·a·pher·na·lia** (păr'ə-fər-nāl'yə, -fə-nāl'-yə) n. **1.** Personal belongings. **2.** Equipment; gear.

**par·a·phrase** (păr'ə-frāz') n. A restatement in other words. —**par'a·phrase'** v.

**par·a·ple·gi·a** (păr'ə-plē'jē-ə, -jə) n. Paralysis of the lower half of the body. —**par·a·ple'gic** adj. & n.

**par·a·site** (păr'ə-sīt') n. An often harmful organism that lives on or in a different organism.

**par·a·sol** (păr'ə-sôl', -sōl') n. A light umbrella.

**par·a·troops** (păr'ə-trōōps') pl.n. Infantry trained and equipped to parachute. —**par'a·troop'er** n.

**par·boil** (pär'boil') v. To cook partially.

**par·cel** (pär'səl) n. **1.** A bundle; package. **2.** A portion or plot of land. —v. To divide into portions.

**parch** (pärch) v. **1.** To make or become very dry, esp. by heat. **2.** To make thirsty.

**par·don** (pärd'n) v. **1.** To forgive. **2.** To excuse. —n. The act of pardoning. —**par'don·a·ble** adj. —**par'don·a·bly** adv.

**pare** (pâr) v. **pared, paring.** To peel.

**par·ent** (pâr'ənt) n. A father or mother. —**par'ent·age** n. —**pa·ren'tal** adj. —**par'ent·hood'** n.

**pa·ren·the·sis** (pə-rĕn'thə-sĭs) n., pl. **-ses.** One of a pair of upright curved lines, ( ), used to mark off additional remarks in printing and writing. —**par'en·thet'ic, par'en·thet'i·cal** adj. —**par'en·thet'i·cal·ly** adv.

**par·fait** (pär-fā') n. A frozen dessert.

**pa·ri·ah** (pə-rī'ə) n. A social outcast.

**par·ish** (păr'ĭsh) n. An administrative part of a diocese. —**pa·rish'ion·er** n.

**par·i·ty** (păr'ə-tē) n., pl. **-ties. 1.** Equality. **2.** Similarity. **3.** A level for farm-product prices, maintained by governmental support.

**park** (pärk) n. Enclosed grounds for recreational use. —v. To leave (a vehicle) for a time in a certain location.

**par·ka** (pär'kə) n. A hooded jacket.

# P-16

**par·ley** (pär′lē) n., pl. **-leys.** A conference, esp. between opponents. **—par′ley** v.

**par·lia·ment** (pär′lə-mənt) n. A legislative body. **—par·lia·men·ta·ry** adj.

**par·lor** (pär′lər) n. **1.** A room for the entertainment of visitors. **2.** A room designed for some special function or business.

**pa·ro·chi·al** (pə-rō′kē-əl) adj. Of a parish. **—pa·ro′chi·al·ly** adv.

**par·o·dy** (păr′ə-dē) n., pl. **-dies.** A comic imitation of a work of literature or music. **—par′o·dy** v.

**pa·role** (pə-rōl′) n. The early release of a prisoner on condition of good behavior. **—pa·role′** v. **—pa·rol·ee′** n.

**par·ox·ysm** (păr′ək-sĭz′əm) n. A sudden outburst. **—par·ox·ys′mal** adj.

**par·quet** (pär-kā′) n. A floor made of inlaid pieces of wood in a design.

**par·rot** (păr′ət) n. A bird having a hooked bill, brightly colored plumage, and sometimes the ability to mimic speech. —v. To repeat without understanding.

**par·si·mo·ny** (pär′sə-mō′nē) n. Unusual frugality. **—par·si·mo′ni·ous** adj.

**par·son** (pär′sən) n. A clergyman. **—par′son·age** n.

**part** (pärt) n. **1.** A portion or division of a whole. **2.** Duty. —v. To divide. —adv. Partially. —adj. Not full or complete. **—part′ly** adv.

**par·take** (pär-tāk′) v. **-took, -taken, -taking.** To take or be given a portion. **—par·tak′er** n.

**par·tial** (pär′shəl) adj. **1.** Incomplete. **2.** Prejudiced. **3.** Especially fond. **—par·ti·al′i·ty** n. **—par′tial·ly** adv.

**par·tic·i·pate** (pär-tĭs′ə-pāt′) v. **-pated, -pating.** To join or share with others. **—par·tic′i·pant** n. **—par·tic·i·pa′tion** n.

**par·ti·ci·ple** (pär′tĭ-sĭp′əl) n. A form of a verb that can function as an adjective or noun. **—par·ti·cip′i·al** adj.

**par·ti·cle** (pär′tĭ-kəl) n. A very small piece; speck.

**par·tic·u·lar** (pär-tĭk′yə-lər) adj. **1.** Of a single person, group, or thing. **2.** Worthy of note. **3.** Concerned with details; fussy. —n. An individual item, fact, or detail. **—par·tic′u·lar·ly** n. n. adv.

**par·ti·san** (pär′tə-zən) n. **1.** A supporter of a cause, etc. **2.** A guerrilla. **—par′ti·san** adj. **—par′ti·san·ship** n.

**par·ti·tion** (pär-tĭsh′ən) n. **1.** A dividing something into parts. **2.** A partial wall dividing a room or larger area.

**part·ner** (pärt′nər) n. A person associated with another in some common activity, esp. in a business. **—part′ner·ship** n.

**par·took** (pär-tŏŏk′). p.t. of partake.

**par·tridge** (pär′trĭj) n. A game bird.

**par·ty** (pär′tē) n., pl. **-ties.** **1.** A social gathering. **2.** A group of persons participating in some common activity. **—par′ty** adj. & v.

**pass** (păs, päs) v. **1.** To go by or ahead; proceed. **2.** To run; extend. **3.** To hand over to someone else. **4.** To move past in time; elapse. **5.** To be communicated, exchanged, transferred, or conveyed. **6.** To come to an end; be terminated. **7.** To undergo (an examination, etc.) with favorable results. **8.** To approve; adopt. —n. **1.** The act of passing. **2.** A narrow passage between mountains. **3.** An authorization to be admitted without charge. **4.** Written leave of absence, esp. from military duty. **5.** A predicament. **—pass′a·ble** adj. **—pass′a·bly** adv.

**pas·sage** (păs′ĭj) n. **1.** The act of passing. **2.** Movement; transit. **3.** The process of elapsing. **4.** A journey. **5.** The right to travel. **6.** A segment of a literary work or musical composition. **—pas′sage·way** n.

**pas·sen·ger** (păs′ən-jər) n. A person traveling in a train, aircraft, ship, etc.

**pas·sion** (păsh′ən) n. **1.** A powerful emotion or appetite. **2.** Sexual desire. **—pas′sion·ate** adj. **—pas′sion·ate·ly** adv.

**pas·sive** (păs′ĭv) adj. **1.** Not active but acted upon. **2.** Accepting without resistance. **—pas′sive·ly** adv. **—pas·siv′i·ty, pas′sive·ness** n.

**pass·port** (păs′pôrt′, -pōrt′, päs′-) n. An official document for traveling abroad.

**past** (păst, päst) adj. **1.** Gone by; over. **2.** Having occurred in an earlier time. **3.** Denoting a verb form used to express action before the time it is expressed. —n. **1.** The time before the present. **2.** A person's background, career, etc. **3.** A verb form in the past tense. —adv. So as to pass by. —prep. **1.** By and beyond. **2.** Beyond in position, time, extent, or amount.

**paste** (pāst) n. **1.** A smooth, sticky substance used to fasten things together. **2.** A hard, brilliant glass used for artificial gems. —v. **pasted, pasting.** To fasten with paste.

**pas·tel** (pă-stĕl′) n. A delicate hue. **—pas·tel′** adj.

**pas·teur·i·za·tion** (păs′chər-ə-zā′shən) n. The destruction of most disease-producing bacteria in milk, beer, and other liquids by sterilization. **—pas′teur·ize′** v.

**pas·tor** (păs′tər, päs′-) n. A minister.

**peasant**

**P-16**

**pas·tor·al** (păs′tər-əl, păs′-) *adj.* **1.** Of shepherds. **2.** Of the country; rural. **3.** Of a pastor.

**pas·try** (pās′trē) *n., pl.* **-tries.** Baked foods, such as pies or tarts, made with a rich dough.

**pas·ture** (păs′chər) *n.* Land used for grazing. —*v.* **-tured, -turing.** **1.** To put in a pasture. **2.** To graze.

**pat** (păt) *v.* **patted, patting.** To tap gently. —*n.* **1.** A light stroke or tap. **2.** A small mass. —*adj.* Of a set form.

**patch** (păch) *n.* **1.** A piece of material used to cover a hole or worn place. **2.** A small piece or part of anything. —*v.* To put a patch or patches on. — **patch′work′** *n.*

**pat·ent** (păt′ənt) *n.* A grant assuring an inventor the sole right to make, use, and sell an invention. —*adj.* (pā′tənt). **1.** Obvious; plain. **2.** Protected by a patent. —*v.* To obtain a patent on.

**pa·ter·nal** (pə-tûr′nəl) *adj.* **1.** Of a father. **2.** On the father's side of a family. — **pa·ter′ni·ty** *n.*

**path** (păth, päth) *n.* **1.** A track or way made by footsteps. **2.** A course of action or conduct.

**pa·thol·o·gy** (pă-thŏl′ə-jē) *n., pl.* **-gies.** The study of disease. — **path′o·log′i·cal** *adj.* — **path′o·log′i·cal·ly** *adv.* — **pa·thol′o·gist** *n.*

**pa·thos** (pā′thŏs′, -thôs′) *n.* A quality in something or someone that arouses pity. — **pa·thet′ic** *adj.* — **pa·thet′i·cal·ly** *adv.*

**pa·tient** (pā′shənt) *adj.* Capable of bearing affliction, delay, etc., with calmness. —*n.* One under medical treatment. — **pa′tience** *n.* — **pa′tient·ly** *adv.*

**pat·i·na** (păt′ə-nə) *n.* A thin layer of corrosion on copper or bronze.

**pat·i·o** (păt′ē-ō′, pä′tē-ō′) *n., pl.* **-os.** An inner, roofless courtyard.

**pa·tri·arch** (pā′trē-ärk′) *n.* **1.** The paternal leader of a family or tribe. **2.** A venerable old man. — **pa′tri·ar′chal** *adj.*

**pat·ri·mo·ny** (păt′rə-mō′nē) *n., pl.* **-nies.** An inheritance. — **pat′ri·mo′ni·al** *adj.*

**pa·tri·ot** (pā′trē-ət, -ŏt′) *n.* One who loves and defends his country. — **pa′tri·ot′ic** *adj.* — **pa′tri·ot′i·cal·ly** *adv.* — **pa′tri·ot·ism′** *n.*

**pa·trol** (pə-trōl′) *n.* **1.** Moving about an area, esp. for security. **2.** A person or group performing such an action. —*v.* **-trolled, -trolling.** To engage in a patrol.

**pa·tron** (pā′trən) *n.* **1.** A benefactor. **2.** A regular customer. — **pa′tron·age** *n.*

**pa·tron·ize** (pā′trə-nīz′, păt′rə-) *v.* **-ized, -izing.** **1.** To go to regularly as a customer.

**2.** To treat condescendingly. — **pa′tron·iz′er** *n.*

**pat·tern** (păt′ərn) *n.* **1.** A model to be followed in making things. **2.** An artistic or decorative design. —*v.* To make by following a pattern.

**pau·ci·ty** (pô′sə-tē) *n.* Short supply.

**paunch** (pônch, pänch) *n.* The belly, esp. a protruding one. — **paunch′y** *adv.*

**pau·per** (pô′pər) *n.* A very poor person.

**pause** (pôz) *v.* **paused, pausing.** To stop action briefly. —*n.* A temporary stop.

**pave** (pāv) *v.* **paved, paving.** To cover (a road, etc.) with a hard, smooth surface that will bear travel. — **pav′er** *n.*

**pa·vil·ion** (pə-vĭl′yən) *n.* **1.** An ornate tent. **2.** An open structure with a roof, used for amusement or shelter.

**paw** (pô) *n.* The clawed foot of an animal, as a dog or cat. —*v.* To strike, touch, or scrape with a paw.

**pawn** (pôn) *n.* Something given as security for a loan. — **pawn** *v.* — **pawn′shop′** *n.*

**pay** (pā) *v.* **paid, paying.** **1.** To give (money) in exchange for goods or services. **2.** To discharge (a debt). **3.** To yield as return. **4.** To let out (a rope or cable) bit by bit. —*n.* **1.** Salary; wages. **2.** Paid employment. — **pay′a·ble** *adj.* — **pay·ee′** *n.* — **pay′ment** *n.*

**pea** (pē) *n.* A vine with round, edible green seeds.

**peace** (pēs) *n.* **1.** The absence of war or other hostilities. **2.** Calm; tranquillity. — **peace′a·ble** *adj.* — **peace′ful** *adj.* — **peace′ful·ly** *adv.*

**peach** (pēch) *n.* A sweet, juicy fruit with yellowish-pink skin.

**pea·cock** (pē′kŏk′) *n.* The male of a large bird having brilliant blue or green plumage and long tail feathers.

**peak** (pēk) *n.* **1.** A point that projects upward. **2.** The pointed summit of a mountain. **3.** The point of greatest development, value, etc. — **peak** *v.* — **peaked** *adj.*

**peal** (pēl) *n.* A loud sound or series of sounds, as a ringing of bells. —*v.* To resound.

**pea·nut** (pē′nŭt′) *n.* A vine bearing edible nutlike seeds in pods that ripen underground.

**pear** (pâr) *n.* An edible fruit with a rounded base and a tapering stem end.

**pearl** (pûrl) *n.* A smooth, often rounded, lustrous gem formed in the shells of oysters. — **pearl′y** *adj.*

**peas·ant** (pĕz′ənt) *n.* A member of the class of small farmers and farm laborers of

Europe. — **peas'ant·ry** n.

**peat** (pēt) n. Partially carbonized moss or other matter, found in bogs and used as fuel. — **peat'y** adj.

**peb·ble** (pĕb'əl) n. A small stone worn smooth by erosion. — **peb'bly** adj.

**peck**[1] (pĕk) v. To strike with or as with the beak. — n. A stroke or mark made with or as with the beak.

**peck**[2] (pĕk) n. A dry measure, equal to 8 quarts.

**pec·tin** (pĕk'tĭn) n. A substance in ripe fruits, such as apples, used to jell foods, drugs, and cosmetics.

**pec·to·ral** (pĕk'tər-əl) adj. Of the breast or chest.

**pe·cu·liar** (pĭ-kyōōl'yər) adj. 1. Unusual; odd. 2. Distinct and particular. 3. Exclusive. — **pe·cu'li·ar'i·ty** n. — **pe·cu'liar·ly** adv.

**ped·al** (pĕd'l) n. A lever worked by the foot. — adj. Of a foot or footlike part. — v. To operate the pedal or pedals of.

**ped·dle** (pĕd'l) v. **-dled, -dling.** To travel about selling (wares). — **ped'dler** n.

**ped·es·tal** (pĕd'ə-stəl) n. A support or base, as for a column or statue.

**pe·des·tri·an** (pə-dĕs'trē-ən) n. One traveling on foot. — adj. 1. Of pedestrians. 2. Commonplace; ordinary.

**pe·di·at·rics** (pē'dē-ăt'rĭks) n. The branch of medicine that deals with the care and treatment of children. — **pe'di·at'ric** adj. — **pe'di·a·tri'cian** n.

**peek** (pēk) v. To look, peer, glance, or show briefly. — n. A brief or furtive look.

**peel** (pēl) n. The skin or rind, esp. of a fruit. — v. 1. To remove the skin, rind, or bark from. 2. To come off in thin layers. — **peel'er** n.

**peer**[1] (pîr) v. To look intently.

**peer**[2] (pîr) n. 1. An equal. 2. A member of the nobility. — **peer'age** n. — **peer'less** adj.

**peeve** (pēv) v. peeved, peeving. To annoy or make irritable. — **peeve** n. — **pee'vish** adj. — **pee'vish·ly** adv. — **pee'vish·ness** n.

**peg** (pĕg) n. A small cylindrical pin, as of wood, used to fasten things. — v. **pegged, pegging.** To put or insert a peg into.

**pel·let** (pĕl'ĭt) n. A small ball or mass, as of medicine.

**pel·lu·cid** (pə-lōō'sĭd) adj. 1. Transparent. 2. Clear. — **pel·lu'cid·ly** adv.

**pelt**[1] (pĕlt) n. An animal skin.

**pelt**[2] (pĕlt) v. To strike repeatedly with or as with blows or missiles.

**pel·vis** (pĕl'vĭs) n. A basin-shaped, bony structure in the abdomen that supports the backbone. — **pel'vic** adj.

**pen**[1] (pĕn) n. An instrument for writing or drawing with ink. — v. penned, penning. To write.

**pen**[2] (pĕn) n. A small fenced enclosure. — v. penned or pent, penning. To confine in a pen.

**pen·al·ty** (pĕn'əl-tē) n., pl. **-ties.** 1. A punishment for a crime. 2. A handicap or disadvantage. — **pe'nal** adj. — **pe'nal·ize** v.

**pen·ance** (pĕn'əns) n. An act of repentance.

**pen·chant** (pĕn'chənt) n. A strong liking.

**pen·cil** (pĕn'səl) n. A writing implement of graphite encased in wood, etc. — v. To write or mark with a pencil.

**pen·dant** (pĕn'dənt) n. A hanging ornament.

**pend·ing** (pĕn'dĭng) adj. Not yet decided. — prep. Until.

**pen·du·lum** (pĕn'jōō-ləm, pĕn'dyə-, pĕn'də-) n. A suspended mass that swings under the influence of gravity. — **pen'du·lar, pen'du·lous** adj.

**pen·e·trate** (pĕn'ə-trāt') v. **-trated, -trating.** 1. To go or enter into; pierce. 2. To permeate. — **pen'e·tra·ble** adj. — **pen'e·trat'ing·ly** adv. — **pen'e·tra'tion** n.

**pen·guin** (pĕn'gwĭn, pĕng'gwĭn) n. A flightless sea bird having flipperlike wings.

**pen·i·cil·lin** (pĕn'ə-sĭl'ĭn) n. An antibiotic compound used to treat many diseases and infections.

**pen·in·su·la** (pə-nĭn's/y/ə-lə) n. A long projection of land into water. — **pen·in'su·lar** adj.

**pe·nis** (pē'nĭs) n. The male sexual organ.

**pen·i·tent** (pĕn'ə-tənt) adj. Repentant of misdeeds. — **pen'i·tence** n. — **pen'i·tent·ly** adv.

**pen·i·ten·tia·ry** (pĕn'ə-tĕn'shə-rē) n., pl. **-ries.** A prison for those convicted of major crimes.

**pen·nant** (pĕn'ənt) n. A long narrow flag.

**pen·ny** (pĕn'ē) n., pl. **-nies.** A coin, the cent. — **pen'ni·less** adj.

**pen·sion** (pĕn'shən) n. A sum of money paid regularly, esp. to a retired person. — v. To give a pension to. — **pen'sion·er** n.

**pen·sive** (pĕn'sĭv) adj. Deeply thoughtful. — **pen'sive·ly** adv. — **pen'sive·ness** n.

**pent** (pĕnt) v. Alternate p.t. & p.p. of **pen**[2].

**pen·ta·gon** (pĕn'tə-gŏn') n. A plane figure having five sides and five angles. — **pen·tag'o·nal** adj.

**pen·tam·e·ter** (pĕn-tăm'ə-tər) n. A line of verse composed of five metrical feet.

**pe·nu·ri·ous** (pə-n/y/ŏŏr'ē-əs) adj. Miserly. — **pe·nu'ri·ous·ness** n.

**pen·u·ry** (pĕn'yə-rē) n. Extreme poverty.

**peo·ple** (pē'pəl) n. **1.** A body of persons of the same country, culture, etc. **2.** The mass of ordinary persons. **3.** Relatives; family. —v. **-pled, -pling.** To populate.

**pep·per** (pĕp'ər) n. **1.** The berry of a vine, used as a condiment. **2.** The bell-shaped edible fruit of several plants. —v. **1.** To season with pepper. **2.** To sprinkle or spray with many small objects.

**pep·tic** (pĕp'tĭk) adj. Of digestion.

**per·ceive** (pər-sēv') v. **-ceived, -ceiving. 1.** To become aware of the senses. **2.** To understand. — **per·cep'ti·ble** adj. — **per·cep'ti·bly** adv. — **per·cep'tion** n. — **per·cep'tive** adj. — **per·cep'tu·al** adj. — **per·cep'tu·al·ly** adv.

**per cent.** Also **per·cent** (pər-sĕnt'). For or out of each hundred. — **per·cent'age** n.

**perch** (pûrch) n. A rod, branch, etc., serving as a roost for a bird. — **perch** v.

**per·cus·sion** (pər-kŭsh'ən) n. The striking together of two bodies, esp. when noise is produced.

**per·emp·to·ry** (pə-rĕmp'tə-rē) adj. Not admitting denial; imperative. — **per·emp'to·ri·ly** adv. — **per·emp'to·ri·ness** n.

**per·en·ni·al** (pə-rĕn'ē-əl) adj. **1.** Everlasting; perpetual. **2.** In botany, having a life span of more than two years. —n. A perennial plant. — **per·en'ni·al·ly** adv.

**per·fect** (pûr'fĭkt) adj. **1.** Without defect. **2.** Complete. —v. (pər-fĕkt'). To make perfect. — **per·fect'i·ble** adj. — **per·fect'i·bil'i·ty** n. — **per·fec'tion** n. — **per'fect·ly** adv.

**per·fo·rate** (pûr'fə-rāt') v. **-rated, -rating.** To pierce, punch, etc., a hole or holes in. — **per·fo·ra'tion** n. — **per'fo·ra'tor** n.

**per·form** (pər-fôrm') v. **1.** To carry out (an action). **2.** To present or enact (a musical work, dramatic role, etc.) publicly. — **per·form'ance** n. — **per·form'er** n.

**per·fume** (pûr'fyōōm', pər-fyōōm') n. **1.** A fragrant liquid. **2.** A pleasing odor. —v. (pər-fyōōm')-**fumed, -fuming.** To apply or fill with a fragrance.

**per·func·to·ry** (pər-fŭngk'tə-rē) adj. Done with little interest or care. — **per·func'to·ri·ly** adv. — **per·func'to·ri·ness** n.

**per·haps** (pər-hăps') adv. Maybe; possibly.

**per·il** (pĕr'əl) n. **1.** Danger. **2.** Something dangerous. — **per'il·ous** adj. — **per'il·ous·ly** adv.

**pe·rim·e·ter** (pə-rĭm'ə-tər) n. **1.** A closed curve bounding a plane area. **2.** The length of such a boundary.

**pe·ri·od** (pîr'ē-əd) n. **1.** An interval of time.

**2.** A punctuation mark (.) indicating a full stop, placed esp. at the end of sentences. —adj. Of a certain historical age or time.

**pe·ri·od·ic** (pîr'ē-ŏd'ĭk) adj. **1.** Having periods or repeated cycles. **2.** Intermittent. — **pe·ri·od'i·cal·ly** adv.

**pe·ri·od·i·cal** (pîr'ē-ŏd'ĭ-kəl) adj. Periodic. —n. A publication that appears at regular intervals.

**pe·riph·er·y** (pə-rĭf'ə-rē) n., pl. **-ies. 1.** The outermost part within a boundary. **2.** A region immediately beyond a boundary. **3.** A zone constituting an imprecise boundary. **4.** Perimeter. — **pe·riph'er·al** adj. — **pe·riph'er·al·ly** adv.

**per·i·scope** (pĕr'ə-skōp') n. An optical instrument that allows observation of objects that are not in a direct line of sight.

**per·ish** (pĕr'ĭsh) v. To die, esp. in a violent manner.

**per·jure** (pûr'jər) v. **-jured, -juring.** To testify falsely under oath. — **per'jur·er** n. — **per'ju·ry** n.

**per·ma·nent** (pûr'mə-nənt) adj. Fixed and lasting. — **per'ma·nence**, **per'ma·nen·cy** n. — **per'ma·nent·ly** adv.

**per·me·ate** (pûr'mē-āt') v. **-ated, -ating.** To spread or flow throughout; pervade. — **per·me·a·ble** adj. — **per'me·a·bly** adv. — **per'me·a'tion** n.

**per·mis·sion** (pər-mĭsh'ən) n. Consent; authorization. — **per·mis'si·ble** adj. — **per·mis'si·bly** adv.

**per·mis·sive** (pər-mĭs'ĭv) adj. **1.** Granting permission. **2.** Allowing freedom; lenient.

**per·mit** (pər-mĭt') v. **-mitted, -mitting. 1.** To allow. **2.** To afford opportunity to. —n. (pûr'mĭt, pər-mĭt'). A document granting permission.

**per·ni·cious** (pər-nĭsh'əs) adj. **1.** Destructive; evil. **2.** Deadly.

**per·pen·dic·u·lar** (pûr'pən-dĭk'yə-lər) adj. **1.** Intersecting at or forming right angles. **2.** Vertical. — **per'pen·dic'u·lar** n. — **per'pen·dic'u·lar·ly** adv.

**per·pe·trate** (pûr'pə-trāt') v. **-trated, -trating.** To be guilty of; commit. — **per'pe·tra'tion** n.

**per·pet·u·al** (pər-pĕch'ŌŌ-əl) adj. **1.** Lasting forever or for an indefinitely long time. **2.** Ceaselessly repeated. — **per·pet'u·al·ly** adv. — **per·pet'u·ate'** v. — **per·pet'u·a'tion** n. — **per'pe·tu'i·ty** n.

**per·plex** (pər-plĕks') v. To puzzle; bewilder. — **per·plex'i·ty** n.

**per·se·cute** (pûr'sə-kyōōt') v. **-cuted, -cuting.**

To oppress or harass with ill-treatment. —per·se·cu'tion n. —per·se·cu'tor n.

per·se·vere (pûr'sə-vîr') v. -vered, -vering. To persist in or hold to a course, belief, etc., in spite of obstacles. —per'se·ver'ance n.

per·sist (pər-sĭst', -zĭst') v. 1. To hold firmly to some purpose or undertaking, despite obstacles. 2. To last. —per·sist'ence n. —per·sist'ent adj. —per·sist'ent·ly adv.

per·son (pûr'sən) n. 1. A human being. 2. The living body of a human being. 3. The personality of a human being.

per·son·a·ble (pûr'sən-ə-bəl) adj. Pleasing in appearance or personality.

per·son·al (pûr'sən-əl) adj. 1. Of a particular person; private. 2. Done in person. 3. Of a person's movable property. —per'son·al·ize' v.

per·son·al·i·ty (pûr'sən-ăl'ə-tē) n., pl. -ties. The totality of distinctive traits of an individual.

per·son·i·fy (pər-sŏn'ə-fī') v. -fied, -fying. 1. To think of or represent (an idea or inanimate object) as a person. 2. To be the embodiment or example of. —per·son'i·fi·ca'tion n.

per·son·nel (pûr'sən-ĕl') n. The body of persons employed in an organization.

per·spec·tive (pər-spĕk'tĭv) n. 1. The technique of representing objects on a flat surface so that they have the three-dimensional quality as when seen with the eye. 2. A point of view.

per·spi·cac·i·ty (pûr'spĭ-kăs'ə-tē) n. The ability to perceive or understand clearly. —per'spi·ca'cious adj. —per'spi·ca'cious·ly adv.

per·spire (pər-spīr') v. -spired, -spiring. To excrete saline moisture through the pores of the skin; sweat. —per'spi·ra'tion n.

per·suade (pər-swād') v. -suaded, -suading. To cause (someone) to do or believe something by reasoning, arguing, etc. —per·suad'a·ble adj. —per·suad'er n. —per·sua'sion n. —per·sua'sive adj.

per·tain (pər-tān') v. To have reference; relate; belong.

per·ti·na·cious (pûr'tə-nā'shəs) adj. Stubbornly persistent. —per'ti·nac'i·ty n.

per·ti·nent (pûr'tə-nənt) adj. Relevant. —per'ti·nence, per'ti·nen·cy n. —per'ti·nent·ly adv.

per·turb (pər-tûrb') v. To make uneasy or anxious. —per'tur·ba'tion n.

pe·ruse (pə-rōōz') v. -rused, -rusing. To read or examine, esp. with care. —pe·rus'al n.

—pe·rus'er n.

per·vade (pər-vād') v. -vaded, -vading. To spread throughout; permeate. —per·va'sive adj.

per·verse (pər-vûrs') adj. 1. Contrary to what is considered right or good. 2. Willful; obstinate. —per·verse'ly adv. —per·ver'si·ty n.

per·vert (pər-vûrt') v. To cause to turn from the right course of action; corrupt or debase. n. (pûr'vûrt'). Someone who is perverted. —per·ver'sion n. —per·vert'ed adj.

pes·si·mism (pĕs'ə-mĭz'əm) n. A tendency to take a gloomy view of a situation. —pes'si·mist n. —pes'si·mis'tic adj.

pest (pĕst) n. An annoying person or harmful thing; nuisance. —pes'ter v.

pes·ti·lence (pĕs'tə-ləns) n. A fatal epidemic disease. —pes'ti·lent, pes'ti·len'tial adj.

pes·tle (pĕs'əl, pĕs'təl) n. A hand tool for crushing substances in a mortar.

pet (pĕt) n. 1. An animal kept for companionship. 2. A favorite. —adj. 1. Kept as a pet. 2. Especially cherished. —v. petted, petting. To stroke or pat gently; caress.

pet·al (pĕt'l) n. A usually colored leaflike part of a flower. —pet'aled adj.

pe·ti·tion (pə-tĭsh'ən) n. A request, esp. to a person or group in authority, often in a formal document. —pe·ti'tion v. —pe·ti'tion·er n.

pet·ri·fy (pĕt'rə-fī') v. -fied, -fying. To convert (wood or other organic matter) into a stony mass. —pet'ri·fac'tion n.

pe·tro·le·um (pə-trō'lē-əm) n. A yellow-to-black, thick, flammable liquid mixture found principally below the earth's surface, processed for use as natural gas, gasoline, fuel oil, etc.

pet·ty (pĕt'ē) adj. -tier, -tiest. 1. Trivial or insignificant. 2. Narrow-minded; selfish. —pet'ti·ly adv. —pet'ti·ness n.

pet·u·lant (pĕch'ōō-lənt) adj. Irritable; peevish. —pet'u·lance n. —pet'u·lant·ly adv.

pew (pyōō) n. A bench in a church.

pew·ter (pyōō'tər) n. An alloy of tin used for tableware, etc. —pew'ter adj.

phan·tom (făn'təm) n. 1. A ghost; specter. 2. An unreal mental image.

phar·ma·col·o·gy (fär'mə-kŏl'ə-jē) n. The science of drugs.

phar·ma·cy (fär'mə-sē) n., pl. -cies. 1. The preparation and dispensing of drugs. 2. A drugstore. —phar·ma·ceu'ti·cal adj. —phar'ma·cist n.

phar·ynx (făr'ĭngks) n. The section of the digestive tract from the nasal cavities to the larynx, there joining the esophagus.

**phase** (fāz) *n.* **1.** A distinct stage of development. **2.** An aspect; part. —*v.* **phased, phasing.** To carry out by one stage at a time.

**pheas·ant** (fĕz′ənt) *n.* A long-tailed, often brightly colored bird.

**phe·nom·e·non** (fĭ-nŏm′ə-nŏn′) *n.*, *pl.* **-na** or **-nons.** **1.** Any occurrence or fact that is directly perceptible. **2.** An unusual or outstanding person or thing. —**phe·nom′e·nal** *adj.*

**phi·lan·thro·py** (fĭ-lăn′thrə-pē) *n.*, *pl.* **-pies.** **1.** Love of mankind. **2.** A charitable action or institution. —**phil′an·throp′ic** *adj.* —**phil·lan′thro·pist** *n.*

**phi·los·o·phy** (fĭ-lŏs′ə-fē) *n.*, *pl.* **-phies.** **1.** Speculative inquiry concerning the source and nature of human knowledge. **2.** Any system of ideas based on such thinking. **3.** The set of values of an individual, culture, etc. —**phi·los′o·pher** n. —**phil′o·soph′i·cal** adj. —**phil′o·soph′i·cal·ly** adv. —**phi·los′o·phize′** v.

**phlegm** (flĕm) *n.* Mucus from the respiratory tract.

**pho·bi·a** (fō′bē-ə) *n.* An illogical fear of a specific thing or situation. —**pho′bic** *adj.*

**phone** (fōn) —*n.* A telephone. —*v.* **phoned, phoning.** To telephone.

**pho·net·ics** (fə-nĕt′ĭks) *n.* The study of the sounds of speech and their representation by symbols. —**pho·net′ic** *adj.*

**pho·no·graph** (fō′nə-grăf′, -grăf′) *n.* A machine that reproduces sound from a record. —**pho′no·graph′ic** *adj.*

**pho·ny** (fō′nē) *adj.* **-ni·er, -ni·est.** Not genuine; fake. —**pho′ni·ness** *n.* —**pho′ny** *n.*

**phos·pho·res·cence** (fŏs′fə-rĕs′əns) *n.* The generation and emission of light by a living thing. —**phos′pho·resce′** v. —**phos′pho·res′cent** adj.

**phos·pho·rus** (fŏs′fər-əs) *n.* A nonmetallic element used in safety matches, fertilizers, glass, and steel. —**phos·phor′ic** *adj.*

**pho·to·graph** (fō′tə-grăf′, -grăf′) *n.* An image recorded by a camera and reproduced on a photosensitive surface. —*v.* To take a photograph of. —**pho·tog′ra·pher** n. —**pho′to·graph′ic** adj. —**pho·tog′ra·phy** n. —**pho·tog′ra·phy** n.

**pho·to·syn·the·sis** (fō′tō-sĭn′thə-sĭs) *n.* The chemical process by which plants that contain chlorophyll use light to convert carbon dioxide and water to carbohydrates.

**phrase** (frāz) *n.* A sequence of words intended to have meaning. —**phrase** v. —**phras′al** adj.

**phra·se·ol·o·gy** (frā′zē-ŏl′ə-jē) *n.*, *pl.* **-gies.** The way in which words are used; style.

**phy·lum** (fī′ləm) *n.*, *pl.* **-la.** One of the broad categories used in the classification of animals and plants.

**phys·i·cal** (fĭz′ĭ-kəl) *adj.* **1.** Of the body. **2.** Of material things. **3.** Of physics. —**phys′i·cal·ly** *adv.*

**phy·si·cian** (fĭ-zĭsh′ən) *n.* A medical doctor.

**phys·ics** (fĭz′ĭks) *n.* The science of matter and energy and the relations between them. —**phys′i·cist** *n.*

**phys·i·og·no·my** (fĭz′ē-ŏg′nə-mē, -ŏn′ə-mē) *n.*, *pl.* **-mies.** Facial features.

**phys·i·ol·o·gy** (fĭz′ē-ŏl′ə-jē) *n.* The science of life processes, activities, and functions. —**phys′i·o·log′i·cal** adj. —**phys′i·ol′o·gist** n.

**phy·sique** (fĭ-zēk′) *n.* The body, considered in terms of its structure and development.

**pi** (pī) *n.*, *pl.* **pis.** The number 3.1416, representing the ratio of the circumference to the diameter of a circle.

**pi·an·o** (pē-ăn′ō) *n.*, *pl.* **-os.** A musical keyboard instrument with hammers that strike wire strings. —**pi·an′ist** n.

**pic·a·yune** (pĭk′ə-yōōn′) *adj.* Of little value or importance.

**pic·co·lo** (pĭk′ə-lō′) *n.*, *pl.* **-los.** A small flute.

**pick¹** (pĭk) *v.* **1.** To select from a group. **2.** To harvest. **3.** To remove the covering of; pluck. **4.** To break up or pierce with a pointed instrument. —*n.* **1.** A choice or selection. The best part. —**pick′er** n.

**pick²** (pĭk) *n.* A long-handled tool for breaking hard surfaces.

**pick·et** (pĭk′ĭt) *n.* **1.** A pointed stake or spike driven into the ground to secure a tent, tether an animal, etc. **2.** A soldier on guard against enemy approach. **3.** A worker on strike, stationed outside a place of employment. —**pick′et** v. —**pick′et·er** n.

**pick·le** (pĭk′əl) *n.* A food, esp. a cucumber, preserved in brine or vinegar. —**led, -ling.** To preserve in brine or vinegar.

**pic·nic** (pĭk′nĭk) *n.* A meal eaten outdoors on an excursion. —*v.* **-nicked, -nicking.** To go on a picnic. —**pic′nick·er** n.

**pic·ture** (pĭk′chər) *n.* **1.** A painting, drawing, photograph, etc., on a flat surface. **2.** A television or motion picture. —*v.* **-tured, -turing. 1.** To make a picture of. **2.** To form a mental picture of; visualize. —**pic·to′ri·al** adj.

**pic·tur·esque** (pĭk′chə-rĕsk′) *adj.* Striking or interesting; attractive.

**pie** (pī) *n.* A baked pastry shell filled with fruit, meat, etc.

**piece** (pès) *n.* **1.** A unit of a larger quantity; portion. **2.** An artistic work. —*v.*, **pieced, piecing. 1.** To mend by adding a piece to. **2.** To join the pieces of.

**piece-meal** (pès'mèl') *adv.* Gradually. —*adj.* Made or done piece by piece.

**pier** (pîr) *n.* **1.** A platform extending over water, used to moor ships or boats. **2.** A supporting structure.

**pierce** (pîrs) *v.* **pierced, piercing. 1.** To cut with or as with a sharp instrument; stab. **2.** To penetrate through. —**pierc'ing·ly** *adv.*

**pi·e·ty** (pî'ə-tè) *n., pl.* **-ties.** Devotion and reverence.

**pig** (pĭg) *n.* **1.** A hoofed mammal with short legs and a blunt snout, esp. one raised for meat. **2.** An oblong block of metal.

**pi·geon** (pĭj'ən) *n.* A bird with a deep-chested body and short legs.

**pig iron.** Crude iron cast in blocks or pigs.

**pig·ment** (pĭg'mənt) *n.* **1.** A coloring substance or matter. **2.** A substance that produces color in plant or animal tissue.

**pig·men·ta·tion** (pĭg'mən-tā'shən) *n.* Coloration of tissues by pigment.

**pile¹** (pīl) *n.* **1.** A quantity of objects in a heap. **2.** A large accumulation or quantity. **3.** A nuclear reactor. —*v.* **piled, piling.** To stack in or form a pile.

**pile²** (pīl) *n.* A heavy beam driven into the earth as a support.

**pile³** (pīl) *n.* The nap of certain fabrics, as velvet, etc.

**pil·fer** (pĭl'fər) *v.* To steal; filch. —**pil'fer·age** *n.*—**pil'fer·er** *n.*

**pil·grim** (pĭl'grĭm, -grəm) *n.* A traveler, esp. one who goes to a holy place. —**pil'grim·age** *n.*

**pill** (pĭl) *n.* A medicine tablet to be taken by mouth.

**pil·lage** (pĭl'ĭj) *v.* **-laged, -laging.** To plunder. —*n.* Spoils. —**pil'lag·er** *n.*

**pil·lar** (pĭl'ər) *n.* A vertical support; a column.

**pil·low** (pĭl'ō) *n.* A cloth case stuffed with feathers, foam, etc., used to cushion the head or as a decoration. —*v.* **1.** To rest (one's head) on or as on a pillow. **2.** To act as a pillow for.

**pi·lot** (pî'lət) *n.* **1.** One who operates or is licensed to operate an aircraft or a ship. **2.** One who guides or directs. —*v.* To serve as the pilot of. —*adj.* Serving as a model for future development.

**pimp** (pĭmp) *n.* A procurer. —*v.* To procure.

**pim·ple** (pĭm'pəl) *n.* A small swelling of the skin. —**pim'pled, pim'ply** *adj.*

**pin** (pĭn) *n.* **1.** A short, straight, stiff piece of wire with a sharp point, used for fastening. **2.** Anything like a pin in shape or use. **3.** An ornament fastened to the clothing with a pin or clasp. —*v.* **pinned, pinning. 1.** To fasten with or as with a pin or pins. **2.** To hold fast; immobilize.

**pin·cers** (pĭn'sərz) *n.* A grasping tool having a pair of jaws and pivoted handles.

**pinch** (pĭnch) *v.* **1.** To squeeze between the thumb and a finger, the jaws of a tool, etc. **2.** To bind (a part of the body) painfully. **3.** To be miserly. —*n.* **1.** The act of pinching. **2.** An amount that can be held between thumb and forefinger. **3.** A difficult circumstance.

**pine¹** (pīn) *n.* A cone-bearing evergreen tree.

**pine²** (pīn) *v.* **pined, pining.** To suffer intense longing.

**pine·ap·ple** (pīn'ăp-əl) *n.* A tropical plant with swordlike leaves and a large edible fruit.

**pink** (pĭngk) *n.* **1.** A plant with fragrant flowers, related to the carnation. **2.** Light red. **3.** The highest degree. —**pink, pink'ish** *adj.*

**pin·na·cle** (pĭn'ə-kəl) *n.* **1.** A tall, pointed formation. **2.** The highest point; summit.

**pint** (pīnt) *n.* **1.** A unit of liquid measure equal to 16 fluid ounces. **2.** A unit of dry measure equal to ¹/₂ quart.

**pi·o·neer** (pî'ə-nîr') *n.* **1.** One who first enters or settles a region. **2.** An innovator in any field. —*v.* **pi·o·neer'** *v.*

**pi·ous** (pî'əs) *adj.* Reverently and earnestly religious; devout. —**pi'ous·ly** *adv.* —**pi'ous·ness** *n.*

**pipe** (pīp) *n.* **1.** A tubular conveyance for a fluid or gas. **2.** A tube of wood or clay with a small bowl at one end, used for smoking. **3. a.** A wind instrument, such as a flute. **b.** A tube in an organ. —*v.* **piped, piping. 1.** To convey (liquid or gas) by pipes. **2.** To play (a tune) on pipes. —**pip'er** *n.*

**pi·quant** (pē'kənt, -kănt', pē·kănt') *adj.* Pleasantly pungent. —**pi'quan·cy** *n.*

**pique** (pēk) *n.* Resentment caused by wounded feelings. —*v.*, **piqued, piquing. 1.** To cause resentment. **2.** To provoke; arouse.

**pi·rate** (pî'rĭt) *n.* A person who robs ships at sea or plunders the land from the sea. —**pi'ra·cy** *n.* —**pi'rate** *v.*

**pir·ou·ette** (pĭr'ŏŏ-ět') *n.* A full turn of the body on the toes. —**pir'ou·ette'** *v.*

**pis·til** (pĭs'tĭl) *n.* The seed-bearing reproductive organ of a flower.

**pis·tol** (pĭs′təl) n. A small gun held and fired with one hand.

**pis·ton** (pĭs′tən) n. A cylinder that fits into a larger cylinder and moves back and forth under fluid pressure.

**pit¹** (pĭt) n. A hole in the ground. **2.** An indentation in the skin, esp. one left by disease. **3.** The musicians' section in front of a stage. —v. **pitted, pitting. 1.** To make holes or scars in. **2.** To set in competition; match.

**pit²** (pĭt) n. The seed of certain fruits, as a peach or cherry; stone. —v. **pitted, pitting.** To remove the pits from.

**pitch¹** (pĭch) n. A dark, sticky substance obtained from coal tar, etc., used for water-proofing, roofing, etc.

**pitch²** (pĭch) v. **1.** To throw; hurl. **2.** To put up, as a tent. **3.** To fix the level of. **4.** To plunge; fall, esp. forward. **5.** To dip bow and stern alternately, as a ship in rough seas. —n. **1.** An act or instance of pitching. **2. a.** Any downward slant. **b.** The degree of such a slant. **3.** The quality of a musical tone by which someone can judge it to be high or low. **4.** A set talk designed to persuade.

**pitch·er** (pĭch′ər) n. A container for liquids, with a handle, and a spout for pouring.

**pitch·fork** (pĭch′fôrk′) n. A large fork with prongs, used to pitch hay and break ground.

**pit·e·ous** (pĭt′ē-əs) adj. Exciting pity; pathetic.

**pith** (pĭth) n. **1.** The spongelike substance in plant stems. **2.** An essential part. **3.** Force; strength. —**pith′y** adj.

**pit·i·a·ble** (pĭt′ē-ə-bəl) adj. Arousing pity. —**pit′i·a·bly** adv.

**pit·y** (pĭt′ē) n., pl. **-ies. 1.** Sorrow or grief for another's suffering. **2.** A cause for regret. —v. **-ied, -ying.** To feel sorry (for). —**pit′i·ful** adj. —**pit′i·ful·ly** adv. —**pit′i·less** adj. —**pit′i·less·ness** n. —**pit′y·ing·ly** adv.

**piv·ot** (pĭv′ət) n. A short shaft about which another part turns or swings. —v. To turn on or as if on a pivot. —**piv′ot·al** adj.

**plac·ard** (plăk′ärd′, -ərd) n. A poster for public display.

**pla·cate** (plā′kāt′, plăk′āt′) v. **-cated, -cating.** To allay the anger of; appease. —**pla·ca′tion** n.

**place** (plās) n. **1.** A portion of space. **2.** A dwelling; residence. **3.** A position of a person or thing as occupied by a substitute. **4.** A position in a series; standing. —v. **placed, placing. 1.** To put in place; position; set. **2.** To rank (someone or something) in order.

**plac·id** (plăs′ĭd) adj. Calm or composed. —**plac′id·ly** adv.

**pla·gia·rize** (plā′jə-rīz′) v. **-rized, -rizing.** To use (the ideas or writings of another) as one's own. —**pla′gia·rism** n. —**pla′gia·riz′er** n.

**plague** (plāg) n. **1.** An infectious, usually fatal, epidemic disease. **2.** A cause for annoyance. —v. **plagued, plaguing.** To harass or annoy.

**plaid** (plăd) n. Cloth with a checked pattern.

**plain** (plān) adj. **1.** Open to view; clear. **2.** Easily understood. **3.** Straightforward. **4.** Not mixed with other substances; pure. **5.** Unsophisticated; simple. —n. A level, treeless area of land. —adv. In a clear or intelligible manner. —**plain′ly** adv. —**plain′ness** n.

**plain·tiff** (plān′tĭf) n. The party that institutes a suit in a court of law.

**plain·tive** (plān′tĭv) adj. Mournful. —**plain′tive·ly** adv. —**plaint** n.

**plait** (plāt, plăt) n. A braid. —v. To braid.

**plan** (plăn) n. **1.** A detailed method for the accomplishment of an object. **2.** A drawing made to scale. —v. **planned, planning.** To make a plan or plans. —**plan′ner** n.

**plane¹** (plān) n. **1.** A flat or level surface. **2.** A level of development. **3.** An airplane.

**plane²** (plān) n. A tool for smoothing wood. —v. **planed, planing.** To smooth or finish with a plane.

**plan·et** (plăn′ət) n. A celestial body illuminated by a star around which it revolves, esp. one of the nine that orbit the sun. —**plan·e·tar′y** adj.

**plan·e·tar·i·um** (plăn′ə-târ′ē-əm) n. A device for projecting images of celestial bodies onto the ceiling of a dome.

**plank** (plăngk) n. **1.** A thick piece of lumber. **2.** One of the principles of a political party. —v. To cover with planks.

**plant** (plănt, plänt) n. **1.** A living thing that differs from an animal by its ability to make its own food and its inability to move from place to place. **2.** A factory. —v. **1.** To place in the ground to grow. **2.** To sow or supply with or as if with seeds or plants. —**plant′er** n.

**plan·ta·tion** (plăn-tā′shən) n. A large estate or farm.

**plas·ma** (plăz′mə) n. The clear, yellowish fluid portion of blood or lymph. —**plas·mat′ic, plas′mic** adj.

**plas·ter** (plăs′tər, pläs′-) n. A paste that hardens to a smooth solid used for coating walls, etc. —v. **1.** To cover with plaster. **To**

cover conspicuously. — **plas'ter·er** *n.*

**plas·tic** (plăs'tĭk) *adj.* **1.** Capable of being shaped or formed; pliable. **2.** Produced by shaping or modeling. —*n.* A material that can be molded, cast, etc., into shapes and films or drawn into filaments. — **plas·tic'i·ty** *n.*

**plate** (plāt) *n.* **1.** A shallow dish from which food is eaten. **2.** Dishes and other articles covered with gold or silver. **3.** A thin, flat sheet of metal. **4.** A support fitted to the gums to anchor artificial teeth. —*v.* **plated, plating.** **1.** To cover with a thin layer of metal. **2.** To armor. — **plat'ed** *adj.*

**pla·teau** (plă·tō') *n.* An elevated, level expanse of land.

**plat·form** (plăt'fôrm') *n.* **1.** A floor or horizontal surface higher than an adjoining area. **2.** A declaration of principles, as by a political party.

**plat·i·num** (plăt'ə-nəm) *n.* A silver-white metallic chemical element.

**pla·toon** (plə-tōōn') *n.* A subdivision of a military company.

**plat·ter** (plăt'ər) *n.* A large, shallow dish or plate for serving food.

**plau·dit** (plô'dĭt) *n.* An expression of praise.

**plau·si·ble** (plô'zə-bəl) *adj.* Appearing true or reasonable. — **plau·si·bil'i·ty, plau·si·ble·ness** *n.* — **plau'si·bly** *adv.*

**play** (plā) *v.* **1.** To have fun; amuse oneself. **2.** To take part in (a game or sport). **3.** To act in a drama. **4.** To perform on (a musical instrument). **5.** To move lightly or irregularly. —*n.* **1.** A dramatic work or its performance. **2.** Activity for enjoyment or recreation. **3.** A manner of playing a game or sport. **4.** Free movement, as of mechanical parts. — **play'er** *n.* — **play'ful** *adj.* — **play'ful·ly** *adv.*

**play·wright** (plā'rīt') *n.* One who writes plays.

**pla·za** (plă'zə, plăz'ə) *n.* A public square in a town or city.

**plea** (plē) *n.* **1.** An appeal or urgent request. **2.** An excuse.

**plead** (plēd) *v.* **pleaded** or **pled, pleading.** **1.** To appeal earnestly; implore. **2.** To give as an excuse or defense. **3.** To put forward a plea in a court of law. **4.** To argue (a case) in a law court. — **plead'er** *n.*

**pleas·ant** (plĕz'ənt) *adj.* Pleasing; agreeable. — **pleas'ant·ly** *adv.* — **pleas'ant·ness** *n.*

**please** (plēz) *v.* **pleased, pleasing.** **1.** To give enjoyment or satisfaction to. **2.** To be willing to. — **pleas'er** *n.* — **pleas'ing·ly** *adv.*

**pleas·ure** (plĕzh'ər) *n.* **1.** Enjoyment; satisfaction. **2.** Preference or wish. — **pleas'ur·a·ble** *adj.* — **pleas'ur·a·bly** *adv.*

**pleat** (plēt) *n.* A fold in cloth made by doubling the material upon itself.

**pleb·i·scite** (plĕb'ə-sīt', -sĭt) *n.* A direct vote by an entire people on a public issue.

**pled** (plĕd). Alternate *p.t.* & *p.p.* of **plead.**

**pledge** (plĕj) *n.* **1.** A solemn promise. **2.** Something given or held as security in a loan, contract, etc. —*v.* **pledged, pledging. 1.** To promise solemnly. **2.** To bind by a pledge. **3.** To deposit as security.

**plen·ty** (plĕn'tē) *n.* A large amount; abundance. — **plen'ti·ful** *adj.* — **plen'ti·ful·ly** *adv.*

**pleth·o·ra** (plĕth'ər-ə) *n.* Excess.

**pli·a·ble** (plī'ə-bəl) *adj.* **1.** Easily bent. **2.** Easily influenced. — **pli'a·bil'i·ty** *n.*

**pli·ant** (plī'ənt) *adj.* Pliable. — **pli'an·cy** *n.*

**pli·ers** (plī'ərz) *pl.n.* A tool with a pair of pivoted jaws, used for holding, bending, cutting, etc.

**plight** (plīt) *n.* A condition of difficulty or danger.

**plod** (plŏd) *v.* **plodded, plodding. 1.** To walk heavily or with great effort. **2.** To work monotonously. — **plod'der** *n.* — **plod'ding·ly** *adv.*

**plot** (plŏt) *n.* **1.** A small piece of ground. **2.** The series of actions or events in a novel, play, etc. **3.** A secret plan. —*v.* **plotted, plotting. 1.** To represent graphically, as on a chart. **2.** To plan secretly. — **plot'ter** *n.*

**plow** (plou) *n.* A farm implement used for breaking up soil and cutting furrows. **2.** An implement of similar function, as a snow-plow. — **plow** *v.*

**pluck** (plŭk) *v.* **1.** To pull off or out; pick. **2.** To sound (the strings of an instrument) by pulling them. —*n.* **1.** The act of plucking. **2.** Resourceful courage; spirit. — **pluck'y** *adj.*

**plug** (plŭg) *n.* **1.** An object used to stop a hole. **2.** A fitting, commonly with metal socket prongs, used to make electric connections. — **plug** *v.*

**plum** (plŭm) *n.* **1.** A smooth-skinned, fleshy fruit. **2.** Something desirable.

**plumb·ing** (plŭm'ĭng) *n.* The pipes and fixtures of a water or sewage system. — **plumb'er** *n.*

**plume** (plōōm) *n.* **1.** A feather, esp. a showy one. **2.** Something resembling a feather. —*v.* **plumed, pluming.** To decorate with or as with plumes. — **plum'age** *n.*

**plum·met** (plŭm'ĭt) *v.* To drop straight down; plunge.

**plump** (plŭmp) *adj.* Rounded and full in form; chubby. —*v.* To make or become rounded. —**plump'ly** *adv.* —**plump'ness** *n.*

**plun·der** (plŭn'dər) *v.* To rob, esp. by force; pillage. —*n.* Stolen property; booty. —**plun'der·er** *n.*

**plunge** (plŭnj) *v.* **plunged, plunging. 1.** To throw oneself forcefully into a substance or place. **2.** To enter suddenly into a given state or activity. **3.** To descend steeply. —**plung'er** *n.*

**plu·ral** (plŏŏr'əl) *adj.* Of or composed of more than one. —*n.* **1.** The plural number or form of a word. **2.** A word in this form. —**plu·ral'i·ty** *n.* —**plu'ral·ly** *adv.*

**plus** (plŭs) *prep.* **1.** Added to. **2.** Increased by. —*adj.* **1.** Of addition. **2.** Positive. —*n.* An addition or a positive quantity.

**plush** (plŭsh) *n.* A fabric with a thick pile. —*adj.* Luxurious.

**Plu·to** (plŏŏ'tō) *n.* The 9th planet from the sun.

**ply¹** (plī) *n., pl.* **plies.** A layer or strand of which rope, yarn, etc., is composed.

**ply²** (plī) *v.* **plied, plying. 1.** To engage in (a trade or task). **2.** To traverse (a route) regularly. **3.** To keep supplying. **4.** To use or handle (a tool, etc.).

**pneu·mat·ic** (n/y/ŏŏ-măt'ĭk) *adj.* Of air or another gas.

**pneu·mo·nia** (n/y/ŏŏ-mōn'yə) *n.* A disease marked by inflammation of the lungs.

**poach¹** (pōch) *v.* To cook in simmering liquid.

**poach²** (pōch) *v.* To trespass on another's property in order to hunt or fish. —**poach'er** *n.*

**pock·et** (pŏk'ĭt) *n.* **1.** A pouch sewn onto a garment with one edge open. **2.** A receptacle or cavity. —*adj.* **1.** Suitable for being carried in a pocket. **2.** Small. —*v.* To place in a pocket.

**pock·et·book** (pŏk'ĭt-bŏŏk') *n.* **1.** A purse. **2.** A paperback.

**pod** (pŏd) *n.* A seed case, as of a pea, that splits open.

**po·di·a·try** (pə-dī'ə-trē) *n.* The treatment of foot ailments. —**po·di'a·trist** *n.*

**po·di·um** (pō'dē-əm) *n., pl.* **-dia** (-dē-ə) or **-ums.** A platform for a lecturer, etc.

**po·em** (pō'əm, -ĭm) *n.* A work of poetry. —**po'et** *n.*

**po·et·ry** (pō'ĭ-trē) *n.* **1.** Verse as distinguished from prose. **2.** The art or work of a poet. —**po·et'ic, po·et'i·cal** *adj.* —**po·et'i·cal·ly** *adv.*

**poign·ant** (poin'yənt, poi'nənt) *adj.* **1.** Keenly distressing. **2.** Affecting; touching. —**poign'an·cy** *n.* —**poign'ant·ly** *adv.*

**point** (point) *n.* **1.** The sharp end of something. **2.** An extension of land projecting into water. **3.** A dot or period. **4.** A position or place. **5.** A specific moment in time. **6.** An essential or primary factor. **7.** A purpose; reason. —*v.* **1.** To aim. **2.** To indicate with or as with the finger. —**point'ed** *adj.* —**point'ed·ly** *adv.* —**point'ed·ness** *n.* —**point'er** *n.* —**point'less** *adj.* —**point'less·ly** *adv.*

**poise** (poiz) *v.* **poised, poising.** To balance or be balanced. —*n.* **1.** Balance. **2.** Composure.

**poi·son** (poi'zən) *n.* A substance that causes injury or death. —*v.* To give poison to. —**poi'son·ous** *adj.*

**poke** (pōk) *v.* **poked, poking.** To push, thrust, or jab. —**poke** —*n.* —**pok'er** *n.*

**pole¹** (pōl) *n.* **1.** Either extremity of an axis that intersects a sphere. **2.** Either point at the ends of a magnet where the force is strongest. —**po'lar** *adj.* —**po·lar'i·ty** *n.*

**pole²** (pōl) *n.* A long piece of wood or other material.

**po·lice** (pə-lēs') *n., pl.* **-lice.** A governmental department that maintains order and enforces the law. —*v.* **-liced, -licing.** To guard or patrol to maintain order. —**po·lice'man** *n.* —**po·lice'wom'an** *n.*

**pol·i·cy¹** (pŏl'ə-sē) *n., pl.* **-cies.** A method or course of action followed by a government, an individual, etc.

**pol·i·cy²** (pŏl'ə-sē) *n., pl.* **-cies.** A written contract of insurance.

**pol·ish** (pŏl'ĭsh) *v.* To make or become smooth or shiny, as by rubbing. —*n.* **1.** Shininess of surface. **2.** A substance used to polish a surface. —**pol'ish·er** *n.*

**po·lite** (pə-līt') *adj.* **-liter, -litest.** Having or showing good manners; courteous. —**po·lite'ly** *adv.* —**po·lite'ness** *n.*

**pol·i·tics** (pŏl'ə-tĭks) *n.* **1.** The art or science of government. **2.** The policies or affairs of a government. **3. a.** The conducting of political affairs. **b.** The profession of a person so involved. —**po·lit'i·cal** *adj.* —**po·lit'i·cal·ly** *adv.* —**pol·i·ti'cian** *n.*

**poll** (pōl) *n.* **1.** The casting and registering of votes in an election. **2.** Often **polls.** The place where votes are cast and counted. **3.** A survey made to determine public opinion. —**poll** —*v.* —**poll'er** *n.*

**pol·len** (pŏl'ən) *n.* The powderlike material produced by flowering plants, the male element in fertilization. —**pol'li·nate** *v.*

— pol'li·na'tion n.

**pol·lute** (pə-lōōt') v. -luted, -luting. To make harmful to living things, esp. by means of waste that contaminates air, soil, or water. — pol·lut'ant n. — pol·lu'tion n.

**po·lyg·a·my** (pə-lĭg'ə-mē) n. The practice of having more than one spouse at one time. — po·lyg'a·mist n. — po·lyg'a·mous adj.

**po·lyph·o·ny** (pə-lĭf'ə-nē) n. The combination of two or more independent melodic parts. — pol'y·phon'ic adj.

**pomp** (pŏmp) n. Magnificent or stately display.

**pomp·ous** (pŏm'pəs) adj. Self-important; pretentious. — pom·pos'i·ty, pom'pous·ness n. — pom'pous·ly adv.

**pond** (pŏnd) n. A small body of water.

**pon·der** (pŏn'dər) v. To think or consider carefully. — pon'der·er n.

**pon·der·ous** (pŏn'dər-əs) adj. Having great weight; unwieldy.

**pon·tiff** (pŏn'tĭf) n. 1. The pope. 2. A bishop. — pon·tif'i·cal adj.

**po·ny** (pō'nē) n., pl. -nies. A small horse.

**pool¹** (pōōl) n. 1. A small pond. 2. A puddle of any liquid.

**pool²** (pōōl) n. 1. A grouping of resources for mutual benefit. 2. A game played on a billiard table. —v. To combine (money, etc.) for mutual benefit.

**poor** (pŏŏr) adj. 1. Having little money. 2. Inferior. 3. Pitiable. — poor'ly adv.

**pop** (pŏp) v. popped, popping. To make or cause to make a sudden sharp, explosive sound. —n. 1. A sudden sharp, explosive sound. 2. A carbonated beverage.

**pope** (pōp) n. Often **Pope**. The head of the Roman Catholic Church.

**pop·u·lace** (pŏp'yə-lĭs) n. The common people.

**pop·u·lar** (pŏp'yə-lər) adj. 1. Widely liked or appreciated. 2. Of the people at large. 3. Widespread. — pop'u·lar'i·ty n. — pop'u·lar·ize' v. — pop'u·lar·ly adv.

**pop·u·late** (pŏp'yə-lāt') v. -lated, -lating. To live in; inhabit. — pop'u·la'tion n.

**por·ce·lain** (pôrs'lĭn, pōrs'-, pôr'sə-lĭn, pōr'sə-) n. A hard, translucent ceramic; china.

**porch** (pôrch, pōrch) n. A roofed platform at an entrance to a building.

**pore** (pôr, pōr) n. A tiny opening, esp. in skin or a leaf.

**pork** (pôrk, pōrk) n. The meat of a pig, used as food.

**por·nog·ra·phy** (pôr-nŏg'rə-fē) n. Indecent literature or art. — por'no·graph'ic adj.

**po·rous** (pôr'əs, pōr'-) adj. Having pores into or through which a gas or liquid can pass. — po·ros'i·ty, po'rous·ness n.

**port¹** (pôrt, pōrt) n. A town having a harbor where ships may dock.

**port²** (pôrt, pōrt) n. The left side of a ship or aircraft. —adj. On the port.

**port·a·ble** (pôr'tə-bəl, pōr'-) adj. Easily carried or moved. — port·a·bil'i·ty n.

**por·tal** (pôrt'l, pōrt'l) n. A doorway or entrance.

**por·tend** (pôr-tĕnd', pōr-) v. To serve as an advance indication of.

**por·tent** (pôr'tĕnt', pōr-) n. 1. An indication of something about to occur. 2. Great or ominous significance. — por·ten'tous adj.

**por·ter** (pôr'tər, pōr'-) n. 1. A railroad attendant. 2. A doorman.

**port·fo·li·o** (pôrt-fō'lē-ō', pōrt-) n., pl. -os. 1. A portable case for holding papers, etc. 2. The office or post of a minister of state.

**por·tion** (pôr'shən, pōr'-) n. 1. A part of a whole. 2. A share. —v. To divide into parts or shares.

**por·trait** (pôr'trĭt, -trāt', pōr'-) n. A painting, photograph, etc., of a person. — por'trai·ture n.

**por·tray** (pôr-trā', pōr-) v. To show by a picture, words, or a dramatic role. — por·tray'al n.

**pose** (pōz) v. posed, posing. 1. To hold a position, as in modeling. 2. To affect a particular attitude. 3. To propound. — pose n.

**po·si·tion** (pə-zĭsh'ən) n. 1. A place or location. 2. A point of view. 3. Status; rank. 4. A job. —v. To place.

**pos·i·tive** (pŏz'ə-tĭv) adj. 1. Expressing affirmation; favorable. 2. Absolutely certain. 3. Confident. 4. Of a quantity greater than zero. 5. Of the opposite of something negative. 6. Tending to attract electrons. 7. Indicating the presence of a disease or microorganism. —n. 1. A positive answer. 2. A photographic image in which the lights and darks appear as they do in nature. 3. The uncompared degree of an adjective or adverb. 4. A positive number. — pos'i·tive·ly adv. — pos'i·tive·ness n.

**pos·sess** (pə-zĕs') v. 1. To have or own. 2. To have as an attribute. 3. To have knowledge of. 4. To exert control over; dominate. — pos·ses'sion n. — pos·ses'sive adj. — pos·ses'sive·ly adv. — pos·ses'sive·ness n. — pos·ses'sor n.

**pos·si·ble** (pŏs'ə-bəl) adj. Capable of happening, existing, or being accomplished. —**pos·si·bil·i·ty** *n.* —**pos·si·bly** *adv.*

**post¹** (pōst) *n.* A stake set upright in the ground to serve as a marker or support. —*v.* To put up (an announcement) in a place of public view.

**post²** (pōst) *n.* **1.** A military base where troops are stationed. **2.** A position or station. —*v.* **1.** To assign to a position or station. **2.** To put forward; present.

**post³** (pōst) *v.* **1.** To mail (a letter). **2.** To inform of the latest news.

**post·age** (pō'stĭj) *n.* The charge for mailing something.

**post·al** (pōst'l) *adj.* Of the post office or mail service.

**post·er** (pō'stər) *n.* A large placard.

**pos·te·ri·or** (pŏ-stîr'ē-ər, pō-) *adj.* **1.** Located behind. **2.** Following in time.

**pos·ter·i·ty** (pŏ-stěr'ə-tē) *n.* Descendants.

**post·hu·mous** (pŏs'chōō-məs) *adj.* **1.** Occurring after one's death. **2.** Born after the death of the father. —**post'hu·mous·ly** *adv.*

**post office** A governmental office where mail is sorted, stamps are sold, etc.

**post·pone** (pōst-pōn', pōs-pōn') *v.* -**poned**, -**poning.** To delay until a future time. —**post·pone'ment** *n.*

**post·script** (pōst'skrĭpt', pōs'skrĭpt') *n.* A message added at the end of a letter after the writer's signature.

**pos·tu·late** (pŏs'chōō-lāt') *v.* -**lated**, -**lating.** To assume with no proof. —**pos'tu·late** *n.* —**pos·tu·la'tion** *n.*

**pos·ture** (pŏs'chər) *n.* A characteristic way of bearing one's body; carriage. —*v.* -**tured**, -**turing.** To assume an exaggerated pose.

**pot** (pŏt) *n.* **1.** A round, deep container, as for cooking. **2.** A container in which plants are grown. **3.** The total amount staked by all the players in one hand of a card game. —**pot** *v.*

**po·tas·si·um** (pə-tăs'ē-əm) *n.* A soft, silver-white, light metallic element.

**po·ta·to** (pə-tā'tō) *n.*, *pl.* -**toes.** The starchy, edible tuber of a cultivated plant.

**po·tent** (pōt'nt) *adj.* **1.** Powerful. **2.** Able to perform sexually. —**po'ten·cy** *n.* —**po'tent·ly** *adv.*

**po·ten·tial** (pə-těn'shəl) *adj.* Possible but not yet realized; latent. —*n.* Capacity for further growth. —**po·ten'ti·al·i·ty** *n.* —**po·ten'tial·ly** *adv.*

**po·tion** (pō'shən) *n.* A drink or dose of liquid.

**pot·ter·y** (pŏt'ə-rē) *n.*, *pl.* -**ies.** Ware, such as

vases, pots, etc., shaped from clay and hardened by heat. —**pot'ter** *n.*

**pouch** (pouch) *n.* **1.** A flexible receptacle used for carrying various things. **2.** A saclike structure.

**poul·try** (pōl'trē) *n.* Domestic fowls.

**pound¹** (pound) *n.*, *pl.* **pound** or **pounds.** A unit of weight equal to 16 ounces.

**pound²** (pound) *v.* **1.** To strike heavily; hammer. **2.** To pulverize or crush.

**pound³** (pound) *n.* An enclosure for stray animals.

**pour** (pôr, pōr) *v.* To flow or cause to flow.

**pov·er·ty** (pŏv'ər-tē) *n.* **1.** The condition of being poor. **2.** A lack or deficiency.

**pow·der** (pou'dər) *n.* **1.** A substance consisting of pulverized particles. **2.** A preparation in this form, as a cosmetic, medicine, etc. —*v.* **1.** To pulverize. **2.** To apply powder to. —**pow'der·y** *adj.*

**pow·er** (pou'ər) *n.* **1.** The ability to act effectively. **2.** Strength; might. **3.** The ability to exercise control; authority. **4.** Mechanical energy derived from water, fuel, wind, etc. —*v.* To supply with power, esp. mechanical power. —**pow'er·ful** *adj.* —**pow'er·ful·ly** *adv.* —**pow'er·less** *adj.* —**pow'er·less·ly** *adv.* —**pow'er·less·ness** *n.*

**prac·ti·ca·ble** (prăk'tĭ-kə-bəl) *adj.* Feasible. —**prac'ti·ca·bil'i·ty** *n.*

**prac·ti·cal** (prăk'tĭ-kəl) *adj.* **1.** Acquired through practice or action. **2.** Capable of being used. **3.** Designed to serve a purpose; useful. **4.** Level-headed. —**prac'ti·cal'i·ty** *n.* —**prac'ti·cal·ly** *adv.*

**prac·tice** (prăk'tĭs) *v.* -**ticed**, -**ticing.** **1.** To do or perform (something) habitually. **2.** To work on over and over in order to learn or acquire a skill. **3.** To work at (a profession). —**prac'tice** *n.* —**prac'ti·tion·er** *n.*

**prag·mat·ic** (prăg-măt'ĭk) *adj.* Dealing with facts or actual occurrences; practical. —**prag·mat'i·cal·ly** *adv.* —**prag'ma·tism** *n.*

**prai·rie** (prâr'ē) *n.* An extensive area of flat grassland.

**praise** (prāz) *n.* **1.** An expression of approval or admiration. **2.** The act of acclaiming, honoring, or exalting. —**praise** *v.*

**prance** (prăns, prăns) *v.* **pranced**, **prancing.** To move about in a lively manner; strut. —**prance** *n.* —**pranc'er** *n.*

**prank** (prăngk) *n.* A mischievous trick. —**prank'ster** *n.*

**prat·tle** (prăt'l) *v.* -**tled**, -**tling.** To talk meaninglessly; babble. —**prat'tle** *n.*

**pray** (prā) *v.* **1.** To address a prayer to a

deity. **2.** To beg earnestly.

**prayer** (prár) *n.* **1.** A reverent petition made to God. **2.** The act of praying. —**prayer'ful** *adj.* —**prayer'ful·ly** *adv.*

**preach** (prēch) *v.* **1.** To deliver (a sermon). **2.** To advocate. —**preach'er** *n.*

**pre·car·i·ous** (prĭ-kâr'ē-əs) *adj.* Dangerously insecure, unsafe, or uncertain. —**pre·car'i·ous·ly** *adv.* —**pre·car'i·ous·ness** *n.*

**pre·cau·tion** (prĭ-kô'shən) *n.* An action taken in advance to protect against possible failure or danger. —**pre·cau'tion·ar·y** *adj.*

**pre·cede** (prĭ-sēd') *v.* **-ceded, -ceding.** To come before in time, place, or rank. —**pre·ced'ence** *n.*

**prec·e·dent** (prĕs'ə-dənt) *n.* An act or instance that can be used as an example in dealing later with similar cases.

**pre·cept** (prē'sĕpt') *n.* A rule or principle of action or conduct.

**pre·cinct** (prē'sĭngkt) *n.* **1.** A part of a city patrolled by a police unit. **2.** An election district. **3.** Often **precincts.** A place marked off by definite boundaries.

**pre·cious** (prĕsh'əs) *adj.* **1.** Valuable. **2.** Beloved. **3.** Affectedly dainty. —**pre'cious·ly** *adv.*

**prec·i·pice** (prĕs'ə-pĭs) *n.* A very steep or overhanging cliff.

**pre·cip·i·tate** (prĭ-sĭp'ə-tāt') *v.* **-tated, -tating.** **1.** To hurl downward. **2.** To cause to happen before anticipated. **3.** To condense, as vapor into rain or snow, and drop. —*adj.* (-tĭt, -tāt'). Moving or acting rapidly and heedlessly. —*n.* (-tāt', -tĭt). A solid separated from a solution. —**pre·cip'i·tate·ly** *adv.* —**pre·cip'i·ta'tion** *n.*

**pre·cip·i·tous** (prĭ-sĭp'ə-təs) *adj.* **1.** Like a precipice; very steep. **2.** Precipitate. —**pre·cip'i·tous·ly** *adv.* —**pre·cip'i·tous·ness** *n.*

**pre·cise** (prĭ-sīs') *adj.* **1.** Clearly expressed. **2.** Correct. **3.** Distinct; very. —**pre·cise'ly** *adv.* —**pre·cise'ness, pre·ci'sion** *n.*

**pre·clude** (prĭ-klōōd') *v.* **-cluded, -cluding.** To prevent.

**pre·co·cious** (prĭ-kō'shəs) *adj.* Showing skills at an earlier age than is usual. —**pre·co'cious·ness, pre·coc'i·ty** *n.*

**pre·cur·sor** (prĭ-kûr'sər, prē'kûr'sər) *n.* **1.** A forerunner. **2.** A predecessor.

**pred·a·tor** (prĕd'ə-tər, -tôr') *n.* An animal that preys upon others. —**pred'a·to·ry** *adj.*

**pred·e·ces·sor** (prĕd'ə-sĕs'ər, prē'də-) *n.* One who precedes another.

**pre·dic·a·ment** (prĭ-dĭk'ə-mənt) *n.* A troublesome, embarrassing, or dangerous situa-

tion.

**pred·i·cate** (prĕd'ə-kāt') *v.* **-cated, -cating.** **1.** To base or establish (a concept or action). **2.** To declare; assert. —*n.* (-kĭt). The part of a sentence or clause that tells something about the subject. —**pred'i·ca'tion** *n.* —**pred'i·ca'tive** *adj.*

**pre·dict** (prĭ-dĭkt') *v.* To foretell; prophesy. —**pre·dict'a·ble** *adj.* —**pre·dic'tion** *n.* —**pre·dic'tor** *n.*

**pre·di·lec·tion** (prĕd'ə-lĕk'shən, prē'də-) *n.* A preference.

**pre·dom·i·nate** (prĭ-dŏm'ə-nāt') *v.* **-nated, -nating.** **1.** To be most numerous, important, or outstanding. **2.** To have authority or power; prevail. —**pre·dom'i·nance** *n.* —**pre·dom'i·nant** *adj.* —**pre·dom'i·nant·ly** *adv.* —**pre·dom'i·nate·ly** *adv.*

**pre·em·i·nent** (prē-ĕm'ə-nənt) *adj.* Superior to all others; outstanding. —**pre·em'i·nence** *n.* —**pre·em'i·nent·ly** *adv.*

**pre·empt** (prē-ĕmpt') *v.* To take possession of before others can. —**pre·emp'tion** *n.* —**pre·emp'tive** *adj.*

**pref·ace** (prĕf'ĭs) *n.* An introduction to a book, speech, etc. —**pref'ace** *v.* —**pref·a·to·ry** *adj.*

**pre·fect** (prē'fĕkt') *n.* A high administrative official. —**pre·fec'ture** *n.*

**pre·fer** (prĭ-fûr') *v.* **-ferred, -ferring.** To like better. —**pref'er·a·ble** *adj.* —**pref'er·a·bly** *adv.* —**pref'er·ence** *n.* —**pref'er·en'tial** *adj.*

**pre·fix** (prē'fĭks') *n.* A form put before a word, changing the meaning. —*v.* To add at the beginning or front.

**preg·nant** (prĕg'nənt) *adj.* **1.** Carrying a developing fetus within the uterus. **2.** Full of meaning or significance. —**preg'nan·cy** *n.*

**prej·u·dice** (prĕj'ə-dĭs) *n.* **1.** A preconceived opinion; bias. **2.** Detriment or injury. —**prej'u·dice** *v.* —**prej'u·di'cial** *adj.*

**pre·lim·i·nar·y** (prĭ-lĭm'ə-nĕr'ē) *adj.* Introductory; prefatory. —*n., pl.* **-ies.** Something antecedent or preparatory.

**prel·ude** (prĕl'yōōd', prē'lōōd') *n.* A preliminary part; preface.

**pre·ma·ture** (prē'mə-chŏŏr', -t/y/ŏŏr') *adj.* Occurring before the usual time. —**pre·ma·ture'ly** *adv.* —**pre·ma·ture'ness, pre·ma·tu'ri·ty** *n.*

**pre·med·i·tate** (prē-mĕd'ə-tāt') *v.* **-tated, -tating.** To arrange or plot in advance. —**pre·med'i·ta'tion** *n.* —**pre·med'i·ta'tor** *n.*

**pre·mier** (prē'mē·ər, prĭ-mîr') *adj.* Chief. —*n.* (prĭ-mîr'). A prime minister.

**pre·mière** (prĭ-mîr') *n.* The first public

presentation of a movie, etc.

**prem·ise** (prĕm′ĭs) n. **1.** A proposition upon which an argument is based. **2. premises.** Land and the buildings on it.

**pre·mi·um** (prē′mē-əm) n. **1.** A prize. **2.** A bonus. **3.** The amount paid for an insurance policy.

**pre·mo·ni·tion** (prē′mə-nĭsh′ən, prĕm′ə-) n. **1.** An advance warning. **2.** A foreboding. —**pre·mon′i·to·ry** adj.

**pre·oc·cu·py** (prē-ŏk′yə-pī′) v. **-pied, -pying.** To engross. —**pre·oc′cu·pa′tion** n.

**pre·pare** (prĭ-pâr′) v. **-pared, -paring. 1.** To make or get ready. **2.** To put together. —**prep′a·ra′tion** n. —**pre·par′a·to·ry** adj. —**pre·par′ed·ness** n.

**prep·o·si·tion** (prĕp′ə-zĭsh′ən) n. A word that indicates the relation of a noun to a verb, an adjective, or another noun. —**prep′o·si′tion·al** adj.

**pre·pos·ter·ous** (prĭ-pŏs′tər-əs) adj. Absurd.

**pre·req·ui·site** (prē-rĕk′wə-zĭt) n. Required as a prior condition to something. —**pre·req′ui·site** n.

**pre·rog·a·tive** (prĭ-rŏg′ə-tĭv) n. An exclusive right or privilege.

**pre·scribe** (prĭ-skrīb′) v. **-scribed, -scribing. 1.** To impose or direct. **2.** To order the use of (a drug, remedy, etc.). —**pre·scrip′tion** n. —**pre·scrip′tive** adj.

**pres·ence** (prĕz′əns) n. **1.** The condition of being present. **2.** Immediate nearness. **3.** Personal appearance; bearing.

**pres·ent¹** (prĕz′ənt) n. **1.** A period in time between past and future; now. —adj. **1.** Occurring now. **2.** Being at hand. **3.** Of a verb form expressing current time.

**pre·sent²** (prĭ-zĕnt′) v. **1.** To introduce. **2.** To exhibit or display. **3.** To give or offer. —n. present (prĕz′ənt). A gift. —**pre·sent′a·ble** adj. —**pre·sent′a·bly** adv. —**pres′en·ta′tion** n.

**pre·sen·ti·ment** (prĭ-zĕn′tə-mənt) n. A premonition.

**pre·serve** (prĭ-zûrv′) v. **-served, -serving. 1.** To protect. **2.** To keep in unchanged condition. **3.** To treat or prepare so as to prevent decay. —n. **1.** Often **preserves.** Fruit cooked with sugar. **2.** An area for the protection of wildlife or natural resources. —**pres′er·va′tion** n. —**pre·serv′a·tive** adj. & n. —**pre·serv′er** n.

**pre·side** (prĭ-zīd′) v. **-sided, -siding.** To act as chairman.

**pres·i·dent** (prĕz′ə-dənt, -dĕnt′) n. **1.** Often

**President.** The chief executive of a republic. **2.** The chief officer of a corporation, etc. —**pres′i·den·cy** n. —**pres′i·den′tial** adj.

**press** (prĕs) v. **1.** To exert weight or force (against). **2.** To iron (clothing). **3.** To embrace. **4.** To urge on. **5.** To require haste. **6.** To put forward insistently. **7.** To push forward. —n. **1.** A machine or device that applies pressure. **2.** A printing press. **3.** A printing or publishing establishment. **4.** Printed matter, esp. newspapers and periodicals. **5.** A crowding forward. **6.** The urgency of business, etc. —**press′ing** adj.

**pres·sure** (prĕsh′ər) n. **1.** The application of continuous force on one body by another. **2.** A compelling influence. **3.** Urgent claim or demand. —v. **-sured, -suring.** To force.

**pres·sur·ize** (prĕsh′ə-rīz′) v. **-ized, -izing.** To maintain normal air pressure in (an aircraft, etc.). —**pres′sur·i·za′tion** n.

**pres·tige** (prĕ-stēzh′, -stēj′) n. Prominence or influential status. —**pres·ti′gious** adj.

**pre·sume** (prĭ-zōōm′) v. **-sumed, -suming. 1.** To take for granted. **2.** To venture; dare. —**pre·sum′a·ble** adj. —**pre·sum′a·bly** adv.

**pre·sump·tion** (prĭ-zŭmp′shən) n. **1.** Arrogant or offensive behavior. **2.** An assumption or supposition. —**pre·sump′tu·ous** adj. —**pre·sump′tu·ous·ly** adv. —**pre·sump′tu·ous·ness** n.

**pre·sup·pose** (prē′sə-pōz′) v. To assume. —**pre′sup·po·si′tion** n.

**pre·tend** (prĭ-tĕnd′) v. **1.** To make believe. **2.** To claim falsely; profess. **3.** To put forward a claim. —**pre·tend′er** n. —**pre·tense′** n.

**pre·ten·sion** (prĭ-tĕn′shən) n. A doubtful claim. **2.** Showy behavior. —**pre·ten′tious** adj. —**pre·ten′tious·ly** adv. —**pre·ten′tious·ness** n.

**pre·text** (prē′tĕkst′) n. An excuse.

**pret·ty** (prĭt′ē) adj. **-tier, -tiest. 1.** Pleasing or attractive. **2.** Excellent; fine; good. —adv. To a fair degree; somewhat. —v. **-tied, -tying.** To make pretty. —**pret′ti·ly** adv. —**pret′ti·ly** adv. —**pret′ti·ness** n.

**pre·vail** (prĭ-vāl′) v. **1.** To be victorious. **2.** To be most common or frequent. **3.** To persuade.

**prev·a·lent** (prĕv′ə-lənt) adj. Widely existing or commonly occurring. —**prev′a·lence** n. —**prev′a·lent·ly** adv.

**pre·var·i·cate** (prĭ-vâr′ə-kāt′) v. **-cated, -cating.** To speak evasively or lie. —**pre·var′i·ca′tion** n. —**pre·var′i·ca′tor** n.

**pre·vent** (prĭ-vĕnt′) v. **1.** To keep from happening; avert. **2.** To hinder; impede.

# P-16

**preview**

—pre·vent'a·ble, pre·vent'i·ble adj. —pre·ven'-tion n. —pre·ven'tive, pre·ven'ta·tive adj. & n.

**pre·view** (prē'vyōō') n. Also **pre·vue.** An advance showing of a motion picture, etc.

**pre·vi·ous** (prē'vē·əs) adj. Existing or occurring earlier. —**pre'vi·ous·ly** adv.

**prey** (prā) n. 1. An animal hunted or caught for food. 2. A victim. —v. 1. To seize as prey. 2. To victimize. 3. To plunder.

**price** (prīs) n. 1. The sum of money asked or given for something. 2. Value or worth. —v. **priced, pricing.** 1. To fix a price for. 2. To find out the price of. —**price'less** adj. —**price'less·ly** adv. —**price'less·ness** n.

**prick** (prĭk) n. 1. A small mark or puncture. 2. Something that punctures, as a thorn, pin, etc. —**prick** v.

**prick·le** (prĭk'əl) n. 1. A small spine or thorn. 2. A stinging sensation. —**prick'le** v. —**prick'ly** adj.

**pride** (prīd) n. 1. Self-respect. 2. Satisfaction over one's accomplishments or possessions. 3. A cause or source of this. 4. Conceit; arrogance. 5. A group of lions. —v. **prided, priding.** To esteem (oneself) for. —**pride'ful** adj.

**priest** (prēst) n. A clergyman. —**priest'hood'** n. —**priest'ly** adj.

**prim** (prĭm) adj. **primmer, primmest.** Precise, neat, or proper to the point of affectation. —**prim'ly** adv. —**prim'ness** n.

**pri·ma·ry** (prī'mĕr'ē, -mə-rē) adj. 1. First in time, order, or importance. 2. Fundamental. —n., pl. **-ries.** A preliminary election for nominating political-party candidates. —**pri·mar'i·ly** adv.

**pri·mate** (prī'māt) n. 1. A mammal of the group that includes the monkeys, apes, and man. 2. A bishop of high rank.

**prime** (prīm) adj. First in quality, degree, or sequence. —n. 1. The earliest stage of something. 2. The period of ideal or peak condition. —v. **primed, priming.** To make ready; prepare for operation. —**prim'al** adj.

**prim·er**[1] (prĭm'ər) n. 1. An elementary reading textbook. 2. A basic handbook.

**prim·er**[2] (prī'mər) n. 1. A device for setting off an explosive. 2. An undercoat of paint, etc., used to prime a surface.

**prim·i·tive** (prĭm'ĭ-tĭv) adj. 1. Of an early stage of development, evolution, etc. 2. Of an early stage in the evolution of human culture. —**prim'i·tive** n. —**prim'i·tive·ly** adv.

**prince** (prĭns) n. A male member of a royal family. —**prince'ly** adj. —**prin·cess** fem.n.

**prin·ci·pal** (prĭn'sə·pəl) adj. First in impor-

tance; chief. —n. 1. The head of a school. 2. A main participant, as in a play, business deal, etc. 3. Capital as distinguished from revenue or interest. 4. One who empowers another to act for him. —**prin'ci·pal·ly** adv.

**prin·ci·pal·i·ty** (prĭn'sə·păl'ə·tē) n., pl. **-ties.** A territory ruled by a prince or princess.

**prin·ci·ple** (prĭn'sə·pəl) n. 1. A basic truth or law. 2. An ethical standard. —**prin'ci·pled** adj.

**print** (prĭnt) n. 1. A mark made by pressure. 2. Something marked with an impression. 3. a. Lettering or other impressions produced in ink. b. The state or form of matter so produced. 4. A design or picture reproduced by printing. 5. A photographic copy. —v. 1. To reproduce by means of inked type, plates, etc., on a paper surface. 2. To publish. 3. To write in characters similar to those used in print. 4. To produce (a photograph) from a negative. —**print'a·ble** adj. —**print'er** n.

**pri·or** (prī'ər) adj. 1. Preceding in time or order. 2. Preceding in importance. —**pri·or'i·ty** n.

**prism** (prĭz'əm) n. A transparent solid used to refract light or break it up into a spectrum. —**pris·mat'ic** adj.

**pris·on** (prĭz'ən) n. A place of confinement for criminals. —**pris'on·er** n.

**pris·tine** (prĭs'tēn', prĭs·tēn') adj. 1. Primitive or original. 2. Pure.

**pri·vate** (prī'vĭt) adj. 1. Belonging to a particular person or persons. 2. Secret; confidential. —n. A soldier of the lowest rank. —**pri'va·cy** n. —**pri'vate·ly** adv.

**pri·va·tion** (prī·vā'shən) n. Lack of the basic necessities of life.

**priv·i·lege** (prĭv'ə·lĭj) n. A special immunity or benefit. —**priv'i·leged** adj.

**prize** (prīz) n. 1. Something won in a competition, etc. 2. Anything worth striving for. —v. **prized, prizing.** To value highly.

**prob·a·ble** (prŏb'ə·bəl) adj. 1. Likely to happen. 2. Apparently true; plausible. —**prob'a·bil'i·ty** n. —**prob'a·bly** adv.

**pro·ba·tion** (prō·bā'shən) n. A trial period for testing a person's behavior, etc. —**pro·ba'tion·al, pro·ba'tion·ar·y** adj.

**probe** (prōb) n. 1. An instrument used to explore a wound or body cavity. 2. An investigation. —**probe** v.

**prob·lem** (prŏb'ləm) n. A question or situation that presents uncertainty or difficulty. —**prob'lem·at'i·cal** adj.

**pro·ceed** (prō·sēd', prə-) v. 1. To advance

# project

or continue. **2.** To undertake and carry on some action. **3.** To issue forth. **4.** To take legal action. — **pro·ce'dure** n. — **pro·ce'dur·al** adj.

**pro·ceeds** (prō'sēdz') pl.n. Profits.

**proc·ess** (prŏs'ĕs', prō'sĕs') n. **1.** A system of operations in the production of something. **2.** A series of actions that bring about a particular result. **3.** Ongoing movement; progression. **4. a.** A court summons or writ. **b.** The entire course of a judicial proceeding. —v. **1.** To put through the steps of a prescribed procedure. **2.** To prepare or convert by subjecting to some special process. — **proc'es·sor, proc'ess·er** n.

**pro·ces·sion** (prə-sĕsh'ən) n. A group of persons, vehicles, etc., moving along in an orderly manner.

**pro·claim** (prō-klām', prə-) v. To announce officially and publicly. — **pro·claim'er** n. — **proc'la·ma'tion** n.

**pro·cliv·i·ty** (prō-klĭv'ə-tē) n., pl. **-ties.** A natural inclination.

**pro·cras·ti·nate** (prō-krăs'tə-nāt', prə-) v. **-nated, -nating.** To put off doing something. — **pro·cras'ti·na'tion** n. — **pro·cras'ti·na'tor** n.

**pro·cre·ate** (prō'krē-āt') v. **-ated, -ating.** To beget or reproduce. — **pro·cre·a'tion** n. — **pro'- cre·a'tive** adj. — **pro'cre·a'tor** n.

**pro·cure** (prō-kyŏŏr', prə-) v. **-cured, -curing. 1.** To obtain; acquire. **2.** To bring about. **3.** To act as go-between in sexual intrigues. — **pro·cur'er** n. — **pro·cure'ment** n.

**prod** (prŏd) v. **prodded, prodding. 1.** To jab or poke. **2.** To urge or goad. — **prod** n.

**prod·i·gal** (prŏd'ĭ-gəl) adj. **1.** Wasteful; extravagant. **2.** Profuse; lavish. — **prod'i·gal** n. — **prod'i·gal'i·ty** n.

**pro·di·gious** (prə-dĭj'əs) adj. **1.** Enormous. **2.** Extraordinary. — **pro·di'gious·ly** adv. — **pro·di'gious·ness** n. — **prod'i·gy** n.

**pro·duce** (prə-d/y/ōōs', prō-) v. **-duced, -ducing. 1.** To bring forth; yield. **2.** To manufacture. **3.** To cause or give rise to. **4.** To bring forward; exhibit. —n. (prŏd'- yōōs, prō'dyōōs') Something produced; a product, esp. fruits and vegetables. — **pro·duc'er** n. — **pro·duc'tion** n. — **pro·duc'tive** adj. — **pro·duc·tiv'i·ty** n.

**prod·uct** (prŏd'əkt) n. **1.** Anything produced by labor. **2.** The result obtained by performing multiplication.

**pro·fane** (prō-fān', prə-) adj. **1.** Blasphemous. **2.** Secular. — **pro·fane'** v. — **pro·fan'i·ty** n.

**pro·fess** (prə-fĕs', prō-) v. **1.** To declare openly. **2.** To claim knowledge of. **3.** To make a show of; pretend. — **pro·fessed'** adj. — **pro·fess'ed·ly** adv.

**pro·fes·sion** (prə-fĕsh'ən) n. **1.** An occupation that requires training and specialized study. **2.** A declaration.

**pro·fes·sion·al** (prə-fĕsh'ən-əl) adj. **1.** Of a profession. **2.** Engaged in one of the learned professions, as law. **3.** Participating for pay in a sport. — **pro·fes'sion·al** n. — **pro·fes'sion·al·ly** adv.

**pro·fes·sor** (prə-fĕs'ər) n. A college teacher of the highest rank. — **pro·fes·so'ri·al** adj. — **pro·fes'sor·ship'** n.

**pro·fi·cient** (prə-fĭsh'ənt) adj. Skillful; expert. — **pro·fi'cien·cy** n. — **pro·fi'cient·ly** adv.

**pro·file** (prō'fīl') n. A side view, esp. of the human head.

**prof·it** (prŏf'ĭt) n. **1.** A benefit. **2.** The net return received on a business undertaking. —v. **1.** To make a profit. **2.** To benefit. — **prof'it·a·bil'i·ty** n. — **prof'it·a·ble** adj. — **prof'- it·a·bly** adv. — **prof'it·less** adj.

**prof·li·gate** (prŏf'lĭ-gĭt, -gāt') adj. **1.** Dissolute. **2.** Recklessly extravagant. — **prof'li·ga·cy** n. — **prof'li·gate** n.

**pro·found** (prə-found', prō-) adj. **1.** Of a great depth; deep. **2.** Wise and full of insight. **3.** Deeply felt or held. **4.** Total; absolute. — **pro·found'ly** adv. — **pro·fun'di·ty** n.

**pro·fuse** (prə-fyōōs', prō-) adj. Copious or abundant. — **pro·fuse'ly** adv. — **pro·fu'sion, pro·fuse'ness** n.

**prog·e·ny** (prŏj'ə-nē) n. Offspring.

**prog·no·sis** (prŏg-nō'sĭs) n., pl. **-ses.** A medical prediction of the course of a disease.

**pro·gram** (prō'grăm', -grəm) n. **1.** A listing of events for a public presentation. **2.** A schedule. **3.** Instructions coded for a computer. —v. **-grammed** or **-gramed, -gramming** or **-graming. 1.** To include in a program. **2.** To provide (a computer) with instructions. — **pro·gram·mat'ic** adj. — **pro'gram'mer** n.

**prog·ress** (prŏg'rĕs', -rəs) n. **1.** Movement toward a goal. **2.** Development. **3.** Steady improvement. —v. **pro·gress** (prə-grĕs'). **1.** To advance; proceed. **2.** To improve. — **pro·gres'sion** n. — **pro·gres'sive** adj.

**pro·hib·it** (prō-hĭb'ĭt) v. **1.** To forbid by authority. **2.** To prevent. — **pro·hib'i·tive** adj. — **pro'hi·bi'tion** n.

**proj·ect** (prŏj'ĕkt', -ĭkt) n. An undertaking requiring concerted effort. —v. **pro·ject** (prə-jĕkt'). **1.** To protrude. **2.** To throw forward. **3.** To plan. — **pro·jec'tion** n. — **pro·jec'tor** n.

**pro·jec·tile** (prə-jĕk′təl, -tīl′) n. An object, as a bullet, projected with force.

**pro·le·tar·i·at** (prō′lə-târ′ē-ĭt) n. The class of industrial wage earners. — **pro′le·tar′i·an** n.

**pro·lif·ic** (prō-lĭf′ĭk) adj. Producing in abundance.

**prom·e·nade** (prŏm′ə-nād′, -näd′) n. **1.** A leisurely walk; stroll. **2.** A public place for such walking. — **prom′e·nade′** v.

**prom·i·nent** (prŏm′ə-nənt) adj. **1.** Projecting outward. **2.** Conspicuous. **3.** Widely known; eminent. — **prom′i·nence** n. — **prom′i·nent·ly** adv.

**pro·mis·cu·ous** (prə-mĭs′kyoō-əs) adj. Indiscriminate, esp. in sexual relations. — **prom′is·cu′i·ty**, **pro·mis′cu·ous·ness** n. — **pro·mis′cu·ous·ly** adv.

**prom·ise** (prŏm′ĭs) n. **1.** A declaration assuring that one will or will not do something. **2.** Indication of future excellence or success. —v. **-ised**, **-ising**. **1.** To pledge assurance. **2.** To afford a basis for expecting.

**prom·on·to·ry** (prŏm′ən-tôr′ē, -tōr′ē) n., pl. **-ries.** A high ridge jutting out into water.

**pro·mote** (prə-mōt′) v. **-moted**, **-moting**. **1.** To raise in position or rank. **2.** To contribute to the progress or growth of; further. **3.** To urge the adoption of; advocate. **4.** To attempt to sell or popularize. — **pro·mot′er** n. — **pro·mo′tion** n. — **pro·mo′tion·al** adj.

**prompt** (prŏmpt) adj. **1.** On time. **2.** Done without delay. —v. **1.** To press into action; incite. **2.** To give rise to; inspire. **3.** To assist with a reminder; remind. — **prompt′er** n. — **prompt′i·tude**, **prompt′ness** n. — **prompt′ly** adv.

**prone** (prōn) adj. **1.** Lying flat, esp. with the front downward. **2.** Tending; inclined. — **prone′ness** n.

**prong** (prŏng, prông) n. A pointed part, as a tine of a fork.

**pro·noun** (prō′noun′) n. A word that functions as a substitute for a noun.

**pro·nounce** (prə-nouns′) v. **-nounced**, **-nouncing**. **1.** To utter (a word or speech sound). **2.** To state officially; declare. — **pro·nounce′ment** n. — **pro·nun′ci·a′tion** n.

**pro·nounced** (prə-nounst′) adj. Strongly marked; distinct.

**proof** (proōf) n. **1.** The evidence establishing the validity of an assertion. **2.** The alcoholic strength of a liquor. —adj. Fully resistant.

**prop** (prŏp) n. A support or stay. — **prop** v.

**prop·a·gan·da** (prŏp′ə-găn′də) n. Material disseminated by the supporters of a doctrine.

**prop·a·gate** (prŏp′ə-gāt′) v. **-gated**, **-gating**.

**1.** To reproduce or cause to reproduce. **2.** To spread information about. — **prop′a·ga′tion** n. — **prop′a·ga′tor** n.

**pro·pel** (prə-pĕl′) v. **-pelled**, **-pelling**. To cause to move or continue in motion. — **pro·pel′lant** n. — **pro·pel′ler** n.

**pro·pen·si·ty** (prə-pĕn′sə-tē) n., pl. **-ties.** An inclination; tendency.

**prop·er** (prŏp′ər) adj. **1.** Suitable; fitting. **2.** Correct; exact. **3.** Designating a noun that is the name of a particular person, place, or thing. — **prop′er·ly** adv. — **prop′er·ness** n.

**prop·er·ty** (prŏp′ər-tē) n., pl. **-ties.** **1.** A possession or possessions. **2.** A characteristic trait or quality. — **prop′er·tied** adj.

**proph·e·cy** (prŏf′ə-sē) n., pl. **-cies.** **1.** A prediction. **2.** The utterance of a prophet. — **proph′e·sy′** v.

**proph·et** (prŏf′ĭt) n. **1.** One who speaks by divine inspiration. **2.** A predictor. — **pro·phet′ic** adj.

**pro·pi·tious** (prə-pĭsh′əs) adj. Favorable; suitable. — **pro·pi′tious·ly** adv.

**pro·po·nent** (prə-pō′nənt) n. An advocate.

**pro·por·tion** (prə-pôr′shən, -pōr′shən) n. **1.** A part considered in relation to the whole. **2.** Harmonious relation. **3.** Often **proportions.** Dimensions; size. —v. **1.** To adjust so that proper relations are attained. **2.** To form with symmetry. — **pro·por′tion·al** adj. — **pro·por′tion·al·ly** adv. — **pro·por′tion·ate** adj.

**pro·pose** (prə-pōz′) v. **-posed**, **-posing**. **1.** To suggest. **2.** To intend. **3.** To make an offer, esp. of marriage. — **pro·pos′al** n. — **pro·pos′er** n. — **pro·po·si′tion** n.

**pro·pound** (prə-pound′) v. To put forward for consideration. — **pro·pound′er** n.

**pro·pri·e·tor** (prə-prī′ə-tər) n. An owner. — **pro·pri′e·tar′y** adj. — **pro·pri′e·tor·ship′** n.

**pro·pri·e·ty** (prə-prī′ə-tē) n., pl. **-ties.** Appropriateness.

**pro·pul·sion** (prə-pŭl′shən) n. A driving force. — **pro·pul′sive** adj.

**prose** (prōz) n. Ordinary writing as distinguished from poetry.

**pros·e·cute** (prŏs′ə-kyoōt′) v. **-cuted**, **-cuting**. **1.** To initiate and conduct court action against. **2.** To persist in so as to complete. — **pros′e·cu′tion** n. — **pros′e·cu′tor** n.

**pros·pect** (prŏs′pĕkt′) n. **1.** A chance for success. **2.** A potential customer or candidate. **3.** An outlook. —v. To explore, esp. for mineral deposits. — **pro·spec′tive** adj. — **pros′-pec′tor** n.

**pros·per** (prŏs′pər) v. To be successful. — **pros·per′i·ty** n. — **pros′per·ous** adj.

**pros·ti·tute** (prŏs′tə-t/y/o͞ot′) n. A whore.
—v. **-tuted, -tuting.** To offer (oneself or another) for sexual hire. — **pros′ti·tu′tion** n.

**pros·trate** (prŏs′trāt′) v. **-trated, -trating.**
1. To kneel or lie face down, as in adoration or submission. 2. To exhaust. —adj. 1. Lying flat. 2. Exhausted. — **pros·tra′tion** n.

**pro·tect** (prə-tĕkt′) v. To keep from harm or injury; guard. — **pro·tec′tion** n. — **pro·tec′tive** adj. — **pro·tec′tor** n.

**pro·tein** (prō′tēn, -tē-ĭn) n. Any of a group of compounds that occur in all living matter and are essential for the growth and repair of animal tissue.

**pro·test** (prə-tĕst′, prō-tĕst′, prō′tĕst′) v.
1. To object to (something). 2. To affirm solemnly. —n. (prō′tĕst′). 1. The act of protesting. 2. A solemn objection. — **prot′es·ta′tion** n. — **pro·test′er** n.

**Prot·es·tant** (prŏt′ĭs-tənt) n. A Christian belonging to a sect descending from those that seceded from the Church of Rome.
— **Prot′es·tant·ism′** n.

**pro·to·plasm** (prō′tə-plăz′əm) n. A substance constituting the living matter of plant and animal cells.

**pro·trude** (prō-tro͞od′) v. **-truded, -truding.**
To push outward; project. — **pro·tru′sion** n.

**proud** (proud) adj. 1. Feeling satisfaction. 2. Haughty; arrogant. 3. Majestic; magnificent. — **proud′ly** adv.

**prove** (pro͞ov) v. **proved, proved** or **proven** (pro͞o′vən), **proving.** 1. To establish the truth of by argument or evidence. 2. To try out; test. 3. To turn out. — **prov′a·ble** adj. — **prov′er** n.

**prov·erb** (prŏv′ûrb′) n. A short, common saying that illustrates a truth. — **pro·ver′bi·al** adj.

**pro·vide** (prə-vīd′) v. **-vided, -viding.** 1. To furnish; supply. 2. To make ready; prepare. 3. To serve as. — **pro·vid′er** n.

**prov·i·dent** (prŏv′ə-dənt, -dĕnt′) adj. Providing for future needs. — **prov′i·den′tial** adj. — **prov′i·den·tial·ly** adv. — **prov′i·dent·ly** adv.

**prov·ince** (prŏv′ĭns) n. 1. An administrative or political unit of a country. 2. An area of interest. — **pro·vin′cial** adj.

**pro·vi·sion** (prə-vĭzh′ən) n. 1. The act of supplying or fitting out. 2. That which is supplied. 3. A preparatory measure. 4. **provisions.** A stock of necessary supplies, esp. food. 5. A stipulation. —v. To supply with provisions.

**pro·vi·sion·al** (prə-vĭzh′ən-əl) adj. Provided for the time being. — **pro·vi′sion·al·ly** adv.

**pro·voke** (prə-vōk′) v. **-voked, -voking.** 1. To incite to anger. 2. To incite to action. — **prov′o·ca′tion** n. — **pro·voc′a·tive** adj. — **pro·voc′a·tive·ly** adv.

**prow·ess** (prou′ĭs) n. Bravery and resourcefulness.

**prowl** (proul) v. To roam stealthily, as in search of prey. — **prowl** n. — **prowl′er** n.

**prox·im·i·ty** (prŏk-sĭm′ə-tē) n. Nearness; closeness.

**prox·y** (prŏk′sē) n., pl. **-ies.** An agent.

**prude** (pro͞od) n. One who is excessively modest or proper. — **prud′er·y** n. — **prud′ish** adj. — **prud′ish·ness** n.

**pru·dence** (pro͞od′əns) n. Wisdom in handling practical matters. — **pru′dent, pru·den′tial** adj. — **pru′dent·ly, pru·den′tial·ly** adv.

**prune** (pro͞on) v. **pruned, pruning.** To cut branches, etc., from (a tree or plant).

**pru·ri·ent** (pro͝or′ē-ənt) adj. Obsessively interested in sexual matters. — **pru′ri·ence** n.

**pry**[1] (prī) v. **pried, prying.** To look curiously or inquisitively; snoop.

**pry**[2] (prī) v. **pried, prying.** To move with a lever. —n., pl. **pries.** A lever.

**psalm** (säm) n. A sacred song; hymn. — **psalm′ist** n.

**pseu·do·nym** (so͞o′də-nĭm′) n. A fictitious name.

**psy·che** (sī′kē) n. The human mind or soul. — **psy′chic** adj.

**psy·chi·a·try** (sĭ-kī′ə-trē, sī-) n. The medical treatment of mental illness. — **psy·chi·at′ric** adj. — **psy·chi′a·trist** n.

**psy·cho·a·nal·y·sis** (sī′kō-ə-năl′ə-sĭs) n. 1. A system of psychotherapy. 2. A theory of human psychology. — **psy′cho·an′a·lyst** n. — **psy′cho·an′a·lyt′ic, psy′cho·an′a·lyt′i·cal** adj. — **psy′cho·an′a·lyze′** v.

**psy·chol·o·gy** (sī-kŏl′ə-jē) n., pl. **-gies.** 1. The science of mental processes and behavior. 2. The behavioral characteristics of an individual or a group. — **psy′cho·log′i·cal** adj. — **psy·chol′o·gist** n.

**psy·cho·sis** (sī-kō′sĭs) n., pl. **-ses.** A severe mental disorder. — **psy·chot′ic** n. & adj.

**psy·cho·ther·a·py** (sī′kō-thĕr′ə-pē) n. The psychological treatment of mental, emotional, and nervous disorders. — **psy′cho·ther′a·pist** n.

**pu·ber·ty** (pyo͞o′bər-tē) n. The stage of development when an individual becomes physiologically capable of reproduction.

**pub·lic** (pŭb′lĭk) adj. 1. Of the community or the people. 2. Widely known. —n. The people. — **pub′lic·ly** adv.

**pub·li·ca·tion** (pŭb'lĭ-kā'shən) *n.* **1.** The process of publishing. **2.** Published material.

**pub·lic·i·ty** (pŭ-blĭs'ə-tē) *n.* Public interest or notice. — **pub'li·cist** *n.* — **pub'li·cize'** *v.*

**pub·lish** (pŭb'lĭsh) *v.* **1.** To prepare and issue (printed material) for public distribution or sale. **2.** To announce to the public. — **pub'lish·er** *n.*

**pud·dle** (pŭd'l) *n.* A small pool of liquid.

**pu·er·ile** (pyōō'ər-ĭl, pyōōr'ĭl, -īl', pwĕr'ĭl, -ĭl') *adj.* Immature; childish.

**puff** (pŭf) *n.* **1.** A short, forceful discharge, as of smoke or air. **2.** A swelling. **3.** Something that is light or inflated, as pastry. — **puff** *v.* — **puff'i·ness** *n.* — **puff'y** *adj.*

**pug·na·cious** (pŭg-nā'shəs) *adj.* Eager to fight; aggressive. — **pug·nac'i·ty** *n.*

**pull** (pŏŏl) *v.* **1.** To apply force so as to draw something toward the force. **2.** To move with force. **3.** To tug; jerk. — *n.* **1.** The action or process of pulling. **2.** Force exerted in pulling. **3.** Something used for pulling, as a handle. **4.** Special influence.

**pul·ley** (pŏŏl'ē) *n., pl.* **-leys.** A wheel with a grooved rim in which a pulled rope or chain is run, used esp. for lifting weight.

**pul·mo·nar·y** (pŏŏl'mə-nĕr'ē, pŭl'-) *adj.* Of the lungs.

**pulp** (pŭlp) *n.* **1.** A soft, moist mass. **2.** The soft, moist part of fruit, a tooth, etc. — **pulp'y** *adj.*

**pul·pit** (pŏŏl'pĭt, pŭl'-) *n.* An elevated platform used by a clergyman.

**pulse** (pŭls) *n.* The throbbing of arteries produced by the regular contractions of the heart. — *v.* **pulsed, pulsing.** To throb. — **pul'sate'** *v.* — **pul·sa'tion** *n.*

**pul·ver·ize** (pŭl'və-rīz') *v.* **-ized, -izing.** To crush or grind to a powder.

**pump** (pŭmp) *n.* A device used to move something, as a liquid or gas, from one place or container to another. — *v.* To move with or as with a pump.

**pun** (pŭn) *n.* A play on words. — *v.* **punned, punning.** To make a pun.

**punch¹** (pŭnch) *n.* A tool for piercing or stamping. — *v.* To perforate with a punch.

**punch²** (pŭnch) *v.* **1.** To hit, as with the fist. **2.** To herd (cattle). — *n.* A blow with the fist. — **punch'er** *n.*

**punc·til·i·ous** (pŭngk-tĭl'ē-əs) *adj.* Attentive to details of formal conduct. — **punc·til'i·ous·ly** *adv.*

**punc·tu·ate** (pŭngk'chōō-āt') *v.* **-ated, -ating.**

**1.** To provide (a text) with periods, commas, etc., to clarify meaning. **2.** To interrupt periodically. — **punc'tu·a'tion** *n.*

**punc·ture** (pŭngk'chər) *v.* **-tured, -turing.** **1.** To pierce. **2.** To deflate by or as by piercing. — *n.* **1.** An act of puncturing. **2.** A hole made by puncturing.

**pun·gent** (pŭn'jənt) *adj.* **1.** Sharp and acrid to taste or smell. **2.** Biting; caustic. — **pun'gen·cy** *n.* — **pun'gent·ly** *adv.*

**pun·ish** (pŭn'ĭsh) *v.* **1.** To subject to a penalty for an offense. **2.** To inflict a penalty for (an offense). **3.** To injure; hurt. — **pun'ish·a·ble** *adj.* — **pun'ish·ment** *n.* — **pu'ni·tive** *adj.*

**pu·ny** (pyōō'nē) *adj.* **-nier, -niest.** Weak. — **pu'ni·ly** *adv.* — **pu'ni·ness** *n.*

**pu·pil¹** (pyōō'pəl) *n.* A student.

**pu·pil²** (pyōō'pəl) *n.* The opening in the iris of the eye.

**pup·pet** (pŭp'ĭt) *n.* A small figure moved by strings or by hand.

**pur·chase** (pûr'chĭs) *v.* **-chased, -chasing.** To buy. — *n.* **1.** That which is bought. **2.** The act of buying. — **pur'chas·er** *n.*

**pure** (pyōōr) *adj.* **purer, purest.** **1.** Free from foreign elements, impurities, etc.; not mixed. **2.** Chaste. — **pure'ly** *adv.* — **pure'ness, pu'ri·ty** *n.* — **pu'ri·fi·ca'tion** *n.* — **pu'ri·fy'** *v.*

**purge** (pûrj) *v.* **purged, purging.** **1.** To purify. **2.** To rid of sin. **3.** To rid (a nation, etc.) of persons considered undesirable. **4.** To cause evacuation of the bowels. — **pur·ga'tion** *n.* — **pur'ga·tive** *adj. & n.* — **purge** *n.*

**pu·ri·tan** (pyōōr'ə-tən) *n.* One who advocates strict religious and moral discipline. — **pu·ri·tan'i·cal** *adj.* — **pu·ri·tan'i·cal·ly** *adv.*

**pur·ple** (pûr'pəl) *n.* A bluish-red color. — **pur'ple** *adj.* — **pur'plish** *adj.*

**pur·port** (pər-pôrt', -pōrt', pûr'pôrt', -pōrt') *v.* **1.** To claim. **2.** To give the impression of being. — *n.* (pûr'pôrt', -pōrt'). Meaning or significance. — **pur·port'ed·ly** *adv.*

**pur·pose** (pûr'pəs) *n.* **1.** The intended result; goal; aim. **2.** Determination; resolution. — *v.* **-posed, -posing.** To resolve or intend. — **pur'pose·ful** *adj.* — **pur'pose·ly** *adv.*

**purse** (pûrs) *n.* **1.** A small pouch for carrying money. **2.** A sum of money offered as a present or prize.

**pur·sue** (pər-sōō') *v.* **-sued, -suing.** **1.** To follow in an effort to overtake. **2.** To engage in (a vocation, hobby, etc.). — **pur·su'ance** *n.* — **pur·su'er** *n.* — **pur·suit'** *n.*

**pur·vey** (pər-vā', pûr'vā') *v.* To supply or

furnish. — **pur·vey'ance** n. — **pur·vey'or** n.

**pus** (pŭs) n. A yellowish-white fluid formed in infected tissue.

**push** (po͝osh) v. 1. To exert force against (an object) to move it. 2. To shove. —n. 1. The act of pushing; a thrust. 2. A vigorous effort. — **push'er** n.

**put** (po͝ot) v. put, putting. 1. To place; set. 2. To assign; attribute. 3. To impose or levy. 4. To express or state. 5. To apply.

**pu·tre·fy** (pyōō'trə-fī') v. -fied, -fying. To decompose; decay. — **pu'tre·fac'tion** n. — **pu'trid** adj.

**puz·zle** (pŭz'əl) v. -zled, -zling. 1. To bewilder; perplex. 2. To ponder over a problem. —n. 1. A device that tests ingenuity. 2. Perplexity; bewilderment. — **puz'zle·ment** n. — **puz'zler** n.

**pyg·my** (pĭg'mē) n., pl. -mies. Also **pig·my**. One of unusually small size. —adj. Unusually small.

**pyr·a·mid** (pĭr'ə-mĭd) n. A solid figure with a polygonal base and triangular faces meeting in a common vertex. —v. To increase rapidly. — **py·ram'i·dal** adj.

**pyre** (pīr) n. A pile of wood, esp. for burning a corpse.

**py·ro·ma·ni·a** (pī'rō-mā'nē-ə, -mān'yə) n. The uncontrollable impulse to start fires. — **py'ro·ma'ni·ac'** adj. & n.

# Q

**q, Q** (kyōō) n. The 17th letter of the English alphabet.

**quack**[1] (kwăk) n. The sound of a duck. — **quack** v.

**quack**[2] (kwăk) n. One who pretends to have knowledge, esp. in medicine; charlatan. — **quack** adj. — **quack'er·y** n.

**quad·ran·gle** (kwŏd'răng'gəl) n. 1. A plane figure with four sides and four angles. 2. A courtyard bordered by buildings.

**quad·rant** (kwŏd'rənt) n. 1. The fourth part of a circle, an arc of 90°. 2. An early instrument for measuring altitudes.

**quad·ri·lat·er·al** (kwŏd'rə-lăt'ər-əl) n. A four-sided plane figure. —adj. Four-sided.

**qua·drille** (kwə-drĭl', kwŏ-, kə-) n. A square dance for four couples.

**quad·ru·ped** (kwŏd'rŏo-pĕd) n. A four-

footed animal.

**quad·ru·ple** (kwŏ-drŏo'pəl, -drŭp'əl, kwŏd'-rŏo-pəl) adj. 1. Having four parts. 2. Multiplied by four. —n. A number four times as much as another. —v. -pled, -pling. To increase fourfold.

**quaff** (kwŏf, kwăf, kwôf) v. To drink heartily. — **quaff** n. — **quaff'er** n.

**quag·mire** (kwăg'mīr', kwŏg'-) n. A bog with a soft, muddy surface.

**quail**[1] (kwāl) n., pl. **quail** or **quails**. A small, short-tailed chickenlike bird.

**quail**[2] (kwāl) v. To lose courage.

**quaint** (kwānt) adj. Agreeably odd. — **quaint'ly** adv. — **quaint'ness** n.

**quake** (kwāk) v. quaked, quaking. 1. To tremble. 2. To shiver, as with emotion. —n. An earthquake.

**qual·i·fy** (kwŏl'ə-fī') v. -fied, -fying. 1. To describe. 2. To be or make competent for a position, office, etc. 3. To limit. 4. To modify. — **qual'i·fi·ca'tion** n.

**qual·i·ty** (kwŏl'ə-tē) n., pl. -ties. 1. A characteristic; a property. 2. The essential nature. 3. Degree of excellence. — **qual'i·ta'tive** adj. — **qual'i·ta'tive·ly** adv.

**qualm** (kwäm, kwôm) n. 1. A feeling of sickness. 2. Doubt or misgiving.

**quan·ti·ty** (kwŏn'tə-tē) n., pl. -ties. 1. A number or amount. 2. A considerable amount. — **quan'ti·ta'tive** adj. — **quan'ti·ta'tive·ly** adv.

**quar·an·tine** (kwôr'ən-tēn', kwŏr'-) n. Isolation to prevent the spread of a disease. —v. -tined, -tining. To place in quarantine.

**quar·rel** (kwôr'əl, kwŏr'-) n. An angry dispute. —v. To argue or disagree. — **quar'rel·some** adj.

**quar·ry**[1] (kwôr'ē, kwŏr'ē) n., pl. -ries. Any object of pursuit.

**quar·ry**[2] (kwôr'ē, kwŏr'ē) n. An open pit from which stone is obtained. —v. -ried, -rying. To dig from a quarry.

**quart** (kwôrt) n. A unit of liquid and dry measure equal to two pints.

**quar·ter** (kwôr'tər) n. 1. One of four equal parts. 2. A coin equal to one fourth of the dollar. 3. Mercy. 4. **quarters**. A place of residence. —v. 1. To divide into four equal parts. —adj. Being one of four equal parts.

**quar·ter·ly** (kwôr'tər-lē) adj. 1. Made up of four parts. 2. Occurring at three-month intervals. —n., pl. -lies. A quarterly publication. —adv. In or by quarters.

**quar·ter·mas·ter** (kwôr'tər-măs'tər, -mäs'-tər) n. 1. A military officer responsible for supplies. **2.** A naval officer responsible for navigation.

**quar·tet** (kwôr-tĕt′) *n.* **1.** A group or set of four, esp. of musicians. **2.** A musical composition for four instruments.

**quartz** (kwôrts) *n.* A hard, crystalline mineral found in granite or as pure crystals.

**qua·sar** (kwā′zär′, -sär′, -zər, -sər) *n.* A starlike celestial object that emits radio waves.

**quash**¹ (kwŏsh) *v.* To set aside or annul.

**quash**² (kwŏsh) *v.* To suppress completely.

**qua·si** (kwā′zī′, -sī′, kwä′zē, -sē) *adv.* To some degree; almost. —*adj.* Resembling.

**qua·ver** (kwā′vər) *v.* **1.** To tremble. **2.** To speak in a quivering voice. —*n.*

**quea·sy** (kwē′zē) *adj.* **-sier, -siest. 1.** Nauseated. **2.** Uneasy. —**quea′si·ness** *n.*

**queen** (kwēn) *n.* **1.** A female monarch. **2.** The wife or widow of a king. **3.** A playing card bearing the figure of a queen. **4.** The fertile female of bees, ants, etc. —**queen′li·ness** *n.* —**queen′ly** *adj.*

**queer** (kwîr) *adj.* **1.** Strange; peculiar. **2.** Eccentric. —**queer′ly** *adv.*

**quell** (kwĕl) *v.* **1.** To put down forcibly. **2.** To pacify.

**quench** (kwĕnch) *v.* **1.** To put out; extinguish. **2.** To slake; satisfy.

**que·ry** (kwîr′ē) *n., pl.* **-ries.** A question. —**que′ry** *v.*

**quest** (kwĕst) *n.* A search.

**ques·tion** (kwĕs′chən) *n.* **1.** An expression of inquiry that invites a reply. **2.** A controversial subject. **3.** A difficult matter; problem. **4.** A proposal under discussion. **5.** Uncertainty; doubt. —*v.* **1.** To ask a question. **2.** To interrogate. **3.** To express doubt about.

**ques·tion·a·ble** (kwĕs′chən-ə-bəl) *adj.* **1.** Uncertain. **2.** Of dubious morality.

**ques·tion·naire** (kwĕs′chə-nâr′) *n.* A printed set of questions.

**queue** (kyoō) *n.* A line of people awaiting a turn. —**queue** *v.*

**quib·ble** (kwĭb′əl) *v.* **-bled, -bling.** To make petty objections or objections. —**quib′ble** *n.* —**quib′bler** *n.*

**quick** (kwĭk) *adj.* **1.** Speedy. **2.** Prompt. **3.** Alert; keen. **4.** Hasty. —**quick** *adv.* —**quick′ly** *adv.* —**quick′ness** *n.*

**quick·en** (kwĭk′ən) *v.* **1.** To make or become more rapid; accelerate. **2.** To come to life. **3.** To excite and stimulate.

**quick·sand** (kwĭk′sănd′) *n.* A shifting mass of loose sand and water that yields easily to

weight.

**quick·sil·ver** (kwĭk′sĭl′vər) *n.* The element mercury.

**qui·es·cent** (kwĭ-ĕs′ənt, kwē-) *adj.* Calm or still; inactive. —**qui·es′cence** *n.* —**qui·es′cent·ly** *adv.*

**qui·et** (kwī′ĭt) *adj.* **1.** Silent. **2.** Still. **3.** Untroubled; peaceful. **4.** Restrained. —*n.* Tranquillity; repose. —*v.* To become or cause to become quiet. —**qui′et·ly** *adv.* —**qui′et·ness** *n.* —**qui′e·tude** *n.*

**quill** (kwĭl) *n.* **1.** A large, stiff feather. **2.** A sharp spine, as of a porcupine.

**quilt** (kwĭlt) *n.* A padded bed covering.

**qui·nine** (kwī′nīn′) *n.* A bitter alkaloid used to treat malaria.

**quin·tes·sence** (kwĭn-tĕs′əns) *n.* The purest form or the essence of something.

**quin·tet** (kwĭn-tĕt′) *n.* **1.** A group or set of five, esp. of musicians. **2.** A musical composition for five instruments.

**quin·tu·ple** (kwĭn-t/y-/oō′pəl, -tŭp′əl, kwĭn′-tōō-pəl) *adj.* **1.** Having four parts. **2.** Multiplied by five. —*n.* A number five times as much as another. —*v.* **-pled, -pling.** To increase fivefold.

**quip** (kwĭp) *n.* A witty or sarcastic remark. —**quip** *v.*

**quirk** (kwûrk) *n.* **1.** A sudden turn or twist. **2.** A peculiarity or eccentricity. —**quirk′i·ness** *n.*

**quit** (kwĭt) *v.* **quit, quitting. 1.** To leave abruptly. **2.** To relinquish. **3.** To stop. —**quit′ter** *n.*

**quite** (kwīt) *adv.* **1.** Completely. **2.** Actually; really. **3.** Somewhat.

**quiv·er** (kwĭv′ər) *v.* To shake; tremble; vibrate. —**quiv′er** *n.*

**quiz** (kwĭz) *v.* **quizzed, quizzing. 1.** To question closely. **2.** To test by posing questions. —*n., pl.* **quizzes. 1.** A questioning. **2.** A short test. —**quiz′zer** *n.*

**quiz·zi·cal** (kwĭz′ĭ-kəl) *adj.* **1.** Puzzled. **2.** Comical; odd.

**quo·rum** (kwôr′əm, kwŏr′-) *n.* The minimum number of members who must be present for the valid transaction of business.

**quo·ta** (kwō′tə) *n.* **1. a.** An allotment. **b.** A production assignment. **2.** The maximum number of persons who may be admitted.

**quote** (kwōt) *v.* **quoted, quoting. 1.** To repeat the words of (another). **2.** To cite. **3.** To state (a price). —**quo·ta′tion** *n.* —**quote** *n.*

**quo·tient** (kwō′shənt) *n.* The quantity resulting from division of one quantity by another.

# R

**r, R** (är) *n.* The 18th letter of the English alphabet.

**rab·bi** (răb'ī) *n.* A Jewish spiritual leader. —**rab·bin'i·cal** *adj.* —**rab'bin·ate'** *n.*

**rab·ble** (răb'əl) *n.* A mob.

**rab·id** (răb'ĭd) *adj.* Fanatical. —**rab'id·ly** *adv.*

**race**[1] (rās) *n.* **1.** A distinct human population with a common origin. **2.** A distinct variety, esp. of plants or animals.

**race**[2] (rās) *n.* **1.** A contest of speed. **2.** A contest for supremacy. **3.** Steady onward movement. —*v.* **raced, racing. 1.** To compete in a race. **2.** To rush. **3.** To run an engine too swiftly. —**rac'er** *n.*

**ra·cial** (rā'shəl) *adj.* **1.** Of an ethnic group. **2.** Arising from differences between ethnic groups. —**ra'cial·ly** *adv.* —**ra'cism'** *n.* —**rac'ist** *n. & adj.*

**rack** (răk) *n.* **1.** A stand to various articles. **2.** A toothed bar that meshes with another toothed structure, such as a pinion or gearwheel. **3.** An instrument of torture. —*v.* **1.** To torture. **2.** To torment. **3.** To strain with great effort.

**rack·et**[1] (răk'ĭt) *n.* Also **rac·quet.** A light bat with a netted hoop, used in games.

**rack·et**[2] (răk'ĭt) *n.* **1.** An uproar; noise. **2.** An illegal or dishonest business. —**rack'et·eer'** *n.*

**ra·dar** (rā'där) *n.* A method of detecting distant objects by reflecting radio waves off their surfaces.

**ra·di·ate** (rā'dē-āt') *v.* **-ated, -ating. 1.** To emit (heat, light, atomic particles, etc.), esp. in the form of rays. **2.** To glow or beam. **3.** To spread out from a center. —**ra'di·ant** *n.* —**ra'di·a'tion** *n.* —**ra'di·a'tor** *n.*

**rad·i·cal** (răd'ĭ-kəl) *adj.* **1.** Going to the root or source; fundamental; drastic. **2.** Favoring revolutionary changes. —*n.* **1.** One who advocates political or social revolution. **2.** A group of atoms that is only stable as part of a compound. —**rad'i·cal·ism'** *n.* —**rad'i·cal·ly** *adv.*

**ra·di·i** *pl. of* **radius.**

**ra·di·o** (rā'dē-ō) *n., pl.* **-os.** The use of electromagnetic waves to transmit electric signals without wires. **2.** The equipment used for transmitting or receiving radio signals. —**ra'di·o** *v.*

**ra·di·o·ac·tiv·i·ty** (rā'dē-ō-ăk'tĭv'ə-tē) *n.* **1.** The process or property by which atomic nuclei emit radiation. **2.** The radiation released. —**ra'di·o·ac'tive** *adj.*

**ra·di·ol·o·gy** (rā'dē-ŏl'ə-jē) *n.* The medical use of radiation, esp. of x rays. —**ra'di·ol'o·gist** *n.*

**ra·di·um** (rā'dē-əm) *n.* A rare, highly radioactive metallic element.

**ra·di·us** (rā'dē-əs) *n., pl.* **-dii** (-dē-ī') *or* **-uses.** A straight line from the center of a circle to the circumference. —**ra'di·al** *adj.*

**raf·fle** (răf'əl) *n.* A lottery in which people buy chances on a prize. —**raf'fle** *v.*

**raft** (răft, räft) *n.* A flat, floating structure of planks, logs, etc.

**raft·er** (răf'tər, räf'-) *n.* A sloping beam that supports a roof.

**rag** (răg) *n.* A scrap of cloth. —**rag'ged** *adj.* —**rag'ged·ness** *n.*

**rage** (rāj) *n.* **1.** Violent anger. **2.** A fad. —*v.* **raged, raging. 1.** To show violent anger. **2.** To continue with great violence. **3.** To spread unchecked.

**raid** (rād) *n.* A surprise attack. —**raid** *v.* —**raid'er** *n.*

**rail** (rāl) *n.* **1.** A horizontal bar supported by vertical posts. **2.** A banister, fence, etc., made of rails. **3.** A bar used as a track for railroad cars. **4.** The railroad.

**rail·road** (rāl'rōd') *n.* **1.** A road made of parallel steel rails, providing a track for trains. **2.** A system of transportation using tracks, stations, trains, etc.

**rain** (rān) *n.* **1.** Condensed atmospheric vapor falling to earth in drops. **2.** Rainy weather. —*v.* To fall or release as rain. —**rain'fall'** *n.* —**rain'y** *adj.*

**rain·bow** (rān'bō') *n.* An arc-shaped spectrum of colors seen in the sky, caused by sunlight refracted by rain drops.

**raise** (rāz) *v.* **raised, raising. 1.** To elevate; lift. **2.** To make erect. **3.** To build. **4.** To cause to appear. **5.** To increase in amount, worth, degree, etc. **6.** To breed or rear. **7.** To collect. **8.** To cause (dough) to puff up. —*n.* **1.** An act of raising or increasing. **2.** An increase in salary.

**rake** (rāk) *n.* A long-handled implement with teeth, used to gather leaves and grass. —**rake** *v.*

**ral·ly** (răl'ē) *v.* **-lied, -lying. 1.** To call or join together. **2.** To reassemble. **3.** To recover (one's strength). —*n., pl.* **-lies. 1.** A mass assembly. **2.** A renewal of strength.

**ram** (răm) *n.* **1.** A male sheep. **2.** A device used to batter or crush. —*v.* **rammed, ramming. 1.** To crash or smash into. **2.** To cram; stuff.

**ram·ble** (răm'bəl) *v.* **-bled, -bling. 1.** To wander aimlessly; stroll or roam. **2.** To follow a winding course. **3.** To speak or write with many digressions. —*n.* A leisurely stroll. —**ram'bler** *n.*

**ramp** (rămp) *n.* A sloping passage connecting different levels.

**ram·page** (răm'pāj) *n.* Violent, frenzied behavior. —*v.* (răm-pāj') **-paged, -paging.** To move about ferociously.

**ran** (răn). *p.t. of* **run.**

**ranch** (rănch) *n.* A large farm for raising cattle, etc. —*v.* To work on a ranch. —**ranch'er** *n.*

**ran·cid** (răn'sĭd) *adj.* Having the disagreeable odor or taste of spoiled fats and oils.

**ran·cor** (răng'kər) *n.* Bitter resentment. —**ran'cor·ous** *adj.*

**ran·dom** (răn'dəm) *adj.* Having no pattern or objective; haphazard. —**ran'dom·ly** *adv.*

**rang** (răng). *p.t. of* **ring.**

**range** (rānj) *n.* **1.** The extent of perception, knowledge, experience, or ability. **2.** The extent of variation. **3.** Open grazing land. **4.** A series of mountains. **5.** A stove. —*v.* **ranged, ranging. 1.** To arrange in order, esp. in rows. **2.** To classify. **3.** To roam freely. **4.** To vary. —**rang'er** *n.*

**rank** (răngk) *n.* **1.** Relative standing in a group. **2.** Official or eminent position. **3.** A row, line, or series. —*v.* **1.** To place in or form a row. **2.** To hold a particular rank.

**ran·sack** (răn'săk') *v.* **1.** To search thoroughly. **2.** To pillage.

**ran·som** (răn'səm) *n.* **1.** The release of a person in return for payment. **2.** The price demanded or paid. —**ran'som** *v.*

**rap** (răp) *v.* **rapped, rapping. 1.** To strike quickly and lightly. **2.** To talk. —*n.* **1.** A knock. **2.** A criticism. **3.** A talk.

**rape** (rāp) *n.* The crime of forcing a person to submit to sexual intercourse. —**rape** *v.* —**rap'ist** *n.*

**rap·id** (răp'ĭd) *adj.* Very fast; swift. —*n.* Often **rapids.** A fast-moving part of a river. —**ra·pid'i·ty** *n.* —**rap'id·ly** *adv.*

**rapt** (răpt) *adj.* Absorbed; engrossed.

**rap·ture** (răp'chər) *n.* Ecstasy. —**rap'tur·ous** *adj.*

**rare** (râr) *adj.* **rarer, rarest. 1.** Unusual. **2.** Special. **3.** Cooked a short time. —**rare'ly** *adv.* —**rare'ness, rar'i·ty** *n.*

**ras·cal** (răs'kəl) *n.* **1.** A dishonest person. **2.** A mischievous person. —**ras'cal·ly** *adj.*

**rash[1]** (răsh) *adj.* Too bold or hasty; reckless. —**rash'ly** *adv.* —**rash'ness** *n.*

**rash[2]** (răsh) *n.* A skin eruption.

**rasp** (răsp, räsp) *v.* **1.** To file or scrape with a coarse file. **2.** To speak in a grating voice. **3.** To grate upon; irritate. —**rasp** *n.* —**rasp'ing·ly** *adv.* —**rasp'y** *adj.*

**rat** (răt) *n.* A long-tailed rodent larger than a mouse.

**rate** (rāt) *n.* **1.** A measure of a part to a whole; proportion. **2. a.** A payment. **b.** A cost per unit. **3.** Level of quality. —**rated, rating. 1.** To calculate the value of. **2.** To classify or be classified.

**rath·er** (răth'ər, rä'thər) *adv.* **1.** Preferably. **2.** Somewhat. **3.** On the contrary.

**rat·i·fy** (răt'ə-fī') *v.* **-fied, -fying.** To give formal sanction to. —**rat'i·fi·ca'tion** *n.*

**ra·tio** (rā'shō, rā'shē-ō') *n., pl.* **-tios.** Proportion; rate.

**ra·tion** (răsh'ən, rā'shən) *n.* A fixed portion or allowance. —*v.* **1.** To supply with. **2.** To restrict or limit.

**ra·tion·al** (răsh'ən-əl) *adj.* **1.** Having or using the ability to reason. **2.** Based upon reason; logical. —**ra·tion·al'i·ty** *n.* —**ra'tion·al·ly** *adv.*

**rat·tle** (răt'l) *v.* **-tled, -tling. 1.** To make a succession of short, sharp sounds. **2.** To fluster. —*n.* **1.** Short, rapid sounds. **2.** A baby's toy.

**rau·cous** (rô'kəs) *adj.* Rough-sounding; harsh. —**rau'cous·ly** *adv.* —**rau'cous·ness** *n.*

**rav·age** (răv'ĭj) *v.* **-aged, -aging.** To destroy or devastate. —*n.* Heavy destruction. —**rav'ag·er** *n.*

**rave** (rāv) *v.* **raved, raving. 1.** To speak wildly or incoherently. **2.** To speak about enthusiastically. —*n.* An enthusiastic review; praise.

**rav·el** (răv'əl) *v.* To separate the threads of (cloth); fray.

**ra·ven** (rā'vən) *n.* A large crowlike bird. —*adj.* Black and shiny.

**rav·en·ous** (răv'ən-əs) *adj.* Extremely hungry. —**rav'en·ous·ly** *adv.*

**ra·vine** (rə-vēn') *n.* A deep, narrow gorge.

**rav·ish** (răv'ĭsh) *v.* **1.** To rape. **2.** To enrapture or entrance. —**rav'ish·ing** *adj.*

**raw** (rô) *adj.* **1.** Uncooked. **2.** In a natural condition. **3.** Untrained. **4.** Cold and damp. **5.** Sore; inflamed. —**raw'ness** *n.*

# 183 recognize

**ray** (rā) *n.* **1.** A narrow beam of light. **2.** A trace; hint. **3.** A line or part extending from a point.

**raze** (rāz) *v.* razed, razing. To tear down or demolish.

**ra·zor** (rā′zər) *n.* A sharp-edged instrument for shaving.

**reach** (rēch) *v.* **1.** To extend. **2.** To touch or take hold of, esp. with the hand. **3.** To arrive at. **4.** To amount to; achieve. —*n.* **1.** The act of stretching out a bodily part. **2.** The extent something can reach.

**re·act** (rē-ăkt′) *v.* **1.** To act in response to. **2.** To be affected by circumstances. —**re·ac′tion** *n.*

**read** (rēd) *v.* read (rĕd), reading. **1.** To comprehend the meaning of (something written). **2.** To utter aloud (something written). **3.** To learn by reading. **4.** To indicate or register. —**read·a·bil′i·ty** *n.* —**read′a·ble** *adj.* —**read′er** *n.*

**read·y** (rĕd′ē) *adj.* -ier, -iest. **1.** Prepared or available. **2.** Willing. —**read′i·ly** *adv.* —**read′i·ness** *n.*

**re·al** (rē′əl, rēl) *adj.* **1.** Existing in fact or actuality. **2.** Genuine; authentic. —*adv.* Very. —**real′ly** *adv.*

**real estate.** Land and anything on it, as natural resources, buildings, etc.

**re·al·i·ty** (rē-ăl′ĭ-tē) *n., pl.* -ties. **1.** The quality or state of being real; actual existence. **2.** The totality of things that actually exist. —**re′al·ism** *n.* —**re′al·ist** *n.* —**re′al·is′tic** *adj.* —**re′al·is′ti·cal·ly** *adv.*

**re·al·ize** (rē′ə-līz′) *v.* -ized, -izing. **1.** To comprehend completely; grasp. **2.** To make real; achieve. **3.** To obtain as profit. —**re′al·iz′a·ble** *adj.* —**re·al·i·za′tion** *n.*

**realm** (rĕlm) *n.* **1.** A kingdom. **2.** A field of interest or expertise.

**reap** (rēp) *v.* To harvest by cutting. —**reap′er** *n.*

**rear**[1] (rîr) *n.* The back part. —*adj.* Of or at the rear.

**rear**[2] (rîr) *v.* **1.** To care for during youth; bring up. **2.** To build. **3.** To rise on the hind legs, as a horse.

**rea·son** (rē′zən) *n.* **1.** The cause or motive for an action, decision, or conviction. **2.** The capacity for rational thinking. —*v.* **1.** To think or argue logically. **2.** To reach a conclusion by logical thinking. —**rea′son·a·ble** *adj.* —**rea′son·a·bly** *adv.*

**re·bate** (rē′bāt′) *n.* A return of part of an amount paid. —**re′bate′** *v.*

**re·bel** (rĭ-bĕl′) *v.* -belled, -belling. **1.** To

engage in armed revolt against a government. **2.** To defy any authority. —*n.* reb·el (rĕb′əl). One who rebels. —*adj.* Of rebels. —**re·bel′lion** *n.* —**re·bel′lious** *adj.*

**re·buff** (rĭ-bŭf′) *n.* A blunt repulse or refusal. —*v.* **1.** To refuse bluntly. **2.** To drive back; repel.

**re·buke** (rĭ-byōōk′) *v.* -buked, -buking. To criticize sharply; scold. —**re·buke′** *n.*

**re·call** (rĭ-kôl′) *v.* **1.** To call back. **2.** To remember or recollect. **3.** To cancel; take back. —**re·call′** *n.*

**re·ca·pit·u·late** (rē′kə-pĭch′ōō-lāt′) *v.* -lated, -lating. To review; summarize. —**re′ca·pit′u·la′tion** *n.*

**re·cede** (rĭ-sēd′) *v.* -ceded, -ceding. **1.** To move back; ebb. **2.** To slope backward.

**re·ceipt** (rĭ-sēt′) *n.* **1.** Often receipts. The amount of something received. **2.** A written acknowledgment that something has been received.

**re·ceive** (rĭ-sēv′) *v.* -ceived, -ceiving. **1.** To take or acquire. **2.** To experience. **3.** To admit or welcome. **4.** To accept electromagnetic signals, as in radio, telegraphy, etc. —**re·ceiv′er** *n.* —**re·cep′tion** *n.* —**re·cep′tive** *adj.* —**re·cip′i·ent** *n.*

**re·cent** (rē′sənt) *adj.* Of a time immediately prior to the present. —**re′cent·ly** *adv.*

**re·cep·ta·cle** (rĭ-sĕp′tə-kəl) *n.* A container.

**re·cess** (rē′sĕs′, rĭ-sĕs′) *n.* **1.** A temporary halt of activities. **2.** A small hollow. —*v.* **1.** To make a recess in. **2.** To suspend for recess.

**re·ces·sion** (rĭ-sĕsh′ən) *n.* A temporary economic decline.

**rec·i·pe** (rĕs′ə-pē′) *n.* A set of directions for making something, esp. food.

**re·cip·ro·cate** (rĭ-sĭp′rə-kāt′) *v.* -cated, -cating. **1.** To give or take mutually or in response. **2.** To show or feel in response. —**re·cip′ro·cal** *adj.* —**re·cip′ro·ca′tion** *n.* —**rec′i·proc′i·ty** *n.*

**re·cite** (rĭ-sīt′) *v.* -cited, -citing. **1.** To repeat aloud something memorized. **2.** To enumerate. —**rec′i·ta′tion** *n.*

**reck·less** (rĕk′lĭs) *adj.* Without care or caution; rash. —**reck′less·ly** *adv.* —**reck′less·ness** *n.*

**reck·on** (rĕk′ən) *v.* **1.** To count or compute. **2.** To consider.

**re·cline** (rĭ-klīn′) *v.* -clined, -clining. To sit or lean back; lie down. —**re·clin′er** *n.*

**rec·og·nize** (rĕk′əg-nīz′) *v.* -nized, -nizing. **1.** To identify or perceive from past experience. **2.** To admit the acquaintance of.

greet. **3.** To acknowledge. — **rec′og·ni′tion** n. — **rec′og·niz′a·ble** adj. — **rec′og·niz′a·bly** adv.

**re·coil** (rĭ-koil′) v. **1.** To spring back. **2.** To shrink back in fear or disgust. — **re′coil′** n.

**rec·ol·lect** (rĕk′ə-lĕkt′) v. To remember. — **rec′ol·lec′tion** n.

**rec·om·mend** (rĕk′ə-mĕnd′) v. **1.** To commend as worthy or desirable. **2.** To advise. — **rec′om·men·da′tion** n.

**rec·on·cile** (rĕk′ən-sīl′) v. -ciled, -ciling. **1.** To re-establish friendship between. **2.** To settle, as a dispute. **3.** To be or make resigned to. **4.** To make compatible. — **rec′on·cil′a·ble** adj. — **rec′on·cil′i·a′tion** n.

**rec·ord** (rĕk′ərd) n. **1.** A written account; document. **2.** The best performance known. **3.** A disk coded to reproduce sound. —v. **re·cord** (rĭ-kôrd′). **1.** To write down for preservation. **2.** To register (sound) in permanent form on a record or a tape. — **re·cord′er** n.

**re·count** (rĭ-kount′) v. To narrate; relate.

**re·course** (rē′kôrs′, -kōrs′, rĭ-kôrs′, -kōrs′) n. A turning to or request for aid.

**re·cov·er** (rĭ-kŭv′ər) v. **1.** To get back. **2.** To regain health. — **re·cov′er·a·ble** adj. — **re·cov′er·y** n.

**rec·re·a·tion** (rĕk′rē-ā′shən) n. Refreshment through diverting activity; play. — **rec′re·a′tion·al** adj.

**re·cruit** (rĭ-krōōt′) v. To engage or enlist as a soldier or supporter. —n. A new member of a military force or an organization. — **re·cruit′er** n. — **re·cruit′ment** n.

**rec·tan·gle** (rĕk′tăng′gəl) n. A parallelogram with a right angle. — **rec·tan′gu·lar** adj.

**rec·ti·fy** (rĕk′tə-fī′) v. -fied, -fying. To set right; correct. — **rec′ti·fi·ca′tion** n.

**rec·tor** (rĕk′tər) n. **1.** A clergyman in charge of a parish. **2.** The principal of certain schools, esp. religious institutions. — **rec′to·ry** n.

**rec·tum** (rĕk′təm) n. The lower end of the large intestine. — **rec′tal** adj.

**re·cu·per·ate** (rĭ-k/y/ōō′pə-rāt′) v. -ated, -ating. To regain health; recover. — **re·cu′per·a′tion** n.

**re·cur** (rĭ-kûr′) v. -curred, -curring. To happen again. — **re·cur′rent** adj. — **re·cur′rent·ly** adv.

**red** (rĕd) n. A color like blood. —adj. redder, reddest. **1.** Having such a color. **2.** Ruddy; flushed. — **red′den** v. — **red′dish** adj. — **red′ness** n.

**re·deem** (rĭ-dēm′) v. **1.** To recover ownership of by paying a sum. **2.** To pay off. **3.** To

fulfill. **4.** To make amends for. **5.** To save from sin. — **re·deem′a·ble** adj. — **re·deem′er** n. — **re·demp′tion** n.

**re·duce** (rĭ-d/y/ōōs′) v. -duced, -ducing. **1.** To lessen in extent, amount, etc.; diminish. **2.** To break down into basic components. **3.** To bring into a given condition or state. **4.** To lose weight. — **re·duc′i·ble** adj. — **re·duc′tion** n.

**re·dun·dant** (rĭ-dŭn′dənt) adj. **1.** Superfluous. **2.** Repetitive.

**re·du·pli·ca·tion** (rĭ-d/y/ōō′plə-kā′shən) n.

**reed** (rēd) n. **1.** A tall, hollow-stemmed marsh grass. **2.** A vibrating strip in certain musical instruments.

**reef** (rēf) n. A ridge of rock, sand, or coral near the surface of water.

**reek** (rēk) v. To give off a strong or unpleasant odor.

**reel¹** (rēl) n. A spool or frame that turns on an axis, used for winding rope, fishing line, etc. — **reel** v.

**reel²** (rēl) v. To stagger, lurch, or sway.

**re·fer** (rĭ-fûr′) v. -ferred, -ferring. **1.** To direct to a source for help or information. **2.** To attribute to. **3.** To submit to an authority for decision. **4.** To direct the attention of. **5.** To allude. — **ref′er·ence** n. — **re·fer′ral** n.

**ref·er·ee** (rĕf′ə-rē′) n. **1.** One to whom something is referred; an arbitrator. **2.** An umpire. — **ref′e·ree′** v.

**re·fine** (rĭ-fīn′) v. -fined, -fining. **1.** To purify, as sugar, petroleum, ore, etc. **2.** To make or become polished, cultured, etc. **3.** To improve. — **re·fine′ment** n. — **re·fin′er·y** n.

**re·flect** (rĭ-flĕkt′) v. **1.** To throw back (heat, light, or sound). **2.** To mirror. **3.** To think seriously. **4.** To bring blame or reproach, esp. as a result of one's actions. — **re·flec′tion** n. — **re·flec′tive** adj.

**re·flex** (rē′flĕks′) adj. Designating an involuntary action or response. —n. An involuntary response to a stimulus.

**re·flex·ive** (rĭ-flĕk′sĭv) adj. Designating a verb having an identical subject and direct object. — **re·flex′ive** n.

**re·form** (rĭ-fôrm′) v. **1.** To improve. **2.** To abolish abuses in. —n. A change for the better. — **ref′or·ma′tion** n. — **re·form′er** n.

**re·fract** (rĭ-frăkt′) v. To deflect heat, light, or sound waves at the boundary between two mediums. — **re·frac′tion** n. — **re·frac′tive** adj.

**re·frain¹** (rĭ-frān′) v. To hold oneself back.

**re·frain²** (rĭ-frān′) n. A recurrent verse in a song or poem.

**re·fresh** (rĭ-frĕsh′) v. **1.** To revive, as with food, drink, etc. **2.** To renew by stimulation. —**re·fresh′er** n. —**re·fresh′ing** adj. —**re·fresh′·ment** n.

**re·frig·er·ate** (rĭ-frĭj′ə-rāt′) v. -ated, -ating. To cool or freeze. —**re·frig·er·a′tion** n. —**re·frig′er·a′tor** n.

**ref·uge** (rĕf′yōōj) n. **1.** Protection or shelter; sanctuary. **2.** Anything to which one may turn for help. —**ref′u·gee′** n.

**re·fund** (rĭ-fŭnd′, rē′fŭnd′) v. To return or repay. —n. (rē′fŭnd′). A repayment of funds.

**re·fuse¹** (rĭ-fyōōz′) v. -fused, -fusing. To decline to do, accept, give, or allow. —**re·fus′al** n.

**ref·use²** (rĕf′yōōs) n. Trash; rubbish.

**re·fute** (rĭ-fyōōt′) v. -futed, -futing. To prove false; disprove. —**ref·u·ta′tion** n.

**re·gal** (rē′gəl) adj. Royal. —**re′gal·ly** adv.

**re·gale** (rĭ-gāl′) v. -galed, -galing. **1.** To delight. **2.** To entertain sumptuously.

**re·gard** (rĭ-gärd′) v. **1.** To observe closely. **2.** To consider in a particular way. **3.** To view or admire. **4.** To concern or refer to. **5.** To take into account. —n. **1.** Attention; concern. **2.** Respect or affection. **3.** **regards.** Good wishes. **4.** Reference.

**re·gard·less** (rĭ-gärd′lĭs) adj. In spite of everything; anyway.

**re·gime** (rā-zhēm′, rĭ-) n. A system of management of government.

**reg·i·ment** (rĕj′ə-mənt) n. An infantry unit. —v. (rĕj′ə-mĕnt′). **1.** To systematize. **2.** To force uniformity and discipline upon. —**reg′i·men′tal** adj. —**reg′i·men·ta′tion** n.

**re·gion** (rē′jən) n. An area; district. —**re′gion·al** adj. —**re′gion·al·ly** adv.

**reg·is·ter** (rĕj′ĭ-stər) n. **1.** A formal record or list. **2.** A device to regulate the flow of heated or cooled air into a room. **3.** The range of a voice or instrument. —v. **1.** To enter in a register. **2.** To indicate. **3.** To have one's name placed on a voting list. —**reg′is·trar′** n. —**reg′is·tra′tion** n. —**reg′is·try** n.

**re·gress** (rĭ-grĕs′) v. To go backward to a previous condition. —**re·gres′sive** adj. —**re·gres′sion** n.

**re·gret** (rĭ-grĕt′) v. -gretted, -gretting. **1.** To feel sorry or disappointed about. **2.** To mourn. —n. **1.** An expression of grief or disappointment. **2. regrets.** A courteous declining to accept an invitation. —**re·gret′ful** adj. —**re·gret′ful·ly** adv. —**re·gret′ta·ble** adj. —**re·gret′ta·bly** adv.

**reg·u·lar** (rĕg′yə-lər) adj. **1.** Customary or

normal. **2.** Symmetrical. **3.** Conforming to set procedure or principle. **4.** Orderly. **5.** Occurring at fixed intervals; periodic. **6.** Of the permanent army of a nation. —n. A soldier in the permanent army. —**reg′u·lar′i·ty** n. —**reg′u·lar·ly** adv.

**reg·u·late** (rĕg′yə-lāt′) v. -lated, -lating. **1.** To control according to a rule. **2.** To adjust. —**reg′u·la′tion** n. —**reg′u·la·to′ry** adj. —**reg′u·la′tor** n.

**re·ha·bil·i·tate** (rē′hə-bĭl′ĭ-tāt′) v. -tated, -tating. **1.** To restore to good condition. **2.** To reinstate. —**re′ha·bil′i·ta′tion** n. —**re′ha·bil′i·ta′tive** adj.

**re·hearse** (rĭ-hûrs′) v. -hearsed, -hearsing. To practice in preparation for a performance. —**re·hears′al** n.

**reign** (rān) n. **1.** The exercise of sovereign power. **2.** The term of a sovereign's rule. —v. To rule with sovereign power.

**re·im·burse** (rē′ĭm-bûrs′) v. -bursed, -bursing. **1.** To repay. **2.** To compensate, as for money spent. —**re′im·burse′ment** n.

**rein** (rān) n. **1.** Often **reins.** Two narrow straps attached to a bridle and used to control a horse. **2.** Any means of restraint. To check or hold back.

**re·in·force** (rē′ĭn-fôrs′, -fōrs′) v. -forced, -forcing. To strengthen; support. —**re·in·force′ment** n.

**re·in·state** (rē′ĭn-stāt′) v. -stated, -stating. To restore to a previous position. —**re′in·state′ment** n.

**re·it·er·ate** (rē-ĭt′ə-rāt′) v. -ated, -ating. To say over again. —**re·it·er·a′tion** n.

**re·ject** (rĭ-jĕkt′) v. **1.** To refuse; repudiate. **2.** To refuse to grant; deny. **3.** To discard; throw away. —n. (rē′jĕkt′). Something rejected. —**re·jec′tion** n.

**re·joice** (rĭ-jois′) v. -joiced, -joicing. To feel or fill with joy.

**re·lapse** (rĭ-lăps′) v. -lapsed, -lapsing. To return to a former state, esp. illness. —n. (rē′lăps′, rĭ-lăps′). The act of relapsing.

**re·late** (rĭ-lāt′) v. -lated, -lating. **1.** To tell. **2.** To have reference to. **3.** To be connected by kinship. —**re·la′tion** n. —**re·la′tion·al** adj. —**re·la′tion·ship′** n.

**rel·a·tive** (rĕl′ə-tĭv) adj. **1.** Considered in comparison to something else. **2.** Dependent upon something else for significance. —n. One related by kinship. —**rel′a·tive·ly** adv. —**rel·a·tiv′i·ty** n.

**re·lax** (rĭ-lăks′) v. **1.** To make or become loose. **2.** To relieve from strain. **3.** To rest. —**re·lax·a′tion** n.

**re·lay** (rē′lā, rĭ-lā′) n. A fresh group, as of workers, to relieve others. —v. To pass or send along from one group to another.

**re·lease** (rĭ-lēs′) v. -leased, -leasing. 1. To set free; liberate. 2. To unfasten. —n. 1. The act of releasing or state of being released. 2. A device releasing a mechanism.

**rel·e·gate** (rĕl′ə-gāt′) v. -gated, -gating. 1. To consign to a lower position, etc. 2. To assign to a particular category. —rel′e·ga′tion n.

**re·lent** (rĭ-lĕnt′) v. To become gentler in attitude; abate. —re·lent′less adj. —re·lent′less·ly adv. —re·lent′less·ness n.

**rel·e·vant** (rĕl′ə-vənt) adj. Pertinent. —rel′e·vance, rel′e·van·cy n.

**re·lieve** (rĭ-lēv′) v. -lieved, -lieving. 1. To alleviate; ease. 2. To free from pain, anxiety, etc. 3. To aid. 4. To free from duty by providing a substitute. 5. To make less monotonous. —re·lief′ n.

**re·lig·ion** (rĭ-lĭj′ən) n. An organized system of beliefs and rituals centering on a supernatural being or beings. —re·lig′ious adj.

**re·lin·quish** (rĭ-lĭng′kwĭsh) v. 1. To let go. 2. To surrender; renounce.

**rel·ish** (rĕl′ĭsh) n. 1. An appetite for something. 2. A spicy condiment. —v. To take pleasure in.

**re·luc·tant** (rĭ-lŭk′tənt) adj. Unwilling. —re·luc′tance n. —re·luc′tant·ly adv.

**re·ly** (rĭ-lī′) v. -lied, -lying. —rely on (or upon). 1. To depend. 2. To trust confidently. —re·li′a·bil′i·ty n. —re·li′a·ble adj. —re·li′ance n. —re·li′ant adj.

**re·main** (rĭ-mān′) v. 1. To continue without change. 2. To stay or be left over. 3. To endure or persist. —re·main′der n.

**re·mark** (rĭ-märk′) v. 1. To say casually; comment. 2. To take notice of. —n. 1. Notice; mention. 2. A comment. —re·mark′a·ble adj. —re·mark′a·bly adv.

**rem·e·dy** (rĕm′ĭ-dē) n., pl. -dies. Something that relieves, cures, or corrects. —v. -died, -dying. 1. To relieve or cure. 2. To rectify. —re·me′di·al adj.

**re·mem·ber** (rĭ-mĕm′bər) v. 1. To recall to or retain in the mind. 2. To give (someone) a gift, tip, etc. —re·mem′brance n.

**re·mind** (rĭ-mīnd′) v. To cause to remember. —re·mind′er n.

**rem·i·nisce** (rĕm′ə-nĭs′) v. -nisced, -niscing. To recollect and tell of past experiences. —rem′i·nis′cence n. —rem′i·nis′cent adj.

**re·miss** (rĭ-mĭs′) adj. Negligent.

**re·mit** (rĭ-mĭt′) v. -mitted, -mitting. 1. To send (money). 2. To pardon; forgive. 3. To di-

minish; abate. —re·mis′sion n. —re·mit′tance n.

**rem·nant** (rĕm′nənt) n. 1. Something left over. 2. A surviving trace.

**re·morse** (rĭ-môrs′) n. Anguish for past misdeeds; bitter regret. —re·morse′ful adj. —re·morse′less adj.

**re·mote** (rĭ-mōt′) adj. -moter, -motest. 1. Far away. 2. Slight. 3. Aloof. —re·mote′ly adv. —re·mote′ness n.

**re·move** (rĭ-mōōv′) v. -moved, -moving. 1. To move from one place to another. 2. To take away. 3. To dismiss from office. —n. Distance apart. —re·mov′a·ble adj. —re·mov′al n.

**re·mu·ner·ate** (rĭ-myōō′nə-rāt′) v. -ated, -ating. To pay for goods, work, etc. —re·mu′ner·a′tion n. —re·mu′ner·a′tive adj.

**ren·ais·sance** (rĕn′ə-säns′, -zäns′) n. A rebirth; revival.

**ren·der** (rĕn′dər) v. 1. To submit. 2. To give or make available. 3. To represent in art. 4. To liquefy (fat) by heating. —ren·di′tion n.

**ren·e·gade** (rĕn′ə-gād′) n. 1. An apostate. 2. An outlaw.

**re·nege** (rĭ-nĭg′, -nĕg′, -nēg′) v. -neged, -neging. To break a promise or commitment.

**re·new** (rĭ-n/yōō′) v. 1. To make as if new again; restore. 2. To resume. 3. To replenish. —re·new′a·ble adj. —re·new′al n.

**re·nounce** (rĭ-nouns′) v. -nounced, -nouncing. 1. To give up a (title or activity), esp. formally. 2. To reject; disown. —re·nounce′ment n. —re·nun′ci·a′tion n.

**ren·o·vate** (rĕn′ə-vāt′) v. -vated, -vating. To renew; repair. —ren′o·va′tion n.

**re·nown** (rĭ-noun′) n. Fame. —re·nowned′ adj.

**rent** (rĕnt) n. Periodic payment for the use of another's property. —v. To pay for and use (another's property). —rent′al n.

**re·pair** (rĭ-pâr′) v. 1. To restore to sound condition. —n. 1. The work of repairing. 2. General condition.

**re·peal** (rĭ-pēl′) v. To revoke or annul officially. —re·peal′ n.

**re·peat** (rĭ-pēt′) v. To say or do again. —n. 1. The act of repeating. 2. Something repeated. —re·peat′ed·ly adv.

**re·pel** (rĭ-pĕl′) v. -pelled, -pelling. 1. To drive back; ward off. 2. To cause aversion in. —re·pel′lent adj. & n.

**re·pent** (rĭ-pĕnt′) v. To feel regret or penitence for (what one has done or failed to do). —re·pen′tance n. —re·pen′tant adj.

**re·per·cus·sion** (rē′pər-kŭsh′ən) n. 1. An indirect effect or result. 2. A reciprocal action; rebound.

**rep·e·ti·tion** (rĕp'ə-tĭsh'ən) n. **1.** The act of repeating. **2.** Something repeated. —**rep'e·ti'tious** adj. —**rep·e·ti'tious·ly** adv. —**re·pet'i·tive** adj. —**re·pet'i·tive·ly** adv.

**re·place** (rĭ-plās') v. **1.** To put back in place. **2.** To take the place of. —**re·place'ment** n.

**rep·li·ca** (rĕp'lə-kə) n. A copy; duplicate.

**re·ply** (rĭ-plī') v. -**plied, -plying.** To answer. —n., pl. -**plies.** An answer; response.

**re·port** (rĭ-pôrt') n. **1.** An account, usually prepared in organized form. **2.** Rumor. **3.** An explosive noise. —v. **1.** To present an account of. **2.** To tell about; relate. **3.** To complain about to the proper authorities. **4.** To gather information for news stories. **5.** To present oneself. —**re·port'er** n.

**rep·re·hen·si·ble** (rĕp'rĭ-hĕn'sə-bəl) adj. Deserving censure; blameworthy. —**rep're·hen'si·bly** adv.

**rep·re·sent** (rĕp'rĭ-zĕnt') v. **1.** To stand for; symbolize. **2.** To depict; portray. **3.** To serve as the agent for. **4.** To act as a spokesman for, esp. in a legislative body. —**rep're·sen·ta'tion** n. —**rep're·sen'ta·tive** n. & adj.

**re·press** (rĭ-prĕs') v. **1.** To restrain. **2.** To suppress. **3.** To force (memories, ideas, or fears) into the subconscious mind. —**re·pres'sion** n. —**re·pres'sive** adj.

**re·prieve** (rĭ-prēv') v. -**prieved, -prieving.** To postpone or cancel punishment. —n. A postponement; respite.

**re·proach** (rĭ-prōch') v. To blame. —n. **1.** Blame. **2.** Disgrace; shame. —**re·proach'ful** adj.

**re·pro·duce** (rē'prə-d/y/ōōs') v. -**duced, -ducing. 1.** To produce a copy of. **2.** To produce offspring. —**re'pro·duc'tion** n. —**re'pro·duc'tive** adj.

**re·proof** (rĭ-prōōf') n. A rebuke.

**re·prove** (rĭ-prōōv') v. -**proved, -proving.** To rebuke; chide. —**re·prov'ing·ly** adv.

**rep·tile** (rĕp'tĭl, -tīl') n. A cold-blooded vertebrate, such as a snake, turtle, or lizard. —**rep·til'i·an** adj. & n.

**re·pub·lic** (rĭ-pŭb'lĭk) n. A political order that has no monarch and is based on a constitutional form of government, esp. a democratic one. —**re·pub'li·can** adj. & n.

**re·pu·di·ate** (rĭ-pyōō'dē-āt') v. -**ated, -ating. 1.** To reject the validity of. **2.** To disown. —**re·pu'di·a'tion** n.

**re·pug·nant** (rĭ-pŭg'nənt) adj. Distasteful; repulsive. —**re·pug'nance** n.

**re·pulse** (rĭ-pŭls') v. -**pulsed, -pulsing.** To repel; reject. —n. **1.** The act of repulsing.

**2.** Rejection; refusal. —**re·pul'sion** n.

**re·pul·sive** (rĭ-pŭl'sĭv) adj. Causing extreme dislike; disgusting. —**re·pul'sive·ly** adv. —**re·pul'sive·ness** n.

**rep·u·ta·tion** (rĕp'yə-tā'shən) n. **1.** The estimation in which one is held by the public. **2.** A specific character or trait.

**re·pute** (rĭ-pyōōt') v. -**puted, -puting.** To assign a reputation to; consider. —n. **1.** Reputation. **2.** A good reputation. —**re·put'a·ble** adj. —**rep'u·ta·bly** adv. —**re·put'ed** adj.

**re·quest** (rĭ-kwĕst') v. To ask for. —n. **1.** An expressed desire. **2.** Something asked for.

**re·quire** (rĭ-kwīr') v. -**quired, -quiring. 1.** To need. **2.** To demand. —**re·quire'ment** n.

**req·ui·site** (rĕk'wĭ-zĭt) adj. Required. —n. A necessity; something essential. —**req'ui·si'tion** n. & v.

**res·cue** (rĕs'kyōō) v. -**cued, -cuing.** To save, as from danger. —n. An act of saving. —**res'cu·er** n.

**re·search** (rĭ-sûrch', rē'sûrch) n. Diligent investigation or inquiry. —**re·search'** v. —**re·search'er** n.

**re·sem·ble** (rĭ-zĕm'bəl) v. -**bled, -bling.** To have a similarity to. —**re·sem'blance** n.

**re·sent** (rĭ-zĕnt') v. To feel indignant at. —**re·sent'ful** adj. —**re·sent'ful·ly** adv. —**re·sent'ment** n.

**re·serve** (rĭ-zûrv') v. -**served, -serving. 1.** To save; hold back. **2.** To set apart for a particular person or use, as land or accommodations. —n. **1.** Something saved for future use. **2.** Reticence; discretion. **3.** Often **reserves.** The part of an army subject to call in an emergency. —**res'er·va'tion** n. —**re·served'** adj.

**res·er·voir** (rĕz'ər-vwär', -vwôr', -vôr') n. **1.** A body of water stored for use. **2.** A lake or chamber for storing a fluid. **3.** A large supply of something built up over a period of time.

**re·side** (rĭ-zīd') v. -**sided, -siding.** To live or dwell. —**re·sid'er** n.

**res·i·dence** (rĕz'ə-dəns, -dĕns') n. **1.** A dwelling. **2.** The act or duration of residing somewhere. —**res'i·dent** n. —**res'i·den'tial** adj.

**re·sign** (rĭ-zīn') v. **1.** To submit (oneself); acquiesce. **2.** To give up (a position). —**res'ig·na'tion** n. —**re·signed'** adj.

**re·sil·ience** (rĭ-zĭl'yəns) n. Also **re·sil·ien·cy. 1.** The ability to recover quickly, as from illness. **2.** Elasticity. —**re·sil'ient** adj.

**re·sist** (rĭ-zĭst') v. **1.** To work against; op-

# R-18

**resolution**                                   188

pose. **2.** To withstand. — **re·sis'tance** n. — **re·sist'er** n.

**res·o·lu·tion** (rĕz'ə-lōō'shən) n. **1.** Determination. **2.** A course of action decided upon. **3.** A formal decision put before an assembly. **4.** Outcome or solution. — **res'o·lute'** adj. — **res'o·lute'ly** adv.

**re·solve** (rĭ-zŏlv') v. -solved, -solving. **1.** To decide firmly; intend. **2.** To decide by formal vote. **3.** To solve. — n. **1.** Firmness of purpose; resolution. **2.** A determination or decision. — **re·solv'a·ble** adj. — **re·solved'** adj.

**res·o·nance** (rĕz'ə-nəns) n. The intensification and prolongation of a tone by vibration; echoing. — **res'o·nant** adj.

**re·sort** (rĭ-zôrt') v. To seek assistance; have recourse. — n. **1.** A place frequented for recreation. **2.** A recourse.

**re·sound** (rĭ-zound') v. **1.** To reverberate. **2.** To sound loudly; ring. — **re·sound'ing** adj. — **re·sound'ing·ly** adv.

**re·source** (rē'sôrs, rĭ-sôrs') n. **1.** A supply that can be drawn upon. **2.** An ability to deal with or adapt to a situation. **3.** Often **resources.** Available capital; assets. — **re·source'ful** adj. — **re·source'ful·ness** n.

**re·spect** (rĭ-spĕkt') v. **1.** To hold in esteem. **2.** To relate or refer to. — n. **1.** Esteem. **2.** A particular feature or detail. **3.** Reference. — **re·spect'a·bil'i·ty** n. — **re·spect'a·ble** adj. — **re·spect'a·bly** adv. — **re·spect'ful** adj. — **re·spect'ful·ly** adv. — **re·spect'ful·ness** n.

**re·spire** (rĭ-spīr') v. -spired, -spiring. To inhale and exhale; breathe. — **res'pi·ra'tor** n. — **res'pi·ra'tor** n.

**re·spond** (rĭ-spŏnd') v. **1.** To answer. **2.** To act in return. **3.** To react positively. — **re·sponse'** n. — **re·spon'sive** adj. — **re·spon'sive·ly** adv. — **re·spon'sive·ness** n.

**re·spon·si·ble** (rĭ-spŏn'sə-bəl) adj. **1.** Involving the ability or authority to act on one's own. **2.** Reliable. **3.** Accountable; answerable. — **re·spon'si·bil'i·ty** n. — **re·spon'si·bly** adv.

**rest¹** (rĕst) n. **1.** Cessation from work, activity, or motion. **2.** Ease or refreshment resulting from sleep or relaxation. — v. **1.** To refresh (oneself). **2.** To be still, quiet, or inactive. **3. a.** To be supported. **b.** To place or lay. **4.** To depend. — **rest'ful** adj. — **rest'less** adj. — **rest'less·ly** adv. — **rest'less·ness** n.

**rest²** (rĕst) n. Remainder. — v. To be or continue to be.

**res·tau·rant** (rĕs'tər-ənt, -tə-ränt') n. A place where meals are served to the public.

**re·store** (rĭ-stôr', -stōr') v. -stored, -storing.

**1.** To bring back into existence or use. **2.** To bring back to a previous condition; renovate. **3.** To reinstate. **4.** To give back. — **res'to·ra'tion** n. — **re·stor'er** n.

**re·strain** (rĭ-strān') v. **1.** To control; check. **2.** To limit; confine. — **re·straint'** n.

**re·strict** (rĭ-strĭkt') v. To keep within limits. — **re·stric'tion** n. — **re·stric'tive** adj.

**re·sult** (rĭ-zŭlt') v. **1.** To occur or exist as a consequence. **2.** To end in a particular way. — n. The consequence; outcome. — **re·sul'tant** adj.

**re·sume** (rĭ-zōōm') v. -sumed, -suming. **1.** To continue after interruption. **2.** To take again. — **re·sump'tion** n.

**re·sus·ci·tate** (rĭ-sŭs'ə-tāt') v. -tated, -tating. To revive. — **re·sus'ci·ta'tion** n.

**re·tail** (rē'tāl') n. The sale of goods to the consumer. — **re·tail'** v. & adj. — **re·tail'er** n.

**re·tain** (rĭ-tān') v. **1.** To keep. **2.** To continue to practice, employ, etc. **3.** To hire by paying a fee. **4.** To remember. — **re·tain'er** n. — **re·ten'tion** n. — **re·ten'tive** adj.

**re·tal·i·ate** (rĭ-tăl'ē-āt') v. -ated, -ating. To return like for like, esp. evil. — **re·tal'i·a'tion** n. — **re·tal'i·a·to'ry** adj.

**ret·i·cent** (rĕt'ĭ-sənt) adj. Not inclined to speak out; reserved. — **ret'i·cence** n.

**re·tire** (rĭ-tīr') v. -tired, -tiring. **1.** To go or go to bed. **2.** To withdraw from business or public life. — **re·tired'** adj. — **re·tire'ment** n.

**re·tort** (rĭ-tôrt') v. **1.** To reply. **2.** To present a counterargument. — n. A quick, incisive reply.

**re·tract** (rĭ-trăkt') v. **1.** To disavow. **2.** To draw back. — **re·tract'a·ble** adj. — **re·trac'tion** n.

**re·treat** (rĭ-trēt') n. **1.** A withdrawal, esp. of a military force. **2.** A quiet, private place; refuge. — v. To withdraw.

**re·trieve** (rĭ-trēv') v. -trieved, -trieving. **1.** To regain. **2.** To fetch. **3.** To bring back game, as a dog does. — **re·triev'a·ble** adj. — **re·triev'al** n.

**ret·ro·ac·tive** (rĕt'rō-ăk'tĭv) adj. Applying to a period prior to enactment.

**ret·ro·spect** (rĕt'rə-spĕkt') n. A review of the past. — **ret'ro·spec'tive** adj. — **ret'ro·spec'tive·ly** adv.

**re·turn** (rĭ-tûrn') v. **1.** To go or come back. **2.** To respond. **3.** To send or put back. **4.** To yield (profit or interest). — n. **1.** The act of returning. **2.** Something brought or sent back. **3.** Often **returns.** A profit or yield. **4.** Often **returns.** The vote in an election. — **re·turn'a·ble** adj.

**re·un·ion** (rē-yōōn'yən) *n.* A gathering of a group whose members have been separated.

**re·veal** (rĭ-vēl') *v.* **1.** To disclose. **2.** To bring to view; expose. —**rev·e·la'tion** *n.*

**rev·eil·le** (rĕv'ə-lē) *n.* The morning bugle call to awaken soldiers.

**rev·el** (rĕv'əl) *v.* **1.** To enjoy greatly. **2.** To party riotously; carouse. —*n.* A noisy festivity. —**rev'el·er** *n.* —**rev'el·ry** *n.*

**re·venge** (rĭ-vĕnj') *v.* **-venged, -venging.** To retaliate; avenge. —*n.* Vengeance; retaliation. —**re·venge'ful** *adj.*

**rev·e·nue** (rĕv'ə-n/yōō) *n.* Income, esp. of a government.

**re·ver·ber·ate** (rĭ-vûr'bə-rāt') *v.* **-ated, -ating.** To re-echo. —**re·ver·ber·a'tion** *n.*

**re·vere** (rĭ-vîr') *v.* **-vered, -vering.** To regard with awe or great respect. —**rev'er·ence** *n.* —**rev'er·end** *adj.* —**rev'er·ent** *adj.* —**rev'er·en'tial** *adj.*

**re·verse** (rĭ-vûrs') *adj.* **1.** Turned backward. **2.** Causing backward movement. —*n.* **1.** The opposite of something. **2.** The back or rear of something. **3.** A defeat; misfortune. —*v.* **-versed, -versing. 1.** To turn to or in the opposite direction. **2.** To revoke or annul (a decision or decree). —**re·ver'sal** *n.* —**re·vers'i·ble** *adj.*

**re·vert** (rĭ-vûrt') *v.* To return to a former condition, practice, or belief.

**re·view** (rĭ-vyōō') *v.* **1.** To look over again. **2.** To look back on. **3.** To examine critically. **4.** To write a critical evaluation on (a new work or performance). —*n.* **1.** A re-examination. **2.** A retrospective survey. **3.** A re-studying of subject matter. **4.** An inspection or examination for evaluation. **5.** A report estimating the quality of a work or performance. —**re·view'er** *n.*

**re·vise** (rĭ-vīz') *v.* **-vised, -vising.** To change or modify; update. —**re·vi'sion** *n.*

**re·vive** (rĭ-vīv') *v.* **-vived, -viving. 1.** To bring back to consciousness. **2.** To regain vigor or spirit. **3.** To restore to use. —**re·viv'al** *n.*

**re·voke** (rĭ-vōk') *v.* **-voked, -voking.** To annul by withdrawing.

**re·volt** (rĭ-vōlt') *v.* **1.** To rebel against authority. **2.** To fill or be filled with disgust. —*n.* An uprising; rebellion.

**rev·o·lu·tion** (rĕv'ə-lōō'shən) *n.* **1. a.** Orbital motion about a point or an axis. **b.** A single complete cycle of such motion. **2.** A momentous or complete change. **3.** A political overthrow brought about from within. —**rev'o·lu'tion·ar'y** *adj. & n.* —**rev'o·lu'tion·ize'** *v.*

**re·volve** (rĭ-vŏlv') *v.* **-volved, -volving. 1.** To

turn or go round; rotate. **2.** To recur in cycles.

**re·volv·er** (rĭ-vŏl'vər) *n.* A pistol having a revolving cylinder with several cartridge chambers.

**re·vul·sion** (rĭ-vŭl'shən) *n.* A change in feeling, esp. to disgust.

**re·ward** (rĭ-wôrd') *n.* **1.** Recompense for service, conduct, etc. **2.** Money offered for some special service. —*v.* To give a reward to, esp. in return for.

**rhet·o·ric** (rĕt'ər-ĭk) *n.* The art of effective use of language. —**rhe·tor'i·cal** *adj.*

**rhi·noc·er·os** (rī-nŏs'ər-əs) *n.* A large, thick-skinned mammal with a horned snout.

**rhyme** (rīm). Also **rime.** *n.* **1.** Correspondence of end sounds of words or lines of verse. **2.** A poem with this correspondence. —*v.* **rhymed, rhyming.** To form a rhyme.

**rhythm** (rĭth'əm) *n.* Any kind of movement with a regular recurrence of strong and weak elements, esp. in music or verse. —**rhyth'mic, rhyth'mi·cal** *adj.* —**rhyth'mi·cal·ly** *adv.*

**rib** (rĭb) *n.* **1.** One of the long, curved bones extending from the spine to the breastbone. **2.** A riblike part used for support.

**rib·bon** (rĭb'ən) *n.* A strip of fine fabric.

**rice** (rīs) *n.* A cereal grass having a starchy edible seed.

**rich** (rĭch) *adj.* **1.** Possessing great wealth. **2.** Valuable. **3.** Elaborate. **4.** Plentiful; abundant. —**rich'ly** *adv.* —**rich'ness** *n.*

**rich·es** (rĭch'ĭz) *pl.n.* Wealth.

**rid** (rĭd) *v.* **rid** or **ridded, ridding.** To free from something; clear away. —**rid'dance** *n.*

**rid·den** (rĭd'n). *p.p. of* **ride.**

**rid·dle¹** (rĭd'l) *v.* **-dled, -dling.** To pierce with numerous holes.

**rid·dle²** (rĭd'l) *n.* A puzzling question or problem.

**ride** (rīd) *v.* **rode, ridden, riding. 1.** To be conveyed by an animal or vehicle. **2.** To sit on or in and drive. **3.** To be supported upon. —*n.* A journey by any means of conveyance. —**rid'er** *n.*

**ridge** (rĭj) *n.* **1.** A long, narrow land elevation. **2.** Any narrow raised strip. —*v.* **ridged, ridging.** To mark with or form into ridges.

**rid·i·cule** (rĭd'ə-kyōōl') *n.* Derision; mockery. —*v.* **-culed, -culing.** To make fun of; deride.

**ri·dic·u·lous** (rĭ-dĭk'yə-ləs) *adj.* Absurd or preposterous. —**ri·dic'u·lous·ly** *adv.* —**ri·dic'u·lous·ness** *n.*

**ri·fle¹** (rī'fəl) *n.* A shoulder firearm with a bore that has spiral grooves. —*v.* **-fled, -fling.**

To cut spiral grooves within (a gun barrel).
**ri·fle²** (rī'fəl) v. **-fled, -fling. 1.** To search with intent to steal. **2.** To rob.

**rig** (rĭg) v. **rigged, rigging. 1.** To fit out; equip. **2.** To equip (a ship) with ropes, chains, and tackle. **3.** To make in an expedient manner. **4.** To manipulate dishonestly. —n. **1.** The arrangement of masts, spars, and sails on a sailing vessel. **2.** A vehicle with one or more horses harnessed to it. **3.** The special apparatus used for drilling oil wells.

**right** (rīt) adj. **1.** In accordance with justice or law; proper. **2.** Factual; correct. **3.** Sound or normal. **4.** Of the side that faces east when a person or thing faces north. —n. **1.** That which is just, legal, proper, or fitting. **2.** The right-hand side. **3. the Right.** Political conservatives. **4.** That which is due to anyone by law or nature. —adv. **1.** Directly. **2.** Properly; correctly. **3.** Exactly. **4.** Immediately. **5.** Completely. —v. **1.** To stand or set upright. **2.** To redress. —**right'ful** adj. —**right'ful·ly** adv. —**right'ful·ness** n. —**right'ly** adv. —**right'ness** n.

**right·eous** (rī'chəs) adj. Virtuous; upright. —**right'eous·ly** adv. —**right'eous·ness** n.

**rig·id** (rĭj'ĭd) adj. **1.** Stiff; inflexible. **2.** Not moving; fixed. **3.** Severe; harsh. —**rig·id'i·ty** n.

**rig·or** (rĭg'ər) n. **1.** Strictness or severity, as judgment. **2.** A hardship. —**rig'or·ous** adj. —**rig'or·ous·ly** adv.

**rim** (rĭm) n. **1.** A border or edge. **2.** The outer part of a wheel around which a tire is fitted. —v. **rimmed, rimming.** To furnish with a rim.

**rind** (rīnd) n. A tough covering, as the skin of some fruits.

**ring¹** (rĭng) n. **1.** A circular object with a vacant circular center. **2.** A small circular band worn on a finger. **3.** Any circular band. **4.** An area in which prize fights, exhibitions, etc., are held. **5.** A group of persons acting privately. —v. To encircle.

**ring²** (rĭng) v. **rang, rung, ringing. 1.** To give forth a clear, resonant sound. **2.** To cause (a bell, chimes, etc.) to sound. **3.** To call (someone) on the telephone. —n. **1.** The sound created by a bell, etc. **2.** A telephone call.

**rinse** (rĭns) v. **rinsed, rinsing. 1.** To wash lightly. **2.** To remove (soap, dirt, etc.) with water. —n. **1.** The act of washing lightly. **2.** A solution used in conditioning or tinting the hair.

**ri·ot** (rī'ət) n. A disturbance created by a

mob. —v. To take part in a riot. —**ri'ot·er** n. —**ri'ot·ous** adj. —**ri'ot·ous·ly** adv.

**rip** (rĭp) v. **ripped, ripping. 1.** To tear. **2.** To remove by pulling. —n. A torn or split place.

**ripe** (rīp) adj. Fully developed; mature. —**rip'en** v. —**ripe'ness** n.

**rip·ple** (rĭp'əl) v. **-pled, -pling. 1.** To form small waves. **2.** To rise and fall gently in tone or volume. —n. **1.** A small wave. **2.** An indistinct vibrating sound.

**rise** (rīz) v. **rose, risen** (rĭz'ən) **rising. 1.** To stand up. **2.** To get out of bed. **3.** To ascend. **4.** To increase in amount, value, etc. **5.** To appear above the horizon. —**rise** n.

**risk** (rĭsk) n. The possibility of loss or danger. —v. To expose to loss or damage. —**risk'y** adj.

**rit·u·al** (rĭch'ōō·əl) n. **1.** The prescribed form for a solemn ceremony. **2.** A body of ceremonies, esp. religious. —**rit'u·al** adj. —**rit'u·al·ly** adv.

**ri·val** (rī'vəl) n. One who competes against another for the same object. —adj. Competing. —v. **1.** To attempt to equal or surpass. **2.** To equal; be a match for. —**ri'val·ry** n.

**riv·er** (rĭv'ər) n. A large natural stream of water.

**riv·et** (rĭv'ĭt) n. A bolt or pin used to fasten metal plates together. —v. **1.** To fasten with a rivet. **2.** To engross (the attention).

**road** (rōd) n. **1.** An open way for the passage of vehicles. **2.** A course toward the achievement of something.

**roam** (rōm) v. To travel aimlessly; wander.

**roar** (rôr) v. **1.** To utter a loud, deep sound. **2.** To express with a roar. **3.** To laugh loudly. —n. **1.** A loud, deep sound. **2.** Loud laughter.

**roast** (rōst) v. **1.** To cook with dry heat. **2.** To expose to great heat. —n. A cut of meat for roasting. —**roast'er** n.

**rob** (rŏb) v. **robbed, robbing. 1.** To steal (from). **2.** To deprive of unlawfully. —**rob'ber** n. —**rob'ber·y** n.

**robe** (rōb) n. **1.** A long, loose, flowing garment. **2.** A blanket or covering. —v. **robed, robing.** To dress in a robe.

**rob·in** (rŏb'ĭn) n. A red-breasted songbird.

**ro·bot** (rō'bət, rŏb'ət) n. A manlike mechanical device.

**ro·bust** (rō·bŭst', rō'bŭst) adj. Healthy and strong; vigorous. —**ro·bust'ly** adv. —**ro·bust'ness** n.

**rock¹** (rŏk) n. A hard natural mass of mineral matter; stone. —**rock'y** adj.

**rock²** (rŏk) v. **1.** To move or sway from side

to side. **2.** To shake violently.

**rock·et** (rŏk'ĭt) n. **1.** A device propelled by ejection of matter, esp. matter produced by internal gaseous combustion. **2.** A rocket-propelled explosive weapon. —v. To move swiftly.

**rod** (rŏd) n. **1.** A thin piece or pole of metal, wood, etc. **2.** A metal bar in a machine. **3.** A linear measure equal to 5.5 yards or 5.03 meters.

**rode** (rōd). p.t. of **ride**.

**ro·dent** (rōd'ənt) n. A gnawing mammal, as a mouse, squirrel, or beaver.

**role** (rōl) n. Also **rôle**. **1.** A character played by an actor. **2.** A function.

**roll** (rōl) v. **1.** To move by turning over and over. **2.** To move on wheels. **3.** To gain momentum. **4.** To wrap round upon itself. **5.** To enfold in a covering. **6.** To spread or flatten with a roller. **7.** To form in a ball. —n. **1.** Something rolled up in the form of a cylinder. **2.** A list of names. **3.** A small rounded bread or cake. **4.** A swaying or rocking motion.

**rol·lick·ing** (rŏl'ĭ-kĭng) adj. High-spirited; boisterous.

**ro·mance** (rō-măns', rō'măns) n. **1.** A fictitious tale of adventure. **2.** A sentimental novel dealing with love. **3.** A love affair.

**ro·man·tic** (rō-măn'tĭk) adj. **1.** Expressive of personal feelings and sentiment. **2.** Given to feelings of love. **3.** Conducive to romance. **4.** Imaginative but impractical. **5.** Imaginary. —n. A romantic person. —**ro·man'ti·cal·ly** adv. —**ro·man'ti·cize'** v.

**roof** (rōōf, rŏŏf) n. **1.** The top covering of a building. **2.** The upper part of the mouth. —v. To cover with a roof.

**room** (rōōm, rŏŏm) n. **1.** Space. **2.** An area of a building set off by walls. —v. To occupy a room; lodge. —**room'er** n. —**room'mate'** n.

**roost** (rōōst) n. A perch on which birds rest at night. —v. To rest or sleep on a perch.

**roost·er** (rōōs'tər) n. The adult male domestic fowl.

**root**[1] (rōōt, rŏŏt) n. **1.** The underground portion of a plant. **2.** The embedded part of an organ, as a tooth, hair, etc. **3.** An essential element; core. **4.** Origin. **5.** A number that when multiplied by itself an indicated number of times equals a specified number. —v. **1.** To put forth roots. **2.** To implant by or as by roots.

**root**[2] (rōōt, rŏŏt) v. To dig with or as with the snout.

**rope** (rōp) n. A flexible, heavy cord. —v. **roped, roping**. **1.** To fasten with rope. **2.** To enclose with a rope. **3.** To lasso.

**rose**[1] (rōz) n. **1.** A prickly plant with showy, fragrant flowers. **2.** Dark pink.

**rose**[2] (rōz). p.t. of **rise**.

**ros·y** (rō'zē) adj. **-ier, -iest. 1.** Having the pink or red color of a rose. **2.** Cheery; optimistic. **3.** Flushed; bright. —**ros'i·ly** adv.

**rot** (rŏt) v. **rotted, rotting**. To decompose; decay. —n. **1.** The process of rotting. **2.** Decay. —**rot'ten** adj. —**rot'ten·ly** adv. —**rot'ten·ness** n.

**ro·tate** (rō'tāt') v. **-tated, -tating. 1.** To turn on an axis. **2.** To alternate in sequence. —**ro'ta·ry** adj. —**ro·ta'tion** n. —**ro·ta'tion·al** adj. —**ro'ta·tor** n.

**rouge** (rōōzh) n. **1.** A red cosmetic for the cheeks or lips. **2.** A reddish polishing powder for metal. —v. **rouged, rouging**. To color with rouge.

**rough** (rŭf) adj. **1.** Not smooth. **2.** Turbulent. **3.** Not gentle. **4.** In a crude or unfinished state. —v. **1.** To make rough. **2.** To treat roughly. —**rough'en** v. —**rough'ly** adv. —**rough'ness** n.

**rough·age** (rŭf'ĭj) n. The coarse parts of certain foods.

**round** (round) adj. **1.** Spherical; circular; curved. **2.** Complete. **3.** Expressed as a whole number. **4.** Approximate; not exact. —n. **1.** Something round. **2.** A cut of beef. **3.** A complete course, succession, or series. **4.** Often **rounds.** A course of customary actions, duties, etc. **5.** A single outburst of applause. **6.** A single shot. **7.** A period of play in various sports. —v. **1.** To make or become round. **2.** To complete. **3.** To go around. —adv. **1.** Around. **2.** Throughout. —prep. Around. —**round'ness** n.

**round·a·bout** (round'ə-bout') adj. Indirect; circuitous.

**round·ly** (round'lē) adv. **1.** Vigorously; bluntly. **2.** Thoroughly.

**rouse** (rouz) v. **roused, rousing. 1.** To wake up. **2.** To excite; spur.

**rout** (rout) n. **1.** A disorderly flight following defeat. **2.** An overwhelming defeat. —v. **1.** To put to flight. **2.** To defeat overwhelmingly.

**route** (rōōt, rout) n. A road or course for travel. —v. **1.** To send along. **2.** To schedule on a certain route.

**rou·tine** (rōō-tēn') n. **1.** A prescribed procedure. **2.** Customary activities. —adj. **1.** Habitual; regular. **2.** Uninteresting or unoriginal. — **rou·tine·ly** *adv.*

**rove** (rōv) *v.* **roved, roving.** To wander; roam. — **rov·er** *n.*

**row**[1] (rō) *n.* A linear arrangement.

**row**[2] (rō) *v.* **rowed, rowing.** To propel with oars. — *n.* A trip in a rowboat. — **row·er** *n.*

**row**[3] (rou) *n.* A noisy quarrel.

**row·boat** (rō'bōt') *n.* A small boat propelled by oars.

**row·dy** (rou'dē) *n., pl.* **-dies.** A rough, disorderly person. — *adj.* **-di·er, -di·est.** Disorderly; rough.

**roy·al** (roi'əl) *adj.* Of a monarch. — **roy·al·ly** *adv.*

**roy·al·ty** (roi'əl-tē) *n., pl.* **-ties.** **1.** Monarchs and their families collectively. **2.** The power of monarchs. **3.** A share paid to an author, etc. out of the proceeds from the sale of his work.

**rub** (rŭb) *v.* **rubbed, rubbing. 1.** To apply pressure and friction to (a surface). **2.** To contact repeatedly and with friction; scrape. **3.** To become or cause to become irritated. — *n.* **1.** The act of rubbing. **2.** An obstacle.

**rub·ber** (rŭb'ər) *n.* **1.** An elastic material, either natural or synthetic. **2.** Often **rubbers.** A low overshoe. — **rub·ber·y** *adj.*

**rub·bish** (rŭb'ĭsh) *n.* **1.** Garbage; litter. **2.** Nonsense.

**rub·ble** (rŭb'əl) *n.* **1.** Fragments of stone. **2.** Debris.

**ru·by** (rōō'bē) *n., pl.* **-bies. 1.** A deep-red gemstone. **2.** A dark red.

**rud·der** (rŭd'ər) *n.* A hinged plate at the rear of a vessel or aircraft, used for steering.

**rude** (rōōd) *adj.* **ruder, rudest. 1.** Impolite; discourteous. **2.** Makeshift; crude. — **rude·ly** *adv.* — **rude'ness** *n.*

**ru·di·ment** (rōō'də-mənt) *n.* Often **rudiments.** A fundamental element, principle, or skill. — **ru'di·men·ta·ry** *adj.*

**rue** (rōō) *v.* **rued, ruing.** To regret; repent. — **rue'ful** *adj.* — **rue'ful·ly** *adv.*

**ruf·fle** (rŭf'əl) *n.* **1.** A strip of frilled or pleated fabric. **2.** A slight disturbance. — *v.* **-fled, -fling. 1.** To disturb the smoothness or ripple. **2.** To gather into a ruffle. **3.** To fluster.

**rug** (rŭg) *n.* A heavy floor covering of fabric, animal skin, etc.

**rug·ged** (rŭg'ĭd) *adj.* **1.** Rough; irregular. **2.** Hard; severe. **3.** Vigorously healthy. — **rug'ged·ness** *n.*

**ru·in** (rōō'ĭn) *n.* **1.** Total destruction. **2.** Often **ruins.** The remains of something destroyed. — *v.* **1.** To reduce to ruin. **2.** To

harm irreparably. — **ru'in·a'tion** *n.* — **ru'in·ous** *adj.* — **ru'in·ous·ly** *adv.*

**rule** (rōōl) *n.* **1.** Governing power. **2.** A principle that governs conduct or procedure; a regulation. **3.** A standard method. — *v.* **ruled, ruling. 1.** To control; govern. **2.** To decide judicially; decree. **3.** To mark with straight parallel lines. — **rul'ing** *n.*

**rul·er** (rōō'lər) *n.* **1.** One who rules. **2.** A straight-edged strip for drawing straight lines and measuring lengths.

**rum** (rŭm) *n.* An alcoholic liquor distilled from molasses.

**ru·mi·nate** (rōō'mə-nāt') *v.* **-nated, -nating. 1.** To chew cud, as cattle, sheep, and deer do. **2.** To meditate; muse. — **ru'mi·na'tion** *n.* — **ru'mi·nant** *n. & adj.*

**ru·mor** (rōō'mər) *n.* Unverified information; gossip. — *v.* To spread rumor.

**rump** (rŭmp) *n.* **1.** The fleshy hind part of an animal. **2.** The buttocks.

**rum·ple** (rŭm'pəl) *v.* **-pled, -pling.** To wrinkle or crease. — **rum'ply** *adj.*

**run** (rŭn) *v.* **ran, run, running. 1.** To move on foot at a pace faster than walking. **2.** To retreat rapidly. **3.** To hurry. **4.** To take part in a race. **5.** To compete for elected office. **6.** To be in operation. **7.** To manage. **8.** To flow. **9.** To melt. **10.** To extend, stretch, or reach. **11.** To extend in time. **12.** To vary or range in quality, price, size, etc. — *n.* **1.** An act of running. **2.** A point scored in baseball. **3.** Unrestricted freedom or use of a place. **4.** A trip between points on a route. **5.** A movement or flow. **6.** A year or unraveled length in a fabric. **7.** An unbroken series or sequence.

**rung**[1] (rŭng) *n.* **1.** A step of a ladder. **2.** A crosspiece supporting the legs or back of a chair. **3.** A spoke in a wheel.

**rung**[2] (rŭng) *p.p. of* ring.

**run·ner** (rŭn'ər) *n.* **1.** One who runs, as a messenger. **2.** A device in or on which something slides, as the blade of a skate. **3.** A long narrow carpet.

**runt** (rŭnt) *n.* An undersized animal or person.

**rup·ture** (rŭp'chər) *n.* **1.** A breaking open or bursting. **2.** A tear in bodily tissue. — **rup'ture** *v.*

**ru·ral** (rōōr'əl) *adj.* Of the country. — **ru'ral·ly** *adv.*

**ruse** (rōōz) *n.* A trick.

**rush** (rŭsh) *v.* **1.** To move or act swiftly. **2.** To attack; charge. — *n.* **1.** A sudden forward motion. **2.** General haste. **3.** A sudden onslaught.

**rust** (rŭst) n. **1.** A reddish oxide formed on iron by exposure to air and water. **2.** A plant disease caused by parasitic fungi. **3.** Reddish brown. —v. **1.** To corrode. **2.** To deteriorate through inactivity. — **rust′i·ness** n. — **rust′y** adj.

**rus·tic** (rŭs′tĭk) adj. **1.** Rural. **2.** Unsophisticated; simple. —n. A country person. — **rus·tic′i·ty** n.

**rus·tle¹** (rŭs′əl) v. **-tled, -tling.** To make or cause to make soft whispering sounds. — **rus′tle** n. — **rus′tling·ly** adv.

**rus·tle²** (rŭs′əl) v. **-tled, -tling.** To steal cattle. — **rus′tler** n.

**rut** (rŭt) n. **1.** A sunken groove made by the passage of wheels. **2.** A fixed routine.

**ruth·less** (rōōth′lĭs) adj. Having no compassion; merciless. — **ruth′less·ly** adv. — **ruth′less·ness** n.

**rye** (rī) n. **1.** A cereal grass, used in making flour and whiskey. **2.** Whiskey made from rye.

# S

**s, S** (ĕs) n. The 19th letter of the English alphabet.

**Sab·bath** (săb′əth) n. The weekly day of rest, Sunday for most Christians and Saturday for Jews.

**sa·ber** (sā′bər) n. A heavy cavalry sword.

**sab·o·tage** (săb′ə-täzh′) n. Deliberate subversion. — **sab′o·tage′** v. — **sab′o·teur′** n.

**sac** (săk) n. A pouchlike structure.

**sac·cha·rin** (săk′ə-rĭn) n. A sweet powder used as a calorie-free sweetener.

**sac·cha·rine** (săk′ə-rĭn, -rīn′) adj. **1.** Sweet. **2.** Cloying in attitude or character.

**sack¹** (săk) n. A large bag.

**sack²** (săk) v. To loot. — **sack** n.

**sac·ra·ment** (săk′rə-mənt) n. A ceremonial act prescribed by a religion; rite. — **sac′ra·men′tal** adj. — **sac′ra·men′tal·ly** adv.

**sa·cred** (sā′krĭd) adj. **1.** Holy; religious. **2.** Inviolable. — **sa′cred·ly** adv. — **sa′cred·ness** n.

**sac·ri·fice** (săk′rə-fīs′) n. **1.** The offering of something valued, as to a god. **2.** The willing acceptance of a loss. — **-ficed, -ficing. 1.** To offer as a sacrifice. **2.** To forfeit; give up.

— **sac′ri·fic′er** n. — **sac′ri·fi′cial** adj.

**sac·ro·sanct** (săk′rō-săngkt′) adj. Sacred.

**sad** (săd) adj. **sadder, saddest. 1.** Unhappy. **2.** Deplorable. — **sad·den** v. — **sad′ly** adv. — **sad′ness** n.

**sad·dle** (săd′l) n. A leather seat for a rider, as on a horse. —v. **-dled, -dling. 1.** To put a saddle on. **2.** To encumber.

**sa·dism** (sā′dĭz′əm, săd′ĭz′əm) n. Pleasure in cruelty. — **sa′dist** n. — **sa·dis′tic** adj.

**safe** (sāf) adj. **safer, safest. 1.** Not dangerous. **2.** Unhurt. —n. A strongbox. — **safe′ly** adv. — **safe′ty** n.

**sag** (săg) v. **sagged, sagging.** To sink or bend downward; droop. — **sag** n.

**sage** (sāj) n. A venerable wise man. —adj. **sager, sagest.** Wise. — **sage′ly** adv.

**said** (sĕd) p.t. & p.p. of **say.** —adj. Aforementioned.

**sail** (sāl) n. **1.** A length of fabric that catches the wind and so propels a vessel. **2.** A trip in a sailing craft. —v. **1.** To move or travel by means of a sail. **2.** To navigate. **3.** To glide; soar. — **sail′boat′** n.

**sail·or** (sā′lər) n. One who works on a ship.

**saint** (sānt) n. A very holy or unselfish person. — **saint′hood** n. — **saint′li·ness** n. — **saint′ly** adj.

**sake** (sāk) n. **1.** Purpose. **2.** Benefit.

**sal·ad** (săl′əd) n. A dish consisting of a mixture of raw vegetables.

**sal·a·ry** (săl′ə-rē, săl′rē) n., pl. **-ries.** A fixed payment for services. — **sal′a·ried** adj.

**sale** (sāl) n. **1.** The exchange of property for money. **2.** Availability for purchase. **3.** An offering of goods, esp. at lowered prices. — **sal′a·ble** adj.

**sales·man** (sālz′mən) n. A man employed to sell things. — **sales′man·ship** n. — **sales′wom′an** fem.n. — **sales′per′son** n.

**sa·li·va** (sə-lī′və) n. The thick, secreted liquid that keeps the mouth and throat moist. — **sal′i·var′y** adj. — **sal′i·vate** v.

**salt** (sôlt) n. **1.** Sodium chloride, used as a food seasoning and preservative. **2.** Flavor or zest. —v. To season or cure with salt. — **salt** adj. — **salt′i·ness** n. — **salt′y** adj.

**sa·lu·tar·y** (săl′yə-tĕr′ē) adj. Beneficial; wholesome.

**sal·u·ta·tion** (săl′yə-tā′shən) n. An expression of greeting.

**sa·lute** (sə-lōōt′) v. **-luted, -luting. 1.** To greet, esp. with a gesture of respect. **2.** To honor. —n. A formal or respectful greeting.

**sal·vage** (săl′vĭj) v. **1.** The rescue of property. **2. a.** The saving of imperiled property. **b.**

The property saved. —v. -vaged, -vaging. To save from loss or destruction. —sal'vage-a-ble adj.

sal-va-tion (săl-vā'shən) n. 1. Deliverance from evil or difficulty. 2. A means of such deliverance. 3. Deliverance from sin; redemption.

salve (săv, säv) n. A medicinal ointment. —v. salved, salving. To soothe.

same (sām) adj. 1. Being the very one. 2. Similar or corresponding. —pron. The same person, thing, or event. —adv. In like manner. —same'ness n.

sam-ple (săm'pəl) n. A part representative of a whole. —v. -pled, -pling. To test or examine by a sample. —sam'pler n.

sanc-ti-fy (săngk'tə-fī') v. -fied, -fying. To make holy; purify. —sanc-ti-fi-ca'tion n. —sanc'ti-fi'er an.

sanc-ti-mo-ni-ous (săngk'tə-mō'nē-əs) adj. Making a pretense of piety. —sanc'ti-mo'ni-ous-ly adv. —sanc'ti-mo'ni-ous-ness, sanc'ti-mo'ny n.

sanc-tion (săngk'shən) n. 1. Authoritative approval. 2. A penalty intended to enforce compliance. —v. To authorize.

sanc-ti-ty (săngk'tə-tē) n., pl. -ties. 1. Saintliness. 2. Sacredness.

sanc-tu-ar-y (săngk'chōō-ĕr'ē) n., pl. -ies. 1. A holy place, as in a church. 2. A refuge or asylum.

sand (sănd) n. Loose particles of disintegrated rock. —v. To sandpaper. —sand'er n. —sand'y adj.

san-dal (săn'dəl) n. A shoe consisting of a sole fastened to the foot by straps.

sand-pa-per (sănd'pā'pər) n. Paper coated with sand, used for smoothing.

sand-wich (sănd'wich, săn'-) n. Slices of bread with a filling between them. —v. To squeeze.

sane (sān) adj. saner, sanest. 1. Of sound mind. 2. Reasonable. —sane'ly adv. —sane'ness n. —san'i-ty n.

sang (săng). p.t. of sing.

san-guine (săng'gwin) adj. Optimistic. —san'guine-ly adv. —san'guine-ness n.

san-i-tar-y (săn'ə-tĕr'ē) adj. 1. Of or used to preserve health. 2. Hygienic. —san'i-tize' v. —san'i-tar'i-ly adv.

san-i-ta-tion (săn'ə-tā'shən) n. 1. Hygiene; cleanliness. 2. Sewage disposal.

sank (săngk) p.t. of sink.

sap[1] (săp) n. 1. The watery fluid in a plant. 2. A fool. —sap'py adj.

sap[2] (săp) v. sapped, sapping. 1. To under-

mine. 2. To weaken gradually.

sap-phire (săf'īr) n. A blue gemstone.

sar-casm (sär'kăz'əm) n. 1. A mocking remark. 2. Scornful irony. —sar-cas'tic adj.

sash (săsh) n. 1. A band worn about the waist or over the shoulder. 2. A frame in which the panes of a window or door are set.

sat (săt). p.t. & p.p. of sit.

sa-tan-ic (sə-tăn'ĭk) adj. 1. Of or suggestive of the Devil. 2. Profoundly cruel or evil. —Sa'tan n. —Sa-tan'i-cal adj.

satch-el (săch'əl) n. A small valise or bag.

sate (sāt) v. sated, sating. To indulge fully; satisfy.

sat-el-lite (săt'l-īt') n. 1. A small body, natural or artificial, orbiting a planet. 2. A nation dominated by another.

sa-ti-ate (sā'shē-āt') v. -ated, -ating. To satisfy fully. —sa'ti-a'tion n. —sa'ti-e'ty n.

sat-in (săt'n) n. A smooth, glossy fabric. —sat'in-y adj.

sat-ire (săt'īr) n. 1. The use of ridicule or comic exaggeration to expose folly or affectation. 2. A story or poem in which this is done. —sa-tir'ic, sa-tir'i-cal adj. —sat'i-rist n. —sat'i-rize v.

sat-is-fy (săt'ĭs-fī') v. -fied, -fying. 1. To fulfill the needs or desires of. 2. To relieve of doubt. 3. To comply with. 4. To pay or compensate. —sat'is-fac'tion n. —sat'is-fac'to-ri-ly adv. —sat'is-fac'to-ry adj.

sat-u-rate (săch'ə-rāt') v. -rated, -rating. To soak or fill to capacity. —sat'u-ra'tion n.

Sat-ur-day (săt'ər-dē, -dā') n. The 7th day of the week.

sauce (sôs) n. 1. A liquid dressing for food. 2. Stewed fruit.

sau-cer (sô'sər) n. A shallow dish for holding a cup.

sau-cy (sô'sē) adj. -cier, -ciest. Impudent. —sau'ci-ly adv. —sau'ci-ness n.

saun-ter (sôn'tər) v. To stroll. —saun'ter n.

sau-sage (sô'sĭj) n. Chopped and seasoned meat stuffed into a casing.

sav-age (săv'ĭj) adj. 1. Not civilized. 2. Ferocious; brutal. —n. 1. An uncivilized person. 2. A brutal person. —sav'age-ly adv. —sav'age-ry n.

save (sāv) v. saved, saving. 1. To rescue from danger. 2. To preserve or safeguard. 3. To store. 4. To spare. —prep. & conj. Except. —sav'er n. —sav'ing adj. & n.

sav-ior (sāv'yər) n. One who saves; rescuer.

sa-vor (sā'vər) n. A taste or aroma. —v. 1. To have a particular savor. 2. To relish. —sa'vor-i-ness n. —sa'vor-y adj.

**saw**[1] (sô) *n.* A cutting tool having a metal blade with a sharp-toothed edge. —*v.* **sawed, sawed** or **sawn** (sôn), **sawing.** To cut with a saw. —**saw'yer** *n.*

**saw**[2] (sô). *p.t.* of **see.**

**sawn** (sôn). Alternate *p.p.* of **saw.**

**say** (sā) *v.* **said, saying. 1.** To utter aloud; speak. **2.** To state or declare. **1.** One's chance to speak. —*n.* **2.** Authority.

**say·ing** (sā'ĭng) *n.* An often repeated expression.

**scab** (skăb) *n.* **1.** A crust over a healing wound. **2.** A strikebreaker. —**scab'by** *adj.*

**scaf·fold** (skăf'ŏld, -ōld) *n.* **1.** A mobile platform for supporting workers. **2.** A platform for executions. —**scaf'fold·ing** *n.*

**scald** (skôld) *v.* **1.** To burn with hot liquid or steam. **2.** To heat almost to the boiling point. —*n.* An injury caused by scalding.

**scale**[1] (skāl) *n.* **1.** One of the small, thin plates covering fishes, reptiles, etc. **2.** A flake. —*v.* **scaled, scaling. 1.** To clear of scales. **2.** To remove or come off in scales. —**scal'y** *adj.*

**scale**[2] (skāl) *n.* **1.** A series of regularly spaced marks, steps, or levels, used in measurement. **2.** A progressive classification. **3.** A series of consecutive musical tones. —*v.* **scaled, scaling. 1.** To climb. **2.** To reproduce or adjust in accordance with a scale.

**scale**[3] (skāl) *n.* Often **scales.** A weighing machine.

**scal·lop** (skŏl'əp, skăl'-) *n.* **1.** An edible marine mollusk. **2.** One of a series of ornamental curves. —*v.* **1.** To border with scallops. **2.** To bake in a casserole with milk or a sauce. —**scal'lop·er** *n.*

**scalp** (skălp) *n.* The skin covering the top of the head. —*v.* **1.** To cut the scalp from. **2.** To sell at an excessive price. —**scalp'er** *n.*

**scal·pel** (skăl'pəl, skăl-pĕl') *n.* A surgical knife.

**scan** (skăn) *v.* **scanned, scanning. 1.** To examine closely. **2.** To look over quickly. **3.** To analyze (verse) into metrical patterns. —*n.* An act of scanning. —**scan'ner** *n.*

**scan·dal** (skăn'dəl) *n.* **1.** Public disgrace. **2.** Outrage; shame. **3.** Gossip. —**scan'dal·ize**' *v.* —**scan'dal·ous** *adj.* —**scan'dal·ous·ly** *adv.*

**scant** (skănt) *adj.* **1.** Barely enough; meager. **2.** Being just short of a specific measure. —**scant'i·ly** *adv.* —**scant'y** *adj.*

**scar** (skär) *n.* A mark left by a healed wound. —*v.* **scarred, scarring.** To mark or become marked with a scar.

**scarce** (skârs) *adj.* **scarcer, scarcest. 1.** Infrequently seen or found. **2.** Not abundant. —**scarce'ness** *n.* —**scar'ci·ty** *n.*

**scarce·ly** (skârs'lē) *adv.* **1.** Barely. **2.** Hardly.

**scare** (skâr) *v.* **scared, scaring.** To frighten. —*n.* **1.** A fright. **2.** Panic. —**scar'y** *adj.*

**scarf** (skärf) *n, pl.* **scarfs** or **scarves.** A piece of cloth worn about the neck or head.

**scar·let** (skär'lĭt) *n.* Vivid red. —**scarlet** *adj.*

**scath·ing** (skā'thĭng) *adj.* Severe. —**scath'ing·ly** *adv.*

**scat·ter** (skăt'ər) *v.* **1.** To disperse. **2.** To distribute loosely.

**scav·enge** (skăv'ĭnj) *v.* **-enged, -enging. 1.** To feed on decaying matter. **2.** To collect or search through (refuse). —**scav'en·ger** *n.*

**scene** (sēn) *n.* **1.** A view. **2.** A setting. **3.** A subdivision of a film or play showing one continuous action. **4.** A display of temper.

**scen·er·y** (sē'nə-rē) *n.* **1.** Landscape. **2.** The painted backdrops on a stage. —**sce'nic** *adj.*

**scent** (sĕnt) *n.* **1.** A distinctive odor. **2.** A perfume. —*v.* **1.** To smell. **2.** To perfume.

**scep·ter** (sĕp'tər) *n.* A staff held by a sovereign.

**sched·ule** (skĕj'ŏol, -ōō-əl, skĕj'əl) *n.* **1.** A list of items, events, or appointments. **2.** A timetable. —*v.* **-uled, -uling. 1.** To enter on a schedule. **2.** To plan for a certain time.

**scheme** (skēm) *n.* **1.** A plan or design. **2.** A plot. —*v.* **schemed, scheming.** To plot. —**sche·mat'ic** *adj.* —**schem'er** *n.*

**schol·ar** (skŏl'ər) *n.* **1.** A learned person. **2.** A student. —**schol'ar·ly** *adj.* —**scho·las'tic** *adj.*

**schol·ar·ship** (skŏl'ər-shĭp') *n.* **1.** Knowledge from study. **2.** Financial assistance to a student.

**school**[1] (skōōl) *n.* **1.** An institution for instruction and learning. **2.** A student body. **3.** A group sharing a unifying belief. —*v.* **1.** To instruct. **2.** To train.

**school**[2] (skōōl) *n.* A group of fish.

**sci·ence** (sī'əns) *n.* **1.** The study of natural phenomena or the knowledge so acquired. **2.** Any branch of knowledge. **3.** An activity requiring study and method. —**sci·en·tif'ic** *adj.* —**sci·en·tif'i·cal·ly** *adv.* —**sci·en·tist** *n.*

**sci·on** (sī'ən) *n.* A descendant.

**scis·sors** (sĭz'ərz) *n.* A cutting implement of two blades joined by a swivel pin.

**scoff** (skôf, skŏf) *v.* To mock at or scorn. —*n.* An expression of scorn. —**scoff'er** *n.*

**scold** (skōld) *v.* To reprimand harshly. —*n.* One who scolds.

**scoop** (skōōp) *n.* **1.** A small, shovellike utensil. **2.** The bucket of a steam shovel or dredge. **3.** An exclusive news story. —*v.* **1.** To take up with a scoop. **2.** To hollow out.

**scope** (skōp) *n.* **1.** A range, as of one's mind. **2.** Opportunity to function.

**scorch** (skôrch) *v.* To burn the surface of. —*n.* A slight or surface burn. — **scorch'ing·ly** *adv.*

**score** (skôr, skōr) *n.* **1.** A notch or incision. **2.** A record of points made. **3.** A result of a test. **4.** A debt. **5.** A group of 20. **6.** The written form of a musical composition. —*v.* scored, scoring. **1.** To mark with lines. **2.** To gain (a point). **3.** To record a score. **4.** To achieve; win. **5.** To assign a grade to. **6.** In music, to arrange. — **scor'er** *n.*

**scorn** (skôrn) *n.* **1.** Contempt. **2.** Derision. —*v.* To treat as contemptible. — **scorn'ful** *adj.* — **scorn'ful·ly** *adv.*

**scoun·drel** (skoun'drəl) *n.* A villain.

**scour** (skour) *v.* **1.** To clean by scrubbing. **2.** To search thoroughly.

**scourge** (skûrj) *n.* **1.** A whip. **2.** A cause of affliction. —*v.* scourged, scourging. **1.** To flog. **2.** To ravage. — **scourg'er** *n.*

**scout** (skout) *n.* One sent in advance to gather information. —*v.* **1.** To reconnoiter. **2.** To observe and evaluate.

**scram·ble** (skrăm'bəl) *v.* -bled, -bling. **1.** To move hurriedly. **2.** To compete frantically. **3.** To mix confusedly. **4.** To fry (eggs) with the yolks and whites mixed. — **scram'ble** *n.* — **scram'bler** *n.*

**scrap** (skrăp) *n.* A fragment or shred. —*v.* scrapped, scrapping. To discard.

**scrape** (skrāp) *v.* scraped, scraping. **1.** To rub forcefully. **2.** To smooth, injure, or remove by rubbing hard. **3.** To amass. —*n.* **1.** The act or result of scraping. **2.** A predicament.

**scratch** (skrăch) *v.* **1.** To make a shallow cut or mark on. **2.** To dig or wound with nails or claws. **3.** To rub (the skin) to relieve itching. **4.** To strike out. —*n.* A mark or wound produced by scratching. — **scratch'y** *adj.*

**scrawl** (skrôl) *v.* To write hastily or illegibly. — **scrawl** *n.*

**scraw·ny** (skrô'nē) *adj.* -nier, -niest. Skinny. — **scraw'ni·ness** *n.*

**scream** (skrēm) *v.* To cry out loudly and shrilly. —*n.* A loud piercing sound.

**screen** (skrēn) *n.* **1.** Something that serves to divide, conceal, or protect. **2.** A window insertion of framed mesh. **3.** A surface upon which a picture is projected for viewing. —*v.*

**1.** To conceal or protect. **2.** To sift out. **3.** To show on a screen.

**screw** (skrōō) *n.* **1.** A naillike metal fastener with incised grooves. **2.** A propeller. —*v.* **1.** To fasten with a screw. **2.** To turn or twist.

**screw·driv·er** (skrōō'drī'vər) *n.* A tool for turning screws.

**scrib·ble** (skrĭb'əl) *v.* -bled, -bling. To write hurriedly and carelessly. — **scrib'ble** *n.* — **scrib'bler** *n.*

**scribe** (skrīb) *n.* A writer.

**script** (skrĭpt) *n.* **1.** Handwriting. **2.** The text of a play, film, etc.

**Scrip·ture** (skrĭp'chər) *n.* Often Scriptures. Sacred writings, esp. the Bible. — **Scrip'tur·al** *adj.*

**scroll** (skrōl) *n.* A rolled document.

**scrounge** (skrounj) *v.* scrounged, scrounging. To forage for. — **scroung'er** *n.*

**scrub**[1] (skrŭb) *v.* scrubbed, scrubbing. To clean by rubbing hard, as with a brush. — **scrub** *n.* — **scrub'ber** *n.*

**scrub**[2] (skrŭb) *n.* Stunted trees or shrubs. — **scrub** *n.* — **scrub'by** *adj.*

**scruff** (skrŭf) *n.* The back of the neck.

**scru·ple** (skrōō'pəl) *n.* An ethical objection. — **scru'pu·lous** *adj.* — **scru'pu·lous·ness** *n.*

**scuff** (skŭf) *v.* To scrape with the feet while walking. —*n.* A worn spot.

**sculp·ture** (skŭlp'chər) *n.* **1.** The art of making statues or other shaped figures. **2.** A statue or other artistically shaped figure. —*v.* -tured, -turing. To create (sculpture) by molding, carving, etc. — **sculpt** *v.* — **sculp'tor** *n.* — **sculp'tress** *fem.n.*

**scum** (skŭm) *n.* Impure matter, esp. on a liquid surface. — **scum'my** *adj.*

**scur·ry** (skûr'ē) *v.* -ried, -rying. To scamper.

**scut·tle** (skŭt'l) *v.* -tled, -tling. **1.** To sink (a ship) deliberately. **2.** To run hastily.

**scythe** (sīth) *n.* A long, curved blade for mowing or reaping. — **scythe** *v.*

**sea** (sē) *n.* **1.** The waters covering most of the earth. **2.** A relatively large body of water completely or partly landlocked. **3.** A vast amount or extent.

**seal**[1] (sēl) *n.* **1.** A stamped emblem or design that indicates approval or authentication. **2.** A device, as a gummed paper, for closing envelopes or packages. —*v.* **1.** To affix a seal to. **2.** To close; make fast. **3.** To settle; conclude.

**seam** (sēm) *n.* **1.** A line formed by sewing together two pieces. **2.** A fissure or wrinkle. **3.** A thin layer, as of coal. —*v.* **1.** To join with a seam. **2.** To mark with lines. — **seam'er** n. — **seam'less** adj.

**sear** (sîr) v. **1.** To wither; dry up. **2.** To burn the surface of.

**search** (sûrch) v. To look through, investigate, or check in hopes of finding something lost or sought. — **search** n. — **search'er** n.

**sea·son** (sē'zən) n. **1.** One of the four equal divisions of the year, spring, summer, autumn, and winter. **2.** A special time of year. —v. **1.** To improve or enhance the flavor of. **2.** To accustom. **3.** To make usable, as by aging. — **sea'son·al** adj.

**seat** (sēt) n. **1.** A surface or place for sitting, as a chair. **2.** The part on which one rests in sitting. **3.** The buttocks. **4.** A location. **5.** Center; capital. —v. **1.** To place in a seat. **2.** To have seats for.

**se·clude** (sĭ-klōōd') v. **-cluded, -cluding.** To set apart; isolate. — **se·clu'sion** n.

**sec·ond**[1] (sĕk'ənd) n. **1.** A unit of time equal to $1/60$ of a minute. **2.** A moment.

**sec·ond**[2] (sĕk'ənd) adj. **1.** Next after the first. **2.** Subordinate. —n. **1.** One that is next after the first. **2.** An assistant or attendant. —v. **1.** To attend; assist. **2.** To endorse (a motion or nomination). — **sec'ond, sec'ond·ly** adv. — **sec'on·dar·y** adj.

**se·cret** (sē'krĭt) adj. **1.** Kept from being generally known. **2.** Operating covertly. —n. Something kept hidden from others. — **se'cre·cy** n. — **se'cre·tive** adj. — **se'cre·tive·ness** n. — **se'cret·ly** adv.

**sec·re·tar·y** (sĕk'rə-tĕr'ē) n., pl. **-ies.** **1.** One employed to handle correspondence and do clerical work. **2.** An officer in charge of records. **3.** An official in charge of a governmental department. **4.** A writing desk. — **sec're·tar'i·al** adj.

**se·crete**[1] (sĭ-krēt') v. **-creted, -creting.** To generate and release (a bodily substance). — **se·cre'tion** n. — **se·cre'to·ry** adj.

**se·crete**[2] (sĭ-krēt') v. **-creted, -creting.** To conceal.

**sect** (sĕkt) n. **1.** A group with the same beliefs within a larger group. **2.** A religious denomination. — **sec·tar'i·an** adj. & n.

**sec·tion** (sĕk'shən) n. A part; portion. —v. To divide into parts. — **section·al** adj.

**sec·tor** (sĕk'tər, -tôr') n. A part; section.

**sec·u·lar** (sĕk'yə-lər) adj. Not pertaining to religion; worldly. — **sec'u·lar·ly** adv.

**se·cure** (sĭ-kyōōr') adj. **-curer, -curest.** **1.** Free from danger; safe. **2.** Free from doubt. **3.** Stable. **4.** Certain. —v. **-cured, -curing.**

**1.** To guard. **2.** To fasten. **3.** To acquire. — **se·cure'ly** adv.

**se·cu·ri·ty** (sĭ-kyŏŏr'ə-tē) n., pl. **-ties.** **1.** Safety. **2.** Confidence. **3.** Something deposited as assurance of the fulfillment of an obligation. **4. securities.** Stocks, bonds, notes, etc.

**se·date** (sĭ-dāt') adj. Serenely deliberate; composed. — **se·date'ly** adv.

**sed·a·tive** (sĕd'ə-tĭv) adj. Having a calming effect. —n. A sedative drug. — **se·da'tion** n.

**sed·en·tar·y** (sĕd'n-tĕr'ē) adj. Characterized by much sitting.

**sed·i·ment** (sĕd'ə-mənt) n. Material that settles to the bottom of a liquid. — **sed'i·men'ta·ry** adj. — **sed'i·men·ta'tion** n.

**se·duce** (sĭ-d/y/ōōs') v. **-duced, -ducing.** **1.** To entice into wrongful behavior. **2.** To induce to have sexual intercourse. — **se·duc'er** n. — **se·duc'tion** n. — **se·duc'tive** adj.

**see**[1] (sē) v. **saw, seen, seeing.** **1.** To perceive with the eye. **2.** To understand. **3.** To regard. **4.** To undergo. **5.** To find out. **6.** To visit. **7.** To escort. **8.** To make sure.

**see**[2] (sē) n. The jurisdiction or office of a bishop.

**seed** (sēd) n., pl. **seeds** or **seed.** **1.** A fertilized plant ovule capable of developing into a new plant. **2.** A source or beginning. **3.** Offspring. —v. **1.** To plant seeds in. **2.** To remove seeds from.

**seed·y** (sē'dē) adj. **-ier, -iest.** **1.** Having many seeds. **2.** Worn and shabby. — **seed'i·ness** n.

**seek** (sēk) v. **sought, seeking.** **1.** To search for. **2.** To try to obtain. **3.** To attempt. — **seek'er** n.

**seem** (sēm) v. To give the impression of being; appear. — **seem'ing** adj. — **seem'ing·ly** adv.

**seen** (sēn) p.p. of **see.**

**seep** (sēp) v. To pass slowly through small openings. — **seep'age** n.

**see·saw** (sē'sô') n. A long, balanced plank that goes up and down when ridden at the ends. — **see'saw'** v.

**seethe** (sēth) v. **seethed, seething.** To churn and foam as if boiling.

**seg·ment** (sĕg'mənt) n. A division or section. —v. (sĕg-mĕnt'). To divide into segments. — **seg'men·tal** adj. — **seg'men·ta'tion** n.

**seg·re·gate** (sĕg'rə-gāt') v. **-gated, -gating.** To isolate from others; keep separate. — **seg're·ga'tion** n.

**seize** (sēz) v. **seized, seizing.** **1.** To take suddenly and forcibly. **2.** To overwhelm. **3.** To confiscate. — **sei'zure** n.

**seldom**

**sel·dom** (sĕl'dəm) adv. Infrequently. — **sel'dom·ness** n.

**se·lect** (sĭ-lĕkt') v. To choose. —adj. 1. Chosen. 2. Of special quality. — **se·lec'tion** n. — **se·lec'tive** adj. — **se·lec'tiv·i·ty** n.

**self** (sĕlf) n., pl. **selves**. 1. One's own being. 2. One's own welfare or advantage.

**self-con·scious** (sĕlf'kŏn'shəs) adj. 1. Excessively conscious of one's appearance or manner. 2. Not natural; stilted. — **self'-con'scious·ly** adv. — **self'-con'scious·ness** n.

**self·ish** (sĕl'fĭsh) adj. Concerned only with oneself; egotistic. — **self'ish·ly** adv. — **self'ish·ness** n.

**self·less** (sĕlf'lĭs) adj. Unselfish. — **self'less·ly** adv. — **self'less·ness** n.

**sell** (sĕl) v. **sold, selling**. 1. To exchange for money. 2. To offer for sale. 3. To be sold or be on sale. — **sell'er** n.

**selves** (sĕlvz). pl. of **self**.

**se·man·tics** (sə-mǎn'tĭks) n. The study of the meanings of words. — **se·man'tic** adj.

**sem·blance** (sĕm'bləns) n. An outward appearance.

**se·men** (sē'mən) n. The male reproductive fluid; sperm. — **sem'i·nal** adj.

**se·mes·ter** (sə-mĕs'tər) n. One of two divisions of an academic year.

**sem·i·co·lon** (sĕm'ĭ-kō'lən) n. A mark of punctuation (;).

**sen·ate** (sĕn'ĭt) n. A legislative and deliberative assembly. — **sen'a·tor** n. — **sen'a·to'ri·al** adj.

**send** (sĕnd) v. **sent, sending**. 1. To cause to be conveyed. 2. To direct to go. 3. To emit. 4. To propel. — **send'er** n.

**se·nile** (sē'nīl', sĕn'īl') adj. 1. Of old age. 2. Weakened, esp. mentally, by old age. — **se·nil'i·ty** n.

**sen·ior** (sēn'yər) adj. 1. Designating the older of two. 2. Above others in rank or length of service. —n. A student in his fourth year of high school or college. — **sen·ior'i·ty** n.

**sen·sa·tion** (sĕn·sā'shən, sən-) n. 1. An impression from a sense organ or a bodily part. 2. Feeling. 3. Heightened public interest and excitement, or an event causing this. — **sen·sa'tion·al** adj. — **sen·sa'tion·al·ism'** n.

**sense** (sĕns) n. 1. Any of the functions of hearing, sight, smell, touch, and taste. 2. Sensation; feeling. 3. Perception. 4. Good judgment. 5. Meaning. —v. **sensed, sensing**. To perceive. — **sense'less** adj. — **sense'less·ly** adv. — **sense'less·ness** n. — **sen'so·ry** adj.

**sen·si·bil·i·ty** (sĕn'sə-bĭl'ə-tē) n., pl. **-ties**.

1. The ability to feel. 2. Delicate sensitivity.

**sen·si·ble** (sĕn'sə-bəl) adj. 1. Perceptible. 2. Aware. 3. Showing good sense. — **sen'si·bly** adv.

**sen·si·tive** (sĕn'sə-tĭv) adj. 1. Responsive to stimulation. 2. Keen; perceptive. 3. Quick to take offense; touchy. 4. Easily irritated. — **sen'si·tive·ly** adv. — **sen'si·tiv'i·ty, sen'si·tive·ness** n.

**sen·su·al** (sĕn'shōō-əl) adj. Of or enjoying physical pleasures. — **sen'su·al'i·ty, sen'su·al·ness** n. — **sen'su·al·ly** adv.

**sen·su·ous** (sĕn'shōō-əs) adj. Of or appealing to the senses. — **sen'su·ous·ly** adv. — **sen'su·ous·ness** n.

**sent** (sĕnt). p.t. & p.p. of **send**.

**sen·tence** (sĕn'təns) n. 1. A grammatical group of words containing a subject and a verb. 2. A legal judgment or punishment. —v. **-tenced, -tencing**. To pass sentence upon. — **sen·ten'tial** adj.

**sen·ti·ment** (sĕn'tə-mənt) n. 1. An opinion or attitude. 2. A feeling. 3. Affection; tenderness. 4. False or conventional emotion. — **sen'ti·men'tal** adj. — **sen'ti·men'tal·ism', sen'ti·men·tal'i·ty** n. — **sen'ti·men'tal·ly** adv.

**sen·try** (sĕn'trē) n., pl. **-tries**. A guard posted to prevent the passage of unauthorized persons.

**sep·a·rate** (sĕp'ə-rāt') v. **-rated, -rating**. 1. To set, keep, or come apart. 2. To differentiate between. —adj. (sĕp'ər-ĭt). 1. Set apart; not connected. 2. Dissimilar; distinct. — **sep'a·ra·ble** adj. — **sep'a·rate·ly** adv. — **sep'a·rate·ness** n. — **sep'a·ra'tion** n.

**Sep·tem·ber** (sĕp-tĕm'bər) n. The 9th month of the year.

**se·pul·cher** (sĕp'əl-kər) n. A burial vault. — **se·pul'chral** adj.

**se·quel** (sē'kwəl) n. 1. A work continuing the narrative of an earlier work. 2. A consequence.

**se·quence** (sē'kwəns) n. 1. Succession. 2. An order of occurrence. 3. A related or continuous series. — **se·quen'tial** adj. — **se·quen'tial·ly** adv.

**ser·e·nade** (sĕr'ə-nād', sĕr'ə-nād') n. Music meant to please or charm a sweetheart or other listener. —v. **-naded, -nading**. To perform a serenade (for). — **ser'e·nad'er** n.

**se·rene** (sə-rēn') adj. Tranquil; dignified. — **se·rene'ly** adv. — **se·ren'i·ty** n.

**serf** (sûrf) n. A feudal farm laborer, owned by a lord. — **serf'dom** n.

**ser·geant** (sär'jənt) n. A low-ranking noncommissioned officer.

**se·ri·al** (sîr′ē-əl) *adj.* Of, forming, or published in a series. —*n.* A work published or produced in installments. — **se′ri·al·ize′** *v.* — **se′ri·al·ly** *adv.*

**se·ries** (sîr′ēz) *n., pl.* **-ries.** A group of related things coming one after another; succession.

**se·ri·ous** (sîr′ē-əs) *adj.* **1.** Grave; sober. **2.** Sincere. **3.** Causing anxiety; critical. — **se′ri·ous·ly** *adv.*

**ser·mon** (sûr′mən) *n.* **1.** A religious speech during a church service. **2.** A long moral lecture.

**ser·pent** (sûr′pənt) *n.* A snake. — **ser′pen·tine′** *adj.*

**ser·vant** (sûr′vənt) *n.* One employed to perform domestic services.

**serve** (sûrv) *v.* **served, serving. 1.** To work for; be a servant to. **2.** To act; function. **3.** To wait on. **4.** To be of assistance to. **5.** To undergo military service. **6.** To meet a need. **7.** To present or deliver. **8.** To put (a ball) in play. —*n.* The right or act of serving in a court game. — **serv′er** *n.*

**serv·ice** (sûr′vĭs) *n.* **1.** The occupation of a servant. **2.** The act of serving. **3.** A government department. **4.** The armed forces. **5.** Maintenance and repairs. **6.** A set of dishes or utensils. —*v.* **-iced, -icing. 1.** To repair; maintain. **2.** To provide services to. — **serv′ice·a·ble** *adj.*

**ser·vile** (sûr′vəl, -vīl′) *adj.* Slavish; submissive. — **ser·vil′i·ty** *n.*

**ses·sion** (sĕsh′ən) *n.* A meeting, as of a class or legislature.

**set¹** (sĕt) *v.* **set, setting. 1.** To put. **2.** To fix, esp. a broken bone. **3.** To arrange tableware upon (a table). **4.** To compose (type). **5.** To prescribe, establish, or assign. **6.** To sit on eggs, as a hen. **7.** To disappear below the horizon. **8.** To harden. —*adj.* **1.** Fixed. **2.** Unyielding. **3.** Ready. —*n.* The act of setting.

**set²** (sĕt) *n.* **1.** A group; collection. **2.** The scenery for a play or motion-picture scene. **3.** An apparatus, esp. a radio or television.

**set·tle** (sĕt′l) *v.* **-tled, -tling. 1.** To arrange or fix definitely. **2.** To establish residence in. **3.** To calm. **4.** To sink or come to rest. **5.** To pay (a debt). **6.** To decide. — **set′tler** *n.*

**set·tle·ment** (sĕt′l-mənt) *n.* **1.** The act of settling. **2.** A colony. **3.** A small community. **4.** An agreement.

**sev·en** (sĕv′ən) *n.* The cardinal number written 7. — **sev′en** *adj.* & *pron.* — **sev′enth** *n.* & *adj.*

**sev·en·teen** (sĕv′ən-tēn′, sĕv′ən-tēn′) *n.* The cardinal number written 17. — **sev·en·teen′** *adj.* & *pron.* — **sev′en·teenth′** *n.* & *adj.*

**sev·en·ty** (sĕv′ən-tē) *n.* The cardinal number written 70. — **sev·en·ti·eth** *n.* & *adj.* — **sev′en·ty** *adj.* & *pron.*

**sev·er** (sĕv′ər) *v.* To separate; cut. — **sev′er·ance** *n.*

**sev·er·al** (sĕv′ər-əl) *adj.* **1.** More than two, but not many. **2.** Single; distinct. —*n.* Several ones; a few. — **sev′er·al·ly** *adv.*

**se·vere** (sə-vîr′) *adj.* **-verer, -verest. 1.** Harsh; stern; strict. **2.** Grave; forbidding. **3.** Plain; unadorned. **4.** Intense; sharp. **5.** Rigorous. — **se·vere′ly** *adv.* — **se·ver′i·ty, se·vere′ness** *n.*

**sew** (sō) *v.* **sewed, sewn** or **sewed, sewing.** To make, repair, or fasten with a needle and thread. — **sew′er** *n.* — **sew′ing** *n.*

**sew·age** (sōō′ĭj) *n.* Waste carried off in sewers.

**sew·er** (sōō′ər) *n.* A pipe or other passageway for carrying off sewage or rain-water.

**sewn** (sōn) Alternate *p.p.* of **sew.**

**sex** (sĕks) *n.* **1.** Either of two divisions of organisms according to reproductive function, male and female. **2.** The urge or instinct to copulate. **3.** Sexual intercourse. — **sex′less** *adj.* — **sex′u·al** *adj.* — **sex·u·al′i·ty** *n.* — **sex′u·al·ly** *adv.* — **sex′u·al·ize** *v.*

**shab·by** (shăb′ē) *adj.* **-bier, -biest. 1.** Threadbare; worn-out. **2.** Wearing worn garments. **3.** Despicable. — **shab′bi·ly** *adv.* — **shab′bi·ness** *n.*

**shack** (shăk) *n.* A small, crudely built cabin.

**shack·le** (shăk′əl) *n.* A metal fastening for restraining a prisoner's ankle or wrist. —*v.* **-led, -ling.** To put shackles on. — **shack′ler** *n.*

**shade** (shād) *n.* **1.** Diminished or partial light, esp. when caused by blocking the sun's rays. **2.** A device to block the sun's rays. **3.** The degree to which a color is darkened. **4.** A slight variation or amount. —*v.* **shaded, shading. 1.** To screen from light. **2.** To change by slight degrees. — **shad′y** *adj.*

**shad·ow** (shăd′ō) *n.* **1.** A darkened area caused by an object blocking rays of light. **2.** Gloom. **3.** A faint indication. —*v.* **1.** To shade. **2.** To follow, esp. in secret. — **shad′ow·er** *n.* — **shad′ow·i·ness** *n.* — **shad′ow·y** *adj.*

**shaft** (shăft) *n.* **1.** The body of a spear or arrow. **2.** A long, narrow object or machine part; bar. **3.** A long, narrow passage.

**shag·gy** (shăg′ē) *adj.* **-gier, -giest.** Bushy and matted. — **shag′gi·ness** *n.*

**shake** (shāk) *v.* **shook, shaken, shaking. 1.** To

move or cause to move to and fro jerkily. **2.** To tremble. **3.** To weaken or discourage. **4.** To clasp (hands or another's hand), as in greeting. —*n.* An act of shaking. —**shak′a·ble,** **shake′a·ble** *adj.* —**shak′er** *n.* —**shak′i·ness** *n.* —**shak′y** *adj.*

**shall** (shăl) *v.* past **should.** —Used as an auxiliary to indicate the future tense.

**shal·low** (shăl′ō) *adj.* Not deep. —*n.* A shallow part of a body of water. —**shal′low·ness** *n.*

**sham** (shăm) *n.* One that is false or counterfeit. —*adj.* Not genuine; counterfeit. —*v.* **shammed, shamming.** To feign.

**sham·bles** (shăm′bəlz) *n.* A scene of complete disorder.

**shame** (shām) *n.* **1.** A painful emotion caused by a sense of guilt, unworthiness, or disgrace. **2.** A dishonor or disgrace. **3.** A great disappointment. —*v.* **shamed, shaming. 1.** To cause to feel shame. **2.** To bring dishonor upon. **3.** To force by making ashamed. —**shame′ful** *adj.* —**shame′ful·ly** *adv.* —**shame′ful·ness** *n.* —**shame′less** *adj.* —**shame′less·ly** *adv.* —**shame′less·ness** *n.*

**sham·poo** (shăm-pōō′) *n.* A sudsy soap, esp. one for the hair. —**sham·poo′** *v.*

**shank** (shăngk) *n.* The lower leg or a similar part.

**shan't, sha'nt** (shănt, shänt). Contractions of *shall not.*

**shape** (shāp) *n.* **1.** The outline of a thing; form. **2.** Developed or definite form. **3.** Condition. —*v.* **shaped, shaping. 1.** To give a form to. **2.** To develop. —**shape′less** *adj.* —**shape′less·ness** *n.* —**shape′ly** *adj.* —**shape′li·ness** *n.*

**share** (shâr) *n.* A part given or due to each participant, member, owner, etc. —*v.* **shared, sharing. 1.** To give out in shares. **2.** To have, use, or experience in common. **3.** To participate. —**shar′er** *n.*

**shark** (shärk) *n.* **1.** A large, voracious fish. **2.** A swindler or cheat.

**sharp** (shärp) *adj.* **1.** Having a thin, keen edge or a fine point. **2.** Abrupt. **3.** Astute. **4.** Alert. **5.** In music, raised a half tone in pitch. —*adv.* **1.** In a sharp manner. **2.** Punctually. —*n.* A musical note raised by a half tone. —**sharp′en** *v.* —**sharp′en·er** *n.* —**sharp′ly** *adv.* —**sharp′ness** *n.*

**shat·ter** (shăt′ər) *v.* To break or burst suddenly into pieces.

**shave** (shāv) *v.* **shaved, shaved** or **shaven** (shā′vən), **shaving. 1.** To remove body hair from with a razor. **2.** To cut thin slices from.

—*n.* The act or result of shaving. —**shav′er** *n.* —**shav′ing** *n.*

**shawl** (shôl) *n.* A cloth for covering a woman's head and shoulders.

**she** (shē) *pron.* The 3rd person sing. pronoun in the nominative case, feminine gender.

**sheaf** (shēf) *n., pl.* **sheaves.** A bundle, esp. of cut grain.

**shear** (shîr) *v.* **sheared, sheared** or **shorn,** **shearing.** To clip off (fleece, hair, etc.).

**shears** (shîrz) *pl.n.* Large-sized scissors.

**sheath** (shēth) *n., pl.* **sheaths.** A long, tight-fitting case, as for the blade of a knife.

**sheathe** (shēth) *v.* **sheathed, sheathing.** To put into a sheath.

**sheaves** (shēvz) *pl.* of **sheaf.**

**shed**[1] (shĕd) *v.* **shed, shedding. 1.** To pour forth. **2.** To diffuse or radiate. **3.** To cast off.

**shed**[2] (shĕd) *n.* A small structure for storage or shelter.

**she'd** (shēd). Contraction of *she had* or *she would.*

**sheen** (shēn) *n.* Shininess.

**sheep·ish** (shēp′ĭsh) *adj.* Embarrassed. —**sheep′ish·ly** *adv.* —**sheep′ish·ness** *n.*

**sheer**[1] (shîr) *v.* To swerve.

**sheer**[2] (shîr) *adj.* **1.** Thin and transparent. **2.** Pure. **3.** Very steep. —**sheer′ly** *adv.* —**sheer′ness** *n.*

**sheet** (shēt) *n.* **1.** A large piece of cloth for covering a bed. **2.** A broad, thin piece, as of paper or glass.

**shelf** (shĕlf) *n., pl.* **shelves** (shĕlvz). **1.** A board fixed at right angles to a wall for holding objects. **2.** A ledge.

**shell** (shĕl) *n.* **1.** A hard outer covering, as of a mollusk, egg, or nut. **2.** A framework. **3.** A narrow racing boat. **4.** A projectile or piece of ammunition. —*v.* **1.** To remove from a shell, pod, etc. **2.** To bombard.

**shel·lac** (shə-lăk′) *n.* A thin varnish. —*v.* **-lacked, -lacking.** To apply shellac.

**shel·ter** (shĕl′tər) *n.* Something that provides cover or protection. —*v.* To provide cover or protection for.

**shelves.** *pl.* of **shelf.**

**shep·herd** (shĕp′ərd) *n.* One that tends sheep. —*v.* To herd, guard, or care for. —**shep′herd·ess** *fem.n.*

**sher·iff** (shĕr′ĭf) *n.* The chief law-enforcement officer in a county.

**shield** (shēld) *n.* **1.** Protective armor carried on the forearm. **2.** Any protective covering. —*v.* To protect or defend.

**shift** (shĭft) *v.* **1.** To move or transfer. **2.** To provide for one's needs. —*n.* **1.** A change,

**shred**

transference, or displacement. **2.** A working period.

**shift·y** (shif'tē) *adj.* **-ier, -iest.** Tricky. — **shift'i·ness** *n.*

**shim·mer** (shim'ər) *v.* To shine with a tremulous light. —*n.* A glimmering. — **shim'mer·y** *adj.*

**shin¹** (shin) *n.* The front part of the leg between knee and ankle. —*v.* **shinned, shinning.** To climb by gripping and pulling with the hands and legs.

**shine** (shīn) *v.* **shone** or **shined, shining. 1.** To emit or reflect light. **2.** To excel. **3.** To aim the beam or glow of. **4.** To make bright by polishing. —*n.* **1.** Brightness. **2.** A polishing. — **shin'i·ness** *n.* — **shin'y** *adj.*

**shin·gle** (shǐng'gəl) *n.* **1.** A piece of wood, asbestos, etc., for roofing or siding. **2.** A small board bearing a sign. —*v.* **-gled, -gling.** To cover with shingles. — **shin'gler** *n.*

**ship** (shǐp) *n.* **1.** Any large vessel for deep-water navigation. **2.** An airplane. —*v.* **shipped, shipping. 1.** To place on a ship. **2.** To transport. —**ship'ment** *n.* — **ship'per** *n.* — **ship'ping** *adj.* & *n.*

**shirk** (shûrk) *v.* To put off or avoid (work or duty). — **shirk'er** *n.*

**shirt** (shûrt) *n.* A garment for the upper body.

**shiv·er** (shǐv'ər) *v.* **1.** To tremble, as from cold. **2.** To shatter. — **shiv'er** *n.*

**shoal** (shōl) *n.* **1.** A shallow. **2.** A school of fish.

**shock** (shŏk) *n.* **1.** A violent collision or impact. **2.** A violent surprise or emotional upset. **3.** An offense to one's sense of propriety. **4.** The sensation of an electric current on the body. —*v.* **1.** To disturb deeply; astonish. **2.** To outrage. **3.** To subject to an electric shock. — **shock'ing** *adj.* — **shock'ing·ly** *adv.*

**shod·dy** (shŏd'ē) *adj.* **-dier, -diest.** Inferior; cheap. — **shod'di·ly** *adv.* — **shod'di·ness** *n.*

**shoe** (shōō) *n.* **1.** A durable covering for the human foot. **2.** A horseshoe. —*v.* **shod, shod** or **shodden, shoeing.** To furnish with shoes.

**shone** (shōn) Alternate *p.t.* & *p.p.* of **shine.**

**shook** (shook). *p.t.* of **shake.**

**shoot** (shōōt) *v.* **shot, shooting. 1.** To hit, wound, or kill with a missile. **2.** To fire. **3.** To move or send forth swiftly. **4.** To project. **5.** To sprout. —*n.* A sprout. — **shoot'er** *n.*

**shop** (shŏp) *n.* **1.** A small retail store. **2.** A business or industrial establishment. —*v.* **shopped, shopping.** To inspect and buy

goods in stores. — **shop'per** *n.*

**shore¹** (shōr, shôr) *n.* Land along the water's edge.

**shore²** (shōr, shôr) *v.* **shored, shoring.** To prop up.

**shorn** (shōrn, shôrn). Alternate *p.p.* of **shear.**

**short** (shôrt) *adj.* **1.** Having little length or height. **2.** Brief. **3.** Lacking; insufficient. **4.** Curt. —*n.* **1.** A short film. **2. shorts.** Short drawers or trousers. **3.** A short circuit. —*v.* To cause a short circuit in. — **short'age** *n.* — **short'en** *v.* — **short'ly** *adv.* — **short'ness** *n.*

**shot¹** (shŏt) *n.* **1.** The firing of a weapon. **2.** *pl.* **shots** or **shot.** A pellet, bullet, etc. **3.** A marksman. **4.** An attempt. **5.** An attempt. **6.** A photograph or single cinematic view. **7.** A hypodermic injection. **8.** A drink of liquor.

**shot²** (shŏt). *p.t.* & *p.p.* of **shoot.**

**should** (shood). *p.t.* of **shall**, used as an auxiliary expressing obligation, necessity, anticipation, contingency, or uncertainty.

**shoul·der** (shōl'dər) *n.* **1.** The part of the body between the neck and the upper arm or forelimb. **2.** The edge of a roadway. —*v.* **1.** To carry on the shoulders. **2.** To push with the shoulder.

**should·n't** (shood'ənt). Contraction of *should not.*

**shout** (shout) *n.* A loud cry. — **shout** *v.* — **shout'er** *n.*

**shove** (shŭv) *v.* **shoved, shoving.** To push roughly or rudely. —*n.* A push. — **shov'er** *n.*

**shov·el** (shŭv'əl) *n.* A digging tool with a handle and a scoop. —*v.* To dig or move with a shovel.

**show** (shō) *v.* **showed, shown** or **showed, showing. 1.** To cause to be seen. **2.** To conduct. **3.** To point out. **4.** To reveal. **5.** To grant. **6.** To instruct. **7.** To be evident. —*n.* **1.** A display. **2.** An appearance. **3.** A public exhibition or entertainment.

**show·er** (shou'ər) *n.* **1.** A brief fall of rain. **2.** An outpouring. **3.** A party held to present gifts. **4.** A bath in which water is sprayed. —*v.* **1.** To spray. **2.** To bestow abundantly. **3.** To pour down. **4.** To bathe in sprayed water.

**shown** (shōn). Alternate *p.p.* of **show.**

**show·y** (shō'ē) *adj.* **-ier, -iest.** Conspicuous; gaudy. — **show'i·ly** *adv.* — **show'i·ness** *n.*

**shrank** (shrăngk). Alternate *p.t.* of **shrink.**

**shred** (shrĕd) *n.* **1.** A long strip torn off. **2.** A small amount. —*v.* **shredded** or **shred, shredding.** To cut into shreds. — **shred'der** *n.*

**shred** (shrĕd) *n.* **1.** A long strip torn off.

**2.** A small amount. —v. **shredded** or **shred, shredding.** To cut into shreds. — **shred'der** n.

**shrewd** (shrōōd) adj. **1.** Discerning; astute. **2.** Cunning. — **shrewd'ly** adv. — **shrewd'ness** n.

**shriek** (shrēk) n. A shrill cry. —v. To utter such a cry.

**shrill** (shril) adj. High-pitched and piercing.

**shrine** (shrīn) n. A saint's tomb or other hallowed place.

**shrink** (shringk) v. **shrank** or **shrunk, shrunk** or **shrunken, shrinking. 1.** To contract; dwindle. **2.** To draw back. — **shrink'age** n.

**shriv-el** (shrĭv'əl) v. To shrink and wrinkle.

**shroud** (shroud) n. **1.** A cloth used to wrap a body for burial. **2.** Something that conceals.

**shrub** (shrŭb) n. A low, many-stemmed woody plant. — **shrub'ber-y** n. — **shrub'by** adj.

**shrug** (shrŭg) v. **shrugged, shrugging.** To raise (the shoulders) as a gesture of doubt or indifference. —n. Such a gesture.

**shrunk** (shrŭngk) Alternate p.t. & p.p. of **shrink.**

**shrunken** (shrŭng'kən) Alternate p.p. of **shrink.**

**shud-der** (shŭd'ər) v. To tremble, as from disgust. — **shud'der** n.

**shuf-fle** (shŭf'əl) v. **-fled, -fling. 1.** To move with a slow, foot-dragging gait. **2.** To mix together. —n. A shuffling gait. — **shuf'fler** n.

**shut** (shŭt) v. **shut, shutting. 1.** To close. **2.** To block passage.

**shut-ter** (shŭt'ər) n. A hinged cover or screen for a window. —v. To furnish or close with a shutter.

**shut-tle** (shŭt'l) n. **1.** A device used in weaving to carry the thread back and forth. **2.** A train, bus, or plane making frequent trips between two points. —v. **-tled, -tling.** To move back and forth.

**shy** (shī) adj. **shier, shiest. 1.** Timid. **2.** Bashful; reserved. **3.** Wary. **4.** Short; lacking. —v. **shied, shying.** To draw back, as from fear or caution. — **shy'ly** adv. — **shy'ness** n.

**sick** (sĭk) adj. **1.** Ill; not well. **2.** Nauseated. **3.** Of or for sick persons. **4.** Morbid. **5.** Disgusted. **6.** Weary. — **sick'en** v. — **sick'en-ing** adj. — **sick'ness** n.

**side** (sīd) n. **1.** A surface, esp. one joining a top and a bottom. **2.** The left or right half. **3.** The adjacent space. **4.** An edge or boundary. **5.** An area separated from another by some feature. **6.** A contending group, team, or opinion. **7.** An aspect. —v. **sided, siding.** To align oneself on or with a side. — **side'ways** adj. & adv.

**siege** (sēj) n. **1.** The surrounding of a place

by an army bent on capturing it. **2.** A prolonged period.

**sieve** (sĭv) n. A strainer or sifter.

**sift** (sĭft) v. **1.** To separate fine particles from coarse ones; strain. **2.** To examine closely. — **sift'er** n.

**sigh** (sī) v. To exhale in a long, deep breath, as in expressing sorrow. —n. The act or sound of sighing.

**sight** (sīt) n. **1.** The ability to see. **2.** The act of seeing. **3.** The field of one's vision. **4.** Something seen. **5.** A device to assist in aiming, as on a gun. —v. **1.** To see. **2.** To aim. — **sight'ed** adj. — **sight'less** adj.

**sign** (sīn) n. **1.** An indication. **2.** A meaningful action or gesture. **3.** A message-bearing board, poster, or placard. **4.** A symbol. —v. **1.** To write (one's name) on. **2.** To hire, transfer, etc., by written contract. — **sign'er** n.

**sig-nal** (sĭg'nəl) n. **1.** A sign or other indicator used to convey a message. **2.** A radio wave. —adj. Remarkable. —v. To make a signal (to).

**sig-na-ture** (sĭg'nə-choor') n. The name of a person as written by himself.

**sig-nif-i-cant** (sĭg-nĭf'ĭ-kənt) adj. **1.** Having a meaning. **2.** Full of meaning. **3.** Important. — **sig-nif'i-cance** n. — **sig-nif'i-cant-ly** adv.

**sig-ni-fy** (sĭg'nə-fī') v. **-fied, -fying. 1.** To denote. **2.** To make known. — **sig-ni-fi-ca'tion** n.

**si-lence** (sī'ləns) n. The absence of sound; stillness. —v. **-lenced, -lencing. 1.** To make silent. **2.** To suppress. — **si'lent** adj. — **si'lent-ly** adv.

**silk** (sĭlk) n. Thread or fabric of lustrous fiber produced by an Asian caterpillar, the silkworm. — **silk'en** adj. — **silk'y** adj.

**sill** (sĭl) n. The horizontal bottom of a window frame.

**sil-ly** (sĭl'ē) adj. **-lier, -liest.** Senseless; scatter-brained. — **sil'li-ness** n.

**sil-ver** (sĭl'vər) n. **1.** A white metallic element valued for jewelry, tableware, and coinage. **2.** Coins of this metal. **3.** Tableware of this metal. **4.** A lustrous gray color. —adj. Of silver. —v. To cover with silver. — **sil'ver-y** adj.

**sim-i-lar** (sĭm'ə-lər) adj. Alike though not identical. — **sim'i-lar'i-ty** n. — **sim'i-lar-ly** adv.

**sim-mer** (sĭm'ər) v. **1.** To cook below or at the boiling point. **2.** To be

**sim-ple** (sĭm'pəl) adj. **-pler, -plest. 1.** Consisting of one thing or part only. **2.** Easy. **3.** Bare; mere. **4.** Plain. **5.** Unaffected.

Straightforward. **7.** Humble or lowly. **8.** Stupid. — **sim·plic'i·ty** *n.* — **sim'ply** *adv.*

**sim·pli·fy** (sĭm'plə-fī') *v.* **-fied, -fying.** To make simpler. — **sim·pli·fi·ca'tion** *n.*

**sim·u·late** (sĭm'yə-lāt') *v.* **-lated, -lating.** To pretend; feign. — **sim·u·la'tion** *n.* — **sim'u·la'tor** *n.*

**si·mul·ta·ne·ous** (sī'məl-tā'nē-əs, sĭm'əl-) *adj.* Happening or done at the same time. — **si'mul·ta·ne·ous·ly** *adv.*

**sin** (sĭn) *n.* A breaking of a religious or moral law. — *v.* **sinned, sinning.** To commit a sin. — **sin'ful** *adj.* — **sin'ful·ness** *n.* — **sin'ner** *n.*

**since** (sĭns) *adv.* **1.** From then until now. **2.** Between then and now. — *prep.* During the time after. — *conj.* **1.** From the time when. **2.** Because; inasmuch as.

**sin·cere** (sĭn-sîr') *adj.* **-cerer, -cerest. 1.** True. **2.** Not hypocritical; honest. — **sin·cere'ly** *adv.* — **sin·cer'i·ty** *n.*

**sin·ew** (sĭn'yōō) *n.* **1.** A tendon. **2.** Muscular power. — **sin'ew·y** *adj.*

**sing** (sĭng) *v.* **sang, sung, singing. 1.** To utter words or sounds in musical tones. **2.** To perform (vocal music). **3.** To proclaim or tell in song. — **sing'er** *n.*

**singe** (sĭnj) *v.* **singed, singeing.** To burn superficially.

**sin·gle** (sĭng'gəl) *adj.* **1.** One only; sole. **2.** Individual. **3.** Designed for one person. **4.** Unmarried. — *n.* **1.** A separate unit; individual. **2.** A one-dollar bill. — *v.* **-gled, -gling.** To separate (with *out*). — **sin'gly** *adv.*

**sin·gu·lar** (sĭng'gyə-lər) *adj.* **1.** Being or denoting only one. **2.** Extraordinary. **3.** Curious; peculiar. — *n.* The grammatical form indicating only one. — **sin·gu·lar'i·ty** *n.* — **sin'gu·lar·ly** *adv.*

**sin·is·ter** (sĭn'ĭ-stər) *adj.* Suggesting veiled evil or menace. — **sin'is·ter·ly** *adv.*

**sink** (sĭngk) *v.* **sank** or **sunk, sunk** or **sunken, sinking. 1.** To submerge beneath the surface of a liquid. **2.** To descend or decline slowly. **3.** To dig or drill. **4.** To worsen or weaken. — *n.* A water basin with a drainpipe. — **sink'a·ble** *adj.* — **sink'er** *n.*

**sip** (sĭp) *v.* **sipped, sipping.** To drink in small quantities. — *n.* A small quantity of liquid sipped.

**si·phon** (sī'fən) *n.* A tube for drawing liquid from one container to a lower one. — *v.* To draw off with a siphon.

**sir** (sûr) *n.* **1.** Often **Sir.** A respectful form of address for a man. **2. Sir.** A title used before the name of baronets and knights.

**sire** (sīr) *n.* A father or forefather. — *v.* **sired,**

**siring.** To beget.

**si·ren** (sī'rən) *n.* A warning device producing a loud wailing noise.

**sis·ter** (sĭs'tər) *n.* **1.** A female having the same mother and father as another. **2.** A female comrade or fellow member. **3.** A nun. — **sis'ter·hood'** *n.* — **sis'ter·ly** *adj.*

**sis·ter-in-law** (sĭs'tər-ĭn-lô') *n., pl.* **sisters-in-law. 1.** The sister of one's spouse. **2.** The wife of one's brother.

**sit** (sĭt) *v.* **sat, sitting. 1.** To rest on the buttocks or hindquarters. **2.** To perch. **3.** To be situated; lie. **4.** To pose. **5.** To be in session. — **sit'ter** *n.*

**site** (sīt) *n.* Location.

**sit·u·a·tion** (sĭch'ōō-ā'shən) *n.* **1.** A location. **2.** A state of affairs. **3.** A job. — **sit'u·ate'** *v.* — **sit'u·a'tion·al** *adj.*

**six** (sĭks) *n.* The cardinal number written 6. — **six** *adj.* & *pron.* — **sixth** *n.* & *adj.*

**six·teen** (sĭk'stēn') *n.* The cardinal number written 16. — **six'teen'** *adj.* & *pron.* — **six'teenth'** *n.* & *adj.*

**six·ty** (sĭk'stē) *n.* The cardinal number written 60. — **six'ti·eth** *n.* & *adj.* — **six'ty** *adj.* & *pron.*

**size** (sīz) *n.* **1.** Physical dimensions; magnitude. **2.** Any of a series of graduated categories of dimension, as for garments. — *v.* **sized, sizing.** To arrange according to size. — **siz'a·ble** *adj.*

**skate** (skāt) *n.* **1.** A bladelike metal runner fixed to a shoe for gliding over ice. **2.** A roller skate. — **skate** *v.* — **skat'er** *n.*

**skel·e·ton** (skĕl'ə-tən) *n.* **1.** The structure of bones that supports the body. **2.** Any structure or framework. — **skel'e·tal** *adj.*

**skep·tic** (skĕp'tĭk) *n.* One who questions or doubts accepted conclusions. — **skep'ti·cal** *adj.* — **skep'ti·cism** *n.*

**sketch** (skĕch) *n.* **1.** A rough drawing or design. **2.** An outline. — *v.* To make a sketch (of). — **sketch'er** *n.* — **sketch'y** *adj.*

**ski** (skē) *n., pl.* **skis.** One of a pair of long, flat runners attached to a boot for gliding over snow. — *v.* To travel on skis. — **ski'er** *n.*

**skid** (skĭd) *n.* **1.** The act of sliding or slipping over a surface. **2.** A plank or log used for sliding or rolling heavy objects. — *v.* **skidded, skidding.** To slip or slide sideways because of loss of traction.

**skill** (skĭl) *n.* **1.** Proficiency; expertness. **2.** An ability or technique. — **skilled** *adj.* — **skill'ful** *adj.* — **skill'ful·ly** *adv.* — **skill'ful·ness** *n.*

**skil·let** (skĭl'ĭt) *n.* A frying pan.

**skim** (skĭm) v. **skimmed, skimming. 1.** To remove (floating matter) from (a liquid). **2.** To glide lightly over. **3.** To glance through quickly.

**skin** (skĭn) n. **1.** The external covering of the body. **2.** An animal pelt. **3.** An outer layer, as the rind of fruit. —v. **skinned, skinning. 1.** To remove skin from. **2.** To bruise.

**skin·ny** (skĭn′ē) adj. **-nier, -niest.** Very thin. —**skin′ni·ness** n.

**skip** (skĭp) v. **skipped, skipping. 1.** To leap or spring lightly (over). **2.** To hop on alternating feet. **3.** To pass from point to point omitting that intervenes. **4.** To omit. —n. An act of skipping. —**skip′per** n.

**skir·mish** (skûr′mĭsh) n. A minor battle. —**skir′mish** v.

**skirt** (skûrt) n. A garment, or part of a garment, that hangs from the waist down. —v. **1.** To pass along the edge of. **2.** To avoid.

**skull** (skŭl) n. The bony framework of the head.

**sky** (skī) n., pl. **skies.** The upper atmosphere.

**slab** (slăb) n. A flat, thick piece.

**slack** (slăk) adj. **1.** Sluggish. **2.** Not busy. **3.** Loose. **4.** Negligent. —v. To slacken. —n. **1.** A lull. **2.** slacks. Trousers for casual wear. —**slack′ness** n.

**slack·en** (slăk′ən) v. **1.** To slow down. **2.** To loosen.

**slain** (slān) p.p. of **slay.**

**slam** (slăm) v. **slammed, slamming.** To strike, hurl, or shut with force and loud noise. —n. A heavy blow or impact.

**slan·der** (slăn′dər) n. The utterance of lies harmful to a person. —v. To utter damaging lies about. —**slan′der·er** n. —**slan′der·ous** adj. —**slan′der·ous·ly** adv.

**slang** (slăng) n. Colorful, often humorous language used in place of standard terms. —**slang′i·ness** n. —**slang′y** adj.

**slant** (slănt, slänt) v. **1.** To incline; slope. **2.** To alter so as to fit a bias. —n. **1.** An incline. **2.** A bias. —**slant′ing·ly** adv.

**slap** (slăp) n. A smacking blow made with the open hand. —v. **slapped, slapping.** To strike with a slap.

**slash** (slăsh) v. **1.** To cut or lash with sweeping strokes. **2.** To reduce drastically. —n. A sweeping stroke or gash. —**slash′er** n.

**slat** (slăt) n. A narrow strip.

**slate** (slāt) n. **1.** A fine-grained, layered rock used for tiles and writing surfaces. **2.** A list of candidates. —v. **slated, slating.** To schedule.

**slaugh·ter** (slô′tər) v. **1.** To kill (animals) for food. **2.** To kill (persons) cruelly. —n. An act of slaughtering.

**slave** (slāv) n. A person, usually a laborer, owned by another. —v. **slaved, slaving.** To work hard. —**slav′er·y** n. —**slav′ish** adj. —**slav′ish·ly** adv. —**slav′ish·ness** n.

**slay** (slā) v. **slew, slain, slaying.** To murder. —**slay′er** n.

**slea·zy** (slē′zē) adj. **-zier, -ziest.** Cheap; shoddy. —**slea′zi·ly** adv. —**slea′zi·ness** n.

**sled** (slĕd) n. A vehicle on runners for moving over ice and snow. —v. **sledded, sledding.** To ride a sled.

**sleek** (slēk) adj. **1.** Glossy. **2.** Neat. —v. To polish. —**sleek′ness** n.

**sleep** (slēp) n. A natural, recurring state of restful unconsciousness. —v. **slept, sleeping.** To be in the state of sleep. —**sleep′er** n. —**sleep′i·ly** adv. —**sleep′i·ness** n. —**sleep′less** adj.

**sleet** (slēt) n. Partially frozen rain. —v. To shower sleet. —**sleet′y** adj.

**sleeve** (slēv) n. The arm of a garment. —**sleeve′less** adj.

**slen·der** (slĕn′dər) adj. **1.** Gracefully slim. **2.** Meager. —**slen′der·ly** adv.

**slept** (slĕpt) p.t. & p.p. of **sleep.**

**slew¹** (slōō) n. A large amount.

**slew²** (slōō) p.t. of **slay.**

**slice** (slīs) n. **1.** A thin, broad piece. **2.** A share. —v. **sliced, slicing. 1.** To cut into slices. **2.** To cut from a larger piece. —**slic′er** n.

**slide** (slīd) v. **slid** (slĭd), **slid** or **slidden** (slĭd′n), **sliding.** To move in smooth, continuous contact with a surface. —n. **1.** A sliding movement. **2.** A playground apparatus for children to slide upon. **3.** An image for projection on a screen. **4.** An avalanche. —**slid′er** n.

**slight** (slīt) adj. **1.** Small; meager. **2.** Insignificant. **3.** Slender. —v. **1.** To treat with disrespect. **2.** To neglect. —n. A snub. —**slight′ly** adv. —**slight′ness** n.

**slim** (slĭm) adj. **slimmer, slimmest. 1.** Slender. **2.** Scant; meager. —v. **slimmed, slimming.** To make or become slim. —**slim′ly** adv. —**slim′ness** n.

**slime** (slīm) n. A moist, sticky substance. —**slim′y** adj.

**sling** (slĭng) n. **1.** A looped strap in which a stone is whirled and then let fly. **2.** A looped rope, band, etc., for supporting, cradling, or hoisting. —v. **slung, slinging.** To hurl from a sling; fling. —**sling′er** n.

**slip¹** (slĭp) v. **slipped, slipping. 1.** To move

quietly. **2.** To slide accidentally. **3.** To escape. **4.** To decline. **5.** To place smoothly and quietly. **6.** To err. —*n.* **1.** The act of slipping. **2.** A slight error. **3.** A docking place for a ship. **4.** A woman's undergarment. —**slip'page** *n.* —**slip'per·y** *adj.*

**slip²** (slĭp) *n.* **1.** A plant cutting. **2.** A small piece of paper.

**slip·per** (slĭp'ər) *n.* A light, low shoe.

**slit** (slĭt) *n.* A long, narrow cut or opening. —*v.* **slit, slitting.** To make a slit in.

**sliv·er** (slĭv'ər) *n.* A slender piece.

**slob·ber** (slŏb'ər) *v.* To drool. —*n.* Saliva running from the mouth.

**slo·gan** (slō'gən) *n.* **1.** A motto. **2.** An often repeated phrase used in advertising.

**slope** (slōp) *v.* **sloped, sloping.** To incline upward or downward. —*n.* Any inclined line or surface.

**slop·py** (slŏp'ē) *adj.* **-pier, -piest.** **1.** Muddy. **2.** Untidy; messy. —**slop'pi·ly** *adv.* —**slop'pi·ness** *n.*

**slot** (slŏt) *n.* A long narrow opening.

**sloth** (slôth, slŏth, slōth) *n.* Laziness. —**sloth'ful** *adj.*

**slouch** (slouch) *n.* **1.** A drooping posture or gait. **2.** A lazy or inept person. —**slouch** *v.*

**slov·en·ly** (slŭv'ən-lē) *adj.* **-lier, -liest.** Untidy; messy. —**slov'en·li·ness** *n.*

**slow** (slō) *adj.* **1.** Moving at a low speed. **2.** Taking a long time. **3.** Registering behind the correct time. **4.** Sluggish. **5.** Stupid. —*v.* To make or become slower. —**slow, slow'ly** *adv.* —**slow'ness** *n.*

**sludge** (slŭj) *n.* **1.** Mire or ooze. **2.** Treated sewage. —**sludg'y** *adj.*

**slug¹** (slŭg) *n.* **1.** A bullet. **2.** A shot of liquor. **3.** A false coin.

**slug²** (slŭg) *v.* **slugged, slugging.** To strike heavily. —**slug'ger** *n.*

**slug·gish** (slŭg'ĭsh) *adj.* Slow; inactive. —**slug'gard** *n.* —**slug'gish·ly** *adv.* —**slug'gish·ness** *n.*

**sluice** (slōōs) *n.* A man-made water channel, or one of the gates regulating the flow through it.

**slum** (slŭm) *n.* A poor, overcrowded residential district.

**slum·ber** (slŭm'bər) *v.* To sleep. —*n.* Sleep. —**slum'ber·er** *n.*

**slump** (slŭmp) *v.* **1.** To decline suddenly; collapse. **2.** To droop or slouch. —**slump** *n.*

**slung** (slŭng) *p.t. & p.p.* of **sling.**

**slunk** (slŭngk) *p.t. & p.p.* of **slink.**

**slur** (slûr) *v.* **slurred, slurring.** **1.** To pass over lightly. **2.** To pronounce indistinctly. **3.** To

disparage. —*n.* A disparaging remark.

**slush** (slŭsh) *n.* Partially melted snow or ice. —**slush'i·ness** *n.* —**slush'y** *adj.*

**sly** (slī) *adj.* **slier** or **slyer, sliest** or **slyest.** **1.** Cunning. **2.** Secretive or underhand. **3.** Roguish. —**sly'ly** *adv.* —**sly'ness** *n.*

**smack¹** (smăk) *v.* **1.** To open (the lips) with a sharp sound. **2.** To kiss or slap noisily. —*n.* **1.** The sound produced by smacking the lips. **2.** A noisy kiss. **3.** A loud slap. —*adv.* Squarely.

**smack²** (smăk) *n.* A savor or hint. —*v.* To have a taste or hint.

**small** (smôl) *adj.* **1.** Little. **2.** Insignificant. **3.** Limited in scope. **4.** Pretty. —**small'ness** *n.*

**smart** (smärt) *v.* To cause or feel a stinging pain. —*n.* A stinging pain. —*adj.* **1.** Mentally alert; bright. **2.** Impertinent. **3.** Fashionable. —**smart'ly** *adv.* —**smart'ness** *n.*

**smash** (smăsh) *v.* **1.** To break into pieces. **2.** To throw violently so as to shatter. **3.** To destroy; wreck. —*n.* **1.** The act or sound of smashing. **2.** A collision or crash. —**smash'er** *n.*

**smear** (smîr) *v.* **1.** To daub with a sticky or greasy substance. **2.** To soil. **3.** To vilify. —*n.* **1.** A smudge or blot. **2.** Slander.

**smell** (smĕl) *v.* **1.** To perceive by odor. **2.** To have an odor. **3.** To stink. —*n.* **1.** The olfactory sense. **2.** Odor. —**smell'y** *adj.*

**smelt** (smĕlt) *v.* To melt (ores), separating the metallic constituents. —**smelt'er** *n.*

**smile** (smīl) *n.* A happy or amused facial expression formed by an upward curving of the mouth. —*v.* **smiled, smiling.** **1.** To form a smile. **2.** To express favor or approval.

**smirk** (smûrk) *v.* To smile archly or complacently. —**smirk** *n.*

**smite** (smīt) *v.* **smote, smitten, smiting.** **1.** To strike. **2.** To afflict. —**smit'er** *n.*

**smog** (smŏg, smôg) *n.* Fog mixed with smoke. —**smog'gy** *adj.*

**smoke** (smōk) *n.* The vapor rising from burning material. —*v.* **smoked, smoking.** **1.** To emit smoke **2.** To draw in and exhale the smoke of tobacco or the like. **3.** To preserve by exposure to smoke. —**smok'er** *n.* —**smok'i·ness** *n.* —**smok'y** *adj.*

**smol·der** (smōl'dər) *v.* **1.** To burn with no flame. **2.** To burn or exist inwardly.

**smooth** (smōōth) *adj.* **1.** Not irregular or

rough. **2.** Agreeable; mild. **3.** Easy. *—v.* To make or become smooth. *— smooth'er n. — smooth'ly adv. — smooth'ness n.*

**smote** (smōt). *p.t.* of **smite.**

**smoth-er** (smŭ*th*'ər) *v.* **1.** To suffocate. **2.** To suppress. **3.** To cover heavily.

**smudge** (smŭj) *v.* **smudged, smudging.** To smear or blur. *—n.* A smear. *— smudg'y adj.*

**smug** (smŭg) *adj.* **smugger, smuggest.** Complacent or self-satisfied. *— smug'ly adv. — smug'ness n.*

**smug-gle** (smŭg'əl) *v.* **-gled, -gling.** **1.** To import or export illegally. **2.** To convey secretly. *— smug'gler n.*

**snack** (snăk) *n.* A light meal.

**snag** (snăg) **1.** A sharp projection. **2.** An unforeseen obstacle. *—v.* **snagged, snagging.** To get caught by a snag. *— snag'gy adj.*

**snail** (snāl) *n.* A mollusk with a spirally coiled shell.

**snake** (snāk) *n.* A legless, long-bodied reptile. *—v.* **snaked, snaking.** To move or twist like a snake.

**snap** (snăp) *v.* **snapped, snapping.** **1.** To make or cause to make a sharp cracking sound. **2.** To break suddenly. **3.** To bite or seize suddenly. **4.** To speak sharply. *—n.* **1.** A sharp cracking sound. **2.** A sudden break. **3.** A clasp or other fastening device. **4.** Briskness. **5.** A simple task. *—adj.* Abrupt. *— snap'per n. — snap'pish adj. — snap'py adj.*

**snare** (snâr) *n.* **1.** A small noose for trapping 'birds, etc. **2.** A trap; pitfall. *— snare v.*

**snarl**[1] (snärl) *v.* **1.** To growl with bared teeth. **2.** To speak angrily. *— snarl n. — snarl'y adj.*

**snarl**[2] (snärl) *n.* A tangle. *— snarl v. — snarl'y adj.*

**snatch** (snăch) *v.* To seize or grab. *—n.* **1.** The act of snatching. **2.** A brief period. **3.** A fragment. *— snatch'er n.*

**sneak** (snēk) *v.* To move, give, or take in a stealthy way. *—n.* **1.** A cowardly or under-hand person. **2.** A stealthy move. *— sneak'i-ness n. — sneak'y adj.*

**sneer** (snîr) *n.* A contemptuous raising of the upper lip. *— sneer v. — sneer'er n.*

**sneeze** (snēz) *v.* **sneezed, sneezing.** To expel breath in an explosive, involuntary action. *— sneeze n.*

**snick-er** (snĭk'ər) *n.* A snide, partly stifled laugh. *— snick'er v.*

**snide** (snīd) *adj.* **1.** Slyly derogatory. **2.** Mean.

**sniff** (snĭf) *v.* To inhale a short, audible breath through the nose. *— sniff n. — sniff'er n.*

**snipe** (snīp) *v.* **sniped, sniping.** To shoot at an enemy from a concealed place. *— sni'per n.*

**snob** (snŏb) *n.* One who is convinced of his social or other superiority. *— snob'ber-y n.*

**snoop** (snōōp) *v.* To pry. *—n.* One who pries. *— snoop'er n. — snoop'y adj.*

**snore** (snōr, snôr) *v.* **snored, snoring.** To breathe noisily while sleeping. *— snore n. — snor'er n.*

**snort** (snôrt) *v.* To force air noisily through the nostrils. *— snort n. — snort'er n.*

**snout** (snout) *n.* An animal's projecting nose or facial part.

**snow** (snō) *n.* White ice crystals falling from the sky. *—v.* To fall as snow. *— snow'y adj.*

**snub** (snŭb) *v.* **snubbed, snubbing.** To slight, as by ignoring. *— snub n. — snub'ber n.*

**snuff**[1] (snŭf) *n.* Finely pulverized tobacco for snorting up the nostrils.

**snuff**[2] (snŭf) *v.* To extinguish (a candle).

**snug** (snŭg) *adj.* **snugger, snuggest.** **1.** Cozy. **2.** Close-fitting or compact. *— snug, snug'ly adv. — snug'ness n.*

**so** (sō) *adv.* **1.** In the manner indicated. **2.** To the degree expressed. **3.** Therefore. **4.** Thereabouts. **5.** Also. **6.** Then. **7.** Indeed. *—adj.* True; factual. *— so.* For that reason.

**soak** (sōk) *v.* **1.** To wet, as by immersing. **2.** To absorb. **3.** To be immersed. **4.** To permeate. *— soak'er n.*

**soap** (sōp) *n.* A cleansing agent. *—v.* To cover with soap. *— soap'i-ly adv. — soap'i-ness n. — soap'y adj.*

**soar** (sôr, sōr) *v.* To rise or fly upward.

**sob** (sŏb) *v.* **sobbed, sobbing.** To weep convulsively. *— sob n. — sob'bing-ly adv.*

**so-ber** (sō'bər) *adj.* **1.** Not drunk. **2.** Serious or grave. Plain. *—v.* To make or become sober. *— so'ber-ly adv. — so'ber-ness, so-bri'e-ty n.*

**so-cia-ble** (sō'shə-bəl) *adj.* Friendly; companionable. *— so'cia-bil'i-ty n. — so'cia-ble-ness n. — so'cia-bly adv.*

**so-cial** (sō'shəl) *adj.* **1.** Living in groups. **2.** Of human society. **3.** Sociable. *—n.* A social gathering. *— so'cial-ly adv.*

**so-cial-ism** (sō'shə-lĭz'əm) *n.* Public ownership of factories, farms, etc. *— so'cial-ist n. & adj. — so'cial-is'tic adj.*

**so-cial-ize** (sō'shə-līz') *v.* **-ized, -izing.** **1.** To place under public ownership. **2.** To take part in social activities. *— so'cial-i-za'tion n.*

**so-ci-e-ty** (sə-sī'ə-tē) *n., pl.* **-ties. 1. a.** The

totality of human relationships. **b.** A human community sharing a culture. **2.** The fashionable social class. **3.** Companionship. **4.** A cultural or charitable organization.

**so·ci·ol·o·gy** (sō'sē-ŏl'ə-jē, sō'shē-) n. The study of human societies. —**so'ci·ol'o·gist** n.

**sock**[1] (sŏk) n. A short stocking.

**sock**[2] (sŏk) v. To punch. —**sock** n.

**sock·et** (sŏk'ĭt) n. A cavity that receives an inserted part.

**sod** (sŏd) n. Grass-covered surface soil. —v. **sodded, sodding.** To cover with sod.

**so·da** (sō'də) n. Carbonated water or a soft drink containing it.

**so·fa** (sō'fə) n. A long couch with a back and arms.

**soft** (sôft, sŏft) adj. **1.** Not hard or firm; yielding. **2.** Not loud. **3.** Gentle; mild. **4.** Tender. **5.** Easy. **6.** Not alcoholic. —adv. Gently. —**soft'en** v. —**soft'en·er** n. —**soft'ly** adv. —**soft'ness** n.

**sog·gy** (sŏg'ē) adj. **-gier, -giest.** **1.** Soaked. **2.** Humid; sultry. —**sog'gi·ly** adv. —**sog'gi·ness** n.

**soil** (soil) n. Earth; ground. —v. **1.** To make or become dirty. **2.** To tarnish.

**so·lar** (sō'lər) adj. Of the sun.

**sold** (sōld). p.t. & p.p. of **sell.**

**sol·der** (sŏd'ər, sŏd'-) n. A fusible alloy used to join metallic parts. —v. To join or repair with solder.

**sole**[1] (sōl) n. **1.** The undersurface of the foot. **2.** The undersurface of a shoe. —v. **soled, soling.** To furnish with a sole.

**sole**[2] (sōl) adj. Single; only. —**sole'ly** adv.

**sol·emn** (sŏl'əm) adj. **1.** Earnest; grave. **2.** Formal. Gloomy. —**so·lem'ni·ty,** (sŏl'-) **emn·ness** n. —**sol'emn·ly** adv.

**so·lic·it** (sə-lĭs'ĭt) v. **1.** To seek to obtain. **2.** To entreat. —**so·lic'i·ta'tion** n. —**so·lic'i·tor** n.

**so·lic·i·tous** (sə-lĭs'ə-təs) adj. Concerned; attentive. —**so·lic'i·tous·ly** adv. —**so·lic'i·tude,** so·lic'i·tous·ness n.

**sol·id** (sŏl'ĭd) adj. **1.** Not liquid or gaseous. **2.** Not hollow. **3.** Of a single substance. **4.** Three-dimensional. **5.** Continuous. **6.** Strongly constructed. **7.** Firm; substantial. —n. **1.** A solid substance. **2.** A three-dimensional figure. —**sol·id'i·ty,** sol·id'ness n. —**sol'id·ly** adv.

**sol·i·dar·i·ty** (sŏl'ə-dăr'ə-tē) n. Unity.

**sol·i·tar·y** (sŏl'ə-tĕr'ē) adj. **1.** Existing or being alone. **2.** Single; sole. —**sol'i·tar'i·ness** n. —**sol'i·tude'** n.

**so·lo** (sō'lō) n., pl. **-los.** A musical composition for one performer. —v. To perform alone. —adj. & adv. —**so'lo·ist** n.

**sol·stice** (sŏl'stəs, sōl'-) n. Either of two times of the year when the sun takes the most northerly or most southerly path across the sky.

**sol·u·ble** (sŏl'yə-bəl) adj. **1.** Capable of being dissolved. **2.** Capable of being solved. —**sol'u·bil'i·ty** n. —**sol'u·bly** adv.

**so·lu·tion** (sə-loō'shən) n. **1.** A liquid with a substance mixed evenly and stably in it. **2.** The solving of a problem. **3.** An answer.

**solve** (sŏlv) v. **solved, solving.** To find an answer. —**solv'a·ble** adj.

**sol·vent** (sŏl'vənt) adj. **1.** Able to pay debts. **2.** Capable of dissolving another substance. —n. A liquid capable of dissolving another substance. —**sol'ven·cy** n.

**som·ber** (sŏm'bər) adj. **1.** Dark; gloomy. **2.** Melancholy. —**som'ber·ly** adv.

**some** (sŭm) adj. **1.** Certain. **2.** Being unknown or unnamed. —pron. An unspecified number or portion. —adv. Approximately.

**some·bod·y** (sŭm'bŏd'ē, -bŭd'ē, -bə-dē) pron. An unspecified person. —n. A person of importance.

**some·one** (sŭm'wŭn', -wən) pron. Some person.

**some·thing** (sŭm'thĭng) pron. An unspecified thing.

**some·times** (sŭm'tīmz') adv. Now and then.

**some·where** (sŭm'hwěr') adv. At, in, or to an unspecified place.

**son** (sŭn) n. A male offspring.

**song** (sŏng, sông) n. **1.** Sound produced by singing. **2.** A brief musical composition for singing. —**song'ful** adj.

**son·ic** (sŏn'ĭk) adj. Of sound or its propagation.

**son-in-law** (sŭn'ĭn-lô') n., pl. **sons-in-law.** The husband of one's daughter.

**soon** (soōn) adv. **1.** In the near future. **2.** Promptly. **3.** Early.

**soothe** (soōth) v. **soothed, soothing.** **1.** To calm. **2.** To ease or relieve. —**sooth'er** n.

**so·phis·ti·cat·ed** (sə-fĭs'tĭ-kā'tĭd) adj. **1.** Experienced, esp. in matters of taste; worldly. **2.** Complicated or refined. —**so·phis'ti·cate** n. —**so·phis'ti·ca'tion** n.

**soph·o·more** (sŏf'ə-môr') n. A second-year student.

**so·pran·o** (sə-prăn'ō, -prä'nō) n., pl. **-os.** The highest natural human voice. —**so·pran'o** adj.

**sor·cer·y** (sôr'sər·ē) n. Witchcraft. —**sor'cer·er** n. —**sor'cer·ess** fem.n.

**sor·did** (sôr′dĭd) *adj.* **1.** Filthy; squalid. **2.** Vile; selfish. —**sor′did·ly** *adv.* —**sor′did·ness** *n.*

**sore** (sôr, sōr) *adj.* sorer, sorest. **1.** Painful; tender. **2.** Grievous. —*n.* An open skin lesion. —**sore′ly** *adv.* —**sore′ness** *n.*

**sor·row** (sôr′ō, sŏr′ō) *n.* **1.** Mental suffering because of injury or loss. **2.** A misfortune. —*v.* To feel sorrow; grieve. —**sor′row·ful** *adj.* —**sor′row·ful·ly** *adv.*

**sor·ry** (sôr′ē, sŏr′ē) *adj.* -rier, -riest. **1.** Feeling sympathy or regret. **2.** Poor; paltry.

**sort** (sôrt) *n.* A class; kind. —*v.* To arrange according to class, kind, or size.

**sought** (sôt). *p.t.* & *p.p.* of **seek.**

**soul** (sōl) *n.* **1.** The essential, spiritual, or immortal part of a person. **2.** A person. **3.** Essence; core. **4.** Deep feeling. —**soul′ful** *adj.* —**soul′ful·ness** *n.* —**soul′less** *adj.* —**soul′less·ness** *n.*

**sound¹** (sound) *n.* A vibratory disturbance capable of being heard. —*v.* **1.** To make or cause to make a sound. **2.** To seem to be.

**sound²** (sound) *adj.* **1.** In good condition. **2.** Reliable. **3.** Sensible. **4.** Thorough; complete. —**sound′ly** *adv.* —**sound′ness** *n.*

**sound³** (sound) *n.* A wide strait or inlet of the ocean. —*v.* **1.** To measure the depth of (water). **2.** To ascertain or test the opinions of. —**sound′ing** *n.*

**soup** (sōōp) *n.* A liquid food prepared from meat, fish, or vegetable stock.

**sour** (sour) *adj.* **1.** Having a sharp or acid taste. **2.** Spoiled. **3.** Bad-tempered. —*v.* To make or become sour. —**sour′ly** *adv.* —**sour′ness** *n.*

**source** (sôrs, sōrs) *n.* **1.** A point of origin. **2.** One that supplies information.

**south** (south) *n.* **1.** The direction to the left of an observer facing the sunset. **2.** The S part of any country or region. —*adj.* & *adv.* In, to, or from the south. —**south′er·ly** *adj.* & *adv.* —**south′ern** *adj.* —**south′ern·er** *n.* —**south′ward, south′wards** *adv.* & *adj.*

**south·east** (south-ēst′) *n.* The direction or region halfway between south and east. —*adj.* & *adv.* To, from, or in the southeast. —**south′east′er·ly** *adj.* & *adv.* —**south′east′ern** *adj.*

**south·west** (south-wĕst′) *n.* The direction or region halfway between south and west. —*adj.* To, from, or in the southwest. —**south′west′er·ly** *adj.* & *adv.* —**south′west′ern** *adj.*

**sou·ve·nir** (sōō′və-nîr′) *n.* Something kept as a remembrance.

**sov·er·eign** (sŏv′ər-ən) *n.* The chief of state in a monarchy. —*adj.* **1.** Supreme. **2.** Independent. —**sov′er·eign·ty** *n.*

**sow¹** (sō) *v.* sowed, sown (sōn) or sowed, sowing. **1.** To plant (seed). **2.** To strew with seed. —**sow′er** *n.*

**sow²** (sou) *n.* An adult female pig.

**space** (spās) *n.* **1.** The expanse in which all things exist. **2.** A distance or area; extent. **3.** A gap. **4.** A period of time. —*v.* spaced, spacing. To arrange with spaces between.

**spa·cious** (spā′shəs) *adj.* Having much space. —**spa′cious·ly** *adv.* —**spa′cious·ness** *n.*

**spade¹** (spād) *n.* A digging tool having a flat blade, esp. with a tapered point. —*v.* spaded, spading. To dig with a spade.

**spade²** (spād) *n.* A playing card marked with a black, inverted heart.

**span** (spăn) *n.* **1.** The extent between two points. **2.** A bridge. **3.** A period of time. —*v.* spanned, spanning. To reach or extend over.

**spank** (spăngk) *v.* To slap on the buttocks. —**spank** *n.*

**spare** (spâr) *v.* spared, sparing. **1.** To save or relieve from pain, trouble, etc. **2.** To use frugally. **3.** To do without. —*adj.* sparer, sparest. **1.** Extra. **2.** Meager; lean. —*n.* A replacement reserved for future use. —**spare′ness** *n.*

**spark** (spärk) *n.* **1.** A glowing particle, as one thrown off from a fire. **2.** A flash of light. **3.** A seed; germ. —*v.* **1.** To give off sparks. **2.** To set in motion.

**spar·kle** (spär′kəl) *v.* -kled, -kling. **1.** To give off flashes of light; glitter. **2.** To give off gas bubbles. —*n.* **1.** A small spark. **2.** Vivacity. **3.** A giving off of gas bubbles. —**spar′kler** *n.*

**sparse** (spärs) *adj.* sparser, sparsest. Not dense; widely spaced. —**spar′si·ty** *n.*

**spasm** (spăz′əm) *n.* **1.** A sudden, involuntary muscular contraction. **2.** A sudden burst. —**spas·mod′ic** *adj.*

**spas·tic** (spăs′tĭk) *adj.* Continuously contracting. —*n.* A person suffering from chronic spasms. —**spas′ti·cal·ly** *adv.*

**spat¹** (spăt). *p.t.* & *p.p.* of **spit.**

**spat²** (spăt) *n.* A brief, petty quarrel. —**spat** *v.*

**spa·tial** (spā′shəl) *adj.* Also **spa·cial.** Of or involving space.

**spawn** (spôn) *n.* **1.** The eggs of fish, frogs, etc. **2.** Offspring. —*v.* **1.** To produce spawn. **2.** To bring forth.

**speak** (spēk) *v.* spoke, spoken, speaking. **1.** To utter words; talk. **2.** To express. **3.** To make a speech. **4.** To converse in (a language). —**speak′er** *n.*

**spear** (spîr) *n.* A sharply pointed weapon

with a long shaft. —v. To pierce with a spear.
**spe·cial** (spĕsh'əl) adj. 1. Exceptional. 2. Peculiar. 3. Having a specific function, application, etc. 4. Additional. —n. Something special. —**spe'cial·ly** adv.

**spe·cial·ize** (spĕsh'ə-līz') v. -ized, -izing. 1. To employ oneself in a special study or activity. 2. To adapt to a specific environment or function. —**spe'cial·ist** n. —**spe'cial·i·za'tion** n. —**spe'cial·ty** n.

**spe·cies** (spē'shēz, -sēz) n., pl. **species.** Kind; type, esp. of organisms.

**spe·cif·ic** (spə-sĭf'ĭk) adj. Explicit; definite; detailed. —n. A distinct thing; item. —**spe·cif'i·cal·ly** adv.

**spec·i·fy** (spĕs'ə-fī') v. -fied, -fying. 1. To state explicitly. 2. To describe or design in full detail. —**spec'i·fi·ca'tion** n.

**spec·i·men** (spĕs'ə-mən) n. A representative part or thing for study; example.

**speck** (spĕk) n. A small spot or bit. —v. To mark with specks.

**spec·ta·cle** (spĕk'tə-kəl) n. 1. A public display. 2. A marvel or curiosity. 3. **spectacles.** Eyeglasses.

**spec·tac·u·lar** (spĕk-tăk'yə-lər) adj. Visually striking; showy.

**spec·ta·tor** (spĕk'tā-tər) n. An observer or onlooker.

**spec·ter** (spĕk'tər) n. A ghost. —**spec'tral** adj.

**spec·trum** (spĕk'trəm) n., pl. **-tra** or **-trums.** A broad sequence or range, esp. of light separated into its constituent colors.

**spec·u·late** (spĕk'yə-lāt') v. -lated, -lating. 1. To reflect. 2. To conjecture; guess. 3. To take risks for financial profits. —**spec'u·la'tion** n. —**spec'u·la·tive** adj.

**speech** (spēch) n. 1. The faculty or manner of speaking. 2. Vocal communication. 3. A public address. —**speech'less** adj.

**speed** (spēd) n. 1. Rate of motion. 2. Swiftness. 3. Rapid movement. —v. **sped** or **speeded, speeding.** 1. To move rapidly. 2. To accelerate. 3. To drive at an illegal rate of speed. —**speed'ing** adj. n. —**speed'y** adj.

**spell¹** (spĕl) v. 1. To name in order the letters of (a word). 2. To mean. —**spell'er** n.

**spell²** (spĕl) n. 1. A magic formula. 2. Fascination. 3. A bewitched state.

**spell³** (spĕl) n. 1. A short period of time. 2. A short turn of work. —v. To relieve (someone) from work.

**spend** (spĕnd) v. **spent, spending.** 1. To pay out (money). 2. To wear out. 3. To pass (time). —**spend'er** n.

**sperm** (spûrm) n. 1. A male reproductive cell. 2. Semen.

**sphere** (sfîr) n. 1. A ball; globe. 2. An environment; range. —**spher'i·cal** adj. —**spher'i·cal·ly** adv.

**spice** (spīs) n. 1. An aromatic substance, as cinnamon or pepper, used as flavoring. 2. Zest. —**spice** v. —**spic'i·ly** adv. —**spic'i·ness** n. —**spic'y** adj.

**spig·ot** (spĭg'ət) n. A faucet.

**spike** (spīk) n. 1. A heavy nail. 2. A sharp-pointed projection. —v. **spiked, spiking.** 1. To secure or pierce with a spike. 2. To thwart.

**spill** (spĭl) v. **spilled** or **spilt** (spĭlt), **spilling.** 1. To cause to run or fall out of a container. 2. To shed (blood). 3. To cause to fall. —n. 1. An act of spilling. 2. A fall.

**spin** (spĭn) v. **spun, spinning.** 1. To draw out and twist fibers into thread. 2. To form (a thread, web, etc.) by forcing out a substance. 3. To rotate rapidly; whirl. —n. 1. A swift whirling motion. 2. A short ride. —**spin'ner** n. —**spin'ning** adj. & n.

**spine** (spīn) n. 1. The long row of bones along the back. 2. A thorn, prickle, or quill. —**spi'nal** adj. —**spine'less** adj. —**spin'y** adj.

**spi·ral** (spī'rəl) n. The path of a point moving around a center at an increasing or decreasing distance. —adj. 1. Moving in a spiral. 2. Coiling. —v. To move in a spiral. —**spi'ral·ly** adv.

**spire** (spīr) n. The top part of a steeple or other tapering structure.

**spir·it** (spĭr'ĭt) n. 1. The soul. 2. A supernatural being. 3. An individual. 4. Mood; feelings. 5. Vivacity and courage. 7. The essential meaning or feeling. 8. **spirits.** Alcoholic liquor. —v. To carry off secretly. —**spir'it·ed** adj. —**spir'it·less** adj.

**spir·i·tu·al** (spĭr'ĭ-chōō-əl) adj. 1. Of the spirit. 2. Sacred. —n. A black religious folk song. —**spir'i·tu·al·i·ty** n. —**spir'i·tu·al·ly** adv.

**spit¹** (spĭt) n. Saliva. —v. **spat** or **spit, spitting.** To eject from the mouth.

**spit²** (spĭt) n. 1. A pointed rod on which meat is impaled for broiling. 2. A narrow point of land. —v. **spitted, spitting.** To fix on a spit.

**spite** (spīt) n. Malicious ill will. —**in spite of.** Regardless of. —v. **spited, spiting.** To hurt maliciously. —**spite'ful** adj. —**spite'ful·ly** adv.

**splash** (splăsh) v. 1. To dash or scatter (a liquid). 2. To dash liquid upon. —n. 1. A flying mass of liquid. 2. A mark produced by scattered liquid. —**splash'er** n.

**splen·did** (splĕn'dĭd) adj. 1. Brilliant. 2.

Magnificent. — **splen'did·ly** adv. — **splen'dor** n.

**splice** (splīs) v. **spliced, splicing.** To join at the ends. — n. A joint. — **splic'er** n.

**splin·ter** (splĭn'tər) n. A sharp, slender piece. — v. To break into splinters.

**split** (splĭt) v. **split, splitting.** 1. To break, burst, or rip apart. 2. To disunite. 3. To divide and share. — n. 1. The act or result of splitting. 2. A breach or rupture. — adj. Divided.

**splurge** (splûrj) n. An extravagant expense. — **splurge** v.

**spoil** (spoil) v. **spoiled, spoiling.** 1. To damage. 2. To overindulge so as to harm the character. 3. To decay. — n. **spoils.** Plunder. — **spoil'age** n. — **spoil'er** n.

**spoke¹** (spōk) n. One of the rods that connect the hub and rim of a wheel.

**spoke²** (spōk) p.t. of **speak.**

**spo·ken** (spō'kən) p.p. of **speak.**

**sponge** (spŭnj) n. 1. A primitive marine animal. 2. This animal's porous absorbent skeleton or a substitute, used in bathing, cleaning, etc. — v. **sponged, sponging.** 1. To wipe or clean with a sponge. 2. To live off others. — **spong'er** n. — **spon'gy** adj.

**spon·sor** (spŏn'sər) n. 1. One who vouches or assumes responsibility for another. 2. A television or radio advertiser. — **spon'sor** v. — **spon'sor·ship** n.

**spon·ta·ne·ous** (spŏn-tā'nē-əs) adj. 1. Happening without external cause. 2. Voluntary. 3. Natural and unstudied. — **spon·ta·ne'i·ty,** **spon·ta'ne·ous·ness** n. — **spon·ta'ne·ous·ly** adv.

**spool** (spool) n. A cylinder upon which thread is wound.

**spoon** (spoon) n. A shallow bowl on a handle, used in eating food. — v. To lift or scoop with a spoon.

**spore** (spôr, spōr) n. A reproductive cell of a fern, fungus, or bacterium.

**sport** (spôrt, spōrt) n. 1. An active pastime or diversion, esp. a game. 2. Light mockery. 3. A funloving person. — v. 1. To play; frolic. 2. To display. — adj. For sports. — **sport'y** adj.

**sports·man** (spôrts'mən, spōrts'-) n. 1. A participant in sports. — **sports'man·like** adj. — **sports'man·ship** n. — **sports'wom·an** fem.n.

**spot** (spŏt) n. 1. A particular place. 2. A mark or stain. — v. **spotted, spotting.** 1. To mark with spots. 2. To detect; locate. — **spot'less** adj. — **spot'ter** n. — **spot'ty** adj.

**spouse** (spous, spouz) n. One's husband or wife.

**spout** (spout) v. 1. To gush forth. 2. To

speak volubly. — n. 1. A pipe through which liquid is released. 2. A continuous stream.

**sprain** (sprān) n. A painful wrenching of the ligaments of a joint. — **sprain** v.

**sprang** (sprăng) p.t. of **spring.**

**sprawl** (sprôl) v. To lie or spread out awkwardly. — **sprawl** n. — **sprawl'er** n.

**spray¹** (sprā) n. 1. A mass of dispersed droplets. 2. a. A fine jet of liquid that releases such jets. b. A pressurized container. — v. 1. To disperse (a liquid) in a spray. 2. To apply a spray to. — **spray'er** n.

**spray²** (sprā) n. A leafy or flowery branch.

**spread** (sprĕd) v. **spread, spreading.** 1. To open; stretch. 2. To move farther apart. 3. To distribute over a surface. 4. To extend. 5. To disseminate. — n. 1. The act of spreading. 2. An expanse. 3. A range. 4. A cloth covering. 5. A food to spread. — **spread'er** n.

**sprig** (sprĭg) n. A twig or shoot.

**spring** (sprĭng) v. **sprang** or **sprung, sprung, springing.** 1. To leap. 2. To emerge suddenly. 3. To arise; develop. 4. To set in motion. 5. To disclose suddenly. — n. 1. An elastic device, as a coil of wire. 2. Elasticity; resilience. 3. The act of springing. 4. A natural fountain or flow of water. 5. A source. 6. The season between winter and summer. — **spring'y** adj.

**sprin·kle** (sprĭng'kəl) v. **-kled, -kling.** 1. To scatter in drops. 2. To rain lightly. — n. A light rainfall. — **sprin'kler** n.

**sprint** (sprĭnt) n. A short race run at top speed. — v. To run at top speed. — **sprint'er** n.

**sprout** (sprout) v. To begin to grow. — n. A bud or shoot.

**spruce** (sproos) adj. **sprucer, sprucest.** Neat or dapper. — v. **spruced, sprucing.** To make or become spruce.

**sprung** (sprŭng) p.p. & alternate p.t. of **spring.**

**spun** (spŭn) p.t. & p.p. of **spin.**

**spur** (spûr) n. 1. A spiked device on a rider's heel to urge the horse forward. 2. An incentive or goad. 3. A pointed projection. 4. A lateral extension. — v. **spurred, spurring.** To urge on.

**spurn** (spûrn) v. To reject disdainfully. — **spurn'er** n.

**spurt** (spûrt) n. A sudden gush. — v. 1. To burst forth. 2. To squirt.

**sput·ter** (spŭt'ər) v. 1. To spit out small particles. 2. To make a sporadic coughing noise. — **sput'ter** n. — **sput'ter·er** n.

**spy** (spī) n., pl. **spies.** One who secretly

watches, esp. to obtain intelligence. —v. **spied, spying.** **1.** To act as a spy. **2.** To see.

**squab-ble** (skwŏb′əl) n. A trivial quarrel. — **squab′ble** v.

**squad** (skwŏd) n. A small group or team.

**squal-id** (skwŏl′ĭd) adj. Filthy and cluttered. — **squal′id-ly** adv. — **squal′id-ness**, **squal′or** n.

**squan-der** (skwŏn′dər) v. To spend wastefully.

**square** (skwâr) n. **1.** A rectangle having four equal sides. **2.** An instrument for drawing right angles. **3.** The product of a number multiplied by itself. **4. a.** An open area at a street intersection. **b.** A block. —adj. **squarer, squarest.** **1.** Having four equal sides and four right angles. **2.** Forming a right angle. **3.** Honest. **4.** Settled. —v. **squared, squaring.** **1.** To cut to a square shape. **2.** To settle. **3.** To raise (a number) to the second power. **4.** To conform. — **square′ly** adv. — **square′ness** n.

**squash** (skwŏsh, skwôsh) v. **1.** To flatten; crush. **2.** To suppress. —n. **1.** The act of squashing. **2.** A game played in a walled court with a racket.

**squat** (skwŏt) v. **1.** To sit on one's heels. **2.** To settle on unoccupied land without legal claim. —adj. **squatter, squattest.** Short and thick. —n. The posture of squatting. — **squat′ter** n.

**squeak** (skwēk) v. **1.** To make a brief, thin, shrill cry or sound. — **squeak** n. — **squeak′y** adj.

**squeal** (skwēl) v. **1.** To make a loud, shrill cry or sound. **2.** To turn informer. — **squeal** n. — **squeal′er** n.

**squeam-ish** (skwē′mĭsh) adj. Easily nauseated or disgusted. — **squeam′ish-ly** adv. — **squeam′ish-ness** n.

**squeeze** (skwēz) v. **squeezed, squeezing.** **1.** To press hard. **2.** To extract by applying pressure. **3.** To cram. —n. An act of squeezing. — **squeez′er** n.

**squelch** (skwĕlch) v. To suppress or silence. —n. A crushing reply.

**squint** (skwĭnt) v. To look with the eyes partly closed. — **squint** n. — **squint′er** n.

**squirm** (skwûrm) v. To twist about; writhe. — **squirm′er** n. — **squirm′y** adv.

**squirt** (skwûrt) v. To eject liquid in a thin swift stream. — **squirt** n.

**stab** (stăb) v. **stabbed, stabbing.** To pierce or wound with a pointed weapon. —n. **1.** A thrust with a pointed weapon. **2.** An attempt.

**sta-ble¹** (stā′bəl) adj. **-bler, -blest.** **1.** Resistant to sudden change. **2.** Maintaining equilibrium. — **sta-bil′i-ty** n. — **sta′bi-li-za′tion** n. — **sta′bi-lize′** v. — **sta′bi-liz′er** n.

**sta-ble²** (stā′bəl) n. A building for domestic animals, esp. horses. —v. **-bled, -bling.** To keep in a stable.

**stack** (stăk) n. **1.** A pile arranged in layers. **2.** A chimney. —v. To arrange in a stack.

**sta-di-um** (stā′dē-əm) n. A large, often unroofed structure for athletic events.

**staff** (stăf) n. **1.** pl. **staffs** or **staves.** A rod or stick. **2.** pl. **staffs.** A group of assistants or employees. **3.** pl. **staves.** The set of lines on which music is written. —v. To provide with employees.

**stage** (stāj) n. **1.** A raised platform, esp. one for theatrical performances. **2.** The theater. **3.** A leg of a journey. **4.** A step in development. —v. **staged, staging.** **1.** To present on a stage. **2.** To carry out.

**stag-ger** (stăg′ər) v. **1.** To move or cause to move unsteadily; totter. **2.** To overwhelm. **3.** To arrange in alternating time periods. —n. A tottering or reeling motion. — **stag′ger-er** n.

**stag-nant** (stăg′nənt) adj. **1.** Foul from standing still. **2.** Inactive; sluggish.

**stag-nate** (stăg′nāt′) v. **-nated, -nating.** To lie inactive. — **stag-na′tion** n.

**staid** (stād) adj. Grave; sober.

**stain** (stān) v. **1.** To discolor or spot. **2.** To disgrace. **3.** To color with a penetrating dye. —n. **1.** A spot or smudge. **2.** A disgrace. **3.** A dye. — **stain′er** n. — **stain′less** adj.

**stair** (stâr) n. **1.** Often **stairs.** A staircase. **2.** One of a flight of steps.

**stair-case** (stâr′kās′) n. A flight of steps.

**stake** (stāk) n. **1.** A pointed stick for driving into the ground. **2.** Often **stakes.** Money risked in a bet. **3.** A share or interest. —v. **staked, staking.** **1.** To mark the limits of. **2.** To gamble or risk. **3.** To finance.

**stale** (stāl) adj. **staler, stalest.** **1.** Having lost freshness. **2.** Unoriginal.

**stalk¹** (stôk) n. A plant stem.

**stalk²** (stôk) v. **1.** To walk with a stiff, haughty, or menacing gait. **2.** To track (game). — **stalk′er** n.

**stall** (stôl) n. A small compartment or booth. —v. To stop or delay.

**stal-lion** (stăl′yən) n. An uncastrated adult male horse.

**stal-wart** (stôl′wərt) adj. Sturdy and brave.

**stam-mer** (stăm′ər) v. To speak with involuntary pauses and repetitions; stutter. — **stam′mer** n. — **stam′mer-er** n.

**stamp** (stămp) v. **1.** To bring the foot down upon forcibly. **2.** To imprint or impress with a mark. **3.** To affix a stamp to. **4.** To cut out with a die. —n. **1.** The act of stamping. **2.** A mark or seal. **3.** A piece of gummed paper, as for postage. **4. a.** An implement used to impress or cut out. **b.** The impression thus formed.

**stam·pede** (stăm·pēd') n. A sudden headlong rush, as of startled animals. —v. **-peded, -peding.** To rush in a stampede.

**stance** (stăns) n. **1.** Manner of standing. **2.** Attitude.

**stanch** (stănch, stänch) v. To check the flow of.

**stand** (stănd) v. **stood, standing. 1.** To take or maintain an upright position on the feet. **2.** To place or be placed upright. **3.** To remain stable or unchanged. **4.** To tolerate; endure. **5.** To rank. **6.** To hold an opinion. —n. **1.** A fixed position. **2.** A halt or stop. **3.** A platform or other place for standing. **4.** A counter, rack, or pedestal. **5.** A growth of trees.

**stan·dard** (stăn'dərd) n. **1.** A flag or banner. **2.** A measure of value; criterion. **3.** A degree or level. — **stan'dard** adj.

**stan·dard·ize** (stăn'dər·dīz') v. **-ized, -izing.** To cause or adapt to fit a standard. — **stan'dard·i·za'tion** n.

**stand·ing** (stăn'dĭng) n. **1.** Status. **2.** Length of time. —adj. **1.** Upright. **2.** Permanent. **3.** Stagnant.

**stank** (stăngk) p.t. of **stink.**

**sta·ple¹** (stā'pəl) n. **1.** A major commodity or product. **2.** A major part. **3.** Fiber. — **sta'ple** adj.

**sta·ple²** (stā'pəl) n. A U-shaped metal loop with pointed ends, used esp. as a paper fastener. — **sta'ple** v. — **sta'pler** n.

**star** (stär) n. **1.** A relatively stationary celestial object visible at night as a point of light. **2.** A graphic design with radiating points. **3.** A superior performer. **4.** A leading actor. **5.** An asterisk. — v. **starred, starring. 1.** To mark with a star. **2.** To play the leading role. — **star'ry** adj.

**star·board** (stär'bərd) n. The right-hand side of a ship or aircraft as one faces forward. — **star'board** adj. & adv.

**starch** (stärch) n. A food substance found in corn, potatoes, and wheat, and used in powdered form as a fabric stiffener. —v. To stiffen with starch. — **starch'y** adj.

**stare** (stâr) v. **stared, staring.** To look with a steady gaze. — **stare** n.

**stark** (stärk) adj. **1.** Utter; extreme. **2.** Bare; bleak. —adv. Utterly. — **stark'ly** adv. — **stark'ness** n.

**start** (stärt) v. **1.** To begin. **2.** To set in motion. **3.** To move suddenly. —n. **1. a.** A beginning. **b.** A place or time of beginning. **2.** A position of advantage. **3.** A sudden movement. — **start'er** n.

**star·tle** (stär'tl) v. **-tled, -tling.** To cause to jump, as in fright.

**starve** (stärv) v. **starved, starving. 1.** To die or cause to die from hunger. **2.** To suffer or cause to suffer from hunger. — **star·va'tion** n.

**state** (stāt) n. **1.** Condition. **2.** Stage; phase. **3.** A nation. **4.** National policy or power; government. **5.** A political unit of a federation. **6.** Ceremony. —v. **stated, stating.** To declare. — **state'hood** n.

**state·ly** (stāt'lē) adj. **-lier, -liest.** Dignified; formal. — **state'li·ness** n.

**state·ment** (stāt'mənt) n. **1.** The act of stating. **2.** An account.

**states·man** (stāts'mən) n. A political leader. — **states'man·like** adj. — **states'man·ship** n.

**stat·ic** (stăt'ĭk) adj. **1.** Having no motion. **2.** Caused by accumulation of electric charge. —n. Random noise produced in a radio or television receiver. — **stat'i·cal·ly** adv.

**sta·tion** (stā'shən) n. **1.** A position. **2.** A center of operations. **3.** A transportation depot. **4.** Social status. **5.** A place for radio or television transmission. —v. To post.

**sta·tion·ar·y** (stā'shə·nĕr'ē) adj. Fixed; not moving.

**sta·tion·er·y** (stā'shə·nĕr'ē) n. **1.** Writing materials and office supplies. **2.** A store that sells stationery.

**sta·tis·tic** (stə·tĭs'tĭk) n. **1.** Any numerical datum. **2. statistics** (takes sing. v.). The interpretation of numerical data. — **sta·tis'ti·cal** adj. — **stat·is·ti'cian** n.

**stat·ue** (stăch'ōō) n. A sculpted form or likeness. — **stat'u·esque'** adj.

**stat·ure** (stăch'ər) n. **1.** A person's height. **2.** Status; reputation.

**stat·us** (stā'təs, stăt'əs) n. **1.** Legal condition. **2.** A relative position; rank. **3.** A state of affairs.

**stat·ute** (stăch'ōōt) n. A law.

**stat·u·to·ry** (stăch'ə·tôr'ē, -tōr'ē) adj. Enacted, regulated, or defined by statute.

**staunch** (stônch, stänch) adj. Firm and steadfast. — **staunch'ly** adv. — **staunch'ness** n.

**stave** (stāv) n. **1.** One of the wooden strips that form the sides of a barrel. **2.** A staff.

**staved** or **stove, staving.** **1.** To break a hole in. **2.** To ward off.

**staves** (stāvz). Alternate *pl.* of **staff.**

**stay**[1] (stā) *v.* **1.** To remain. **2.** To stop. **3.** To wait. **4.** To endure. **5.** To postpone. —*n.* **1.** A stop or visit. **2.** A postponement.

**stay**[2] (stā) *v.* To prop up. —*n.* A support or brace.

**stead·y** (stĕd'ē) *adj.* **-ier, -iest.** **1.** Firm. **2.** Unfaltering. **3.** Calm. —*v.* **-ied, -ying.** To make or become more steady. — **stead'i·ly** *adv.* — **stead'i·ness** *n.*

**steak** (stāk) *n.* A slice of meat, usually beef.

**steal** (stēl) *v.* **stole, stolen, stealing.** **1.** To take without right or permission. **2.** To get or effect secretly. **3.** To move stealthily.

**stealth** (stĕlth) *n.* Covert action; furtiveness. — **stealth'i·ly** *adv.* — **stealth'i·ness** *n.* — **stealth'y** *adj.*

**steam** (stēm) *n.* **1.** Water vapor. **2.** Energy. —*v.* **1.** To emit steam. **2.** To expose to steam, as in cooking. — **steam'y** *adj.*

**steed** (stēd) *n.* A horse.

**steel** (stēl) *n.* A hard, malleable alloy of iron and carbon. —*v.* To make hard or strong. — **steel·ed** *adj.* — **steel'y** *adj.*

**steep**[1] (stēp) *adj.* **1.** Sharply sloping. **2.** Excessive. — **steep'en** *v.* — **steep'ly** *adv.* — **steep'ness** *n.*

**steep**[2] (stēp) *v.* **1.** To soak in liquid. **2.** To saturate. — **steep'er** *n.*

**stee·ple** (stē'pǝl) *n.* A tall tower.

**steer**[1] (stir) *v.* **1.** To guide; direct. **2.** To drive; move.

**steer**[2] (stir) *n.* A young ox.

**stem**[1] (stĕm) *n.* **1.** A supporting or connecting plant part; stalk. **2.** A stemlike part, as of a pipe. **3.** The prow of a vessel. —*v.* **stemmed, stemming.** **1.** To derive or develop (from). **2.** To make headway against. — **stem'less** *adj.*

**stem**[2] (stĕm) *v.* **stemmed, stemming.** To stop or hold back.

**stench** (stĕnch) *n.* A foul odor.

**ste·nog·ra·phy** (stǝ-nŏg'rǝ-fē) *n.* Writing in shorthand. — **ste·nog'ra·pher** *n.* — **sten'o·graph'ic** *adj.*

**step** (stĕp) *n.* **1.** A single movement of the foot in walking. **2.** A manner or rhythm of walking. **3.** A short distance. **4.** One of the horizontal surfaces in a stairway. **5.** One of a series of actions. **6.** A stage. **7.** A level; rank; degree. —*v.* **stepped, stepping.** **1.** To put the foot down (on). **2.** To walk.

**ster·e·o·type** (stĕr'ē-ǝ-tīp', stîr'-) *n.* A conventional, oversimplified conception.

**ster·ile** (stĕr'ǝl) *adj.* **1.** Incapable of reproducing. **2.** Unproductive. **3.** Free from germs. — **ste·ril'i·ty** *n.* — **ster'il·i·za'tion** *n.* — **ster'il·ize** *v.* — **ster'il·iz'er** *n.*

**ster·ling** (stûr'lĭng) *n.* **1.** British money. **2.** An alloy of 92.5% silver. —*adj.* **1.** Of sterling. **2.** Of the highest quality.

**stern**[1] (stûrn) *adj.* **1.** Unyielding. **2.** Grave or severe. — **stern'ly** *adv.*

**stern**[2] (stûrn) *n.* The rear part of a ship.

**stew** (st/y/ōō) *v.* To cook (food) by boiling slowly. —*n.* A dish cooked by stewing, esp. a mixture of meat and vegetables.

**stew·ard** (st/y/ōō'ǝrd) *n.* **1.** One who manages another's property or other affairs. **2.** One in charge of provisions and dining arrangements. **3.** A servant on a ship or airplane. — **stew'ard·ess** *fem.n.*

**stick** (stĭk) *n.* **1.** A long, slender piece of wood, esp. a tree branch. **2.** A cane or baton. —*v.* **stuck, sticking.** **1.** To pierce. **2.** To fasten or attach. **3.** To adhere; cling. **4.** To become fixed or obstructed. **5.** To put or thrust. **6.** To burden. **7.** To persist.

**stick·y** (stĭk'ē) *adj.* **-ier, -iest.** **1.** Adhesive. **2.** Muggy. — **stick'i·ly** *adv.* — **stick'i·ness** *n.*

**stiff** (stĭf) *adj.* **1.** Not flexible. **2.** Excessively formal. **3.** Not fluid. **4.** Strong or steady. **5.** Difficult. **6.** Severe. — **stiff'en** *v.* — **stiff'en·er** *n.* — **stiff'ly** *adv.* — **stiff'ness** *n.*

**sti·fle** (stī'fǝl) *v.* **-fled, -fling.** **1.** To smother or suffocate. **2.** To suppress. — **sti'fler** *n.*

**still**[1] (stĭl) *adj.* **1.** Silent; quiet. **2.** Without movement. —*n.* A single photograph. —*adv.* **1.** Now as before. **2.** Even. **3.** Nevertheless. —*conj.* Nevertheless. —*v.* **1.** To make or become still. **2.** To allay; calm. — **still'ness** *n.*

**still**[2] (stĭl) *n.* An apparatus for distilling liquids, particularly alcohols.

**stilt·ed** (stĭl'tĭd) *adj.* Pompous. — **stilt'ed·ly** *adv.*

**stim·u·late** (stĭm'yǝ-lāt') *v.* **-lated, -lating.** To excite. — **stim'u·lant** *adj. & n.* — **stim'u·la'tion** *n.*

**stim·u·lus** (stĭm'yǝ-lǝs) *n., pl.* **-li.** **1.** Anything causing a response. **2.** A spur; goad. — **stim'u·la'tive** *adj. & n.*

**sting** (stĭng) *v.* **stung, stinging.** **1.** To pierce with a sharp-pointed structure or organ. **2.** To cause or feel sharp pain. —*n.* **1.** A wound or pain caused by stinging. — **sting'er** *n.*

**stin·gy** (stĭn'jē) *adj.* **-gier, -giest.** Giving or spending reluctantly. — **stin'gi·ly** *adv.* — **stin'gi·ness** *n.*

**stink** (stĭngk) *v.* **stank** or **stunk, stunk, stinking.** To give off a strong foul odor. —*n.* A strong

**stint** 214

offensive odor. — **stink'er** n.

**stint** (stĭnt) v. **1.** To be sparing with. **2.** To be frugal. —n. A period of duty. — **stint'er** n.

**stip·u·late** (stĭp'yə-lāt') v. **-lated, -lating.** To specify as a condition. — **stip'u·la'tion** n. — **stip'u·la'tor** n.

**stir** (stûr) v. **stirred, stirring. 1.** To mix with circular motions of an implement. **2.** To change or move slightly. **3.** To rouse; excite. **4.** To affect strongly. —n. **1.** An act of stirring. **2.** A commotion. — **stir'rer** n. — **stir'ring** adj. — **stir'ring·ly** adv.

**stir·rup** (stûr'əp, stĭr'-) n. A flat-based loop to support a rider's foot.

**stitch** (stĭch) n. **1.** A single complete movement in sewing, knitting, etc. **2.** A sudden sharp pain. —v. To sew. — **stitch'er** n.

**stock** (stŏk) n. **1.** A supply, esp. of goods kept on hand. **2.** Domestic animals. **3.** The capital of a business, or shares of ownership in a business. **4.** Ancestry. **5.** A related group; family. **6. stocks.** A pillory. **7.** A supporting structure or frame. **8.** Broth. **9.** A regional theater. —v. To supply. —adj. **1.** Kept regularly available. **2.** Commonplace.

**stock·ing** (stŏk'ĭng) n. A close-fitting covering for the foot and leg.

**stock·y** (stŏk'ē) adj. **-ier, -iest.** Short and solidly built. — **stock'i·ness** n.

**stodg·y** (stŏj'ē) adj. **-ier, -iest.** Pompous; stuffy. — **stodg'i·ly** adv. — **stodg'i·ness** n.

**sto·ic** (stō'ĭk) adj. Also **sto·i·cal.** Indifferent to emotion or pain; impassive. —n. A stoic person. — **sto'i·cal·ly** adv. — **sto'i·cism'** n.

**stoke** (stōk) v. **stoked, stoking.** To stir up or tend (a fire). — **stok'er** n.

**stole¹** (stōl) n. A woman's long scarf worn about the shoulders.

**stole²** (stōl). p.t. of **steal.**

**sto·len** (stō'lən). p.p. of **steal.**

**stol·id** (stŏl'ĭd) adj. Impassive. — **sto·lid'i·ty** n. — **stol'id·ly** adv.

**stom·ach** (stŭm'ək) n. **1.** A saclike digestive organ below the esophagus. **2.** The abdomen or belly. **3.** An appetite. —v. To tolerate; endure.

**stomp** (stŏmp, stômp) v. To tread heavily (on).

**stone** (stōn) n. **1.** Solid mineral matter; rock. **2.** A piece of rock. **3.** A seed with a hard covering. **4.** A mineral concretion as in the kidney. —v. **stoned, stoning.** To pelt or kill with stones. — **stone** adj. — **ston'y** adj.

**stood** (stood). p.t. & p.p. of **stand.**

**stool** (stool) n. **1.** A backless and armless single seat. **2.** A bowel movement.

**stoop** (stoop) v. **1.** To bend from the waist. **2.** To debase oneself. —n. The act of stooping.

**stop** (stŏp) v. **stopped, stopping. 1.** To close (an opening). **2.** To obstruct. **3.** To halt or cease. **4.** To visit briefly. —n. **1.** An end or pause. **2.** A stay. **3.** A place stopped at. **4.** An obstruction. — **stop'page** n. — **stop'per** n.

**store** (stôr, stōr) n. **1.** A place where goods are offered for sale; a shop. **2.** A reserve supply. —v. **stored, storing. 1.** To put away for future use. **2.** To deposit for safekeeping. — **stor'age** n.

**storm** (stôrm) n. **1.** Strong winds accompanied by rain or snow. **2.** A violent, sudden attack. —v. **1.** To rain or snow violently. **2.** To rage. **3.** To attack suddenly. — **storm'y** adj.

**sto·ry¹** (stôr'ē, stōr'ē) n., pl. **-ries. 1.** The narrating of an event or series of events. **2.** A short fictional narrative; tale. **3.** A plot. **4.** An explanation, esp. a false one.

**sto·ry²** (stôr'ē) n., pl. **-ries.** A horizontal division of a building, from floor to ceiling.

**stout** (stout) adj. **1.** Bold or brave. **2.** Strong; sturdy. **3.** Corpulent. — **stout'ly** adv. — **stout'ness** n.

**stove¹** (stōv) n. An apparatus for cooking or heating.

**stove²** (stōv). Alternate p.t. & p.p. of **stave.**

**stow** (stō) v. To store away. — **stow·a·way'** n.

**strad·dle** (străd'l) v. **-dled, -dling. 1.** To sit astride (of). **2.** To appear to favor both sides of an issue. — **strad'dle** n.

**strag·gle** (străg'əl) v. **-gled, -gling. 1.** To stray behind. **2.** To spread out irregularly. — **strag'gler** n. — **strag'gly** adj.

**straight** (strāt) adj. **1.** Extending continuously without curving. **2.** Erect. **3.** Direct and candid. **4.** Unbroken. **5.** Accurate. **6.** Unmodified or undiluted. —adv. In a straight line or manner. — **straight'en** v. — **straight'ness** n.

**straight·for·ward** (strāt-fôr'wərd) adj. Honest; candid. — **straight·for'ward·ness** n.

**strain¹** (strān) v. **1.** To pull or stretch to the breaking point. **2.** To exert or strive to the utmost. **3.** To injure by overexertion. **4.** To filter. —n. **1.** The act of straining. **2.** A great effort, exertion, or tension. — **strain'er** n.

**strain²** (strān) n. **1.** A group of the same ancestry. **2.** A kind; sort. **3.** A streak; trace. **4.** A melody.

**strait** (strāt) n. **1.** A narrow passage of water. **2.** Often **straits.** A position of difficulty or need. —*adj.* **1.** Narrow. **2.** Strict.

**strand**[1] (strănd) *n.* A beach. —*v.* **1.** To drive aground, as a ship. **2.** To leave in a helpless position.

**strand**[2] (strănd) *n.* **1.** A fiber or filament in a rope, cable, etc. **2.** A string.

**strange** (strānj) *adj.* **stranger, strangest. 1.** Unfamiliar. **2.** Extraordinary. **3.** Peculiar. **4.** Exotic. — **strange'ly** *adv.* — **strange'ness** *n.*

**stran-ger** (strān'jər) *n.* **1.** A person one does not know. **2.** A newcomer.

**stran-gle** (străng'gəl) *v.* **-gled, -gling.** To kill by choking or suffocating. — **stran'gler** *n.* — **stran'gu-late'** *v.* — **stran'gu-la'tion** *n.*

**strap** (străp) *n.* A long, narrow strip for binding or securing objects. —*v.* **strapped, strapping.** To fasten with a strap. — **strap'less** *adj.*

**stra-ta.** *pl.* of **stratum.**

**strat-a-gem** (străt'ə-jəm) *n.* A trick or artifice.

**strat-e-gy** (străt'ə-jē) *n., pl.* **-gies. 1.** The planning of military operations. **2.** A plan of action; scheme. — **stra-te'gic** *adj.* — **strat'e-gist** *n.*

**stra-tum** (strā'təm, străt'-, străt'əm) *n., pl.* **-ta** (-tə). One of several parallel layers. — **stra'tal** *adj.*

**straw** (strô) *n.* **1.** Stalks of threshed grain. **2.** A slender tube for sucking up a liquid. — **straw** *adj.*

**stray** (strā) *v.* **1.** To wander. **2.** To go astray. **3.** To digress. —*n.* One that has strayed, esp. a lost domestic animal. —*adj.* **1.** Straying. **2.** Lost. **3.** Scattered.

**streak** (strēk) *n.* **1.** A long, bold line or mark. **2.** A trait. **3.** An unbroken series or period. —*v.* **1.** To mark with a streak. **2.** To rush. — **streak'i-ness** *n.* — **streak'y** *adj.*

**stream** (strēm) *n.* **1.** A body of running water. **2.** A current or flow. —*v.* **1.** To flow in a stream. **2.** To pour forth. — **stream'er** *n.*

**stream-er** (strē'mər) *n.* A long, narrow banner or strip.

**stream-lined** (strēm'līnd') *adj.* **1.** Designed to offer the least resistance to fluid flow. **2.** Improved in efficiency. — **stream'line'** *v.*

**street** (strēt) *n.* A public road in a city or town.

**strength** (strĕngkth, strĕngth) *n.* **1.** Physical or moral power. **2.** Durability. **3.** Capability. **4.** Effective or binding force. **5.** Degree of concentration; intensity. **6.** An asset. — **strength'en** *v.* — **strength'en-er** *n.*

**stren-u-ous** (strĕn'yōō-əs) *adj.* **1.** Requiring great effort. **2.** Energetic. — **stren'u-ous-ly**

*adv.* — **stren'u-ous-ness** *n.*

**stress** (strĕs) *n.* **1.** Emphasis. **2.** Special force and loudness with which a syllable is spoken. **3.** Physical pressure. **4.** Mental or emotional strain. —*v.* **1.** To place emphasis on; accent. **2.** To strain.

**stretch** (strĕch) *v.* **1.** To lengthen by pulling. **2.** To extend. **3.** To make taut. **4.** To strain. **5.** To prolong. —*n.* **1.** The act of stretching. **2.** Elasticity. **3.** An expanse. **4.** A continuous period of time. —*adj.* Elastic. — **stretch'a-ble** *adj.*

**strew** (strōō) *v.* **strewed, strewn** (strōōn) or **strewed, strewing.** To scatter; sprinkle.

**strick-en** (strĭk'ən). Alternate *p.p.* of **strike.** —*adj.* Struck or affected.

**strict** (strĭkt) *adj.* **1.** Exact. **2.** Complete; absolute. **3.** Exacting. **4.** Devout. — **strict'ly** *adv.* — **strict'ness** *n.*

**stride** (strīd) *v.* **strode** (strōd), **stridden** (strĭd'n), **striding.** To walk vigorously with long steps. —*n.* **1.** The act of striding. **2.** A long step. — **strid'er** *n.*

**strife** (strīf) *n.* Violent or bitter dissension.

**strike** (strīk) *v.* **struck, struck** or **stricken, striking. 1.** To hit sharply. **2.** To collide with. **3.** To launch an attack. **4.** To afflict. **5.** To impress or stamp. **6.** To sound. **7.** To produce by friction. **8.** To eliminate. **9.** To find; reach. **10.** To assume (a pose). **11.** To quit working in support of labor demands. —*n.* **1.** An act of striking. **2.** An attack. **3.** A cessation of work by employees. — **strik'er** *n.*

**string** (strĭng) *n.* **1.** A cord thicker than thread. **2.** A long, thin line. **3.** A set of objects threaded together. **4. strings.** The instruments of the violin family. —*v.* **strung, stringing. 1.** To furnish with a string. **2.** To thread on a string. **3.** To arrange in a series. **4.** To stretch out. — **string'i-ness** *n.* — **string'y** *adj.*

**strip**[1] (strĭp) *v.* **stripped, stripping. 1.** To undress. **2.** To remove covering, etc., from. **3.** To deprive.

**strip**[2] (strĭp) *n.* A long, narrow piece.

**stripe** (strīp) *n.* **1.** A long, narrow band of a distinctive color. **2.** Sort; kind. —*v.* **striped, striping.** To mark with stripes. — **striped** *adj.*

**strive** (strīv) *v.* **strove** (strōv), **striven** (strĭv'ən) or **strived, striving. 1.** To exert much effort. **2.** To contend. — **striv'er** *n.*

**strode** (strōd). *p.t.* of **stride.**

**stroke** (strōk) *n.* **1.** An impact; blow; strike. **2.** An act of striking. **3.** Apoplexy. **4.** An inspired idea or act. **5.** A single completed movement, as in swimming or rowing. **7.** A

# stroll

single mark made by a pen or other marking implement. **8.** A light caressing movement. —v. **stroked, stroking.** To rub lightly, as with the hand; caress.

**stroll** (strōl) v. To walk leisurely. — **stroll** n. — **stroll'er** n.

**strong** (strông) adj. **1.** Powerful; forceful. **2.** In sound health. **3.** Solid. **4.** Intense. — **strong'ly** adv.

**strove** (strōv) p.t. of **strive.**

**struck** (strŭk) p.t. & p.p. of **strike.**

**struc-ture** (strŭk'chər) n. **1.** Organization; design. **2.** Something constructed, esp. a building or part. —v. **-tured, -turing.** To give structure to. — **struc'tur-al** adj. — **struc'tur-al-ly** adv.

**strug-gle** (strŭg'əl) v. **-gled, -gling. 1.** To exert energy; strive. **2.** To fight; wrestle. **3.** To contend. —n. **1.** Strenuous effort. **2.** A fight. **3.** Contention. — **strug'gler** n.

**strung** (strŭng) p.t. & p.p. of **string.**

**strut** (strŭt) v. **strutted, strutting.** To walk conceitedly. —n. **1.** A stiff, self-important gait. **2.** A bar or rod used to strengthen a framework. — **strut'ter** n. — **strut'ting-ly** adv.

**stub** (stŭb) n. A short blunt end remaining after something has been removed. —v. **stubbed, stubbing.** To strike (one's toe or foot).

**stub-born** (stŭb'ərn) adj. **1.** Obstinate. **2.** Persistent. — **stub'born-ly** adv. — **stub'born-ness** n.

**stuck** (stŭk) p.t. & p.p. of **stick.**

**stud¹** (stŭd) n. **1.** An upright post in the framework of a wall. **2.** A small projecting knob. **3.** A small ornamental button. —v. **studded, studding.** To provide with studs.

**stud²** (stŭd) n. A male animal kept for breeding.

**stu-dent** (st/y/ōo'dənt) n. One who studies.

**stu-di-o** (st/y/ōo'dē-ō) n., pl. **-os. 1.** An artist's workroom. **2.** A single-room apartment. **3.** A room or building for motion-picture, television, or radio productions.

**stu-di-ous** (st/y/ōo'dē-əs) adj. **1.** Devoted to study. **2.** Diligent. — **stu'di-ous-ly** adv.

**stud-y** (stŭd'ē) v. **-ied, -ying. 1.** To seek knowledge of. **2.** To inquire into. **3.** To examine closely. —n., pl. **-ies. 1.** The process of studying. **2.** A branch of knowledge. **3.** A treatise. **4.** A room for studying. — **stud'i-er** n.

**stuff** (stŭf) n. **1.** Substance; material. **2.** Unspecified objects; things. —v. **1.** To pack tightly; fill up. **2.** To cram. — **stuff'ing** n.

**stuff-y** (stŭf'ē) adj. **-ier, -iest. 1.** Lacking

sufficient ventilation. **2.** Stodgy. — **stuff'i-ness** n.

**stum-ble** (stŭm'bəl) v. **-bled, -bling. 1. a.** To trip and almost fall. **b.** To proceed unsteadily. **2.** To come upon accidentally. — **stum'ble** n. — **stum'bler** n. — **stum'bling-ly** adv.

**stump** (stŭmp) n. A part left after the rest has been cut off. —v. To perplex. — **stump'er** n. — **stump'y** adj.

**stun** (stŭn) v. **stunned, stunning. 1.** To daze or render senseless. **2.** To shock. **3.** To impress vividly. — **stun'ning** adj.

**stung** (stŭng) p.t. & p.p. of **sting.**

**stunk** (stŭngk) p.p. & alternate p.t. of **stink.**

**stunt¹** (stŭnt) v. To check the growth of. — **stunt'ed** adj.

**stunt²** (stŭnt) n. A feat or spectacle.

**stu-pe-fy** (st/y/ōo'pə-fī') v. **-fied, -fying. 1.** To dull the senses of. **2.** To amaze; astonish. — **stu'pe-fa'cient** adj. & n. — **stu'pe-fac'tion** n.

**stu-pen-dous** (st/y/ōo-pĕn'dəs) adj. Tremendous; overwhelming. — **stu-pen'dous-ly** adv.

**stu-pid** (st/y/ōo'pĭd) adj. **1.** Lacking intelligence; dull. **2.** Senseless; pointless. — **stu-pid'i-ty** n. — **stu'pid-ly** adv.

**stu-por** (st/y/ōo'pər) n. Mental confusion; daze. — **stu'por-ous** adj.

**stur-dy** (stûr'dē) adj. **-dier, -diest.** Durable; strong. — **stur'di-ly** adv. — **stur'di-ness** n.

**stut-ter** (stŭt'ər) v. To speak with a spasmodic hesitation or repetition of sounds. — **stut'ter** n. — **stut'ter-er** n.

**sty¹** (stī) n., pl. **sties.** An enclosure for pigs.

**sty²** (stī) n., pl. **sties** or **styes.** An inflammation on the rim of an eyelid.

**style** (stīl) n. **1.** The way in which something is said or done. **2.** A kind; sort. **3.** A distinctive quality; individuality. **4.** Elegance. **5.** A fashion. —v. **styled, styling. 1.** To name. **2.** To design. — **styl'ish** adj. — **sty-lis'tic** adj.

**suave** (swäv, swāv) adj. Smoothly gracious; urbane. — **suave'ly** adv. — **suav'i-ty, suave'ness** n.

**sub-due** (səb-d/y/ōo') v. **-dued, -duing. 1.** To conquer. **2.** To bring under control. **3.** To make less intense.

**sub-ject** (sŭb'jĭkt) adj. **1.** Under the power of another. **2.** Inclined; liable. **3.** Dependent; contingent. —n. **1.** One under the power of another. **2.** A citizen. **3.** A person or thing being spoken of or studied; topic. **4.** The part of a sentence that denotes the

**sugar**

doer of the action. —*v.* (səb-jĕkt′). **1.** To subjugate. **2.** To cause to undergo. — **sub-jec′tion** *n.*

**sub-jec-tive** (səb-jĕk′tĭv) *adj.* **1.** Mental. **2.** Particular to a given individual; personal. — **sub-jec′tive-ly** *adv.* — **sub-jec′tive-ness, sub′jec-tiv′i-ty** *n.*

**sub-lime** (sə-blīm′) *adj.* Exalted; lofty. — **sub-lime′ly** *adv.*

**sub-ma-rine** (sŭb′mə-rēn′, sŭb′mə-rēn′) *adj.* Beneath the water surface. —*n.* A ship capable of operating submerged.

**sub-merge** (səb-mûrj′) *v.* **-merged, -merging.** To place or go under water. — **sub-mer′gence, sub-mer′sion** *n.* — **sub-mer′gi-ble** *adj.* — **sub-mer′gi-bil′i-ty** *n.*

**sub-mit** (səb-mĭt′) *v.* **-mitted, -mitting. 1.** To yield (oneself) to the authority of another; give in. **2.** To offer as a proposition. — **sub-mis′sion** *n.* — **sub-mis′sive** *adj.*

**sub-or-di-nate** (sə-bôr′də-nĭt) *adj.* **1.** Lower in rank. **2.** Subject to another's authority. —*n.* One that is subordinate. —*v.* (-nāt′) **-nated, -nating.** To make subordinate. — **sub-or′di-na′tion** *n.*

**sub-scribe** (səb-skrīb′) *v.* **-scribed, -scribing. 1.** To pledge or contribute (a sum of money). **2.** To place or contribute (a sum of money). **2.** To express approval (with *to*). **3.** To receive or attend by advance purchase (with *to*). — **sub-scrib′er** *n.* — **sub-scrip′tion** *n.*

**sub-sid-i-ar-y** (səb-sĭd′ē-ăr′ē) *adj.* **1.** Assisting. **2.** Secondary. —*n., pl.* **-ies.** A company formed by another.

**sub-si-dy** (sŭb′sə-dē) *n., pl.* **-dies.** Monetary assistance. — **sub′si-dize′** *v.*

**sub-sist** (səb-sĭst′) *v.* To exist. — **sub-sis′tence** *n.*

**sub-stance** (sŭb′stəns) *n.* **1.** Matter or a single kind of matter. **2.** The essence; gist. **3.** Density; body.

**sub-stan-tial** (səb-stăn′shəl) *adj.* **1.** Having substance; material. **2.** Real. **3.** Solidly built. **4.** Ample; considerable. — **sub-stan′tial-ly** *adv.*

**sub-sti-tute** (sŭb′stə-t/y̅o̅o̅t′) *n.* A replacement. —*v.* **-tuted, -tuting. 1.** To put or use in place of another. **2.** To take the place of another. — **sub′sti-tu′tion** *n.*

**sub-ter-ra-ne-an** (sŭb′tə-rā′nē-ən) *adj.* Underground.

**sub-tle** (sŭt′l) *adj.* **-tler, -tlest. 1.** Slight; elusive. **2.** Keen. **3.** Skillfully muted or restrained. **4.** Crafty. — **sub′tle-ness, sub′tle-ty** *n.* — **sub′tly** *adv.*

**sub-tract** (səb-trăkt′) *v.* To take away; deduct. — **sub-trac′tion** *n.*

**sub-urb** (sŭb′ûrb) *n.* A town or district

outlying a city. — **sub-ur′ban** *adj.* — **sub-ur′-ban-ite′** *n.*

**sub-vert** (səb-vûrt′) *v.* **1.** To undermine and overthrow. **2.** To corrupt. — **sub-ver′sion** *n.* — **sub-ver′sive** *adj. & n.* — **sub-vert′er** *n.*

**sub-way** (sŭb′wā′) *n.* An underground urban railroad.

**suc-ceed** (sək-sēd′) *v.* **1.** To follow or come after. **2.** To be successful. — **suc-ces′sor** *n.*

**suc-cess** (sək-sĕs′) *n.* **1.** The achievement of something desired or attempted. **2.** Fame or prosperity. **3.** One that succeeds. — **suc-cess′ful** *adj.* — **suc-cess′ful-ly** *adv.*

**suc-ces-sion** (sək-sĕsh′ən) *n.* **1.** The process of following in order. **2.** A series; sequence. — **suc-ces′sion-al** *adj.* — **suc-ces′sive** *adj.* — **suc-ces′sive-ly** *adv.*

**suc-cu-lent** (sŭk′yə-lənt) *adj.* Juicy. — **suc′cu-lence, suc′cu-len-cy** *n.* — **suc′cu-lent-ly** *adv.*

**suc-cumb** (sə-kŭm′) *v.* **1.** To yield. **2.** To die.

**such** (sŭch) *adj.* **1.** Of this or that kind. **2.** Of so great a degree or quality. —*pron.* Such a one or ones.

**suck** (sŭk) *v.* **1.** To draw (liquid) into the mouth. **2.** To draw in, as by suction. **3.** To draw nourishment from with the mouth. —*n.* The act of sucking. — **suck′er** *n.*

**suck-le** (sŭk′əl) *v.* **-led, -ling.** To feed at the breast or udder.

**suc-tion** (sŭk′shən) *n.* The pulling force of a partial vacuum. — **suc′tion** *adj.*

**sud-den** (sŭd′n) *adj.* **1.** Without warning; abrupt. **2.** Rash. **3.** Quick. — **sud′den-ly** *adv.* — **sud′den-ness** *n.*

**suds** (sŭdz) *pl.n.* Foam; lather. — **suds′y** *adj.*

**sue** (so̅o̅) *v.* **sued, suing. 1.** To bring suit against. **2.** To appeal.

**suf-fer** (sŭf′ər) *v.* **1.** To feel pain or distress. **2.** To experience. **3.** To endure. **4.** To allow. — **suf′fer-a-ble** *adj.* — **suf′fer-ance** *n.* — **suf′fer-er** *n.* — **suf′fer-ing** *adj. & n.* — **suf′fer-ing-ly** *adv.*

**suf-fice** (sə-fīs′) *v.* **-ficed, -ficing.** To be adequate.

**suf-fi-cient** (sə-fĭsh′ənt) *adj.* Enough. — **suf-fi′cien-cy** *n.* — **suf-fi′cient-ly** *adv.*

**suf-fix** (sŭf′ĭks′) *n.* An affix added to the end of a word to form a new word.

**suf-fo-cate** (sŭf′ə-kāt′) *v.* **-cated, -cating. 1.** To kill by cutting off oxygen. **2.** To die from lack of air. **3.** To deprive of fresh air. — **suf′fo-ca′tion** *n.*

**suf-frage** (sŭf′rĭj) *n.* The right of voting.

**sug-ar** (sho̅o̅g′ər) *n.* A sweet, crystalline carbohydrate. —*v.* To coat or sweeten with sugar. — **sug′ar-y** *adj.*

**sug·gest** (səg-jěst′, sə-jěst′) v. **1.** To offer for consideration; propose. **2.** To evoke. **3.** To imply. — **sug·ges′tion** n. — **sug·ges′tive** adj.

**su·i·cide** (s/y/ōo′ĭ-sīd′) n. **1.** The act of intentionally killing oneself. **2.** One who commits suicide. — **su′i·ci′dal** adj.

**suit** (sōot) n. **1.** A coat and matching trousers or skirt. **2.** Any of the four sets of playing cards. **3.** Any proceeding in a court of law to recover a right or claim. — v. **1.** To be or make appropriate; fit or adapt. **2.** To satisfy.

**suit·a·ble** (s/y/ōo′tə-bəl) adj. Appropriate. — **suit′a·bil′i·ty** n. — **suit′a·bly** adv.

**suit·case** (s/y/ōot′kās′) n. A rectangular, flat piece of luggage.

**suite** (swēt) n. **1.** A series of connected rooms. **2.** A matched set, as of furniture.

**sulk** (sŭlk) v. To be sullenly aloof or withdrawn. — n. A mood of sulking. — **sulk′i·ly** adv. — **sulk′i·ness** n. — **sulk′y** adj.

**sul·len** (sŭl′ən) adj. Broodingly ill-humored; morose. — **sul′len·ly** adv. — **sul′len·ness** n.

**sul·try** (sŭl′trē) adj. **-tri·er, -tri·est. 1.** Hot and humid. **2.** Heated, as with passion. — **sul′tri·ness** n.

**sum** (sŭm) n. **1.** The amount obtained from adding. **2.** The aggregate. **3.** An amount of money. **4.** A summary. — v. **summed, summing.** To summarize.

**sum·ma·ry** (sŭm′ə-rē) adj. **1.** Condensed; concise. **2.** Hasty. — n., pl. **-ries.** A condensation; outline. — **sum·mar′i·ly** adv. — **sum′ma·rize′** v. — **sum·ma′tion** n.

**sum·mer** (sŭm′ər) n. The warmest season, between spring and autumn. — **sum′mer,** **sum′mer·y** adj.

**sum·mit** (sŭm′ĭt) n. The highest point.

**sum·mon** (sŭm′ən) v. **1.** To call together. **2.** To send for. **3.** To call forth; muster.

**sum·mons** (sŭm′ənz) n., pl. **-mons·es.** A call or order to come, esp. to a court.

**sump·tu·ous** (sŭmp′chōo-əs) adj. Lavish. — **sump′tu·ous·ly** adv. — **sump′tu·ous·ness** n.

**sun** (sŭn) n. **1.** The central star of the solar system. **2.** The heat and light emitted by the sun. — v. **sunned, sunning.** To expose to or bask in the sun's rays. — **sun′ny** adj.

**Sun·day** (sŭn′dē, -dā′) n. The first day of the week.

**sun·dry** (sŭn′drē) adj. Various.

**sung** (sŭng). p.p. of **sing.**

**sunk** (sŭngk). p.p. & alternate p.t. of **sink.**

**sunk·en** (sŭng′kən) Alternate p.p. of **sink.** — adj. **1.** Depressed or hollowed. **2.** Submerged.

**sun·rise** (sŭn′rīz′) n. The rising of the sun.

**sup** (sŭp) v. **supped, supping.** To dine.

**su·per** (sōo′pər) n. A superintendent. — adj. Excellent.

**su·perb** (sŏo-pûrb′, sə-) adj. Of unusually high quality.

**su·per·cil·i·ous** (sōo′pər-sĭl′ē-əs) adj. Disdainful; arrogant. — **su′per·cil′i·ous·ly** adv. — **su′per·cil′i·ous·ness** n.

**su·per·fi·cial** (sōo′pər-fĭsh′əl) adj. **1.** On or near the surface. **2.** Seeing only the obvious; shallow. **3.** Trivial. — **su′per·fi′ci·al′i·ty, su′per·fi′cial·ness** n. — **su′per·fi′cial·ly** adv.

**su·per·flu·ous** (sŏo-pûr′flōo-əs) adj. Beyond what is required; unnecessary. — **su·per′flu·ous·ly** adv. — **su·per′flu·i·ty, su·per′flu·ous·ness** n.

**su·per·in·tend** (sōo′pər-ĭn-těnd′) v. To supervise; manage. — **su′per·in·ten′dence** n.

**su·per·in·ten·dent** (sōo′pər-ĭn-těn′dənt) n. **1.** A supervisor. **2.** A janitor.

**su·pe·ri·or** (sə-pîr′ē-ər) adj. **1.** Higher in rank, nature, or authority. **2.** Of great value or excellence. **3.** Haughty. — n. One who surpasses another, as in rank. — **su·pe′ri·or′i·ty** n.

**su·per·la·tive** (sŏo-pûr′lə-tĭv) adj. Of the highest order or degree. — n. The highest degree. — **su·per′la·tive·ly** adv. — **su·per′la·tive·ness** n.

**su·per·nat·u·ral** (sōo′pər-năch′ər-əl) adj. Not attributable to natural forces. — **su′per·nat′u·ral·ly** adv.

**su·per·son·ic** (sōo′pər-sŏn′ĭk) adj. Of or at a speed greater than that of sound.

**su·per·sti·tion** (sōo′pər-stĭsh′ən) n. Any belief, practice, or rite unreasoningly upheld by faith in magic, chance, or dogma. — **su′per·sti′tious** adj.

**su·per·vise** (sōo′pər-vīz′) v. **-vised, -vising.** To direct the performance of (workers or work). — **su′per·vi′sion** n. — **su′per·vi′sor** n. — **su′per·vi′so·ry** adj.

**sup·per** (sŭp′ər) n. An evening meal.

**sup·ple** (sŭp′əl) adj. **-pler, -plest. 1.** Readily bent. **2.** Limber. — **sup′ple·ness** n.

**sup·ple·ment** (sŭp′lə-mənt) n. Something added. — v. To provide a supplement to. — **sup′ple·men′tal, sup′ple·men′ta·ry** adj.

**sup·pli·cate** (sŭp′lĭ-kāt′) v. **-cated, -cating. 1.** To ask for humbly. **2.** To beseech. — **sup′pli·ant** adj. & n. — **sup′pli·cant** adj. & n. — **sup′pli·ca′tion** n.

**sup·ply** (sə-plī′) v. **-plied, -plying. 1.** To provide; furnish. **2.** To fill. — n., pl. **-plies. 1.** An amount available; stock. **2.** Often **sup-**

219

S-19

**plies.** Stored materials. —**sup·pli'er** n.

**sup·port** (sə-pôrt', -pōrt') v. **1.** To hold up or in position. **2.** To provide with necessities; maintain. **3.** To help prove. **4.** To defend; advocate. —n. **1.** The act of supporting. **2.** A prop. **3.** Maintenance or subsistence. —**sup·port'er** n. —**sup·port'ive** adj.

**sup·pose** (sə-pōz') v. **-posed, -posing. 1.** To assume to be true. **2.** To believe probable. **3.** To expect or require. —**sup'po·si'tion** n.

**sup·press** (sə-prĕs') v. **1.** To subdue; crush. **2.** To curtail or prohibit the activities of. **3.** To hold back; check. —**sup·pres'sion** n. —**sup·pres'sive** adj.

**su·preme** (sə-prēm') adj. Greatest in authority, rank, or importance. —**su·prem'a·cy** n. —**su·preme'ly** adv.

**sure** (shŏŏr) adj. **surer, surest. 1.** Certain. **2.** Having no doubt; confident. **3.** Dependable. **4.** Bound; destined. —adv. Undoubtedly. —**sure'ly** adv.

**surf** (sûrf) n. Foamy water caused by the breaking of waves against the shore.

**sur·face** (sûr'fəs) n. **1.** The outer or topmost boundary or layer. **2.** Outward appearance. —v. **-faced, -facing. 1.** To give a surface to. **2.** To rise to the surface. —**sur'face** adj.

**sur·feit** (sûr'fĭt) v. To feed or supply to fullness or excess. —n. **1.** Overindulgence. **2.** An excessive amount.

**surge** (sûrj) v. **surged, surging. 1.** To move in a great wave. **2.** To increase suddenly. —n. A sudden increase or onrush.

**sur·geon** (sûr'jən) n. A physician specializing in surgery.

**sur·ger·y** (sûr'jə-rē) n., pl. **-ies. 1.** Medical operations. **2.** An operating room or laboratory. —**sur'gi·cal** adj.

**sur·ly** (sûr'lē) adj. **-lier, -liest.** Sullenly rude. —**sur'li·ness** n.

**sur·mise** (sər-mīz') v. **-mised, -mising.** To guess. —n. A guess.

**sur·name** (sûr'nām') n. One's family name.

**sur·pass** (sər-păs', -päs') v. **1.** To go beyond; transcend. **2.** To exceed. —**sur·pass'ing** adj.

**sur·plus** (sûr'pləs) adj. Being in excess. —n. A quantity in excess.

**sur·prise** (sər-prīz') v. **-prised, -prising. 1.** To encounter; to astonish; amaze. —n. **1.** Amazement or wonder. **2.** An unexpected thing. —**sur·pris'er** n.

**sur·ren·der** (sə-rĕn'dər) v. **1.** To yield possession of. **2.** To give oneself up. —**sur·ren'der** n.

**sur·rep·ti·tious** (sûr'əp-tĭsh'əs) adj. Stealthy; secret. —**sur·rep·ti'tious·ly** adv.

**sur·round** (sə-round') v. **1.** To encircle; ring. **2.** To confine on all sides.

**sur·round·ings** (sə-roun'dĭngz) pl.n. The things or the area around one.

**sur·vey** (sər-vā', sûr'vā') v. **1.** To examine broadly or systematically. **2.** To determine the boundaries, area, or elevation of land. —n. (sûr'vā'). **1.** A detailed inspection. **2.** A general view. **3.** The process of surveying. —**sur·vey'al** n. —**sur·vey'or** n.

**sur·vive** (sər-vīv') v. **-vived, -viving. 1.** To remain alive or in existence. **2.** To outlive. —**sur·viv'al** n. —**sur·vi'vor** n.

**sus·cep·ti·ble** (sə-sĕp'tə-bəl) adj. **1.** Readily affected. **2.** Liable; prone. **3.** Impressionable. —**sus·cep'ti·bil'i·ty** n. —**sus·cep'ti·bly** adv.

**sus·pect** (sə-spĕkt') v. **1.** To mistrust. **2.** To surmise. **3.** To think guilty without proof. —n. (sŭs'pĕkt'). One who is suspected. —adj. Doubtful.

**sus·pend** (sə-spĕnd') v. **1.** To bar or exclude for a period. **2.** To interrupt temporarily. **3.** To defer; put off. **4.** To hang loosely. —**sus·pen'sion** n.

**sus·pense** (sə-spĕns') n. Anxious uncertainty. —**sus·pense'ful** adj.

**sus·pi·cion** (sə-spĭsh'ən) n. **1.** The act of suspecting. **2.** Distrust; doubt. **3.** A trace. —**sus·pi'cious** adj. —**sus·pi'cious·ly** adv.

**sus·tain** (sə-stān') v. **1.** To prolong. **2.** To supply with necessities. **3.** To keep up; support. **4.** To suffer. **5.** To affirm the validity of. —**sus·tain'a·ble** adj.

**sus·te·nance** (sŭs'tə-nəns) n. **1.** Maintenance. **2.** Nourishment.

**su·ture** (sōō'chər) n. A surgical stitch or stitching, as of a wound. —v. **-tured, -turing.** To join surgically.

**swab** (swŏb). Also **swob.** n. **1.** A piece of absorbent material for cleansing or applying medicine. **2.** A mop. —v. **swabbed, swabbing.** To clean or treat with a swab.

**swad·dle** (swŏd'l) v. **-dled, -dling.** To wrap (a baby) in strips of cloth.

**swag·ger** (swăg'ər) v. **1.** To walk insolently; strut. **2.** To brag. —**swag'ger** n. —**swag'ger·er** n.

**swal·low** (swŏl'ō) v. **1.** To pass (food) from the mouth into the stomach. **2.** To consume. **3.** To suppress. —n. **1.** The act of swallowing. **2.** The amount swallowed.

**swam** (swăm). p.t. of **swim.**

**swamp** (swŏmp, swômp) n. Land saturated with water; marsh. —v. **1.** To drench or sink in water. **2.** To overwhelm. —**swamp'i·ness**

*n.* — **swamp'y** *adj.*

**swap** (swăp) *v.* **swapped, swapping.** To trade; exchange. — **swap** *n.* — **swap'per** *n.*

**swarm** (swôrm) *n.* **1.** A large mass of insects or other small organisms. **2.** A throng. — *v.* **1.** To move in a swarm. **2.** To teem.

**swarth·y** (swôr'thē) *adj.* **-ier, -iest.** Dark-skinned. — **swarth'i·ness** *n.*

**swat** (swăt) *v.* **swatted, swatting.** To slap. — **swat** *n.* — **swat'ter** *n.*

**sway** (swā) *v.* **1.** To swing from side to side. **2.** To vacillate. **3.** To influence. — *n.* **1.** A gentle swinging. **2.** Power; influence.

**swear** (swâr) *v.* **swore, sworn, swearing. 1.** To make a solemn declaration or promise. **2.** To curse. **3.** To assert under oath. **4.** To administer a legal oath to. — **swear'er** *n.*

**sweat** (swĕt) *v.* **sweated** or **sweat, sweating. 1.** To perspire. **2.** To work long and hard. — *n.* **1.** Perspiration. **2.** Condensed moisture on a surface. **3.** Strenuous labor. — **sweat'y** *adj.*

**sweat·er** (swĕt'ər) *n.* A knitted garment worn on the upper body.

**sweep** (swēp) *v.* **swept, sweeping. 1.** To clean or clear with a broom. **2.** To brush. **3.** To carry or blow away. **4.** To move or traverse powerfully. **5.** To move emotionally. **6.** To extend; reach. — *n.* **1.** An act or motion of sweeping. **2.** A range or extent. — **sweep'er** *n.* — **sweep'ing** *n.*

**sweet** (swēt) *adj.* **1.** Having a sugary taste. **2.** Pleasing or charming. **3.** Fresh. — *n.* A candy or other sweet food. — **sweet'en** *v.* — **sweet'en·er** *n.* — **sweet'ly** *adv.* — **sweet'ness** *n.*

**swell** (swĕl) *v.* **swelled, swelled** or **swollen, swelling. 1.** To expand; bulge. **2.** To increase. **3.** To fill with an emotion, as pride. — *n.* **1.** A bulge. **2.** A long wave. — *adj.* Fine; excellent.

**swell·ing** (swĕl'ĭng) *n.* An enlargement or increase. **2.** A swollen area on the body.

**swel·ter·ing** (swĕl'tər·ĭng) *adj.* Oppressively hot.

**swept** (swĕpt). *p.t. & p.p.* of **sweep.**

**swerve** (swûrv) *v.* **swerved, swerving.** To turn abruptly aside. — **swerve** *n.*

**swift** (swĭft) *adj.* **1.** Fast; fleet. **2.** Quick; prompt. — **swift'ly** *adv.* — **swift'ness** *n.*

**swill** (swĭl) *v.* To drink greedily. — *n.* Liquid animal feed. — **swill'er** *n.*

**swim** (swĭm) *v.* **swam, swum, swimming. 1.** To propel oneself through water by bodily movements. **2.** To be flooded. **3.** To feel giddy. — *n.* A period or instance of swim-ming.

**swin·dle** (swĭnd'l) *v.* **-dled, -dling.** To cheat or defraud. — *n.* A fraud. — **swin'dler** *n.*

**swine** (swīn) *n., pl.* **swine.** A pig. — **swin'ish** *adj.*

**swing** (swĭng) *v.* **swung, swinging. 1.** To move back and forth. **2.** To turn in place, as on a hinge. **3.** To aim a blow. **4.** To manage successfully. — *n.* **1.** A rhythmic back-and-forth movement. **2.** A sweeping blow or stroke. **3.** A seat suspended from above for playful swinging. — **swing'er** *n.*

**switch** (swĭch) *n.* **1.** A slender stick for whipping. **2.** A device used to break or open an electrical circuit. **3.** A change; shift. — *v.* **1.** To shift, transfer, or change. **2.** To turn (an electric appliance) on or off. — **switch'er** *n.*

**switch·board** (swĭch'bôrd', -bōrd') *n.* A panel containing electrical switches.

**swiv·el** (swĭv'əl) *n.* A pivot or other fastening that permits free turning. — *v.* To turn on or as on a swivel.

**swol·len** (swōl'ən). Alternate *p.p.* of **swell.**

**swoon** (swōōn) *v.* To faint. — *n.* A fainting spell.

**sword** (sôrd) *n.* A weapon having a long blade.

**swore** (swôr). *p.t.* of **swear.**

**sworn** (swôrn). *p.p.* of **swear.**

**swum** (swŭm). *p.p.* of **swim.**

**swung** (swŭng). *p.t. & p.p.* of **swing.**

**syc·o·phant** (sĭk'ə-fənt) *n.* A flatterer. — **syc'o·phan·cy** *n.*

**syl·lab·i·cate** (sĭ-lăb'ə-kāt') *v.* **-cated, cating.** To divide into syllables. — **syl·lab'i·ca'tion** *n.* — **syl·lab'i·ty** *n.*

**syl·la·ble** (sĭl'ə-bəl) *n.* A single uninterrupt ed sound forming part of a word or an entire word. — **syl·lab'ic** *adj.*

**sym·bol** (sĭm'bəl) *n.* Something that represents something else. — **sym·bol'ic** *adj.* — **sym·bol'i·cal·ly** *adv.* — **sym'bol·ism** *n.* — **sym'bol·ize** *v.*

**sym·me·try** (sĭm'ə-trē) *n.* Correspondence between parts on opposite sides of a dividing line; balance. — **sym·met'ri·cal** *adj.*

**sym·pa·thize** (sĭm'pə-thīz') *v.* **-thized, -thizing.** To feel or express sympathy. — **sym'pa·thiz'er** *n.*

**sym·pa·thy** (sĭm'pə-thē) *n., pl.* **-thies. 1.** Sameness of feeling; mutual understanding. **2.** Pity; compassion. **3.** Agreement; approval. — **sym'pa·thet'ic** *adj.*

**sym·pho·ny** (sĭm'fə-nē) *n., pl.* **-nies. 1.** A long orchestral composition. **2.** A full orchestra. — **sym·phon'ic** *adj.*

**syn·a·gogue** (sĭn'ə-gŏg') *n.* A building for Jewish worship.

**syn·chro·nize** (sĭn'krə-nīz', sĭng'-) *v.* **-nized, -nizing. 1.** To make or be simultaneous. **2.** To set at the same time or rate. — **syn'chro·ni·za'tion** — **syn'chro·niz'er** *n.*

**syn·di·cate** (sĭn'dĭ-kĭt) *n.* An association of related businesses.

**syn·o·nym** (sĭn'ə-nĭm') *n.* A word having a meaning similar to that of another.

**syn·tax** (sĭn'tăks') *n.* The way words are put together to form phrases and sentences. — **syn·tac'tic, syn·tac'ti·cal** *adj.*

**syn·the·sis** (sĭn'thə-sĭs) *n.* The combining of separate elements to form a whole. — **syn'the·size'** *v.*

**syn·thet·ic** (sĭn-thĕt'ĭk) *adj.* Artificial. — **syn·thet'i·cal·ly** *adv.*

**sy·ringe** (sə-rĭnj', sĭr'ĭnj) *n.* A medical instrument used to inject fluids.

**syr·up** (sûr'əp, sĭr'-) *n.* Also **sir·up.** A thick, sweet liquid. — **syr'up·y** *adj.*

**sys·tem** (sĭs'təm) *n.* **1.** A group of inter-related elements forming a whole. **2.** The human body. **3.** A set of interrelated ideas, rules, laws, etc. **4.** A deliberate procedure; method. **5.** Orderliness. — **sys'tem·at'ic** *adj.* — **sys'tem·at'i·cal·ly** *adv.* — **sys'tem·a·tize'** *v.*

# T

**t, T** (tē) *n.* The 20th letter of the English alphabet.

**tab** (tăb) *n.* **1.** A flap or short strip. **2.** A bill or check.

**ta·ble** (tā'bəl) *n.* **1.** An article of furniture having a flat surface set on legs. **2.** An orderly display of data. — *v.* **-bled, -bling. 1.** To place on a table. **2.** To postpone.

**ta·ble·spoon** (tā'bəl-spōōn') *n.* **1.** A large spoon for serving food. **2.** A household cooking measure.

**tab·u·late** (tăb'yə-lāt') *v.* **-lated, -lating.** To arrange in a table or list. — **tab'u·lar** *adj.* — **tab'u·la'tion** *n.*

**tac·i·turn** (tăs'ə-tûrn') *adj.* Habitually untalk-ative; uncommunicative. — **tac'i·tur'ni·ty** *n.*

**tack** (tăk) *n.* **1.** A short, flat-headed nail. **2.** The course of a ship in relation to the position of its sails. **3.** A course of action.

— *v.* **1.** To fasten with a tack. **2.** To change the course of a vessel.

**tack·le** (tăk'əl) *n.* **1.** Fishing equipment. **2.** An apparatus for raising weights. — *v.* **-led, -ling. 1.** To take on; deal with. **2.** To seize and throw to the ground.

**tact** (tăkt) *n.* The ability to handle a delicate situation. — **tact'ful** *adj.* — **tact'less** *adj.*

**tac·tics** (tăk'tĭks) *n.* (takes sing. v.). The technique of securing strategic objectives, esp. in the deployment of military forces. — **tac'ti·cal** *adj.* — **tac·ti'cian** *n.*

**tag** (tăg) *n.* A strip of paper, etc., attached as identification or a label. — *v.* **tagged, tagging.** To label or identify with a tag.

**tail** (tāl) *n.* **1.** An elongated appendage at the hind part of an animal. **2.** Something resem-bling an animal's tail. **3.** The bottom, rear, or hindmost part of anything. — *v.* To keep under surveillance. — *adj.* At or from the rear.

**tai·lor** (tā'lər) *n.* One who makes or repairs garments. — *v.* To make or adapt for a particular purpose.

**taint** (tānt) *v.* **1.** To stain or dishonor. **2.** To infect or spoil. — *n.* **1.** A moral defect. **2.** An infecting touch, influence, or tinge.

**take** (tāk) *v.* **took, taken** (tā'kən), **taking. 1.** To get possession of; seize. **2.** To grasp. **3.** To lead or convey to another place. **4.** To remove. **5.** To assume upon oneself. **6.** To select; choose. **7.** To travel by. **8.** To oc-cupy. **9.** To require. **10.** To accept. **11.** To endure. **12.** To interpret or react to. **13.** To subtract. **14.** To have the intended effect. — *n.* The amount taken. — **tak'er** *n.*

**take·off** (tāk'ôf', -ŏf') *n.* **1.** The act of leaving the ground. **2.** An imitative cari-cature.

**tale** (tāl) *n.* **1.** A story. **2.** A lie.

**tal·ent** (tăl'ənt) *n.* A natural or acquired ability; aptitude.

**talk** (tôk) *v.* **1.** To articulate words. **2.** To converse; discuss. **3.** To speak. **4.** To gossip. **5.** To confer or negotiate. — *n.* **1.** Speech; conversation. **2.** An informal speech. **3.** Hearsay, rumor, or speculation. **4.** A con-ference or parley; negotiation. — **talk'a·tive** *adj.* — **talk'er** *n.*

**tall** (tôl) *adj.* Having greater than ordinary height; high.

**tal·ly** (tăl'ē) *n., pl.* **-lies. 1.** A notched stick used to keep a count. **2.** A reckoning or score. — *v.* **-lied, -lying. 1.** To reckon or count. **2.** To correspond; agree.

**tame** (tām) *adj.* **tamer, tamest. 1.** Not wild;

domesticated. **2.** Insipid; flat. —*v.* **tamed,
taming. 1.** To domesticate. **2.** To subdue.

**tam·per** (tăm′pər) *v.* **1.** To interfere in a harmful manner. **2.** To engage in underhand or illegal dealings. —**tam′per·er** *n.*

**tan** (tăn) *v.* **tanned, tanning. 1.** To convert (hide) into leather. **2.** To make or become brown by exposure to the sun. —*n.* A light brown. —*adj.* **tanner, tannest. 1.** Of the color tan. **2.** Having a sun tan. —**tan′ner** *n.* —**tan′ner·y** *n.*

**tan·gent** (tăn′jənt) *adj.* Touching but not intersecting. —*n.* **1.** A line, curve, or surface touching but not intersecting another. **2.** A sudden digression or change of course.

**tan·ger·ine** (tăn′jə-rēn′) *n.* An orangelike fruit with easily peeled skin.

**tan·gi·ble** (tăn′jə-bəl) *adj.* **1.** Discernible by touch. **2.** Real; concrete. —**tan′gi·bil′i·ty** *n.* —**tan′gi·bly** *adv.*

**tan·gle** (tăng′gəl) *v.* **-gled, -gling. 1.** To intertwine in a confused mass. **2.** To be or become entangled. —*n.* **1.** A confused, intertwined mass. **2.** A confused state or condition.

**tank** (tăngk) *n.* **1.** A large container for fluids. **2.** An enclosed, heavily armored combat vehicle.

**tank·er** (tăng′kər) *n.* A ship, plane, or truck constructed to transport oil.

**tan·ta·lize** (tăn′tə-līz′) *v.* **-lized, -lizing.** To tease or torment by repeatedly showing something unobtainable.

**tan·trum** (tăn′trəm) *n.* A fit of bad temper.

**tap¹** (tăp) *v.* **tapped, tapping.** To strike gently. —**tap** *n.*

**tap²** (tăp) *n.* **1.** A faucet. —*v.* **tapped, tapping. 1.** To pierce in order to draw off liquid. **2.** To draw (liquid) from.

**tape** (tāp) *n.* A narrow strip of fabric, paper, plastic, etc. —*v.* **taped, taping. 1.** To bind or wrap with tape. **2.** To record (sound) on magnetic tape.

**ta·per** (tā′pər) *n.* **1.** A slender candle. **2.** A gradual decrease or lessening in thickness, loudness, etc. —*v.* To decrease or lessen in thickness, loudness, etc.

**tape recorder.** A device for recording and playing back sound on magnetic tape. —**tape′·re·cord′** *v.*

**tap·es·try** (tăp′ĭ-strē) *n., pl.* **-tries.** A heavy textile with a woven design, used as a wall hanging.

**tar** (tär) *n.* A black, oily liquid distilled from wood, coal, or peat. —*v.* **tarred, tarring.** To coat with tar.

**tar·dy** (tär′dē) *adj.* **-dier, -diest.** Late. —**tar′di·ly** *adv.* —**tar′di·ness** *n.*

**tar·get** (tär′gĭt) *n.* **1.** A marked object that is shot at to test accuracy. **2.** Anything aimed at. **3.** A desired goal.

**tar·iff** (tăr′ĭf) *n.* **1.** A list of duties on imported or exported goods. **2.** A duty of this kind.

**tar·nish** (tär′nĭsh) *v.* **1.** To make or become discolored. **2.** To taint. —**tar′nish** *n.*

**tar·ry** (tăr′ē) *v.* **-ried, -rying.** To delay; linger.

**tart¹** (tärt) *adj.* **1.** Agreeably sour. **2.** Caustic; cutting. —**tart′ly** *adv.* —**tart′ness** *n.*

**tart²** (tärt) *n.* A small pie with a sweet filling.

**task** (tăsk, täsk) *n.* **1.** A piece of assigned work. **2.** A difficult undertaking. —**task′mas′ter** *n.*

**tas·sel** (tăs′əl) *n.* An ornament consisting of a bunch of loose threads knotted at one end.

**taste** (tāst) *v.* **tasted, tasting. 1.** To distinguish the flavor of by taking into the mouth **2.** To eat or drink a small quantity of. **3.** To have a distinct flavor. —*n.* **1.** The sense that distinguishes different flavors with the tongue. **2.** The act of tasting. **3.** A small quantity eaten or tasted. **4.** A personal preference. **5.** Discernment of what is excellent or appropriate. —**taste′ful** *adj.* —**taste′ful·ly** *adv.* —**taste′less** *adj.* —**tast′er** *n.* —**tast′y** *adj.*

**tat·tle** (tăt′l) *v.* **-tled, -tling. 1.** To reveal another's secrets. **2.** To gossip. —**tat′tler** *n.*

**tat·too** (tă-tōō′) *n.* A permanent mark made on the skin by pricking and dyeing. —**tat·too′** *v.*

**taught** (tôt) *p.t. & p.p.* of **teach.**

**taunt** (tônt) *v.* To jeer mockingly. —**taunt** *n.* —**taunt′er** *n.*

**taut** (tôt) *adj.* Stretched tight; tense. —**taut′ly** *adv.* —**taut′ness** *n.*

**tav·ern** (tăv′ərn) *n.* A saloon or inn.

**tax** (tăks) *n.* **1.** Compulsory payment by persons and businesses for the support of a government. **2.** An excessive demand; a strain. —*v.* **1.** To place a tax on. **2.** To make excessive demands. —**tax′a·ble** *adj.* —**tax·a′tion** *n.* —**tax′ing·ly** *adv.*

**tax·i** (tăk′sē) *n., pl.* **-is** or **-ies.** An automobile that carries passengers for a fare. —*v.* **-ied, -iing** or **-ying. 1.** To be transported by taxi. **2.** To move slowly on the ground before takeoff or after landing. Used of an aircraft.

**tea** (tē) *n.* **1.** The dried leaves of an Asian shrub, steeped in boiling water to make a beverage. **2.** The beverage thus prepared. **3.** An afternoon social gathering.

# tend

**teach** (tēch) v. **taught, teaching. 1.** To impart knowledge to. **2.** To instruct in. — **teach′er** n.

**team** (tēm) n. **1.** Two or more harnessed draft animals. **2.** A group of players in a game. **3.** A group organized to work together. —v. To join in a team.

**tear¹** (târ) v. **tore, torn, tearing. 1.** To pull apart. **2.** To make (an opening) by ripping. **3.** To lacerate. **4.** To extract forcefully; wrench. **5.** To divide; disunite. **6.** To move fast; rush. —n. A rip or rent.

**tear²** (tîr) n. **1.** A drop of the clear saline liquid that lubricates the eyeball. **2. tears.** The act of weeping. — **tear′ful** adj.

**tease** (tēz) v. **teased, teasing. 1.** To annoy; vex. **2.** To make fun of; bait. **3.** To fluff up, as hair. —n. One given to playful mocking. — **teas′er** n.

**tea·spoon** (tē′spōōn′) n. **1.** A small spoon. **2.** A household cooking measure.

**tech·ni·cal** (tĕk′nĭ-kəl) adj. **1.** Of the mechanical or industrial arts. **2.** Specialized. **3. a.** Theoretical. **b.** Scientific. — **tech′ni·cal·ly** adv.

**tech·nique** (tĕk-nēk′) n. **1.** The systematic procedure by which a task is accomplished. **2.** The degree of skill in performance. — **tech·ni′cian** n.

**tech·nol·o·gy** (tĕk-nŏl′ə-jē) n., pl. **-gies. 1.** The application of science in industry or commerce. **2.** The methods and materials thus used. — **tech′no·log′i·cal** adj. — **tech′no·log′i·cal·ly** adv. — **tech·nol′o·gist** n.

**te·di·ous** (tē′dē-əs) adj. Tiresome and long; boring. — **te′di·ous·ly** adv. — **te′di·um** n.

**teeth** (tēth) pl. of **tooth.**

**teethe** (tēth) v. **teethed, teething.** To grow teeth.

**tel·e·gram** (tĕl′ə-grăm′) n. A message sent by telegraph.

**tel·e·graph** (tĕl′ə-grăf′, -grăf′) n. A communications system that sends or receives messages by means of electric impulses carried through a wire. —v. To transmit (a message) by telegraph. — **tel′e·graph′ic** adj. — **te·leg′ra·phy** n.

**te·lep·a·thy** (tə-lĕp′ə-thē) n. Communication by scientifically unknown means. — **tel′e·path′ic** adj.

**tel·e·phone** (tĕl′ə-fōn′) n. An electrical device that transmits voice or acoustic signals to remote locations. —v. **-phoned, -phoning.** To communicate by telephone. — **tel′e·phon′ic** adj.

**tel·e·scope** (tĕl′ə-skōp′) n. An arrangement of lenses that permits observation of distant objects. —v. **-scoped, -scoping. 1.** To slide together in overlapping sections. **2.** To compress inward. — **tel′e·scop′ic** adj.

**tel·e·vi·sion** (tĕl′ə-vĭzh′ən) n. **1.** The transmission of moving images with accompanying sounds by electronic means. **2.** The receiving apparatus used in this process. — **tel′e·vise′** v.

**tell** (tĕl) v. **told, telling. 1.** To narrate. **2.** To express with words; communicate. **3.** To notify. **4.** To command. **5.** To identify.

**te·mer·i·ty** (tə-mĕr′ə-tē) n. Rashness; foolish boldness.

**tem·per** (tĕm′pər) v. **1.** To modify; moderate. **2.** To harden (a metal). —n. **1.** A state of mind or emotions; disposition. **2.** Composure. **3.** Irascibility; rage. — **tem′pered** adj.

**tem·per·a·ment** (tĕm′prə-mənt, tĕm′pər-ə-) n. **1.** An individual's manner of thinking, behaving, and reacting; disposition. **2.** Excessive irritability. — **tem′per·a·men′tal** adj.

**tem·per·ance** (tĕm′pər-əns, tĕm′prəns) n. **1.** Moderation or self-restraint. **2.** Abstinence from alcoholic liquors.

**tem·per·ate** (tĕm′pər-ĭt, tĕm′prĭt) adj. **1.** Moderate; restrained. **2.** Not extreme in climate.

**tem·per·a·ture** (tĕm′pər-ə-chōōr′, tĕm′prə-) n. **1.** The degree of hotness or coldness of a body or environment. **2.** Fever.

**tem·pest** (tĕm′pĭst) n. A violent storm. — **tem·pes′tu·ous** adj.

**tem·ple¹** (tĕm′pəl) n. A place of worship.

**tem·ple²** (tĕm′pəl) n. The flat region on either side of the forehead.

**tem·po** (tĕm′pō) n., pl. **-pos. 1.** The speed at which music is to be played. **2.** A rate of activity.

**tem·po·rar·y** (tĕm′pə-rĕr′ē) adj. Lasting for a limited time. — **tem′po·rar′i·ly** adv.

**tempt** (tĕmpt) v. **1.** To entice. **2.** To be attractive to; provoke. **3.** To incline or dispose strongly. — **temp·ta′tion** n. — **tempt′er** n. — **tempt′ress** fem.n.

**ten** (tĕn) n. The cardinal number written 10. — **ten** adj. & pron. — **tenth** n. & adj.

**te·na·cious** (tə-nā′shəs) adj. **1.** Persistent; stubborn. **2.** Cohesive or adhesive. **3.** Retentive. — **te·nac′i·ty** n.

**ten·an·cy** (tĕn′ən-sē) n., pl. **-cies. 1.** Possession or occupancy by rent. **2.** The period of such occupancy. — **ten′ant** n.

**tend¹** (tĕnd) v. **1.** To be disposed or inclined. **2.** To be likely.

**tend²** (tĕnd) v. **1.** To look after. **2.** To serve at.

**ten·den·cy** (tĕn'dən-sē) n., pl. **-cies.** An inclination to think or act in a certain way; bent.

**ten·der¹** (tĕn'dər) adj. **1.** Delicate; fragile. **2.** Young and vulnerable. **3.** Frail; weak. **4.** Sensitive or sore. **5.** Gentle and loving. — **ten'der·ly** adv. — **ten'der·ness** n.

**ten·der²** (tĕn'dər) n. **1.** A formal offer. **2.** Money. —v. To offer formally.

**ten·don** (tĕn'dən) n. A band of tough, fibrous tissue that connects a muscle with its bony attachment.

**ten·et** (tĕn'ĭt) n. A fundamental principle or dogma.

**ten·nis** (tĕn'ĭs) n. A game played with rackets and a light ball on a court divided by a net.

**ten·or** (tĕn'ər) n. **1.** Flow of meaning; gist. **2.** The highest adult male voice.

**tense¹** (tĕns) adj. **tenser, tensest. 1.** Taut; strained. **2.** Nerve-racking. —v. **tensed, tens·ing.** To make or become tense. — **tense'ness** n.

**tense²** (tĕns) n. Any inflected form of a verb that indicates the time of the action.

**ten·sion** (tĕn'shən) n. **1.** A stretching or being stretched. **2.** Mental strain. **3.** A strained relation. **4.** Suspense.

**tent** (tĕnt) n. A portable shelter, as of canvas.

**ten·ta·tive** (tĕn'tə-tĭv) adj. **1.** Of an experimental nature. **2.** Uncertain. — **ten'ta·tive·ly** adv.

**ten·u·ous** (tĕn'yōō-əs) adj. **1.** Slender or thin; rarefied. **2.** Not substantial; flimsy. — **ten'u·ous·ly** adv. — **ten'u·ous·ness** n.

**ten·ure** (tĕn'yər, -yōōr') n. **1.** The holding of something, as an office; occupation. **2.** The period of holding.

**tep·id** (tĕp'ĭd) adj. Lukewarm.

**term** (tûrm) n. **1.** A limited or fixed period of time. **2.** A word having a precise meaning. **3. terms.** Conditions or stipulations. —v. To designate; name.

**ter·mi·nal** (tûr'mə-nəl) adj. **1.** Of or at the end. **2.** Concluding; final. —n. **1.** A terminating point, limit, or part. **2.** A point at which a connection to an electrical component is made. **3.** A railroad or bus station. — **ter'mi·nal·ly** adv.

**ter·mi·nate** (tûr'mə-nāt') v. **-nated, -nating.** To end or conclude. — **ter'mi·na'tion** n.

**ter·race** (tĕr'ĭs) n. **1.** A porch or balcony. **2.** A patio. **3.** A raised level of earth with sloping sides.

**ter·rain** (tə-rān', tĕ-) n. A tract of land.

**2.** The physical character of land.

**ter·res·tri·al** (tə-rĕs'trē-əl) adj. **1.** Of the earth or its inhabitants. **2.** Living or growing on land.

**ter·ri·ble** (tĕr'ə-bəl) adj. **1.** Causing fear; dreadful. **2.** Intense; severe. **3.** Very bad. — **ter'ri·bly** adv.

**ter·rif·ic** (tə-rĭf'ĭk) adj. **1.** Terrifying. **2.** Splendid. **3.** Very great. — **ter·rif'i·cal·ly** adv.

**ter·ri·fy** (tĕr'ə-fī') v. **-fied, -fying.** To fill with terror. — **ter'ri·fy'ing·ly** adv.

**ter·ri·to·ry** (tĕr'ə-tôr'ē, -tōr'ē) n., pl. **-ries. 1.** A region. **2.** The land and waters of a state. **3.** A part of a nation not yet accorded statehood. — **ter'ri·to'ri·al** adj.

**ter·ror** (tĕr'ər) n. Intense fear. — **ter'ror·ize'** v.

**ter·ror·ism** (tĕr'ər-ĭz'əm) n. The political use of terror and intimidation. — **ter'ror·ist** n. & adj.

**terse** (tûrs) adj. **terser, tersest.** Concise. — **terse'ly** adv. — **terse'ness** n.

**test** (tĕst) n. **1.** A means of examination or proof. **2.** A series of questions designed to determine knowledge. — **test** v.

**tes·ti·cle** (tĕs'tĭ-kəl) n. A testis.

**tes·ti·fy** (tĕs'tə-fī') v. **-fied, -fying.** To give evidence under oath.

**tes·ti·mo·ni·al** (tĕs'tə-mō'nē-əl) n. **1.** A written affirmation of another's character. **2.** A tribute for a person's achievement.

**tes·ti·mo·ny** (tĕs'tə-mō'nē) n., pl. **-nies. 1.** A declaration or affirmation of fact or truth. **2.** Supporting evidence; proof.

**tes·tis** (tĕs'tĭs) n., pl. **-tes.** The male reproductive gland.

**text** (tĕkst) n. **1.** The main body of a printed work. **2.** A textbook. — **tex'tu·al** adj.

**text·book** (tĕkst'bŏŏk') n. A book used in teaching a particular subject.

**tex·tile** (tĕks'tīl', -tĭl) n. Cloth; fabric, esp. woven. —adj. Of textiles or their manufacture.

**tex·ture** (tĕks'chər) n. **1.** The appearance and feel of a fabric. **2.** The structure of a substance; grain. — **tex'tur·al** adj.

**than** (thăn) conj. **1.** —Used to introduce the second element of a comparison or inequality. **2.** —Used with the sense of "beyond" with adverbs of degree or quantity.

**thank** (thăngk) v. To express gratitude to. — **thank'ful** adj. — **thank'less** adj.

**that** (thăt) adj., pl. **those** (thōz). **1.** Being the one singled out. **2.** Being the one further removed. —pron., pl. **those. 1. a.** The one designated. **b.** The less immediate one.

—Used as a relative pronoun to introduce a clause. 3. Something. —adv. To such an extent. —conj. —Used to introduce a subordinate clause stating a fact, wish, consequence, or reason.

**thaw** (thô) v. 1. To melt. 2. To become more friendly. —n. 1. The process of thawing. 2. A period during which ice and snow melt.

**the**[1] (thē before a vowel; thə before a consonant). The definite article, used before nouns that denote particular specified persons or things.

**the**[2] (thē before a vowel; thə before a consonant) adv. To that extent.

**the-a-ter** (thē′ə-tər) n. Also **the-a-tre**. 1. A building for the presentation of dramas, motion pictures, etc. 2. Dramatic literature or performance. —the-at′ri-cal adj.

**theft** (thĕft) n. The act or an instance of stealing.

**their** (thâr). The possessive form of they.

**theirs** (thârz). The possessive form of they.

**them** (thĕm) pron. The objective case of they.

**theme** (thēm) n. 1. A topic of discourse. 2. The subject of an artistic work. 3. A short essay. 4. The main melody. —the-mat′ic adj.

**them-selves** (thĕm′sĕlvz′, thəm′-) pron. The reflexive form of they.

**then** (thĕn) adv. 1. At that time in the past. 2. Next in time, space, or order. 3. At another time. 4. In that case; accordingly. 5. Besides. 6. Yet. —adj. Being so at that time.

**the-ol-o-gy** (thē-ŏl′ə-jē) n., pl. **-gies**. The study of the nature of God and religious truth. —the-o-lo′gi-an n. —the-o-log′i-cal adj.

**the-o-ry** (thē′ə-rē, thîr′ē) n., pl. **-ries**. 1. A system of assumptions, accepted principles, and rules of procedure devised to analyze, predict, or explain a set of phenomena. 2. Speculation. 3. Hypothesis or supposition. —the-o-ret′i-cal adj. —the-o-ret′i-cal-ly adv.

**ther-a-py** (thĕr′ə-pē) n., pl. **-pies**. The treatment of illness or disability. —ther-a-peu′tic adj. —ther′a-pist n.

**there** (thâr) adv. 1. At or in that place. 2. To that place; thither.

**there-fore** (thâr′fôr′, -fōr′) adv. & conj. Consequently; hence.

**ther-mal** (thûr′məl) adj. Of or by heat.

**ther-mom-e-ter** (thər-mŏm′ə-tər) n. An instrument for measuring temperature.

**ther-mo-stat** (thûr′mə-stăt′) n. A device that automatically regulates temperature.

**these.** pl. of **this**.

**the-sis** (thē′sĭs) n., pl. **-ses**. 1. A proposition maintained by argument. 2. An essay written to obtain an academic degree.

**they** (thā) pron. The 3rd person pl. pronoun in the nominative case.

**they'd** (thād). Contraction of they had or they would.

**they'll** (thāl). Contraction of they will.

**they're** (thâr). Contraction of they are.

**they've** (thāv). Contraction of they have.

**thick** (thĭk) adj. 1. Relatively great in depth or in extent from side to side. 2. Dense; concentrated. 3. Having a viscous consistency. 4. Abounding. 5. Pronounced; heavy. 6. Stupid. —thick′en v. —thick′ly adv. —thick′ness n.

**thief** (thēf) n., pl. **thieves**. One who steals. —thiev′er-y n.

**thigh** (thī) n. The portion of the leg between the hip and the knee.

**thim-ble** (thĭm′bəl) n. A small cuplike guard to protect the finger while sewing.

**thin** (thĭn) adj. thinner, thinnest. 1. Having a small distance between opposite sides. 2. Lean or slender. 3. Sparse. 4. Not heavy in consistency. 5. Lacking substance; flimsy. —v. thinned, thinning. To make or become thin or thinner. —thin′ly adv. —thin′ness n.

**thing** (thĭng) n. 1. Something that exists; an entity. 2. A real object. 3. A creature. 4. **things**. Possessions. 5. A thought or notion.

**think** (thĭngk) v. thought, thinking. 1. To formulate in the mind. 2. To ponder. 3. To reason. 4. To believe. 5. To remember. 6. To imagine. 7. To devise or invent. 8. To consider. —think′er n.

**third** (thûrd) n. 1. The ordinal number 3 in a series. 2. One of 3 equal parts. —adj. 1. Next after second. 2. Being one of 3 equal parts. —adv. In the 3rd place, rank, or order. —third′ly adv.

**thirst** (thûrst) n. 1. A need or desire to drink. 2. A craving. —v. 1. To feel a need to drink. 2. To have a strong craving. —thirst′y adj.

**thir-teen** (thûr-tēn′) n. The cardinal number written 13. —thir-teen′ adj. & pron. —thir′teenth′ n. & adj.

**thir-ty** (thûr′tē) n. The cardinal number written 30. —thir′ty adj. & pron. —thir′ti-eth n. & adj.

**this** (thĭs) pron., pl. these (thēz). 1. The person or thing present, nearby, or just mentioned. 2. What is about to be said. 3. The one nearer than another or compared with the other. —adj., pl. these. 1. Being just mentioned or present. 2. Being nearer than or compared with another. **3.** Being about to be stated or described. —*adv.* To this extent.

**tho·rax** (thôr'ăks, thōr'-) *n.* The part of the body between the neck and the diaphragm. —**tho·rac·ic** *adj.*

**thorn** (thôrn) *n.* A sharp spine protruding from a plant stem. —**thorn·y** *adj.*

**thor·ough** (thûr'ō) *adj.* **1.** Fully done; finished. **2.** Complete; absolute. **3.** Careful. —**thor·ough·ly** *adv.* —**thor·ough·ness** *n.*

**thor·ough·bred** (thûr'ō-brĕd', thûr'ə-) *adj.* Bred of pure stock. —**thor·ough·bred** *n.*

**thor·ough·fare** (thûr'ō-fâr', thûr'ə-) *n.* A main road or public highway.

**those.** *pl.* of **that.**

**though** (thō) *conj.* **1.** Despite the fact that. **2.** However. —*adv.* However; nevertheless.

**thought** (thôt). *p.t.* & *p.p.* of **think.** —*n.* **1.** The act of thinking. **2.** An idea. **3.** Consideration; concern. **4.** A trifle. —**thought·ful** *adj.* —**thought·less** *adj.*

**thou·sand** (thou'zənd) *n.* The cardinal number written 1,000. —**thou·sand** *adj.* & *pron.* —**thou·sandth** *adj.* & *n.*

**thrash** (thrăsh) *v.* **1.** To beat or flog. **2.** To defeat utterly. **3.** To move wildly. —**thrash·ing** *n.*

**thread** (thrĕd) *n.* **1.** A fine cord of a fibrous material. **2.** A spiral ridge on a screw, nut, or bolt. —*v.* **1.** To pass one end of a thread through the eye of (a needle). **2.** To pass cautiously through. **3.** To machine a thread on (a screw, nut, or bolt).

**threat** (thrĕt) *n.* **1.** An expression of an intention to inflict pain, injury, etc. **2.** One regarded as a possible danger. —**threat·en** *v.*

**three** (thrē) *n.* The cardinal number written 3. —**three** *adj.* & *pron.*

**thresh** (thrĕsh) *v.* To remove the grain or seeds. —**thresh·er** *n.*

**thresh·old** (thrĕsh'ōld', thrĕsh'hōld') *n.* **1.** The piece of wood or stone beneath a door. **2.** An entrance or starting point.

**threw** (thrōo). *p.t.* of **throw.**

**thrice** (thrīs) *adv.* Three times.

**thrift** (thrĭft) *n.* Economy; frugality. —**thrift·y** *adj.*

**thrill** (thrĭl) *v.* To feel or cause to feel a sudden intense sensation. —*n.* That which produces great excitement. —**thrill·er** *n.*

**thrive** (thrīv) *v.* **thrived, thriving. 1.** To prosper. **2.** To grow vigorously; flourish.

**throat** (thrōt) *n.* The front portion of the neck.

**throb** (thrŏb) *v.* **throbbed, throbbing.** To beat or vibrate strongly. —**throb** *n.*

**throne** (thrōn) *n.* The chair occupied by a sovereign, bishop, etc.

**throng** (thrông) *n.* A crowd; a multitude. —*v.* To crowd into.

**throt·tle** (thrŏt'l) *n.* **1. a.** A valve in an internal-combustion engine that regulates the amount of fuel entering the cylinders. **b.** A similar valve in a steam engine regulating the amount of steam. **2.** A lever or pedal controlling this valve. —*v.* **-tled, -tling. 1.** To regulate the speed of (an engine) with a throttle. **2.** To strangle; choke. —**throt·tler** *n.*

**through** (thrōo) *prep.* **1.** In one side and out another side of. **2.** In the midst of. **3.** By way of. **4.** By means of. **5.** From the beginning to the end of. **6.** Finished with. —*adv.* **1.** From one end to another. **2.** From beginning to end. **3.** To a conclusion. —*adj.* **1.** Passing from one end to another. **2.** Unobstructed. **3.** Finished; done.

**through·out** (thrōo-out') *prep.* In or during every part of. —*adv.* **1.** Everywhere. **2.** During the entire duration.

**throw** (thrō) *v.* **threw, thrown** (thrōn), **throwing. 1.** To propel; fling. **2.** To perplex. **3.** To move (a controlling lever). —**throw** *n.*

**thrust** (thrŭst) *v.* **1.** To push forcibly. **2.** To stab. —*n.* **1.** A forceful shove. **2.** A driving force or pressure, esp. in a jet engine. **3.** A stab.

**thud** (thŭd) *n.* A dull sound. —*v.* **thudded, thudding.** To make such a sound.

**thug** (thŭg) *n.* A ruffian; hoodlum.

**thumb** (thŭm) *n.* The short first digit of the hand. —*v.* To hitchhike.

**thun·der** (thŭn'dər) *n.* The explosive sound resulting from the electrical discharge of lightning. —*v.* **1.** To produce thunder. **2.** To utter loudly. —**thun·der·bolt** *n.* —**thun·der·cloud** *n.* —**thun·der·ous** *adj.*

**Thurs·day** (thûrz'dē, -dā') *n.* The 5th day of the week.

**thus** (thŭs) *adv.* **1.** In this way. **2.** To this extent; so. **3.** Therefore; consequently.

**thwart** (thwôrt) *v.* To prevent; frustrate.

**tic** (tĭk) *n.* A facial twitch.

**tick** (tĭk) *n.* A recurring clicking sound, esp. that made by a clock. —**tick** *v.*

**tick·et** (tĭk'ĭt) *n.* **1.** A paper slip indicating right of admission. **2.** An identifying tag. **3.** A list of candidates endorsed by a political party. **4.** A summons. —*v.* To attach a tag to.

**tick·le** (tĭk'əl) *v.* **-led, -ling. 1.** To tingle. **2.** To touch (the body) lightly, causing laughter or twitching movements. **3.** To tease or amuse.

—*n.* The act or sensation of tickling. —**tick′-lish** *adj.*

**tide** (tīd) *n.* **1.** The periodic rise and fall of the surface of oceans. **2.** A tendency or trend. —**tid′al** *adj.*

**tid-ings** (tī′dĭngz) *pl.n.* Information; news.

**ti-dy** (tī′dē) *adj.* **-dier, -diest.** Orderly and neat. —*v.* **-died, -dying.** To put in order. —**ti′di-ly** *adv.* —**ti′di-ness** *n.*

**tie** (tī) *v.* **tied, tying. 1.** To fasten with a cord, rope, etc. **2.** To draw together and knot. **3.** To equal (an opponent) in a contest. —*n.* **1.** Something used to tie. **2.** A bond. **3.** A necktie. **4.** A beam or rod that joins parts. **5.** An equality of scores, etc.

**tier** (tîr) *n.* One of a series of rows placed one above another.

**ti-ger** (tī′gər) *n.* A large carnivorous Asian cat. —**ti′gress** *fem.n.*

**tight** (tīt) *adj.* **1.** Impermeable, esp. by water or air. **2.** Fastened or closed securely. **3.** Taut. **4.** Snug. **5.** Closely contested. —*adv.* Firmly; securely. —**tight′en** *v.* —**tight′ly** *adv.* —**tight′ness** *n.*

**tile** (tīl) *n.* A slab of baked clay for covering walls, floors, and roofs. —*v.* **tiled, tiling.** To cover with tiles.

**till**[1] (tĭl) *v.* To prepare (land) for planting.

**till**[2] (tĭl) *prep.* Until. —*conj.* Until.

**tilt** (tĭlt) *v.* To slope or cause to slope; incline; tip. —*n.* **1.** A slant; slope. **2.** A verbal duel.

**tim-ber** (tĭm′bər) *n.* **1.** Wooded land. **2.** Wood for building. **3.** A wooden beam.

**tim-bre** (tĭm′bər, tăm′-) *n.* The distinguishing quality of an individual sound.

**time** (tīm) *n.* **1.** A continuum in which events occur; duration. **2.** An interval; a period of time. **3.** Often **times.** A span of years. **4.** An opportune or designated moment. **5.** An occasion. **6.** The rate of speed of a measured activity. **7.** The beat of musical rhythm. —*adj.* **1.** Of time. **2.** Of installment buying. —*v.* **timed, timing. 1.** To set the time for; schedule. **2.** To regulate for orderly sequence. **3.** To record the speed or duration of. —**time′less** *adj.* —**time′ly** *adj.* —**tim′er** *n.*

**time-ta-ble** (tīm′tā′bəl) *n.* A table listing the arrival and departure times of trains, buses, etc.

**tim-id** (tĭm′ĭd) *adj.* **1.** Hesitant or fearful. **2.** Shy. —**ti-mid′i-ty** *n.* —**tim′id-ly** *adv.*

**tim-or-ous** (tĭm′ər-əs) *adj.* Apprehensive; timid.

**tin** (tĭn) *n.* **1.** A malleable metallic element

used to coat other metals to prevent corrosion. **2.** A tin container. —*v.* **tinned, tinning. 1.** To coat with tin. **2.** To pack in tins; can. —**tin′ny** *adj.*

**tin-der** (tĭn′dər) *n.* Readily combustible material. —**tin′der-box′** *n.*

**tine** (tīn) *n.* A pointed prong, as of a fork.

**tinge** (tĭnj) *v.* **tinged, tinging** or **tinging. 1.** To color slightly. **2.** To affect slightly. —*n.* A faint trace.

**tin-gle** (tĭng′gəl) *v.* **-gled, -gling.** To have a prickling sensation. —**tin′gle** *n.* —**tin′gly** *adj.*

**tin-kle** (tĭng′kəl) *v.* **-kled, -kling.** To make or cause to make light metallic sounds. —**tin′kle** *n.*

**tint** (tĭnt) *n.* **1.** A shade of a color. **2.** A slight coloration. —*v.* To give a tint to.

**ti-ny** (tī′nē) *adj.* **-nier, -niest.** Extremely small.

**tip**[1] (tĭp) *n.* **1.** An end or extremity. **2.** A piece fitted to the end of something. —*v.* **tipped, tipping.** To furnish with a tip.

**tip**[2] (tĭp) *v.* **tipped, tipping. 1.** To knock over. **2.** To tilt. —*n.* A slant or tilt.

**tip**[3] (tĭp) *n.* **1.** A sum of money given for services rendered. **2.** Useful information. —**tip** —*v.* —**tip′per** *n.*

**ti-rade** (tī′rād′, tĭ-rād′) *n.* A long, harshly critical speech.

**tire**[1] (tīr) *v.* **tired, tiring. 1.** To make or become weary. **2.** To make or become bored. —**tire′less** *adj.* —**tire′some** *adj.*

**tire**[2] (tīr) *n.* A round, usually rubber covering for a wheel.

**tis-sue** (tĭsh′o͞o) *n.* **1.** Cellular matter in organisms. **2.** A soft, absorbent piece of paper. **3.** A thin paper used for packing. **4.** A fine sheer cloth, as gauze.

**ti-tle** (tīt′l) *n.* **1.** A name given to a book, painting, etc. **2.** A formal appellation, as of rank. **3. a.** In law, the right of possession or control. **b.** The evidence of this, as a deed. **4.** In sports, a championship. —*v.* **-tled, -tling.** To give a title to. —**tit′u-lar** *adj.*

**tit-ter** (tĭt′ər) *v.* To utter a nervous giggle. —**tit′ter** *n.*

**to** (to͞o; *unstressed* tə) *prep.* **1.** Toward. **2.** As far as. **3.** Until. **4.** For or of. **5.** As compared with.

**toad** (tōd) *n.* A froglike, mostly land-dwelling amphibian.

**toast**[1] (tōst) *v.* To heat and brown (bread, rolls, etc.). —*n.* Sliced bread heated and browned. —**toast′er** *n.*

**toast**[2] (tōst) *n.* **1.** A person or thing in whose honor persons drink. **2.** The act of proposing such an honor. —*v.* To make a toast.

**to·bac·co** (tə-băk′ō) n., pl. **-cos** or **-coes**. **1.** A plant having broad leaves used chiefly for smoking. **2.** The processed leaves of this plant.

**to·bog·gan** (tə-bŏg′ən) n. A long, runner-less sled.

**to·day** (tə-dā′) adv. **1.** On the present day. **2.** At the present time. —n. The present day, time, or age.

**tod·dle** (tŏd′l) v. **-dled, -dling.** To walk with short, unsteady steps. —**tod′dler** n.

**toe** (tō) n. **1.** One of the digits of the foot. **2.** The forward part of something worn on the foot.

**to·geth·er** (tə-gĕth′ər) adv. **1.** In or into a single group or place. **2.** In total. **3.** Simultaneously. **4.** In harmony or cooperation.

**toil** (toil) v. To work strenuously. —n. Exhausting labor.

**toi·let** (toi′lĭt) n. **1.** A disposal apparatus used to receive body waste. **2.** A bathroom. **3.** The act or process of grooming and dressing oneself.

**to·ken** (tō′kən) n. **1.** A sign; symbol. **2.** A keepsake. **3.** A metal disk used as a substitute for currency. —adj. Done as an indication or pledge.

**told** (tōld). p.t. & p.p. of **tell.**

**tol·er·a·ble** (tŏl′ər-ə-bəl) adj. **1.** Endurable. **2.** Adequate; passable. —**tol′er·a·bly** adv.

**tol·er·ance** (tŏl′ər-əns) n. **1.** The capacity for respecting the opinions or practices of others. **2.** The capacity to endure hardship, pain, etc. —**tol′er·ant** adj.

**tol·er·ate** (tŏl′ə-rāt′) v. **-ated, -ating. 1.** To allow; permit. **2.** To respect the opinions, practices, or behavior of others. **3.** To put up with. —**tol·er·a′tion** n.

**toll**[1] (tōl) n. **1.** A fixed tax, as for passage across a bridge. **2.** A charge for a service, as a telephone call.

**toll**[2] (tōl) v. To sound (a bell) slowly at regular intervals. —**toll** n.

**tom·a·hawk** (tŏm′ə-hôk′) n. A light ax used by North American Indians.

**tomb** (tōōm) n. A vault for the dead.

**to·mor·row** (tə-môr′ō, -mŏr′ō). Also **to·mor·row.** v. The day following today. —adv. On the day following today.

**ton** (tŭn) n. **1.** A unit of weight equal to 2,240 pounds; long ton. **2.** A unit of weight equal to 2,000 pounds; short ton.

**tone** (tōn) n. **1.** A distinct sound. **2.** Quality of sound. **3.** Manner of expression. **4.** A general quality or atmosphere. **5.** A color or shade of color. **6.** Normal muscular firmness. —**to′nal** adj.

**tongs** (tŏngz, tôngz) n. (often takes sing. v.). A two-armed grasping device.

**tongue** (tŭng) n. **1.** The fleshy muscular organ in the mouth. **2.** Anything resembling a tongue. **3.** A spoken language.

**ton·ic** (tŏn′ĭk) n. Anything that invigorates.

**to·night** (tə-nīt′) adv. On the present night. —n. This night.

**ton·sil** (tŏn′səl) n. A mass of tissue between the mouth and pharynx.

**too** (tōō) adv. **1.** In addition. **2.** Excessively. **3.** Very.

**took** (tōōk). p.t. of **take.**

**tool** (tōōl) n. **1.** A hand instrument. **2.** A mechanical device. **3.** A servile helper; stooge. —v. To form or work with a tool.

**tooth** (tōōth) n., pl. **teeth. 1.** A hard, bonelike structure rooted in the jaw. **2.** A toothlike structure or projection. —**toothed** adj.

**top** (tŏp) n. **1.** The uppermost part, point, or end. **2.** A lid or cap. **3.** The highest rank or degree. —adj. Of, at, or forming the top. —v. **topped, topping. 1.** To go over the top of. **2.** To surpass.

**top·ic** (tŏp′ĭk) n. A subject treated in a speech, essay, or conversation.

**to·pog·ra·phy** (tə-pŏg′rə-fē) n., pl. **-phies. 1.** The art of representing on a map the physical configuration of a place or region. **2.** The features of a place or region. —**to·pog′ra·pher** n. —**top′o·graph′ic, top′o·graph′i·cal** adj.

**top·ple** (tŏp′əl) v. **-pled, -pling. 1.** To push over. **2.** To fall.

**torch** (tôrch) n. A portable light or flame.

**tore** (tôr, tōr). p.t. of **tear**[1].

**tor·ment** (tôr′mĕnt′) n. Great pain or anguish. —v. (tôr-mĕnt′). **1.** To afflict with great pain or anguish. **2.** To annoy or harass. —**tor·men′tor** n.

**torn** (tôrn, tōrn). p.p. of **tear**[1].

**tor·na·do** (tôr-nā′dō) n., pl. **-does** or **-dos.** A funnel-shaped, whirling, destructive storm.

**tor·pe·do** (tôr-pē′dō) n., pl. **-does.** A cigar-shaped, self-propelled underwater projectile. —v. To attack with a torpedo.

**tor·pid** (tôr′pĭd) adj. Sluggishly inactive; lethargic. —**tor′por** n.

**tor·rent** (tôr′ənt, tŏr′-) n. **1.** A turbulent, rapid stream. **2.** A raging flood. —**tor·ren′tial** adj.

**tor·rid** (tôr′ĭd, tŏr′-) adj. **1.** Parched by the sun. **2.** Scorching.

**tor·so** (tôr′sō) n., pl. **-sos** or **-si.** The trunk of the human body.

**tort** (tôrt) *n.* A wrongful act for which a civil suit can be brought.

**tor·toise** (tôr′təs) *n.* A turtle, esp. a land turtle.

**tor·tu·ous** (tôr′chōō-əs) *adj.* **1.** Winding; twisting. **2.** Complex.

**tor·ture** (tôr′chər) *n.* **1.** The intentional infliction of severe pain. **2.** Pain or mental anguish. —*v.* **-tured, -turing.** To subject to torture.

**toss** (tôs, tŏs) *v.* **1.** To throw or be thrown to and fro. **2.** To throw lightly. **3.** To flip a coin to decide something. —*n.* An act of tossing.

**to·tal** (tōt′l) *n.* The whole amount. —*adj.* Complete; utter. —*v.* **1.** To find the sum of. **2.** To amount to. —**to·tal′i·ty** *n.* —**to′tal·ly** *adv.*

**tote** (tōt) *v.* **toted, toting.** To carry.

**tot·ter** (tŏt′ər) *v.* **1.** To sway as if about to fall. **2.** To walk unsteadily.

**touch** (tŭch) *v.* **1.** To cause a part of the body to come in contact with so as to feel. **2.** To be or come into contact. **3.** To tap lightly. **4.** To come up to; equal. **5.** To move or affect. —*n.* **1.** The act of touching. **2.** The sense by which bodily contact is registered. **3.** The sensation from contact. **4.** A mark or effect left by a specific contact. **5.** A small amount. **6.** A knack.

**touch·down** (tŭch′doun′) *n.* In football, a scoring play worth six points.

**tough** (tŭf) *adj.* **1.** Strong and resilient. **2.** Hard to cut or chew. **3.** Rugged. **4.** Difficult; demanding. **5.** Having a determined will. —**tough′en** *v.* —**tough′ness** *n.*

**tour** (tŏŏr) *n.* **1.** A trip with visits to different places. **2.** A brief trip to or through a place. **3.** A period of duty at a single place. —*v.* To make a tour of. —**tour′ism** *n.* —**tour′ist** *n.*

**tour·na·ment** (tŏŏr′nə-mənt, tûr′-) *n.* A contest composed of a series of games.

**tour·ni·quet** (tŏŏr′nĭ-kĭt, -kā′, tûr′-) *n.* A bandage or other device to stop bleeding.

**tou·sle** (tou′zəl) *v.* **-sled, -sling.** To rumple.

**tow** (tō) *v.* To pull along behind by a chain or line. —*n.* **1.** An act of towing or being towed. **2.** Something being towed.

**to·ward** (tôrd, tōrd, tə-wôrd′) *prep.* Also **to·wards. 1.** In the direction of. **2.** With regard to. **3.** In furtherance of.

**tow·el** (tou′əl) *n.* An absorbent cloth or paper used for drying.

**tow·er** (tou′ər) *n.* A tall building or part of a building. —*v.* To rise to a great height.

**town** (toun) *n.* A population center smaller than a city.

**town·ship** (toun′shĭp′) *n.* A subdivision of

a county. **2.** A public land surveying unit of 36 square miles.

**tox·ic** (tŏk′sĭk) *adj.* **1.** Of a toxin. **2.** Harmful; poisonous. —**tox·ic′i·ty** *n.*

**tox·in** (tŏk′sĭn) *n.* A poisonous organic substance.

**toy** (toi) *n.* A thing to play with. —*v.* To trifle (*with*). —*adj.* **1.** Designed as a toy. **2.** Very small.

**trace** (trās) *n.* **1.** A visible sign of the former presence of something. **2.** A touch. **3.** A minute quantity. —*v.* **traced, tracing. 1.** To follow the trail of. **2.** To locate or discover. **3.** To sketch. **4.** To copy by following lines seen through transparent paper.

**tra·che·a** (trā′kē-ə) *n.* An air-carrying tube descending from the larynx to the bronchi.

**track** (trăk) *n.* **1.** A mark, as a footprint; a trace. **2.** A path, route, or course. **3.** A road laid out for racing. **4.** A set of parallel rails for a train. —*v.* To follow; trail.

**tract**[1] (trăkt) *n.* **1.** An expanse of land. **2.** A system of related bodily organs.

**tract**[2] (trăkt) *n.* A propaganda pamphlet.

**tract·a·ble** (trăk′tə-bəl) *adj.* Easily controlled.

**trac·tion** (trăk′shən) *n.* **1.** The act of drawing or of being drawn. **2.** Adhesive friction.

**trac·tor** (trăk′tər) *n.* A vehicle designed for pulling machinery.

**trade** (trād) *n.* **1.** An occupation; a craft. **2.** The business of buying and selling commodities; commerce. **3.** An exchange. —*v.* **traded, trading. 1.** To buy and sell. **2.** To exchange. —**trad′er** *n.* —**trades′man** *n.*

**trade·mark** (trād′märk′) *n.* A registered name, symbol, or other device identifying a product.

**tra·di·tion** (trə-dĭsh′ən) *n.* **1.** The passing down of elements of a culture from generation to generation. **2.** A set of cultural customs and usages. —**tra·di′tion·al** *adj.* —**tra·di′tion·al·ly** *adv.*

**traf·fic** (trăf′ĭk) *n.* **1.** The commercial exchange of goods; trade. **2.** The passage of persons or vehicles through travel routes. **3.** The amount, as of vehicles, in transit. —*v.* **-ficked, -ficking.** To carry on trade in. —**traf′fick·er** *n.*

**trag·e·dy** (trăj′ə-dē) *n., pl.* **-dies. 1.** A dramatic work dealing with human misfortune and profound unhappiness. **2.** A disastrous event. —**trag′ic, trag′i·cal** *adj.* —**trag′i·cal·ly** *adv.*

**trail** (trāl) *v.* **1.** To drag or allow to drag behind. **2.** To follow the trail of; track. **3.** To

**trailer**

become gradually fainter. —*n.* **1.** Something that trails, esp. something that hangs loose and long. **2.** A mark, trace, or scent left. **3.** A path.

**trail·er** (trā′lər) *n.* **1.** One that trails. **2.** A large vehicle or van drawn by a truck or automobile and sometimes used as a home.

**train** (trān) *n.* **1.** Something that follows or is drawn along behind. **2.** A staff of followers; retinue. **3.** A line of moving persons, vehicles, etc. **4.** A string of connected railroad cars. **5.** A succession of related events or thoughts. —*v.* **1.** To make or become proficient with instruction. **2.** To prepare physically. **3.** To focus (on); aim. —**train′a·ble** *adj.* —**train·ee′** *n.* —**train′er** *n.* —**train′ing** *n.*

**trait** (trāt) *n.* A distinguishing feature.

**trai·tor** (trā′tər) *n.* One who betrays his country, a cause, etc., esp. one who has committed treason. —**trai′tor·ous** *adj.*

**tramp** (trămp) *v.* **1.** To walk with a heavy step. **2.** To travel on foot. —*n.* **1.** The sound of heavy walking or marching. **2.** A walking trip. **3.** A vagrant.

**trance** (trăns) *n.* A hypnotic, semiconscious, or ecstatic state.

**tran·quil** (trăng′kwəl) *adj.* Peaceful; calm. —**tran·quil′li·ty, tran·quil′i·ty** *n.* —**tran′quil·ize′, tran′quil·lize′** *v.*

**tran·scend** (trăn-sĕnd′) *v.* **1.** To exist above and independent of. **2.** To rise above; surpass. —**tran·scen′dent** *adj.*

**tran·scribe** (trăn-skrīb′) *v.* -scribed, -scribing. To write or type a copy of. —**tran′script** *n.* —**tran·scrip′tion** *n.*

**trans·fer** (trăns-fûr′, trăns′fər) *v.* -ferred, -ferring. To convey or change from one person or place to another. —*n.* **1.** The act or means of transferring. **2.** Any person or thing transferred. —**trans·fer′a·ble** *adj.* —**trans·fer′ence** *n.*

**trans·form** (trăns-fôrm′) *v.* **1.** To change markedly in appearance. **2.** To change the nature or function of. —**trans′for·ma′tion** *n.*

**trans·fu·sion** (trăns-fyōō′zhən) *n.* The injection of whole blood, plasma, etc., into the blood stream.

**trans·gress** (trăns-grĕs′, trănz-) *v.* **1.** To go beyond (a limit). **2.** To violate (a law). —**trans·gres′sion** *n.* —**trans·gres′sor** *n.*

**tran·sient** (trăn′shənt, -zhənt, -zē-ənt) *adj.* **1.** Passing away with time; transitory. **2.** Passing through from one place to another. —*n.* One that is transient. —**tran′sience** *n.* —**tran′sient·ly** *adv.*

**tran·sis·tor** (trăn-zĭs′tər, trăn-sĭs′-) *n.* An

electrical device used for amplification, switching, etc.

**tran·sit** (trăn′sĭt, -zĭt) *n.* **1.** Passage; crossing. **2.** The conveying of persons or goods, esp. on a local transportation system.

**tran·si·tion** (trăn-zĭsh′ən, -sĭsh′ən) *n.* The changing or passing from one form, state, or place to another. —**tran·si′tion·al** *adj.*

**tran·si·tive** (trăn′sə-tĭv, trăn′zə-) *adj.* Designating a verb that requires a direct object.

**tran·si·to·ry** (trăn′sə-tôr′ē, -tōr′ē, trăn′zə-) *adj.* Brief; short-lived.

**trans·late** (trăns-lāt′, trănz-, trăns′lāt′, trănz′-) *v.* -lated, -lating. **1.** To express or render in another language. **2.** To explain. —**trans·lat′a·ble** *adj.* —**trans·la′tion** *n.* —**trans·la′tor** *n.*

**trans·lu·cent** (trăns-lōō′sənt, trănz-) *adj.* Letting light pass through diffusely. —**trans·lu′cence, trans·lu′cen·cy** *n.*

**trans·mis·sion** (trăns-mĭsh′ən, trănz-) *n.* **1.** The act of transmitting. **2.** Something transmitted. **3.** An assembly or system of gears linking an engine to a driving axle.

**trans·mit** (trăns-mĭt′, trănz-) *v.* -mitted, -mitting. **1.** To send or pass along. **2.** To cause to spread. **3.** To impart by heredity. **4.** To send (a signal). —**trans·mis′si·ble, trans·mit′ta·ble** *adj.* —**trans·mit′tal** *n.* —**trans·mit′ter** *n.*

**tran·som** (trăn′səm) *n.* A small window above a door or another window.

**trans·par·ent** (trăns-pâr′ənt, -pâr′ənt) *adj.* Letting light pass through without distortion; clear.

**tran·spire** (trăn-spīr′) *v.* -spired, -spiring. **1.** To become known; come to light. **2.** To happen; occur.

**trans·port** (trăns-pôrt′, -pōrt′) *v.* **1.** To carry from one place to another. **2.** To enrapture. —*n.* (trăns′pôrt′). **1.** The act of transporting; conveyance. **2.** A vehicle used to transport. —**trans′por·ta′tion** *n.*

**trans·pose** (trăns-pōz′) *v.* -posed, -posing. **1.** To change the order of. **2.** In music, to write or perform (a composition) in a different key. —**trans·po·si′tion** *n.*

**trans·verse** (trăns-vûrs′, trănz′, trăns′vûrs′, trănz′-) *adj.* Lying across; crosswise. —**trans·verse′** *v.* —**trans·verse′ly** *adv.*

**trap** (trăp) *n.* **1.** A device for catching animals. **2.** A stratagem for tricking an unsuspecting person. —*v.* trapped, trapping. To catch in a trap. —**trap′per** *n.*

**tra·peze** (tră-pēz′) *n.* A short swinglike bar used for acrobatics.

**trash** (trăsh) n. Garbage. — **trash'y** adj.

**trau·ma** (trou'mə, trô'-) n. 1. A wound, esp. one produced by sudden physical injury. 2. An emotional shock. — **trau·mat'ic** adj. — **trau'ma·tize'** v.

**tra·vail** (trə-vāl', trăv'āl') n. 1. Strenuous exertion. 2. Agony; anguish. 3. The labor of childbirth. — v. 1. To toil. 2. To labor in childbirth.

**trav·el** (trăv'əl) v. 1. To go from one place to another. 2. To be transmitted. — n. The act of traveling. — **trav'el·er** n.

**trav·erse** (trăv'ərs, trə-vûrs') v. -ersed, -ersing. 1. To travel across or through. 2. To extend across. — n. A structural crosspiece. — adj. Lying across.

**trav·es·ty** (trăv'ĭ-stē) n., pl. -ties. A grotesque parody. — v. -tied, -tying. To make a travesty of.

**trawl** (trôl) n. A large fishing net towed along the sea bottom. — v. To fish with a trawl. — **trawl'er** n.

**tray** (trā) n. A flat, shallow receptacle for carrying, holding, etc.

**treach·er·ous** (trĕch'ər-əs) adj. 1. Disloyal. 2. Not dependable. 3. Dangerous. — **treach'er·y** n.

**tread** (trĕd) v. trod, trodden or trod, treading. 1. To walk on. 2. To press beneath the foot; stamp. — n. 1. The act or manner of treading. 2. The horizontal part of a staircase step. 3. The grooved face of an automobile tire.

**trea·son** (trē'zən) n. Violation of allegiance toward one's country or sovereign. — **trea'son·a·ble** adj. — **trea'son·ous** adj.

**treas·ure** (trĕzh'ər) n. 1. Accumulated wealth in the form of valuables. 2. One considered precious. — v. -ured, -uring. To value highly.

**treas·ur·y** (trĕzh'ə-rē) n., pl. -ies. 1. A place where private or public funds are kept. 2. A governmental department in charge of public revenue. — **treas'ur·er** n.

**treat** (trēt) v. 1. To act or behave toward. 2. To regard or consider. 3. To deal with. 4. To entertain. 5. To subject to a process. 6. To give medical aid to. — n. 1. Something paid for by another. 2. A special delight; pleasure. — **treat'er** n. — **treat'ment** n.

**trea·tise** (trē'tĭs) n. A formal written account on some subject.

**trea·ty** (trē'tē) n., pl. -ties. A formal agreement between two or more states.

**tre·ble** (trĕb'əl) adj. 1. Triple. 2. In music, of the highest range. — n. In music, the highest part, voice, instrument, or range; soprano.

— v. -led, -ling. To triple. — **treb'ly** adv.

**tree** (trē) n. A tall woody plant with a single main trunk.

**trem·ble** (trĕm'bəl) v. -bled, -bling. To shake involuntarily; quiver. — **trem'ble** n.

**tre·men·dous** (trĭ-mĕn'dəs) adj. 1. Awesome; terrible. 2. a. Enormous. b. Wonderful. — **tre·men'dous·ly** adv.

**trem·or** (trĕm'ər) n. 1. A vibration. 2. An involuntary trembling; shiver.

**trem·u·lous** (trĕm'yə-ləs) adj. 1. Trembling; shaking. 2. Timid; fearful.

**trench** (trĕnch) n. A deep furrow or ditch.

**trench·ant** (trĕn'chənt) adj. Keen; incisive. — **trench'ant·ly** adv.

**trend** (trĕnd) n. 1. A direction or course. 2. A tendency.

**trep·i·da·tion** (trĕp'ə-dā'shən) n. A state of apprehension.

**tres·pass** (trĕs'pəs, -păs') v. 1. To invade the property or rights of another. 2. To commit an offense. — n. 1. The act of trespassing. 2. An offense. — **tres'pass·er** n.

**tres·tle** (trĕs'əl) n. 1. A horizontal bar held up by legs and used as a support. 2. A framework of such construction for supporting a bridge.

**tri·al** (trī'əl, trīl) n. 1. A legal examination of evidence in a judicial procedure. 2. The act of testing and trying. 3. An attempt. 4. Suffering or adversity. 5. A test of patience or endurance. — adj. Made or done during a test.

**tri·an·gle** (trī'ăng'gəl) n. A plane figure with three angles. — **tri·an'gu·lar** adj.

**tribe** (trīb) n. 1. A social organization or division. 2. A group having a common distinguishing characteristic. — **trib'al** adj. — **tribes'man** n.

**trib·u·la·tion** (trĭb'yə-lā'shən) n. 1. Great affliction. 2. A cause of such affliction.

**tri·bu·nal** (trī-byōō'nəl, trĭ-) n. A court of justice.

**trib·u·tar·y** (trĭb'yə-tĕr'ē) adj. 1. Subsidiary. 2. Paying tribute. — n., pl. -ies. A stream or river flowing into a larger one.

**trib·ute** (trĭb'yōōt) n. 1. A gift or act as acknowledgment of respect. 2. A payment, often forced, from one nation to another as acknowledgment of submission.

**trick** (trĭk) n. 1. A deception; stratagem. 2. A prank. 3. A knack or ability. 4. All the cards played in a single round. — v. To swindle or cheat; deceive. — **trick'er·y** n. — **trick'y** adj.

**tri·en·ni·al** (trī-ĕn'ē-əl) adj. 1. Occurring

every third year. **2.** Lasting three years. —*n.* A third anniversary.

**tri·fle** (trī′fəl) *n.* **1.** Something of little value. **2.** A small amount. —*v.* -**fled, -fling. 1.** To deal with something as if it were of little value. **2.** To deal insincerely with someone. — **tri′fler** *n.* — **tri′fling** *adj.*

**trig·ger** (trĭg′ər) *n.* **1.** The lever pressed to discharge a firearm. **2.** A device to release a mechanism. **3.** A stimulus. —*v.* To initiate; set off.

**trill** (trĭl) *n.* **1.** A fluttering sound. **2.** In music, the rapid alternation of two tones. —*v.* To sound, sing, or play with a trill.

**tril·lion** (trĭl′yən) *n.* The cardinal number represented by 1 followed by 12 zeros. — **tril′lion** *adj. & pron.* — **tril′lionth** *n. & adj.*

**trim** (trĭm) *v.* **trimmed, trimming. 1.** To make neat by clipping or pruning. **2.** To ornament; decorate. **3. a.** To adjust (the sails and yards). **b.** To balance (a ship). —*n.* **1.** Appearance; condition. **2.** Ornamentation. **3.** The readiness or balance of a ship. —*adj.* **trimmer, trimmest.** In good or neat order. — **trim′ly** *adv.* — **trim′mer** *n.* — **trim′ness** *n.*

**trin·i·ty** (trĭn′ə-tē) *n., pl.* -**ties. 1.** Any three parts in union. **2. Trinity.** The three-person godhead of orthodox Christian belief.

**trin·ket** (trĭng′kĭt) *n.* **1.** Any small ornament, esp. a piece of jewelry. **2.** A trivial thing.

**tri·o** (trē′ō) *n., pl.* -**os. 1.** A group of three. **2. a.** A musical composition for three performers. **b.** The people who perform this composition.

**trip** (trĭp) *n.* **1.** A journey. **2.** A stumble. —*v.* **tripped, tripping. 1.** To stumble or cause to stumble. **2.** To move quickly or nimbly.

**trip·le** (trĭp′əl) *adj.* **1.** Of three parts. **2.** Thrice multiplied. —*v.* -**led, -ling.** To make or become three times as great. — **trip′ly** *adv.*

**trip·li·cate** (trĭp′lĭ-kĭt) *adj.* Triple. —*n.* One of a set of three copies.

**tri·pod** (trī′pŏd′) *n.* A three-legged stool, support, etc.

**trite** (trīt) *adj.* **triter, tritest.** Overused and commonplace; lacking originality. — **trite′-ness** *n.*

**tri·umph** (trī′əmf) *v.* **1.** To be victorious. **2.** To rejoice over a victory. —*n.* **1.** Victory; success. **2.** Exultation derived from victory. — **tri·um′phal** *adj.* — **tri·um′phant** *adj.* — **tri·um′-phant·ly** *adv.*

**triv·et** (trĭv′ĭt) *n.* A metal stand under a hot dish.

**triv·i·al** (trĭv′ē-əl) *adj.* **1.** Trifling. **2.** Ordinary. — **triv′i·a** *pl.n.* — **triv′i·al′i·ty** *n.* — **triv′i·al·ly** *adv.*

**trod** (trŏd) *p.t. & alternate p.p.* of **tread.**

**trod·den** (trŏd′n). *p.p.* of **tread.**

**trol·ley** (trŏl′ē) *n., pl.* -**leys. 1.** A streetcar. **2.** A carriage suspended from an overhead track.

**trom·bone** (trŏm-bōn′, trəm-, trŏm′bōn′) *n.* A low-pitched brass musical instrument. — **trom·bon′ist** *n.*

**troop** (trōōp) *n.* **1. a.** A group of people, animals, or things. **2. troops.** Military units. —*v.* To move as a throng. — **troop′er** *n.*

**tro·phy** (trō′fē) *n., pl.* -**phies.** A prize received as a symbol of victory.

**trop·ic** (trŏp′ĭk) *n.* **1.** One of two latitudes N and S of the equator that are the boundaries of the Torrid Zone. **2. tropics.** The region of the earth's surface lying between these latitudes. — **trop′i·cal** *adj.*

**trot** (trŏt) *n.* **1.** A gait of a four-footed animal. **2.** A gait faster than a walk. —*v.* **trotted, trotting. 1.** To move at a trot. **2.** To proceed rapidly. — **trot′ter** *n.*

**trou·ble** (trŭb′əl) *n.* **1.** Severe distress, affliction, or danger. **2.** A disturbance or annoyance. **3.** Pain, disease, or malfunction. —*v.* -**led, -ling. 1.** To afflict with pain or discomfort. **2.** To perturb. **3.** To inconvenience. **4.** To take pains. — **trou′ble·some** *adj.*

**trough** (trôf, trŏf) *n.* **1.** A long, narrow receptacle, esp. for water or feed for animals. **2.** A long, narrow depression.

**troupe** (trōōp) *n.* A company, esp. of touring performers. — **troup′er** *n.*

**trou·sers** (trou′zərz) *pl.n.* A two-legged outer garment covering the body from the waist to the ankles.

**trow·el** (trou′əl) *n.* **1.** A flat-bladed hand tool for spreading cement, mortar, etc. **2.** A small gardening implement with a scoop-shaped blade.

**tru·ant** (trōō′ənt) *n.* One who is absent without permission, esp. from school. —*adj.* **1.** Absent without leave. **2.** Lazy or neglectful. — **tru′an·cy** *n.*

**truce** (trōōs) *n.* An agreement to cease hostilities temporarily.

**truck** (trŭk) *n.* **1.** A heavy automotive vehicle for transporting loads. **2.** A two-wheeled hand barrow. —*v.* To transport by or drive a truck.

**truc·u·lent** (trŭk′yə-lənt) *adj.* **1.** Savage and cruel; fierce. **2.** Defiant. — **truc′u·lence** *n.*

**trudge** (trŭj) *v.* **trudged, trudging.** To walk wearily; plod. —*n.* A long, tedious walk. — **trudg′er** *n.*

**true** (trōō) *adj.* **truer, truest. 1.** Consistent with fact. **2.** Correct. **3.** Genuine. **4.** Faithful. —*adv.* **1.** Rightly; truthfully. **2.** Exactly. —**tru'ly** *adv.*

**tru·ism** (trōō'iz'əm) *n.* An obvious truth.

**trum·pet** (trŭm'pĭt) *n.* A brass instrument consisting of a long tube ending in a flared bell. —*v.* **1.** To play a trumpet. **2.** To give forth a resounding call. —**trum'pet·er** *n.*

**trun·cate** (trŭng'kāt') *v.* **-cated, -cating.** To shorten by cutting. —**trun·ca'tion** *n.*

**trunk** (trŭngk) *n.* **1.** The main stem of a tree. **2.** The human body excluding the head and limbs. **3.** A main body of anything. **4.** A large packing case used as luggage or for storage. **5.** A covered compartment of an automobile. **6.** A flexible snout, esp. of an elephant. **7. trunks.** Shorts worn for swimming or athletics.

**truss** (trŭs) *n.* **1.** A supportive device worn to prevent enlargement of a hernia. **2.** A framework used to support a roof, bridge, etc. —*v.* **1.** To tie up or bind. **2.** To support with a truss.

**trust** (trŭst) *n.* **1.** Firm reliance; confident belief. **2.** Custody; care. **3.** One committed into the care of another. **4.** The condition of having confidence placed in one; responsibility. **5.** Future hope. **6.** A legal title to property held by one party for the benefit of another. **7.** An often monopolistic combination of firms. —*v.* **1.** To rely; depend. **2.** To hope. **3.** To expect; assume. **4.** To believe. **5.** To entrust. **6.** To extend credit to. —*adj.* Maintained in trust. —**trust'ful** *adj.* —**trust'wor'thy** *adj.*

**trus·tee** (trŭs·tē') *n.* **1.** A person holding and administering a trust. **2.** A member of a board that directs an institution. —**trus·tee'ship'** *n.*

**truth** (trōōth) *n., pl.* **truths. 1.** Conformity to knowledge, fact, etc. **2.** Fidelity to a standard. **3.** Reality. **4.** A true statement. **5.** Sincerity; integrity. —**truth'ful** *adj.* —**truth'ful·ly** *adv.* —**truth'ful·ness** *n.*

**try** (trī) *v.* **tried, trying. 1.** To test. **2. a.** To examine by judicial process. **b.** To put on trial. **3.** To subject to great strain; tax. **4.** To attempt. —*n., pl.* **tries.** An attempt; effort. —**try'ing** *adj.*

**tryst** (trĭst) *n.* **1.** An agreement between lovers to meet. **2.** The arranged meeting place.

**tub** (tŭb) *n.* **1.** A round, open, flat-bottomed vessel. **2.** A bathtub.

**tu·ba** (t/y/ōō'bə) *n.* A large brass musical

wind instrument.

**tube** (t/y/ōōb) *n.* **1.** A hollow cylinder for fluids. **2.** A flexible cylindrical container for pigments, toothpaste, etc. —**tu'bu·lar** *adj.*

**tu·ber** (t/y/ōō'bər) *n.* A swollen, usually underground stem, as a potato. —**tu'ber·ous** *adj.*

**tuck** (tŭk) *v.* **1.** To make folds in. **2.** To turn in the end or edge of. **3.** To draw in; contract. —*n.* A flattened pleat or fold.

**Tues·day** (t/y/ōōz'dē, -dā') *n.* The 3rd day of the week.

**tuft** (tŭft) *n.* A cluster of yarn, hair, grass, etc., held or growing close together.

**tug** (tŭg) *v.* **tugged, tugging. 1.** To pull at vigorously. **2.** To move by pulling with great effort. —*n.* **1.** A strong pull. **2.** A tugboat.

**tug·boat** (tŭg'bōt') *n.* A powerful small boat for towing larger vessels.

**tu·i·tion** (t/y/ōō·ĭsh'ən) *n.* A fee for instruction.

**tum·ble** (tŭm'bəl) *v.* **-bled, -bling. 1.** To perform acrobatic feats. **2.** To fall or roll over end. **3.** To fall headlong. **4.** To cause to fall; bring down. —*n.* A fall.

**tum·bler** (tŭm'blər) *n.* **1.** An acrobat. **2.** A drinking glass having no handle or stem. **3.** The part in a lock that engages the bolt.

**tu·mid** (t/y/ōō'mĭd) *adj.* **1.** Swollen. **2.** Bombastic. —**tu·mid'i·ty** *n.*

**tu·mor** (t/y/ōō'mər) *n.* A noninflammatory bodily growth.

**tu·mult** (t/y/ōō'mŭlt) *n.* Din and commotion. —**tu·mul'tu·ous** *adj.*

**tun·dra** (tŭn'drə) *n.* A treeless area of arctic regions.

**tune** (t/y/ōōn) *n.* **1.** A simple arrangement of pleasing musical tones. **2.** Correct musical pitch or agreement with respect to pitch. **3.** Harmony. —*v.* **tuned, tuning. 1.** To put into tune. **2.** To adjust for maximum performance. **3.** To adjust a radio or television receiver to receive signals. —**tune'ful** *adj.*

**tune-up** (t/y/ōōn'ŭp') *n.* An adjustment of an engine.

**tun·nel** (tŭn'əl) *n.* An underground passage. —*v.* To make a tunnel.

**tur·ban** (tûr'bən) *n.* A headdress made of a scarf wound around the head.

**tur·bu·lent** (tûr'byə·lənt) *adj.* **1.** Violently agitated; stormy. **2.** Causing disturbance; unruly. —**tur·bu·lence** *n.*

**tu·reen** (t/y/ōō·rēn') *n.* A broad, covered dish for serving soups, stews, etc.

**turf** (tûrf) *n.* Surface ground covering of grass and roots.

# T-20

**turgid**

**tur·gid** (tûr′jĭd) adj. **1.** Swollen. **2.** Overornate.

**tur·key** (tûr′kē) n., pl. **-keys.** A large edible North American bird.

**tur·moil** (tûr′moil) n. Utter confusion; agitation.

**turn** (tûrn) v. **1.** To rotate; revolve. **2.** To shape (something) on a lathe. **3.** To change the position of. **4.** To upset; nauseate. **5.** To change the direction of. **6.** To make a course around. **7.** To direct (the attention, interest, etc.) toward or away from. **8.** To change. **9.** To become. **10.** To depend upon. **11.** To change color. **12.** To sour; ferment. —n. **1.** A rotation; revolution. **2.** A change of direction. **3.** A departure or deviation. **4.** An opportunity to do something determined by a scheduled order. **5.** Natural inclination. **6.** A short excursion. **7.** A single wind or convolution.

**turn·pike** (tûrn′pīk′) n. A road, esp. a wide highway with tollgates.

**turn·stile** (tûrn′stīl′) n. A device used to control passage, consisting of revolving horizontal arms projecting from a central post.

**tur·pen·tine** (tûr′pən-tīn′) n. A thin, volatile oil from certain pine trees, used as a paint thinner, solvent, etc.

**tur·pi·tude** (tûr′pə-t/y/ōōd′) n. Depravity.

**tur·quoise** (tûr′kwoiz′, -koiz′) n. **1.** A bluegreen mineral valued as a gemstone. **2.** Bluish green.

**tur·ret** (tûr′ĭt) n. **1.** A small tower-shaped projection on a building. **2.** A projecting armored structure, usually rotating, for mounted guns.

**tur·tle** (tûr′tl) n. A reptile with the body enclosed in a shell.

**tusk** (tŭsk) n. A long pointed tooth, as of an elephant or walrus.

**tu·te·lage** (t/y/ōō′tə-lĭj) n. **1.** Guardianship. **2.** Instruction.

**tu·tor** (t/y/ōō′tər) n. A private instructor. —v. To act as a tutor to. —**tu·to′ri·al** adj.

**twang** (twăng) v. **1.** To emit or cause to emit a sharp, vibrating sound. **2.** To utter with a nasal sound. —n. **1.** A sharp, vibrating sound. **2.** A nasal tone of voice. —**twang′y** adj.

**tweed** (twēd) n. A rough-textured woolen fabric. —**tweed′y** adj.

**tweez·ers** (twē′zərz) pl.n. A small pincerlike tool.

**twelve** (twĕlv) n. The cardinal number written 12. —**twelve** adj. & pron. —**twelfth** n. & adj.

**twen·ty** (twĕn′tē) n. The cardinal number written 20. —**twen′ty** adj. & pron. —**twen′ti·eth** n. & adj.

**twice** (twīs) adv. Two times; doubled.

**twig** (twĭg) n. A small branch.

**twi·light** (twī′līt′) n. **1.** The time interval during which the sun is at a small angle below the horizon. **2.** The illumination of the atmosphere during this interval.

**twin** (twĭn) n. **1.** One of two offspring born at the same birth. **2.** One of two identical things. —**twin** adj.

**twine** (twīn) v. **twined, twining.** **1.** To twist together. **2.** To encircle. —n. A strong cord of threads twisted together.

**twinge** (twĭnj) n. A sharp and sudden physical or emotional pain.

**twin·kle** (twĭng′kəl) v. **-kled, -kling.** To shine with slight, intermittent gleams. —n. **1.** A slight, intermittent gleam of light. **2.** A sparkle of delight in the eye.

**twirl** (twûrl) v. To spin. —**twirl** n.

**twist** (twĭst) v. **1.** To entwine (two or more threads) so as to produce a single strand. **2.** To coil about. **3.** To impart or assume a spiral shape. **4.** To turn or break by turning. **5.** To wrench or sprain. **6.** To distort the meaning of. **7.** To rotate or turn. —n. **1.** A spin or twirl. **2.** A spiral curve or turn. **3.** A sprain or wrench. **4.** An unexpected change. —**twist′er** n.

**twitch** (twĭch) v. To move or cause to move jerkily. —n. A sudden involuntary muscular movement.

**two** (tōō) n. The cardinal number written 2. —**two** adj. & pron.

**ty·coon** (tī-kōōn′) n. A wealthy and powerful businessman.

**tyke** (tīk) n. A small child.

**type** (tīp) n. **1.** A category of persons or things sharing common distinguishing characteristics. **2.** One belonging to such a category. **3.** An example. **4. a.** A small metal block bearing a raised character, used in printing. **b.** Such pieces collectively. —v. **typed, typing.** **1.** To typewrite. **2.** To classify.

**type·writ·er** (tīp′rī′tər) n. A keyboard machine that prints characters on paper. —**type′write′** v.

**ty·phoon** (tī-fōōn′) n. A severe tropical hurricane of the western Pacific.

**typ·i·cal** (tĭp′ĭ-kəl) adj. **1.** Exhibiting · the characteristics peculiar to a kind or category. **2.** Characteristic. —**typ′i·cal·ly** adv.

**typ·i·fy** (tĭp′ə-fī′) v. **-fied, -fying.** To serve as an example of.

**ty·pog·ra·phy** (tĭ-pŏg'rə-fē) n. 1. The composition of printed material from movable type. 2. The arrangement and appearance of such matter. —**ty·pog'ra·pher** n. —**ty'po·graph'i·cal** adj.

**tyr·an·ny** (tĭr'ə-nē) n., pl. -nies. 1. A government in which a single ruler wields absolute power. 2. Absolute power, esp. when exercised unjustly or cruelly. 3. A cruel or despotic act. —**ty·ran'ni·cal** adj. —**tyr'an·nize'** v.

**ty·rant** (tī'rənt) n. 1. A harsh, cruel, despotic ruler; an oppressor. 2. Any despotic person.

**ty·ro** (tī'rō) n., pl. -ros. A beginner.

# U

**u, U** (yōō) n. The 21st letter of the English alphabet.

**u·biq·ui·tous** (yōō-bĭk'wə-təs) adj. Being everywhere at the same time. —**u·biq'ui·tous·ly** adv. —**u·biq'ui·ty** n.

**ud·der** (ŭd'ər) n. The mammary organ of cows, goats, etc.

**ug·ly** (ŭg'lē) adj. -lier, -liest. 1. Unsightly. 2. Repulsive or offensive. —**ug'li·ness** n.

**u·ku·le·le** (/yōō'kə-lā'lē) n. A small four-stringed guitar.

**ul·cer** (ŭl'sər) n. An inflammatory lesion, as on the skin. —**ul'cer·ate'** v.

**ul·na** (ŭl'nə) n., pl. -nae (-nē) or -nas. The forearm bone on the side opposite the thumb. —**ul'nar** adj.

**ul·te·ri·or** (ŭl'tîr'ē-ər) adj. 1. Beyond what is evident or admitted. 2. Beyond or outside a certain area or region. —**ul'te'ri·or·ly** adv.

**ul·ti·mate** (ŭl'tə-mĭt) adj. 1. Final; conclusive. 2. Fundamental; elemental. —**ul'ti·mate·ly** adv.

**ul·ti·ma·tum** (ŭl'tə-mā'təm, -mä'təm) n., pl. -tums or -ta. A final demand or offer.

**ul·tra·vi·o·let** (ŭl'trə-vī'ə-lĭt) adj. Of the range of radiation wavelengths beyond violet in the visible spectrum to the x-ray region. —**ul'tra·vi'o·let** n.

**um·bil·i·cus** (ŭm'bĭl'ĭ-kəs, ŭm'bə-lī'kəs) n. The navel. —**um·bil'i·cal** adj.

**um·brage** (ŭm'brĭj) n. Offense.

**um·brel·la** (ŭm'brĕl'ə) n. A device consisting of a cloth cover on a collapsible frame mounted on a handle, for protection from the weather.

**um·pire** (ŭm'pīr) n. A judge, esp. one who rules in sports. —**um'pire** v.

**un·ac·count·a·ble** (ŭn'ə-koun'tə-bəl) adj. Inexplicable; mysterious. —**un'ac·count'a·bly** adv.

**un·ac·cus·tomed** (ŭn'ə-kŭs'təmd) adj. Unfamiliar or unusual.

**un·af·fect·ed** (ŭn'ə-fĕk'tĭd) adj. Natural; sincere. —**un'af·fect'ed·ly** adv.

**u·nan·i·mous** (yōō-nǎn'ə-məs) adj. 1. Sharing the same opinion. 2. Based on complete agreement. —**u'na·nim'i·ty** n. —**u·nan'i·mous·ly** adv.

**un·as·sum·ing** (ŭn'ə-sōō'mĭng) adj. Modest. —**un'as·sum'ing·ly** adv.

**un·bound·ed** (ŭn'boun'dĭd) adj. Having no limits. —**un'bound'ed·ly** adv.

**un·bowed** (ŭn'boud') adj. Not subdued.

**un·bur·den** (ŭn'bûrd'n) v. To relieve, as from a burden.

**un·can·ny** (ŭn'kǎn'ē) adj. -nier, -niest. 1. Arousing wonder and fear; strange. 2. So perceptive as to seem supernatural. —**un'can'ni·ly** adv.

**un·cer·tain** (ŭn'sûrt'n) adj. 1. Doubtful; not sure. 2. Not definite; vague. 3. Subject to change; variable. —**un'cer'tain·ly** adv. —**un'cer'tain·ty** n.

**un·civ·il** (ŭn'sĭv'əl) adj. Impolite; rude. —**un'civ'il·ly** adv.

**un·cle** (ŭng'kəl) n. 1. The brother of one's mother or father. 2. The husband of one's aunt.

**un·con·scion·a·ble** (ŭn'kŏn'shən-ə-bəl) adj. Unreasonable; immoderate; excessive. —**un'con'scion·a·bly** adv.

**un·con·scious** (ŭn'kŏn'shəs) adj. 1. Without conscious awareness, esp. psychological rather than physiological. 2. Temporarily lacking consciousness. —**un'con'scious·ly** adv. —**un'con'scious·ness** n.

**un·couth** (ŭn'kōōth') adj. 1. Not refined; crude. 2. Awkward.

**unc·tu·ous** (ŭngk'chōō-əs) adj. 1. Oily; greasy. 2. Showing excessive sincerity, courtesy, etc. —**unc'tu·ous·ly** adv. —**unc'tu·ous·ness** n.

**un·daunt·ed** (ŭn'dôn'tĭd, -dän'tĭd) adj. Resolute; fearless. —**un'daunt'ed·ly** adv.

**un·de·ni·a·ble** (ŭn'dĭ-nī'ə-bəl) adj. 1. Irrefutable. 2. Excellent. —**un'de·ni'a·bly** adv.

**un·der** (ŭn'dər) prep. 1. In a lower position or place than. 2. Beneath the surface of. 3. Less than; smaller than. —**un'der** adj. & adv.

**un·der·cov·er** (ŭn'dər-kŭv'ər) adj. Secret.

**un·der·cut** (ŭn'dər-kŭt') v. **1.** To make a cut under or below. **2.** To sell at a lower price than (a competitor). — **un'der·cut'** n.

**un·der·de·vel·oped** (ŭn'dər-dĭ-vĕl'əpt) adj. **1.** Immature. **2.** Economically backward.

**un·der·dog** (ŭn'dər-dôg', -dŏg') n. One who is expected to lose a contest.

**un·der·go** (ŭn'dər-gō') v. **1.** To experience; be subjected to. **2.** To endure; suffer.

**un·der·grad·u·ate** (ŭn'dər-grăj'ŏo-ĭt) n. A college student who has not yet received a degree.

**un·der·ground** (ŭn'dər-ground') adj. **1.** Below the surface of the earth. **2.** Hidden; secret. —n. A clandestine subversive organization. —adv. **1.** Below the surface of the earth. **2.** In secret; stealthily.

**un·der·hand** (ŭn'dər-hănd') adj. Deceitful; sneaky. —adv. Slyly; secretly.

**un·der·hand·ed** (ŭn'dər-hăn'dĭd) adj. Sly; secret; underhand. — **un'der·hand'ed·ly** adv. — **un'der·hand'ed·ness** n.

**un·der·mine** (ŭn'dər-mīn') v. **1.** To dig a tunnel beneath. **2.** To weaken or impair by or as if by wearing away.

**un·der·neath** (ŭn'dər-nēth') adv. In a place beneath; below. —prep. Beneath; below; under.

**un·der·stand** (ŭn'dər-stănd') v. **-stood, -standing.** To perceive and comprehend the nature and significance of; know. — **un'der·stand'a·ble** adj.

**un·der·stand·ing** (ŭn'dər-stăn'dĭng) n. **1.** Comprehension; discernment. —adj. Compassionate and sympathetic.

**un·der·stood** (ŭn'dər-stŏod') adj. **1.** Agreed upon. **2.** Not expressed in writing; implied.

**un·der·study** (ŭn'dər-stŭd'ē) n., pl. **-ies.** A performer trained to substitute for the regular performer.

**un·der·take** (ŭn'dər-tāk') v. **1.** To take upon oneself. **2.** To pledge or commit oneself to doing (something).

**un·der·tak·er** (ŭn'dər-tā'kər) n. One who prepares the dead for burial or cremation and makes funeral arrangements.

**un·der·world** (ŭn'dər-wûrld') n. The part of society engaged in crime and vice.

**un·do** (ŭn'dŏo') v. **1.** To reverse; cancel; annul. **2.** To untie or loosen. **3.** To ruin or destroy.

**un·doubt·ed** (ŭn'dou'tĭd) adj. Accepted as beyond question. — **un·doubt'ed·ly** adv.

**un·due** (ŭn'd'y/ŏo') adj. **1.** Excessive. **2.** Not just, proper, or legal — **un·du'ly** adv.

**un·du·late** (ŭn'jŏo-lāt', ŭn'd/y/ə-) v. **-lated,**

-lating. To move or cause to move in a smooth wavelike motion. — **un'du·lant** adj. — **un'du·la'tion** n.

**un·earth** (ŭn'ûrth') v. To bring to public notice; reveal.

**un·eas·y** (ŭn'ē'zē) adj. **1.** Lacking ease, comfort, etc. **2.** Awkward in manner; constrained. — **un'eas'i·ly** adv. — **un'eas'i·ness** n.

**un·e·quiv·o·cal** (ŭn'ĭ-kwĭv'ə-kəl) adj. Clear; plain. — **un·e·quiv·o·cal·ly** adv.

**un·err·ing** (ŭn'ûr'ĭng, -ĕr'ĭng) adj. Consistently accurate; without error. — **un·err'ing·ly** adv.

**un·ex·pect·ed** (ŭn'ĭk-spĕk'tĭd) adj. Coming without warning; unforeseen. — **un'ex·pect'ed·ly** adv. — **un'ex·pect'ed·ness** n.

**un·fail·ing** (ŭn'fā'lĭng) adj. **1.** Inexhaustible. **2.** Constant; reliable. — **un'fail'ing·ly** adv.

**un·fair** (ŭn'fâr') adj. Not fair, right, or just. — **un'fair'ly** adv. — **un'fair'ness** n.

**un·faith·ful** (ŭn'fāth'fəl) adj. **1.** Disloyal. **2.** Not reflecting the original contents; inaccurate. — **un'faith'ful·ly** adv. — **un'faith'ful·ness** n.

**un·fit** (ŭn'fĭt') adj. **1.** Inappropriate. **2.** Unqualified. **3.** Not in good health. — **un'fit'ly** adv. — **un'fit'ness** n.

**un·fold** (ŭn'fōld') v. **1.** To open and spread out. **2.** To reveal or be revealed gradually.

**un·for·tu·nate** (ŭn'fôr'chə-nĭt) adj. **1.** Causing misfortune; disastrous. **2.** Regrettable; deplorable. —n. A victim of disaster, poverty, etc. — **un'for'tu·nate·ly** adv. — **un'for'tu·nate·ness** n.

**un·friend·ly** (ŭn'frĕnd'lē) adj. Not disposed to friendship; hostile. — **un'friend'li·ness** n.

**un·god·ly** (ŭn'gŏd'lē) adj. **-lier, -liest.** **1.** Not revering God. **2.** Sinful; wicked. **3.** Outrageous. — **un'god'li·ness** n.

**un·guent** (ŭng'gwənt) n. Salve; ointment.

**un·hap·py** (ŭn'hăp'ē) adj. **1.** Sad. **2.** Unlucky. **3.** Inappropriate. — **un'hap'pi·ly** adv. — **un'hap'pi·ness** n.

**un·ho·ly** (ŭn'hō'lē) adj. **1.** Not consecrated. **2.** Wicked; immoral. **3.** Outrageous.

**u·ni·corn** (yŏo'nə-kôrn') n. A fabled horselike creature with a single horn on its forehead.

**u·ni·form** (yŏo'nə-fôrm') adj. **1.** Consistent. **2.** Being the same everywhere; identical. —n. An outfit identifying those who wear it as members of a special group, organization, etc. — **u'ni·for'mi·ty, u'ni·form'ness** n. — **u'ni·form'ly** adv.

**u·ni·fy** (yŏo'nə-fī') v. **-fied, -fying.** To make into a unit; consolidate. — **u'ni·fi·ca'tion**

— u'ni·ti'er n.

**u·ni·lat·er·al** (yōō'ni-lăt'ər-əl) adj. **1.** Of only one side. **2.** Having only one side. — **u'ni·lat'er·al·ly** adv.

**un·im·peach·a·ble** (ŭn'ĭm-pē'chə-bəl) adj. Beyond doubt or reproach. — **un'im·peach'a·bly** adv.

**un·ion** (yōōn'yən) n. **1.** The act of uniting. **2.** A combination; an alliance or confederation. **3.** A labor organization for the purpose of serving class interests with respect to wages, etc. — adj. Of a union, esp. a labor union. — **un'ion·i·za'tion** n. — **un'ion·ize'** v.

**u·nique** (yōō-nēk') adj. Being the only one, esp. in kind, excellence, etc. — **u·nique'ly** adv. — **u·nique'ness** n.

**u·ni·son** (yōō'nə-sən, -zən) n. Agreement; concord.

**u·nit** (yōō'nĭt) n. A thing, group, person, etc., regarded as part of a whole.

**u·nite** (yōō-nīt') v. **united, uniting.** To bring together or become joined, formed, or combined into a unit.

**u·ni·ty** (yōō'nə-tē) n., pl. **-ties. 1.** The state of being one. **2.** Accord, as of aims, feelings, etc.; agreement.

**u·ni·ver·sal** (yōō'nə-vûr'səl) adj. **1.** Of, for, done by, or affecting all. **2.** Of the universe; cosmic. — **u'ni·ver·sal'i·ty** n. — **u'ni·ver'sal·ly** adv.

**u·ni·verse** (yōō'nə-vûrs') n. All the matter and space that exists, considered as a whole.

**u·ni·ver·si·ty** (yōō'nə-vûr'sə-tē) n., pl. **-ties.** An institution that includes a graduate school, professional schools, and an undergraduate division.

**un·kempt** (ŭn'kĕmpt') adj. Messy.

**un·less** (ŭn-lĕs') conj. Except on the condition that.

**un·like** (ŭn'līk') adj. Different; dissimilar.

**un·like·ly** (ŭn'līk'lē) adj. **1.** Improbable. **2.** Likely to fail. — **un'like'li·hood, un'like'li·ness** n.

**un·load** (ŭn'lōd') v. **1.** To remove the load or cargo from. **2.** To remove the charge from (a firearm). **3.** To dispose of.

**un·nerve** (ŭn'nûrv') v. **-nerved, -nerving.** To cause to lose courage, composure, etc.

**un·pack** (ŭn'păk') v. **1.** To remove the contents of (a suitcase, etc.). **2.** To empty from a container.

**un·rav·el** (ŭn'răv'əl) v. **1.** To undo (a knitted fabric). **2.** To solve.

**un·rest** (ŭn'rĕst') n. Uneasiness; disquiet.

**un·ru·ly** (ŭn'rōō'lē) adj. **-ier, -liest.** Difficult to discipline or control. — **un'ru'li·ness** n.

**un·set·tled** (ŭn'sĕt'əld) adj. **1.** Disordered; disturbed. **2.** Not determined or resolved.

**un·sight·ly** (ŭn'sīt'lē) adj. Offensive to look at; not attractive. — **un'sight'li·ness** n.

**un·tan·gle** (ŭn'tăng'gəl) v. **1.** To disentangle. **2.** To clarify; resolve.

**un·tie** (ŭn'tī') v. **1.** To undo or loosen (a knot). **2.** To free from something that binds or restrains.

**un·til** (ŭn-tĭl') prep. **1.** Up to the time of. **2.** Before a specified time. — conj. **1.** Up to the time that. **2.** Before. **3.** To the point or extent that.

**un·to** (ŭn'tōō) prep. To.

**un·told** (ŭn'tōld') adj. **1.** Not revealed. **2.** Without limit.

**un·to·ward** (ŭn'tôrd', -tōrd') adj. **1.** Unfortunate. **2.** Hard to control.

**un·true** (ŭn'trōō') adj. **1.** False. **2.** Disloyal. — **un·truth'** n. — **un·truth'ful** adj. — **un·truth'ful·ness** n.

**un·used** (ŭn'yōōzd') adj. **1.** Not used or never having been used. **2.** Not accustomed.

**un·u·su·al** (ŭn'yōō'zhōō-əl) adj. Not usual, common, or ordinary.

**un·veil** (ŭn'vāl') v. **1.** To remove a veil from. **2.** To disclose or reveal.

**un·wield·y** (ŭn'wēl'dē) adj. **-ier, -iest.** Difficult to carry or handle because of shape or size.

**un·wind** (ŭn'wīnd') v. **1.** To open (something rolled up). **2.** To become free of tension, etc.

**un·wise** (ŭn'wīz') adj. Lacking wisdom; foolish. — **un'wise'ly** adv.

**un·wit·ting** (ŭn'wĭt'ĭng) adj. **1.** Not knowing; unaware. **2.** Not intended or intentional. — **un'wit'ting·ly** adv.

**un·wont·ed** (ŭn'wŏn'tĭd, -wōn'tĭd, -wŭn'tĭd) adj. Not habitual or ordinary.

**un·wor·thy** (ŭn'wûr'thē) adj. **1.** Not deserving. **2.** Not suiting or befitting. — **un'wor'thi·ness** n.

**up** (ŭp) adv. **1.** From a lower to a higher position. **2.** In or toward a higher position. **3.** From a reclining to an upright position. **4.** Out of bed. — prep. **1.** Toward or at a point farther along. **2.** In a direction toward the source of. — n. A rise or ascent. — v. **upped, upping.** To increase or improve.

**up·braid** (ŭp'brād') v. **1.** To scold or chide vehemently. — **up'braid'er** n.

**up·heav·al** (ŭp'hē'vəl) n. A sudden and violent disruption.

**up·hill** (ŭp'hĭl') adj. Going up a hill or slope. — n. (ŭp'hĭl'). An upward incline. — adv.

**up·hold** (ŭp-hōld´) v. To support.

**up·hol·ster** (ŭp-hōl´stər) v. To supply furniture with stuffing, covering fabric, etc. —**up·hol·ster·er** n. —**up·hol·ster·y** n.

**up·keep** (ŭp´kēp´) n. Maintenance in proper condition.

**up·lift** (ŭp-lĭft´) v. To raise to a higher social, intellectual, or moral level. —**up·lift** n.

**up·on** (ə-pŏn´, ə-pôn´) prep. On.

**up·per** (ŭp´ər) adj. Higher in place, position, or rank. —**up´per·most** adj.

**up·right** (ŭp´rīt´) adj. **1.** Erect. **2.** Morally respectable; honorable. —**up´right·ness** n.

**up·ris·ing** (ŭp´rī´zĭng) n. A revolt; insurrection.

**up·roar** (ŭp´rôr´, -rōr´) n. Noisy excitement and confusion; tumult. —**up·roar´i·ous** adj. —**up·roar´i·ous·ly** adv.

**up·set** (ŭp-sĕt´) v. -**set**, -**set·ting**. **1.** To overturn or capsize; tip over. **2.** To disturb the usual or normal functioning of. **3.** To distress or perturb mentally or emotionally. **4.** To defeat unexpectedly. —n. (ŭp´sĕt´) **1. a.** An act of upsetting. **b.** The condition of being upset. **2.** A disturbance, disorder, or agitation. **3.** A game or contest in which the favorite is defeated. —adj. (ŭp-sĕt´). **1.** Overturned; capsized. **2.** Disordered; disturbed. **3.** Distressed; distraught; agitated. —**up·set´ter** n.

**up·shot** (ŭp´shŏt´) n. The final result or outcome.

**up·stairs** (ŭp´stârz´) adv. In, on, or to an upper floor; up the stairs. —n. (ŭp´stârz´). A floor above the ground level. —adj. (ŭp´stârz´). Of an upper floor or floors.

**up·start** (ŭp´stärt´) n. A person who attains sudden wealth or prominence, esp. one who becomes arrogant.

**up tight.** Also **up·tight** (ŭp´tīt´). Tense; nervous.

**up·ward** (ŭp´wərd) adv. Also **up·wards.** In, to, or toward a higher place, level, or position. —adj. Ascending.

**u·ra·ni·um** (yŏŏ-rā´nē-əm) n. A heavy radioactive metallic element.

**U·ra·nus** (yŏŏr´ə-nəs, yŏŏ-rā´nəs) n. The 7th planet from the sun.

**ur·ban** (ûr´bən) adj. Of a city or city life. —**ur·ban·i·za´tion** n. —**ur·ban·ize´** v.

**ur·bane** (ûr´bān´) adj. Polite; suave. —**ur·bane´ly** adv. —**ur·ban´i·ty** n.

**ur·chin** (ûr´chĭn) n. A small, mischievous, or needy boy.

**urge** (ûrj) v. urged, urging. **1.** To push, force, or drive onward; impel. **2.** To plead with; exhort. —n. An irresistible desire, etc.

**ur·gent** (ûr´jənt) adj. Calling for immediate action or attention; pressing. —**ur´gen·cy** n. —**ur´gent·ly** adv.

**u·ri·nate** (yŏŏr´ə-nāt´) v. -**nated**, -**nating**. To excrete urine. —**u´ri·na´tion** n.

**u·rine** (yŏŏr´ĭn) n. A solution containing wastes extracted by the kidneys and excreted from the body.

**urn** (ûrn) n. **1.** A vase with a pedestal. **2.** A pot used for serving tea or coffee.

**us** (ŭs) pron. The objective case of we.

**us·age** (yŏŏ´sĭj, -zĭj) n. **1.** The act or manner of using something. **2.** Customary practice; habitual use. **3.** The actual way the elements of a language are used, interrelated, or pronounced.

**use** (yŏŏz) v. used, using. **1.** To employ for some purpose. **2.** To consume or expend. **3.** To make a habit of. **4.** To exploit. —n. (yŏŏs). **1.** The act of using. **2.** Usage. **3.** The goal, object, or purpose for which something is used. —**us´a·ble** adj. —**us´a·ble·ness** n. —**use´ful** adj. —**use´ful·ly** adv. —**use´ful·ness** n. —**use´less** adj. —**use´less·ly** adv. —**use´less·ness** n. —**us´er** n.

**ush·er** (ŭsh´ər) n. One who escorts people to their seats, as in a theater. —**ush´er** v.

**u·su·al** (yŏŏ´zhŏŏ-əl) adj. **1.** Ordinary or normal. **2.** Habitual or customary. —**u·su·al·ly** adv. —**u´su·al·ness** n.

**u·surp** (yŏŏ-sûrp´, -zûrp´) v. To seize and hold without legal right. —**u·sur·pa´tion** n. —**u·surp·er** n.

**u·su·ry** (yŏŏ´zhə-rē) n., pl. -ries. The lending of money at an exorbitant rate of interest. —**u·su·rer** n. —**u·su´ri·ous** adj.

**u·ten·sil** (yŏŏ-tĕn´səl) n. An instrument or container, esp. one used in a kitchen.

**u·ter·us** (yŏŏ´tər-əs) n. An organ of female mammals that holds the fertilized ovum during the development of the fetus. —**u·ter·ine** adj.

**u·til·i·tar·i·an** (yŏŏ-tĭl´ə-târ´ē-ən) adj. Useful or practical.

**u·til·i·ty** (yŏŏ-tĭl´ə-tē) n., pl. -ties. **1.** Usefulness. **2.** A public service, such as electricity, water, etc.

**u·til·ize** (yŏŏ´tə-līz´) v. -ized, -izing. To put to use. —**u´til·i·za´tion** n.

**ut·most** (ŭt´mōst´) adj. Of the highest or greatest degree, amount, or intensity. —n. The maximum.

**u·to·pi·a** (yŏŏ-tō´pē-ə) n. A condition or place of perfection.

**ut·ter**[1] (ŭt'ər) v. To express audibly; pronounce; say. — **ut'ter·ance** n. — **ut'ter·er** n.

**ut·ter**[2] (ŭt'ər) adj. Complete; absolute. — **ut'ter·ly** adv.

**u·vu·la** (yoo'vyə-lə) n. The small mass of tissue that hangs from the soft palate. — **u'vu·lar** adj.

**v, V** (vē) n. The 22nd letter of the English alphabet.

**va·cant** (vā'kənt) adj. **1.** Empty. **2.** Not occupied. **3.** Expressionless; blank. — **va'can·cy** n. — **va'cant·ly** adv.

**va·cate** (vā'kāt') v. **-cated, -cating.** To cease to occupy or hold; give up; leave.

**va·ca·tion** (vā-kā'shən) n. An interval of time devoted to rest or relaxation from work, study, etc. — v. To take or spend a vacation. — **va·ca'tion·er** n.

**vac·ci·nate** (văk'sə-nāt') v. **-nated, -nating.** To inoculate with a disease-producing agent to immunize against a disease. — **vac'ci·na'tion** n. — **vac·cine'** n.

**vac·il·late** (văs'ə-lāt') v. **-lated, -lating. 1.** To oscillate. **2.** To change one's mind often; waver. — **vac'il·la'tion** n. — **vac'il·la'tor** n.

**va·cu·i·ty** (vă-kyoo'ə-tē) n., pl. **-ties. 1.** Emptiness. **2.** Emptiness of mind; stupidity. — **vac'u·ous** adj. — **vac'u·ous·ly** adv.

**vac·u·um** (văk'yoo-əm, -yoom) n. **1.** A space that is empty of matter. **2.** A void.

**vag·a·bond** (văg'ə-bŏnd') n. A person who wanders from place to place; vagrant. — **vag'a·bond** adj.

**va·gi·na** (və-jī'nə) n. The passage leading from the uterus to the outside of the body. — **vag'i·nal** adj.

**va·grant** (vā'grənt) n. A person who wanders from place to place and lives by begging, etc.; tramp. — **va'gran·cy** n. — **va'grant** adj.

**vague** (vāg) adj. **vaguer, vaguest. 1.** Not clearly expressed. **2.** Lacking definite form or character. — **vague'ly** adv. — **vague'ness** n.

**vain** (vān) adj. **1.** Unsuccessful; futile. **2.** Conceited. — **vain'ly** adv. — **vain'ness** n.

**val·iant** (văl'yənt) adj. Brave or courageous. — **val'iance, val'ian·cy** n. — **val'iant·ly** adv.

**val·id** (văl'ĭd) adj. **1.** Well-grounded; sound.

**2.** Having legal force. — **val'i·date'** v. — **val'i·da'tion** n. — **va·lid'i·ty** n.

**va·lise** (və-lēs') n. A small piece of hand luggage.

**val·ley** (văl'ē) n., pl. **-leys.** A region of lowland between mountains or hills.

**val·or** (văl'ər) n. Courage; bravery. — **val'or·ous** adj. — **val'or·ous·ly** adv.

**val·u·a·ble** (văl'yoo-ə-bəl, văl'yə-) adj. **1.** Having high monetary or material value. **2.** Of importance, use, or service. — n. Often **valuables.** A valuable possession. — **val'u·a·bly** adv.

**val·ue** (văl'yoo) n. **1.** Monetary or material worth. **2.** Worth or importance; merit. **3.** A worthwhile principle or quality. — v. **-ued, -uing. 1.** To estimate the worth of; appraise. **2.** To prize; esteem. — **val'u·a'tion** n.

**valve** (vălv) n. A device that regulates gas or liquid flow.

**van** (văn) n. A covered truck for transporting goods, etc.

**van·dal** (văn'dl) n. One who maliciously destroys property. — **van'dal·ism'** n.

**vane** (vān) n. A thin wooden or metal plate that pivots on a spindle, used esp. to indicate wind direction.

**van·guard** (văn'gärd') n. **1.** The foremost position in an army or fleet. **2.** The leading position in a trend or movement.

**van·ish** (văn'ĭsh) v. To disappear or become invisible.

**van·i·ty** (văn'ə-tē) n., pl. **-ties.** Excessive pride; conceit.

**van·quish** (văng'kwĭsh, văn'-) v. To defeat thoroughly; subjugate. — **van'quish·er** n.

**van·tage** (văn'tĭj) n. Something providing superiority or advantage.

**vap·id** (văp'ĭd) adj. Insipid; flat.

**va·por** (vā'pər) n. **1.** Any fine particles of matter in the air, as mist, fumes, etc. **2.** The gaseous state of a substance. — **va'por·ize'** v. — **va'por·iz·er** n. — **va'por·ous** adj. — **va'por·ous·ness** n.

**var·i·a·ble** (vâr'ē-ə-bəl) adj. **1.** Subject to variation; changeable. **2.** Fickle. — n. Something that varies. — **var'i·a·bil'i·ty, var'i·a·ble·ness** n. — **var'i·a·bly** adv.

**var·i·a·tion** (vâr'ē-ā'shən) n. **1.** The act, process, or result of varying; change or deviation. **2.** The extent or degree of such change. **3.** Something that is slightly different from another of the same type.

**var·i·e·gat·ed** (vâr'ē-ə-gā'tĭd) adj. Having a variety of colors.

**va·ri·e·ty** (və-rī'ə-tē) n., pl. **-ties. 1.** Diversity.

**2.** A number of different kinds of things; assortment. **3.** A kind, sort, or form.

**var·i·ous** (vâr'ē-əs) *adj.* **1.** Of different kinds. **2.** More than one; several. — **var'i·ous·ly** *adv.*

**var·nish** (vär'nĭsh) *n.* An oil-based liquid that dries with a hard, glossy finish. — *v.* **varnish** *v.*

**var·y** (vâr'ē) *v.* **-ied, -y·ing. 1.** To cause or undergo change. **2.** To give variety to; diversify. **3.** To differ. — **var'i·ance** *n.* — **var'i·ant** *adj.* & *n.*

**vase** (vās, vāz, väz) *n.* An open container for holding flowers.

**vast** (văst, väst) *adj.* Very great in size; immense. — **vast'ly** *adv.* — **vast'ness** *n.*

**vat** (văt) *n.* A tank or tub used for storing liquids.

**vault¹** (vôlt) *n.* **1.** An arched structure forming a ceiling or roof. **2.** An arched room, esp. an underground storeroom or burial chamber. — *v.* To construct or cover with a vault.

**vault²** (vôlt) *v.* To jump or leap over. — *n.* A leap. — **vault'er** *n.*

**veal** (vēl) *n.* The meat of a calf.

**veer** (vîr) *v.* To change direction; swerve. — **veer** *n.*

**veg·e·ta·ble** (vĕj'tə-bəl, vĕj'ə-tə-) *n.* **1.** A plant cultivated for an edible part, as roots, leaves, etc. **2.** A plant as distinguished from an animal or mineral. — *adj.* Of plants.

**veg·e·tate** (vĕj'ə-tāt') *v.* **-tat·ed, -tat·ing. 1.** To grow as a plant does. **2.** To lead a passive existence.

**veg·e·ta·tion** (vĕj'ə-tā'shən) *n.* **1.** The process of vegetating. **2.** Plant life collectively. — **veg'e·ta'tive** *adj.*

**ve·he·ment** (vē'ə-mənt) *adj.* **1.** Intense or ardent. **2.** Strong or violent. — **ve'he·mence** *n.* — **ve'he·ment·ly** *adv.*

**ve·hi·cle** (vē'ĭ-kəl) *n.* A device for carrying passengers, goods, etc.; conveyance. — **ve·hic'u·lar** *adj.*

**veil** (vāl) *n.* **1.** A piece of thin fabric worn over the head or face. **2.** Anything that covers or conceals. — **veil** *v.*

**vein** (vān) *n.* **1.** A blood vessel through which blood returns to the heart. **2.** A branching structure forming a leaf's framework or an insect's wing. **3.** Style or mode of expression. — *v.* To fill or mark with veins.

**ve·loc·i·ty** (və-lŏs'ə-tē) *n., pl.* **-ties.** Rapidity or speed.

**vel·vet** (vĕl'vĭt) *n.* A fabric having a smooth, dense pile. — *adj.* Made of or resembling velvet. — **vel'vet·y** *adj.*

**ve·nal** (vē'nəl) *adj.* Corrupt or corruptible. — **ve·nal'i·ty** *n.*

**ve·neer** (və-nîr') *n.* **1.** A thin surface layer covering an inferior material. **2.** A surface show. — *v.* To cover with a veneer.

**ven·er·a·ble** (vĕn'ər-ə-bəl) *adj.* Worthy of reverence or respect. — **ven'er·a·bil'i·ty** *n.* — **ven'er·ate** *v.* — **ven'er·a'tion** *n.*

**ve·ne·re·al** (və-nîr'ē-əl) *adj.* Of or transmitted by sexual intercourse.

**venge·ance** (vĕn'jəns) *n.* Retaliation or retribution.

**venge·ful** (vĕnj'fəl) *adj.* Desiring or seeking vengeance; vindictive. — **venge'ful·ly** *adv.* — **venge'ful·ness** *n.*

**ven·om** (vĕn'əm) *n.* **1.** A poisonous secretion of some animals, esp. some snakes or spiders. **2.** Malice; spite. — **ven'om·ous** *adj.*

**vent** (vĕnt) *n.* An opening for the passage of liquids or gases. — *v.* **1.** To give expression to. **2.** To provide with a vent.

**ven·ti·late** (vĕn'tl-āt') *v.* **-lat·ed, -lat·ing. 1.** To admit fresh air into. **2.** To expose to public discussion. — **ven'ti·la'tion** *n.* — **ven'ti·la'tor** *n.*

**ven·tri·cle** (vĕn'trĭ-kəl) *n.* A cavity or chamber in an organ, esp. either of the main chambers of the heart. — **ven·tric'u·lar** *adj.*

**ven·ture** (vĕn'chər) *n.* A speculative or risky undertaking. — *v.* **-tured, -tur·ing. 1.** To risk; stake. — **ven'tur·er** *n.* — **ven'ture·some, ven'tur·ous** *adj.*

**Ve·nus** (vē'nəs) *n.* The 2nd planet from the sun.

**ve·ra·cious** (və-rā'shəs) *adj.* Honest; truthful. — **ve·ra'cious·ness, ve·rac'i·ty** *n.*

**verb** (vûrb) *n.* A word functioning to express existence, action, or occurrence.

**ver·bal** (vûr'bəl) *adj.* **1.** Of words. **2.** Expressed in speech. **3.** Word for word; literal. **4.** Of a verb. — *n.* A verb functioning as a noun, adjective, or adverb. — **ver'bal·ize** *v.* — **ver'bal·i·za'tion** *n.* — **ver'bal·ly** *adv.*

**ver·bose** (vər-bōs') *adj.* Wordy. — **ver·bose'ly** *adv.* — **ver·bose'ness, ver·bos'i·ty** *n.*

**ver·dict** (vûr'dĭkt) *n.* **1.** The decision reached by a jury. **2.** A conclusion or judgment.

**ver·i·fy** (vĕr'ə-fī') *v.* **-fied, -fy·ing. 1.** To prove the truth of. **2.** To test the truth of. — **ver'i·fi'a·ble** *adj.* — **ver'i·fi·ca'tion** *n.*

**ver·i·ta·ble** (vĕr'ə-tə-bəl) *adj.* Unquestionable; true. — **ver'i·ta·bly** *adv.*

**ver·i·ty** (vĕr'ə-tē) *n.* Truth.

**ver·mil·ion** (vər-mĭl'yən) *n.* A bright red. — **ver·mil'ion** *adj.*

**ver·min** (vûr'mĭn) *n., pl.* **vermin.** A small destructive animal, as a cockroach or rat.

— **ver'min·ous** adj.

241    **vile**

V-22

**ver·nac·u·lar** (vər-năk′yə-lər) n. **1.** The spoken language of a country or region. **2.** The idiom of a profession, etc. — **ver·nac′u·lar** adj.

**ver·sa·tile** (vûr′sə-təl) adj. **1.** Capable of doing many things well. **2.** Having varied uses. — **ver′sa·til′i·ty** n.

**verse** (vûrs) n. **1.** A line of poetry. **2.** A stanza. **3.** Poetry. **4.** A division of a Biblical chapter. — **ver′si·fy** v.

**ver·sion** (vûr′zhən, -shən) n. **1.** A description or account. **2.** A translation.

**ver·te·bra** (vûr′tə-brə) n., pl. **-brae** (-brē) or **-bras.** A bone or segment of cartilage of the spinal column. — **ver′te·bral** adj.

**ver·te·brate** (vûr′tə-brāt′, -brĭt) adj. **1.** Having a backbone or spinal column. **2.** Of vertebrates. — n. A vertebrate animal.

**ver·ti·cal** (vûr′tĭ-kəl) adj. At right angles to the horizon. — n. A vertical line, plane, circle, etc. — **ver′ti·cal·ly** adv.

**ver·y** (vĕr′ē) adv. **1.** Extremely; exceedingly. **2.** Truly. **3.** Precisely. — adj. **1.** Absolute; utter. **2.** Identical; selfsame. **3.** Mere. **4.** Actual.

**ves·sel** (vĕs′əl) n. **1.** A container. **2.** A ship. **3.** A bodily duct, canal, etc., for the flow of fluid.

**vest** (vĕst) n. A sleeveless garment worn over a shirt. — v. **1.** To dress, esp. in ecclesiastical robes. **2.** To place (authority, power, etc.) in the control of.

**ves·ti·bule** (vĕs′tə-byōōl′) n. An entrance hall; lobby. — **ves·tib′u·lar** adj.

**ves·tige** (vĕs′tĭj) n. A remaining trace, sign, or part. — **ves·tig′i·al** adj.

**vest·ment** (vĕst′mənt) n. A garment, esp. a robe, gown, etc., worn by a clergyman.

**vet·er·an** (vĕt′ər-ən, vĕt′rən) n. A person of long experience in an activity, esp. a former member of the armed forces. — **vet′er·an** adj.

**vet·er·i·nar·i·an** (vĕt′ər-ə-nâr′ē-ən, vĕt′rə-) n. A doctor qualified to treat animals. — **vet′er·i·nar′y** adj. & n.

**ve·to** (vē′tō) n., pl. **-toes. 1.** The power or right, esp. of a chief executive, to reject a bill passed by a legislature. **2.** A prohibition or rejection. — ve·to v.

**vex** (vĕks) v. To irritate or annoy. — **vex·a′tion** n. — **vex·a′tious** adj.

**vi·a·ble** (vī′ə-bəl) adj. Capable of living or developing. — **vi·a·bil′i·ty** n.

**vi·brant** (vī′brənt) adj. **1.** Of vibration; vibrating. **2.** Energetic or active. — **vi′bran·cy** n. — **vi′brant·ly** adv.

**vi·brate** (vī′brāt′) v. **-brated, -brating. 1.** To move or cause to move back and forth rapidly. **2.** To produce a sound; resonate. — **vi·bra′tion** n. — **vi′bra·to·ry** adj.

**vic·ar** (vĭk′ər) n. **1.** A clergyman in charge of a parish. **2.** A substitute or deputy. — **vic′ar·age** n.

**vi·car·i·ous** (vī-kâr′ē-əs, vĭ-) adj. **1.** Endured or done by one person substituting for another. **2.** Felt or undergone as if taking part in the experience or feelings of another. — **vi·car′i·ous·ly** adv. — **vi·car′i·ous·ness** n.

**vice**[1] (vīs) n. **1.** An immoral practice or habit. **2.** Corruption.

**vice**[2] (vīs) adj. Substituting for; deputy.

**vi·cin·i·ty** (vĭ-sĭn′ə-tē) n., pl. **-ties.** A nearby region or place.

**vi·cious** (vĭsh′əs) adj. **1.** Cruel; mean; malicious. **2.** Marked by evil or vice; wicked. **3.** Savage and dangerous. — **vi′cious·ly** adv. — **vi′cious·ness** n.

**vi·cis·si·tude** (vĭ-sĭs′ə-t / y / ōōd′) n. **1.** Changeability. **2.** vicissitudes. A sudden or unexpected change in a person's life.

**vic·tim** (vĭk′tĭm) n. **1.** A living creature sacrificed to a deity. **2.** One harmed or killed by accident, disease, etc. **3.** A person who is tricked, swindled, etc. — **vic′tim·ize** v. — **vic′tim·i·za′tion** n.

**vic·tor** (vĭk′tər) n. The winner in a war, contest, struggle, etc. — **vic·to′ri·ous** adj. — **vic′to·ry** n.

**vid·e·o** (vĭd′ē-ō′) adj. Of television. — n. **1.** The visual part of a televised broadcast. **2.** Television.

**vie** (vī) v. **vied, vying.** To contend or compete.

**view** (vyōō) n. **1.** An examination or inspection. **2.** The act of seeing something; sight. **3.** An opinion. **4.** Range of sight. **5.** A scene or vista. **6.** An aspect, as from a particular position or angle. **7.** An aim; intention. — v. **1.** To look at; see. **2.** To examine or inspect. **3.** To regard or consider. — **view′less** adj. — **view′point** n.

**vig·il** (vĭj′əl) n. A period of alert watchfulness, esp. at night.

**vig·i·lant** (vĭj′ə-lənt) adj. On the alert; watchful. — **vig′i·lance** n.

**vig·or** (vĭg′ər) n. **1.** Active physical or mental strength. **2.** Effectiveness or force. — **vig′or·ous** adj. — **vig′or·ous·ly** adv. — **vig′or·ous·ness** n.

**vile** (vīl) adj. **viler, vilest. 1.** Miserable; wretched. **2.** Morally low or base. **3.** Hateful. **4.** Unpleasant or objectionable. — **vile′ness** n.

**vil·i·fy** (vĭl′ə-fī′) v. **-fied, -fying.** To defame; denigrate. — **vil′i·fi·ca′tion** n.

**vil·lage** (vĭl′ĭj) n. **1.** A community smaller than a town. **2.** The inhabitants of a village. — **vil′lag·er** n.

**vil·lain** (vĭl′ən) n. An evil person; scoundrel. — **vil′lain·ous** adj. — **vil′lain·y** n.

**vin·di·cate** (vĭn′dĭ-kāt′) v. **-cated, -cating. 1.** To clear of accusation, blame, etc. **2.** To justify. — **vin′di·ca′tion** n. — **vin′di·ca′tor** n.

**vin·dic·tive** (vĭn-dĭk′tĭv) adj. Showing a desire for revenge; vengeful. — **vin·dic′tive·ly** adv. — **vin·dic′tive·ness** n.

**vine** (vīn) n. A plant whose stem is supported by climbing, twining, or creeping.

**vin·e·gar** (vĭn′ĭ-gər) n. An acid liquid obtained by fermentation, used as a flavoring and preservative.

**vine·yard** (vĭn′yərd) n. Ground planted with cultivated grapevines.

**vi·nyl** (vī′nəl) n. A tough, flexible plastic.

**vi·o·la** (vē-ō′lə, vī-) n. A musical instrument of the violin family. — **vi·o′list** n.

**vi·o·late** (vī′ə-lāt′) v. **-lated, -lating. 1.** To break (a law or regulation); disregard. **2.** To profane; desecrate. **3.** To rape. — **vi′o·la′tion** n. — **vi′o·la′tor** n.

**vi·o·lent** (vī′ə-lənt) adj. **1.** Displaying great physical force or rough action. **2.** Showing great emotional force. **3.** Severe; harsh. — **vi′o·lence** n. — **vi′o·lent·ly** adv.

**vi·o·let** (vī′ə-lĭt) n. **1.** A plant with usually purplish-blue flowers. **2.** A bluish purple. — **vi′o·let** adj.

**vi·o·lin** (vī′ə-lĭn′) n. A stringed instrument played with a bow. — **vi′o·lin′ist** n.

**vir·gin** (vûr′jĭn) n. One who has not experienced sexual intercourse. — adj. **1.** Chaste. **2.** In a pure or natural state. — **vir′gin·al** adj. — **vir·gin′i·ty** n.

**vir·ile** (vĭr′əl) adj. **1.** Having masculine strength and vigor. **2.** Of male sexual functions. — **vi·ril′i·ty** n.

**vir·tu·al** (vûr′chōō-əl) adj. Existing in effect though not in actual fact. — **vir′tu·al·ly** adv.

**vir·tue** (vûr′chōō) n. **1.** Moral excellence and righteousness. **2.** Chastity. **3.** A beneficial quality. — **vir′tu·ous** adj. — **vir′tu·ous·ly** adv. — **vir′tu·ous·ness** n.

**vir·tu·o·so** (vûr′chōō-ō′sō) n., pl. **-sos** or **-si.** A person with masterly skill or technique, esp. in music. — **vir′tu·os′i·ty** n.

**vir·u·lent** (vĭr′y/ə-lənt) adj. **1.** Extremely poisonous or harmful, as a disease. **2.** Bitterly hostile. — **vir′u·lence** n. — **vir′u·lent·ly** adv.

**vi·rus** (vī′rəs) n. A submicroscopic disease-causing agent. — **vi′ral** adj.

**vi·sa** (vē′zə) n. An authorization stamped on a passport, permitting travel within a country or region.

**vis·cid** (vĭs′ĭd) adj. Thick and sticky; resembling glue. — **vis·cos′i·ty, vis′cous·ness** n. — **vis′cous** adj.

**vise** (vīs) n. Also **vice.** A clamping device used to hold work in position, as in carpentry.

**vis·i·ble** (vĭz′ə-bəl) adj. **1.** Capable of being seen. **2.** Apparent. — **vis′i·bil′i·ty** n. — **vis′i·bly** adv.

**vi·sion** (vĭzh′ən) n. **1.** The sense of sight. **2.** Unusual or supernatural perception. **3.** A mental image produced by the imagination.

**vi·sion·ar·y** (vĭzh′ən-ĕr′ē) adj. **1.** Of vision or the nature of a vision. **2.** Not practicable. — n., pl. **-ies. 1.** One who has visions. **2.** One who has impractical ideas.

**vis·it** (vĭz′ĭt) v. **1.** To go to see for business, pleasure, etc. **2.** To afflict; assail. — n. **1.** An act of visiting. **2.** A stay or call as a guest. — **vis′i·tor** n.

**vi·sor** (vī′zər) n. **1.** A piece on the front of a cap that shades the eyes. **2.** The movable front part of a helmet.

**vis·u·al** (vĭzh′ōō-əl) adj. **1.** Of the sense of sight. **2.** Capable of being seen; visible. — **vis′u·al·ly** adv.

**vis·u·al·ize** (vĭzh′ōō-ə-līz′) v. **-ized, -izing.** To form a mental image of. — **vis′u·al·i·za′tion** n.

**vi·tal** (vī′tal, vĭt′l) adj. **1.** Of life. **2.** Necessary for life. **3.** Having great importance; essential. — **vi′tal·ly** adv.

**vi·tal·i·ty** (vī-tăl′ĭ-tē) n., pl. **-ties. 1.** The capacity to grow; living force. **2.** Vigor; energy.

**vi·ta·min** (vī′tə-mən) n. Any organic substance found in plants and animals, essential for life maintenance and growth.

**vit·re·ous** (vĭt′rē-əs) adj. Of glass; glassy.

**vi·tu·per·ate** (vī-t/y/ōō′pə-rāt′, vĭ-) v. **-ated, -ating.** To revile or berate. — **vi·tu′per·a′tion** n. — **vi·tu′per·a′tive** adj.

**vi·va·cious** (vĭ-vā′shəs, vī-) adj. Animated; lively. — **vi·va′cious·ly** adv. — **vi·vac′i·ty** n.

**viv·id** (vĭv′ĭd) adj. **1.** Perceived as bright and distinct; brilliant. **2.** Full of the freshness of immediate experience. — **viv′id·ly** adv. — **viv′id·ness** n.

**viv·i·sect** (vĭv′ĭōōsĕkt′) v. To dissect a living animal, esp. for scientific investigation. — **viv′i·sec′tion** n.

**vo·cab·u·lar·y** (vō-kăb′yə-lĕr′ē) n., pl. **-ies.**

**1.** A list of words, usually arranged alphabetically. **2.** All the words of a language. **3.** The words used by a particular person, profession, etc.

**vo·cal** (vō′kəl) *adj.* **1.** Of or produced by the voice. **2.** Meant to be sung. **3.** Speaking freely; outspoken. — **vo′cal·ist** *n.* — **vo′cal·ize′** *v.* — **vo′cal·ly** *adv.*

**vo·ca·tion** (vō-kā′shən) *n.* A profession, trade, or occupation. — **vo·ca′tion·al** *adj.*

**vo·cif·er·ous** (vō-sĭf′ər-əs) *adj.* Making an outcry; clamorous. — **vo·cif·er·ous·ly** *adv.* — **vo·cif′er·ous·ness** *n.*

**vogue** (vōg) *n.* **1.** The current fashion, practice, etc. **2.** Popularity.

**voice** (vois) *n.* **1.** The sound produced by the vocal organs. **2.** This sound used in singing. **3.** A medium of expression. **4.** The right to express a choice or opinion. **5.** A verb form indicating the relation between the subject and the action the verb expresses. — *v.* **voiced, voicing.** To express or utter; give voice to. — **voice′less** *adj.*

**void** (void) *adj.* **1.** Empty. **2.** Having no legal force. **3.** Ineffective; useless. — *n.* **1.** An empty space. **2.** A feeling of emptiness, loneliness, or loss. — *v.* **1.** To invalidate or annul. **2.** To empty.

**vol·a·tile** (vŏl′ə-tĭl) *adj.* **1.** Changing to vapor readily at normal temperature. **2.** Changeable, esp. fickle or explosive. — **vol′a·til′i·ty** *n.*

**vol·ca·no** (vŏl-kā′nō) *n., pl.* **-noes** or **-nos.** **1.** A vent in the earth through which molten lava and hot gases are thrown forth. **2.** A mountain formed by the material thrown forth. — **vol·can′ic** *adj.*

**vo·li·tion** (və-lĭsh′ən) *n.* The power of choosing; the will. — **vo·li′tion·al** *adj.*

**vol·ley** (vŏl′ē) *n., pl.* **-leys.** The simultaneous discharge of a number of missiles. — **vol′ley** *v.*

**volt** (vōlt) *n.* A unit of electronic potential or electromotive force. — **volt′age** *n.*

**vol·u·ble** (vŏl′yə-bəl) *adj.* Talking easily; fluent; glib. — **vol·u·bil′i·ty** *n.* — **vol′u·bly** *adv.*

**vol·ume** (vŏl′yōōm, -yəm) *n.* **1.** A book. **2.** One book of a set. **3.** The measure or size of a three-dimensional object. **4.** Quantity; amount. **5.** The loudness of a sound. — **vo·lu′mi·nous** *adj.* — **vo·lu′mi·nous·ly** *adv.*

**vol·un·tar·y** (vŏl′ən-tĕr′ē) *adj.* **1.** Arising from an act of choice. **2.** Acting by choice or guarantee of reward. — **vol′un·tar′i·ly** *adv.*

**vol·un·teer** (vŏl′ən-tîr′) *n.* **1.** One who performs or gives services of his own free will. **2.** A person who enlists in the armed forces. — *v.* To give or offer of one's own accord.

**vo·lup·tu·ous** (və-lŭp′chōō-əs) *adj.* **1.** Of sensual pleasures. **2.** Full in form. — **vo·lup′tu·ous·ly** *adv.* — **vo·lup′tu·ous·ness** *n.*

**vom·it** (vŏm′ĭt) *v.* To eject (the contents of the stomach) through the mouth. — *n.* Matter ejected from the stomach.

**vo·ra·cious** (vô-rā′shəs, vō-, və-) *adj.* **1.** Greedy for food; ravenous. **2.** Too eager; avid. — **vo·rac′i·ty, vo·ra′cious·ness** *n.*

**vor·tex** (vôr′tĕks′) *n.* A flow of fluid that rotates around an axis.

**vote** (vōt) *n.* **1.** A formal expression of preference for a candidate or a proposed resolution. **2.** The result of an election, referendum, etc. **3.** Suffrage. — *v.* **voted, voting.** To express preference by a vote. — **vot′er** *n.*

**vouch** (vouch) *v.* **1.** To supply assurance; verify. **2.** To give or serve as a guarantee. — **vouch′er** *n.*

**vow** (vou) *n.* A solemn pledge. — *v.* To promise or pledge solemnly.

**vow·el** (vou′əl) *n.* **1.** A speech sound made by the relatively free passage of breath through the larynx and mouth. **2.** A letter that represents such a sound.

**voy·age** (voi′ĭj) *n.* A long journey to a distant place. — *v.* **-aged, -aging.** To travel. — **voy′ag·er** *n.*

**vul·gar** (vŭl′gər) *adj.* **1.** Ill-bred. **2.** Obscene; offensive. **3.** Of the common people. — **vul′gar·i·ty** *n.* — **vul′gar·ly** *adv.*

**vul·ner·a·ble** (vŭl′nər-ə-bəl) *adj.* **1.** Capable of being harmed or injured. **2.** Easily affected or hurt. — **vul′ner·a·bil′i·ty** *n.*

# W

**w, W** (dŭb′əl-yōō, -yōō) *n.* The 23rd letter of the English alphabet.

**wad** (wŏd) *n.* **1.** A small soft mass. **2.** A compressed ball. — *v.* **wadded, wadding.** To pad or stuff. — **wad′ding** *n.*

**wad·dle** (wŏd′l) *v.* **-dled, -dling.** To walk with a swaying motion. — *n.* A waddling gait. — **wad′dler** *n.*

**wade** (wād) *v.* **waded, wading.** **1.** To walk through water. **2.** To make one's way arduously.

**wa·fer** (wā′fər) *n.* A thin, crisp biscuit.

**waf·fle** (wŏf′əl) *n.* A batter cake baked in a

2-sided griddle.

**waft** (wăft; wäft) *v.* To carry gently through the air. —*n.* **1.** An odor or whiff. **2.** A light breeze.

**wag** (wăg) *v.* **wagged, wagging.** To move repeatedly to and fro. —*n.* **wag** *n.*

**wage** (wāj) *n.* Pay; salary. —*v.* **waged, waging.** To carry on (a war or campaign).

**wa·ger** (wā'jər) *n.* A bet. —*v.* To bet.

**wag·on** (wăg'ən) *n.* **1.** A 4-wheeled vehicle with a large rectangular body. **2.** A child's low 4-wheeled carriage.

**waif** (wāf) *n.* A homeless child.

**wail** (wāl) *v.* **1.** To grieve audibly; to lament. **2.** To make a high-pitched mournful sound. —**wail** *n.*

**waist** (wāst) *n.* **1.** The part of the body between the ribs and the pelvis. **2.** A middle part of a garment. —**waist'line** *n.*

**wait** (wāt) *v.* **1.** To remain in anticipation. **2.** To delay. **3.** To serve or attend, as a clerk or waitress. —*n.* The act of or time spent waiting.

**wait·er** (wā'tər) *n.* A man who waits on table. —**wait'ress** *fem.n.*

**waive** (wāv) *v.* **waived, waiving.** To relinquish voluntarily. —**waiv'er** *n.*

**wake¹** (wāk) *v.* **woke** or **waked, waking. 1.** To awaken or rouse from sleep. **2.** To stir up. —*n.* A vigil beside a corpse. —**wak'en** *n.*

**wake²** (wāk) *n.* The track left in water by a moving boat.

**walk** (wôk) *v.* To go or cause to go on foot. —*n.* **1.** The act of walking. **2.** A slow gait. **3.** A sidewalk, path, etc. —**walk'er** *n.*

**wall** (wôl) *n.* **1.** A vertical structure forming an inner partition or exterior siding of a building. **2.** Something resembling a wall. —*v.* To enclose, divide, or fortify with or as if with a wall.

**wal·let** (wŏl'ĭt) *n.* A small, flat case for paper money, cards, etc.

**wal·lop** (wŏl'əp) *v.* To beat soundly; thrash. —*n.* A severe blow.

**wal·low** (wŏl'ō) *v.* **1.** To roll about in water, mud, etc. **2.** To luxuriate.

**wal·nut** (wôl'nŭt', -nət) *n.* **1.** An edible nut with a hard shell. **2.** A tree bearing such nuts. **3.** The hard, dark wood of this tree.

**wal·rus** (wôl'rəs, wŏl'-) *n., pl. -ruses* or *-rus.* A large, tusked Arctic marine mammal.

**waltz** (wôlts) *n.* A dance in triple time. —*v.* To dance a waltz. —**waltz'er** *n.*

**wan** (wŏn) *adj.* Pale; sickly. —**wan'ly** *adv.*

**wan·der** (wŏn'dər) *v.* **1.** To roam aimlessly. **2.** To go astray. **3.** To think or express

oneself incoherently. —**wan'der·er** *n.*

**wane** (wān) *v.* **waned, waning.** To decrease gradually. —*n.* A decline or dwindling.

**want** (wŏnt, wônt) *v.* **1.** To lack. **2.** To desire. **3.** To need or require. —*n.* **1.** Poverty. **2.** A need or desire. —**want'ing** *adj.*

**wan·ton** (wŏn'tən) *adj.* **1.** Lewd. **2.** Maliciously cruel. **3.** Freely extravagant; capricious. —**wan'ton·ly** *adv.* —**wan'ton·ness** *n.*

**war** (wôr) *n.* **1.** Armed conflict. **2.** Active antagonism or hostility. —*v.* **warred, warring.** To wage war. —**war'fare** *n.*

**war·ble** (wôr'bəl) *v.* **-bled, -bling.** To sing with trills, as a bird. —**war'ble** *n.*

**ward** (wôrd) *n.* **1.** An administrative division of a city. **2.** A division in a hospital, prison, etc. **3.** In law, a person placed under the care of a guardian or court. —*v.* To turn aside; repel.

**war·den** (wôrd'n) *n.* **1.** The administrative official of a prison. **2.** An official who enforces certain laws and regulations.

**ward·robe** (wôrd'rōb') *n.* **1.** A clothes cabinet or closet. **2.** Garments collectively, as of one person.

**wares** (wârz) *pl.n.* Goods for sale.

**warm** (wôrm) *adj.* **1.** Moderately hot. **2.** Preserving or imparting heat. **3.** Having a sensation of bodily heat, as from exercise. **4.** Enthusiastic. **5.** Cordial. **6.** Loving. —*v.* To make or become warm. —**warm'ly** *adv.* —**warmth** *n.*

**warn** (wôrn) *v.* **1.** To make aware of potential danger. **2.** To admonish. —**warn'ing** *n. & adj.*

**warp** (wôrp) *v.* **1.** To twist or become twisted out of shape. **2.** To corrupt. —*n.* A distortion or twist.

**war·rant** (wôr'ənt, wŏr'-) *n.* **1.** Authorization or certification. **2.** Justification for an action. **3.** A writ, esp. a judicial writ, authorizing something. —*v.* **1.** To guarantee. **2.** To deserve. **3.** To authorize.

**war·ran·ty** (wôr'ən-tē, wŏr'-) *n., pl. -ties.* **1.** An official authorization. **2.** A guarantee.

**wart** (wôrt) *n.* A small, hard growth on the skin. —**wart'y** *adj.*

**war·y** (wâr'ē) *adj.* **-ier, -iest.** Cautious; watchful. —**war'i·ly** *adv.* —**war'i·ness** *n.*

**was** (wŏz, wŭz; *unstressed* wəz). 1st and 3rd person sing. past indicative of **be.**

**wash** (wŏsh, wôsh) *v.* **1.** To cleanse using water or other liquid and usually soap. **2.** To flow over or past. **3.** To carry away or erode. —*n.* **1.** The act of cleansing. **2.** Articles to be washed. **3.** A light hue. **4.** The surge of water

**weight**

or waves. — **wash'a·ble** adj. — **wash'ing** n.

**wash·er** (wŏsh'ər, wôsh'-) n. **1.** A small perforated disk of metal or rubber placed beneath a nut to relieve friction, etc. **2.** A machine for washing.

**was·n't** (wŏz'ənt, wŭz'-) Contraction of *was not.*

**wasp** (wŏsp, wôsp) n. A stinging insect.

**waste** (wāst) v. **wasted, wasting. 1.** To use carelessly; squander. **2.** To become weak. **3.** To fail to take advantage of. —n. **1.** An unnecessary expenditure. **2.** Destruction. **3.** A useless by-product or remainder. —adj. Worthless or useless. — **waste'ful** adj. — **waste'ful·ly** adv. — **waste'ful·ness** n.

**watch** (wŏch) v. **1.** To observe carefully. **2.** To guard or tend. —n. **1.** Careful, continuous observation. **2.** A period of observation or guard duty. **3.** A guard or watchman. **4.** A small timepiece. **5.** A period of duty on a ship. — **watch'ful** adj. — **watch'man** n.

**wa·ter** (wô'tər, wŏt'ər) n. **1.** A clear, tasteless liquid essential for life. **2.** Any form of water, as rain. **3.** Any body of water. —v. **1.** To pour water upon. **2.** To supply with drinking water. **3.** To dilute. **4.** To discharge fluid. — **wa'ter·fall** n. — **wa'ter·y** adj.

**watt** (wŏt) n. A unit of electric power. — **watt'age** n.

**wave** (wāv) v. **waved, waving. 1.** To move or cause to move back and forth in the air. **2.** To signal by waving the hand. **3.** To curve. —n. **1.** A ridge on the surface of water. **2.** A curve or curl. **3.** A back and forth movement. **4.** A surge. — **wav'y** adj.

**wa·ver** (wā'vər) v. **1.** To sway. **2.** To hesitate. **3.** To fluctuate.

**wax** (wăks) n. **1.** A natural, semisolid, heat-sensitive substance, as beeswax. **2.** A substance found in the ears. —v. To coat with wax. — **wax'en, wax'y** adj.

**way** (wā) n. **1.** A road or path. **2.** A course of action. **3.** A method. **4.** A mode of living. **5.** A distance. **6.** A direction. —adv. **1.** Far. **2.** Away.

**way·ward** (wā'wərd) adj. **1.** Willful. **2.** Erratic. — **way'ward·ly** adv. — **way'ward·ness** n.

**we** (wē) pron. The 1st person pl. pronoun in the nominative case.

**weak** (wēk) adj. **1.** Lacking strength; frail. **2.** Lacking strength of character. **3.** Unsound; deficient. — **weak'en** v. — **weak'ly** adj. & adv. — **weak'ness** n.

**wealth** (wĕlth) n. **1.** A great quantity of possessions or resources. **2.** A profusion.

— **wealth'y** adj.

**weap·on** (wĕp'ən) n. An instrument used in combat. — **weap'on·ry** n.

**wear** (wâr) v. **wore, worn, wearing. 1.** To be clothed in. **2.** To bear. **3.** To impair by use. **4.** To fatigue. —n. **1.** The act of wearing; use. **2.** Clothing. **3.** Gradual impairment or diminution. — **wear'er** n.

**wea·ry** (wîr'ē) adj. **-rier, -riest. 1.** Tired. **2.** Bored or resigned. —v. **-ried, -rying.** To make or become weary. — **wea'ri·ly** adv. — **wea'ri·ness** n. — **wea'ri·some** adj.

**wea·sel** (wē'zəl) n. A small carnivorous mammal. —v. To be evasive.

**weath·er** (wĕth'ər) n. Atmospheric conditions as temperature, moisture, etc. —v. **1.** To expose to or show the effects of weather. **2.** To pass through safely; survive.

**weave** (wēv) v. **wove, woven, weaving. 1.** To interlace threads into cloth. **2.** To construct by interlacing. **3.** To wind or curve in and out. —n. The pattern or method of weaving. — **weav'er** n.

**web** (wĕb) n. **1.** A woven fabric. **2.** A latticed structure. **3.** A threadlike structure spun by spiders. **4.** A complex network. **5.** A membranous tissue between the toes of ducks, frogs, etc. — **webbed** adj.

**wed** (wĕd) v. **wedded, wed** or **wedded, wedding. 1.** To marry. **2.** To unite. — **wed'ding** n. — **wed'lock** n.

**we'd** (wēd). Contraction of *we had, we should,* and *we would.*

**wedge** (wĕj) n. **1.** A V-shaped piece of metal or wood for splitting, securing, etc. **2.** Anything shaped like a wedge. —v. **wedged, wedging. 1.** To split or fix in place with a wedge. **2.** To crowd into a limited space.

**Wednes·day** (wĕnz'dē, -dā') n. The 4th day of the week.

**weed** (wēd) n. A troublesome or useless plant. —v. **1.** To remove weeds from. **2.** To eliminate as unsuitable. — **weed'er** n. — **weed'y** adj.

**week** (wēk) n. A period of seven days. — **week'day** n. — **week'end** n. — **week'ly** adv., adj. & n.

**weep** (wēp) v. **wept, weeping. 1.** To mourn (with *for*). **2.** To shed (tears). — **weep'er** n. — **weep'ing** n.

**weigh** (wā) v. **1.** To measure the weight of. **2.** To consider or ponder. **3.** To burden (with *down*). **4.** To have a specific weight. **5.** To be important. — **weigh'er** n.

**weight** (wāt) n. **1.** A measure of the heaviness or mass of an object. **2.** A system of unit measures of heaviness or mass. **3.** Burden; oppressiveness. **4.** Preponderance. **5.** Influence; importance. —*v.* To add heaviness to. —**weight′y** *adj.*

**weird** (wîrd) *adj.* Strange; uncanny. —**weird′ness** *n.*

**wel·come** (wĕl′kəm) *adj.* **1.** Received with hospitality. **2.** Gratifying. **3.** Permitted to do or enjoy. —*n.* A cordial reception. —*v.* **-comed, -coming. 1.** To greet cordially. **2.** To accept gladly.

**weld** (wĕld) *v.* To join (metals) by heat and pressure. —**weld′er** *n.*

**wel·fare** (wĕl′fâr′) *n.* **1.** Well-being. **2.** Public relief.

**well¹** (wĕl) *n.* **1.** A deep hole dug to obtain water, oil, etc. **2.** A vertical opening through floors, as for stairs. **3.** A source to be drawn upon. —*v.* To rise or surge.

**well²** (wĕl) *adv.* **better, best. 1.** Satisfactorily. **2.** With skill. **3.** Properly. **4.** Favorably. **5.** Thoroughly. —*adj.* **1.** Satisfactory. **2.** In good health. **3.** Fortunate; good. —*interj.* Expressive of surprise.

**we'll** (wĕl) Contraction of *we will* and *we shall.*

**welt** (wĕlt) *n.* **1.** A strip stitched into a shoe between the sole and upper. **2.** A decorative or supporting cord sewn into a seam. **3.** A bump on the skin from a blow or allergy.

**wend** (wĕnd) *v.* To proceed along.

**went** (wĕnt). *p.t.* of **go.**

**wept** (wĕpt). *p.t.* & *p.p.* of **weep.**

**were** (wûr). **1.** Pl. & 2nd person sing. of the past indicative of **be. 2.** Past subjunctive of **be.**

**we're** (wîr). Contraction of *we are.*

**wer·en't** (wûrnt, wûr′ənt). Contraction of *were not.*

**west** (wĕst) *n.* **1.** The direction opposite that of the earth's rotation. **2.** Often **West.** The W part of any country or region. **3. West.** Europe and the W Hemisphere; the Occident. —*adj.* & *adv.* To, from, or in the west. —**west′er·ly** *adj.* & *adv.* —**west′ern, West′ern** *adj.* —**west′ern·er, West′ern·er** *n.* —**west′ward** *adv.* & *adj.*

**wet** (wĕt) *adj.* **wetter, wettest. 1.** Covered or saturated with a liquid. **2.** Not yet dry. **3.** Rainy. —*n.* **1.** Moisture. **2.** Rainy weather. —*v.* **wetted, wetting.** To make or become wet.

**we've** (wēv). Contraction of *we have.*

**whale** (hwāl) *n.* A large fishlike marine mammal. —*v.* **whaled, whaling.** To hunt whales.

**wharf** (hwôrf) *n., pl.* **wharves** or **wharfs.** A

place for loading or mooring vessels.

**what** (hwŏt, hwŭt; *unstressed* hwət) *pron.* **1.** Which thing or one. **2.** That which. —*adj.* **1.** Which one. **2.** Whatever. **3.** How great. —*adv.* **1.** How. **2.** Why (with *for*). —**what·ev′er** *pron. & adj.*

**wheat** (hwēt) *n.* The grain of a cereal plant, ground for flour.

**wheel** (hwēl) *n.* A solid disk or spoked ring that turns around a center axle. —*v.* **1.** To move on wheels. **2.** To turn around.

**wheeze** (hwēz) *v.* **wheezed, wheezing.** To breathe with a hoarse whistling sound. —*n.* A wheezing breath. —**wheez′y** *adj.*

**whelp** (hwĕlp) *n.* A young offspring of a dog, wolf, etc. —*v.* To bear whelps.

**when** (hwĕn) *adv.* At what time. —*conj.* **1.** At the time that. **2.** Since. —**when·ev′er** *adv. & conj.*

**whence** (hwĕns) *adv.* From where. —*conj.* From which.

**where** (hwâr) *adv.* **1.** To, at, or in what place. **2.** In what situation. —*conj.* **1.** At what or which place. **2.** In or to a place in which. **3.** Wherever. —*pron.* Which place. —*n.* The place or occasion.

**where·as** (hwâr-ăz′) *conj.* **1.** Inasmuch as. **2.** While on the contrary.

**whet** (hwĕt) *v.* **whetted, whetting. 1.** To sharpen; hone. **2.** To stimulate. —**whet′stone** *n.*

**wheth·er** (hwĕth′ər) *conj.* **1.** If it is so that. **2.** In case. **3.** Either.

**which** (hwĭch) *pron.* **1.** What one. **2.** The particular one. **3.** Whichever. —*adj.* **1.** What particular one. **2.** Whichever. —**which·ev′er** *pron. & adj.*

**whiff** (hwĭf) *n.* **1.** A slight gust. **2.** A breath of air, smoke, etc. —*v.* **1.** To be carried in gusts. **2.** To breathe in. **3.** To sniff.

**while** (hwīl) *n.* A period of time. —*conj.* **1.** As long as. **2.** Whereas. —*v.* **whiled, whiling.** To spend (time) pleasantly.

**whim** (hwĭm) *n.* **1.** A capricious idea. **2.** An impulse.

**whim·per** (hwĭm′pər) *v.* To cry or sob softly. —*n.* A whine.

**whim·si·cal** (hwĭm′zĭ-kəl) *adj.* Capricious; playful. —**whim′si·cal·ly** *adv.*

**whine** (hwīn) *v.* **whined, whining. 1.** To complain in an annoying fashion. **2.** To produce a sustained high-pitched noise. —**whine** *n.* —**whin′y** *adj.*

**whip** (hwĭp) *v.* **whipped, whipping. 1.** To strike with repeated strokes; flog. **2.** To move quickly. **3.** To beat (cream or eggs).

4. To defeat. —*n.* 1. A flexible instrument for whipping. 2. A legislator charged by his party with insuring attendance. — **whip'per** *n.*

**whir** (hwûr) *v.* **whirred, whirring.** To move with a buzzing sound. —*n.* A buzzing sound.

**whirl** (hwûrl) *v.* 1. To revolve or spin rapidly. 2. To move rapidly. —*n.* 1. A spinning motion. 2. Confusion; tumult.

**whisk** (hwĭsk) *v.* 1. To move or cause to move with quick, sweeping motions. 2. To whip (eggs or cream). —*n.* 1. A small broom. 2. A kitchen utensil for whipping.

**whisk·er** (hwĭs'kər) *n.* 1. **whiskers.** A man's facial hair. 2. A bristle near the mouth of certain animals.

**whis·key** (hwĭs'kē) *n., pl.* **-keys.** Also **whis·ky** *pl.* **-kies.** An alcoholic liquor distilled from grain.

**whis·per** (hwĭs'pər) *v.* 1. To speak softly. 2. To tell secretly. —*n.* 1. Soft speech. 2. A soft, rustling sound.

**whis·tle** (hwĭs'əl) *v.* **-tled, -tling.** To make a high-pitched, often musical sound by forcing air through pursed lips or a device. 1. A device for making whistling sounds. 2. A whistling sound. — **whis'tler** *n.*

**white** (hwīt) *n.* 1. The color of snow. 2. The white part of something, as the albumen of an egg. —*adj.* **whiter, whitest.** 1. Of the color white. 2. Pale. 3. Having light skin. — **whit·en** *v.* — **white'ness** *n.* — **whit'ish** *adj.*

**whith·er** (hwĭth'ər) *adv.* 1. To what place. 2. To whatever place.

**whit·tle** (hwĭt'l) *v.* **-tled, -tling.** 1. To cut or pare shavings from (wood). 2. To reduce gradually. — **whit'tler** *n.*

**who** (hōō) *pron.* 1. What or which person. 2. The person that. — **who·ev'er** *pron.*

**whole** (hōl) *adj.* 1. Complete. 2. Not divided; intact. 3. In mathematics, integral; not fractional. —*n.* 1. All the parts of a thing. 2. A complete entity. — **whole'ness** *n.* — **whol'ly** *adv.*

**whole·sale** (hōl'sāl') *n.* The sale of goods in quantity, as for resale. —*adj.* 1. Of or engaged in the sale of goods at wholesale. 2. Extensive and indiscriminate. — **whole'sal·er** *n.*

**whole·some** (hōl'səm) *adj.* Healthy. — **whole'some·ly** *adv.* — **whole'some·ness** *n.*

**whom** (hōōm). The objective case of **who.** — **whom·ev'er** *pron.*

**whose** (hōōz). The possessive form of **who.**

**why** (hwī) *adv.* 1. For what reason. 2. Because of which. —*n.* The cause or intention.

**wick** (wĭk) *n.* A cord of fibers, as in a candle, that draws up fuel to the flame.

**wick·ed** (wĭk'ĭd) *adj.* 1. Vicious; depraved. 2. Harmful. — **wick'ed·ly** *adv.* — **wick'ed·ness** *n.*

**wide** (wīd) *adj.* **wider, widest.** 1. Extensive; broad. 2. Of great scope. 3. Fully open. 4. Landing away from a desired goal. —*adv.* 1. Extensively. 2. Completely. — **wide'ly** *adv.* — **wid'en** *v.* — **wide'ness** *n.*

**wid·ow** (wĭd'ō) *n.* A woman whose husband has died. — **wid'ow·er** *masc.n.*

**width** (wĭdth, wĭth) *n.* The measurement of something from side to side; breadth.

**wield** (wēld) *v.* 1. To handle (a weapon, etc.). 2. To exercise (power).

**wife** (wīf) *n., pl.* **wives.** A married woman. — **wife'ly** *adj.*

**wig** (wĭg) *n.* A hairpiece.

**wig·gle** (wĭg'əl) *v.* **-gled, -gling.** To move or cause to move quickly from side to side.

**wild** (wīld) *adj.* 1. Not domesticated or cultivated. 2. Reckless. 3. Disordered. 4. Violent. 5. Demented. —*n.* An uninhabited or uncultivated region. — **wild, wild'ly** *adv.* — **wild'ness** *n.*

**wil·der·ness** (wĭl'dər·nĭs) *n.* A wild or desolate region.

**wile** (wīl) *n.* A cunning or seductive manner or stratagem.

**will**[1] (wĭl) *n.* 1. The mental faculty of deciding upon a course of action; volition. 2. An intention or wish. 3. Attitude toward others. 4. Determination. 5. A declaration specifying the disposition of one's possessions after death. —*v.* 1. To decide upon. 2. To bequeath.

**will**[2] (wĭl) *v.* —Used to indicate (often with future reference) willingness, intention, etc. 2. To wish. — **will'ing** *adj.* — **will'ing·ly** *adv.* — **will'ing·ness** *n.*

**will·ful** (wĭl'fəl) *adj.* Also **wil·ful.** 1. Deliberate. 2. Obstinate. — **will'ful·ly** *adv.* — **will'ful·ness** *n.*

**wilt** (wĭlt) *v.* To make or become limp.

**wi·ly** (wī'lē) *adj.* **-lier, -liest.** Guileful; calculating. — **wi'li·ness** *n.*

**win** (wĭn) *v.* **won, winning.** 1. To achieve victory. 2. To receive as a prize. 3. To gain the support of. —*n.* A victory. — **win'ner** *n.*

**wince** (wĭns) *v.* **winced, wincing.** To shrink, as in pain. —*n.* A wincing movement.

**wind**[1] (wĭnd) *n.* 1. Moving air. 2. Respiration; breath. —*v.* To cause to be out of breath. — **wind'y** *adj.*

**wind**[2] (wīnd) *v.* **wound, winding.** 1. To wrap

(something) around an object. **2.** To turn repeatedly, as a crank.

**wind·fall** (wind'fôl') *n.* **1.** Something blown down. **2.** An unexpected piece of good fortune.

**wind·mill** (wind'mil') *n.* A mill that runs on wind.

**win·dow** (win'dō) *n.* A wall opening that admits light or air, usually framed and spanned with glass. — **win'dow·pane** *n.*

**wind·pipe** (wind'pīp') *n.* The trachea.

**wind·shield** (wind'shēld') *n.* A framed glass shield in the front of a vehicle.

**wine** (win) *n.* The fermented juice of grapes or other fruits.

**wing** (wing) *n.* **1.** An organ of flight, as of a bird, bat, etc. **2.** A winglike structure. **3.** A side projection of an airplane. **4.** An extension of a house, building, etc. —*v.* **1.** To fly. **2.** To wound superficially.

**wink** (wingk) *v.* **1.** To close and open (the eyelid) deliberately. **2.** To twinkle. —*n.* The act of winking.

**win·ning** (win'ing) *adj.* **1.** Successful; victorious. **2.** Charming. —*n.* **1.** The act of one that wins. **2.** winnings. Something won, esp. money.

**win·some** (win'səm) *adj.* Pleasant; charming. — **win'some·ly** *adv.* — **win'some·ness** *n.*

**win·ter** (win'tər) *n.* The coldest season of the year. —*adj.* Of, like, or occurring in winter. — **win'try, win'ter·y** *adj.*

**wipe** (wip) *v.* **wiped, wiping.** **1.** To rub, as with a cloth, in order to clean or dry. **2.** To remove by rubbing. — **wip'er** *n.*

**wire** (wir) *n.* **1.** A pliable metallic strand or rod. **2.** A telegram. Made of wire. —*v.* **wired, wiring.** **1.** To connect or provide with a wire. **2.** To send a telegram to.

**wir·y** (wir'ē) *adj.* **-ier, -iest.** **1.** Wirelike; kinky. **2.** Slender but tough.

**wis·dom** (wiz'dəm) *n.* **1.** Understanding and knowledge. **2.** Common sense; judgment.

**wise** (wiz) *adj.* **wiser, wisest.** **1.** Judicious. **2.** Prudent; sensible. **3.** Shrewd. **4.** Having knowledge or information. **5.** Arrogant. — **wise'ly** *adv.*

**wish** (wish) *n.* **1.** A desire. **2.** Something desired. —*v.* **1.** To desire; want. **2.** To express wishes for. — **wish'ful** *adj.* — **wish'ful·ly** *adv.*

**wisp** (wisp) *n.* **1.** A small bunch or tuft. **2.** A faint streak, as of smoke. — **wisp'y** *adj.*

**wist·ful** (wist'fəl) *adj.* Melancholy. — **wist'·ful·ly** *adv.* — **wist'ful·ness** *n.*

**wit** (wit) *n.* **1.** Understanding; resourceful-ness. **2.** The ability to express perceptions in an ingeniously humorous manner. **3.** One with this ability.

**witch** (wich) *n.* A person who practices sorcery. — **witch'craft** *n.*

**with** (with, with) *prep.* **1.** Accompanying. **2.** Next to. **3.** Possessed of. **4.** In support of. **5.** By the means of. **6.** And; plus. **7.** Against.

**with·draw** (with-drô', with-) *v.* **-drew, -drawn, -drawing.** **1.** To take back. **2.** To draw back; retreat. — **with·draw'al** *n.*

**with·drawn** (with-drôn', with-) *adj.* Shy.

**with·er** (with'ər) *v.* **1.** To dry up or shrivel. **2.** To fade; droop.

**with·hold** (with-hōld') *v.* **-held, -holding.** To refrain from giving or permitting.

**with·in** (with-in', with-) *adv.* **1.** Inside. **2.** Inwardly. —*prep.* **1.** Inside. **2.** Inside the fixed limits of.

**with·out** (with-out', with-) *adv.* Outside. —*prep.* **1.** Lacking. **2.** With none of.

**with·stand** (with-stănd', with-) *v.* **-stood, -standing.** To resist or endure.

**wit·ness** (wit'nis) *n.* **1.** One who has seen something. **2.** A sign. **3.** One called upon to testify before a court. —*v.* **1.** To see. **2.** To testify. **3.** To attest to by signing one's name.

**wit·ty** (wit'ē) *adj.* **-tier, -tiest.** Cleverly humorous. — **wit'ti·ly** *adv.* — **wit'ti·ness** *n.*

**wives** (wivz). *pl.* of **wife.**

**wiz·ard** (wiz'ərd) *n.* A magician. — **wiz'ard·ry** *n.*

**wiz·ened** (wiz'ənd) *adj.* Shriveled.

**wob·ble** (wŏb'əl) *v.* **-bled, -bling.** **1.** To move erratically from side to side. **2.** To vacillate. — **wob'ble** *n.* — **wob'bly** *adj.*

**woe** (wō) *n.* **1.** Deep sorrow. **2.** Misfortune. — **woe'ful** *adj.* — **woe'ful·ly** *adv.*

**woke** (wōk). *p.t.* of **wake.**

**wolf** (woolf) *n., pl.* **wolves.** A carnivorous mammal related to the dog. —*v.* To eat voraciously.

**wom·an** (woom'ən) *n., pl.* **women** (wim'in). A female human being. — **wom'an·hood** *n.* — **wom'an·li·ness** *n.* — **wom'an·ly** *adj.*

**womb** (woom) *n.* The uterus.

**won** (wŭn). *p.t.* & *p.p.* of **win.**

**won·der** (wŭn'dər) *n.* **1.** A marvel. **2.** Awe. **3.** Curiosity or doubt. —*v.* **1.** To feel awe or admiration. **2.** To be curious. — **won'der·ful** *adj.* — **won'drous** *adj.*

**wont** (wônt, wŏnt, wŭnt) *adj.* **1.** Accustomed. **2.** Apt or likely. —*n.* Usage or custom. — **wont'ed** *adj.*

**won't** (wōnt). Contraction of *will not.*

**woo** (woo) *v.* **1.** To seek the affection of, esp.

with hopes of marrying. **2.** To entreat.

**wood** (wŏŏd) *n.* **1.** The tough substance beneath the bark of trees. **2.** Such a substance used for building material or fuel. **3.** Often **woods.** A forest. —*adj.* Made of wood. —**wood'ed** *adj.* —**wood'y** *adj.*

**wood-cut** (wŏŏd'kŭt') *n.* A print made from an engraved piece of wood.

**wood-en** (wŏŏd'n) *adj.* **1.** Made of wood. **2.** Lifeless. **3.** Clumsy.

**wood-wind** (wŏŏd'wĭnd') *n.* Any of a group of musical wind instruments. —**wood'wind'** *adj.*

**wood-work** (wŏŏd'wûrk') *n.* Wooden interior fittings.

**wool** (wŏŏl) *n.* **1.** Dense, soft, curly hair, esp. of a sheep. **2.** A material or garment made of wool. **3.** A woollike substance. —**wool** *adj.* —**wool'en** *adj.* & *n.* —**wool'ly** *adj.*

**word** (wûrd) *n.* **1.** A combination of sounds or letters that symbolizes a meaning. **2.** A discourse or talk. **3.** A promise. **4.** News. **5. words.** A dispute. —*v.* To express in words.

**word-y** (wûr'dē) *adj.* **-ier, -iest.** Using more words than necessary. —**word'i-ly** *adv.* —**word'i-ness** *n.*

**wore** (wôr, wōr) *p.t.* of **wear.**

**work** (wûrk) *n.* **1.** Toil; labor. **2.** Employment. **3.** A duty or task. **4.** Something produced as a result of effort. **5. works** (takes sing. *v.*) A factory, plant, etc. **6. works.** Machinery. —*v.* **1.** To labor. **2.** To be employed. **3.** To operate. **4.** To prove successful. **5.** To change or move, esp. by repeated movement. **6.** To cause; bring about. **7.** To solve (an arithmetic problem). **8.** To make productive. **9.** To excite. —**work'a-ble** *adj.* —**work'er** *n.* —**work'man** *n.* —**work'man-like'** *adj.* —**work'man-ship'** *n.*

**world** (wûrld) *n.* **1.** The earth. **2.** The universe. **3.** Mankind. **4.** A particular part of the earth. **5.** A sphere, realm, or kingdom. **6.** A large amount.

**world-ly** (wûrld'lē) *adj.* **-lier, -liest. 1.** Secular. **2.** Sophisticated or cosmopolitan. —**world'li-ness** *n.*

**worm** (wûrm) *n.* **1.** An invertebrate with a long, flexible body. **2.** A contemptible person. **3. worms.** An intestinal infestation with worms. —*v.* **1.** To move with the crawling motion of a worm. **2.** To elicit deviously. **3.** To cure of intestinal worms. —**worm'y** *adj.*

**worn** (wôrn, wōrn) *p.p.* of **wear.**

**wor-ry** (wûr'ē) *v.* **-ried, -rying. 1.** To feel or cause to feel uneasy or troubled. **2.** To grasp and tug at repeatedly. —*n., pl.* **-ries. 1.**

Anxiety. **2.** A source of concern. —**wor'ri-er** *n.* —**wor'ri-some** *adj.*

**worse** (wûrs). **1.** *compar.* of **bad. 2.** *compar.* of **ill.** —*adj.* **1.** More inferior. **2.** More unfavorable. —*n.* Something that is worse. —*adv.* In a worse way. —**wors'en** *v.*

**wor-ship** (wûr'shĭp) *n.* **1.** The reverence accorded a deity. **2.** The prayers by which this is expressed. **3.** Ardent devotion. —*v.* **-shiped** or **-shipped, -shiping** or **-shipping. 1.** To honor as a deity. **2.** To love devotedly. **3.** To participate in religious worship. —**wor'ship-er** *n.* —**wor'ship-ful** *adj.*

**worst** (wûrst). **1.** *superl.* of **bad. 2.** *superl.* of **ill.** —*adj.* **1.** Most inferior. **2.** Most unfavorable. —*n.* Something that is worst. —*adv.* In the worst manner. —*v.* To defeat.

**worth** (wûrth) *n.* **1.** Value or importance. **2.** The material value of something. **3.** The quantity of something that can be purchased for a specific sum. —*adj.* **1.** Equal in value to. **2.** Deserving of. —**worth'less** *adj.* —**worth'less-ness** *n.* —**worth'while'** *adj.*

**wor-thy** (wûr'thē) *adj.* **-thier, -thiest. 1.** Having merit or value. **2.** Honorable. **3.** Deserving. —*n., pl.* **-thies.** A worthy person. —**wor'thi-ly** *adv.* —**wor'thi-ness** *n.*

**would** (wŏŏd) *p.t.* of **will.**

**would-n't** (wŏŏd'ənt). Contraction of *would not.*

**wound**[1] (wŏŏnd) *n.* An injury, esp. a cut. —*v.* To inflict a wound upon.

**wound**[2] (wound) *p.t.* & *p.p.* of **wind**[2].

**wove** (wōv) *p.t.* of **weave.**

**wo-ven** (wō'vən) *p.p.* of **weave.**

**wrack** (răk) *n.* Damage or destruction.

**wran-gle** (răng'gəl) *v.* **-gled, -gling. 1.** To dispute angrily. **2.** To obtain by argument. —*n.* A dispute. —**wran'gler** *n.*

**wrap** (răp) *v.* **wrapped** or **wrapt, wrapping. 1.** To arrange or fold about. **2.** To cover or envelop. —*n.* An outer garment. —**wrap'per** *n.* —**wrap'ping** *n.*

**wrath** (răth, räth) *n.* **1.** Violent, resentful anger. **2.** Retribution. —**wrath'ful** *adj.* —**wrath'ful-ly** *adv.*

**wreak** (rēk) *v.* To inflict (vengeance or punishment).

**wreath** (rēth) *n., pl.* **wreaths. 1.** A ring of flowers or leaves. **2.** Something resembling this.

**wreck** (rēk) *v.* **1.** To destroy or dismantle. **2.** To bring to ruin. —*n.* **1.** The state of being wrecked. **2.** Something in a worn-out state. —**wreck'age** *n.* —**wreck'er** *n.*

**wrench** (rĕnch) *n.* **1.** A forcible twist. **2.** An

injury from straining. **3.** A tool with jaws for gripping. —*v.* **1.** To twist forcibly. **2.** To sprain.

**wrest** (rĕst) *v.* **1.** To obtain by or as by pulling violently. **2.** To usurp.

**wres·tle** (rĕs'əl) *v.* **-tled, -tling. 1.** To contend by attempting to throw one's opponent. **2.** To struggle with. —**wres'tler** *n.* —**wres'tling** *n.*

**wretch** (rĕch) *n.* **1.** An unfortunate person. **2.** A despicable person.

**wretch·ed** (rĕch'ĭd) *adj.* **1.** Pitiable; woeful. **2.** Contemptible. **3.** Inferior. —**wretch'ed·ly** *adv.* —**wretch'ed·ness** *n.*

**wrig·gle** (rĭg'əl) *v.* **-gled, -gling. 1.** To squirm. **2.** To insinuate oneself by sly means. —**wrig'gle** *n.* —**wrig'gly** *adj.*

**wring** (rĭng) *v.* **wrung, wringing. 1.** To twist and squeeze; compress. **2.** To extract by twisting. —**wring'er** *n.*

**wrin·kle** (rĭng'kəl) *n.* A small furrow or crease. —*v.* **-kled, -kling. 1.** To make a wrinkle in. **2.** To become wrinkled. —**wrin'kly** *adj.*

**wrist** (rĭst) *n.* The junction between the hand and arm.

**writ** (rĭt) *n.* A written order issued by a court.

**write** (rīt) *v.* **wrote, written, writing. 1.** To form (letters, etc.) with a pen, pencil, etc. **2.** To compose, esp. as an author. **3.** To communicate by writing. —**writ'er** *n.*

**writhe** (rīth) *v.* **writhed, writhing.** To twist, as in pain.

**writ·ten** (rĭt'n) *p.p.* of **write.**

**wrong** (rông, rŏng) *adj.* **1.** Not correct. **2.** Contrary to conscience or law. **3.** Not suitable. **4.** Out of order; awry. —*adv.* **1.** Erroneously. **2.** Unjustly. —*n.* **1.** That which is wrong. **2.** The condition of being wrong. —*v.* To treat unjustly. —**wrong'do'er** *n.* —**wrong'do'ing** *n.* —**wrong'ful** *adj.* —**wrong'ful·ly** *adv.* —**wrong'ly** *adv.*

**wrote** (rōt) *p.t.* of **write.**

**wrought** (rôt) *adj.* **1.** Put together. **2.** Shaped by hammering.

**wrung** (rŭng) *p.t.* & *p.p.* of **wring.**

**wry** (rī) *adj.* **wrier** or **wryer, wriest** or **wryest. 1.** Twisted, as facial features. **2.** Dryly humorous. —**wry'ly** *adv.*

# XYZ

**x, X** (ĕks) *n.* The 24th letter of the English alphabet.

**xe·non** (zē'nŏn') *n.* A colorless, odorless, highly unreactive gaseous element.

**xen·o·phobe** (zĕn'ə-fōb') *n.* One unduly fearful of strangers or foreigners. —**xen·o·pho'bi·a** *n.* —**xen·o·pho'bic** *adj.*

**x ray. 1.** A relatively high-energy photon with a very short wavelength. **2.** Also **X ray.** A photograph taken with x rays. —**x'-ray'** *v.* & *adj.*

**xy·lo·phone** (zī'lə-fōn') *n.* A musical percussion instrument consisting of a mounted row of graduated wooden bars played with two small mallets.

**y, Y** (wī) *n.* The 25th letter of the English alphabet.

**yacht** (yät) *n.* A small sailing vessel, used for pleasure cruises or racing. —**yachts'man** *n.*

**ya·hoo** (yä'hōō, yä'-) *n.* A crude or brutish person.

**yak** (yăk) *n.* A long-haired Asian ox.

**yam** (yăm) *n.* The edible potatolike root of a tropical vine.

**yank** (yăngk) *v.* To pull suddenly; jerk. —*n.* A sudden vigorous pull; a jerk.

**Yan·kee** (yăng'kē) *n.* A native or inhabitant of a New England or N state of the U.S. —**Yan'kee** *adj.*

**yap** (yăp) *v.* **yapped, yapping. 1.** To bark sharply; yelp. **2.** To talk noisily or stupidly. —*n.* A sharp, shrill bark; yelp.

**yard¹** (yärd) *n.* **1.** A measure of length equal to 3 feet or 0.9144 meter. **2.** A long spar used to support a sail.

**yard²** (yärd) *n.* **1.** A tract of ground adjacent to a building. **2.** An enclosed area used for a specific purpose.

**yard·age** (yär'dĭj) *n.* An amount measured in yards.

**yard·stick** (yärd'stĭk') *n.* **1.** A measuring stick one yard in length. **2.** A standard; criterion.

**yarn** (yärn) *n.* **1.** A continuous strand of twisted threads of wool, etc. **2.** A long story.

**yaw** (yô) *v.* To deviate from the intended course, as a ship. —*n.* The action of yawing.

**yawl** (yôl) *n.* A two-masted sailing vessel.

**yawn** (yôn) *v.* To open the mouth wide from drowsiness or boredom. —*n.* An act of yawning.

**yea** (yā) *adv.* Yes; aye. —*n.* An affirmative vote.

**year** (yîr) *n.* A period of time consisting of 365 days. —**year′ly** *adj. & adv.*

**year·ling** (yîr′lĭng) *n.* An animal that is one year old.

**yearn** (yûrn) *v.* To have a strong or deep desire. —**yearn′ing** *n.*

**yeast** (yēst) *n.* A fungus capable of fermenting carbohydrates, used esp. as a leavening agent. —**yeast′y** *adj.*

**yell** (yĕl) *v.* To cry out loudly. —*n.* **1.** A loud cry; a shriek; shout. **2.** A rhythmic cheer uttered in unison.

**yel·low** (yĕl′ō) *n.* A color resembling that of ripe lemons. —*adj.* **1.** Of the color yellow. **2.** Cowardly. —**yel′low·ish** *adj.*

**yellow jacket.** A small yellow and black wasp.

**yelp** (yĕlp) *v.* To utter a sharp, short cry. —*n.* A sharp, short cry or bark.

**yen** (yĕn) *n.* A yearning; a longing.

**yes** (yĕs) *adv.* Expressive of affirmation, agreement, or consent. —*n.* An affirmative reply or vote.

**yes·ter·day** (yĕs′tər-dā′, -dē) *n.* The day before the present day. —*adv.* On the day before the present day.

**yet** (yĕt) *adv.* **1.** At this time; now. **2.** Thus far. **3.** In the time remaining; still. **4.** Besides; in addition. —*conj.* Nevertheless; and despite this.

**yew** (yōō) *n.* An evergreen tree or shrub with poisonous berries.

**yield** (yēld) *v.* **1.** To give forth; produce. **2.** To furnish or give in return. **3.** To relinquish or concede. **4.** To surrender; submit. **5.** To give way, as to pressure, force, or persuasion. —*n.* **1.** The amount yielded. **2.** The profit obtained from investment; a return.

**yo·del** (yōd′l) *v.* To sing so that the voice fluctuates between the normal chest voice and a falsetto. —*n.* A song that is yodeled.

**yo·ga** (yō′gə) *n.* A Hindu discipline aimed at training the consciousness for a state of perfect spiritual insight. —**yo′gi** *n.*

**yo·gurt** (yō′gərt, -gŏŏrt′) *n.* Also **yo·ghurt.** A custardlike food prepared from curdled milk.

**yoke** (yōk) *n.* A crossbar that encircles the necks of a pair of draft animals. —*v.* **yoked, yoking.** To fit or join with a yoke.

**yo·kel** (yō′kəl) *n.* A country bumpkin.

**yolk** (yōk) *n.* The yellow inner mass of an egg.

**yon·der** (yŏn′dər) *adv.* Over there.

**yore** (yôr, yōr) *n.* Time long past.

**you** (yōō) *pron.* The 2nd person sing. or pl. pronoun in the nominative or objective case.

**you'd** (yōōd) Contraction of *you had* or *you would.*

**you'll** (yōōl) Contraction of *you will* or *you shall.*

**young** (yŭng) *adj.* **1.** In the early period of life; not old. **2.** Vigorous or fresh. —*n.* **1.** Young persons collectively; youth. **2.** Offspring. —**young′ster** *n.*

**your** (yōŏr, yôr, yōr; *unstressed* yər). The possessive form of *you.*

**you're** (yōŏr; *unstressed* yər). Contraction of *you are.*

**yours** (yōŏrz, yôrz, yōrz). The possessive form of *you.*

**your·self** (yōŏr-sĕlf′, yôr-, yər-) *pron.*, *pl.* **-selves.** The reflexive form of *you.*

**youth** (yōōth) *n.*, *pl.* **youths. 1.** The condition of being young. **2.** An early period of development. **3. a.** Young people collectively. **b.** A young person. —**youth′ful** *adj.* —**youth′ful·ness** *n.*

**you've** (yōōv) Contraction of *you have.*

**yowl** (youl) *v.* To howl; wail. —*n.* A howl; a wail.

**yuc·ca** (yŭk′ə) *n.* A tall New World plant with a cluster of white flowers.

**z, Z** (zē) *n.* The 26th letter of the English alphabet.

**za·ny** (zā′nē) *n.*, *pl.* **-nies.** A clown; buffoon. —*adj.* **-nier, -niest. 1.** Clownish; droll. **2.** Silly; absurd.

**zeal** (zēl) *n.* Enthusiastic and diligent devotion. —**zeal′ous** *adj.* —**zeal′ous·ly** *adv.* —**zeal′ous·ness** *n.*

**zeal·ot** (zĕl′ət) *n.* One who is fanatically committed.

**ze·bra** (zē′brə) *n.* A striped, horselike African mammal.

**Zeit·geist** (tsīt′gīst′) *n.* The spirit and outlook characteristic of a period.

**Zen** (zĕn) *n.* A school of Buddhism that asserts that enlightenment can be attained through meditation rather than through the scriptures.

**ze·nith** (zē′nĭth) *n.* **1.** The celestial point that is directly above the observer. **2.** Any culmination or high point. — **ze′nith·al** *adj.*

**zeph·yr** (zĕf′ər) *n.* **1.** The west wind. **2.** A gentle breeze. **3.** Any of various light, soft fabrics or yarns.

**zep·pe·lin** (zĕp′ə-lĭn) *n.* A rigid airship or dirigible.

**ze·ro** (zîr′ō, zē′rō) *n., pl.* **-ros** or **-roes**. **1.** The numerical symbol "0." **2.** A number indicating the absence of any or all units under consideration. **3.** The lowest point. **4.** Nothing; nil.

**zest** (zĕst) *n.* **1.** Piquancy; charm. **2.** Spirited enjoyment; gusto. — **zest′ful** *adj.*

**zig·zag** (zĭg′zăg′) *n.* A line that proceeds by sharp turns in alternating directions. — *adj.* Having or moving in a zigzag. — *adv.* In a zigzag manner or pattern. — *v.* **-zagged, -zagging.** To form into or move in a zigzag.

**zinc** (zĭngk) *n.* A bluish-white, lustrous metallic element.

**zing** (zĭng) *n.* A brief high-pitched humming sound. — **zing** *v.*

**zin·ni·a** (zĭn′ē-ə) *n.* An annual plant with variously colored flowers.

**zip** (zĭp) *n.* **1.** A brief sharp, hissing sound. **2.** Alacrity; speed. — *v.* **zipped, zipping. 1.** To move swiftly. **2.** To fasten with a zipper.

**zip·per** (zĭp′ər) *n.* A fastening device consisting of interlocking rows of teeth on adjacent edges controlled by a sliding tab.

**zith·er** (zĭth′ər) *n.* A stringed musical instrument with a flat sounding box.

**zo·di·ac** (zō′dē-ăk′) *n.* **1.** An imaginary band of the celestial sphere that represents the path of the principal planets. **2.** In astrology, this band divided into 12 equal parts called signs, each bearing the name of the constellation for which it was named. — **zo·di′a·cal** *adj.*

**zom·bie** (zŏm′bē) *n.* **1.** A corpse revived by a voodoo spell. **2.** One who behaves like an automaton.

**zone** (zōn) *n.* **1.** An area, region, or division distinguished from adjacent parts by some distinctive feature. **2.** Any of the five regions of the surface of the earth divided according to prevailing climate. **3.** A division of an area or territory.

**zoo** (zōō) *n.* A park in which living animals are kept and exhibited.

**zo·ol·o·gy** (zō-ŏl′ə-jē) *n.* The biological science of animals. — **zo′o·log′i·cal** *adj.* — **zo·ol′o·gist** *n.*

**zoom** (zōōm) *v.* **1.** To climb suddenly and sharply in an airplane. **2.** To move about rapidly; swoop.

**zuc·chi·ni** (zōō-kē′nē) *n., pl.* **-ni.** A narrow, green-skinned variety of squash.

# PUNCTUATION

The rules of punctuation listed in this section, although far from comprehensive, cover the most important usages.

## Dash

Three kinds of dashes are commonly used in printed materials: The en dash (–) is used: Between numbers, dates, and places, to denote extent, duration, etc. It represents the word *to*: *1935–37*; *the New York–London flight*; *opened from 9–5:30*.

The em dash (—) is used:

**1.** To mark a sudden break or abrupt change in thought in a sentence: *She said — and no one contradicted her — "The windows need washing."*

**2.** Before and after parenthetical material for the sake of clarity or emphasis: *Two of the other players — Connors and Nastase — watched the first match.*

**3.** Before a summarizing statement: *Gravel, sand, and clay — these are important shore deposits.*

**4.** Before the name of an author or source at the end of a quotation: *"To be or not to be"— Shakespeare.*

The two-em dash (——) is used: To indicate the omission of a word, letters in a word, numbers, etc.: *"Such an idea can hardly be called ——." Dear Dr. M ——.*

*Note:* Three styles of typewritten dashes are commonly used: (1) a single mark with a space on each side (a usual form, especially in tabulations); (2) two marks with a space on each side (most commonly used nowadays); (3) two marks with no space on each side (printers' preferred style). In preparing manuscript for composition the kind of dash wanted should be carefully specified.

## Exclamation Point

The exclamation point is used:

To mark surprise, incredulity, admiration, or other strong emotion: *What! How beautiful! "Excellent!" he shouted. Who shouted, "All aboard!" O Lord, save Thy people!*

## Comma

The comma is used:

**1.** To separate independent clauses joined by a coordinate or correlative conjunction (as *and, but, for, nor,* and *or*): *It snowed yesterday, and today the road is closed.*

**2.** To separate independent clauses not joined by a conjunction when the clauses are short, closely related, and have no commas within: *I came, I saw, I conquered.*

**3.** After a dependent clause that precedes the main clause: *If there is any error, please let us know.*

**4.** To set off a nonrestrictive clause, phrase, or word: *Joan Smith, who lives next door, is ill.* (But *not* in the case of a restrictive clause as in: *The girl who lives next door is ill.*)

**5.** To set off parenthetical expressions, whether words, phrases, or clauses: *Our host, Bill Martin, is an excellent cook.*

**6.** To set off words or phrases expressing contrast: *Mr. Smith, not Mr. Jones, was elected.*

**7.** To set off transitional words and expressions (as *in short, of course*) or conjunctive adverbs (as *however, consequently, therefore*): *We found, in short, many errors in his work. Your question, however, remained unanswered.*

**8.** After expressions that introduce an example or illustration (as *namely, i.e., for example*): *Some of the presidential candidates, i.e., Jackson, Church, Bayh, are also senators.*

**9.** To separate words, phrases, or clauses in a series: *Mary, Louise, and Rachel are sisters. He stalked out of the room, turned around, came back, and resumed the argument.*

**10.** To separate two words or figures that might otherwise be misunderstood: *To Mary, Louise was very kind. Instead of hundreds, thousands came.*

**11.** To separate two adjectives that modify the same noun and can be interchanged in position: *an eager, restless young man.* (But *not* in: *three silver spoons; a rare second chance.*)

**12.** To set off a short direct quotation: *He said, "Now or never."*

**13.** To set off a word or phrase in direct address: *Please go, Mary, I'm tired.*

**14.** To indicate the omission of a word or words: *Then we had much, now nothing.*

**15.** After a statement followed by a direct question: *You are sure, are you not?*

**16.** To set off items in dates, addresses, names of places: *She was born on June 5, 1936, at 64 Chestnut Street, Boston, Massachusetts.*

**17.** To separate a proper name from a title: *Phillip Smith, Esq.*

**18.** After the salutation in informal correspondence: *Dear Mary,*

**19.** After the complimentary close of a letter: *Very truly yours,*

**20.** To separate an inverted name or phrase: *Jones, Edith.*

**21.** To separate thousands, millions, etc., in numbers of four or more digits: *5,256; 1,000,000.*

# Period

The period is used:

1. To mark the end of a sentence or sentence fragment that is neither exclamatory nor interrogatory: *Lobsters are crustaceans. Do not be late.*

2. After some abbreviations: *U.S.A.; Dr.*

3. Before a decimal and between dollars and cents in figures: *.90 pounds; 14.5 feet; $9.95.*

# Colon

The colon is used:

1. To introduce a series: *Four items were sold: a painting, two sculptures, and a rare book.*

2. To introduce a clause or phrase that extends, illustrates, or amplifies preceding matter: *Forestry is not an outdoor sport: it is a science.*

3. To introduce formally any material that forms a complete sentence, question, or quotation: *A topic came up for discussion: Which monetary policy should be pursued?*

4. After a salutation in formal correspondence: *Dear Sir:*

5. In expressing clock time: *2:40.*

6. In Biblical and bibliographic references: *Luke 4:3; Boston: Houghton Mifflin Company.*

7. To separate book titles and subtitles: *The Strong Brown God: The Story of the Niger River.*

8. In ratios: *Mix oil and vinegar in the proportion 3:1.*

# Question Mark

The question mark is used:

1. To mark the end of a direct query, even if not in the form of a question: *"Did she do it?" he asked. Can the money be raised? is the question.*

2. To express uncertainty or doubt: *Pocahontas (1595?–1617), American Indian princess; The mail clerk said the book weighed 50 (?) pounds.*

# Quotation Marks

Double quotation marks are used:

1. To enclose direct quotations: *"Karen," asked Kathy, "why are you singing?"*

2. To enclose titles of speeches or lectures, articles, short poems, short stories, chapters of books, songs, short musical compositions, radio and TV programs: *a lecture entitled "The Atomic Era"; The article "The Gypsies" appeared in the last issue. She read Shirley Jackson's "The Lottery" and Keats's "Ode to a Grecian Urn." Review the chapter "Money and Banking." The chorus sang "God Bless America." We watched ABC's "Happy Days."*

**3.** To enclose coined words, slang expressions, or ordinary words, etc., used ironically or in some other arbitrary way: *references to the "imperial Presidency" of Richard Nixon; George Herman "Babe" Ruth; His report was "bunk."*

## Semicolon

The semicolon is used:

**1.** To separate clauses containing commas: *Richard Smith, president of the National Bank, was also a director of Acme Lumber Co.; Harvey Jones, chairman of the board of Williams & Sons, was also on the board of American Steel Co. No, sir; I do not recall.*

**2.** To separate independent clauses joined by conjunctive adverbs: *The foreman praised his work highly; therefore he was given a raise.*

**3.** To separate statements that are too closely related to be written as separate sentences, and also contrasting statements: *War is destructive; peace, constructive.*

## Brackets

Brackets, in pairs, are used:

**1.** To indicate a word or phrase that is extraneous, incidental, or explanatory, especially within quoted material: *The emperor [Napoleon] ordered him to leave. She wrote: "I recieved [sic] your package."*

**2.** To set off parenthetical material within other parenthetical material: *Act of August 5, 1882 (ch. 4, sec. [or §] 284).*

## Apostrophe

The apostrophe is used:

**1.** To form the possessive case of nouns and some pronouns: *the man's hat; men's clothes; Mars' satellites; each other's books; someone's coat; somebody else's package.*

**2.** To indicate the omission of figures or letters: *don't; it's; class of '32.*

**3.** To form the plural of letters, figures, and symbols: *the 1930's; three R's; 2 by 4's; dot the i's; 8's; &'s.*

## Parentheses

Parentheses are used:

**1.** To set off nonessential, supplementary, or explanatory material: *She bought three dresses for £10 (a little less than $20.00). The result (see fig. 2) proves your theory. Ms. Jones belongs to the Portland (Ore.) Chamber of Commerce.*

**2.** To enclose parenthetical material where the interruption is too great to be indicated by commas: *You can find it neither in American catalogues (at any rate, not in Sears') nor in European.*

**3.** To enclose letters or numbers in a series: *The order of deliveries will be*

(a) mail, (b) groceries, and (c) laundry, if any. The cars are (1) old-fashioned, (2) still in good condition, and (3) quite expensive.

## PROOFREADERS' MARKS

| Instruction | Mark in Margin | Mark in Type |
|---|---|---|
| Delete | (dele) | the ~~good~~ word |
| Insert indicated material | good | the ʌ word |
| Let it stand | (stet) | the good word |
| Make capital | (cap) | the ≡word |
| Make lower case | (lc) | the Word |
| Set in small capitals | (sc) | See word |
| Set in italic type | (ital) | The word is word |
| Set in roman type | (rom) | the (word) |
| Set in boldface type | (bf) | the entry **word** |
| Set in lightface type | (lf) | the entry good |
| Transpose | (tr) | the woʳd / the word |
| Close up space | ⌒ | the wo rd |
| Delete and close up space | (⌒) | the word |
| Spell out | (sp) | (2) words |
| Insert space | # | the word |
| period | ⊙ | This is the word ʌ |
| comma | ⌄ | words ʌ words, words |
| hyphen | = / = / = = | word for word test |

| Instruction | Mark in Type | Mark in Margin |
|---|---|---|
| colon | The following words ʌ | ⊙ |
| semicolon | Scan the words skim the words. | ;/ |
| apostrophe | Johnʌs words | ⌄ |
| quotation marks | the word word | ⌄/⌄ |
| parentheses | The word is in parentheses. | (/) |
| brackets | He read from the Word the Bible. | [/] |
| en dash | 1964 1972 | -N- |
| em dash | The dictionary how often it is needed belongs in every home. | -M- |
| Start paragraph | "Where is it?" "It's on the shelf." | ¶ |
| Move left | the word | ⊏ |
| Move right | the word | ⊐ |
| Align | the word / the word | ‖ |
| Wrong font | the word | (wf) |
| Broken type | the word | X |

# WEIGHTS AND MEASURES

## Length

| U.S. Customary Unit | U.S. Equivalents | Metric Equivalents |
|---|---|---|
| inch | 0.083 foot | 2.54 centimeters |
| foot | ⅓ yard. 12 inches | 0.3048 meter |
| yard | 3 feet. 36 inches | 0.9144 meter |
| rod | 5½ yards. 16½ feet | 5.0292 meters |
| mile (statute, land) | 1,760 yards. 5,280 feet | 1.609 kilometers |
| mile (nautical international) | 1.151 statute miles | 1.852 kilometers |

## Area

| U.S. Customary Unit | U.S. Equivalents | Metric Equivalents |
|---|---|---|
| square inch | 0.007 square foot | 6.4516 square centimeters |
| square foot | 144 square inches | 929.030 square centimeters |
| square yard | 1,296 square inches. 9 square feet | 0.836 square meter |
| acre | 43,560 square feet. 4,840 square yards | 4,047 square meters |
| square mile | 640 acres | 2.590 square kilometers |

## Volume or Capacity

| U.S. Customary Unit | U.S. Equivalents | Metric Equivalents |
|---|---|---|
| cubic inch | 0.00058 cubic foot | 16.387 cubic centimeters |
| cubic foot | 1,728 cubic inches | 0.028 cubic meter |
| cubic yard | 27 cubic feet | 0.765 cubic meter |

259

| U.S. Customary Liquid Measure | U.S. Equivalents | Metric Equivalents |
|---|---|---|
| fluid ounce | 8 fluid drams. 1.804 cubic inches | 29.573 milliliters |
| pint | 16 fluid ounces. 28.875 cubic inches | 0.473 liter |
| quart | 2 pints. 57.75 cubic inches | 0.946 liter |
| gallon | 4 quarts. 231 cubic inches | 3.785 liters |
| barrel | varies from 31 to 42 gallons, established by law or usage | |

| U.S. Customary Dry Measure | U.S. Equivalents | Metric Equivalents |
|---|---|---|
| pint | ½ quart. 33.6 cubic inches | 0.551 liter |
| quart | 2 pints. 67.2 cubic inches | 1.101 liters |
| peck | 8 quarts. 537.605 cubic inches | 8.810 liters |
| bushel | 4 pecks. 2,150.42 cubic inches | 35.238 liters |

| British Imperial Liquid and Dry Measure | U.S. Customary Equivalents | Metric Equivalents |
|---|---|---|
| fluid ounce | 0.961 U.S. fluid ounce. 1.734 cubic inches | 28.412 milliliters |
| pint | 1.032 U.S. dry pints. 1.201 U.S. liquid pints. 34.678 cubic inches | 568.26 milliliters |

| British Imperial Liquid and Dry Measure | U.S. Customary Equivalents | Metric Equivalents |
|---|---|---|
| quart | 1.032 U.S. dry quarts. 1.201 U.S. liquid quarts. 69.354 cubic inches | 1.136 liters |
| gallon | 1.201 U.S. gallons. 277.420 cubic inches | 4.546 liters |
| peck | 554.84 cubic inches | 0.009 cubic meter |
| bushel | 1.032 U.S. bushels. 2,219.36 cubic inches | 0.036 cubic meter |

## Weight

| U.S. Customary Unit (Avoirdupois) | U.S. Equivalents | Metric Equivalents |
|---|---|---|
| grain | 0.036 dram. 0.002285 ounce | 64.79891 milligrams |
| dram | 27.344 grains. 0.0625 ounce | 1.772 grams |
| ounce | 16 drams. 437.5 grains | 28.350 grams |
| pound | 16 ounces. 7,000 grains | 453.59237 grams |
| ton (short) | 2,000 pounds | 0.907 metric ton (1,000 kilograms) |
| ton (long) | 1.12 short tons. 2,240 pounds | 1.016 metric tons |

| Apothecary Weight Unit | U.S. Customary Equivalents | Metric Equivalents |
|---|---|---|
| scruple | 20 grains | 1.296 grams |
| dram | 60 grains | 3.888 grams |
| ounce | 480 grains. 1.097 avoirdupois ounces | 31.103 grams |
| pound | 5,760 grains. 0.823 avoirdupois pound | 373.242 grams |

# GUIDE TO THE METRIC SYSTEM

## Length

| Unit | Number of Meters | Approximate U.S. Equivalent |
|---|---|---|
| myriameter | 10,000 | 6.2 miles |
| kilometer | 1,000 | 0.62 mile |
| hectometer | 100 | 109.36 yards |
| dekameter | 10 | 32.81 feet |
| meter | 1 | 39.37 inches |
| decimeter | 0.1 | 3.94 inches |
| centimeter | 0.01 | 0.39 inch |
| millimeter | 0.001 | 0.04 inch |

## Area

| Unit | Number of Square Meters | Approximate U.S. Equivalent |
|---|---|---|
| square kilometer | 1,000,000 | 0.3861 square mile |
| hectare | 10,000 | 2.47 acres |
| are | 100 | 119.60 square yards |
| centare | 1 | 10.76 square feet |
| square centimeter | 0.0001 | 0.155 square inch |

## Volume

| Unit | Number of Cubic Meters | Approximate U.S. Equivalent |
|---|---|---|
| dekastere | 10 | 13.10 cubic yards |
| stere | 1 | 1.31 cubic yards |
| decistere | 0.10 | 3.53 cubic feet |
| cubic centimeter | 0.000001 | 0.061 cubic inch |

## Capacity

| Unit | Number of Cubic Liters | Approximate U.S. Equivalents Dry | Liquid |
|---|---|---|---|
| kiloliter | 1,000 1.31 cubic yards | | |
| hectoliter | 100 3.53 cubic feet | 2.84 bushels | |
| dekaliter | 10 0.35 cubic foot | 1.14 pecks | 2.64 gallons |
| liter | 1 61.02 cubic inches | 0.908 quart | 1.057 quarts |
| deciliter | 0.10 6.1 cubic inches | 0.18 pint | 0.21 pint |
| centiliter | 0.01 0.6 cubic inch | | 0.338 fluid ounce |
| milliliter | 0.001 0.06 cubic inch | | 0.27 fluidram |

## Mass and Weight

| Unit | Number of Grams | Approximate U.S. Equivalent |
|---|---|---|
| metric ton | 1,000,000 | 1.1 tons |
| quintal | 100,000 | 220.46 pounds |
| kilogram | 1,000 | 2.2046 pounds |
| hectogram | 100 | 3.527 ounces |
| dekagram | 10 | 0.353 ounce |
| gram | 1 | 0.035 ounce |
| decigram | 0.10 | 1.543 grains |

## Mass and Weight

| Unit | Number of Grams | Approximate U.S. Equivalent |
|---|---|---|
| centigram | 0.01 | 0.154 grain |
| milligram | 0.001 | 0.015 grain |

# METRIC CONVERSION CHART — APPROXIMATIONS

| When You Know | Multiply By | To Find |
|---|---|---|

## Length

| millimeters | 0.04 | inches |
| centimeters | 0.4 | inches |
| meters | 3.3 | feet |
| meters | 1.1 | yards |
| kilometers | 0.6 | miles |

## Area

| square centimeters | 0.16 | square inches |
| square meters | 1.2 | square yards |
| square kilometers | 0.4 | square miles |
| hectares (10,000m$^2$) | 2.5 | acres |

## Mass and Weight

| grams | 0.035 | ounce |
| kilograms | 2.2 | pounds |
| tons (1000kg) | 1.1 | short tons |

| When You Know | Multiply By | To Find |
|---|---|---|

## Volume

| | | |
|---|---|---|
| milliliters | 0.03 | fluid ounces |
| liters | 2.1 | pints |
| liters | 1.06 | quarts |
| liters | 0.26 | gallons |
| cubic meters | 35 | cubic feet |
| cubic meters | 1.3 | cubic yards |

## Temperature (exact)

| | | |
|---|---|---|
| Celsius temp. | 9/5, +32 | Fahrenheit temp. |
| Fahrenheit temp. | −32, 5/9 x remainder | Celsius temp. |

| When You Know | Multiply By | To Find |
|---|---|---|

## Length

| | | |
|---|---|---|
| inches | 2.5 | centimeters |
| feet | 30 | centimeters |
| yards | 0.9 | meters |
| miles | 1.6 | kilometers |

## Area

| | | |
|---|---|---|
| square inches | 6.5 | square centimeters |
| square feet | 0.09 | square meters |
| square yards | 0.8 | square meters |
| square miles | 2.6 | square kilometers |
| acres | 0.4 | hectares |

| When You Know | Multiply By | To Find |
|---|---|---|

## Mass and Weight

| When You Know | Multiply By | To Find |
|---|---|---|
| ounces | 28 | grams |
| pounds | 0.45 | kilograms |
| short tons (2000 lb) | 0.9 | tons |

## Volume

| When You Know | Multiply By | To Find |
|---|---|---|
| fluid ounces | 30 | milliliters |
| pints | 0.47 | liters |
| quarts | 0.95 | liters |
| gallons | 3.8 | liters |
| cubic feet | 0.03 | cubic meters |
| cubic yards | 0.76 | cubic meters |

# STATES OF THE UNITED STATES

| State | Capital | Admitted to the Union | Population |
|---|---|---|---|
| Alabama | Montgomery | 1819 | 3,444,165 |
| Alaska | Juneau | 1959 | 302,173 |
| Arizona | Phoenix | 1912 | 1,772,482 |
| Arkansas | Little Rock | 1836 | 1,923,295 |
| California | Sacramento | 1850 | 19,953,134 |
| Colorado | Denver | 1876 | 2,207,259 |
| Connecticut* | Hartford | 1788 | 3,032,217 |
| Delaware* | Dover | 1787 | 548,104 |
| Florida | Tallahassee | 1845 | 6,789,443 |
| Georgia* | Atlanta | 1788 | 4,589,575 |
| Hawaii | Honolulu | 1959 | 769,913 |
| Idaho | Boise | 1890 | 713,008 |
| Illinois | Springfield | 1818 | 11,113,976 |
| Indiana | Indianapolis | 1816 | 5,193,669 |

*One of the thirteen original states

| State | Capital | Admitted to the Union | Population |
|---|---|---|---|
| Iowa | Des Moines | 1846 | 2,825,041 |
| Kansas | Topeka | 1861 | 2,249,071 |
| Kentucky | Frankfort | 1792 | 3,219,311 |
| Louisiana | Baton Rouge | 1812 | 3,643,180 |
| Maine | Augusta | 1820 | 993,663 |
| Maryland* | Annapolis | 1788 | 3,922,399 |
| Massachusetts* | Boston | 1788 | 5,689,170 |
| Michigan | Lansing | 1837 | 8,875,083 |
| Minnesota | St. Paul | 1858 | 3,805,069 |
| Mississippi | Jackson | 1817 | 2,216,912 |
| Missouri | Jefferson City | 1821 | 4,677,399 |
| Montana | Helena | 1889 | 694,409 |
| Nebraska | Lincoln | 1867 | 1,483,791 |
| Nevada | Carson City | 1864 | 488,738 |
| New Hampshire* | Concord | 1788 | 737,681 |
| New Jersey* | Trenton | 1787 | 7,168,164 |
| New Mexico | Santa Fe | 1912 | 1,016,000 |
| New York* | Albany | 1788 | 18,241,266 |
| North Carolina* | Raleigh | 1789 | 5,082,059 |
| North Dakota | Bismarck | 1889 | 617,761 |
| Ohio | Columbus | 1803 | 10,652,017 |
| Oklahoma | Oklahoma City | 1907 | 2,559,253 |
| Oregon | Salem | 1859 | 2,091,385 |
| Pennsylvania* | Harrisburg | 1787 | 11,793,909 |
| Rhode Island* | Providence | 1790 | 946,723 |
| South Carolina* | Columbia | 1788 | 2,590,516 |
| South Dakota | Pierre | 1889 | 666,257 |
| Tennessee | Nashville | 1796 | 3,924,164 |
| Texas | Austin | 1845 | 11,196,730 |
| Utah | Salt Lake City | 1896 | 1,059,273 |
| Vermont | Montpelier | 1791 | 444,732 |
| Virginia* | Richmond | 1788 | 4,648,494 |
| Washington | Olympia | 1889 | 3,409,169 |
| West Virginia | Charleston | 1863 | 1,744,237 |
| Wisconsin | Madison | 1848 | 4,417,933 |
| Wyoming | Cheyenne | 1890 | 332,416 |

*One of the thirteen original states